MODERN IRELAND
1600–1972

R. F. FOSTER

MODERN IRELAND
1600–1972

ALLEN LANE
THE PENGUIN PRESS

To Dermot, and in memory of Nuala

ALLEN LANE
THE PENGUIN PRESS

Published by the Penguin Group
27 Wrights Lane, London W8 5TZ, England
Viking Penguin Inc., 40 West 23rd Street, New York, New York 10010, USA
Penguin Books Australia Ltd, Ringwood, Victoria, Australia
Penguin Books Canada Ltd, 2801 John Street, Markham, Ontario, Canada L3R 1B4
Penguin Books (NZ) Ltd, 182–190 Wairau Road, Auckland 10, New Zealand

Penguin Books Ltd, Registered Offices: Harmondsworth, Middlesex, England

First published 1988
9 10 8

Copyright © R. F. Foster, 1988

The acknowledgements on pp. xii–xiii constitute an extension of this copyright page

British Library Cataloguing in Publication Data

Foster, R. F. (Robert Fitzroy), 1949–
    Modern Ireland 1600–1972.
    1. Ireland, 1600–1972
    I. Title
    941.5

ISBN 0–7139–9010–4

Library of Congress Catalog Card No.: 88–61902

CONTENTS

List of Maps

List of Tables

List of Figures

PREFACE

The tradition of writing the 'story of Ireland' as a morality tale, invented around the seventeenth century and retained (with the roles of hero and villain often reversed) until the twentieth, has been abandoned over the last generation. A vast number of special studies have appeared, revolutionizing long-held views in several key areas. These have been followed by some masterly books that are not general histories but present general arguments: riveting for those who know the basic material already and have been reared on the orthodoxies that they question.[1] Where straightforward modern narratives exist, however, they tend to cover short periods, an inevitable response to the influx of so much new material, or to provide a schematic political-constitutional survey, invariably owing a large, and sometimes unacknowledged, debt to the pioneering work of J. C. Beckett.[2]

This book does not compete with either genre. It is not an exhaustive catalogue of events or record of administrations; these sequences are more easily accessible in volumes specifically devoted to such things.[3] Nor, however, is it a series of thematic reflections, though these occur. The intention is to provide a narrative with an interpretive level, stressing themes as much as events, and concentrating on areas that have come under recent re-evaluation – often with the effect of liberating them from the Anglocentric obsession that once led the study of Irish political and economic history so far astray.

Much of Irish history as usually conceived concerns what did *not* happen: the theme of the missed chance, usually of reconciliation with, or complete separation from, England. Allied to this approach are the events that historians used to feel *ought* not to have happened and have therefore – in a sense – denied. 'Placed between memory and hope, the race will never conquer what it desires, and it will never discover what it regrets,'[4] wrote one of the romantic observers who have laid so many false trails for interpreters of Irish history. This book is an attempt to clarify some of the realities behind such supposed desires and regrets over the period since 1600.

Note on the Text

Reference notes, indicated by Arabic numerals, have been kept to a minimum and will be found at the end of the book. Roman numerals, sequential in each chapter, refer to the biographical and textual notes that appear at the foot of the relevant page.

ACKNOWLEDGEMENTS

I owe the completion of this book to the kindness and patience of many people: the following obligations are the most outstanding.

From the beginning, the debt I have owed to my wife, Aisling, for her support, encouragement and criticism has been immeasurable and heartfelt. For advice and help in planning the project, I am deeply grateful to Gabriele Annan, Jonathan Allison, Fanny Blake, Peter Carson, Giles Gordon, David Kewley, Georgina Morley, Thaddeus O'Sullivan, Donna Poppy, Malise Ruthven, Marina Warner, Eileen Webster and James White. For hospitality that enabled me to write large sections in undisturbed surroundings, my thanks to Natasha Hicks, Noelle Hodgkinson Bellier, Sheila Sheehan, David and Martina Thomson, Tim and Catriona Williams, and – repeatedly – Terence de Vere White and Victoria Glendinning.

The Nuffield Foundation and the Wolfson Trust provided invaluable financial help that enabled research and secretarial assistance at a time when such things are in very short academic supply. Without the sterling help of the late Jenny Bray the manuscript would have taken years longer to complete; without Joe Spence, whose voice may be heard in the biographical footnotes, it would never have been completed at all.

This work owes much to other historians, but it owes most of all to those who read it in whole or in part: Joe Spence once more, Toby Barnard, Marianne Elliott, Paul Bew, Charles Townshend, Margaret Windham Heffernan and especially Tom Dunne – an inspiration throughout. Their generosity, advice and friendship is greatly appreciated; the errors and obstinate misinterpretations are all my own.

Finally, three people who indirectly influenced the making of this book did not live to see it completed. Theo Moody not only taught me Irish history throughout my undergraduate and postgraduate careers, but remained a formative influence in the years of friendship that followed. Leland Lyons, first through his books and then as a friend and mentor, helped me in more ways than I can count. Most bitterly missed of all is my much loved mother-in-law, Nuala O'Conor Donelan, whose ironic interrogations and first-class mind clarified much about Irish history (and a great deal else). This book is dedicated to her and to my father-in-law, Dermot, for their unfailing encouragement and friendship through my years of studying and teaching history.

R. F. Foster
London, December 1987

For permission to reproduce material from the following copyright works, the author and publisher gratefully acknowledge the following:

C. S. Andrews, *Man of No Property*, Mercier Press; J. H. Andrews, 'Geography and Government in Elizabethan Ireland', *Irish Geographical Studies in Honour of E. Estyn Evans*, N. Stephens and R. E. Glasscock (editors), Department of Geography, Queen's University, Belfast; Elizabeth Bowen, *Bowen's Court*, Virago Press; J. Bowman, *De Valera and the Ulster Question 1917–73*, Oxford University Press; N. Browne, *Against the Tide*, Gill & Macmillan; Daniel Corkery, *The Hidden Ireland*, Gill & Macmillan; L. M. Cullen, *An Economic History of Ireland since 1660*, B. T. Batsford; R. Dudley Edwards, *An Atlas of Irish History*, Methuen London and the Irish Stationery Office; G. and D. FitzGerald, *The Memoirs of Desmond FitzGerald*, Routledge & Kegan Paul; D. Fitzpatrick, 'The Geography of Irish Nationalism 1910–21', The Past and Present Society, 175 Banbury Road, Oxford; D. Fitzpatrick, *Politics and Irish Life 1913–21: Provincial Experience of War and Revolution*, Gill & Macmillan; Lady Augusta Gregory, *Our Irish Theatre*, Colin Smythe Ltd; Desmond Hamill, *Pig in the Middle: The British Army in Northern Ireland 1969–84*, Methuen London; D. W. Harkness, *Northern Ireland since 1920*, The Educational Company of Ireland; K. T. Hoppen, *Elections, Politics and Society in Ireland 1832–85*, Oxford University Press; J. H. Johnson, 'Harvest Migration from Nineteenth-century Ireland', The Institute of British Geographers; R. Lawton, 'Irish Immigration to England and Wales in the Mid-nineteenth Century', *Irish Geography*, The Geographical Society of Ireland; T. W. Moody, F. X. Martin and F. J. Byrne (editors), *A New History of Ireland, Vol. III* and *A New History of Ireland, Vol. IX*, Oxford University Press; J. Mokyr, *Why Ireland Starved: A Quantitative and Analytical History of the Irish Economy 1800–1850*, Allen & Unwin; C. Ó Gráda, 'Demographic Adjustment and Seasonal Migration in Nineteenth-century Ireland'; Ernie O'Malley, *On Another Man's Wound*, Cormac O'Malley and the Anvil Press; A. T. Q. Stewart, *The Ulster Crisis*, Faber & Faber;

J. M. Synge, *Collected Works. Vol. II: Prose*, A. Price (editor), Oxford University Press; D. Thomson and M. McGusty (editors), *The Irish Journals of Elizabeth Smith 1840–50*, Oxford University Press; C. Townshend, *Political Violence in Ireland: Government and Resistance since 1848*, Oxford University Press; M S autobiography of Alfred Webb, Historical Committee of the Religious Society of Friends in Ireland; W. B. Yeats, *Purgatory* and *Autobiographies*, M. B. Yeats and Macmillan & Co. Ltd.

PART ONE

PROLOGUE

==

VARIETIES OF
IRISHNESS

I

==

WHEN DOES MODERN Irish history begin? The dates of reigns, administrations and battles provide convenient markers. In 1541 Henry VIII assumed the title 'King of Ireland', which had technically been a 'lordship' of the English Crown since the twelfth-century conquest. The change of title signified a commitment to effective and total rule. In 1601 the Irish rebels and their Spanish allies were routed at the battle of Kinsale; in 1607 the great leader of Gaelic Ireland, Hugh O'Neill,[i] went into exile. But nothing began, or ended, thus neatly: the English colonial presence in Ireland remained superimposed upon an ancient identity, alien and bizarre. Even as the tensions of early modern Europe manifested themselves in Ireland, and as English authority established itself throughout the island, the incompleteness of conquest remained the salient truth. In 1600, as later, Ireland was characterized by a fragmented polity: varieties of peoples, defining their 'Irishness' differently, many of whom denied the legitimacy of the official state apparatus and lived indifferently outside its writ.

In 1600 resistance to the Tudor reconquest was at a pivotal point. The last great Gaelic counter-attack under Hugh O'Neill, Earl of Tyrone, was challenging the imposition of Englishness: according to the acute observer Fynes Moryson,[ii] the rebellion was 'at its greatest

[i] Hugh O'Neill (*c.* 1540–1616): born in Dungannon; reared in England in the 'new religion'; served in the English army in Ireland from 1568; lamented his countrymen's unwillingness to accept English ways; became second Earl of Tyrone, 1585; proclaimed a traitor; led the Irish victoriously at the battle of Yellow Ford, 1598; compromised Essex with Elizabeth by his smooth talking, 1599; less successful with Mountjoy, who defeated him at Kinsale, 1601; submission accepted, March 1603; received at the court of James I but chose to lead the 'flight of the earls', 1607; resided at Rome, where, according to popular sources, he eventually succumbed to death by melancholy.

[ii] Fynes Moryson (1566–1630): chief secretary to Mountjoy in Ireland, 1600–1603, and in England, 1603–6; second volume of his *Itinerary* (three volumes, 1617) of travels

strength', though it was just about to crumble. In 1600 Spanish help was on the seas, but it would misfire within the year; and in Mountjoy,[iii] the new Lord Deputy from England, O'Neill would meet his nemesis. But to look at Ireland then, in the last year of Elizabeth and just before the final Gaelic collapse, would form a fairer picture than in the devastation and demoralization of 1603 or 1604: the rich 'survey' literature of late Elizabethan observers helps us anatomize Irish life as it appeared at the beginning of 1600, when O'Neill, renegade Elizabethan and restored Ulster chieftain, set off on a peregrination south, in probable imitation of the old High Kings, and following the precisely articulated practice of Gaelic society whereby a lord exacted institutionalized hospitality from his dependants.

O'Neill, too, is an appropriate focus, for he represents the Janus-face of Ireland, whose ambivalence and elusiveness exhausted contemporaries and historians alike. 'I am quite tired with pursuing Tyrone through all his shifts and devices,' wrote William Camden[iv] primly. Waging war in 1600, he was at once the last Gaelic hero and the first temporizing Irish politician. 'He built up his own military machine, relying on both English and Irish methods';[1] while resisting the English encroachments of local government and metropolitan influence on Ulster, he fought surrounded by Scotch bodyguards and foreign servants. Originally chieftain with English support and an English earldom, in 1595 he claimed an Irish title, 'The O'Neill', by Gaelic ritual; in 1598 he spread native resistance into the southern province of Munster, west to Connacht, and even into the English-dominated Pale, that eastern strip running from Dundalk to Dublin. In 1601 Mountjoy would show a fine comprehension of symbol by breaking into pieces the pre-Christian stone at Tullahogue upon which the

through Europe deals with the history and topography of Ireland and was published separately, 1637; obtained a licence to publish a supplement to the *Itinerary*, 1626, but this remained in manuscript form.

iii Charles Blount (1563–1606): educated at Oxford; succeeded as eighth Lord Mountjoy, 1594; replaced Essex as Lord Deputy of Ireland, 1600; successfully commanded the English forces that drove the rebels from the Pale, 1601–3; continued to advise on Irish affairs under James I; created Earl of Devonshire and Master of the Ordnance, 1603.

iv William Camden (1551–1623): born in London of modest descent; a decade of research and perambulations through every English county resulted in *Britannia*, 1586; published Giraldus Cambrensis's *Topographia Hibernica* and *Expugnatio Hibernica*, 1602; *Annales ... regnante Elizabetha ... ad annum 1589*, 1615. A religious controversialist, it is his antipathy to Catholicism, rather than an inherent sense of racial superiority, that colours his pictures of Ireland.

O'Neills were inaugurated; but in 1600 O'Neill of Tyrone was spoken of in Europe, and treated with, as 'Prince of Ireland'.

When the stone at Tullahogue was smashed, O'Neill was attacked where he had finally (not without hesitation) taken up his ground: the defence of Gaelic Ireland. This should not be confused with later conceptions of national politics: palatinate status for Ulster, at this point intractably Gaelic, would probably have satisfied him. By 1600 European developments in politics and religion implied the possibility of a more widespread rebellion against English rule in Ireland, with religion as a rallying-cry. But Irish local realities made this purely rhetorical.

II

Those local realities can only be understood in terms of the Irish landscape. Elizabethan cartography shows its unfamiliarity: there was no real map of the Donegal coast until 1602–3. Surveyors carried out their trade in danger of life and limb. To the native Irish, the literal representation of the country was less important than its poetic dimension. In traditional bardic culture, the terrain was studied, discussed and referenced: every place had its legend and its own identity. *Dindsenchas*, the celebration of place-names, was a feature of this poetic topography; what endured was the mythic landscape, providing escape and inspiration.

None the less, O'Neill's progress south in January 1600 was made at a time when travel for its own sake was rare and troublesome, even in the notoriously mobile society of the Gaelic lordships. He came down through Westmeath in the centre of the island, turning aside to discipline the O'Carroll lands for disloyalty; by February he was in Munster with the Earl of Desmond, a member of the old Norman Fitzgerald family, now thoroughly Hibernicized. Passing by the lands of the Earl of Ormond (Hiberno-Norman also, but loyal to the Crown), O'Neill burned part of Kilkenny town: his sojourn in Cork saw further punitive expeditions, but he also received submissions from local chiefs and preached a holy war against the English. During this parade of authority, Mountjoy, the new Deputy, landed; O'Neill contemptuously evaded him and withdrew across the great central Bog of Allen to Ulster, inflicting 'a great dishonour' on the Deputy and the Queen.

It was a demonstration that not only the Irish chiefs were disloyal to English authority: it was opposed by the very lie of the land. Wood, bog, lake and mountain concealed and sustained resistance, and Elizabethan soldiers hated the terrain with vehemence. It had never been plotted out, as the Normans did with post-Conquest England: information about the number of ploughlands in each county was only vaguely determined, and the measurement unit itself was variously defined. Maps existed, but they were chiefly used for the identification of dominant families in key localities: the shiring of counties, still in process of completion, may have been partly intended to neutralize the regional loyalties of the native Irish and to subdue the terrain itself. The civil landscape of east Munster or the midlands was mild, rich and mouth-watering to English observers and colonial investors; but even there, the administration found itself unable to 'read' the country. Their assumption that most of the farmland was unenclosed may, for instance, have been based on an inability to recognize traditional boundaries; a 'ditch' in Ireland still means the exact opposite to what it signifies in England. And where the grazing ended, herds, flocks and men could disappear into the mountains, the bogs, even the lakes, which secreted fortified island dwellings, and most of all the woods.

Irish woods were famous: varied, dense and impenetrable to the unfamiliar. Willow, birch, hazel, pine, alder, oak, elm and ash were predominant, though the concentration varied: yew woods in Cork, oak in the south-east. Beech and sycamore followed later; gorse and hawthorn really flourished only when the woods were cleared, and rampant exotica like fuchsia and arbutus were a later development still. In 1600 the woods covered about one-eighth of the country; they were gradually being cleared, and by the late sixteenth century commentators were already noticing the lack of good mature timber. This was of great economic importance: pipe staves and barrelling were vital products. Specialized work in wood was widespread (Galway was famous for boat-builders), though stonemasons had to be imported; the woods were also the basis of the great glass industry in Cork and Waterford that was just beginning. Other industries rose and fell with the availability of timber; and with the decline of the wood, distinctively Irish fauna, like goshawks, deer and wolves, declined too.

Dymmok[v] in 1600 described Leinster, the most developed province,

[v] John Dymmok (*fl.* 1600): probably an English attendant upon Essex as Lord Lieutenant of Ireland, 1599; his political and topographical *Treatise of Ireland* (manuscript c. 1600; published 1842), dedicated to 'Sir Edmunde Carye', contains an eyewitness account of the Anglo-Irish confrontations of the summer of 1599.

as still heavily wooded; but the tendency of observers was to exaggerate, since they generally judged the woods from a military point of
view. Certainly the river valleys and the eastern slopes of the mountain
ranges were thickly forested. Bogs presented similar opportunities to
rebels, who could pick their way across; they lay on upland and
lowland, and provided summer pasturage for migrating herds. The
mobility of the Irish on their watery terrain surprised the English.
Communication was by water as much as by land, and fords were
used rather than bridges; roads were not much attended to. The vehicles
used reflected this: in the country the wheelless slide-car, which was
good for bogs; in towns the two-wheeled cart and block-wheel car.

Even the nature of the separate provinces seemed changing and
uncertain. In 1600 Ulster was synonymous with wildness and untamed
Gaelicism: separate by nature and geography, least inhabited, least
developed economically, least urbanized. On the other hand, in the
late medieval era, the western province of Connacht had become
anything but a remote backwater: it was characterized by economic
activity and cultural vitality. In the following years both these stereotypes would be reversed, as administrative conquest and plantation
made their mark. In the early 1600s north Armagh and south-east
Antrim were already being 'landscaped' into village patterns by the
building of Big Houses – a process that would dictate much of the
shape of rural Ireland. Already in Munster the ambitious planter
Richard Boyle[vi] had tried to mould the countryside round Lismore to
the English fashion: a 'lordly mansion', surrounded by a stocked
deer-park, selected fruit-orchards, fish-ponds, stud-farms, eyries, a
meticulously constructed rabbit-warren. This was to him as important
as forest-clearing, castle- and town-building, iron-smelting and the
foundation of almshouses. Estate formation would leave its mark on
the countryside, but the nature of the land, elusive and intractable as
ever, would assert its own stubborn patterns.

III

Landscape expressed the incompleteness of conquest, and the same
perception preoccupied those observers whose writings created the

[vi] Richard Boyle (1566–1647): first ('great') Earl of Cork; profited greatly as Clerk
of the Council for Munster under Carew; Privy Councillor, 1606; Lord Justice of

image of Elizabethan Ireland for their contemporaries, Spenser,[vii] Moryson, Dymmok, Gernon[viii] and Payne.[ix] Their accounts, written to prove a point, reflected distrust not only of the Gaelic chieftains who controlled the land to the west and the north, but also of the 'Old English', the descendants of the Anglo-Norman conquerors. Those in possession of great estates in the midlands and south-west, like the Earl of Desmond, had shown themselves to be as unreliable as O'Neill. Even within the Pale around Dublin, the Anglicized ethos maintained only a precarious position. Moryson, travelling round Ireland with Mountjoy, felt that English rulers had weakened the authority of the Lord Deputy as royal representative, and of the Irish government in general, by their readiness to 'grant suits and rewards to many of the Irish in England'. There was a continuing tension between policy on the ground and at court. 'Nothing is more dangerous than middle counsels, which England of old too much practised in Ireland.'[2] After 1600 a draconian new emphasis would make itself felt.

Between the Gaelic lordships and the Pale a constant tension existed. The policy under Henry VIII sixty years before, of regranting their lands to Irish chieftains on English tenures and English terms, had not really imposed a new dispensation; the Irish lords entered in and out

Ireland, 1629; Lord High Treasurer, 1631; subsequently an implacable enemy to Wentworth. Fathered a large and gifted family, including Richard, first Earl of Burlington, Roger, first Earl of Orrery, and the scientist Robert. Survived rebellion, many accusations of corruption and political vicissitudes. Epitome of the Elizabethan settler–adventurer.

[vii] Edmund Spenser (1552–99): born in London; secretary to Lord Grey de Wilton in Ireland, 1580; clerk in the Irish Court of Chancery, 1581; granted the 3,000 acre estate of Kilcolman, County Cork, 1586, where he wrote much of The Faerie Queene (first three books 1590; second three, 1596); appointed Secretary to the Council of Munster, 1588, and Sheriff of Cork, 1598; saw Kilcolman Castle attacked and burned in the attempt of the sugán Earl of Desmond to repossess his forefathers' lands, October 1598; escaped to London, where he died three months later. His View of the Present State of Ireland (written 1596; published 1633) is that of the Elizabethan Englishman, believing Irish nationality had to be uprooted by the sword.

[viii] Luke Gernon (c. 1580–c. 1670): admitted to Lincoln's Inn, 1604; appointed second Justice of Munster, 1619; wrote his Discourse of Ireland, 1620; a friend of the 'great' Earl of Cork; left Limerick during the rebellion of 1641, having been deprived of his £3,000 estate; received an annual pension from Cromwell, 1653, which was continued by Ormond in the 1660s.

[ix] Robert Payne (fl. 1589): a native of Nottinghamshire and sometime resident of Poynes-End, County Cork; his Brief Description of Ireland, 1589, reported on the state of the country after the suppression of the Desmond rebellion, 1583, with a view to encouraging Englishmen to accept government inducements to settle in Munster.

of treaties as easily with the royal government as with each other. Even from the government's point of view, it amounted to a tentative and formal arrangement, rather than an alteration of practice. Here, as elsewhere, conquest was nominal. This was borne out, at another level, by the way that Gaelic patterns survived within the Pale, in peasant society. Nor can the Pale itself be neatly defined as a separate ethos coinciding with a geographical area; Pale practice, in agriculture and law, can be found outside that eastern strip, in areas like Cavan. In many ways the power of the local overlord, Gaelic or feudal, was a more important determining factor than geographical or ethnic considerations. This, too, signalled the incompleteness of conquest. And by 1600, faced with the most serious resistance yet, the English official mind had come to conceive of the Pale as a moving colonial frontier, which should be pressed outwards.

What remained to be conquered was the social and cultural equivalent of that alien and intriguing landscape: the equally intractable Gaelic way of life. The Elizabethan mind found the native Irish – described as 'mere', in the sense of 'pure' rather than 'inferior' – incomprehensible, and rapidly took refuge in the analysis of barbarism. It is a commonplace that the Romans never colonized Ireland; but the more germane point to make is that while Christianity had affected religion, it had not moulded social structure. Priests in Ireland enjoyed respect and status, but social authority lay in other hands. The Jesuit officers of the European Counter-Reformation, already active in Ireland by 1600, found Gaelic Catholicism in some ways unrecognizable. Society was based on the *tuath*, a tribal or kindred unit of land, not usually more than 300 or 400 square miles. 'Clans' did not exist in the Scots sense of areas homogeneously populated by one family. Identity and coherence were dictated by commitment to the land: some kings ritually 'wedded' their domains, like Venetian doges. Within the *tuath*, chieftain, freemen and serfs sustained a mobile structure of client relationships; these were replicated in the links between chieftains and their overlords.

There were parallels with feudalism (clientage, association for defence), and the system existed quite comfortably alongside feudal practices that came in with conquest. But the great and significant difference, emblematic of all that seemed odd in Irish society, was the contractual and terminable nature of such arrangements. The ultimate nature of authority was essentially temporary; a chieftain had no right of inheritance in his land, which passed by election among his kindred within a four-generation family group. This was the system of 'tanistry' so condemned by English observers. And a client could attach himself for protection, by a money payment, to a chieftain outside his *tuath*: while a chieftain's freedom of action was actually restricted by reliance on levies, as well as dependence on ritual observance (only an O'Cahan, for instance, could inaugurate an O'Neill). Fluidity, in a word, ruled. Land was often repartitioned among the family group: holdings could be fragmented and then reconstructed by purchase, with a complex mortgaging system leading to lengthy lawsuits. Though local autonomies were vital, the main social and institutional features of the Gaelic system were surprisingly consistent over the country as a whole. But 'Gaelicism' itself was a spectrum, not a clear demarcation.

What struck English observers was the fluidity of a structure where the social foundations of authority and even property were redefined in every generation; and they rationalized this as anarchy. In fact, while raiding of rivals was frequent, and violence could erupt at the great gatherings held twice a year to transact business, Gaelic society was well adapted to the mobile Irish way of life and to the powerful Irish sense of family. It was an aristocratic culture, where the lowborn were of little account, and where a chief's authority was sustained by a complex, archaic and variable system of levies and taxation in kind, which presented yet another obstacle to the imposition of English systems. An income was also provided by the chief's demesne, set aside from the family land repartitioned on his death. This practice of corporate and redivisible proprietorship, loosely called 'gavelkind' by the English, was to be outlawed in 1606, along with tanistry. But the attitudes and ethos that it reflected could not be legislated out of existence.

If it was a violent society, the violence was ritualized with a certain sophistication. The *Life of Red Hugh O'Donnell*[x] is a contemporary text that, while written in deliberately archaic language, reflects the contemporary *beau idéal* of Gaelic sovereignty; it thus describes the first year of Red Hugh's kingship in 1592:

He proceeded to govern his principality as was right, preventing theft and evil deeds, banishing rogues and robbers, executing everyone who was plundering

---

[x] Red Hugh O'Donnell (*c.* 1571–1602): born in County Donegal into the increasingly anti-English Tyrconnell family; captured by Perrot and imprisoned in Dublin Castle, 1587; successfully escaped, 1591; inaugurated The O'Donnell, 1592; shared in the Irish victory at Yellow Ford, 1598; defeated Clifford at the Curlews, 1599; yielded to the impetuosity of the Spanish commander Don Juan d'Aquila, which led to the Irish defeat at Kinsale, 1601; sought further aid from Philip III of Spain; received graciously but to no effect; poisoned with the cognizance, if not at the instigation, of Sir George Carew.

and robbing, so that it was not necessary for each one to take care of his herds of cattle but only to bed them down on straw and litter, and the country was without guard or protector, without plundering one by the other, and two enemies slept in the one bed, for fear did not allow them to remember their wrongs against each other. Hugh passed the first year in the very beginning of his sovereignty having large followings, holding meetings, being generous, joyous, roaming, restless, quarrelsome, aggressive, and he was advancing every year in succession till the end of his life came.[3]

Though dues for land were often exacted in the form of military service, the tradition of war as sport went back to the great cattle raids of Gaelic storytelling; and Irish warfare was fairly limited, elitist and restricted. The anarchy that might seem implied by Gaelic social and legal practice was held in check by the power of tradition, respect for the legal classes and the authority of effective overlords. There were also law-enforcement mechanisms of local custom, at least one of which would have a very long-lived resonance indeed. This was the practice of 'fasting upon' an enemy to force him to arbitration – in effect, going on a hunger strike outside his door.

The Elizabethan wars, however, brought a new kind of reality to these archaic ideals. In some ways, Irish forces were well adapted for the new circumstances, being equipped with fast, light horsemen and an unrivalled knowledge of the territory. Nor were they reliant solely on 'barbarous cries' and mutilation of corpses, their frightening stock-in-trade. The professional expertise of the Scots–Irish 'gallowglasses' and the mobile 'kernes' (Spenser's 'rakehelly horseboys') was impress-ive: by 1600 they were already wielding firearms. O'Neill had moder-nized Irish warfare by using the Gaelic practice of military services ('bonnaght') to build up a trained militia. But they could not adapt to campaigns waged by sieges and forts, as 1601 would demonstrate, with the disastrous affair of the Spanish intervention at Kinsale.

IV

Kinsale would turn the tide against the Gaelic revival that seemed to be sweeping back the encroachment of Anglicization in 1600. Caught between the conflicting currents was the element in Irish life most emblematic of the mixed polity and the uncertainty of conquest: those descendants of the first conquerors now known as the Old English, inhabiting mainly the towns and the Pale.[xi] It is significant that in his royal progress of 1600 O'Neill was supported by Desmond, but Ormond remained an officer of the Crown; for at this point the Old English faced both ways. Their position is vital. As descendants of the old colony, differentiated by stock and culture from the Gaelic Irish, they could have occupied the position of an elite group mediating between English monarch and Irish subjects – in which case, differences of language and culture might have counted for less. But their own position was so odd, and their authority so fragmented, that they never achieved this defined status. And at this very point, the hardening and institutionalizing of religious differences compounded their alienation.

To observers like Moryson, the disloyalty of a grandee like Desmond, while scandalous, was inevitable, for it seemed self-evident that the customs of the country had corrupted the old settler stock. They even sent their children out to be fostered with Gaelic families. 'Lord, how quickly doth that country alter men's natures!' wrote Spenser.[4] The Old English were already finding themselves considered 'Irish' in England, to their annoyance. But Irish they were, if not Gaelic. The typical Old Englishry were not great lords with Norman names. They might have been professional gentry families in the Pale, monopolizing legal offices, socially ambitious, sending their sons to the Inns of Court in London. The concept of 'degeneracy' levelled by Spenser and Moryson sits oddly on them, for they were preoccupied by civility and the values of the Pale. When the distinguished English Jesuit Edmund Campion stayed in such a household, he was deeply impressed. Richard Stanihurst,[xii] the son of the house, described his stock as 'Anglo-Hibernici', 'so completely disassociated from the ancient Hibernici that the humblest colonist resident in the English province would not give his daughter in marriage to even the most noble Irish chieftain'. But the records do not bear him out. Beyond

---

[xi] The use of this term may be slightly anachronistic for 1600. A text like *Advertisements for Ireland*, 1623, distinguishes between 'the English–Irish' and 'Irish gentlemen of the English Pale' like the Dillons. 'The English of Irish birth' remained a general term up to this time, 'Old English' occurring as an adjective rather than as a noun. 'Anglo-Irish', often in Latin, also appears. But for clarity's sake, the term 'Old English' will be adopted here from 1600 on.

[xii] Richard Stanihurst (1547–1618): born in Dublin; educated at Oxford; contributed a description of Ireland to Holinshed's *Chronicles*, 1577; translator of Virgil's *Aeneid*, 1582; published *De Rebus in Hibernia Gestis*, 1584, which was condemned as maliciously misrepresenting Irish character, and a life of St Patrick, 1587. Under the influence of Campion, became a Catholic around 1580, but he continued to maintain a friendly correspondence with his nephew, Ussher.

the Pale, Old English families like the Barrys and Roches of Cork had become completely Gaelicized. Religious polarization and relations with the new wave of Tudor settlers would drive the rest unwillingly towards *rapprochement* with the Gaelic Irish in the ensuing period.

Already, in 1600, the Old English were being precipitated into an identity crisis by English policy – which meant the government's ideas of Anglocentricism as much as the aggressive spirit of Protestantism. Between the sixteenth century and the seventeenth, the Old English moved from a position where they lacked any active principle of self-determination, being simply 'the English of Irish birth', to the achievement of a coherence based on the unifying force of religion.[5] The progression was not, however, as simple as it sounds; and it was not clearly recognized at the time. The degrees by which the Old English were differentiated from an 'English' identity were gradual and halting enough for perception of their exclusion to be equally uneven. What finally helped crystallize the process was that in the new reign after 1603, the reins of government were returned to local hands – but offered to Protestants only.

The 'New English', against whom these Old English were uncomfortably defined, were the landowners introduced by the Tudors in a number of ventures at plantation. Plans to install colonists on lands forfeited by the Church or the Fitzgeralds had been mooted from the 1520s. An effort had been made in King's County and Queen's County under Mary; Sidney[xiii] had pioneered a venture in the 1560s; the Ards peninsula in County Down was colonized in the 1570s. Frequent schemes of an authoritarian and centralized nature were circulated throughout the sixteenth century, often with an American connection: the ideal was the transplantation of English ways, across the Irish Sea no less than over the Atlantic. The sixteenth-century settlement initiative in Munster and elsewhere had lasted more tenaciously than contemporaries (and many later historians) allowed. It had been, after all, a large-scale undertaking, involving major population movement and large-scale resources of the state. By 1602 renewal plans were in the air; by 1622 there were probably 12,000 settlers resident in the colonized Munster lands.

[xiii] Henry Sidney (1529–86): lifelong friend and counsellor of Edward VI; knighted, 1550; Vice-Treasurer of Ireland, 1556, Lord Justice in the Deputy's absence, 1558–9, exhibiting great skill in holding Shane O'Neill in check; thrice Lord Deputy of Ireland, 1565–78; his government centred on colonization schemes; lost court favour but was again considered for Ireland, 1582. By far the ablest of Elizabeth's able band of Irish governors.

In general, of course, the great expansion of settler stock came in the seventeenth century. In 1600, less than 2 per cent of the population of Ireland was of Scots or English descent; by the early 1700s the proportion had soared to 27 per cent. Thus the diversification, as well as the growth, of the Irish population after 1600 should be noted. But in 1600 one can discern the existence of a Protestant yeomanry and artisanate, part of the New English settlement, to be found in Wicklow, Wexford and Armagh, as well as Cork and Waterford. It is a component of the Irish population underestimated by the 1660 'poll tax', which went by status and ignored many labourers and small farmers. These Protestant communities declined from the early nineteenth century, but their existence explains much of the dynamics of seventeenth- and eighteenth-century history.

They do not supply the emblematic figures of New English settlement; the personification of the planter is traditionally Richard Boyle, Earl of Cork, exemplar of the New English entrepreneurs arriving at the beginning of our period. Boyle built a great fortune and reared a huge family; based in Cork but influential in London, his own identity became oddly confused. He wanted to have his children 'bred in England and abroad in the world, and not to have their youth infected with the leaven of Ireland';[6] but he became increasingly 'Irish' in his own identification and attitudes, sending out his children to Gaelic families for fostering, though only to those within his patronage system. (Some New English landowners took rapidly to using Irish wet-nurses.) Yet the New English remained apart, and not only for religious reasons; they were preoccupied by their relations with the Crown and with each other, resenting Dublin officials as much as native Irish and Old English, cultivating estates and making money with aggressive energy, and passing on to their children the mingled insecurity and self-congratulation of the parvenu as well as the garrison values of the frontier. Within that planter culture were the seeds of what would later be known as Anglo-Irishness.

CHAPTER ONE

'WILD SHAMROCK MANNERS': IRELAND IN 1600

I

UPON THE INCONSTANT landscape that so preoccupied the Elizabethan observers, these several components – Gaelic Irish, Old English and New English – imposed the forms of their various domestic and economic patterns of life. The ravages of war and the impermanence of native materials like wood, mud, wattle and thatch meant that medievalism in Irish architecture essentially lasted until the mid-seventeenth century. In 1600 the classic large dwellings were still the tall, narrow fortified castles described by Gernon, with a hall upstairs; a large dining room of less substantial materials was sometimes attached at ground level. In some towns, there was stone-building of great substance (Rothe House, still to be seen in Kilkenny, dates from 1594 to 1604). But large houses in the English style were rare; the great Butler house at Carrick (officially dated 1565, though possibly up to forty years later) 'is exactly like hundreds of buildings in Northamptonshire or the Cotswolds, but like no other in Ireland'.[1] And even it, inevitably, is attached to a massive and pre-existing castle. From the 1590s the first Irish country 'houses' begin to evolve, in the form of Rathfarnham Castle, but even these are fortified. From 1600 there is a discernibly Irish style of house, though far less elegant and coherent than it would become. The English or Scotch 'imported' styles to be found in plantation areas are less interesting and lasted less well. The castle would take a hundred years to become the country house; even then, the name of 'castle' would sometimes misleadingly linger on, affording the English some contemptuous amusement at Irish pretensions. But the derivation is often manifestly demonstrated, even today, in the modest eighteenth-century farmhouse grafted on to the shell of a late medieval keep: a palimpsest of conquest.

The dwellings of the native Irish were more transient in their materials; though the wooden hall of a chieftain's fort could be impressive enough, contemporary observers spent more time decrying the mud and wattle cabins of the lower orders. Gaelic architecture, in any case, reflected the loosely knit, mobile structure of pastoral society, with large-scale internal migration for summer pasturage, as well as the extremely low density of population around 1600. Rurally, there were less than twenty inhabitants per square mile. The population has recently been estimated as 1,400,000, but this is probably too high; a figure nearer one million seems more likely. Though it would double over the seventeenth century, the country was at this point devastated by war and famine; County Galway was described in 1600 as 'unpeopled'. This crisis, taken with the mobility of the population, makes estimation extremely difficult. But from 1600 a sustained demographic growth is evident, accelerated first by changes in diet and then by a decline in mortality.

The vast majority of this population was rurally based. Towns were not characteristic of Gaelic lordships, except for episcopal centres and the odd exception of the O'Reillys' settlement at Cavan. Urbanization was to come: of the 117 municipal corporations existing in 1692, 80 were created after 1603, and then more often for political than economic or demographic reasons. Where a borough was created, it could indicate an ambitious landlord, an entrepreneurial colonist or a new industry; or simply the need to pack a parliament. The towns existing in 1600 were often imposed on older foundations or sited at a port or estuary. Franchises and liberties were extensive by English standards. Their freemen tended to be aristocratic merchants rather than craftsmen: Old English burgher families or local gentry who had migrated inside the walls. There were Gaelic merchant families, too: the Ronaynes of Cork or the Kirwans of Galway. But the nature of urbanized society was essentially defined against threats from outside.

Towns were usually protected by a complex system of walls, like Waterford or – to take an example still evident today – Fethard, County Tipperary. Inside, stone and brickwork were on the increase; but thatched buildings were still to be found. Ports had their quays guarded by moles and castles. The gates of Cork were kept on constant guard. The sixteenth-century plantations in Leix and Offaly had produced uneasy settlements called Philipstown and Maryborough, which twentieth-century Gaelicization would render as Daingean and Portlaoise; though intended as market-towns with borough status, in 1600 they were still essentially garrisons.

The towns of more ancient growth were also seen as distinctively 'English' or at least non-Gaelic; but they were also noted for their independence and pretensions, and they exaggerated their 'Englishness' for political effect. In fact, though Moryson assumed they were invariably founded by the English or Normans, they could as easily originate in Viking or monastic settlement. Moryson also suspected townsmen of secretly favouring O'Neill's rebels; but the general English tendency was to equate urbanization with the advance of Anglicization and 'civility'.

This, however, underrated the idiosyncratic and rather embattled nature of most Irish towns, as well as their strong Old English identity. Both characteristics appear striking, even in a cursory survey of Irish towns in 1600. Dublin was still a timber-built city; Gernon described it as an inferior version of Bristol. It had already developed suburbs, though the wealthy lived within the walls; developments like Trinity College had been founded outside the perimeter, to the east. It was the focus of a coastal communications system despite its barred harbour (large ships unloaded at Ringsend). Camden and Stanihurst describe it conventionally as 'royal', strong, well-defended and populous, but its great days were to come. Cork had, then as now, its own jealously guarded identity; a solid, compact town, its inhabitants were noted by Moryson for their inbreeding and by Gernon for their papistry, though it had strong English connections. Dingle, now a beautiful but remote Kerry fishing-village, was of primary importance in 1600, with a merchant population and a municipal organization. It sustained important commercial links with Bristol and Bordeaux. Visitors noted the massively built houses and the splendid main street, with gates at each end to open and close in times of war; traces of both remain.

Waterford, by some reckoning the second city of the realm in 1600, possessed a famous harbour and quay; but a chequered career in the O'Neill wars deprived her of status, and the city charter was to be withheld from 1617 to 1626. Commercially, the town remained Ireland's gateway to Europe; ships of 300 tons rode at the quayside in the city centre. Stanihurst found the people wary, cautious and prosperous. To the west of Waterford, the port of Youghal had been boosted through the activities of the surrounding plantation, but it never achieved great importance. On the other hand, Limerick, on the Shannon estuary, surprised visitors by some grand buildings; from early on it was divided into an 'Irish' and 'English' town, clearly differentiated on maps. Gernon found the unity and spaciousness of its architecture 'like the colleges of Oxford, so magnificent that at my first entrance it did amaze me'.[2] He was less impressed on further acquaintance. Galway was even more important: again, an English identification was traditional, but its identity was more cosmopolitan than any other Irish town, retaining strong links through trade, and even settlement, with Portugal and Andalusia – an influence evident even in the town's buildings. Its great days were essentially in the sixteenth century, when a large-scale commerce in wine conferred prosperity and autonomy; by the early seventeenth century it remained, in Campion's words, 'a proper neat city at seaside', and it still is.

It is no coincidence that all these towns were situated on the coast. Inland there were no important cities, with the resounding exception of Kilkenny: universally praised by visitors as Anglicized, though in Gernon's description it sounds almost Italian, with its marble-fronted buildings and houses supported by pillars and arches that provided a cloistered pavement at ground level. Rich and powerful, Kilkenny was run by a small oligarchy of merchant families. The other obvious exception in this survey of Irish towns in 1600 concerns Ulster; and here, too, the reasons are evident. In that year Moryson described the episcopal centre of Armagh as 'altogether ruinated' by the ravages of the O'Neill wars; while Drogheda was only being developed, due to the recent military offensive into Ulster, and Belfast was as yet of no importance except as a garrison. The shire town was Carrickfergus, and, though it was a vital centre of distribution, its chief importance was also military. For Ulster, urbanization would come with plantation.

With towns widely distributed and strongly differentiated from their surrounding areas, Ireland remained overwhelmingly an agricultural country. The picture of Irish farming round about 1600 is preserved in the fulminations of observers, who described 'primitive' practices like attaching ploughs to horses' tails, drinking blood from living cattle, burning out oats rather than threshing them and living a 'nomadic' life of mobile pasturage. Much of this was inaccurate. Tail-ploughing was used only for reworking land that had already been opened, winnowing out stones; first ploughing was done by the heavy harness plough. Oat-burning had much to be said for it, given Irish conditions; the drinking of cattle's blood, mixed with milk, was a commonplace in pastoral societies (as among the Masai or, as Spenser pointed out, the Scythians). Most importantly, Irish dairying was not 'nomadic'; this is to misinterpret the practice of transhumance, or 'booleying' – the moving of herds to upland pasture in the summer. There, as elsewhere, the proponents of 'civility' saw only what they wanted to see.

They also inveighed against the wetness of Irish pastures, the need for drainage schemes, the diseases bred by marshes. But the mildness of the climate, the fish-filled rivers, the rich pastureland, captured their imaginations; so did the 'gardens full of rosemary, laurel and sweet herbs, which the cold of England often destroyeth'.[3] Though pasturage dominated the agricultural economy, grazing was often integrated with tillage (as on the stubble after harvest); oats, barley and rye were most common, but there were also important grain-growing areas in the south-east. In 1600, however, these were devastated by war: people lived on imported rye and saltfish, while food prices fluctuated wildly. With plantation in the early seventeenth century, orchards spread. Tillage was prominent in the Pale and Leinster; though contemporaries believed the land was not much enclosed, they may have been misled. County Kilkenny, famously Anglicized, was certainly one exception, Leix another. Similarly, Dymmok's statement that manuring was little used should not be taken at face value; it was certainly intensively practised in some areas, and arable land was used as winter pasture, fertilizing it for the spring.

Most criticized of all, however, was the uncertainty of landholding, both inside and outside the Gaelic system, which seemed to English observers to discourage consistent agricultural methods as well. The fourteenth-century Gaelic reconquest had swept away many feudal impositions, and both Gaelic and English systems continued through-out the seventeenth century, often coexisting on the same estate. Gaelic conventions regarding traditional gale-days for the settlement of rent, for instance, eventually took over completely. In Anglo-Norman areas and the Pale, the various medieval forms of tenure were by 1600 replaced by two systems: the leasing of farms on fixed rents, usually for twenty-one years, and the custom of letting land on a sharecropping basis, one-third or one-half, which was in effect an approximation to Gaelic practice. In these areas, there was a general consolidation of ownership, with a predominance of fairly large proprietors, and feudal duties carefully defined in areas like County Carlow. But in Gaelic areas, tillage took the form of small open fields farmed by strips; the size of holdings, and even the denominations of land measurement, varied greatly from area to area. Partible and corporate inheritance complicated matters even further. This fluidity, like the practice of summer 'booleying', disturbed the authorities for reasons that were military and administrative rather than economic.

Cattle, in fact, represented wealth, and were treated accordingly; they were not only used as units of value, but were stolen or mutilated as a demonstration of aggressive intent against enemies or interlopers. In this sense, a link runs from the cattle raids of Gaelic myth down to the 'houghing' in land agitations of the nineteenth and even twentieth century. A powerful chieftain could possess several thousand head. The great mystique of Irish horses was already notable, though they were considered unsuitable for rough work. By 1600 goats were already appearing in large numbers, and pig-keeping was becoming important; though the great expansion in pig-farming was brought about, like so much else, by the introduction of the potato, which revolutionized their feeding.

Patterns of agricultural activity and the prevalence of certain forms of livestock were accurately reflected in the Irish diet, which was based on milk and meat: pork, lean beef and variants of milk-foods, like the soured milk drink 'bonyclabber', blenched at by English travellers. Bread was seasonally absent but not unknown, as some travellers assumed. With their griddle-cakes, mutton, curds and buttermilk, the food of the native Irish in 1600 would have been rather like that in pastoral regions of India today. The dietetic balance was good, and descriptions of the people's physique bear this out: well-shaped, agile, rarely overweight. English observers were surprised that the rich and various resources of fish and wildfowl were not tapped by the natives: fishing, for instance, tended to be monopolized by foreigners. During the Desmond wars, an English soldier found Burrishoole on Clew Bay 'the best fishing place for herring and salmon in Ireland; where a ship of 500 tons could ride close to the shore, and frequented annually by fifty Devonshire fishing smacks, the owners of which paid tribute to the O'Malleys'.[4] Similarly, though surrounded by deer, the Irish were not great eaters of venison, nor great hunters. Although the Normans introduced cereals and pulses, the preference in the Gaelic diet was for raw salads of watercress. Variety was available for those with access to plenty: at Lecale, County Down, in 1620, a group of English officers feasted on brawn with mustard, muscatel wine, stuffed geese, pies of venison and game, tarts of marrow, and plums with 'coagulated milk' (curds or yoghurt?), cheese and sweetmeats, followed by the universally praised Irish whiskey.

Like the local diet, native patterns of life may seem healthier now than they did to those Elizabethan travellers who made it their business to be appalled. As in other peasant communities, life was lived in close proximity to farm animals, who often shared living quarters with their owners. These dwellings were constructed of clay, turf-sod and branches, and were built in a variety of shapes; an elliptical ground-plan, with rounded walls for extra support, was common. Old-style lake-dwellings and fortified enclosures were still to be found in 1600. However, stone-built houses, with lime-washed interior walls, were increasingly adopted: buildings on a more modest scale than the great tower-houses described above. And while fortifications were part of every edifice built to last, their defensive properties were in reality often quite limited; they reflected a subconscious insecurity as much as any more serious intent.

As this picture will indicate, the Irish economy in 1600 was of a fairly primitive nature, geared towards subsistence. Trade was crippled by war and coinage debasement; moreover, the lack of consistent trade figures for the end of the sixteenth century prevents a quantitative assessment of value and volume. Even an impressionistic survey, however, reveals features of interest. There are indications of vitality – commerce would revive with surprising speed – and of a certain degree of internationalism. In 1599 at least one contemporary observer thought Ireland could be a great entrepôt for trade between northern and southern Europe.[5] The wine trade was a vehicle for much activity; vitally important at this time, there was much legislation, and litigation, regarding questions of importation and taxation. War, and the troubled international situation, meant that in 1600 imports from Spain were uncharacteristically low; but Irish buyers were to be found sampling and purchasing vintages in Bordeaux and Andalusia. The wine business was often organized by family networks, with younger sons being planted out abroad. Shipowning was just beginning on a large scale.

Where official calculations of Ireland's commercial potential arose, however, they were usually accompanied by reservations as to whether Irish development might harm English interests. Most of Ireland's trade was, traditionally, the export of agricultural produce to England, and secondarily to Iberia and France. The trade in live cattle across the Irish Sea had commenced, and there was a flourishing, if generally illicit, trade in foodstuffs; Elizabethan restrictions were intended to keep sufficient food in Ireland to feed the army. Corn exports varied with prices in England as well as scarcity at home; in 1600, in any case, wholesale destruction of crops by the army had led to severe scarcity. Fish were another vital export – salmon, herrings and hake, as well as saltfish and oysters – but fisheries were embarking upon a decline in 1600, owing to the migration of shoals to Newfoundland. The other principal export was hides: marten, kid, fox, otter and wolf as well as cattle. Here, too, however, the outlook in 1600 was uncertain; prices had been rising fast, a process that reflected the thinning of the forests that sustained the most valuable wild animals (martens were rare already). For the same reason, the oak-bark necessary for tanning was increasingly difficult to come by. More obviously, the booming export trade in timber, both staves and crude wood, was running down a natural resource faster than it could be replenished.

Textiles were something of a special case. Wool exports, which would become very important, were restricted under an erratic licensing system in the sixteenth century, as was linen yarn. By 1601 the linen cloth-making industry had lapsed almost completely, yarn being the major product. Some made-up woollen cloth was exported: the famous rough friezes and the controversial Irish mantle, which, though seen as tailored for the concealment of iniquity, was evidently in demand in England. But from about 1590 the export of raw wool predominated, while English cloth figured largely in imports, along with wine, salt, iron and manufactured or luxury products. The export of raw materials and the import of manufactured goods would remain characteristic (with the notable exception of glass). Indeed, the exports that were declining in 1600 – hawks, horses, hounds, corn, wolfskins – represented the old Ireland, and those that were rising – timber, glass, tallow, victuals, live cattle – presaged the economic future.

II
===

The political system under which Ireland operated as a Tudor kingdom could appear exiguous, since the country was not a political entity and the extent of conquest itself remained a shifting and uncertain variable – but it was expanding. At the head of the administration was the Lord Deputy, who, according to Moryson, never stayed long enough in the country to do good.

For magistrates often changed like hungry flies suck more blood, and as the devil rageth more because his time is short, so these magistrates, fearing soon to be recalled, are not so much bent to reform the commonwealth, the fruit whereof should be reaped by the successor, as they are vigilant to enrich themselves and their followers. Neither indeed can that crafty and subtle nation be well known to any governor by few years' experience.[6]

The Deputy presided over a Privy Council of the Chancellor and Law Officers, the 'Common Council' formed by the addition of some magnates, and a 'Great Council' that was effectively made up of the same groupings as the parliament but drawn only from the Pale. Following the Geraldine rebellion in the 1530s, Henry VIII's officials had done what they could through the Reformation and Anglicization; but policy had often shifted. Provincial councils and presidencies, while attempted, never really took root; local factions remained dominant, and the ensuing calculations and manipulations may go a long way to explain even such upheavals as the great Desmond rebellion. English governments used local struggles 'to lend a rough and ready stability to Irish politics, somewhat akin to the untidy but relatively efficient two-party system of modern democracies'.[7]

For this reason and others, to contemporary writers it seemed that Ireland was not being governed as a conquered country. The policy of encouraging one chief against another was criticized: thus, it was felt, Hugh O'Neill had been unwisely elevated at the outset of his career. The country, after all, was nominally subject to English law, law officers had been established, parliamentary representation arranged. Since the constitutional redefinitions of the 1540s, Ireland was a 'sovereign kingdom', not a 'lordship'; this, along with the policy of surrender and regrant of Gaelic lands, was intended to impose stability. The act of 1541, whereby the King of England was also to be King of Ireland, was an initiative taken by the Irish Council, not by royal ambition; the hope was that mercurial local alliances would now be directed enduringly towards the Crown and its favours. In fact, by 1600 (and following the experiment of provincial presidencies), local authorities were resurgent; and, though the end of the war would see the resumption of authority by central government, this end-result bore little resemblance to the blue-prints of the constitutional reformers sixty years before.

The position of the Irish parliament reflected these developments. It was not subject to the English Parliament, but had since 1495 been controlled by the Crown under 'Poynings' Law'.[i] By 1600 the Catholic Old English were using it to protect their position against antagonistic Lord Deputies trying to rush through legislation inimical to their interests. In 1541 the Irish parliament had even included a small Gaelic

[i] Introduced by Sir Edward Poynings in December 1494, 'Poynings' Law' prevented the Irish parliament from meeting without royal licence and provided that all parliamentary business must first be approved by the King's Deputy and his Council in Ireland *and* by the King and his Council in England. In the early seventeenth century it was sometimes used by the Anglo-Irish opposition against the executive; by the eighteenth century the 'patriots' were utilizing it as a convenient constitutional grievance.

component; with the spread of the Reformation, the adherence of the Old English to Rome, the key fact of sixteenth-century Irish politics, meant that there was a potential opposition to royal policy within the parliament. After 1613, however, parliament was tightly packed with Protestants, due to the creation of plantation boroughs.

Moreover, in 1600 geographical realities distorted the constitutional picture. Though its bills, legal, administrative, fiscal and private, technically applied to all Ireland, the parliament really affected only the Pale. In 1600 no parliament had been convened for fourteen years, and it would be another thirteen before one was summoned again, though even then, the continuity between the two would be striking. In 1603, however, Sir John Davies[ii] proposed the summoning of a parliament that would show the completion of the English conquest of Ireland and promise a new era of just and orderly rule. Such a step was intended, also, to symbolize the final extirpation of the Gaelic social and political system.

By 1600 the development of local government, too, reflected a falling off from mid-sixteenth-century ambitions. Justices of the Peace had declined into desuetude even by that date; and sheriffs were not very active outside the Pale. The very notion of counties was an alien form of administrative unit, introduced under Anglo–Norman administration. Formally, the shiring of the country was on the edge of completion in 1600; even Ulster had been nominally shired in 1585, and Wicklow, the last region to be thus demarcated, would be shired in 1606. Sometimes a pre-existing territorial unit was used, sometimes not. Either way, the new system became only very slowly operational. The subdivision of counties into baronies and townlands did, on the other hand, follow indigenous boundaries; these could remain disputed and uncertain, even though they became the basis for land grants. Outside the Pale an imperfect perception of Irish geography remained.

The distinction between that uneasy enclave and Ireland beyond similarly held good for matters like finance. Governmental receipts and profits were largely restricted to the Pale; customs and taxation

[ii] John Davies (*c.* 1570–1626): author of writings flattering Elizabeth and James; Irish Solicitor-General, 1603; knighted, 1607; *Discovery of the True Causes Why Ireland was Never Entirely Subdued until the Beginning of His Majesty's Reign*, 1612, promised that Ireland would henceforth be a fruitful Canaan, not a stricken Egypt; Speaker of the Irish parliament of 1615, which repealed the statutes of Kilkenny; *Reports of Cases*, 1615, contains a wealth of Irish legal, historical and antiquarian information; returned to the English Parliament, 1619, and assiduously opposed measures that might have injured Irish trade.

collection were often alienated to local authorities. There were constant
fiscal wrangles between Dublin and London. As for the judiciary,
although judges enforced laws on circuit, it is very doubtful how far
their writ ran outside the counties around Dublin. There, common
law courts were in operation; sheriffs made their 'tourn'; special justices
and commissions were appointed from time to time. Local jurisdictions
could be exercised by 'liberties' and towns; taxation rights might be
assumed by a great lord like Ormond. But the idea that English law
applied to the whole island remained a fiction, formally adhered to by
the government in Dublin.

After 1603 the English system spread more easily, with assizes reaching into the north and west. But the old Gaelic observance of Brehon
law continued to have some influence despite theoretical condemnations. The Court of Chancery had even enforced Brehon judgments
in the sixteenth century; and local custom had been found to have the
force of law. The courts may have occasionally made awards and fines
for homicide, in the Gaelic fashion, even in the early 1600s. Kinship
links made the securing of impartial juries almost impossible. There as
elsewhere, the intractable old identity remained beneath the English
imposition: sometimes working with it, more often counteracting it;
in English eyes, representing an unaccountable adherence to a way of
life that was impractical, outmoded and undesirable.

III

These were the attitudes that presented English observers with a constant conundrum. How could the Irish be both savage and subtle? Both
warlike and lazy? At once evidently 'inferior', yet possessed of an
ungovernable pride? Cowardly, yet of legendary fortitude in the face
of death? Socially primitive, but capable of complex litigation? To
Moryson, even the names they held 'rather seemed the names of
devouring giants than Christian subjects'. They were dirty, lazy, dis-
honest and violent. Their laws were unethical and inequitable. Yet
these 'corrupt customs' had invariably fascinated and drawn in the
English who settled in Ireland, 'degenerating' them. For this reason,
the forms of Irish social and legal life were the subject of much adverse
commentary.

Gaelic society revolved around the laws of the *tuath* – a commitment
to extended family groupings that carried great emotional charge.

Thus, though the Irish practice of fostering out their children into other families had parallels in contemporary England, what struck observers was the exceptional depth of the bond created: foster-brothers owed each other a deeper commitment than natural siblings. The family could thus be extended in deliberate directions: another mechanism to this end was the custom of 'naming' fathers, whereby a woman might claim paternity, often noble, for her child at any stage of his minority, binding him to a father he had not previously known. The convention of tanistry, the election of leaders, might be interpreted in this context, too, with the organization of the family group strengthening itself through redefinition in every generation.

This symbolized the flexibility that was so characteristic of Gaelic institutions. Tenancies at will, chiefs living by levies and impositions, mobile pasture-farming, were all instanced by English observers as conducive to lawlessness. Partible inheritance, even subdividing and reapportioning the family castle from generation to generation, was equally shocking. In fact, from 1585, with the Composition of Connacht,[iii] Irish lords at all levels were building up personal estates on the English pattern; and poor farmers were declining from joint owners into tenants. By 1600 English observers were probably exaggerating the lack of fixed tenancies. In any case, where wealth was itself mobile, in the form of cattle, rather than stable, in the form of land, such arrangements often benefited the tenant. But in English eyes the whole system looked like a celebration of anarchy.

The same description would fit the English perception of the Irish legal system, the Brehon laws. These were practised by a hereditary caste of jurists, a concept that infuriated professionally minded English observers. With their archaic divinations of pragmatic principles and their complex system of fines, the Brehon laws imposed a powerful obstacle to the spread of English law; they sustained an underground existence even in post-Elizabethan times and represented an intuitive, archaic and subtle pattern of life.

To some observers, the foreign nature of this society was appealing, with its wild, often beautiful scenery and a style of life both convivial and bizarre. The harpists, storytellers, even the professional gamblers, imparted an exotic flavour to travels in Gaelic lands. The English

[iii] A negotiated settlement between the government and the Connacht lords in 1585, whereby the latter agreed to replace the previous haphazard cess by specific charges and rents to the Crown based upon an accurately assessed survey of their land, and to abolish Irish jurisdictions and the landholding practices that they entailed.

soldiers, whose feasting at Lecale has been described, were visited by 'maskers of the Irish gentry' who borrowed the style of roving gambling entertainers.

They entered in this order: first a boy, with lighted torch; then two beating drums; then the maskers, two and two; then another torch. One of the maskers carried a dirty pocket-handkerchief with ten pounds in it, not of bullion but of the new money lately coined, which has the harp on one side and the royal arms on the other. They were dressed in shirts with many ivy leaves sewn on here and there over them, and had over their faces masks of dog-skin with holes to see out of, and noses made of paper; their caps were high and peaked (in the Persian fashion) and were also of paper, and ornamented with the same leaves.[8]

Exoticism manifested itself in long hair, curious jewellery and flowing clothes. Fashions varied throughout the country, especially in headgear: beaver hats with velvet and lace in prosperous Kilkenny, furred caps in Waterford. However, by 1620, according to Gernon, the 'better sort' were dressed like the English, except for the notorious mantle, that convenient symbol of duplicity, beneath whose folds anything could be concealed. Gernon similarly saw Irish trews and the uncorseted dress of the women as a deliberate flaunting of sexual temptations.

Such judgements, especially regarding the behaviour of women, were affected by English reactions to the fact that Irish women drank alcohol, presided at feasts and – to English discomfiture – greeted strangers with a social kiss. They could also keep their own names after marriage, and divorce was easy under Brehon law, with damages materialistically reckoned. The prevalence of probationary marriage and voluntary affiliation ('naming' a father) also conditioned English impressions; marriage and kinship were not what they were in England (judging by twentieth-century survivals in Donegal and Tory Island, a wife sometimes continued to live in her natal home). There was no taboo on sexual relations within degrees of affinity that would have been frowned upon by English law (or Roman Catholic practice: Jesuits in Ireland found themselves issuing many dispensations on this score). All agreed that, though Irish children were brought up without discipline, Irish women were authoritative within the home, and often outside it; but though some believed that sexual licence was common among married women, which surprised one observer 'on account of the climate', others, like Gernon, found Irish women unreserved but chaste. By and large, observers emphasized national characteristics of sensuality and vehemence.

These qualities were celebrated by the great tradition of Irish bardic culture: the poets sang of heroes and love, which to the English looked like glorifying robbery and licentiousness. Culture seemed to work against civility, wrote Moryson: 'Alas! how unlike unto Orpheus, who, with his sweet harp and wholesome precepts of poetry, laboured to reduce the rude and barbarous people from living in woods to dwell civilly in towns and cities, and from wild riot to moral conversation!'[9] The perverseness of bardic influence was all the more infuriating to the English because of the extent of their social power. A thirteenth-century poet remarked that immortality was conferred by poets rather than by gods, and this attitude remained. The practice of poetry provided a more everyday power, too, as borne out by an incident of 1599 matter of factly described in the contemporary *Life of Red Hugh O'Donnell*. O'Donnell's army, travelling through Thomond, takes some cattle from the land of the poet Maoilín Óg, as from everybody else through whose lands they passed. The poet comes to O'Donnell, 'displays his knowledge and talent in the presence of the prince', and recites him a poem: 'recompense for his cattle and flocks was given to the poet with an increase and he took leave of O'Donnell and left him his blessing'.

Like Brehons, and even doctors, the craft of poetry was hereditary; the presentation of the poetry was archaic and formal, though it retained a devastating directness of expression. By 1600 the poets were capable of attaching themselves to Old English patrons; some of the poetry of this period is even composed by Old English poets. They could be hired to write *against* the native Irish, and some were cynically prepared to do so. This was a real power: if O'Donnell had not restored Maoilín Óg's cattle to him, and had not left with his blessing, the alternative would have been very serious indeed. A bardic attack was not so much a satire as a curse in verse; so much feared were the poets that some Elizabethan observers thought they were possessed of occult powers.

By 1600 bardic poetry was lamenting the passing of the old Gaelic order; but even among the Munster poets, the themes are dispossession and insecurity rather than oppression. The politicization of Irish poetry came later, and remained a debatable subject; literary convention and political necessity combine to make the evidence of the poetry very equivocal indeed. But its vividness remains undimmed, and so does its power for contemporaries.

Exotic social behaviour, bizarre familial customs, the magical power of poetry – all predisposed the English to view the Irish as pagan; and the state of the Church in Ireland seemed to bear them out. Catholicism had been adhered to, and Protestantism not much noticed; time and again Moryson and others reiterated that Irish Catholics were 'taught it is no sin to break faith with us', a belief that would endure among Irish Protestants. The Irish traditions of asceticism, monasticism and popular respect for the clergy were well-adapted to maintaining the old faith – the laxity of local priests notwithstanding. Church lands were part of the archaic structure of landholding, devolving upon episcopal tenants with powerful local families, the much-discussed 'coarbs' and 'erenachs'. Moreover, under the Tudors the Reformed Church was inseparably connected with the Anglicizing process. Protestantism never really took root; though in making the point, it should not be forgotten how cautious and uneven the dissemination of the Reformation was, even in England. Ireland could in some ways be seen simply as an extreme case.

By 1605 all dioceses would have royally appointed bishops, though the last bishop recognized by Pope *and* Crown died only in 1603. In 1604 Davies wrote:

The churches are ruined and fallen down to the ground in all parts of the Kingdom. There is no divine service, no christening of children, no receiving of the sacrament, no Christian meeting or assembly, no, not once a year; in a word, no more demonstration of religion than among Tartars or cannibals.[10]

Davies had an axe to grind. But clerical abuses remained a commonplace, or so it was supposed, and religious practice only tentatively followed Anglican communion rather than Catholic mass. Ireland was, in fact, just about to become a battleground of the Counter-Reformation.

The 'holy war' for Pope against heretic had been proclaimed by James Fitzmaurice Fitzgerald[iv] twenty years before, in the Desmond rebellion, but this was not typical. Though there had been a tradition within the Irish Church of 'Rome-running' with complaints against the English, this was not as yet fused with a political identity or a sense of Irishness. In 1596 the Ulster chiefs did ask for 'liberty of conscience or at least immunity from harassment for their clergy'; but this was not an inseparable part of the package, and in any case the Pope

---

[iv] James Fitzmaurice Fitzgerald (*c.* 1530–79): cousin of the fifteenth Earl of Desmond; fought on the Continent before returning to rally the Irish to oppose the Elizabethan settlers in Munster, 1570; unsuccessfully sought assistance for the Irish cause at the French and Spanish courts but favourably received at Rome, 1578; led the small invasion force that landed at Dingle, July 1579; killed in a private skirmish with his cousin, Theobald Burke, on his way to rally disaffection in the north.

withheld support from O'Neill. It was generally accepted that the Gaelic identity went with a lax and archaic Catholicism. But the central fact of Anglo-Irish politics was evident by 1600: the Old English were obviously going to adhere to Roman Catholicism.

Religion would thus become one conduit of anti-English feeling, and eventually of national identity. The Irish language was in a similar position. Moryson found an antipathy among the Irish to speaking English, even when they could: at an earlier stage of rebellion, Shane O'Neill[v] was too proud 'to writhe his mouth in clattering English'. It could be an index of loyalty; O'Donnell, invading Connacht in 1595, 'spared no male between fifteen and sixty years old who was unable to speak Irish'. To speak the language was seen early on as an anti-English identification, though Spenser, Campion and others were intellectually interested in it. Like long hair, the bestowal of Gaelic names was taken as the deliberate articulation of a refusal to conform.

In any case, the spread of the English language was uneven. English was the language generally spoken in Leinster by 1600, but legislation shows an ever-present fear of Irish swamping it. The parliament of 1613–15 contained some members who could speak no English. The evidence for this time shows the two languages interpenetrating each other; the metamorphosis of Irish names and place-names in the early seventeenth century arose from the varying stabs at transposing them into English legal documents (within Irish orthography, spelling was regular and consistent). In 1610 Richard Boyle's small son Roger interpreted Irish for him. Trinity College, whose ethos was characterized by Anglicization and Elizabethan puritanism, allowed for speaking and teaching in Irish. But, by and large, the Gaelic tongue was associated with Gaelic resistance and eventually with Catholicism as well – a process instituted by the officers of the Counter-Reformation in Ireland, who deliberately used demotic Irish rather than the classical bardic language.

This process raises the important issue of Irish education. Lay schools had opened after the dissolution of the monasteries; grammar schools

[v] Shane O'Neill (c. 1530–67), rightly called 'The Proud': son of Con, first Earl of Tyrone; elected The O'Neill, 1559, with Elizabeth's authorization; revoked, 1560; summoned to London to submit, 1562, he persuaded the Queen to accept his rights and titles; destroyed the Scottish settlements of the MacDonnells in Antrim, taking Sorley Boy prisoner, 1564–5; invaded the Pale and burned Armagh, 1566; defeated by Hugh Dubh O'Donnell at Lough Swilly, 1567; sought refuge in Cushendun with the MacDonnells; they murdered him. The antithesis of Hugh O'Neill, having no English qualities, not even the language.

and a university were set up by 1600. But the religious divide characterized all educational developments; Trinity College was, as has been said, essentially a Reformation institution with a puritan complexion, anti-Catholic and anti-Gaelic. The Gaelic identity held to its old modes of clerical learning. Moryson remarked in an aside: 'I have seen the chief of a sept ride, with a gentleman of his own name (and so learned he spoke Latin) running barefooted by his stirrup'. What struck him was the indignity borne by the 'gentleman'; but bare feet mattered less in Ireland, and it seems more noteworthy to us that he spoke Latin. John Harrington[vi] provides a more celebrated vignette: the idyllic picture of Hugh O'Neill entertaining at a 'fern table and fern forms, spread under the stately canopy of heaven', discussing Ariosto with his guest, his little sons and their tutor. Stanihurst shows us Irish students sprawled out on straw, learning 'to speak Latin like a vulgar language, learned in their common schools of leechcraft and law'. In a more Anglicized mode, Payne visited a grammar school in Limerick where he saw 'one hundred and threescore scholars, most of them speaking good and perfect English, for that they have used to construe the Latin into English.'

In Gaelic Ireland two syndromes were established by 1600 that would last: the practice of studying for the priesthood abroad (notably in Salamanca), and the prevalence of peripatetic Catholic primary schoolmasters. 'Alternative' educational processes helped reinforce alternative patterns of thought, and drove the wedge between English and Irish perceptions even deeper. Language was a vehicle for this: exaggerations, strange uses of words, deliberate pleasure in paradox, were noted with irritation by Moryson and others – the Irish use of the word 'murdered' to signify 'injured', for instance. A failure of communication established itself early on; that awkward English–Irish interaction that the novelist Elizabeth Bowen would describe as 'a mixture of showing-off and suspicion, worse than sex'. Not only were concepts of society different; the Irish affected to dwell in a different abstract world as well. Moryson thought they mixed superstition with Christian rituals and believed in werewolves. Speed's map of 1610 repeated from Giraldus Cambrensis details such as the existence in

[vi] John Harrington (1561–1612): twice dismissed from court under charge to grow more sober; translator of Ariosto's *Orlando Furioso*, 1591; knighted by Essex during his Irish expedition, before presenting the Queen with a chronicle of his patron's time-wasting; sought Irish employment again, under James, enclosing with his application a view of the state of Ireland in 1605 that counselled a conciliatory policy towards the natives. Said of Ireland: 'I think my very genius doth in a sort lead me to that country.'

Ireland of 'islands some full of angels, some full of devils'. And above all, the natives were calculating and plausible. Gernon found them 'servile, crafty and inquisitive after news, the symptoms of a conquered nation', and Moryson recorded that Mountjoy kept an Irish fool, but 'we found him to have craft of humouring every man to attain his own ends, and to have nothing of a natural fool'.

The Tudor state, preoccupied by the priority of uniformity, could not stomach this complex, intuitive and protean way of life. Though it was certainly archaic and inadequate in many ways, judged as an effective form of social organization, it also had qualities of dynamism and sophistication that might have made it capable of adaptation. But by 1600 the gulf was too wide for that.

The strength of the English reaction against Ireland's lack of 'civility' stemmed partly from Protestantism, partly from English nationalism, and partly from the spice of attraction mixed with the repulsion roused by what John Derricke[vii] called 'their wild shamrock manners'. Irish *mores* could be useful to the conquest, as in the easy alliance of chiefs against each other: the English ambition was, after all, to create a stable landowning aristocracy as well as English law and a docile Church. But more potent was, first, the dangerous fascination that 'wild shamrock manners' had for those who had settled in the country; and second, the fact that the picture of Irish habits observed by English visitors coincided with contemporary anthropological ideas of savagery.

Thus Gaelic society was measured against a 'standard of outlandish reference', providing an index of comparison for observation of American Indians and Africans on the Gambia River. The English saw the world of cattle-raids, Brehons and poets as arrogantly archaic and deliberately mystifying: a world at once bogus and perverse, which could only be civilized by means of plantation. Moryson, Spenser and Camden tried to find classical and barbarian parallels for the Irish, the Scythians being a particular favourite, but comparisons were usually less dignified. Moryson compared staying with the Irish to venturing into a wild beast's cave, where any other animal 'might perhaps find meat, but not without danger to be ill entertained, perhaps devoured of his insatiable host'.

[vii] John Derricke (*fl.* 1578): perhaps employed making the Great Seal of Ireland, 1557. His *Image of Irelande*, 1581, is divided into allegorical and historical sections; dedicated to Sir Philip Sidney, its hero is Sir Henry, his father. In his prefatory epistle, Derricke urges his readers to understand that his unflattering but veracious pictures of the native Irish (woodkerne) should not be allowed to reflect adversely on the Irish nobility and gentry who remain loyal to the Queen.

Moryson, however, like so many others, was generalizing from the experience of O'Neill's Ulster in the final stages of a devastating war. Others, like Harrington and Payne, were obviously attracted to the strange country in which they found themselves. There was an heroic, bizarre, seductive and oddly subtle twist to Irish life, echoed, some thought, in the natives' misplaced admiration for sophistry. For some, as David Quinn has shown, there was a brief glimpse of Arcadia. For all his criticism, Spenser saw it thus:

And sure it is yet a most beautiful and sweet country as any is under heaven, seamed throughout with many goodly rivers replenished with all sorts of fish most abundantly, sprinkled with many very sweet islands and goodly lakes like little inland seas, that will carry even ships upon their waters, adorned with goodly woods fit for building of houses and ships so commodiously, as that if some princes in the world had them, they would soon hope to be lords of all the seas, and ere long of all the world also full of very good ports and havens opening upon England and Scotland, as inviting us to come unto them, to see what excellent commodities that country can afford, besides the soil itself most fertile, fit to yield all kind of fruit that shall be committed thereinto; and lastly, the heavens most mild and temperate, though somewhat more moist than the parts towards the west.[11]

It was felt by many that country and people were attractive enough for 'civility' to become established. Stanihurst, anti-Gaelic in 1577 ('Description' in Holinshed's *Chronicles*), had changed his views by 1584 (*De Rebus in Hibernia Gestis*): by then, he wanted to clear up erroneous ideas 'that the Irish have cast off all humanity, that they wander scattered and dispersed through very dense woods, and generally that they live unrestrainedly in a rough and uncivilized fashion'. This conversion was an extreme development of Old English alienation; he would eventually become an adherent of Hugh O'Neill. In a less committed mould, however, there was still at the end of the sixteenth century a strain in Tudor official thought regarding Ireland that was moderate, if assimilationist. But those on the ground – Humphrey Gilbert,[viii] the legendary Lord Grey de Wilton,[ix] even Sir

[viii] Humphrey Gilbert (*c.* 1539–83): served under Sir Henry Sidney in Ireland, 1566–7, assisting in an unsuccessful attempt to establish an English colony in Ulster; charged to complete the ruthless pacification of Munster, 1569; knighted, 1570; served under Perrot in Ireland, 1579.

[ix] Arthur Grey (1536–93): succeeded as fourteenth Baron Grey de Wilton, 1562; considered for the position of Irish Lord Deputy, 1571, but spared 'that unlucky place' until 1580; on arrival, chased James Eustace's rebels into the Wicklow mountains against the advice of those experienced in Irish warfare; disastrously defeated and

John Perrot[x] – implicitly argued for extirpating the unstable elements in Irish society. This is reflected in the nature of Elizabethan warfare, which took a horrific toll of civilians in order to deprive the Irish of food, succour and recruits. The scorched-earth policy in Munster after the Desmond wars called forth Spenser's famous and chilling description of the rebel remnant: 'out of every corner of the woods and glens they came, creeping forth upon their hands, for their legs would not bear them. They looked like anatomies of death; they spake like ghosts crying out of their graves.' The description, it should be noted, is given in praise of the effectiveness of Spenser's preferred form of warfare.

Though scorched earth had been advocated since the 1530s, massacres like those perpetuated by Grey and the elder Essex[xi] were probably an innovation; Grey was censured by contemporaries for his brutality. Irish life was, none the less, seen by many of the 'civilizers' as of little account. Mountjoy, a humane man, devastated Ulster in 1601; the ensuing descriptions of starvation and cannibalism made unbearable reading even then. The strategy was spoliation: 'when plough and breeding of cattle shall cease, then will the rebellion end'.

Possibly these tactics were encouraged by the fact that the Munster economy had recovered with remarkable speed after similar devastation in the 1580s. But a stronger reason lies in the fact that rationalizations of the Irish as a population of beasts and vermin appear in the literature from the end of the sixteenth century – feelings that escalated after the attempted Spanish invasion in 1601. The official

forced back to Dublin; massacred the garrison at Smerwick, 1580; repeatedly requested to be recalled; plea granted, 1582.

[x] Sir John Perrot (1527–92): reluctantly became the first President of Munster, 1571; his troops' mutiny prevented the annihilation of Fitzgerald months before his submission, 1573; Elizabeth commissioned his plan for the government of Ireland, 1581; appointed Lord Deputy of Ireland, 1584; sought to govern Ulster with a strong garrison while encouraging the plantation of Munster; seized hostages from the Irish chiefs to ensure their loyalty; unsuccessful attempts to suspend Poynings' Law and establish an Irish College, 1585, involved him in quarrels with Archbishop Loftus and the English party in Ireland; contrived reports of disloyalty led to his recall, 1588; convicted of treason, 1592, he died before sentence was executed.

[xi] Walter Devereux (1541–76): created Earl of Essex, 1572; volunteered to undertake the colonization of 'wild' Ulster, 1573; his methods, treachery and slaughter; appointed Earl Marshal of Ireland, 1575; months later the vacillating Queen declared the Ulster scheme moribund; his evacuation was accompanied by the massacre at Rathlin Island; reappointed Earl Marshal, 1576, but immediately contracted the dysentery that caused his death. In his will he left money for the fortification of the Pale. His sanguinary Irish policy was not unique, but none of his contemporaries practised it so wantonly.

view continued to stress that it was not a war of 'conquest'; the country was already loyal; a few 'unnatural and barbarous rebels' needed to be 'rooted out'. Yet theoretical suggestions were being made in 1599 for transferring the Irish population *as a whole*, to provide a helot class in England; and when Mountjoy was appointed in 1600, his plan was to make Ireland 'a razed table' upon which the Elizabethan state could transcribe a neat pattern.

By now, anti-Catholicism was strongly reinforcing the 'civilizing' ethos: the Irish were pagan as well as savage. It should be remembered that even after 1603, the great bulk of the land would still be in the hands of Catholic owners; sovereignty, not expropriation, was still the keynote of official policy. The next forty years would see a reversal of ownership, while occupancy remained comparatively stable: an ironic repetition of Gaelic patterns, whereby 'theoretical ownership and actual possession' might only rarely be the same thing.

In 1600 this process was not yet happening. But the concept of the Irish as savages to be civilized or extirpated had in some quarters taken root, and the grisly sportiveness of Essex's massacre on Rathlin Island bears this out. Moryson produced an argument, in rather defensive terms, that blamed Irish ills on Gaelic perverseness. 'They abhor from all things that agree with English civility. Would any man judge these to be born of English parents, or will any man blame us for not esteeming or employing them as English who scorn to be so reputed?'[12] But the results of such an approach troubled even Froude, most bloodthirsty of Victorian historians. Nor were all Moryson's contemporaries so sure. Francis Bacon, for one, was advising, even in 1602, that the Irish be treated evenhandedly and impartially, 'as if they were one nation' with England. This would remain the panacea of reforming unionists throughout the history of the troubled connection. But it begged the question of different kinds of Irishness, and of the enduring and influential nature of Irish difference. For Ireland, like Marco Polo's China, would prove time and again 'a sea that salts all rivers that run into it'.

CHAPTER TWO

'NATIONALISM' AND RECUSANCY

I

A NARRATIVE OF Irish history beginning in 1600 would encounter almost at once a classic Irish defeat, for the last of Elizabeth's Irish wars involved the subduing of Hugh O'Neill's great rebellion, a process that began with the battle of Kinsale. In fact, the most striking thing about the Irish resistance after the high point of 1600 was how quickly it collapsed. Two conclusions can be drawn: first, that the flinty strategist Mountjoy and his aide Carew[i] exposed how superficial the 'modernization' of O'Neill's army was. An encounter like Mountjoy's attempt to force his way into Ulster by the Moyry Pass demonstrated the Irish talent for ambuscade and brilliant skirmishing. But the confused events at the little port of Kinsale, County Cork, in December 1601, showed that once O'Neill was put in the offensive position, the unwieldy Spanish-inspired formations adopted by his infantry were unable to cope with frontal assault.

The second lesson to be drawn from Mountjoy's success is that O'Neill's strength was essentially based in Ulster. Munster had been quickly reduced by Carew and even by his predecessor, the younger Essex,[ii] despite the latter's fate at the hands of historians as well as of

---

[i] George Carew (1555–1629): left Oxford for the Irish army, 1574; chosen to describe the difficulties of Irish government to the Queen, 1587; Master of the Irish Ordnance, 1588–92; as President of Munster, 1600, lent the greatest support to Mountjoy in the suppression of Tyrone's revolt; reported on the possibility of resettling Ulster, 1609–10, and reform of the Irish army and revenue, 1611; tirelessly collated the massive collection of his Irish papers, which inspired Stafford's *Pacata Hibernia*, 1632.

[ii] Robert Devereux (1566–1601): became second Earl of Essex, 1576; never a statesman, but the supreme Elizabethan courtier and soldier; reached his apotheosis as the hero of Cadiz, 1596; fell swiftly from royal favour thereafter; sent to Ireland as Lord Lieutenant, April 1599; returned to England, having contravened all the Queen's

Elizabeth: this was what had prompted O'Neill's royal progress south in 1600. And from an early point, O'Neill showed himself ready to withdraw and negotiate, having been weakened by splits within the O'Donnell interest, as well as by Mountjoy's success in forcing the submission of chiefs in Wicklow and Monaghan by early 1601.

Finally, the fiasco at Kinsale is significant both because it involved a Spanish invading force, which impressively demonstrated Ireland's occasional importance in Continental strategies; and because the inadequate number of soldiers, their misconceptions of where they should land,[iii] and their speedy capitulation equally indicate the limitations of Spanish commitment. At most a destabilizing tactic in 'England's Netherlands', the invasion was as much a matter of diplomatic pressure as anything else. Though the sight of Spanish soldiers in Cork fulfilled the long-held fears of commentators like Payne and Moryson, and the Ulster lords were known to have offered 'the crown of Ireland' to Philip of Spain in 1595, it was not clear in the Irish context what kind of authority this actually meant. The Spanish were more preoccupied by diplomatic calculations than by demonstrating Catholic solidarity, much less liberating Ireland from English control.

What happened at Kinsale generated its own historiography, both contemporary and subsequent. This is partly because the Irish seemed to throw away their advantage: when O'Neill and O'Donnell eventually travelled south, the glamorous Red Hugh by a famous forced march over ice-bound mountains, Spanish reinforcements were arriving at nearby Castlehaven, and the government forces were being depleted by sickness and desertion. Lack of co-ordination, arguments over precedence and the pusillanimity of the Spanish within the town of Kinsale have all been instanced as reasons for failure. But the more significant lesson to be drawn is the inadequacy of Irish troops for the unprecedented logistics of the situation: Mountjoy's speedy cavalry

orders, five months later; his attempts to justify his actions remaining unheeded, a sense of frustration led him to plot the overthrow of Elizabeth's leading counsellors; this being discovered, he was arrested, sentenced and executed. His downfall can be traced directly to his unsanctioned conferences with O'Neill in Ireland, September 1599.

[iii] Limerick, Galway or even Donegal would by this stage have been safer; the arguments in favour of Munster held good only if the invading force was large enough to operate independently. The Spanish leader had argued for Donegal, but been overridden. The theory was that a large Munster force would distract the Lord Deputy, while a small Donegal invasion would merely bolster up O'Neill in his stronghold.

seized the initiative in the early hours of Christmas Day 1601.[iv] The town surrendered nine days later: the desired peace between England and Spain subsequently followed.

Thus the victory had an important European dimension in terms of Anglo–Spanish relations. But its local importance was utterly decisive. The events at that obscure Cork fishing-town have been interpreted and reinterpreted; various forms of perfidy have been alleged, and classic Irish weaknesses agonizingly rehearsed. The early seventeenth-century historian Geoffrey Keating[v] concluded: 'It was the fault of the Irish themselves – wrangling over petty, worthless claims – which destroyed them at one stroke, and not the armed might of the foreigners.' And for once the affected and archaic language of O'Donnell's biographer, Lughaidh Ó Clérigh, found its appropriate pitch.

Though there fell in that defeat at Kinsale so few of the Irish that they would not miss them after a while, and indeed did not miss even then, yet there was not lost in any defeat in recent times in Ireland so much as was lost there. There was lost there to begin with the one island which was most productive and fruitful, most temperate in heat and cold in the greater part of Europe, in which there was much honey and wheat, with many fish – abounding rivers, waterfalls and estuaries, in which were calm, profitable harbours ... There were lost there all who escaped of the noble freeborn sons of Míl, valiant, impetuous chiefs, lords of territories and tribes, chieftains of districts and cantreds; for it is full certain that there will never be in Erin at any time together people better or more famous than the nobles who were there, and who died afterwards in other countries one after another, after being robbed of their patrimony and of their noble land which they left to their enemies in that defeat. There were lost besides nobility and honour, generosity and great deeds, hospitality and kindliness, courtesy and noble birth, culture and activity, strength and courage, valour and steadfastness, the authority and sovereignty of the Gaels of Ireland to the end of time.

Was this so? Kinsale symbolizes the defeat of an order. But much of this is the purely conventionalized lament of the early seventeenth century; and the process of Gaelic decline cannot be personalized or specified so restrictively. It can as easily be claimed that the Gaelic

[iv] Reckoned by the old-style calendar, which was observed by the English. The Gaelic Irish followed the new Gregorian calendar to demonstrate their independence of English authority and their adherence to Catholic orthodoxy.

[v] Geoffrey Keating [Seathrún Céitinn] (c. 1570–1644): born into an affluent Old English family in County Tipperary; educated in Bordeaux; returned to Ireland as curate of his native parish, 1610; his sermons enlivened by historical fable brought him widespread fame but also the attention of the government; retiring to the glens of Aherlow, he completed *Foras Feasa ar Éirinn*, the first narrative history of Ireland in Irish and the last important work to circulate the country in manuscript form.

world was already doomed, if only through its infiltration by the modernizing influences of the Counter-Reformation, and that O'Neill only championed 'the Gael' when it suited him. Soon after Kinsale he was suing for a pardon, but he found himself unable to agree to the shiring of 'his country', by which he meant Ulster, not Ireland. Red Hugh departed for Spain, and into legend. Mountjoy attacked Ulster with sea-power, interlinked garrisons and economic warfare. But the end of the campaign was accomplished as much by famine as anything else: horrific tales of cannibalism are recorded by more than one contemporary. As Carew ravaged the wilder shores of Kerry, O'Neill withdrew into his farthest recesses; Mountjoy ceremonially broke the crowning-stone of the O'Neills, and Gaelic Ireland's last resistance sputtered out with the end of Elizabeth's reign.

Here again, however, a curious talent for survival came into play. When O'Neill made his formal submission to King James by the Treaty of Mellifont in 1603, he was treated by the new court with extraordinary respect, for a 'rebel'. He retained absolute rights over his lordship and chief dependants, which contradicted the expressed Crown policy that all authority was vested in the King, not overlords. The arrangement was a hasty one, precipitated by the Queen's death, which was known to Mountjoy but concealed from O'Neill. Traditionally, this has been supposed a disadvantage to the latter, who could have hoped for a new deal under King James. But it seems to have disadvantaged Mountjoy, in that it propelled him into agreement; and O'Neill stood his ground on the vital issue of the area to be left under his jurisdiction. He also struck up an unlikely alliance with Mountjoy himself, under whose protection O'Neill travelled to London. When Mountjoy retired to England, he remained a chief advisor on Ireland, and a defender of O'Neill's status in Ulster. His own reputation, after all, stood on the settlement achieved at Mellifont. Mountjoy's death in 1606, in fact, helped precipitate O'Neill's final eclipse, but up to then one can only share the amazement of contemporaries at how reasonably the rebel earl was treated. And this casts some doubts on the apocalyptic interpretation of the events at Kinsale.

II

What is important, however, is the sense of defeat, the psychological trauma, that affected Ireland at large, if not O'Neill in particular. The defeat of O'Neillism gave rise, not only to laments like Keating's and Ó Clérigh's, but also to endless analyses of what had motivated both sides, and where the battle had really been lost and won.[vi] A vitally important part of this process concerns the evaluation of religious inspiration. How decisive had adherence to Catholicism been? O'Neill had preached its importance on his royal progress; his letters to recalcitrants like Barry of Cork played the card of Catholic solidarity. The Spaniards had heavily emphasized it in public pronouncements. The catalogue of Continental seminaries with a strong Irish identification must be remembered here, Salamanca, Alcalá, Douai, Louvain, Paris, as well as the Franciscan friaries of St Anthony's, Louvain, and St Isidore's, Rome. Between such centres and the strongholds of Gaelic Ireland a network of Catholic publicists plied to and fro; emigrant Irish culture was preoccupied by the necessity to renew Catholicism in Ireland. This was also true of exiled Irish lords and their retinues, turning up as clients at Habsburg courts. Most of all, the growing commitment of exiled scholars in Catholic intellectual centres to the memorializing of Irish history established an early connection between Catholic zeal and Gaelic identity that would be seen, at least in retrospect, as 'nationalist'.

But a commitment to Catholic renewal very often meant explicitly criticizing the nature of Gaelic Catholicism; and Old English controversialists argued for the viability of a position that could be both Catholic and loyalist. Moreover, Pope Clement VIII, though his Bull of Indulgence in April 1600 gave O'Neill's followers plenary pardon as for a crusade, was extremely ambivalent about endorsing the Ulster cause – for fear that it could endanger the recusant position, as much as because of the need to procure an open door in relations with England. The entire question of Catholic identification on the part of the Irish needs to be considered in this light.

For reasons that were often disingenuous, government opinion preferred to see things in starker terms. The Queen's Irish Council in 1597, for instance, made its feelings clear.

The rebels stand not as heretofore upon terms of oppression and country grievances, but pretend to recover their ancient land and territories out of the Englishmen's hands, and [strive] for the restoring of the Romish religion, and to cast off English laws and government, and to bring the realm to the tanist law, acknowledging Tyrone to be lieutenant to the Pope and King of Spain.

[vi] Such analysis was returned to whenever new sources were appraised, as after the publication of calendars of state papers in the late nineteenth century or following the historiographical renaissance from the 1940s.

Afterwards, Protestant attitudes set hard, with Catholicism blamed as the primary motive for the rebellion. Thus Barnaby Rich in 1610:

It is popery that hath drawn the people from that confidence and trust that they should have in God ... It is popery that hath alienated the hearts of that people from that faith, fidelity, obedience, love and loyalty that is required in subjects towards their sovereigns. It is popery that hath set afoot so many rebellions in Ireland, that hath cost the lives of multitudes, that hath ruined that whole realm and made it subject to the oppression of thieves, robbers, spoilers, murderers, rebels and traitors.[1]

Others, however, were less certain. The reasons for rebellion given by James, Earl of Desmond,[vii] to Carew in 1601 were recorded:

he allegeth that the causes that moved the dislike of the Munster men against the English government were religion, undertakers encroaching upon gentlemen's lands, the fear of English juries, which passed upon the trial of Irishmen's lives, the receipt of slight evidence upon such arraignment, the general fear conceived of the safety of their lives by the examples of the execution of Redmond Fitzgerald and Connor McCraghe, and the great charge which was yearly exacted ... called the composition rent.[2]

But the order of priority may be Carew's rather than Desmond's; other reasons given under interrogation by Oliver Hussey emphasize taxation and do not mention religion at all. Mountjoy's communications to London often recur to land and titles as causes for rebellion, though few of the Munster rebels gave this as a reason for rising in 1598.

It is clear that religious commitment and a national grievance against foreign rule were considered appropriate topics for rhetoric, especially outside Ireland itself. Within the island, however, where religious grievances did feature, it was often in a rather equivocal or materialistic sense. Much resentment, for instance, focused on the takeover by the Reformed Church of ecclesiastical land, because this removed such holdings from the control of the local lord, which was not the case under the old dispensation. In many areas, discrimination against Catholics is hard to establish, let alone persecution. After the war, recusants

[vii] James Fitzthomas Fitzgerald (d. 1608): remained staunch in his allegiance to the Crown during and after the Desmond rebellion of 1583; finding this did not result in the restoration of his title, rights or territories, he joined the rebels; created Earl of Desmond by O'Neill, 1598, the English party dismissed him as the *sugán*, or straw, earl; distinguished himself at the head of 8,000 clansmen in Munster before being forced into hiding, 1601. Betrayed into the hands of Carew, and attempts were made to use him against the greater rebels; refusing to comply, he was taken to the Tower of London, where he died.

supposedly 'swarmed over' to Munster; this was probably exaggerated, but observance of the Catholic religion was fairly open, and marriages were performed by Catholic priests. There were more Catholic than Protestant landowners; Catholics were made JPs and sheriffs on a large scale; two-thirds of the Limerick JPs were apparently Catholics by the 1620s. Meath by 1622 presents a picture of 'Romish bishop surrogates and priests' living in the houses of the gentry, saying mass openly and anticipating the return of patronages and vicarages.[3] A generalized rhetoric of persecution sits oddly with this picture.

What, then, of the rhetoric of nationalism? One might profitably substitute the idea of 'O'Neillism'. In one of his many overtures to the Crown, the 'great' earl had sought the granting of an authoritative government that would be Irish but under the King. The prejudices of the 'civilizing' mission, not to mention the ambitions of Tudor and Stuart statecraft, ruled that out; even within Ulster, palatinate status was strongly argued against by the lawyers. And Ulster's status was at the core of O'Neill's case. Many native Irish Catholics, as well as Jesuits from the Pale, saw his claims to a wider authority as bogus. The pious regrets expressed by historians about the 'lack of unity' among the Irish chiefs imply that unity was the key for which they were searching; but it was never there in the first place. Even their perceptions of the enemy were oddly confused; Mountjoy, destroying the O'Mores' territory in 1600, was amused to find 'in one of the rebel's houses a picture of Queen Elizabeth fastened up behind the door, and at the other end of the room one of King Philip'.

The claim that those who fought for O'Neill thought they were fighting for 'Ireland' rests upon one kind of rhetoric or another: notably the language of the poetry. This is extremely loaded evidence, constricted as it is by the conventions of traditional expression, and characterized by a spirit described by one historian as 'highly pragmatic, deeply fatalistic, increasingly escapist, and essentially apolitical'.[4] At this very time, the poets took refuge in a revival of the most ancient, archaic and formalized of literary disputes, 'the rivalry between North and South', as the framework in which they would celebrate the culture of a vanishing world.

The word 'foreign' was applied to the English enemy, but it could also be used for anybody who threatened one's lands. Localist, aristocratic archaism was a more dominant motif of the Gaelic consciousness in the early seventeenth century than anything like a national sense of identity; the poets are capable of stating with a robust idealism that the background of *everyone* in Ireland involves immigration and spoliation.

The appeal to the Gaelic ethos was an appeal to the *status quo ante*, not to an ideal of national unity.

The ideology of the Counter-Reformation, absorbed through the channels set up to Catholic Europe, would help to change this; by mid-century a fusion of Catholicism and patriotism was evident in the work of intellectuals like Keating. Whether this can be called 'nationalism' remains debatable. The work of Keating and others was a response to the need to make historical sense of what had happened in Ireland; but it cannot be used as evidence for the motivation behind the O'Neill war. His *Foras Feasa* takes its place with the outpouring of contemporary Irish hagiographies and annals as 'a monument to a doomed civilization',[5] as a contradiction of the anti-Irish works of Spenser, Moryson and Davies, and as a political tract. In Irish life, historiography and poetry did the duty of political manifestos and would continue to do so. In the same way, the work of Catholic writers like O'Sullivan Beare[viii] and Peter Lombard[ix] retrospectively interpreted the war that ended in 1603 as a religious struggle: hagiography and historical annals presented the Irish as Israelites.

In this formalization, a key theme was provided by the 'flight of the earls': the departure of O'Neill with his O'Donnell allies and retinue, to end his life in Continental exile. Far from being an inevitable coda to the disaster at Kinsale and the capitulation at Mellifont, however, this now appears the point at which O'Neill threw it all away. He had retained far more power than anyone expected, but neither he nor the government abided by the arrangement of 1603. The state pressed ahead with shiring the Ulster province, appointing JPs, arranging assizes; there was even pressure for a presidency. For his part, O'Neill made the most of the traditional lordship that he apparently retained and even exploited his near-palatinate position to override the interest

---

[viii] Philip O'Sullivan Beare (*c.* 1590–1660): emigrated to Spain after the fall of the family seat, Dunboy Castle, 1601; educated at Compostella; held a naval commission from Philip II, but preferred to write history. His *Historiae Catholicae Iberniae Compendium* (1621) is essentially an apologia for the O'Neill wars; *Zoilomastix* (1625) asserts Ireland's civility and England's perfidy, and provides a tendentious but useful gazetteer of contemporary Irish intellectual life abroad.

[ix] Peter Lombard (*c.* 1560–1625): son of a Waterford merchant; educated at Westminster (under Camden), Oxford and Louvain; Provost of Cambrai Cathedral, 1594; absentee Archbishop of Armagh and Primate of All-Ireland, 1601–25. His *De Regno Hiberniae Commentarius*, which portrays O'Neill's rebellion as a war in defence of the Catholic faith, was written in 1600 to enlist the Pope's support for the Irish cause; published posthumously, Charles I ordered Wentworth to ensure its suppression, 1633.

of collaterals and favour his own immediate family line. As always, he was a Gaelic traditionalist only so far as it suited him. Mountjoy's successors, Chichester[x] and Davies, were committed to stopping this, for reasons of private interest as well as public policy. The government backed the case of tenants against overlords in Tír Conaill as well, to the discomfiture of Red Hugh's successor, Rory O'Donnell.[xi] By 1607 O'Neill and Davies were locked in a key dispute about the control of O'Cahan's country round Coleraine, the outcome of which was to be decided in London.

But O'Donnell's continued traffickings with the Spanish compromised O'Neill and made his London journey beset with risks. Swiftly determining to cut his losses, he fled to the Continent with O'Donnell in September 1607 – an ill-considered and completely unexpected action. It provided a great historical set-piece and was interpreted symbolically by both sides. The English argument held that the Ulster lords had formally identified themselves as fugitives and outlaws; the Irish, that English rapacity had forced them out. O'Donnell emphasized, in addition, religious persecution; O'Neill, characteristically, did not. His fight was not a defeatist recognition of political impotence; he had adapted with striking effectiveness, blocking the Dublin government's plans and ruthlessly using his English contacts, until com·promised by O'Donnell. But what mattered was the symbolic image of the last great Gaelic chieftain joining the world of the Irish exiles.

Exile would provide a vital dimension in Irish developments during the seventeenth century. By 1614 there were 300 Irish students and 3,000 Irish soldiers in Spanish territories alone; the Old Irish aristocracy were finding lonely homes there, with their descendants entering the ranks of the *hidalgos* under titles like the Conde de Tiron, or de

---

[x] Arthur Chichester (1563–1625): arrived in Ireland, 1597; held commanding positions in the English army throughout the war with O'Neill; an Irish Privy Councillor, 1603; appointed Lord Deputy of Ireland, 1604; vigorous in the enforcement of English law and habit, he was relatively tender in his attempts to lessen the influence of the Roman Church; assisted in the dissemination of an Irish version of the Prayer Book, 1608; became Lord Chichester of Belfast, 1613; required to resign as Lord Deputy for opposing the severe enforcement of the anti-Catholic laws, 1614, but given the dignity of the position of Lord Treasurer of Ireland.

[xi] Rory O'Donnell (1575–1608): younger brother of Red Hugh, whose command he took up at Kinsale, 1601; made his submission, 1602; graciously received by King James and created first Earl of Tyrconnell, 1603; granted the greater part of Donegal, 1604, but feared the government would interfere with his tribal independence and began to plot again; realizing that news of this had reached the authorities, he panicked and fled the country, 1607.

Tirconel, or de Birhaven. The diplomatic and rhetorical necessities of exile and the intellectual developments mentioned already gave a religious and patriotic resonance to the outcome of the O'Neill wars. This helped to conceal both the covert continuities from the Tudor period and the ambivalent complexity of relationships between Old Irish, Old English and the increasingly important New English.

III

At the most basic level, the question preoccupying the government after 1603 was whether Catholics could be trusted. Issues of land ownership and political history were more pressing than doctrinal questions. The Old English advanced arguments in favour of Catholic loyalism, but the Dublin government paid less and less attention. From the time of the Ulster plantation, Protestants constituted the new political elite; segregation took the place of Anglicization. The result was a series of clashes between the still powerful colony and the Dublin administration over the functions of parliament.

This was of more immediate concern than the anti-Catholic issue *per se*; legislation about, for instance, priests quitting the realm was periodically reasserted but rarely enforced. The real priority of the government was to reorganize representation, incorporate new boroughs and Protestantize the personnel of parliament. This produced a decisive, if dependent, Protestant majority in the 1613 parliament, ranged against a largely Old English minority. The embittered opposition between the Old English and the New English interests favoured by the government led to violent scenes and would be sustained for decades.

But it should not be taken to imply an ensuing *rapprochement* between Old English and Old Irish, whose objective interests were not seen as identical. The Old English continued to stake their position on the compatibility of Catholicism and loyalism – which implied, from the beginning, that they were different from their co-religionists 'beyond the Pale'. And this involved a recognition of differences within Irish Catholicism, which the great wave of Counter-Reformation activity from this period helped to exacerbate.

Though the Dublin government would never have believed it, the organization of the Catholic Church in early seventeenth-century Ireland was varied, haphazard, informal and uncoordinated. The papacy was rather embarrassed by Irish overtures: the orthodoxy of international Catholicism was very different from Irish localism. From this time, however, the absentee Primate, Peter Lombard, determined upon reorganization as his first priority, which meant devoting less attention to political activity.

The vagueness and laxity of popular religious practice in Ireland was witnessed by many observers. The very ideas of communion, catechism and confession were – in their Tridentine sense – unfamiliar. Kinship relations predominated over religious identification: irregular marriages were a commonplace, local pilgrimages provided great occasions for general levity, and the Irish celebration of death supplied a very different social activity from those approved of by Counter-Reformation puritanism. The objective of the Counter-Reformation was, in fact, to reform exactly this kind of degeneration at least as much as to resist heresy. 'The spirit of the Counter-Reformation is of course expressed in part in the romantic image of the mendicant missionary conducting outdoor mass on a specially constructed altar-stone,' Aidan Clarke has written,

but it is conveyed with greater authority in the busy programme of Francis Kirwan, as vicar-general of Tuam, making provision for older priests to be properly instructed in church ceremony, rusticating the sinful clergy, suspending the ignorant from pastoral duty, reducing the pluralists to a single parish, endlessly adjudicating the disputes of the laity and arranging to have adulterers publicly whipped.[6]

This was a slow process; in 1631 at least one Catholic bishop was complaining that the clergy 'swaggered' from house to house, 'playing or drinking or vagabonding'. But the offensive launched by reforming Jesuits and others took effect, often ironically borrowing the metaphors of English colonizers. 'A new plantation' of Catholic faith was spoken of, imposed upon a '*tabula rasa*': 'piety flourishes where all had once been a waste, and where even the name of piety was not known'.[7] This version of 'civility' was imposed through provincial synods, which by enforcing Tridentine practices took an implicitly anti-Gaelic line. David Rothe,[xii] quintessential Old English Catholic intellectual,

[xii] David Rothe (1573–1650): born into an Old English family in Kilkenny; educated at Douai; became Vicar-General of Armagh on returning to Ireland, 1609; wrote *Analecta Sacra*, 1610–11 (published 1616–17), a critique of English ecclesiastical policy in Ireland under Elizabeth and James; appointed Bishop of Ossory, 1618, and acknowledged as virtual leader of the Catholic Church in Ireland in the absence of Lombard; came into conflict with Rinuccini in the 1640s, Rothe's Catholicism being Anglo-Irish rather than ultramontane.

believed that Catholicism should 'eliminate barbarous customs, abolish bestial rites, and convert the detestable intercourse of savages into polite manners and a case for maintaining the commonwealth'. Put this way, Catholic revanchism looks less like subversiveness than another facet of the 'civilizing mission'.

What had to be combated was the Gaelic preference for the religious orders and a slack parochial system, rather than an energetic secular clergy. A Gaelic–Old English division within the Church was of long standing. The Franciscans were traditionally pro-Gaelic, while the Jesuits represented Continental reformism and Old English values, as was appreciated even by some Protestant observers. The Catholic Church in Ireland thus developed its own implicit split. Jesuit and Francophile influence established itself through education; the famous school run by White and Flahy in Waterford was actually described as 'a Trojan horse'. The Jesuits even established, briefly, a *soi-disant* 'university' in Dublin. By 1640, however, their influence was largely limited to some secondary schools in the Old English towns. From the 1620s, on the other hand, the hierarchy was filled by pro-Spanish and pro-Gaelic bishops, and the reports of Rinuccini[xiii] after 1641 show that 'Irish' practices continued. But, besides the wakes and the casual marriages (even, occasionally, among priests), this also meant the kind of adaptability, domesticity and flexibility that kept the Irish Church vital and alive.

The new reign was used by some to revert to open observance of Catholicism, and even defiance of the government; while Mountjoy repressed such public observations, private rights remained an open question. Regulars and seculars brought their disputes into the common law courts. By 1633 the Congregatio de Propaganda Fide noted that Ireland was at last plentifully supplied with clergy. Officials on the spot did what they could – removing Waterford's charter in 1618, for instance, for electing recusant officers. But in towns like Navan and Drogheda during the revival of the 1620s, there were public celebrations of high mass and Catholic burial processions that were

---

[xiii] Giovanni Battista Rinuccini (1592–1653): son of a Florentine patrician; Archbishop of Fermo, 1625; papal nuncio to the Irish Confederate Catholics, 1645; opposed all peace proposals that failed to provide for full recognition of Catholicism and the appointment of Catholic Viceroys; allied himself with Owen Roe O'Neill; power began to wane, 1647, and his excommunication of those involved in the truce of April 1648 was not treated seriously; left for Rome, 1649, and was reported to have been severely censured for want of prudence in Ireland, where he had never allowed local circumstances to affect his policy.

attended by most of the community. There is an interesting ambivalence in a dispatch from the Lord Deputy, Falkland,[xiv] in December 1627, about

the traitorous locusts of Rome, by name the Jesuits and Franciscan friars, if not all the friars, none being tolerable unless such secular priests for whose loyalty and forthcoming good security might be given, amongst whom good subjects may be found. But the banishment of the rest is of necessity to be speedy; it may be done safely, and would not be unacceptable to all the moderate papists of the kingdom, who are weary to be robbed, insulted over, and daily endangered by them and their practices, as they are.[8]

Elsewhere he emphasized that 'the seculars and those that adhere to them are generally well affected to the peace of the state'. The clear presumption is that there was a difference between 'good' and 'bad' Catholics.

Examples were made: punitive fines, imprisonments, even death. However, severity was exercised on a sliding scale. Religion could be kept tactfully private, as indicated by the name attached to Catholic churches: 'chapels'. But formal enforcements and occasional pronouncements, like that of July 1605 (reissued in 1611) in which Catholic priests were ordered to quit the realm, helped to put Catholics in organized opposition. And, ironically, this alienation affected the Old English community most sharply, because they were the element most vulnerable to government edicts. In material terms, it might be wondered why they had adhered to Catholicism, since there is evidence that much of the early Reformation appealed to them. But by the early seventeenth century the insensitivity of government policy and the attractive nature of Counter-Reformation Catholicism had bound them closely to Rome, while resistance provided them with a political nucleus and, eventually, a political leadership.

The nature of Irish Protestantism must also be considered. The Protestant Church of Ireland, heavily endowed with land and ensured of an income, ought to have been rich and powerful. But much of its revenues were farmed out, sometimes, ironically, to Catholic land-

[xiv] Henry Cary (d. 1633): knighted, 1616; created Viscount Falkland, 1620; appointed Lord Deputy of Ireland, 1622; inauspiciously proclaimed the banishment of priests from Ireland at the time of the Spanish marriage negotiations, 1623; unskilfully handled the question of the 'Graces' to be offered the Irish nobility for supporting the army in Ireland, 1626–8; increasingly involved in internecine disputes with Lord Chancellor Loftus; recalled, 1629, after charges of bearing false witness, with a view to confiscating and replanting the lands of the Byrnes of Wicklow.

owners, and a good deal of its land was let on uneconomic leases. Episcopal families, rather in the pre-Reformation Irish manner, appropriated appointments and enriched themselves at the expense of the lower clergy. English sinecurists imposed an additional burden. Moreover, the other characteristic of the Church of Ireland was a doctrinal inflexibility that militated against winning converts. Irish-Protestant bishops, like the Irish administration and the Irish Council, took a stronger line than the King did: their tendency was to emphasize immovability and to enjoy their privileged position. On the ground, Protestant organization remained sketchy: by the early 1620s only one parish in six possessed a preaching minister. As late as 1615 Roman Catholics had even clung on to the odd living and church. The Church of Ireland evolved its own identity. Since the 1590s it had possessed its own intellectual foundation in Trinity College, Dublin. In 1613–15 a convocation met to draw up articles, drafted by James Ussher, the Professor of Divinity.[xv] These reflected the Trinity mind in being firmly Anglican, intellectually oriented towards doctrinal disputation, but not much interested in proselytism. Staffed by the New English, the Church of Ireland enjoyed the self-conscious and uneasy privilege of an elite situated in marcher lands. Like the planters it represented, the Church achieved a distinctive character; like them, it represented another version of Irishness, reflected in its anxiety to claim continuity with the Church of St Patrick. But that identity remained firmly attached to the New English ethos.

IV

In these uneasy conditions, the King's government attempted to carry on business, which, as in England, was dominated by short-term

[xv] James Ussher (1581–1656): among the students admitted at the foundation of Trinity College, Dublin, 1594; Trinity's Professor of Divinity, 1607; Bishop of Meath, 1621; Archbishop of Armagh, 1625; obstructed Bedell's Irish bible scheme, 1629; challenged, as a slight upon the independence of a national Church, the attempt to make the Irish Church adopt the Anglican articles, 1634; left Ireland permanently, 1641; Bishop of Carlisle, 1642; preached against the authority of the Westminster Assembly of Divines, 1643; subsequently declined Cromwell's occasional invitations to discuss the state of Protestantism, and practically retired. In his lifetime, his historical and theological scholarship was admired even more than his ecclesiastical statesmanship. His system of chronology placed the Creation at 4004 BC, inaugurating the practice among Irish antiquarians of showing scant respect for time.

expedients to raise money. Both the practice of subsidy and that of parliamentary grants were given a particular twist by Irish conditions. The Old English who assembled for the parliament of 1613–15 had traditionally given that parliament its character, and fought hard to preserve it as their voice. But the new assembly, long called for by Sir John Davies, was convened with the express intention of extending Crown authority over the population as direct subjects of the King; the effective sacking of Sir John Everard, Justice of the King's Bench, for his refusal to take the Oath of Supremacy, indicated the new priority. This was the background to a parliament that stressed the necessity to raise revenue through recusancy fines and subsidy, but ignored pressure to enforce church attendance upon the laity. Proclamations against Jesuits, seminary priests and foreign education were comparatively safe gestures that had little effect in reality.

The other vital characteristic of the 1613 parliament concerned the detailed preparations for packing it with Protestants from new boroughs in Connacht and Ulster. The problem of representation reflected the distribution of land between Old Irish and Old English versus New English planters, but it did not reflect the pattern of religious affiliations among the population at large, since 132 Protestants sat in the Commons to 100 Catholics, nearly all of whom were Old English.

The rusty machinery of parliament worked quite smoothly, after an acrimonious beginning that involved physical struggles over the Speaker's chair, a boycott by the Old English and appeals to London. Hasty reassessments on the part of government produced a smaller Protestant majority; a sense of precedent reasserted itself; and Everard emerged as acknowledged spokesman of the Old English element. The latter used what leverage they had to take up causes like that of the recusant lawyers, debarred from practising unless they took the Oath of Supremacy, and tried to initiate laws suspending the statutory disabilities entailed upon the Irish. They appeared to have fought a successful rearguard action, having been cast by circumstances into an ostensible 'opposition' role versus the government party, who succeeded only in gaining an inadequate subsidy and had to leave the recusant position unchanged. But the Old English by their very participation had condemned themselves to taking part in a process that could only aggrandize the new colonists. Time was against them.

Moreover, the new approach evinced by the 1613 parliament was reflected in a threat to landed property too. The imposition of English property law for Irish lands left very many titles uncertain – Old

English as well as Gaelic. In 1606 a commission was set up to remedy defective titles. Land sales added further complications and so, most of all, did the position of minors who inherited land held from the King. The Court of Wards, in which such matters were decided, became a battleground of old and new definitions of tenure. And this gave the Crown the opportunity, not only to redefine conditions of tenure in a manner profitable to itself, but also to impose the Oath of Supremacy as a condition of inheritance. Chicanery and corruption characterized the processes whereby 'secure' titles were granted to suitors: the royal officials collaborated with the New English interests in redefining the rules. Thus government was increasingly seen to be exercised in one particular interest, while the Crown priority appeared bent on maximizing revenue rather than encouraging loyalty. The farming out of the Irish customs revenue to English interests was also resented; efforts at administrative reform and pruning costs in the early 1620s led nowhere.

What was happening to the government of Ireland was 'Anglicization' – not necessarily in the sense of 'direct rule', because the administrative reins were periodically returned to the hands of local Protestants, but in the sense of governing Ireland with English priorities and in English interests. Part of this strategy meant Protestantization: the Oath of Supremacy was uniformly enforced in the central administration, and the highest offices were reserved specifically for Protestants. And these developments in politics, coupled with the threat to land titles and the effects of the Counter-Reformation in Ireland, completed the politicization of the Old English, the phrase now applied universally to those 'English of Irish birth'.

They were, by the 1620s, firmly entrenched in urban and trade interests, though two and a quarter million acres of profitable land were held among only about 2,000 families; while even the townsmen of the Old English interests had acquired land interests through mortgages. As a social group, they were closely knit, both through their adherence to Catholicism and through interlinked marriage arrangements. They were utterly sure of themselves socially, but they now occupied a political position that was anomalous. James accused them of being 'only half his subjects': where did the other half of their allegiance go? Not, certainly, to Gaelic Ireland; nor, primarily, to the Pope, much less to France or Spain. The two kinds of Catholic ethos in early seventeenth-century Ireland, outlined above, ensured that religion could divide them from their Gaelic fellow-Catholics as easily as it could unite them among themselves. Counter-Reformation

Catholicism reinforced their separateness; it also gave them a sense of European identity and a competing ideology to Protestantism.

None the less, they wished to emphasize their English origin and their loyalism, and they did so by trying to stress a special relationship with the Crown. The problem was that Catholicism was, in the general view, only ambiguously English – an interpretation that seemed borne out by recent history, notably the Gunpowder Plot of 1605. Their position was not always coherent. In a celebrated scene of 1613, James, who loved a disputation, forced three Old English spokesmen to choose between the authority of Pope and King. One denied the Pope's authority to depose a monarch; the second procrastinated, though he eventually agreed after three months' imprisonment; the third opted unequivocally for papal supremacy. This was probably a fair reflection of Old English political opinion in the process of crystallization. It relied, as has been indicated, on a 'special relationship' with the King; but that was not always easy. With Charles, who came to the throne in March 1625, it would apparently become easier. The fate of the Old English was inextricably linked to Stuart fortunes and to the exercise of the royal prerogative on their behalf; at various points through the seventeenth century this would bring dividends. But it turned Irish affairs into a highly contentious issue in English politics; and as the rules of the constitutional game changed, and the role of Parliament in England diverged from the position it continued to hold in Ireland, the Old English options became more and more limited.

V
==

At this point, the financial exigencies of Stuart government threw the vexed question of Irish loyalties into sharp relief. War preparations in England from 1624 meant that Irish defence expenditure had to be funded from Irish resources. And an outside war provided those who protested their loyalty with a lever to exert, as was to be the case again in the late eighteenth century and the early twentieth. In pressing for the right to raise a militia in the Pale, the Old English achieved a surprising degree of success, and the significance of this was lost neither on the New English nor on the Dublin government. But it was not a question of favouring the Old English, more a reflection of the shifts imposed on Crown policy by financial crisis. As in England, extra-parliamentary taxation became the crucial question.

A contemporary, listing the grievances that might produce another Irish rebellion, emphasized that Irish-Catholic disaffection was

not only in respect of their religion, but the oppressions they sustained by the Court of Wards, by licences for Alehouses of aquavitae, ploughmonies, taking away their lands for plantations, the English and Scots so far encroaching upon them as they feared they should in the end be thrust out of all.[9]

More specifically, Old English grievances were epitomized in the discussions from 1626, by which a tentative arrangement was sketched out for the King to render twenty-six 'Matters of Grace and Bounty to Ireland' in return for financial support towards maintaining an expanded army. The suggested concessions included many minor measures, universally applicable, but also some relaxations aimed purely at Catholics – for example, suspension of recusancy fines and the abolition of religious tests for inheritance and appointment to legal office.

Once again, the New English reaction was to feel threatened; and the Dublin government objected to an initiative that had originated so clearly from London. They missed the point that the suggested 'Graces' were in many ways a *pis aller*: a consolation prize instead of the militia that the Old English had not, in the event, been permitted to raise. But to unreconstructed New English opinion, what mattered was that King Charles was bargaining away the purest symbols of Protestant ascendancy. This was pointed out by Ussher and the Archbishop of Cashel. The Dublin government wanted recusancy fines and other discriminating policies slammed home; the King and his advisors, drifting into Continental war, needed to propitiate the potentially disaffected, especially well-off Catholics. And the international situation after the failure of the La Rochelle expedition in late 1627 made Ireland all the more vulnerable.

In January 1628 a delegation of eight Old English spokesmen, with three Protestant settlers, came to England: by May they had agreed with the English Privy Council on a lengthy list of administrative and policy reforms, including an implicit recognition of the right of Catholics to bear arms for self-defence. Moreover, land titles were to be confirmed after sixty years' possession. But recusancy fines were not to be remitted, and the right of Catholics to public office was not allowed. With the rapid increase of Protestant settlement, anti-Catholic feeling was growing. The New English were confirmed in their superior position, and the new settlers obtained the right to secure titles in Ulster whether or not they observed the regulations governing conditions of plantation. This, if nothing else, should serve as a reminder that the 'Graces', and what they were intended to achieve, did not constitute anything as simple as restitution of Catholic rights. For their part, the Irish negotiators agreed to raise £40,000, payable quarterly for each of three years.

The government regarded this bargain as binding on the Irish parliament; the negotiators believed that the Dublin assembly would have to ratify the arrangement. None the less, they set about immediate collection of the first subsidy, leading to much ensuing faction and disagreement in Ireland. From the English side, the King's interpretation of his part of the bargain seemed unreliable and pusillanimous. Yet despite complaint, delays in calling parliament and invocations of Poynings' Law, the first subsidy was paid, and some of the 'Graces' passed into practice, if not the most important. Nevertheless, the anti-Catholic impetus in Dublin gathered momentum.

In 1629 the Lord Deputy, Falkland, though anxious to keep up the *rapprochement*, was authorized, yet again, to proceed against 'disloyal' clergy – meaning, more or less, the regulars. This policy was kept up after his dismissal, facilitated by the restoration of international peace and the ascendancy of the New English policy-makers like Loftus[xvi] and Richard Boyle, heading the government in rather uneasy double harness. Up to this, there had been a shuttlecock policy with regard to lay recusants, varying with government personnel and the state of royal finances. 'Freedom of Catholic worship,' in the words of one authority, 'was restricted by nothing more substantial than a sense of discretion.'[10] This now changed. The religious orders were pursued; recusancy fines were collected; and from 1630 threats to property titles revived, aimed even at so great a personage as the Earl of Ormond. Still more ominous was the circulation of ideas regarding new plantations.

Contemporary Ireland being what it was, one must emphasize yet again the contradictions within the general picture. At this very time, for instance, the Order of Poor Clares was set up in Ireland, moving

---

[xvi] Adam Loftus (*c.* 1568–1643): nephew of the Chancellor–Archbishop of the same name who ensured that he rose swiftly and pluralistically in the Church and in politics; knighted, 1605; Irish Privy Councillor, 1608; Irish Lord Chancellor, 1619; Lord Justice and Viscount Loftus of Ely, 1622; henceforth his power was such that no Lord Deputy could rule comfortably; a five-year vendetta against Falkland, 1624–9, was followed by a period of four years in which Loftus was virtual ruler of Ireland; he seemed to have been chastened when a feud with Wentworth resulted in his imprisonment, 1637–9, but avenged when the Long Parliament chose the arbitrary treatment of Loftus to form part of the eighth article of Wentworth's impeachment.

calmly round the country from one convent to another. And even the Gaelic Irish were, in some cases, returned for the 1634 parliament, and they continued to use constitutional and legal machinery to combat the challenge to their land titles. But events after 1629 show clearly that, if the 'Graces' had ever implied tolerance or pluralism, the New English grip on the Dublin government ensured that such an approach was quickly discounted.

VI
=

If this was the underlying reality of policy in Ireland, it was temporarily concealed by the appointment of a new strong man in 1633: Thomas Wentworth, later Earl of Strafford.[xvii] Wentworth's singlemindedness and decisiveness ensure him his place as one of the foremost English administrators in Ireland, but much of his Irish reputation revolves round more personal issues. One of these concerns his building up of an immense fortune through land investments: 3,500 acres round Clane and Naas in Kildare, where ruins of his vast but uncompleted palace at Jigginstown still dominate the main road to the south, and speculations in Wicklow, obtained with knowledge acquired in the course of the endless intrigues about finding a royal title to the lands of the O'Byrnes. By 1640 he held 34,000 profitable and 23,000 unprofitable acres, and had spent £60,000 on building. Unlike his New English contemporaries, land did not make Wentworth personally rich; his own wealth came from political influence, which enabled him to invest in customs-farming. Ambitions to set up iron manufactures and to monopolize tobacco imports never fulfilled his expectations. The interesting thing about his accumulation of wealth is that it can often be construed as having an eye to Crown profit as much as to his own.

[xvii] Thomas Wentworth (1593–1641): as Lord Deputy of Ireland, 1632–41, he hoped, by 'Thorough government to make every Irishman a loyal and prosperous English citizen'; enforced Laudian articles upon the Irish Church; encouraged some Irish industries but discouraged others to keep Ireland dependent; dissolving the parliament of 1634, without granting the 'Graces' promised his Catholic supporters, he boasted, to the chagrin of the resident governing clique, that the King was absolute in Ireland; created Earl of Strafford, 1640; the grievances of his Irish enemies were eagerly heard by the Long Parliament; of the twenty-eight articles of his impeachment, twenty concerned his Irish administration; ably defending himself, the impeachment was abandoned, and it was under a bill of attainder that he was beheaded.

But contemporaries, dedicatedly amassing Irish fortunes on their own accounts, understandably missed the distinction.

The new Lord Deputy was also distinguished, from the Irish point of view, as the great adversary of Richard Boyle, archetypal new-rich planter: and here he was unintentionally instrumental in forcing the New English interest to coalesce as a political opposition group. This did not break down their celebrated competitiveness, nor the 'personalization of political affairs' that characterized their approach to public life. But the threat that Wentworth seemed to pose to their interests was of great importance. He both despised and exploited the ethos of Irish planter society, in the King's interest and in his own, 'always doing either the unexpected or the unthinkable'.[11] The result was, briefly, that the Old English interest seemed suddenly in the ascendant once more.

In religious policy, Wentworth's line was that of Archbishop Laud;[xviii] and Laudianism in the Irish context had a potentially revolutionary implication, affecting matters of property as much as of conscience. Wentworth trampled on New English sensibilities, taking over the direction of Church affairs from the Primate, working through his chaplain John Bramhall, whom he appointed to the bishopric of Derry, and restoring the property of the Church of Ireland that had been alienated to lay lessees on terms unfavourable to the Church. His declared policy was to settle solvent and competent clergy in the parishes, but the fact that he pressed this unpopular policy hardest in the north, where it was least needed, raised suspicions that his priority was not to reorganize the Church so much as to trim the wings of the planters.

In fact, Wentworth was privately as anti-Catholic as any of them could have wished. But he was prepared publicly, for instance, to meet the Catholic Archbishop of Dublin shortly after his arrival. And he preferred to streamline Protestantism rather than to proceed against Catholics for recusancy fines; here, as elsewhere, he extrapolated from

---

[xviii] William Laud (1573–1645): the King's chief ecclesiastical adviser from 1629; a member of the Irish Committee of the English Privy Council that selected Wentworth for the position of Lord Deputy of Ireland, 1631; Archbishop of Canterbury, 1633; concerned to enforce conformity upon the national Church by countering all Calvinistic taints; successful in Ireland with the assistance of Wentworth, he was constantly at war with the Scottish Church; his love of external order in Church establishments and his approval of Wentworth's occasional toleration of Catholics in Ireland led to the accusations of crypto-popery, which, although ill-founded, were sufficient to lead him to the block when the climate of opinion in England turned against the monarchy.

his English experience, where such a step had proved unprofitable. For revenue, he preferred to try customs reorganization or a subsidy. And this, yet again, threatened the interest of planters as much as of Old English.

Again, it was in line with Church policy in England to restrain ecclesiastical courts from proceeding against Catholic practices in baptism, marriages and burials; so Wentworth acted likewise in Ireland. But, though Church of England canons since 1604 had tended to emphasize continuities and practices assimilable to the Catholic tradition (partly as a way of combating Calvinism), in Ireland the opposite tradition had been stressed. There, anti-Catholicism, and the material insecurity regarding landholding that was inextricably woven into it, were more important than doctrinal differences within Protestantism. Already friendly to Calvinist influence, the Church of Ireland could even put up with Presbyterianism. But it could not assimilate Wentworth.

His religious policies indirectly attacked the New English; his use of the commission for defective titles and the draconian Court of Castle Chamber challenged their interests head-on. Under his regime, the tacit allowances made by common law courts for the dubious nature of many settlers' titles was no longer observed. The much-quoted 'Rule of Thorough' that Wentworth put into practice was a stringent exercise in profit-making, intended for eventual use in England as well: not for the last time, Ireland was being used by an inflexible theoretician to experiment with ideas too radical for immediate English consumption. What mattered in the short term, however, was that these policies worked temporarily to the advantage of the beleaguered Old English.

Wentworth disliked the New English planters, 'a company of men the most intent upon their own ends that ever I met with'. But he needed to summon a parliament to gain statutory support for his financial reorganization and to achieve freedom from the necessity to bargain with local interest-groups. He had to manipulate Poynings' Law in order to exert full control over parliamentary business, but he was also temporarily able to use Old English support. For their part, they used the parliament summoned in July 1634 to get many of the 'Graces' put into law. Wentworth obtained a subsidy, as well as the passing of an important measure that enabled him to transfer the commission for defective land titles from London to Dublin. The significance of this was that he could unilaterally control the granting of secure titles, at a price. But this ambitious policy implied the breakdown of *rapprochement* with the Old English.

They were already alarmed at the delay over admitting the 'Graces' into statute law; and if their religious position had been eased by Wentworth's Laudian policies, their titles were threatened by his plans for asserting royal tenure claims, and still more for plantations in the traditionally Old English area of Galway. By late 1634 the Old English honeymoon was over; Wentworth was wooing the Ulster planters. He had begun, inevitably, to present his difficulties in a Protestant-versus-Catholic framework. Wentworth pressed on with policies of administrative reform to increase Crown revenue, especially regarding land titles and inheritance laws; he arranged subsidies and levied contributions; he showed himself prepared for peremptory and authoritarian action. If the Old English had become disenchanted, the New English could not trust him either; his policies posed implicit threats regarding both land ownership and religious practice. And in Ireland the two were by now inextricably intertwined to form the basis of social and political ascendancy: the result, not only of Stuart policies, but of the traumas and reassessments that followed the collapse of O'Neill's rebellion.

CHAPTER THREE

===

PLANTATION: THEORY
AND PRACTICE

I

===

THE UPHEAVALS OF Irish history from the 1630s must be understood against the background of a country that had been intensively
colonized from the beginning of the century, and earlier; some attempt
must now be made to define this process. The idea of 'plantation' is
inseparable from the notion of 'civility', but rapidly took on a very
different meaning. The history of Munster from the later sixteenth
century involved attempts to plant English virtues in an area that could
yield Irish profits; the early seventeenth saw similar, but far more
coherent, ideas put to the test in Ulster. The differences, however, are
in many ways more enlightening than the similarities.

From the beginning there were varying interpretations of the plantation idea. Was it to be a policy of Anglicization or of colonization?
'Anglicization' presupposed a slow process: part of the destabilizing of
Gaelic society and practices by introducing English modes of law,
tenure and social relations. 'Colonization' indicated a more drastic
approach, amounting at least in theory to tearing Gaelicism out by the
roots. It has been seen that the packing of parliament with Protestants
was carried out by means of colonizing Ulster;[i] this was only one of
the fringe benefits in the minds of those who advocated colonization.
A Protestant population was desired in order that the government
need no longer be dependent upon cajoling the Catholic political
classes: effectively, the Old English. This idea was at least as prominent
as the more abstract notions of importing a civilizing influence. It was
not yet anticipated that the new settlers might prove just as difficult,
in their own way, as the old.

As soon as the O'Neill wars ended, Ulster was destined for plan-

[i] See above, pp. 45, 50.

tation; the initial idea, in line with the generally favourable treatment of the rebels, did not involve dispossession. There was a sense, indeed, in which some of the province was 'planted' already; Scots had been spilling back and forth across the narrow straits since time immemorial, and Antrim and Down were densely Scottish in population. In many ways the Antrim coast was closer to the Scottish mainland than to its own hinterland. From the time of James's accession this process was further formalized by the settlements privately instituted by Hugh Montgomery[ii] and James Hamilton.[iii] A more formal and centralized plan for hitherto Gaelic Ulster was to follow.

The flight of O'Neill and O'Donnell left the way open for the government to inflict confiscation upon other areas of the province; the ensuing rebellion of Sir Cahir O'Doherty[iv] amplified the case, implicating many among the Gaelic gentry. Also at this time the illegitimization of the Brehon laws provided a convenient machinery for dispossessing others besides proven rebels, though it necessitated ignoring the shiring of the province, formally in existence since the 1580s, not to mention the conferring of freeholds in the recent past. In the plans of 1607–8, then, the approach was very much 'colonization' rather than 'Anglicization'.

In theory, the six counties of Armagh, Coleraine, Fermanagh, Tyrone, Cavan and Donegal[v] were to be worked on, producing an ideal pattern of close settlement that would feature urbanization and

[ii] Hugh Montgomery (c. 1560–1636): sixth Laird of Braidstane; knighted, 1605; conceived the idea of plantation of Ards and Clandeboye, which he undertook with Sir James Hamilton, 1610; also with Hamilton, MP for County Down, 1613, and Commissioner for the plantation of County Longford, 1619. A Privy Councillor, 1614; created Viscount Montgomery of the Great Ards, 1622.

[iii] James Hamilton (1559–1643): sent to Dublin by James to report on Anglo-Irish affairs, 1587; fellow of Trinity College, Dublin, 1593; knighted, 1609; the middle years of his Irish career have been noted above; created Viscount Clandeboye and Hamilton, 1622; Privy Councillor, 1634; commander of a troop of horse against the Ulster rebels, 1642.

[iv] Cahir O'Doherty (1587–1608): heir to the lordship of Inishowen; set aside by his uncle on account of his youth, 1600; fostered by the MacDavitts, who promised to serve the state if his patrimony was secured; proclaimed the 'Queen's O'Doherty' and knighted for bravery at Augher, 1602; foreman of the jury that found O'Neill and O'Donnell guilty after their flight, 1607; himself charged with treason and insulted by Sir George Paulet, Governor of Derry; marched on Derry and sacked it, 1608; unsuccessfully attacked Lifford; tracked down and killed by the English forces in County Donegal.

[v] The last two, it should be noted, were not included in the area later demarcated as 'Northern Ireland'. Coleraine included contemporary Derry.

segregation. No Irish tenants were to be allowed on the lands taken over by the major 'undertakers'. The tenure offered would be the simple and desirable arrangement of common socage. The areas were to be carefully demarcated in proportions of 1,000-, 1,500- and 2,000-acre lots. Chief undertakers would be allowed 3,000 acres, on condition that they were resident, settled English or Scottish families, and undertook to bear arms and to build defences. Deserving natives would be carefully treated, and the colonized lands were to provide laboratory conditions for the chemistry of the civilizing process.

The history of Ulster from that time to this was dictated by the fact that these proposals did not work out as intended. Practice rapidly deviated from theory in two vital areas. Segregation proved impracticable; and the size of the units actually granted to undertakers bore little or no relation to the theory.

In a sense, the latter difficulty gave rise to the former. The vast holdings taken over by speculators were dealt with from afar or even resold; administrative problems and the desire for profit meant that native Irish were rapidly accepted as tenants on a rent-paying basis, often simply staying *in situ* and working the land. Much of the initial reason for unmanageably large grants had to do with the classic Anglo-Irish difficulty of semantic misunderstanding. The Irish land unit of a 'balliboe' was reckoned in terms of *value* or productivity, not as a fixed unit of acreage. English surveyors, however, decided to work on the ludicrous underestimate that it averaged sixty acres. Sixteen 'balliboes' made up a 'ballybetagh', the traditional area of a sept's authority; by their arithmetic the commissioners decided that a 'ballybetagh' would equal the 1,000-acre unit called for by plantation theorists.

One effect of this was that the new estates ran curiously close to the old demarcations: this presented the displacement process as a change of ownership rather than as a complete reconstruction of the Gaelic ways. Another outcome was that many holdings, reckoned in terms of 'balliboes' and 'ballybetaghs', turned out to be so large that undertakers relied upon natives staying on – all the more as they were ready to pay high rents for land that was underdeveloped by English standards. Much of Ulster was poorer than Connacht, in contemporary terms, being bog, wood and scrub, and requiring large-scale clearance and fertilization. As early as 1623 the pamphlet *Advertisements for Ireland* could isolate the two drawbacks of the Ulster plantation. One was the 'error of the acre' (the fact that Irish measurements varied from place to place); the other, the fact that Ulster undertakers 'suffered the ruder sort of mere Irish to inhabit their lands because they pay them greater

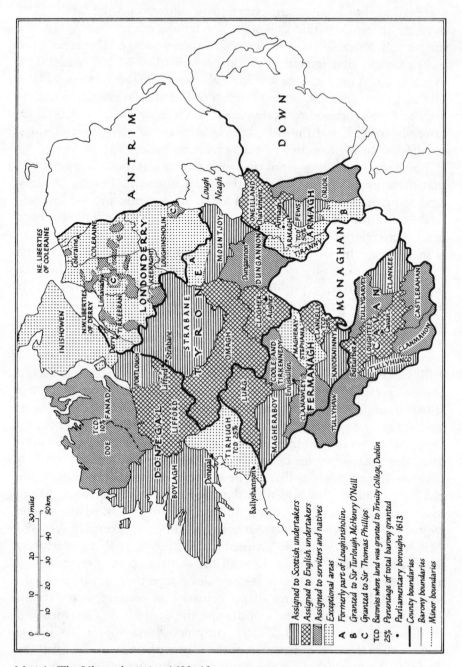

Map 1: *The Ulster plantation 1609–13.*
Source: T. W. Moody, F. X. Martin and F. J. Byrne (editors), *A New History of Ireland.*
Vol. III: Early Modern Ireland 1534–1691.

rents they say than the British will', or at best handed over their proportions to 'footmen and other of their meaner tenants'.

II
==

Many of these misapprehensions and confusions were still in the future in 1610, when the plantation was fully planned by the English and Scottish Privy Councils. Advisors in Ireland like Sir John Davies were prominent; his ideas, favouring sweeping colonization, overcame those of the more cautious Chichester, who preferred gradual Anglicization. By the late summer itinerant commissioners were organizing the disposition of Ulster lands, a process memorably recorded in Davies's letters. The primary question was: who would sign on for the lands that were separated out? To onlookers, the profit motive was what characterized undertakers: it was 'rather an adventure for such as are full, than a setting up of those that are low in means'.[1] But the central planners saw things in stricter terms. The categories of grantees were defined as undertakers (about a hundred in all); 'servitors' (army veterans); favoured natives; the Church; and Trinity College, Dublin. All were expected to inculcate English 'civility' in Ulster. There were two further exceptional cases. The Lord Deputy, who already possessed vast estates in Antrim, was granted the barony of Inishowen; and the City of London took over Coleraine County on the most special terms of all. Though granted the land by central government, the City was expected to provide large-scale capital to fortify towns and to engage in trade.

Servitors and natives were allowed to take on Irish tenants, but they paid higher dues for the privilege. Native tenants were excused the Oath of Supremacy. The position of the natives has preoccupied retrospective commentators, for the original plan might have had some chance of success if the natives had been given far more land and the undertakers far less. 'Deserving' natives were isolated in each area. A few were granted 'great' proportions; more received lesser lots of a few hundred acres. But this was no compensation for a dislocation that could be not only geographical but psychological. This came about through a combination of transplantation and limitation of tenure. Where an Irish grantee did receive a patent, English law often ensured that the arrangement might not be permanent. Thus Art Mac Baron O'Neill, the father of Owen Roe, was removed from his traditional holding of Oneilan and received a new estate of 2,000 acres only during the life of himself and his wife. As it turned out, the notorious Lord Audley[vi] took it over within two years. The classic complaint was that of social *bouleversement*: ancient scions of Gaelic chieftainry working the land their clan had owned. This gave rise to the cliché beloved of later observers, that every Irish peasant considered himself the son of kings.

The majority received nothing and had to adapt as best they could to the new dispensation. An early outline had enjoined that care should be taken to dispose each element of the plantation in an appropriate area: 'that the English and Scottish be next to rivers. The Irish on the plains. The captains and servitors on the borders and near the Irish.' 'Plains' in this context means 'exposed land', where they could be easily watched. The position of the Irish was similarly a special pre-occupation of Chichester's. He believed that the Munster experience had shown that the distribution of natives among settlers did not work. On the other hand, Ulstermen had to stay in their own province, because they would be unwelcome elsewhere. The idea was, then, to confine them in areas that were coastal or exposed. It was *not* part of the plantation theory that they should be deliberately given less productive holdings; but that was how it worked out.

By 1628, with legislation relaxing plantation articles and allowing one-quarter of the land to be held by natives, the practice had been institutionalized whereby they were confined to the poorer land. Protestant farmers were to utilize the deep drumlin soil, later famous for flax production; Catholic demography followed different patterns. Internal population movements and the cumulative effect of established British settlements attracting newcomers exacerbated the process. The Catholic Irish stayed on, in an insecure and grudging position: as plantation tenants they were in most cases formally on sufferance, with the date of their expulsion continually moved forward. Ulster settled into the pattern of native living uneasily adjacent to planter – more typical than the image of the romantic woodkerne preying on colonists from woods and mountains. But the resentment experienced was no less heartfelt, and the fear of displacement no less present. Sir Toby Caulfield sent Chichester this account in June 1610:

[vi] George Touchet (*c.* 1550–1617): sometime Governor of Utrecht; wounded at the siege of Kinsale, 1601; an undertaker in the Ulster plantation, 1610; created Baron Audley of Orier, County Armagh, 1614; became first Earl of Castlehaven, County Cork, 1616.

Reports his ill success in the prosecution of woodkerne. *There is no hope of the* *people* since the news of the plantation divulged by Sir Turlagh McHenry [O'Neill of the Fewes] and the rest lately arrived from England, that it will shortly be many of their cases to be woodkerne out of necessity, no other means being left to them to keep a being in this world than to live as long as they can by scrambling ... They hold discourse among themselves, that if this course [of dispossession] had been taken with them in wartime, it had had some colour of justice; they having been pardoned and their land given them [in 1603], and having lived under law ever since, and being ready to submit themselves to mercy for any offence they can be charged with since their pardoning, they conclude it to be the greatest cruelty that was ever inflicted on any people. Takes leave to assure [the Lord Deputy] there is not a more discontented people in Christendom.[2]

How did the theoreticians of plantation rationalize the process? In the judgement of a lawyer like Davies, the natives had no rights of inheritance: he instanced as proof the unpredictability of 'gavelkind', the looseness of marital ties, the impermanence of farming and husbandry. It was also possible to produce examples of plantation from Roman, Spanish and Scottish history. But the real preoccupation was the imposition of English property law, which invalidated Irish landholding practices. The conditions for Irish undertakers stressed that they 'take no Irish exactions'; they were to use 'tillage and husbandry after the manner of the English Pale'. This was linked with the general policy of 'feudalization' of tenures mentioned above.[vii] Thus, although the Crown pursued a robustly modern approach to the question of leases and feudal duties, undertakers were allowed to erect manors and enjoy feudal jurisdiction and profits on their own account.

Most important, though, was the power, conferred by English law, of redefining titles and ownership; as has been seen, this induced uneasiness among Old English as well as native Irish. Many of the latter who remained in the Ulster plantation found the policies of enforced Anglicization hard to comprehend, let alone adapt to. 'Many natives have answered that it is hard for them to alter their course of living by herds of cattle and creaghting,' wrote Chichester to Davies in March 1609,

and as to the building of castles, or strong houses and bawns, it is for them impossible; none of them, the Neales [O'Neills] and such principal surnames excepted, affect above a ballybetagh, and most of them will be content with two or three balliboes; and for others, he knows whole counties will not content the meanest of them, albeit now they have but their mantle and their sword.[3]

[vii] See above, pp. 19, 50–51.

This indicates how irrelevant was the idea of a settled, demarcated landholding, even to those Irish who were offered one. Some plantation articles were relaxed for native undertakers, who were in any case charged higher rents (which they were, significantly, able to pay). In the early days of the plantation there was a competition for land, and a tendency to offer it on very short leases; a widespread and ill-founded expectation prevailed that land values would rocket as the plantation got under way. Irish tenants, however, were ready to take it on these, or any, terms. The idea of leases was irrelevant; what they cared desperately about was possession.

By 1618 there was much evidence of very general letting and subletting to natives on short leases (even half-yearly renewal) and at high rents. 'A depression in their economic status, not expulsion, was the usual fate of the natives on the [Londonderry] companies' lands';[4] the same picture held in general terms. There was a future refinement, of great importance in later agrarian history. English land law was, theoretically, being introduced at a stroke. But the attempt to settle vast estates with an inadequate number of immigrants meant that Ulster landlords who were short of capital had to acquiesce in tenant practices, like the sale of leases, which were being *suppressed* in England. Even where the desired kind of tenant materialized in Ulster, the terms on which they held their land developed idiosyncratically.

III

The business of settlement got under way rapidly. Undertakers had to be in residence by September 1610, and to have fulfilled their conditions of settlement by Easter 1613. The enterprise attracted those pressed hard by the cost of living, in Scotland as well as in England; those who felt the government owed them something; and those who had made money and wanted to invest it. In the glowing prose of plantation publicists like Bacon, Davies and Philips, the abiding image is that of 'fruitfulness' – meaning not only fertility but profit. A 'new Carthage' would be built or, even more ominously, a 'new Troy'. Salmon-fishing and timber-stocks were legendary; so was the fertility of the valleys and the abundance of the livestock. Hence the readiness of grasping undertakers like Lord Audley to take on far more than they could manage – a process exacerbated by the underestimation of proportions in the first place. Bogs and wildernesses were casually added on, unmeasured, to land grants; commissioners were extremely cavalier (and probably corrupt) in deciding such matters. Wentworth later estimated that the actual estates possessed averaged ten times the acreage patented; this was in several cases no exaggeration.[viii] Maps and surveys were extremely sketchy, despite Davies's claims that 'the most obscure part of the King's dominions is now as well-known and more particularly described than any part of England'. Inaccurate measurement, consolidation and accumulation eventually produced exactly the kind of estates that had not been envisaged.

The same was true of types of colonist. One of the Irish Society's[ix] few recorded attempts at proselytism shows them looking for sober craftsmen and sending over poor boys as apprentices to Derry. But a gloomy report from Chichester in October 1610 was more typical. The English settlers were generally 'plain country gentlemen', tight-fisted and easily scared away; many had already sold or exchanged their portions. The Scots were a tougher proposition, but too ready to use natives to supply their wants and to let land to them. There, as elsewhere, the settlement in practice worked very differently from the plantation idea.

The same was true, of course, elsewhere in Ireland. In Munster the plantation culture had survived the wars. Resettled after the Desmond rebellion, there may have been nearly 5,000 planters resident by 1611. But the eternal contradiction presented itself: the kind of skilled, solid, prosperous artisan settler whom the theorists wanted was exactly the kind who had no need to move to Ireland. The rogues, the vagabonds and the opportunists had. Ireland could be treated as a practice frontier area, a decompression chamber for letting off steam. It is likely that the misfits were those who later moved on to Virginia. The remainder, whatever their origins, were always anxious to define their status. 'We stand more upon place here than in England; here are many start-ups that wealth doth advance from baseness to preferment.'

But on another level, matters proceeded closer to the plan. Plantation

---

[viii] Thus the precinct of Clonkee, County Cavan, actually contained 64,377 acres, but two-thirds of it was formally occupied by four proprietors whose portions supposedly totalled 5,000 acres. And the O'Neill, O'Donnell and Maguire lands set aside for Trinity College, supposed to constitute 10,000 acres, totalled nearly ten times that amount.

[ix] The Irish Society of London was set up in January 1610 as a consortium of City merchant companies who contracted with the government to carry out the plantation of the City of Derry, Coleraine County and the barony of Loughinsholin (hence, of course, 'Londonderry'). See above, p. 63.

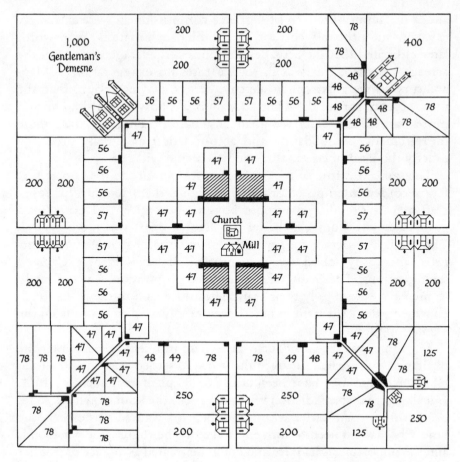

Map 2: *Proposed lay-out of a Munster seignory of 12,000 acres in 1586. Figures within boundaries refer to acreages. The space around the central settlement represents 1,692 acres of arable land, to be divided into allotments. The four blocks of unnumbered strips facing each other across the central church square represent cottages on 5½-acre plots.*
Source: J. H. Andrews, 'Geography and Government in Elizabethan Ireland' in N. Stephens and R. E. Glasscock (editors), *Irish Geographical Studies in Honour of E. Estyn Evans.*

Munster was closely integrated with south-west England, socially as well as economically. An export-led economy, concentrating on wool and cattle, was performing impressively by the 1630s, even if it was based on pastoral developments very far from the ideas of plantation theorists. Ironworks were established and became celebrated (if rather exaggerated). By 1626 the Munster fisheries trade was worth £29,000, the pilchard shoals having obligingly migrated to south-west Ireland from England along with the settlers. And parts of Munster received

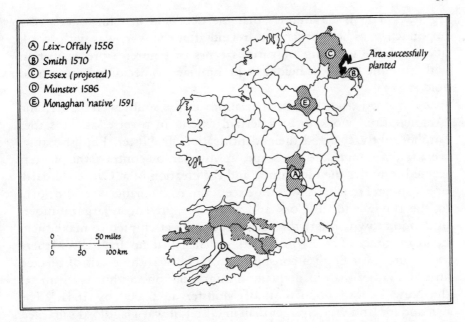

Map 3: *Tudor plantations.*
Source: R. Dudley Edwards, *An Atlas of Irish History.*

the English impress that they still retain – evinced by apple-growing and cider-making no less than by market-towns, timber and mineral industries, cross-breeding with English farm-stock, the building of estate villages and Protestant churches. In a sense, many of those who settled in Munster from Devon or Somerset are more like the migrating gentry of contemporary England than colonists entering a *terra incognita.*

Accordingly, treatment of the natives in Munster followed its own pattern. By 1611 about one-third of the whole plantation area had been returned to native ownership. There was much intermarriage; even Spenser's descendants became Catholic. Up to 1641 relations could be surprisingly relaxed, considering the history of rebellion and dispossession (though Boyle, for one, while prepared to use Catholic lawyers, was too cautious to employ a Catholic doctor).

Elsewhere, plantation articles were not adhered to, though the reformed religion remained the entrée to public life and security of tenure. The residual plantations in Leitrim, Longford, King's County, Queen's County and Wexford did not follow through James's idea of planting; here, as elsewhere, enrichment of the New English was the key theme in what has been called 'a new, predatory form of surrender and regrant'.[5] This is a reminder that the obsession in Chichester's correspondence, as he reorganized Ireland after the war, was with 'weak titles' and the meaning of various types of tenure: a preoccupation with how the land was held, as a preliminary to deciding who would hold it.

It remained true that social relations in the south were easier; and 'Anglicization' worked, to a certain extent, in reverse, as the settler families subtly changed their identification. In Ulster, English names were fastened on to the landscape; in Munster, by contrast, the planters seemed to prefer the old names, and the creation of a 'Castle Bernard' or a 'Mount Trenchard' was the exception. Irish tenants were the norm on the Boyle lands in Cork and were even present in large numbers in Bandon town, where the agent repeatedly attempted to make them build in stone. (The Earl of Cork's claims that no Irish dwelt there were purely for English consumption.) This was the result of relaxed attitudes rather than inadequate immigration; one authority estimates the New English population of Munster at 22,000 by 1641.[6] The demand for land was stronger than in Ulster: it was a landlord's market, with the new ascendancy of Protestant proprietors letting land on short leases. Boyle and others learned to manipulate not only the Irish mortgage system (by which the mortgagee took possession until repaid) but also Irish legal traditions and the Irish predisposition to short leases. Profiteering in pastoral farming was not what plantation theorists had intended, but it fitted well with the nature of Munster land. The Earl of Cork himself was a figure whose grandeur was unequalled, north or south; his own ambivalent position, socially and intellectually, was very much part of the southern settler experience, as he cultivated relations with the great world of English politics from his stronghold in Cork. To men of his position, the Irish Sea was a gangway rather than a barrier.

More typical settlers, perhaps, were the needy gentry bent on making fortunes; if not necessarily the debtors and bigamists of tradition, they certainly exaggerated their social pretensions and saw Munster as an avenue to upward social mobility. In Cork, unlike Ulster, to quote Nicholas Canny, 'the New English were so successful in convincing themselves that their future in Ireland was secure that they did not perceive themselves as an embattled minority'.[7] Much of this depended on a reassuringly symbiotic relationship with the English West Country. But it also indicated a 'conversion environment' where local papists seemed ready to conform to the newcomers' ethos; and the newcomers themselves were prepared to bend a little. Intermarriage was far more common than in Ulster. To slightly later observers, like Sir John Temple, looking back nostalgically over the gulf of the 1641 rising, a hybrid culture seemed to be in the making.

These people of late times were so much civilized by their cohabitation with the English as that the ancient animosities and hatred which the Irish had ever been observed to bear upon the English nation seemed now to be quite deposited and buried in a firm conglutination of their affection and national obligations passed between them. The two nations had now lived together forty years in peace with great security and comfort, which had in a manner consolidated them into one body, knit and compacted together with all those bonds and ligatures of friendship, alliance and consanguinity as might make up a constant and perpetual union betwixt them. Their intermarriages were frequent, gossipred, fostering (relations of much dearness among the Irish) together with all others of tenancy, neighbourhood and service interchangeably passed amongst them. Nay they had made as it were a kind of mutual transmigration into each other's manners, many English being strangely degenerated into Irish affections and customs, and many Irish, especially of the better sort, having taken up the English language, apparel and decent manner of living in their private houses.[8]

Some at least of this was wishful thinking: reminiscences of a golden age occur after every outbreak of disaffection throughout Irish history. And the Reformed religion, in Munster as elsewhere, was still an essential prerequisite for a public career and a safe estate – even if many JPs and sheriffs were Catholic. But there was an element of truth in Temple's encomiums none the less.

Outside Munster and Ulster, the plantation idea was more shallowly rooted, though it was still to be found. By 'discovery' of Crown titles, some enforced planting took place in Wexford after 1610, against organized local resistance. Similar regrants were made, for similar purposes, in the midlands. The scheme was modified, with smaller allotments than in Ulster; and the idea of enforcing British tenants was abandoned. In a sense, the idea was Anglicization rather than colonization: urbanization and English-style farming practices were stressed. But even these modest plans were vitiated by absenteeism.

What did take place in the midlands and west was informal colonization: not a centrally planned scheme, but undertakings by Scots courtiers or Palesmen extending their investment. Instead of importing British tenants, they tried to Anglicize the local communities by example. Building stipulations and religious proselytizing were disregarded in favour of ventures like the Huguenot glassworks near Birr, and some ironworks. Some state-sponsored efforts were combined with a drift of entrepreneurial settlers from elsewhere. Very often, here as in Connacht, 'the plantation idea' simply involved the law being exploited in order to facilitate land investment by New English speculations. But there is evidence from Clanricard and Thomond (east County Galway and Clare) that shows local nobles of Old English stock promoting English colonization, voluntarily reorganizing· their estates on English patterns, and introducing English tenants: possibly an intelligent attempt to accommodate and control the process of change.

Even New English adventurers in the midlands like Matthew De Renzi[x] maintained a curious relationship with the Gaelic world they were supplanting. But insecurity remained rife; in 1630 yet another plantation scheme was floated, threatening Ormond's Tipperary lands, and Connacht was also being considered for development. Even in adjacent counties not specifically 'planted', changes in ownership were being brought about. By 1640 less than half of Monaghan was owned by native families: 'a change brought about not by any total conquest or wholesale plantation but by the gradual and inevitable effect of the English system on an uncomprehending people'.[9] The exception was one barony, Farney, dominated by a Gaelic clan who had astutely learned how to manipulate English ways well before 1600.

IV

The state of the Ulster plantation might seem conveniently gauged by the existence of a valuable survey conducted in 1622; but many of the surveyors had sharp axes to grind, and their reliability cannot be assumed. One of them thought that the British population of the Londonderry lands was declining, but figures from 1628 contradict this. Many areas were affected by centripetal population movements, leading to regional decline; but generally the population rose by 1630, if not dramatically. The Irish population certainly increased; in this and other ways, the continuity rather than the displacement of population is what strikes us now. By 1622, in the six escheated counties of Ulster, there were about 13,000 adults of English stock, concentrated in dense settlement patterns.

[x] Matthew De Renzi (1577–1634): born in Cullen [Cologne?], Germany; traveller, linguist and scribe to Lord Deputy Falkland; obtained grants of land in Counties Westmeath and Wexford, 1622; knighted, 1627; composed an Irish dictionary, grammar and chronology that was completed by his son, Matthew, 1635.

In Down and Antrim there were about 7,500 of Scottish and English stock. There, the plantation had 'taken', but this was not due to Crown planning or a central 'idea'; the reasons lay in the informal settlements of previous years, and in the tradition of coming and going to Scotland. The Ards peninsula had remained part of the marketing hinterland for Stranraer across the channel; in calm weather, merchants came over for the day and traded with their kinfolk who had settled there. Later, when the government took steps against Ulster Presbyterian ministers, their congregations would row across to worship in Scotland, returning the same evening.

Scottish pedlars were a commonplace in Ulster, and by 1630 the Scots monopolized mercantile activity at Derry. Imports, at first mainly building materials, had shifted to clothing, hardware, food-stuffs, spices, tobacco, salt and wine from the Continent. Exports were, inevitably, linen yarn, beef, hides, tallow and wool; more irregularly, butter, pork, salmon and cattle – the latter an increasingly important activity. Coleraine had become a shipbuilding centre, and Derry was a wool staple by 1621. Trade was expanding by 1640, though it was inhibited by a great cash shortage that produced high interest rates and much reliance on barter. Here, again, the contrast with Cork was notable.

The reality of the planters' experience is less easy to itemize than the patterns of their trade. One entry for Pynner's survey of 1618, describing a Londonderry estate taken by the Vintners' Company and leased by them to an agent, expresses the ideal in action:

Vintners'-Hall, 3,210 acres

This is in the hands of Baptist Jones, Esq., who hath built a Bawn of Brick and Lime, 100 feet square, with two round Flankers, and a good Rampart, which is more than any of the rest have done. There are also within the Bawn two good houses, one opposite to the other; the one is 70 feet long, and 25 feet wide, the other is nothing inferior unto it. Near upon the Bawn he hath built 10 good *English* houses of cagework, that be very strong and covered with Tiles; the street very wide, and is to be commanded by the Bawn. All these are inhabited with *English* families and himself, with his Wife and Family be resident therein. There are divers other Houses built upon the Land which are further off; and these do use Tillage plentifully after the *English* manner. He hath made his full Number of Freeholders and Leaseholders; but he being gone into *England*, and tenants at the Assizes, I saw them not. There was good store of Arms in his House, and upon the land 76 men, as I am informed.[10]

Not all conformed as well as Baptist Jones (and even his record elsewhere condemned him as 'a needy, grasping adventurer'[11]). At least as common were accounts of flimsy buildings, scrappy husbandry and

Irish inhabitants. Jones's arrangement with the Vintners bound him not to let land 'to any person or persons whatsoever natives from within the Kingdom of Ireland, nor to any person or persons that shall not have taken the Oaths of Allegiance and Supremacy'. But the Ironmongers' Company claimed to enforce a similar clause, and, thanks to a rare surviving itemization, we know that out of 127 undertenants on their estates, all but nine were Irish.

The record of Baptist Jones none the less conveys the flavour of one Ulster holding. Indenturing with the Vintners, he promised that he would

at his costs and charges ... have and keep in and out upon the premises afore-demised such and so many able men furnished with Corselets, Pikes and Muskets, Powder shot and other armour and Munition for service of his Majesty and for his and their own defence ... as ... the said [Company] and the tenants and occupiers of the premises ... shall be charged or commanded to have in readiness to be showed at musters.[12]

This was important. Accounts of casual butchery at the hands of woodkernes were common enough in the first years, though robbery tended to take over after that – especially of cattle. To take another case-history, we find Sir Ralph Bingley, an important undertaker with estates on Lough Swilly and elsewhere, importing tenantry from England; combining with other ex-military men to form a consortium; and leaving a high proportion of Irish tenants on the lands, far more than the 25 per cent allowed by the royal 'Graces' granted in 1628, though relations between the Irish and the British on his estates were strictly controlled.

A sense of geographical insecurity is inseparable from these arrangements. Though Derry and Coleraine were the key settlements, there were many scattered farms and hamlets in Ulster; and from early on settlers realized the importance of centring towns on them. The classic plantation town involved fortification, houses of brick and lime (as well as cagework) and the central square, or 'diamond'. The famous walls of Derry were completed in 1618 after four years of building, making it one of Ireland's principal fortresses: in plan, 'a distorted ellipse like a battered shield'.[13] But the walls were never really satisfactory, and the town remained vulnerable to attack from the river. In towns like Downpatrick and Dungannon, the tensions of contingent populations were expressed by an 'English Street', an 'Irish Street', a 'Scotch Street'. The question of contiguity remained vital. Catholics were not allowed to settle inside Derry, as a threatening majority; they colonized the

Bogside outside the walls. But they were allowed into Belfast, as a small minority; and towns like Armagh and Cavan retained a strongly native complexion. Armagh, being on Church land, was allowed to take Irish tenants; they became shopkeepers and the town slowly developed a commercial ethos.

Of course, 'borough-making' was an important incentive in the founding of towns. But in building, conditions were carefully laid down for 'defence and decency', with English-style houses and provisions for church, markets, school and sometimes a prison. In Ulster, towns were often allotted functions disproportionate to their size, though their organization was not as sophisticated as Cork plantation towns like Bandon and Mallow. The outlines provided are rather similar to the orders for building in Virginia; American comparisons are, indeed, more relevant than English ones. But urban growth in Ulster was healthier than in contemporary Maryland or Virginia, though there were variations depending on the fortunes of urban patrons. Enniskillen followed the ideal pattern closely; Virginia, County Cavan, did not.

Central to the plantation idea was the notion of an urban network; landlords wanted towns for reasons of profit and security, and the government wanted them for administrative coherence. Settled Ulster was to be a market-oriented economy, helped by improved communications and concentrations of population. But by 1641 towns were less developed than had been hoped, certainly by comparison with contemporary England. Growth had been restricted by the lack of profitable land attached and the scarcity of charitable donations; nor did those who planned them really understand the nature of their hinterlands. The mobility and fluidity of the Irish agricultural population was, as usual, underestimated; many markets established early on were gone by 1641. Urban settlers could themselves adopt peripatetic habits, moving out into the countryside when they had acquired land. For land investment rather than mercantile activity remained the great desideratum of profiteers. Crooked arrangements like that whereby Sir Arthur Chichester and James Hamilton arranged regrants of vast tracts of land around Lough Neagh have supplied much material for historians. But even an estate as great as that founded by Chichester, due to low land values and leasing difficulties never delivered the economic return expected; it provided only a shaky basis to the outward grandeur of the family's life. In profiteering, as in everything else, the actual outcome of the Ulster plantation was very different from the theory that lay behind it.

The urban economy was backward in exchange terms, too, relying on debts and barter rather than on tokens or bills of exchange, at least until 1650. Some small inland towns did succeed in integrating their rural hinterlands, and they became 'the enduring legacy of the urban element in the Ulster plantation'.[14] Commitment to local office was not great; fines had to be levied on those who evaded it. Local government was a complex enough business, with a proliferation of courts arising from manorial rights as well as royal assizes, and the regular civil courts summoned by sheriffs. In the Londonderry plantation accusations of oligarchy and corruption were common, due to the monopolies held by the Irish Society and the City companies. The quarter sessions at Derry dealt with

assault, theft of money and stock, salmon-poaching, ploughing by the tail, breaking the assize of bread, selling drink in unsealed measures, permitting drunkenness, selling wine and bread in a solitary place to outlaws, altering boundaries, refusal to assist constables in bringing prisoners to jail, rescuing prisoners, the acquittal of prisoners by jurors, relieving rebels, murder and treason.

– not to mention living in Irish houses and not repairing roads and bridges. Such a list of offences is as good a way as any of profiling the tensions and the flavour of Ulster life.

It also indicates the strenuous effort to apply English models to Irish ways. But on many levels 'the scheme disguised in a cloak of British nomenclature a remarkable continuity with the pre-existing Gaelic social structure and land division'.[15] Though there were prosecutions for exercising Catholic offices, the observation of the old religion continued openly, with the connivance of local officials. Some priests even rented land; and some planters were accused of bringing over Catholics. Much more notable, however, and ultimately as subversive, was the influx of influential Scotch Calvinists in James's reign. Even in Ulster, many of the 'deserving Irish' of the old dispensation, who had kept or acquired land, participated in the machinery of local government and entered into social relations with the planters. But they occupied a precarious, if distinctive, position, which would be highlighted in the cataclysm of 1641.

In fact, the onset of political crisis in the 1620s coincided with a crisis of administration of the Ulster plantation, centred upon a celebrated dispute regarding the observance by the Londonderry planters of the conditions under which their land had been acquired. It was aggravated by the Scots issue and by Wentworth's suspicions about rival 'farmers' for the companies' lands. But there was also a substantive point, in that the Society's undertaking had always been a special case. Its commitment in Ulster was not really analogous to contemporary joint-stock enterprises in the New World: the Londonderry planters had responded to an initiative from the Crown, and, in fact, were being used by the Crown to carry out Anglicization. Profit-making had been the initial temptation; but once they were committed, the Crown concentrated entirely upon their obligations. And these, as in every other plantation, went by default.

The government expected them to expel Irish tenants, and to rebuild Derry and Coleraine; the undertakers, while prepared to build, were reliant upon the local population. King James reminded them in 1615 that the 'removal of natives' was the 'fundamental reason' of the plantation; but this was never practicable. The incomplete dispossession that did take place created continuing tension; on the Londonderry lands, unlike in Munster, this was symbolized by a war of words. The christening of localities with English names was never accepted; the natives never adopted the name 'Londonderry', thus indicating that they never accepted the legitimacy of the settlement or the right of the settlers to proclaim an 'English' allegiance.[xi]

Surveys in 1611 and 1613 showed a particularly slow rate of progress, exacerbated by administrative extravagance and jobbery as well as local difficulties. The business of plantation had been divided into that conducted by the 'general plantation', run by the City's Irish Society, and twelve separate undertakings in the hands of different companies. From 1615 dire warnings had been issued by the government, who threatened repossession if the plantation articles were not adhered to. But a proclamation of 1618 shows that the government was prepared to settle for levying fines rather than enforcing segregation. And by 1628, as has been seen, the Crown had to agree to planters defaulting even on the vital question of Irish tenants. The inquiry that reported in 1629 filled out the picture. It concentrated upon the planters' acceptance of native residents; threats of expulsion were levelled against those who would not conform to Protestantism and English habits. The lengthy wrangle between City and Court eventually led to the imposition of heavy fines in 1638, and the forfeiting of some lands. But this had more to do with the Crown's desperation for money, and Wentworth's propensity for fishing in troubled waters, than with any real plan to reassert the direction intended by the plantation's architects.

[xi] In 1984 the City Council voted to change the name back to Derry.

Another extraneous factor was the question of unrest among the Scots; and all this was still at issue when the storm broke.

The halting and contentious nature of government-planned colonization adds weight to the argument that the 'real' Ulster plantation was that carried out 'invisibly' by the Scots, both before the initiatives of 1609–10 and later in the century. This would later provide an argument used by Unionists: that Ulster's different nature is immemorial and uncontrollable, and stems from something more basic than English governmental policy. None the less, what must be grasped from the early seventeenth century is the importance of the plantation idea, with its emphasis on segregation and on native unreliability. These attitudes helped Ulster solidify into a different mould. The reliance of the planters upon the Irish, economically, was combined with an obsession about their religious, and therefore political, untrustworthiness. Contemporaries sensed Ulster's edgy quality. 'A rude and remote kingdom,' Boyle described it from Cork as late as 1630; 'the first likely to be wasted . . . if any trouble or insurrection should arise.'[16] Intellectually, this insecurity was expressed in the mentality of settler radicalism. At once austere, exalted and unbending, they were also cantankerous, febrile and prone to hysteria and conspiracy theories. Initially, religion had not been important in dictating the unofficial Scots settlements of Antrim and Down; but settler defensiveness and intolerance fused with anti-establishment Presbyterianism to create a northern mentality very different from the providentialist philosophy of Boyle. Ulster people believed they lived permanently on the edge of persecution; they gloried in covenanting against 'tyranny'; and they were committed to a democracy that extended to the elect alone. These attitudes did not moderate with time.

CHAPTER FOUR

===

CONFEDERATE
IRELAND

I

===

IT WAS NOT ONLY the Ulster plantation that brought about a symbiotic relationship between events in Ireland and in Scotland during the early seventeenth century. For one thing, the Scottish crisis from the late 1630s made it imperative for Wentworth to sustain his decisive and radical role in Irish government; and the ensuing years would see not only a Scottish army in Ireland, but even Irish ambitions to invade Scotland. This theme, of interdependent events in the two countries, is nearly as important as the more obvious interaction between the great constitutional crisis in England and the collapse of government in Ireland.

Indeed, the most striking development in contemporary English history – the extraordinary radicalization of religious and political life from the 1630s to the 1650s – is precisely what did not happen in Ireland. For one thing, the Church of Ireland was already of an Erastian, Calvinist and anti-Catholic cast; there were no urban communities of radical Protestants, where religious sects could take their own direction. Such a development did not appear until the 1640s, and then only in a limited way. By the 1650s a radical policy of social reconstruction had been adopted, on another level. But it took the form of massive expropriation of estates and transplantation of native inhabitants. *This* was the Irish revolution, and its social effects were arguably more long-lived than any other inheritance of the Cromwellian era.

Otherwise, for a parallel with Ireland in the 1640s, one looks not to England but to other European 'conservative' revolts – Bohemia, Catalonia, Portugal – and to·the atmosphere of contemporary Germany. The scenario is one of endless on–off war with shifting lines, wandering detachments, often at cross-purposes with each other, bewildering kaleidoscopes of alliances, miraculous escapes, mysterious envoys bearing charmed lives, and sudden changes of side: and a bloodletting that both invoked and reinforced the bitterest religious dissensions. In Ireland as in Germany, unpaid armies sometimes reached the point of independence from political control. Many of the commanders – Monro,[i] O'Neill[ii] and others – were, indeed, veterans of the Thirty Years War by the time they became involved in the 'Irish Rebellion'; and French agents, at large in Ireland in the mid-1640s, tended to see the situation purely in terms of the rise of Spanish influence in Ireland.

'Such reeling times', a contemporary described them.[1] But when calm was regained at last, it did not come about as a result of an equivocating compromise like the Peace of Augsburg; it was the stillness that follows utter annihilation.

II

The terms of Irish politics in the 1630s remained dictated by Wentworth's manipulations of planter and Old English interests. His policies had divided and ruled, and, while regaining much for the Crown, he alienated both elements. On the one hand, there was the contemptuous attitude to the Old English demands enshrined in the 'Graces'; on the other, his plans for confiscation and plantation, even in Galway, as Old English an enclave as the Pale itself. This brought about an influential backlash from the Galway gentry, and interacted with New English resentment at Wentworth's customs-farming; his position was further undermined by court intrigues in London.

[i] Robert Monro (d. 1680?): the zealous plunderer of many Ulster towns, including Newry, 1642; failed in an attempt to surprise Owen Roe O'Neill at Charlemont, 1643; seized Belfast, 1644; routed by Owen Roe at Benburb, 1646; retreated to Carrickfergus, which was given up to General Monck by the treachery of his own officers, 1648; spent five years in the Tower but often consulted by Cromwell, who remained his protector; permitted to return to Ireland and compound his estates, 1654.

[ii] Owen Roe O'Neill (c. 1590–1649): nephew of the 'great' Hugh O'Neill; spent thirty years in the Spanish military service, 1610–40; accepted an offer to lead the Ulster rebels, April 1642; swore allegiance to the Confederates, November 1642; warm supporter of Rinuccini's ultramontane Irish policies, 1645; achieved the greatest Irish victory of the 1640s at Benburb, 1646; declared an enemy of the Confederacy, 1648; acting with it again in the months before his death, Cromwell's arrival having caused the differences of the Irish leaders to be forgotten. In a decade of faction and strange alliance, Owen Roe had the clearest notion of what he wanted for his country and his Church.

Wentworth's alienation from both elite elements in Irish politics is preserved in the literature of the day; he is the villain of Richard Boyle's diaries as well as of Old English polemical pamphlets. Religion entered the picture, too; his appointment of Laudian Englishmen to Irish bishoprics was deeply resented by the New English, who, having successfully colonized the episcopacy, were now being ousted in their turn. Opposition would thus have been ensured even without doctrinal resentments. ('As for bowing at the name of Jesus, it will not down with them yet,' remarked Wentworth to Laud; 'they have no more joints in their knees for that than an elephant.')

A similarly rough hand was seen in Wentworth's treatment of Galway nobles like the Earl of Clanricarde: commandeering his house to hear depositions in, helping himself to the best grazing, 'casting himself in his riding boots upon very rich beds'. It is symptomatic that Wentworth, when brought to account for this, saw it only in terms of money: he had paid for his retinue. The Old English saw it as an insulting abuse of hospitality on the part of a dictatorial parvenu. His abuse of legal practice regarding the hearing of title-claims was of a piece with this. It showed a different set of social, as well as political, values. And the significance of Wentworth's assault on Connacht titles was that the Old English were being treated as contemptuously as the Old Irish.

None the less he pressed ahead with formalization of the Galway confiscations; but he was slowed down, not only by the resistance of the Clanricardes, father and son, but also by the fact that there were not many takers for a new plantation. Scots were no longer acceptable, and Wentworth's Laudian orientation made Ireland unattractive to Protestant *émigrés*. As late as 1640 the Connacht plantation was still 'notional'; the same was true of Wentworth's confiscations in Clare and Wicklow. The plantation idea also came under fire in Ulster, with the Crown's proceedings against the Londonderry investors. And this brought into focus both the volatility of the planter element in the current crisis, and the connections between them and the escalating opposition to Charles in England. For his part, Charles characteristically took this moment to reverse the priorities of his Irish administration by attempting to utilize the Ulster Irish, under the Earl of Antrim, to mount an attack on the Ulster Scots. This risky plan, which helped ruin the King's reputation in Ireland, may not have been approved of by Wentworth, who believed that it was arming potentially disloyal Catholics: ironically, the very thing that he was to do himself.

The 1620s had, in fact, seen a Catholic revival in Ulster connected with the ambitions of this MacDonnell interest. But Ulster's Scottish identity was expressed in a dominant and defiant nonconformity. While this was not necessarily connected with Scottish politics, the constant contact across the straits was vitally important, and Scots ministers who tangled with episcopal authority could and did come to Ulster for more sympathetic treatment. The Dublin government's campaign against nonconformity in the late 1630s aroused inevitable resistance. In the summer of 1639 Wentworth, notoriously anti-Scottish, imposed an Oath of Abjuration, or 'Black Oath',[iii] in response to the Covenanting movement, and he backed it with the presence of the army.

This is a reminder that by this stage, even in Ireland, Presbyterianism was perceived as a more dangerous threat than Catholicism – at least by Laud and the King. Wentworth had not originated this policy; the threat of an Ulster Scots rebellion was probably exaggerated. But it was there. And the ostensibly successful imposition of Crown power in Ulster coincided with its evident breakdown in Scotland; at this very point Charles backed down before the Scots army at Berwick. The interdependence of events between Ireland and Scotland was sharply apparent once more.

Wentworth subsequently returned to England, where he played a vital part in the crisis of 1640–41: not least because of his emphatic policy of using Irish resources, both soldiers and subsidies, to back up the tactics he suggested to the Crown. Thus he called an Irish parliament for 1640 in which the Protestant-packing strategy was further evident; the representation of Catholics (effectively, Old English) was reduced by one-third from 1634. But *they* were no longer automatically the King's enemies. Subsidies were forthcoming, and Wentworth presented the docility of the parliament as proof of Ireland's loyalty, as well as an example to Westminster. It was none the less an edgy proceeding, leaving Wentworth, now Earl of Strafford, ill and strained when he returned to England in April 1640.

Events in the English Parliament set hard at once in the most unconciliatory direction; while in Ireland, the raising of the planned new army ran into financial difficulties and the Dublin parliament began to show recalcitrance about the government's requirements both

---

[iii] This was an oath imposed on the Ulster Scots, to abjure their covenant and bind them to allegiance to Charles. It was systematically administered to Ulster Scots over the age of sixteen during the summer of 1639 by civil commissioners supported by an imposing military presence.

as regards subsidies and land confiscation. Most importantly, this meant that the interests of Old English and New English were running towards opposing the government. The issues of their disaffection may have been different, but the basis remained the same: Wentworth's domination of centralized government. Inevitably, this reacted with the declared Puritan opposition in England. Just when the King was at the mercy of invading Scots and a hostile Parliament in September 1640, Ireland was not prepared to form the bulwark of support Wentworth had hoped. In fact, Ireland helped provide his nemesis.

The raising of a King's army, and his overweening authority there, were made the basis of the attack on the new Earl of Strafford that ended with his execution in May 1641. During this process, there was constant coming and going between Dublin and London; restrictions on travel between the two countries were lifted to facilitate the gathering and presentation of evidence. In Ireland a concurrent attack was mounted on the Lord Deputy's exploitative financial techniques; all the resentful came together, from the Galway Old English to the Londonderry planters, and Wentworth fell like Lucifer. But the excitement of his impeachment and the change of authority in the Irish government (to the Lords Justices Parsons[iv] and Borlase[v]) merely papered over some substantial cracks in the opposition. Wentworth's successful repudiation of many charges did not save him; and Ireland came to the forefront of public attention, giving both Old English and New English a chance to exert successful pressure on the King.

In the case of the Old English this involved, yet again, the 'Graces', which Charles showed himself ready to confirm, and the Connacht plantation plans, which he was prepared to revoke. But their part in the prosecution of Wentworth was necessarily more muted than that of their temporary allies among the New English. They knew they would need the King's aid again; and they knew that Wentworth's policies towards them were no more than the parliamentary opposition

[iv] William Parsons (c. 1570–1650): became assistant to the Irish Surveyor-General, 1587; succeeded to that office, 1602; active in all major Irish plantations, 1610–20; knighted, 1620; a Privy Councillor, 1623; MP for County Wicklow, 1639; as Lord Justice, 1640–43, accused of stimulating rebellion to excuse further confiscations; opposed attempts to secure a reconciliation between Ormond and the King, for which he was relieved of his justiceship; retired to England, 1648.

[v] John Borlase (1576–1648): knighted, 1606; appointed Master of the Ordnance in Ireland, 1633; Lord Justice of Ireland, 1640, but, bred a soldier and little else, left much of the work to Parsons; superseded by the appointment of Ormond as Lord Lieutenant, 1644.

in England tacitly approved of. Others might, indeed, have treated them even worse. Thus, as events ran to confrontation in England, and the unifying factor of the attack on Wentworth was removed, fissures of religious identification opened wide within the Irish opposition.

That opposition had previously been a close reflection of Ireland's peculiar condition, and Ireland's peculiar grievances – notably regarding titles to land. From the summer of 1641 it was Ireland's peculiar religious mix that came to the fore, with stirrings in Ulster against episcopacy and the favouring of Catholics; and in Dublin a new development appeared as parliamentary opposition was increasingly cast into the mould of a movement for constitutional reform. The main objection was to executive dominance; the chief claim, the parliamentary right to impeach. The position of the King *vis-à-vis* his Irish realm was also called into question. And the position of the Irish parliament was defined by the Old English lawyer–politician, Patrick Darcy,[vi] as one of effective legislative independence.

This was very special pleading indeed, arising from the very special circumstances of these years: ideas whose growth was forced by a combination of events in England and Wentworth's Irish record. But the tradition of political thought that began in the Old Irish opposition is worth some attention. Elements in it would recur in parliamentary independence movements over the next century (and later);[vii] but in the context of the 1630s and 1640s, a more immediate connection might be made with the kind of Continental *politique* theory that searched out a reconciliation between private conscience, political status and a rationale for supporting the established powers. Given the crisis conditions of these years, it was also a way of evading the exertion of authority by the English Parliament – now an increasingly ominous threat.

Theoretical disquisitions were made easier by the hiatus in the practice of government caused by Wentworth's fall. Revenue collection declined; the defective titles commission, the Courts of Castle Chamber and of Wards fell into desuetude; the new army was hesi-

---

[vi] Patrick Darcy (1598–1668): sat for Navan in the Irish parliament of 1634; a member of the supreme council of Confederate Catholics at Kilkenny from 1641 and appointed as a delegate of the general assembly of that body to make peace with Ormond, 1646. His *Argument* against Poynings' Law, published 1643, that no English statute can be enforced upon Ireland unless enacted by an Irish parliament, pre-empted William Molyneux's *Case* by over fifty years and remained the linchpin of constitutional nationalist thought until the fall of Isaac Butt in 1877.

[vii] See below, pp. 144–5, 161–2, 173–4, 247–51, 308–9, 397–9.

tantly disbanded. The King gave way on many concessions regarding legal and administrative practice. But he ignored the Old English opposition's claim, as articulated by Patrick Darcy, for the right of the Irish parliament to initiate legislation – a claim reacted sharply against by both the Dublin government and the New English. The Old English were, after all, a minority in the parliament, thanks to Wentworth's policies in the 1630s; and for all their constitutional theorizing, when the various components of the anti-Wentworth camp split apart the Old English were left conscious of their basic dependence on royal authority. This alone could protect their social position and their religious freedom against the ambition and bigotry of the New English interest. The New English, for their part, were affected by the onset of confrontation in England – as well as keeping themselves in constant expectation of the ancient threat of Catholic insurgency. This was made manifest even sooner than they expected.

III

Lecky,[viii] writing his great history of eighteenth-century Ireland, found he had to begin with a lengthy disquisition on the insurrection of 1641: or, more accurately, with its reputation. What people thought happened in that bloody autumn conditioned events and attitudes in Ireland for generations to come. From 22 October 1641 an attack was launched on Ulster settlers by their native neighbours, especially directed at those outside the walled towns. Lecky's hesitant estimate of 4,000 casualties is too high; a figure of 2,000 may be nearer, but must remain speculative. Retaliatory attacks on Catholics soon added many more fatalities. These figures are arresting enough. But the number of victims killed in the initial 'massacre' rapidly became inflated to fantastic levels, affecting both Irish historiography and Protestant mentality from this time on. In 1662 the Irish parliament declared that 23 October, the day the rebellion was discovered, 'shall be kept and

[viii] W. E. H. Lecky (1838–1903): historian of European ideas and Anglo-Irish realities. His major works on the latter were *Leaders of Public Opinion in Ireland*, 1862, and his twelve-volume *History of England in the Eighteenth Century*, 1878–90, which includes five volumes on Ireland aimed at refuting the calumnies of J. A. Froude upon his countrymen. In Irish terms, always nationally minded, never nationalist; a liberal Unionist, for whom Home Rule threatened not Rome rule but the onset of fatal democracy and consequently the infringement of liberty.

celebrated as an anniversary holy day in this kingdom for ever':
commemorative church services and public demonstrations persisted
into the nineteenth century, memorializing Catholic treachery and
celebrating Protestant deliverance. In Lecky's lifetime a great volume
of contemporary records and reportage was made available, faithfully
reproduced by scholars who still could not avoid taking sides.[2] But the
reliability of contemporary accounts remained suspect – specifically
the thirty-three volumes of 'Depositions' regarding the actions of
insurgents in 1641. These resemble a pornography of violence, and
they may indicate more about contemporary mentality than actual
massacres. The circumstances of their composition, and the uses to
which such evidence was intended to be put, must be borne in mind.
But there is more than enough coincidence of evidence to indicate the
horrific sufferings of non-combatants.

To those involved, the sudden shock was part of the horror. 'The
Irish servant which overnight was undressing his master in Duty, the
next morning was stripping master and mistress with a too-officious
tyranny.'[3] Lookers-on, however, were less surprised – especially after
the event. 'It had been no hard matter to have been a prophet,' wrote
a contemporary in 1643, 'and, standing upon the top of Holyhead, to
have foreseen those black clouds, engendering in the Irish air, which
broke out afterwards into such fearful tempests of blood'.[4] But such
easy wisdom, no less than the vivid picture of the treacherous servant,
obscures the initial nature of the rising.

For those who led the revolt on 22–3 October 1641 were not
the dispossessed natives, driven beyond endurance; nor were they
fanatically Catholic revanchists. They were the Ulster gentry, of Irish
origin, but still possessing land: the 'deserving Irish' whose interests
had survived the plantation. Though victims of psychological displacement, heavily indebted and unable to manipulate their new status
to advantage, the leaders of the conspiracy all fit this mould – Rory
O'More,[ix] Lord Maguire, Sir Phelim O'Neill[x] ('a light, desperate

---

[ix] Rory O'More (fl. 1620–52): main contriver of the 1641 rebellion and chief
mediator between the Ulster Irish and the gentry of the Pale; enlisted the help of
Owen Roe, 1642; commanded the Confederate Catholics in King's and Queen's
Counties, 1643; Owen Roe's mediator with Inchiquin, 1648, and Ormond, 1649;
driven to seek refuge in Innisbofin, 1652; perhaps escaped to Scotland, more likely to
have perished in Ireland.

[x] Phelim O'Neill (c. 1604–53): expelled from the Irish Commons for concerting
the Ulster rebellion, 1641; first commander of the northern forces, but totally eclipsed
by Owen Roe; represented Ulster on the Confederates' supreme council; fought at

young gentleman'). And though their formal demands stressed religious freedom, the statements made by those who joined in, like the O'Reillys of Cavan and the Farrells of Longford, played it down. Throughout, the emphasis fell on threats to land titles, the depredations of the new-style government and – most importantly – a residual loyalty to the King.

This lent the revolt potential political reverberations of great importance. So did the inevitable Continental connection and the rebel hopes, largely unfounded, that they would be joined by what was left of Wentworth's army – its disbandment and redeployment having become an electric political issue. Relying on underground royalist contingency plans, the rebel strategy was for a coup to bring pressure to bear on the Dublin government – not for an apocalyptic war of liberation. With much publicity, they spared Scots settlers, at least in the early stages – a careful political calculation. But the attempt at a synchronized attack on Dublin Castle was short-circuited; and in the north, popular fears and expectations were released that the gentry leaders were unable to control. 'The old leaven still fermented inwardly.'[5]

As the accumulated resentments of thirty years burst out, the insurrection spread through the province, though many of the walled towns, enjoined by so many plantation articles to prepare against just such an eventuality, resisted. Though this had been no St Bartholomew's Day, planned far in advance, the fearful violence of many murders brought about inevitable retaliations and propaganda. Contemporary events in Europe predisposed people to believe, and to retail, the most horrendous stories; the Protestant mind also saw it as judgement on those who had signed the 'Black Oath' imposed by Wentworth. Money and volunteer corps were raised in Scotland to help their beleagured brethren in Ulster – and sent over with royal encouragement. But the question of an actual Scots army going to Ireland was one of great political sensitivity: the strategy provided a volatile new element both with a base and an inevitable claim on confiscated Irish lands. The way was now open for a 'war of the three kingdoms'.

From the Irish point of view, the government defined the outbreak

Benburb and attempted to make peace between the rebels and Ormond, 1646; sought to prevent an alliance of the Lord Lieutenant and Owen Roe, 1648; captured by the Parliament forces, 1653; offered a pardon if he would validate a forged commission from Charles I, authorizing the 1641 rebellion; refused to do so; executed.

of war as a papist jacquerie: an insurrection of the dispossessed, out to claim their own in religious and economic terms. How accurate was this? The early announcement of intentions was moderate: religious and legal grievances were stated, but no really sweeping demands were made. Not being allowed to buy back escheated territory 'doth more discontent them than that plantation rule'. But this was changing radically by early 1642. 'As the leaders became less moderate, their ideas coincided with those of their followers.'[6]

The other area of tension was the putative involvement of English royalists. O'Neill's announcement that they were not in arms against the King set the tone early on. By November, as they marched rather uncertainly south, the insurgents were claiming that they had the King's support. Certainly, at an early stage some of the conspirators believed that the royalist leader Ormond[xi] was represented in their councils; others, that he would join them. The royal commission under the Great Seal of Scotland, authorizing the rebellion and published in November, was certainly a forgery, providing many red herrings for historians, as well as capitalizing on the contemporary panic and credulity about Catholic plots. But the King had been involved in the early soundings that led O'Neill and his associates to believe an insurrection would not be seen as disloyal, and this explains many of their early tactics.

The King's contingency plans had halted at an early stage of co-operation, but enough had passed for Ulstermen, and even Irishmen on the Continent, to believe that royal support would be forthcoming for a 'pre-emptive coup' against the government. Even more bewildering was the ambiguous attitude of the insurgents to the Scots, whose lives and property they were initially at pains to spare – a scruple that

[xi] James Butler (1610–88): entered the Irish parliament on succeeding as twelfth Earl of Ormond and Ossory, 1633; commanded the loyal forces against the Irish rebels, 1641–4; commissioned to negotiate the cessation of hostilities in Ireland, 1643–4; became Lord Lieutenant, 1644; failed to make peace with the Irish rebels, 1646; concluded a truce with Parliament, 1647; treated with the various Irish leaders upon the execution of the King, 1649; crushed by Cromwell, 1649–50; served Charles II in exile, 1651–60; created Duke of Ormond, 1661; reappointed Lord Lieutenant, 1662; ensured the operation of the Acts of Settlement, 1662, and Explanation, 1665; showed rare initiative in his defence of Irish industry, 1663; removed from Irish office, 1669, and treated coldly by the King, 1670–77; reappointed Lord Lieutenant, 1677; kept Ireland quiet during the popish terror, 1678; retired from public life after the accession of James II, 1685. The only actor to remain centre-stage through fifty of the most turbulent years of Irish history, he possessed one gift essential to survival: a talent for loyalty.

disadvantaged them from the tactical point of view. They also claimed they were in league with the Scots Covenanters, obeying royal commands to spare them. The forged commission expressed such an injunction. Part at least of this was pure propaganda, dictated by the need to keep a weather eye on developments in Britain. But they did write private letters emphasizing the need to keep the Scots out of the fray. It made sense to try and buy them off; it also added to the presumption that they were part of a wider movement; and, Catholics or not, they had been inspired by Scottish pressure tactics. 'The Scots have taught us our A B C.'

If the rebels hoped the Ulster Scots would stay aloof, they were disappointed. O'Neill's manifestos were less striking than the obvious threat: and the inevitable engagements that took place helped cast the die. Moreover, such political calculations soon turned out, inevitably, to be far less important than the mobilization of religious feeling, which gained in potency with the progress of events.

None the less, it was the rebels' rhetorical identification with threatened constitutionalism, as much as their rather surprising victory over government forces in late November, that precipitated the leaders of the Old English in the Pale to join them. The political fabric in England was rending apart; and many observers already intuited a connection between the parliamentary opposition in Dublin and the armed rebellion in Ulster. Most importantly, an exclusive religious identification was also taking over: a symbolic conjunction came about of Old English and Old Irish against the Protestant threat. 'To all Catholics of the Roman party, both English and Irish, we wish all happiness, freedom of conscience.'[7] They were shortly calling themselves 'the Catholic army'. But the two cultural traditions, and the two kinds of Catholicism embraced by Old English and Old Irish, created structural pressures towards a split. And the Old English were very conscious that they had entered an alliance, not formed a union.

IV
==

The coalition of forces against the government was still daunting. The official forces were dispersed and scanty; the advantage lay with the rebels, though they were hampered by inadequate equipment. From the English side the decision to raise a Scots army to combat the Ulster rebels was fraught with tension; the disintegration of royal authority dealt a wild card into the game. All in all, reactions to the Irish rebellion precipitated the final resolution of where authority lay, between the Commons and the King. The 10,000 soldiers originally contracted for were eventually raised under Monro; their payment by Parliament became impossible with the advent of civil war in England. As early as December 1641 the idea was mooted of raising money on the security of Irish lands. All calculations were taking place in an atmosphere generated by an avalanche of unsubstantiated reports, often marked by hysterical inventions of names, places, battles and outrages. The reaction in England, understandably, was at once exaggerated and inadequate.

To contemporaries, the unplanned spread of the Irish rebellion was what was most striking – and provided the most evident condemnation of government policy. For their part, the government was violently unconciliatory. The early success of the insurgent forces was reversed by the arrival of Monro's army in April 1642; they were severely disadvantaged when the Continental contact system of the Irish abroad delivered to them a legendary military hero, bearing a legendary name: Owen Roe O'Neill. Subtle, aristocratic, a great figure in the Spanish army, O'Neill was deeply imbued with Continental Catholic zeal; his arrival on the scene is a reminder that Irish events are part of the history of the later Counter-Reformation and the Thirty Years War. While he was capable of fervent royalist rhetoric, it was suspected that he harboured the characteristic O'Neill ambitions on his own account. But his years in exile had not prepared him for the reality of his ancestral Ulster: 'Not only looks like a desert, but like hell, if there could be a hell upon earth.' Nor, with his foreign conditioning, did he understand the ambiguous position of tolerated Catholicism in Ireland: the *politique* approach of the Old English struck him as pusillanimity. O'Neill could still declare that he 'held him no better than a devil who will make any difference [between Old English and Old Irish] but call and term all Irish'. But his influence was inevitably cast on the Old Irish side, and not all his allies were so tolerant.

As the rebellion snowballed, it was joined not only by the Old Irish, but even by the Old English of the southern towns; Kilkenny emerged as the centre of military organization. By the spring of 1642 it was clear that Charles did not support the rebels; he called on them to lay down arms. But the parliamentary faction, now bent on confiscation of rebel lands, was a more formidable opponent. The English Parliament had approved raising £1,000,000 on the security of two and a half million acres of Irish land, to be forfeited after the rebellion, in all four provinces: thus a massive future reallocation of proprietorship was already at stake. And Parliament, rather than the Crown, would be arbiter, though the mechanism of this 'Act for Adventurers' temporarily resolved the deadlock as to who would meet the army's bills.

The rebellion spread unevenly, the rebels 'by reason of their inexperience after forty years' peace fancying the war a pleasant progress and but a change of exercise'. Their inexperience was notable. It was late in the summer of 1642 before O'Neill could begin to build his army, helped by Old English commanders like Thomas Preston[xii] and John Burke. By now, events in England had reached the point of civil war; and the nature of the rebel alliance in Ireland was easier to pin down. The Catholic Church had taken a leading part, backing the insurgent cause as being that of the true faith, while holding back from any overt assumption of control. And clergy and laity came together in Kilkenny in May 1642 to draft an organizational structure.

One great emphasis was the necessity to overcome provincial and cultural rivalries: there was to be no distinction between Old Irish and Old English within the alliance, though overtures from royalists like Ormond tried to stress their different interests, and there was recurrent resentment about, for instance, Old Irish soldiery not being entrusted with access to ammunition and weaponry. The cracks that would broaden into a rift over the issue of peace in 1643 were present from the beginning. For the moment, differences were overcome by the specific allegiance that all swore to the King, and by the fact that the organization was defined as a confederacy of *Irish Catholics*, not an alliance between the two different elements of Old Irish and Old English. But the loyalist ethos of the Old English, anxious from the outset to press on the King the virtues of moderation, was not shared by the Old Irish; nor was it always compatible with the intransigent Continental Catholicism imported with Owen Roe O'Neill.

It was none the less this emphasis that prevailed. Clanricarde's remark that many rebels believed that 'they walked in loyal and warrantable ways' should not be discounted, and nor should their genuine belief that they were acting in the King's essential interests. A strong emphasis

[xii] Thomas Preston (1585–1655): son of the fourth Viscount Gormanston; served in the Spanish service alongside Owen Roe, with whom professional rivalry deepened into personal antipathy; joined the Confederates and chosen commander of its Leinster forces, 1642; defeated by Ormond at New Ross, 1643; later successes were undermined by persistent arguments with Rinuccini and Owen Roe; his army annihilated by the Cromwellians at Dungan's Hill, 1647; allied with Ormond from 1648; defended Waterford and created Viscount Tara, 1650; escaped to France, 1652.

on royalist commitment is discernible in the lines of organization laid down at Kilkenny. Though there was an executive council and a representative assembly, the acute Old English sense that they relied on the King's prerogative prevented them calling it a parliament; they were also anxious to contrast their assembly with what had become of the English Parliament, and with its revolutionary relocation of authority. At the same time, the traditional Old English arguments for legislative independence were readily discernible in the manifestos from Kilkenny. As to the mandate of the Confederate 'government', it was of necessity indefinable; and their authority was not, in the end, answerable even to the assembly they had convened. Whether they liked it or not, they were revolutionaries too. But this did not necessarily make them constitutional radicals.

V
==

There was also another revolutionary party in Ireland: those Parliamentarian Protestants, planters and New English, who supported the Puritan cause in England. The numbers of those openly committed were small, but some planters, like John Clotworthy[xiii] and William Jephson,[xiv] played an important part in English parliamentary politics. By the autumn of 1642 they were intriguing with envoys from Parliament in the Dublin government; Parsons, at least, was sympathetic to their cause. There was, however, a powerful royalist faction in Irish politics, led by Ormond, Old English but impeccably Protestant, thanks to an orphaned upbringing under the Court of Wards. He commanded the royalist forces, and despite an implicit tension between

[xiii] John Clotworthy (d. 1665): a Presbyterian zealot; represented County Antrim, where he was one of the largest landholders, in the parliament of 1634; an opponent and prosecutor of Wentworth and Laud in the Long Parliament; unsuccessful envoy from Parliament to Ormond, 1646; agent for the adventurers and soldiers who sought to be confirmed in their Irish estates after the wars; made favourable terms for them, still better for himself; created first Viscount Masserene, 1660.

[xiv] William Jephson (c. 1615–c. 1659): sat in the Long Parliament; inherited estates in Mallow, County Cork; raised a force that dispersed the insurgents of Waterford, 1641; appointed Governor of Bandon, 1646; chosen by Parliament to dissuade Inchiquin from desertion, he followed that nobleman's example, 1648; lost all military employment and had to appeal to retain his Irish land; represented County Cork at the second Protectorate Parliament, at which he proposed Cromwell be made King, 1656.

him and the Lords Justices, for a year the government authorities in Dublin stayed nominally loyal to Charles. But when negotiations opened for a truce with the rebel Confederates at Kilkenny, it was through Ormond as the King's representative, while the Lords Justices were more concerned with mounting a military offensive against them. The location of authority was universally uncertain.

The Scots army in Ulster was also a variable factor. With the onset of civil war, its ultimate control was in question. It was paid, by and large, by the English Parliament, but subject to conflicting orders from Scotland. O'Neill's arrival had set it back, but it had tied down most of the rebel activity in Ulster; a strategic deadlock set in until the end of the 1640s. Though there was a strong movement to withdraw it for deployment in Britain, most of the army stayed in Ulster, a result of Monro's personal preferences as much as anything else. By mid-1644, however, the Scots army in Ulster was effectively a Covenanting force, in arms for Parliament, against whom any royalist elements grudgingly stood down. In 1644 the Earl of Antrim's scheme to invade Scotland for the royalist cause (or, more accurately, for the old cause of MacDonnell against Campbell) helped Monro to a year of unbroken victories. The vital importance of Scottish influences was further emphasized by the overspill of Scots refugees from the western Highlands to Ulster, many of whom stayed on. The events of the 1640s, which began with a threat to the Ulster plantation, ended by solidifying the Scottish nature of the province, while the question of the Scots army's arrears of pay joined the lengthening list of claims on Irish land as the hastily legalized spoils of war.

Politics in Dublin were also affected by the seismic shifts of these years in England: Charles, with characteristic indecisiveness, finally came round to appointing Ormond Lord Lieutenant in November 1643, which put the Irish government formally in royalist hands. Ormond remains a curiously colourless character for such a prominent figure, despite − or maybe because of − a vast eighteenth-century biography. Though possessed of enviable powers of survival and an unusual political consistency, he was unable to cope with the manipulations that surrounded him, both then and during his return to Irish politics after the Restoration. A King's man, a Protestant and a Butler, related to many of the Confederate leaders, he had to weather an impossible situation.

Much of his energy was spent negotiating for peace with the Confederates, for whom the year's truce arranged from September 1643 was a mixed blessing. It gave O'Neill the chance to consolidate an army, but divided counsels and internal rivalries bedevilled the Confederate military organization; and the truce achieved nothing for Catholic claims, since the King refused their demand for redress of grievances and guarantees against confiscation – effectively, the *status quo ante* Wentworth. From the royalist side the truce turned out to be a propaganda disaster, which could be presented by Parliamentarians as a sell-out to papists. The Covenanting intransigence of Scots, in Ulster as well as Scotland, escalated; even among more moderate Protestants there were considerable defections from the royalist cause.

These results were ironic, since the King's sympathies were anything but pro-Catholic where the Irish were concerned. Considerations of strategy as well as of property would always make them a special case. At this point, too, the question of European influence was about to assume a new importance. The influential Irish at Rome, notably Luke Wadding,[xv] were closely connected with the Confederate cause; papal envoys were already travelling to Kilkenny; and in October 1645 a papal nuncio, Giovanni Battista Rinuccini,[xvi] Archbishop of Fermo, arrived in Ireland.

The atmosphere at Kilkenny, the strange mixture of personnel, the sense of an Irish-Catholic government that might have been, is conveyed in the first impressions of this exotic newcomer.

The evening before my arrival at Kilkenny, I remained at a villa three miles from the town, to give time for all the preparations for my reception. Here I was visited by four noblemen, on the part of the Supreme Council of the Confederation, accompanied by Mr Bellings, who came to welcome me again. One of them, a man of erudition, delivered a short address. As soon as I was in my carriage, we set out, and in the limit of those three miles I was met by all the nobility and all the young men of Kilkenny, with crowds of other persons in different detachments, the leaders of each dismounting to compliment me. The first to arrive was a band of fifty scholars, all however armed with pistols, who, after caracoling around, conveyed their compliments through a youth, who, crowned with laurel and in a richer habit than the rest, recited some verses addressed to me.

Outside the doors of the church of Saint Patrick were assembled the secular

---

[xv] Luke Wadding (1588–1657): born in Waterford; educated in Lisbon and Coimbra; became a Franciscan, 1607; President of the Irish College, Salamanca, 1617; chaplain to the Spanish Ambassador at Rome, 1618; founder of St Isidore's Irish College, Rome, 1625; indirect instigator and director of the Irish rebellion, sending officers and arms to the country, 1641, encouraging Owen Roe to return, 1642, and advising the Pope to send Rinuccini as nuncio, 1645.

[xvi] See above, p. 47.

and regular clergy, who immediately commenced the procession. At the gate the magistrates of the city were in waiting, and amongst them the Vicar-General, who handed me a crucifix to kiss. I then mounted on horseback, wearing the pontifical robe and hat; the poles of my canopy were borne by some of the citizens, who walked uncovered, although it rained. All the way to the cathedral, a distance perhaps not less than the length of the Via Lungara in Rome, was lined with soldiers on foot bearing muskets. In the middle of the city, and at the foot of a very high cross, where a crowd was also assembled, we all stopped, and a youth delivered an oration, after which we moved on till we reached the church. Here, at the door, the Bishop of Ossory [David Rothe], the Ordinary of this place, although of great age, attired in his cope, met me and offered the holy water and incense, and, conducting me to the high altar, delivered an address appropriate to the ceremony. After this I pronounced a solemn benediction and granted the indulgences. Another oration was then made in honour of my arrival.

My first visit to the Supreme Council was in the following manner: General Preston and Lord Muskerry, brother-in-law to Ormond, waited upon me on the part of the Council; upon which I proceeded on foot, accompanied by all the nobility and soldiers under arms, towards the castle, to which, out of compliment to me, the Council had for that day transferred their sitting, and prepared the reception in a hall of great beauty. At the foot of the stairs, I was greeted by four of the Supreme Council, two of whom were the Archbishop of Dublin [Thomas Fleming] and the Archbishop of Cashel [Thomas Walsh]. At the head of the hall was seated Lord Mountgarret, President of the Council. He rose as I approached, but received me without moving from his place. My seat of red damask, decorated with gold, and a little richer than that of the President, was set on his right hand, but so that it principally faced the left side, and indeed both had the appearance of being in the centre. I made a very strong speech in Latin, explaining the sentiments, resolutions, and objects of his Holiness the Pope. Then I caused the Papal brief and the letter of Cardinal Panfilio to be read, and concluded with a few more words; after which I conferred upon them all the Apostolic benediction, which was mentioned in this brief. A reply was delivered by the Bishop of Clogher, standing, and in a short habit. Having taken leave of the President, who did not move from his place, the four gentlemen before-mentioned attended me to the east gate of the castle, and [General] Preston and Lord Muskerry with the same guards escorted me to the door of my house. All this has been carried out, because, as a formal visit must necessarily pass between the President and me, I thought it well to pay him the first one; to him as the head of those to whom I am accredited, and we have been treated on an equality in everything. The entire course of this reception was arranged by Secretary Bellings, to whom, as lately come from Italy and conversant with usages and formalities, the direction of these matters was committed.[8]

But from the very beginning, the Old English were suspicious of Rinuccini and wanted to trim his wings. This made inevitable an alliance between the nuncio and the Old Irish, particularly Owen Roe O'Neill, who had felt cold-shouldered from the start. Thus the Old English–Old Irish division, so carefully denied at the outset, came to the surface. The insurgents always called themselves the 'Confederate Catholics' (the 'Confederation of Kilkenny' is a nineteenth-century invention); this indicates an uneasy alliance of individuals, not a coalition of groups. The Old English especially articulated the grievances of Catholic subjects regarding education, land and the law, relying on royal prerogative to put them right; religious equality was only a reasonable condition of loyalty. They were very far from nationalist revolutionaries, even if increased parliamentary independence was an important part of the package.[xvii] They did not analyse the potential conflict between the demands of Catholicism and royalism: *could* a king who was not a Catholic give them what they asked? A not inaccurate reflection was the opinion of Lord Castlehaven,[xviii] who joined them: 'we hope in time, the storm being passed, to return to our old Government under the King'.

Indeed, the casual circumstances of Castlehaven's commitment to the Confederates are worth quoting:

On my arrival at *Kilkenny*, I found the town very full, and many of my acquaintance all preparing for war. To this end, they had chosen among them-

---

[xvii] Note the 'Reasons which moved ... the Confederate Roman Catholic army to present certain propositions' to Ormond in September 1644, requesting the abolition of laws forbidding the sale of plantation lands.

These clauses do and did nourish division and distinction between his Majesty's subjects: the like was never used in England, nor in any other kingdom. They extend not only to the Old Irish, but likewise, by construction to the Old English. For he that is born in Ireland, though his parents and all his ancestors were aliens, nay if his parents are Indians or Turks, if converted to Christianity is an Irishman as fully as if his subjects were here born for thousands of years, and by the laws of England as capable of the liberties of a subject. Such marks of distinction, being the insteps to trouble and war, are incompatible with peace and quiet.

(J. T. Gilbert, *History of the Irish Confederation and the War in Ireland 1641–9 ... Published from Original Manuscripts*, Dublin, 1882–90, vol. iii, 1885, pp. 301–2.)

[xviii] James Touchet (1617–84): became Baron Audley and third Earl of Castlehaven, 1633; a Catholic, his offers of service to the Irish Lord Deputies were declined, 1641; imprisoned, 1642; escaped to join the Confederates, to whom he gave excellent service under Preston, 1643–6; joined Ormond when Rinuccini refused to accept the peace of 1646; fled to France on Cromwell's arrival in Ireland; served in many Continental campaigns, which are graphically described, alongside his Irish ones, in *Memoirs*, 1680; restored to his lands and dignities during the reign of Charles II, he passed his last years on his Irish estates.

selves, out of the most eminent persons, a council, to which they gave the title of *The supreme council of the confederate Catholics of Ireland*, and formed an oath of *association*, by which all were bound to obey them. They had made four generals for the respective provinces of the kingdom; *Preston*, of *Leinster; Barry*, of *Munster; Owen Roe O'Neill*, of *Ulster;* and one *Burke*, of *Connaught*; and being to give commissions, they caused a seal to be made, which they called the seal of the council.

I was sent for to this council to tell my story, where I gave them a particular account of my adventures; and being asked, what I intended to do? I answered, to get into *France*, and from thence into *England*. Hereupon they told me their condition, and what they were doing for their preservation and natural defence, seeing no distinction made, or safety, but in arms; persuading me to stay with them, being as I was beloved in the country, had three sisters married amongst them, was persecuted on the same score they were, and ruined so, that we had no more to lose but our lives. I took two or three days to think of this proposition, and to examine the *model of government* they had prepared against the meeting of the general assembly, and most particularly their oath of *association* ...

Having spent some time on these thoughts, and at last taken my resolution, I returned to the supreme council, thanked them for their good opinion of me, and engaged myself to run a fortune with them. Whether anger and revenge did not incline me to it, as much as anything else, I cannot certainly resolve. This I well remember, that I considered how I had been used, and seen my house burning as I passed by; besides, that I was a light man, with no charge, and without any hopes of redress from the king, who was then engaged in the intestine war. Now, being thus a confederate, and having taken the oath of *association*, they made me one of the council, and general of the horse under *Preston*.[9]

But it is symptomatic of the divisions among the Confederates that some Old Irish opinion saw Castlehaven as a stool-pigeon sent in by Ormond.

The summer of 1645 was also marked by a twist in the peace negotiations that greatly complicated Ormond's position. The King, defeated and bereft of an army since the battle of Naseby on 14 June, sent the Earl of Glamorgan as a personal envoy to the Confederates; and he apparently promised to concede religious demands and make the arrangement public, the Catholics in return providing an army for the King. When the arrangements were prematurely disclosed, they led to a great crisis. The King's position, without the Irish army that was a supposed quid pro quo of Glamorgan's concessions, was increasingly boxed in; while the concessions he gave were now either meaningless or could not be adhered to. All Ormond could now do was make peace with the Confederates, essentially on Old English terms; it is notable that the arrangements came to be concentrated on their position, and for that reason and others Rinuccini set his already considerable influence against it. The arguments over accepting Ormond's terms show the *politique* approach clashing with ultramontanism.

Rinuccini was backed by Owen Roe O'Neill, the Earl of Antrim and his MacDonnells (whose Scottish adventuring was supported by the nuncio) and even some Old English, including, rather unwillingly, Preston. The Confederates were split; eventually, Rinuccini won and took over the council of the Confederates by a coup. His hand had been strengthened by O'Neill's spectacular victory over Monro at the battle of Benburb; but the significance of this encounter was exaggerated, then and later, by apologists seeking to vindicate Rinuccini's confrontation strategy. What mattered was that, with the failure of the Glamorgan initiative and the ensuing divisions between Old Irish and Old English, the chance of a broad front of Confederates and royalists against the Parliament's forces in Ireland had been lost; and with it, the chance, more considerable than often realized, of Irish events forcing a reversal in the English Civil War.

Ormond was driven back upon negotiations with the Parliamentarians. In June 1647 General Jones arrived at Dublin with a Parliamentarian army of 2,000. The position of the King, by now effectively a prisoner, made the question of where authority resided very doubtful. Ormond handed over Dublin to Jones and retired to England, leaving the Confederates riven by jealousies between Preston and O'Neill, and resentment against Rinuccini. If the Old English had looked for the *status quo ante* Wentworth, the nuncio's hard line demanded the restoration of Catholic rights as before the Reformation, with, as ever, important reservations regarding land ownership. He also presented a proselytizing front: Catholicism on the offensive. Hence his approval of an Irish-Catholic invasion of Scotland. His arrival had confused an already complicated situation.

In one way, matters were simplified by the arrival of Jones and the departure of Ormond. The lines of opposition were now clearly drawn between the parliamentary commissioners' army and the Catholic Confederates. But the Confederates themselves were split between the Old English, still open to royalist overtures from the Queen's party in France, and the Old Irish partisans who thought of the Old English not as fellow-Catholics but as English aliens. Rinuccini himself described them as Henrician or Elizabethan Protestants rather than real Irish Catholics.

These tensions were exacerbated by military reverses and complicated by the re-entry on the scene of Ormond, now negotiating with Confederate envoys in France on behalf of the imprisoned King, and alarming Rinuccini, whose earlier policy had revolved around excluding him. By 1648, indeed, a bewildering number of hands were in the game. Lord Inchiquin,[xix] up to this time the leader of the anti-Confederate forces in Ireland, had become increasingly uneasy under Parliamentarian rule and was moving towards coming out as a King's man. Some remnants of Monro's Scottish army were open to overtures from the royalists as well. But as the possibility of a broad-front policy swam back into view, it was once again torpedoed by the papal nuncio.

Obsessed by the fear of moderating a pure Catholic line, Rinuccini vetoed a draft truce with Inchiquin in April 1648 and withdrew to O'Neill's camp. The council at Kilkenny went ahead and proclaimed a truce with Inchiquin. And it was over this issue, at the end of May, when the Confederates were about to mount a military campaign under Preston, that the nuncio produced the ultimate weapon of papal excommunication against all those who supported the truce with Inchiquin. The propriety of this was much questioned, but it succeeded, if nothing else, in finally destroying any remaining unity between Old English and Old Irish within the Confederates.

This process was solidified by Ormond's return at the end of September 1648. He joined with Inchiquin and opened negotiations with the Confederates about religious concessions. A deadlock over the question of ecclesiastical jurisdiction was suddenly overcome by the news of the Remonstrance of the army in England, calling for the King to be put on trial. The Confederate assembly instantly agreed to Ormond's limited offers, to the chagrin of the bishops left among them. Symbolically, it was an impulse of pure royalism that brought about the formal end of the ill-starred confederacy.

Under the new arrangement, Ormond held the position of Lord

[xix] Murrough O'Brien (1614–74): Gaelic Protestant royalist who returned from the Spanish service, 1639; Vice-President of Munster, 1640; Governor, 1642; sought the presidency of the province from the King, 1644, but was put off; determined to serve the cause that best protected the Protestants of Munster, whose interests he personified; expelled Catholics from the major towns of his province, 1644; submitted to parliament and made President of Munster; massacred the garrison at the Rock of Cashel and defeated Taaffe's army to become master of the south, 1647; sought an alliance with Ormond, 1648; Cromwell forced him into retreat, 1649, and, in causing the solidification of the many warring factions into two monolithic parties, prevented the possibility of further realignment; being stuck with the royalists, followed Ormond to the exiled Stuart court; created Earl of Inchiquin, 1654; contrived a final twist to his tale by converting to Catholicism, 1656.

Lieutenant, appointed by Charles II in exile; ex-Confederate commissioners controlled local authority beneath him. Rinuccini left
Ireland three weeks after the King's execution, refusing to countenance
the new arrangements; O'Neill as a consequence similarly held aloof.
Old Irish intransigence came, again, at a point when royalists, the kirk
party, the Ulster Scots and many ex-Confederates seemed about to
unite against the regicide Parliament. Instead, by a Machiavellian irony
characteristic of the times, the beleaguered Parliamentarian General
Monck in Ulster made a truce, nearly, indeed, an alliance, with Owen
Roe O'Neill. The two extremes came together in repudiating the
middle ground, and Monck received the breathing-space he needed.
The stage was set for the last phase of the war.

Two years later Lord Broghill, son of Richard Boyle and hammer
of the Catholics, sent Henry Ireton some prayers and amulets removed
from the Irish dead after a battle: remarking that his countrymen were
'a people given to destruction, who, though otherwise understanding
enough, let themselves be deluded by ridiculous things, and by more
ridiculous persons'. It was a pithy Cromwellian epitaph for the Confederates, and an indication of Puritanism in the ascendant.

CHAPTER FIVE

CROMWELLIAN IRELAND

I

CROMWELLIAN IRELAND has become a subject of more balanced and analytical historical inquiry than used to be the case; but Oliver Cromwell's[i] record in Ireland is still inextricably identified with massacre and expropriation. His arrival on 15 August 1649 followed the great defeat sustained by Ormond and his new allies at Rathmines, and the disintegration of the royalist revival in Ulster; and he embarked on a brief, famous and much-studied campaign.

The events of the previous year had shown how Irish alliances could dramatically affect the course of events in England. Even at this stage there was the potential for a powerful royal coalition, stretching from the Scots to Inchiquin; and Ormond was still negotiating with Owen Roe O'Neill. Parliamentarian strategy was well aware of this danger; and there was, further, the necessity to make sure of reimbursing those who had invested in the probable reconquest of Irish land. More

---

[i] Oliver Cromwell (1599–1658): changed the face of Irish war, landscape and history; sent into Ireland in 1649 as Commander-in-Chief and Lord Lieutenant, commissioned to enforce the control of Parliament and ensure the progress of the new Protestant land settlement and the transplantation of Catholics; arrived 15 August; declared *civil* liberty for all who had shown 'constant good affection', but *religious* liberty was a contradiction in Cromwellian terms; stormed and massacred Drogheda, 2 September, and Wexford, 2 October, causing a succession of terrified towns to surrender; failed to take Waterford, 2 November to 2 December; published his *Declaration* 'for the undeceiving of deluded and seduced people', January 1650, justifying the new settlement as a godly retribution upon the 'barbarous wretches' who had contrived the rebellion of 1641; caused further towns to submit, including tenacious Clonmel, 10 May; left Ireland, 26 May; became Lord Protector of the Commonwealth of England, 1654; refused the title of King in 1657, but installed as Protector a second time, with the power to appoint his successor. Trod on Irish soil for only nine months, but few men's footprints have been so deeply imprinted upon Irish history and historiography.

publicly emphasized, however, was the rhetoric of vengeance – the mission against infidels, and the settling of the 1641 account. This combined ominously with the nature of Cromwell's Irish army: as much a conscripted infantry bent on plunder as a corps of radicals bearing God's word.

The Cromwellians were also fewer in number than Ormond's forces, especially after he at last made terms with Owen Roe in October; but their coalition was at best uncertain, and Cromwell's tactics were nothing if not decisive. The tone was set by his massacre of the civilian population at Drogheda – a town taken by Inchiquin but with no record of Confederate support. Like the later horror at Wexford, it is one of the few massacres in Irish history fully attested to on both sides; even Edmund Ludlow[ii] saw it as 'extraordinary severity'. Cromwell himself affected to see no need for excusing or palliating the actions of his troops, but his account betrays an uncharacteristically uneasy tone. As with later wartime outrages, the argument was proffered that such tactics saved lives in the long run by acting as a scare tactic; but this, too, has the tone of an *ex post facto* rationalization. Certainly, the supposed atrocities of 1641 were frequently invoked in extenuation; and one of the uncontested events of that year had been the massacre of a garrison at Augher after their submission.

In early November the legendary O'Neill died of a mysterious illness, leaving Ormond reliant on Fabian tactics of withdrawal and evasion – though if he had accepted a pitched battle in the Waterford area later that month, he could have won a much-needed advantage. But already, Cromwell's reputation was fighting his battles for him; fear of pillage and transplantation at best, carnage at worst, was bringing about local capitulations. Plague made its appearance in the towns. Despite the tension of Catholics serving under a Protestant commander, Ormond's supporters achieved at last a desperate unity; but they could not fight demoralization. The final betrayal was Charles II's revocation of support for the Irish forces, made at Dunfermline, which abandoned Ormond and the Irish Catholics. The remnants of confederacy dissolved in bickering. The remaining resistance was led by the inadequate

[ii] Edmund Ludlow (*c.* 1617–92): virtual commander of the army in Ireland between the death of Ireton and the arrival of Fleetwood, in which time, with the capture of Galway, 1652, the conquest was practically completed; refused to acknowledge the Protectorate and retired from public life, 1655; Commander-in-Chief of the Irish army on the re-establishment of the Commonwealth, 1659, promoting many officers of republican sympathies; escaped abroad at the Restoration.

Bishop of Clogher;[iii] significantly, the more resourceful figure of Daniel O'Neill[iv] was ruled out because he was not sufficiently Catholic. And those that fought on were clear that they were prosecuting 'a holy war for religion, king and nation'.[1] Cromwell departed in late May, leaving Ireton to complete the campaign. By the late summer resistance was restricted to guerrilla bands living a 'tory'[v] existence.

The history of Ireland in the ensuing decade of Cromwellian rule has often been passed over, by historians and even by reflective contemporaries, for political reasons as well as lack of evidence. It was for many an interlude more tactfully forgotten; while to historians, the landscape simply appeared an exhausted desert, though that perverse Victorian, J. A. Froude,[vi] persisted in describing it as Ireland's golden age. Parliamentarian representation was restricted to thirty members at Westminster, and the country was governed by parliamentary commissioners under the authority of a Commander-in-Chief – successively Cromwell's sons-in-law Ireton[vii] and Fleetwood,[viii] and then

[iii] Heber MacMahon (1600–1650): educated Douai; ordained Louvain; Bishop of Down and Connor, 1642; Bishop of Clogher, 1643; constant counsellor to Owen Roe and adherent of Rinuccini; became leader of the Ulster forces on Owen Roe's death, although without military training or experience; defeated at Scariffhollis, 1650; wounded, imprisoned and executed. Described by a French envoy as a violent Ulster Catholic, bent on making Ireland a Spanish fief.

[iv] Daniel O'Neill (c. 1612–64): Protestant nephew of Owen Roe; fought with the royalists in England, 1642–5; sent to Ireland to mediate between his uncle and Ormond; leader of the Ulster forces during Owen Roe's illness, 1649, but opposed as his permanent successor by the Roman clerical party; employed in royalist intrigues at home and abroad, 1649–60; made Postmaster-General, 1663, thus becoming the first Gaelic Irishman to hold a prestigious position in the English administration; known as the 'Infallible Subtle'.

[v] Toraidhe, the Irish word for 'raider', was applied from the mid-1640s to the banditti remnants of Irish armies. It later became a satirical sobriquet for political 'outlaws'.

[vi] James Anthony Froude (1818–94): Carlylean chronicler of Protestant heroism and Catholic villainy; had much first-hand experience of Ireland and an exasperated interest in Irish affairs; the chief value of his The English in Ireland in the Eighteenth Century, 1872, written to expose the folly of Gladstonian conciliation, was that it drew forth Lecky's riposte. Believed the most perfect English history was found in Shakespeare.

[vii] Henry Ireton (1611–51): fought at Edgehill, Newbury and Naseby, 1642–5; concerted 'Pride's Purge', with Ludlow, 1648, and signed the King's death warrant, 1649; chief author of the 'Agreement of the People', 1649; Irish Deputy, 1650–51, carrying out the Cromwellian settlement with great industry until struck by fever after the successful siege of Limerick.

[viii] Charles Fleetwood (d. 1692): succeeded Ireton both as Irish Commander and as

his son Henry,[ix] who became the chief influence in the Irish Council well before being appointed Lord Deputy in 1657. The efforts and ideas of these administrators, and the circumstances they worked in, deserve attention; at least initially, they had a positive conception of their role. One parliamentary commissioner described being led by God 'into a strange land, and to act in as strange a work, a work that neither we nor our forefathers knew or heard of: the framing or forming a commonwealth out of a corrupt rude mass'.[2]

They did not, of course, succeed: Irish conditions rapidly moderated evangelical intentions. Much of the Church of Ireland's ethos was compatible enough with Puritanism. Episcopalianism and royalism were diligently rooted out of the Church in Munster, for instance; but local variations defiantly remained, often through clergy being retained by local patrons – guilds and corporations as well as individuals. Ideas of wholesale conversion were circumscribed, not only by uncertainty as to what doctrines were officially acceptable, but also by a deep-rooted idea that the Irish nation was too steeped in guilt to be worth much bother. Despite an effort to proselytize in Irish, the conversion of Catholics was not really attempted, though there were some who crossed over, evidently from fairly cynical motives. As regards propagating the gospel, legislators dragged their feet. The army had, however, imported religious radicalism, and it left a residue behind. In the early years of Cromwellian rule, sects like the Baptists recruited impressively. Fleetwood was a religious Independent, and his tolerance of the Baptists nearly enabled them to take over the country's administration; but Henry Cromwell was more aware of the danger. The general approach towards Protestant sects was fairly tolerant, though a tough line was taken with those Ulster Scots who had turned against Parliament. Even this confrontation ended with the government paying salaries to Ulster Presbyterian ministers, creating a bulwark of

Bridget Cromwell's husband, 1652; Lord Deputy of Ireland, 1654–7, but only nominally from 1655, when he returned to England; a bitter persecutor of Irish Catholics.

[ix] Henry Cromwell (1628–74): followed his father to Ireland and defeated Inchiquin near Limerick, 1650; represented Ireland in the 'barebones' Parliament, 1653; an Irish Councillor and Major General of the Irish forces, 1654; approved of the transplantation of Catholics but opposed the imposition of an Oath of Abjuration upon them, 1657; as Lord Deputy, 1657, and Governor-General of Ireland, 1658–9, he consulted not only his soldiery, as his predecessors had done, but also the 'ancient Protestant inhabitants' of the country; unsuccessfully solicited by the royalists on the death of his father, he retired from public life on the fall of his brother Richard's Protectorate, 1659. Petitioning for the restoration of Irish lands from Charles II, 1660, he successfully pleaded the merits of his government of Ireland.

support for the Commonwealth. Had the Restoration not happened so quickly, they might have been comprehended within a non-episcopal Church of Ireland.

Catholics, of course, were another matter. But the Oath of Abjuration of popery imposed upon recusants seems to have often been ineffective. Under Henry Cromwell, religious moderates were preferred to zealots, and policy followed accordingly. General legislation against 'superstitious observance of Christmas holidays' continued, and Sunday observance remained a preoccupation; but many of the Commonwealth's attempts to 'reform manners' are closer to early legislation against Irish social practice than to any imposition of a Rule by Saints. Plans to ship poor Irish children to England as a servant class also have a familiar ring. Wide-ranging ideas of educational control were mooted, from primary to university level, but they were never really developed. There were some interesting private schemes, like Erasmus Smith's[x] benefaction of lands to found five schools and endow scholarships to Trinity College, which was taken up by the government; but this only really got under way after the Restoration. An elaborate scheme for a second college of the University also came to nothing, though important decisions were taken for the development of Trinity College.[xi]

It is arguable how evident the new experimental and scientific learning was in Cromwellian Ireland. Certainly it was not encouraged by government thinkers, who saw the chief function of education as religious proselytizing and political indoctrination. But a circle of innovative thinkers had already coalesced around Archbishop Ussher in Dublin, like the Dutchmen Arnold and Gerard Boate;[xii,xiii] there was

---

[x] Erasmus Smith (1611–91): merchant and alderman of London; having 'adventured' £300 into the Irish wars, he received 666 acres in County Tipperary, 1652; his estates expanding rapidly, he built schools for the education of the local children 'in the fear of God, and good literature, and to speak the English tongue', 1655; initially run by Presbyterian trustees, the schools were placed, with his consent, under episcopalian supervision by a Royal Charter of 1669.

[xi] See below, pp. 124–5.

[xii] Arnold Boate (c. 1600–c. 1653): Dutch Hebraist and physician; corresponded with Archbishop Ussher on biblical and chronological matters, 1635; became resident in Dublin and, through the Archbishop's influence, acquired an extensive medical practice; became Physician-General to the English forces in Ireland, 1642; returned to the Continent, 1644, but continued to correspond with Ussher, who acknowledged many literary obligations.

[xiii] Gerard Boate (1604–50): brother of the above; settled in London, becoming physician to the King in the 1630s; contributed to a fund that enabled the Dutch to

also the influence of Samuel Hartlib,[xiv] whose admirers and disciples wanted him to be supported by a grant of Irish lands. Boate's great *Natural History of Ireland* had its own proselytizing motivation – to attract settlers – but it was an exacting and distinguished intellectual achievement. William Petty[xv] was another remarkable thinker whose energies were focused on Ireland in these years. Token English intellectuals found employment in the land survey and redistribution, attracted by the idea of Ireland as a *tabula rasa* for new ideas as well as the chance of personal profit; there were also, inevitably, men like Benjamin Worsley[xvi] who arrived full of 'mountain-bellied conceptions' about making gold, manufacturing saltpetre and establishing a universal trade. More importantly, a certain level of planter society, like Robert Boyle[xvii] and his friends, did respond to the initiatives of the new learning, though their identification was often English as much as Irish, and they saw themselves as organizing a 'visible church of philosophers' to lighten the dark corners of a barbarous land.

This may serve as a reminder that, even under the Commonwealth,

subscribe money for the reduction of Ireland, in return for grants of Irish land; compiled a manuscript work on the topography and resources of Ireland for which the statistics were provided by his brother, 1644–5; appointed a doctor of the Dublin Hospital, 1649.

[xiv] Samuel Hartlib (d. *c.* 1670): came to England from Poland, *c.* 1628; an indefatigable writer and theorist of husbandry and education; published Gerard Boate's *The Natural History of Ireland*, 1652; dedicating it to Cromwell and Fleetwood, he professed to publish it 'for the common good of Ireland, and more especially for the benefit of Adventurers and planters there'.

[xv] William Petty (1623–87): came to Ireland as Physician-General of the army and reformed its medical services, 1652; undertook the first scientific cartography of Ireland, known as the 'Down Survey', 1654; supervisor of the settlement, all conflicts over land grants being referred to his survey; acquiesced in the Restoration; knighted, 1662; a founding father of political economy, his most notable tract being *The Political Anatomy of Ireland* (written 1672; published 1691), which describes the country's land, people and politics and analyses the potential of its resources, concluding that only a legislative union could preserve the industries of Ireland from the hostility of a jealous English Parliament; founder and first President of the Dublin Philosophical Society, 1683.

[xvi] Benjamin Worsley (*fl.* 1641–60): Secretary to the Commissioners of Parliament in Ireland, 1653; became Surveyor-General of Ireland, commissioned to present the 'civil survey', 1654; retaining the title, the actual work was undertaken and revolutionized by Petty.

[xvii] Honourable Robert Boyle (1627–91): born in Lismore Castle, County Waterford; son of the 'great' Earl of Cork; educated at Eton and Geneva; a founder of the Royal Society; propounder of 'Boyle's Law' concerning the relation between elasticity and pressure. Deeply religious, he financed the publication of Bedell's Irish Bible, 1686.

there was no union between England and Ireland. There was a separate Irish executive, and economic policies remained independent – free trade did not exist between the two countries. High taxation and unpopular methods of government led at first to resentment among the old settlers. There was a constant shortage of government money but also, especially in the late 1650s, a number of reforming projects. Economic and agricultural prosperity returned by the mid-1650s; traditional onslaughts on the stagnation of the Irish economy under Cromwell can be discounted. If the government was new, many of the old patterns steadily came back into focus.

Most of all, the stubborn structural differences in Irish society remained. The country was not a blank 'white paper', as the ambitious legal reformer John Cook[xviii] had ardently hoped. As Chief Justice in Munster, he planned sweeping legal reorganization, simplifying and modernizing the process of law, as a blueprint for what could be done in England. But, as so often, reorganization remained a matter of theory; the old ways were eventually reinstated for the country as a whole. On every side, there were existent structures to be accommodated. Henry Cromwell grasped this clearly. He set up close links with the New English planter interest, whose names appear prominently in local government and parliamentary returns for the 1650s. Like their new Cromwellian rulers, the pre-Cromwellian planters were pragmatic and moderate about religious practice; but all along they had looked to Cromwell to preserve the privileges of Protestant Ireland. They had come through as the victors.

II

The losers were more immediately apparent: the inhabitants of a devastated and depopulated[xix] land, whose property was now effect-

[xviii] John Cook (d. 1660): appointed by Parliament to prepare the charge and conduct the prosecution of Charles I; appointed Chief Justice of Munster, 1649; granted lands in County Cork, 1653; Justice of the Court of the Upper Bench in Ireland, 1655; arrested by Sir Charles Coote, then anxious to please the royalists, 1660; sent over to London to be tried; condemned and executed.

[xix] The Irish population of *c.* 1650 is hard to estimate. It had certainly dropped; 34,000 soldiers emigrated, and others were conscripted or sold abroad. 'Slave-hunts' certainly happened, though their extent has been exaggerated; there were possibly 12,000 Irish in the West Indies by the late 1660s.

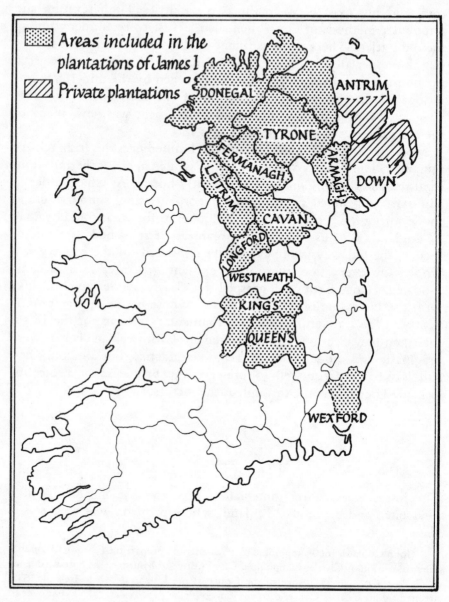

Map 4: *Plantations of James I.*
Source: R. Dudley Edwards, *An Atlas of Irish History.*

Map 5: *Cromwellian and Restoration land confiscations 1653–65.*
Source: R. Dudley Edwards, *An Atlas of Irish History.*

ively up for sequestration. More or less anyone who had been involved with the Confederates, or could be held to have been, was liable to expropriation. However, despite the sweeping scale of the initial condemnations, in reality property was taken as the base-line for punishment; the 'inferior sort' of rebels were pardoned at once. The government policy was not one of drumhead courts martial and widespread sentencing; in any case, most soldiers-in-arms had emigrated. Their aim was far more ambitious and far-reaching: a reconstruction of the entire pattern of land ownership.

For a decade the English Parliament had been allotting Irish land to English investors ('adventurers'), as well as offering land to soldiers in lieu of pay, and using it as security for loans, to prosecute the Irish war. The Acts of 1652–3 defining the guilt of the Irish were prompted by the necessity to make sure enough land was confiscated to meet such obligations. And since many of these obligations were to a discontented soldiery, the situation was very volatile indeed. There was a constant fear that the supply of land would run out, and an unrelenting pressure to accomplish the business quickly. The result was wholesale confiscation on a basis of incomplete knowledge and conjectural calculations of measurement. Even the celebrated 'Down Survey' conducted by William Petty was an underestimation.

Connacht and Clare were the designated areas for transplantation of proprietors who forfeited their lands elsewhere; they were to be settled within a cordon sanitaire imposed by the Shannon and the sea. The reasons for choosing this area were strategic, not economic; Ulster, not Connacht, was still considered the poorest province. Early ideas of a total clearance were abandoned, not for reasons of humanity as much as because of the difficulty of attracting an English yeomanry to replace the evicted peasants. But the notion of radically removing the previous owners was in many ways a new development in the plantation idea.

Those who held land and were expropriated were allocated land in Connacht, theoretically in proportion to what they had lost. It was an endlessly slow process, delayed by desperate petitioning and incomplete surveys, and also by the fact that the new settlers often demanded, and got, land in Sligo, Leitrim and Mayo set aside for the expropriated Irish. Pressure on land was also increased by the more surprising fact that many supposed ex-Confederates, who were not in fact entitled to a pardon, had survived condemnation and were in the market too. Very often they were Old English grandees who had fought with the Confederates and even, in some cases, been sentenced to death. On the other hand, some applicants to whom land was due never received it, because 'the great capital out of which all debts were paid' simply dried up.

By the time this had happened, the great majority of Catholic landowners in all Ireland had been expropriated, and many were resettled on smaller holdings in the west (though sixty-five emerged with estates of over 2,000 acres). A surviving 'List of the Transplanted

Irish 1655–9' has been described by a modern authority as a 'guide to the Roman Catholic landowners of Ireland in the mid-seventeenth century'.

Here will be met representatives of the old aristocracy and minor gentry, lords and ladies of the Pale and elsewhere, knights and baronets, esquires and gentlemen, widowed ladies, grandmothers, orphans and their guardians, aldermen and burgesses of Galway, Limerick and Drogheda, merchants and those of lesser estate as suggested by their acreages – all on the way out.[3]

One generalization that may be risked is that those transplanted were the uninfluential landowners. The great magnates at the top of the landowning social scale, and the 'inferior sort' at the bottom, generally stayed behind. A local study of Meath clearly demonstrates this pattern. In this way the Cromwellian plantation produced a social upheaval within the landowning class, not at large. Certificates for passage to Connacht and applications for dispensation give a vivid, harrowing and elegiac picture. One celebrated appeal, at least to historians, was that of Edmund Spenser's grandson, on whose behalf Cromwell interceded in vain. An interim survey for Wexford shows that 77 per cent of Catholics (by 1641 figures) disappeared as landowners; the remainder got lands in Connacht, on average less than half their original holdings in acres, and stony Connacht acres at that.

The transplanted were replaced throughout Ireland by 'adventurers' and soldiers, settled in mixed plantations. As with Ulster a half-century before, there were extraordinarily vague notions of how much acreage was at issue, and a curiously haphazard method of arriving at allocations. Some adventurers' estates were vast; some drew lots that were more like smallholdings. The plans for settlement can be followed in the huge and untidy assemblage of evidence to be found in the *Books of Survey and Distribution*, compiled to 'discover' the concealment of eligible lands. These have recently been put on computer,[4] and an attempt made to analyse the kind of adventurer who invested in the settlement from early on. Initial hopes for consortiums of the 'London citizens' type had to be abandoned; the riskiness of the venture required that anyone prepared to put up money be accepted. In a great propaganda offensive, investors were sought as far afield as Holland. Putting down the rebellion had cost nearly £3,000,000. The money raised was eventually £306,708 – not even the expected £1,000,000. But it was still a great capital to be repaid.

Attempts to profile the investors are complicated by the fact that land certificates were traded and exchanged; 67 per cent of the original investors failed to claim their land in 1653. Motives for investment were varied – zeal, cupidity, colonial ambition, the need to provide for younger children. Londoners were the predominant element, followed by West Countrymen. The money seems to have come from urban and merchant interests, with some gentry investors. As in previous undertakings, holdings snowballed in size as those who drew small shares sold out. Thus far, there were strong parallels with the plantation of Ulster, particularly the Londonderry involvement.

It is hard to discern a strongly ideological orientation to investment. Those who put money in were often aggressively Parliamentarian, and the project was more or less shunned by the peerage; but there were some large royalist backers. The interests of those who had put money on the chance of Irish land were strongly emphasized throughout the alarms and excursions of the 1640s; one criticism of the Ormond peace of 1643 was that it was 'unjust to the spoiled Protestants and to the English Adventurers'. Pressure was brought throughout for systematic confiscation and colonization whenever the war might end; though the investor influence on policy as such remained indirect. And, in the end, the important fact was that the implementation of the Cromwellian settlement and the attendant confiscations were a matter of state policy rather than entrepreneurial initiative.

The settlement of ex-Cromwellian soldiers was an even more complex subject. Depreciating land values meant that the government wanted to offload debts in this form wherever possible, often on unwilling soldiers. But many private soldiers were owed such small sums, in terms of land values, that they simply got rid of them to officers. The plan to establish a yeomanry of Protestant military veterans was stymied. Initially, about 12,000 ex-soldiers appear as potential settlers: but by about 1670 only 7,500 ex-soldiers had had their lands confirmed by the King.

As with the adventurers, it was the large-scale entrepreneurs who did best. Ex-Cromwellian officers predominate in town corporations from the 1650s and become prominent in the landlord class of the Restoration era. The lottery system of allocation distributed the new settlers throughout Ireland; the average settler–adventurer emerged with a holding of about 700 acres, though some accumulated thousands (and others, while allocated lands on paper, seem never to have claimed them). And as in Ulster, the old inhabitants often stayed on as tenants. By the end of 1655 supposedly not a single 'inhabitant of the Irish nation that knows the country' was left in one Tipperary barony. But in the 'English baronies' of Wexford the names of the old proprietors emerged as the larger tenants of the Restoration era. A local study of Tipperary indicates similar continuities.[5] This could be perceived as threatening, sometimes in subtle ways: the Cork Cromwellian Henry Bowen left a will in 1658 disinheriting his son if he married a daughter of the previous owner of his Farahy estate.

And the agricultural labouring population also remained; all in all, the pattern of replacement was far less total than its architects had hoped. Summing up in 1659, Henry Cromwell wrote:

> There are many deficiencies of lands to adventurers, soldiers, and to persons transplantable by virtue of decrees, many public debts and engagements mentioned in the said act for satisfaction, besides what other public engagements lie upon the Commonwealth to be discharged thereout, which were contracted in the redeeming and reducing this poor land from the enemies thereof.

A more pithy official summing-up described the undertaking as fraught with 'frustration, fraud and injustice'. The zealous plans for socio-religious reconstruction foundered. The ideal of towns free of Catholics, for instance, was never matched by reality, though the diaspora of Catholic merchants had a bad effect on trade. Efforts to attract exotic new Dutch or Huguenot entrepreneurs met with little success. An attempt to give Galway to the city of Gloucester, and thus create a new Londonderry, was a complete failure.

None the less, the collapse of a plan like the one to make Waterford an exclusively Protestant enclave still brought about a change in social demography. Catholics tended to be found in the suburbs, Protestants within the walls – just like an Ulster town. And Dublin did become 'Protestantized', though this was a result of the Confederate wars rather than of Cromwellian policy. It benefited from centralization, aggrandized its trade and grew in population: arguably laying the basis for its emergence as the second city of the British Isles in the eighteenth century. On other levels, too, the religious complexion of ascendancy was completely institutionalized. There was a fairly tolerant approach to Protestant independency; the distinguished history of Irish Quakerism starts at this period. The continuities of the old Church of Ireland, always Puritanically inclined, are clearly identifiable; so is tolerance of Presbyterian elements (as was only necessary, given the volatility of Ulster). Tithes re-emerged for the clergy's sustenance, rather than state salaries. But popery and even 'prelacy' remained, of course, forbidden. Priests were imprisoned and exiled, only very occasionally staying on upon sufferance; what amounted to forced labour camps for clerics had at one stage been set up on the Aran islands. By 1660 they were filtering back into provincial towns; some celebrated survivors re-emerged, like Archbishop O'Reilly.[xx] But, like schoolmasters, they ministered in secret, often deep in the country, around a mass-rock: an appropriate symbol for a rooted and perdurable native faith.

III
===

Cromwellian Ireland lasted a decade, declining to an ignominious close with the Protector's inadequate political heirs. Though many changes were nominal only, landowning and religion now followed a sharp line of demarcation. Would this change with the Restoration?

This partly depended on the extent of royalist commitment to change; and royalists did not automatically oppose plantation. Clarendon, always anti-Irish but probably typical, observed from Paris in 1654 that 'if we can get [Ireland] again, we shall find difficulties removed which a virtuous Prince and more quiet times could never have compassed'. But it was not purely a question of what royalists wanted. As matters turned out, even those who wished to undo the Cromwellian settlement had their hands tied. Royal authority in Ireland depended on the goodwill of the new landowners more than on the loyalty of ex-Confederate Catholics. The fact that under Henry Cromwell the interregnum authorities had depended on the established Protestant planters meant that in Ireland the 'ruling class' was not necessarily tainted with Cromwellianism, and was thus in a more secure position than it might have been. When Ormond, another great survivor, returned as a royalist Viceroy with a ducal title, he grappled hopelessly and unsuccessfully with the competing claims of incumbents and dispossessed. The New English wanted things to stay as they were, and they had influence at court – especially Broghill, now Earl of Orrery. They represented an entrenched Protestant interest that had never been too extreme in religious terms, and was very difficult to

[xx] Edmund O'Reilly (1606–69): educated at Louvain; returned to Ireland, 1641; Governor of Wicklow, 1642; Vicar-General of Dublin, until dismissed under suspicion of betraying Ormond's forces to Michael Jones, 1649; restored, 1650; imprisoned for a murder committed while governor of Wicklow, 1653, but pardoned as a token of thanks for his earlier betrayal of Ormond; retired to Lille; returned as Archbishop of Armagh, 1657; withdrew at the Restoration; returned for the Dublin synod, 1666; entertained by Ormond, who hoped to win his support for the Remonstrance; banished when the Synod rejected it; never returned.

dislodge; and they had allied with Henry Cromwell's men to protect the interests of the Protestant Ascendancy. Old and new Protestants formed the basis of Charles II's first Irish parliament; the adventurers' influence in retaining their Irish land was boosted. Rumour and threats of a Protestant rebellion and an army mutiny deeply concerned the Irish administration. It was inevitable that Charles's declarations of principles on which 'innocent papists' might reclaim their land were so qualified as to be almost useless.

In 1662 an Act of Settlement gave the Crown the right to reorganize the disposition of all confiscated lands, except those held by the Church and Trinity College. 'Innocents', whoever they were, could repossess without arranging compensation for those who had dispossessed them. In fact, matters stayed much as they were; the tribunal set up to adjudicate applications dealt only with claims of 'innocence' and only with a small proportion of these. Out of thousands of applications, 566 decrees of innocence were issued to Catholics, and 141 to Protestants. Those who applied, to judge by their names, were overwhelmingly Anglo-Irish rather than Gaelic. Ironically, had the plantation worked according to plan and the lands been clearly partitioned among adventurers and soldiers, it could have been more easily dismantled; the uncertainty and contradictions in its implementation helped preserve it.

The proceedings were open to much corruption and intervention; many fortunes were made at this as at earlier stages. An Act of Explanation in 1665 enjoined soldiers and adventurers to give up one-third of their holdings in order to compensate those Protestant settlers who had been dispossessed by reinstated Catholics. And through the agency of these Acts, and the courts they set up, a number of Catholics recovered some land – usually aristocrats with access to influence. Enough were left unsatisfied to preserve a potent and smouldering resentment. The age-old issues of land, religion and the manipulation of 'defective titles' remained intertwined, vexing politics and providing profit to lawyers and the Crown. The point may technically be made that the Cromwellian settlement affected 'only a small part of the population':[6] in fact, at most 2,000 families (and their retainers) were actually moved. But to this must be added the psychological displacement of changes of ownership, even where *residence* remained unaltered. The enduring sense was that expressed in Fear Dorcha Ó Mealláin's poem on the exodus to Connacht: a vision of the Gaelic Irish as the Israelites. The salient fact was that Catholics held about 60 per cent of Irish land in 1641; about 9 per cent in 1660; and about 20 per cent after the Restoration settlement. The political influence of Protestants was assured (borough corporations remained in the firm grip of the new settler interest); so, essentially, was their hold on property. Even after 1660, the Catholics' position as landowners was drastically altered. Their status as Catholics was more complex, but just as unenviable.

CHAPTER SIX

===

RESTORATION
IRELAND

I

===

TRADITIONALLY, THE Restoration period in Ireland has been interpreted by historians as an interim between upheavals: a stunned pause after the departure of Cromwell and before the arrival of William. There is much, however, about the nature of life in late seventeenth-century Ireland that demands examination. The static picture of post-war fallout is misleading. The Catholic upper classes hold on to land in the Pale; agriculture, architecture and intellectual life take on a distinctive shape. And there are several anticipations of the ethos usually associated with the eighteenth century: not least, the foundation of a landlord culture.

The special nature of Restoration Ireland is indicated by the interest of contemporaries in analysing it – facilitated by the opportunities for travel in more settled times. Evidence is provided by tourists like Dineley,[i] Brereton (for the 1630s),[ii] and de Rochefort;[iii] and also by

[i] Thomas Dineley (d. 1695): traveller and antiquary; visited Ireland armed with letters of introduction to numerous Protestant 'Big Houses', 1680; wrote *Observations on a Voyage through the Kingdom of Ireland*, 1681, an account of the state of the country, with passing comments on Irish history, which was posthumously published. An edition by James Graves was published in Dublin in 1870 under the auspices of the *Journal of the Kilkenny and South-east of Ireland Archaeological Society*.

[ii] William Brereton (d. 1661): knighted, 1627; MP for Cheshire, 1627–8, and in the Short and Long Parliaments, 1640; commanded the parliamentary army in Cheshire, 1642–9; an adventurer for 6,700 acres in Counties Tipperary and Armagh, which he received in the Cromwellian settlement. Kept a journal of three weeks spent in Ireland, July 1635, which is especially illuminating on Dublin, which he found to be among the 'fairest, richest and best built' of cities, resembling London more than any other town and far exceeding Edinburgh.

[iii] Albert Jouvin, de Rochefort (*fl.* 1668–78): a '*trésorier de France*' and traveller; published *Le Voyager d'Europe*, 1672, which included a description of Ireland in the latter years of Ormond's second viceroyalty.

those like William King,[iv] who wrote 'descriptions' in order to emphasize how things had been before the Catholic threat of the 1680s. But
there is also a new kind of analytical literature from William Petty,
Gerard Boate, William Molyneux[v] and his fellow-contributors to an
abortive *Irish Atlas*. Statistics are estimated energetically, if often
loosely; the late seventeenth-century approach to learning sees Ireland
as a laboratory. There is an intellectual flavour in religious and educational activity; possibly the beginning of what Yeats would call the
'ancient, cold, explosive, detonating impartiality' of the Irish mind.
The nature of Irish life in the later seventeenth century tends to be
obscured by the dramatic confrontation between Catholic James II
and Protestant William of Orange, fought out on Irish battlefields at
the end of the century: the glow of that epic conflagration has cast a
shadow over the world that it consumed.

II
===

Since the spark leapt on the issue of religion, this might be considered
first; and here a curious anomaly presents itself at once. In all the

---

[iv] William King (1650–1729): born in Antrim, of Scottish descent; educated at
Trinity College, Dublin; Dean of St Patrick's, 1689; a founder of the Dublin Philosophical Society; imprisoned for espousing the Williamite cause, 1689–90; published
State of the Protestants of Ireland, 1691, a powerful apologia for the revolution; as Bishop
of Derry from 1691 sought to repress Presbyterianism; supported the Penal Laws of
the parliament of 1695; appointed Archbishop of Dublin, 1703, and henceforth
recognized as the leader of the opposition to the English interest in Ireland ('to a
ridiculous extravagance, national' according to the Lord Lieutenant in 1714); sent
Swift to London to petition for the restoration of the first fruits to the Irish Church,
1701–11, and supported him over 'Wood's halfpence', 1725; passed over for the
primacy on account of his Whiggery, but a Commissioner for the Irish government
on four occasions, 1714–23.

[v] William Molyneux (1656–98): born in Dublin; educated at Trinity College,
Dublin; first Secretary of the Dublin Philosophical Society, 1683; by Ormond's
influence, became Surveyor-General of the King's works, 1684; retired to Chester,
fearing Tyrconnell planned a massacre of Irish Protestants, 1689; returned to become
a Commissioner for army accounts, 1690; sat as MP for Dublin University, 1692–5,
and during the absence of the Lords Justices, 1697–8, shared responsibility for the Irish
government; his inquiries into the effect of English legislation on Irish industry led
him to write the famous *Case of Ireland Stated*, 1698. Purportedly burned by the
common hangman, it is the book rather than its author that has earned a place in
nationalist martyrology.

turmoil of James's policy of 'Catholicization' after 1685, affecting army, judiciary and local administration, the actual position of the Catholic Church was approached very cautiously. And this reflects the ambiguous position it already occupied.

In order to grasp the dynamic of events in Ireland, we have to understand the strength of anti-Catholicism in England. The Act of Supremacy, giving spiritual authority to the King, formally excluded Catholics from civil or military office. Attempts in the 1660s to work out a formula by which Catholics would allow the sovereign temporal authority were condemned by Rome. Given that Catholics were, in the sense of citizens, 'non-persons', the attempts of Old English Catholics in Ireland to find ways in which to demonstrate their 'loyalty' were in a sense irrelevant.

Yet the basic, enormous fact that the vast majority of Irish people *were* Catholics necessitated a considerable amount of double-think. Up to the 1660s Capuchins and Franciscans led an underground life: petitions to Rome show such friars doubling as gardeners and coal-porters in Waterford, for instance. But by about 1670 there was a noticeable degree of relaxation. The Vatican was already taking sound-ings from the English court; Catholic bishops like Oliver Plunkett[vi] come to prominence at this time; the Church was lively, active and increasingly visible. A Catholic schoolmaster was teaching in every parish in Limerick in 1670. Decrees of Catholic synods in the 1670s show a strong effort at social as well as ecclesiastical control; there were determined attempts to restrict the traditional laxity of Gaelic Catholicism. Organizationally, the Church in Ireland was still hap-hazard in keeping parish records; but this was due as much to inefficiency and illiteracy as to penalization. Tridentine standards were still combating Irish ways in the eighteenth century. Petty discerned two kinds of Catholicism in Ireland: that of the poor, with their ancient customs and practices, and 'the richer and better educated sort of them,

[vi] Oliver Plunkett (1629–81): born in Meath, of Old English descent; educated at the Irish College, Rome, 1645; ordained, 1654; remained in Rome as professor of Theology at the Propaganda College and as a general solicitor for Irish causes; returned to Ireland as Archbishop of Armagh, 1670; disputed the seat of the primacy in Ireland with Peter Talbot, Archbishop of Dublin, 1670–78; ultramontane in ecclesiastical politics, but conservative in social philosophy; his preference for Jesuits over Fran-ciscans and his castigation of 'tories' excited the enmity of some co-religionists; generally tolerated by the Castle until 1678 but then accused of instigating the Irish Popish Plot; endured the travesty of a trial in London before being hanged, drawn and quartered. Beatified, 1920; canonized, 1975.

[who] are such Catholicks as are in other places'. The influence of the latter probably lay behind the Church's determined efforts to stop Catholic communities nurturing 'Tories' – 'lawless bandits [who] under the pretence of defending the national rights, infest the country'. This makes it less surprising to find that the local Protestant gentry were on good terms with Catholic bishops like the well-recorded Brenan[vii] of Cashel, and even helped them on occasion.

Policy could none the less shift, and have repercussions that reached down to local level. In 1672, 40 of the 190 pupils at a Jesuit school in Drogheda were Protestant; but within a year it was closed, and Plunkett and Brenan had gone into hiding. A backlash had begun even before the Popish Plot: anti-Catholic prosecutions escalated in England during 1673. And in England, anti-Catholicism took a distinctively anti-Irish cast, often inspired by the evidence of the 1641 'Depositions'. According to a preacher obsessed by the current Catholic *revanche*, his listeners' wives ran the danger of being

prostituted to the lust of every savage bog-trotter, your daughters ravished by goatish monks, your smaller children tossed upon pikes, and torn limb from limb, whilst you have your own bowels ripped up ... or else murdered with some other exquisite torture and holy candles made of your grease (which was done within our memory in Ireland).[1]

Thus the horrific iconography of the Irish rebellion was built into subsequent generations of English anti-Catholicism. The 'Popish Plot' and the ensuing witch-hunts that cost Plunkett his life were part of the same process.

None the less, in Ireland the Church continued to gain; and, given local conditions, a certain amount of coming and going across the religious divide was inevitable. There were even many mixed marriages. Discrimination was still institutionalized in organizations like town guilds, but it was more slackly observed. The irrepressible nature of Irish Catholicism was one reason for its vitality – the 'gaiety and superstitious forms' noted by one disapproving contemporary.

[vii] John Brenan (*c*. 1625–93): born in Kilkenny; entered the Irish College, Rome, 1645; ordained, 1650; returned to Ireland as Bishop of Waterford and Lismore, 1671; raised to the archbishopric of Cashel, 1677; an able administrator, who succeeded in tightening Irish ecclesiastical discipline, and the correspondent who provided the Vatican with the clearest reports they received of the progress and problems of Catholicism in Ireland. The only senior prelate to remain at his station through twenty years of actual and threatened persecution; perhaps the most remarkable priest of the Irish penal era, after Plunkett.

But ambivalences in official policy should not be forgotten either. There was no equivalent in Ireland to the English Test Act of 1672, and there were plenty of precedents for exemptions to the Act of Supremacy. The legal position of Irish Catholics was, in many practical respects, better than that of English Catholics; many fines and penalties fell into abeyance under Charles, and the Catholic hierarchy co-operated openly with the Dublin administration. From James's accession, the Church's position was obviously improved; priests emerged into the public eye and were allowed salaries, though they were not as yet endowed. Protestant superiority remained, in many areas, axiomatic; Catholics continued to occupy a curiously edgy position of formal inferiority combined with tacit toleration. But the ambiguities of their situation reflected the logic of local conditions just as much as the shifts in central policy.

This is especially applicable to the vital area of education. The traditional image of the seventeenth-century Irish-Catholic teacher is that of the scholar abroad – usually a Franciscan. But, as already indicated, the Catholic educational initiative in Ireland itself went as far as a short-lived attempt to set up Jesuit schools in the early 1670s. After 1685 there was a rush to found schools and convents; in 1688 James would order that Jesuits be put in control of government-controlled schools as the opportunities occurred. But even under the previous dispensation, Catholic influence was well-entrenched at local levels.

The educational machine could build on traditions of articulacy and linguistic variety that were noted by many observers. Petty in the 1670s described the use of 'the Latin tongue, very frequent among the poorest Irish, and chiefly in Kerry, most remote from Dublin'. More importantly, attitudes to the Irish language were in a state of transition. Those who wanted to institutionalize a cultural apartheid between ruler and ruled were not particularly worried about the use of Irish in traditionally Gaelic areas. But conciliators and proselytizers saw it as a barrier to reconciling the two Irelands, and wished to invoke Henrician legislation against it. There was no return to the great efforts of Provost Bedell[viii] of Trinity, who had tried to proselytize in Irish (though the

---

[viii] William Bedell (1571–1642): became Provost of Trinity College, Dublin, on Ussher's recommendation, 1627; Bishop of Ardagh and Kilmore, 1629; fought against non-residence, pluralities (he resigned Ardagh, 1633) and his clergy's failure to regard the native Irish as part of their charge; sought Irish-speaking incumbents for every clerical vacancy; spoke feelingly of the outrages against English settlers in 1641, but gave no credence to notions of a massacre; while in the custody of the rebels, he drew up a 'statement of grievances' for them to present to the Lords Justices.

native language continued to be taught in the College, and some chapel services were conducted in it). And the use of English continued to spread. The members of the supreme council at Kilkenny had been unable to read Irish, according to Castlehaven; English was by now the necessary tongue for business, used for utilitarian purposes. *Béarla*, the Irish word for the English language, originally meant something more like 'technical jargon'. Gaelic words were being adapted in their meaning (*Sasanach* doing duty for 'Protestant' as well as 'Englishman'); and, as the English language spread into the Gaelic areas, it became adapted in its turn. Many of the usages of English that are now considered distinctively Irish go back to the late seventeenth century; non-standard tenses, for instance ('I do be...') develop from about 1690.

On a popular level, spoken Irish faded far more quickly than the native languages of Scotland, Wales or Brittany. This was an indication of disruption, penetration, settlement and commercialization, rather than a result of government policy. The language remained in the west and south-west, in pockets along the Waterford coast and elsewhere; strange bastard mixtures of patois survived in north County Dublin and areas of Wexford. But English was becoming the language of everyday things.

A distinction must be made between the patchy survival of the spoken tongue and the sophisticated techniques of literary Gaelic, kept alive by the intellectual powerhouses of the Irish abroad. In these centres, the old language was used for works trying to make sense of the disruptions of Irish history, like Keating's *Foras Feasa ar Éirinn*; it was also used for combating the calumnies of English writers about Ireland, and for catechisms and devotional commentaries. Literary Irish was kept alive abroad for propaganda purposes; it is even possible that much of the 'orally preserved' storytelling that so excited folklorists in the nineteenth and twentieth centuries may originate from literary compositions still being made at this time. Seventeenth-century poetry in Irish, however, is remarkable for the survival of 'occasional' pieces in the ancient tradition – deft masterpieces turned for a particular occasion rather than based on a great theme. This memorialized poetry was a part of life. At the same time, the fashion for tediously stylized and artificial poetic 'disputations' also lasted on; but some commentators at least saw this as fiddling while Rome burned, and a more idiomatic style of accentual poetry is evident from mid-century.

From this point, too, the poetic preoccupation is with the decline of their order, and the need for Catholic and Gaelic unity – often accompanied by the fatal *leitmotif* of loyalty to the Stuarts. Several celebrated Gaelic poets observed and participated in the Confederate wars, notably Piras Féiritéir.[ix] Cromwell, Owen Roe O'Neill, the transplantations, all figure in the poetry of the next generation (interspersed with English words for new English importations). And through haunting refrains like *Séan Ó Duibhir an Ghleanna* comes the memory of a lost world, and the fugitive values of an idealized dispensation now lost for ever.

The Protestant culture that triumphed with Cromwell also had its rifts and contradictions. Under the Restoration the Dissenters of Ulster, though much increased, were also an out-group, and as deliberately difficult as ever. Relations with the Established Church were strained, although from 1672 they were officially, if irregularly, in receipt of a state subsidy, the *regium donum*. Nonconformity in the towns could be economically powerful, as were the Quaker merchants of Cork. By and large, however, Irish Protestantism was identified with the Established Church of Ireland – an intense minority, bent on keeping up their position. By 1672 Petty thought there were only 50,000 members of the Church of Ireland outside the towns; but the wealth of the Church was considerable, reinforced by endowments, an income from tithes and state support. The see of Derry was worth £2,000 a year; and a lack of suitable personnel was not allowed to stand in the way (being 'in a crazed condition' did not prevent one Trinity Fellow succeeding to the rich deanery of Cashel). Though the Restoration period saw some rebuilding of churches, and there were a number of distinguished bishops, the towns, especially Dublin, remained the real preserve of the Church of Ireland; and, as would always be the case, the contrast remained striking between episcopal grandeur and local churches falling into disuse, manned by underpaid clergy who needed to be pluralists in order to survive.

The Cromwellian administration had increased the salaries of ministers, as well as beginning the reorganization of parishes – a work that the Restoration hierarchy episodically tried to continue, without success. But in 1665 a traveller in Kilkenny, looking for the church, was told it was twelve miles off; the locals had one sermon a year, when the minister came to collect tithes. Nearly twenty years later, in Meath, only four churches in forty-two parishes were usable.

[ix] Piras Féiritéir [Peirce Ferriter] (*c.* 1600–1653): Old English gentleman of Kerry; Confederate captain in 1641; maintained the fight until 1652; captured and hanged at the fall of Ross Castle. Epitome of the cultured Anglo-Irishman: the love-poet and music-lover who could turn to martial pursuits when the occasion called.

None the less, the Church of Ireland preserved a certain flavour of its own, and in the seventeenth century it built the foundations of a distinctive intellectual tradition. A strong effort was made to control education, especially in areas with a Nonconformist identity: some notable schools were founded, though in several the teachers were largely Dissenters. Education as a means of social control, often suggested as a theoretical solution to Irish disaffection, was never really embraced in practice. Here as elsewhere, the initiative was left to Roman Catholicism.

In university education, the Church of Ireland enjoyed an automatic monopoly. Trinity College, as the 'University of Dublin' was generally known, reached a low point in the 1640s, as described in its saturnine official history: 'The few entries in the Register of this period mostly relate to the sale of plate; by 1644 the Chancellor was in the Tower awaiting execution, the Vice-Chancellor resident in England, and there was still no Provost.'[2] (The authentically astringent and economic tone should be noted.) In the 1650s there was a cautious revival of fortunes; a number of the Fellows were remarkable for their moderation and elegant political trimming. With the Restoration, the College was expanded and endowed, though a financial crisis arose yet again in the 1680s (the gift of landed estates carried no guarantee that the tenants would actually pay rent). But more importantly, there was a discernible improvement in academic developments after 1660, symbolized by Charles's bequest in that year of Ussher's great library, originally bought by the Cromwellian army for a projected second college. The range of subjects was broadened, with the foundation of chairs in Law, Physics, Oratory and Mathematics, the last encouraged by the government for vocational purposes: soldiers were to learn surveying at the feet of Myles Symner,[x] even if the curriculum remained intellectually old-fashioned.

The proportion of English-born graduates declined between 1661 and 1681, and Trinity became more identifiable with the distinctively Irish-Protestant cast of mind. This was partly composed of an uncompromisingly Puritan ethos – the incumbent of the chair of Divinity being referred to as the 'Professor of Theological Controversies'. It

[x] Miles Symner (c. 1610–86): educated at Trinity College, Dublin, 1626; ordained, c. 1633; chief engineer in the army, holding the rank of Major, c. 1648; became Professor of Mathematics at Trinity College, 1651; Fellow of Trinity College, 1652; also an acting Bursar, c. 1655, and auditor of the College, 1661–81; appointed Commissioner for the distribution of lands on the basis of the 'Down Survey', 1656–9; became Archdeacon of Clogher, 1661, and of Kildare, 1667–70.

also embodied a distinctly Anglican tradition, speaking out strongly against James, and being disciplined for it. Even after 1685, the College got away with refusing to elect Catholic Fellows. But in September 1689 it would be occupied by the Jacobite army as a barracks and a prison: an experience that embattled the flinty Irish-Protestant mind still further.

Trinity distrusted experimentalism, though it had an observatory by 1687, and there was no official place for the new scientific learning there, despite Symner's appointment and the interests of Bedell and Ussher. As in contemporary England, innovative intellectuals had to form their own circles. None the less, there were ways in which the Irish ambience was conducive to the new experimental approach to science. This may be connected with the passion for analysing contemporary Irish society mentioned at the beginning of this chapter; it also meshed with the preoccupations of scientifically minded Prot-estant planters. Practical experiment appealed to them rather than the speculations of antique philosophy. The interests of men like Thomas Molyneux[xi] and the Boates ran to experiments in animal husbandry and veterinary science as well as astronomy and physics. But intellectual experimentalism in Restoration Ireland is focused above all on the protean figure of William Petty.[xii]

Ireland expanded Petty's intellect as well as his fortune; his Kerry estates helped inspire some of his most fertile experimental ideas. If he is the key figure in the intellectual world of Irish science, Molyneux was the leading spirit in the revival of the 1680s that established the Dublin Philosophical Society – following through the tradition of radical intellectualism that is discernible in Cromwellian Ireland thirty years earlier, even if advances in sciences like astronomy had by then been forgotten. It was Molyneux who revived Hartlib's and Symner's ambition to complete Boate's *Natural History of Ireland*, and who began to collect material to this end. While he made no formal claim to con-nection with the earlier generation of intellectuals when founding the Dublin Philosophical Society in 1683, Symner, Robert Wood and most of all Petty were still active, and Petty was the Society's first President.

[xi] Thomas Molyneux (1661–1733): born in Dublin; educated at Trinity College, Dublin, and Leyden; wrote the first scientific *Account of the Irish Elk*, 1696, and a treatise that first asserted that the Giant's Causeway was a natural phenomenon; four times President of the Royal College of Physicians of Ireland, 1702–20; founded Dublin Asylum for the Blind, 1711; state physician, 1715; Professor of Medicine, Trinity College, Dublin, 1717; *Discourse on Danish Forts*, 1725; knighted, 1730.

[xii] For a brief biography that only hints at his intellectual range, see p. 106 above.

The extent to which the intellectual organizations of the 1680s built upon the achievements of the 1650s must remain debatable; it may be true that the later exponents of experimental science were more integrated into Irish life than their predecessors. But there were native traditions of experimental intellectualism in medical science, for example. And it is interesting that membership of the Dublin Philosophical Society was not of an emphatically Puritan complexion; it even included one Roman Catholic. Those who formed the Society tended to be rising men of English or Anglo-Irish backgrounds; they were also, by other criteria, a rather bizarre and 'marginalized' collection of people. They had close connections with English natural philosophy; but, just as much as reacting to Trinity's intellectual conservatism, they were addressing themselves to problems raised by everyday observations on their estates. In intellectual life, as in architecture, Restoration Ireland may show early pointers to the peculiar achievements of eighteenth-century Anglo-Irish culture.

III
===

A picture of economic life in Restoration Ireland is necessarily speculative: it must be inferred from literary evidence that is often blatantly self-interested, and from figures that have survived only erratically. Statistics exist for 1641 and 1665 that conveniently indicate the volume of trade before the Confederate wars and after the Restoration (but before the Great Cattle Act); they indicate considerable expansion, despite the upheavals of the intervening period, especially in exports of sheep and cattle. Under Cromwellian rule there had been prohibitions of export, in order to restock the country, but trade was reputed to have increased greatly by the 1680s. Certainly, prices and labour costs were famously low, and economic activity was observed to have picked up; low commodity prices helped exports, though high interest rates inhibited financial developments. But the general picture is much more uneven and patchy than is often assumed; to take the boom figures for 1650, or the late 1670s, or the mid-1680s, is to present a skewed picture. Most of all, the view of Irish economics as responding in a Pavlovian way to the dictates of exploitative government policy is to oversimplify the nature of economics, then as now.

Irish trade was largely, inevitably and profitably directed to England; trade across St George's Channel often accounted for three-quarters of its total volume. In 1660 Bristol and Chester (and Minehead for cattle) were still the traditional ports for Irish produce, though by 1700 the emphasis had shifted to Liverpool. As ever, the trade involved pastoral products in return for finished goods. In 1665 sheep, cattle (and related products), fish and horses made up over 80 per cent of total Irish exports; specific exports to England were principally cattle, sheep, wool, tallow and hides, while imports were woollen cloth, tobacco, coal, haberdashery, grocery, ironware, silks, linen and hops. In 1683 the list of Irish exports, again in order of importance, was made up of wool, tallow, linen yarn, and lambskins; this alteration in priorities, taken with the overall decrease in volume, and the compensating boom in the butter trade to the Continent, has generally been taken as an indication of the restrictive effect of the prohibiting Cattle Acts.

This will be discussed below, but first the motives of the English government in restricting Irish trade should be examined. There was no specific government policy of keeping the Irish subservient and benefiting the English. The legislation that *did* restrict Irish commerce was largely contingent upon other calculations, often to do with European economy and politics – or else a result of the activity of pressure-groups in the English Parliament, often working against the preferences of the government. The Navigation Acts of the early 1660s, in fact, included Ireland as part of England: Irish trade was not differentiated until the 1670s. Trade between the colonies and Ireland was temporarily excluded, but it flourished when such restrictions were not in force; in any case, colonial exclusions were notoriously easy to evade. The colonies of Irish in the West Indies, notably Trinidad and Montserrat, and the Irish addiction to tobacco, created a ready-made network.

Taking the Irish economy as a whole, the leading authority for the period has concluded, 'the navigation acts do not seem to emerge as of crucial importance';[3] there is even a case to be made that certain Irish products, like linen and provisions, were favoured by commercial restrictions. But government policy had the important, if unintended, effect of marginalizing the smaller ports of the west and south coast; trade was centralized more and more on Cork, Limerick, Waterford and Dublin, while by the end of the century Youghal, Kinsale and Dingle were declining. By 1700 Belfast had replaced Limerick as the fourth port of Ireland, even before the great expansion of the linen industry. The legislation of the 1660s led to the expansion of Ireland's trade with the Continent as well as the colonies; this became more important in the ensuing decades than it ever was again. By 1683 only

30 per cent of Irish exports went to England, compared to 74 per cent in 1665.

The economic adjustments of the eighteenth century, however, would make the Irish and English economies complementary, and Anglo-Irish trade would once more become the central axis of commerce. Even in the 1670s and 1680s England remained the main source of Irish imports (leaving aside Continental wine, brandy and salt). And English credit and banking mechanisms were inevitably used for financing Irish trade, given the primitive state (and prohibitive interest rates) of the Irish economy. Even as late as the 1650s some of the export trade was based on barter. The fact that the English connection was central by the 1690s meant that the embargoes attendant upon the Jacobite and Williamite wars had a drastic effect; exports were decimated until after 1696. When recovery came, it depended greatly upon the buoyant wool market that had been established from the 1660s; this was a chief reason why, by 1700, exports to England had once again become the largest component of Irish trade.

Indeed, the spread of sheep-raising and the increase of wool products characterized the late seventeenth-century Irish economy. Domestic woollen manufacture was still active, with friezes made up and sometimes exported; though techniques were unsophisticated, there was an imaginative use of native dyes. Most of the raw wool, however, was monopolized by export to England, though there was a thriving if illicit trade in wool to the Continent. New fashions, as well as new fabrics, favoured the long Irish wool; prices kept consistently high, even during the Dutch wars. In this context, trade was helped by a statute that was supposedly restrictive: the law forbidding the export of Irish sheep. The result was that English wool production remained inadequate, and manufacturers were reliant on Irish imports. Here was one of the many instances in the Irish context where the history of economic policy is a very different thing from economic history.

The Irish textile industry was effectively limited to wool at this time, though linen manufacturing developed hesitantly from the late seventeenth century on; there were imported communities of linen weavers in the south, and flax was by now a traditional product of the Ulster economy. The basis of the agricultural economy, however, remained cattle; and here again we encounter the questionable effect of English government policy. The great trade in exporting cattle 'on the hoof' was campaigned against in Britain in the 1660s and suspended in the Dutch wars; the Cattle Acts that restricted it have been presented as a deliberate body-blow to the most profitable sector of Irish trade.

But low prices consistently characterized the live export trade, and the importance of cattle export as a profit-making sector has been exaggerated at the best of times. The main effect of the Cattle Acts was probably the diversification of the Irish agricultural economy into saltbeef, butter and sheep, as well as the expansion of Continental and colonial trade mentioned above. The boom in butter exports, in fact, may have largely compensated for the exclusion of live cattle from the English market. Butter was a volatile trade, largely restricted to the Continental market, and subject to fluctuations; nor were beef exports particularly remunerative. But contemporaries exaggerated the economic results of the suspension of the cattle trade and confused them with the effects of war.

What the Cattle Acts *did* help bring about was the interdependent cattle economy within Ireland, symbolized by the great fairs that linked the fattening lands of the midlands and Connacht to the dairying ones where calves and yearlings were reared. What can already be discerned is the division of the agricultural geography into breeding and fattening lands; while the north-east, different in this as in so much else, followed its own pattern of tillage mixed with self-sufficient dairying.

The staples of the Irish economy thus remained what they had been for centuries, though there was some attempt at exploiting novel resources. Ironworks were the classic undertaking for 'improving' landlords; the attempts to establish local iron industries had already created intensive pre-1641 settlement along the river valleys of Cork and Waterford as well as in the midlands. Here again Petty comes to the fore, as the most noted of the ironmasters who helped denude the Kerry mountains of their forests. Inevitably, however, the iron industries were abandoned, and pastoral farming taken up once more; this was not so much a reflection of insufficient commitment to investment and a search for quick returns as a realization of what economic activity best suited a wet climate and a peripheral situation in relation to urban markets. Their abandonment of ironworks, it has been suggested, may illustrate the planters' adaptability and their determination to stay.

The newcomers were also responsible for developing fisheries, most notable in much-planted Munster and on the Foyle. However, the tradition that the native Irish ignored the wealth of fish surrounding them is contradicted by the evidence of poems like a mock-heroic seventeenth-century salutation to the herring's return. It remains true that a commercialized fishing industry did not develop outside some plantation areas; as with much else, the native Irish appreciated their fish but did not capitalize upon them. By the eighteenth century, sea-fish were seen as the food of the poor.

IV

The size of the population sustained by this economy in the late seventeenth century is a subject for endless discussion. Early gener-alizations were based on literary evidence, which emphasized the extent to which the Irish people had been decimated by the Confederate wars. When we try to establish figures, however, all seems notional. We know the Irish population in the very early eighteenth century was between two and a half and three million. The claim that it had reached this level in a very short time is more doubtful, and would put Irish developments out of line with the rest of Europe.

There was immigration, however, though not to a level that would compensate for setbacks through war, plague and emigration. And there was, indubitably, population growth in the latter part of the century. The composition of this growth is worth speculating about. Petty thought that at least 80,000 of the settlers, who left in the upheavals at mid-century, had returned by 1672; he added to this an equal number of new immigrants, probably young and fecund. There was certainly a strong trend of independent settlement after the 1650s that was more durable than sponsored plantation. It was after 1660, too, that really large-scale immigration into Ulster from Scotland began to be sustained. The proportion of the Irish population of Scottish and English blood would be 27 per cent by 1733.

L. M. Cullen, trying to profile the growth rate of the seventeenth-century Irish population, has persuasively argued that it was a good deal higher in 1600 than previously thought, and thus the expansion at the end of the century is less dramatic than often claimed. He has estimated a population of 1,400,000 in 1600, rising to over 2,000,000 by the Confederate wars; though this had dropped back to 1,700,000 by 1672, it recovered to 2,000,000 by 1687. This strong growth trend is often attributed to sustained early marriage – though not as early as used to be thought. Diet variations helped keep the death rate down, too, while young marriages remained the norm even as the average age at marriage increased elsewhere in Europe.

These are generally inductive patterns, looking at evidence like trade and urban growth as well as comparative statistics; further arguments can be adduced from the geographical distribution of the population, especially the immigrant population. Pre-1641 settlement persisted in the midlands and east Leinster, and to a certain extent around Limerick. Wexford and south Wicklow had strong Protestant farming communities, too; but settler society did not recover so well in Munster, partly because the iron industry lost its dynamic there in these years. Settlement areas tended to be 'dependent communities', focused on Protestant families: already the architecture can give pointers to this process. New communities were wooed after 1662 by an 'Act for Encouraging Protestant Strangers in Ireland', which helped bring in business communities of Huguenots and Quakers: the former imported the technique of goldsmithing into Cork from 1660. It should be noted, however, that there was already an energetic Dutch commercial and industrial element in the provinces as well as in Dublin – and, bizarrely, a Dutch Catholic community in Waterford. The mercantile culture of towns like Limerick, Waterford and Cork, which had doubled in size since 1600, was given its peculiar stamp by immigrant communities. And, since the events of the Confederate wars, such towns tended to be demographically divided along religious lines: Protestants within the walls, Catholics outside. Here, as elsewhere, the historical memory of confrontation created divisions that were palpable as well as enduring.

Living standards in late seventeenth-century Ireland were conditioned by the economic and demographic outline already presented. From the 1650s observers invariably stressed the low cost of living, especially in comparison with England; in 1676 Petty calculated labourers' wages at a half of what they were in England. Ireland's devalued currency ($£108\frac{1}{3}$ Irish pounds to $£100$ sterling by 1688) helped the process. But due to high prices for certain agricultural products, farmers did well, while rents stayed low. The depopulation of the 1650s may have been influential here. Petty, again, noted that most people in the country owned a house; while one Daniel O'Brien is recorded as setting aside a vast park around his house 'for mares, colts and deer'.

However, agricultural depressions were recurrent after 1660, due as much to freak weather as to the Dutch wars; there were famine conditions in Ulster, as in Scotland, in 1674–5. Another crisis came in the late 1680s, with epidemics of disease, and a dramatic fall in exports and revenue; agricultural prices accordingly collapsed. The picture is as patchy as for the economy as a whole; there had been an agricultural boom shortly before, with Irish imports banned in Scotland from the late 1670s. Patterns of prosperity, as of demography, were volatile, much as in the American colonies around the same time. Mobility remained the motif – reflected in the enthusiastic patronization of fairs, pilgrimages and horse-races. Even the face of the countryside may have reflected this, with the existence of many more 'villages' than previously supposed, unwalled and temporary but with an economic life of their own.

A variety of settlement and sustained population growth infer some change in patterns of diet, and this can be discerned in the late seventeenth century. Grain cultivation was now widespread, if subject to scarcity and restricted to areas where sunshine coincided with lime-rich soil: the Pale, Wexford and Limerick. Exports were variable, but prices remained low and harvests, evidently, abundant. Where there *was* a wheat economy, population became more dense. Bread was becoming more of a staple, especially in areas influenced by Scots and English settlements, though wheaten bread was still essentially an urban phenomenon (the celebrated 'soda bread' would be a nineteenth-century development).

Otherwise, much in the Irish diet resembled the food recorded by travellers in 1600. Bean cultivation was declining but still known. 'Bonyclabber' was still a staple. Potatoes had added to the variety; consumption and appreciation of them was spreading through all ranks of society, but they were not for keeping long and had not become a basic. It should be noted, though, that by 1688 anti-Irish mobs in England had adopted into their iconography a potato impaled on a stick. The overwhelmingly pastoral economy was reflected in the food people ate. Access to one or two cows was general, and butter featured strongly – for cooking meat in as well as providing the milky messes described in appalled terms by late seventeenth-century travellers, and served with the aggressively unstinting hospitality that was part of the Irish ethos. Diet in Restoration Ireland, in fact, was on the point of changing dramatically, with population expansion and increased commercialization; and signs of the process were already evident by the end of the century.

Imposed on the framework of Irish rural society in the Restoration period was the preoccupation of statisticians (like Petty) and poets alike: a new kind of landlord. Land ownership, and the distribution of Protestants and Catholics, remained much as dictated by the upheavals of the 1650s. But the actual patterns were much complicated by subsequent rearrangements. The anonymous poem *Páirlimint Cloinne Tomáis* is a celebrated contemporary satire, partly on the parvenu landlords but more especially on their tenants; snobbery and elitism seemed to be taking over at all levels. As in America, a new settler–landlord could act the gentleman on a much smaller income than in England, with his origins conveniently obscured. Some of them were anxious to show that they could give their tenants a better deal than the old Gaelic order; but their preoccupation with cultivating an aristocratic ethos, and the limited funds at their disposal for estate investment, rarely gave them a chance.

The genteel poverty of the old chieftains became a poetic cliché from this point on. However, an important sector of the Gaelic upper classes had Continental contact systems to sustain them, and to provide careers for sons and nephews in army, Church and commerce; aristocratic Galway families kept up their links with a cousinage that stretched as far afield as the Irish merchant communities of the West Indies. Of less interest to the poets, but far more numerous, were the nearly landless agricultural labourers, possessing a half-acre holding and possibly some residual grazing rights – the cottier class described by Petty, farming their patches in an obdurately primitive way. They had become, however, a 'settled substratum rather than the labour force for which the settlement had designed them'.[4] A less obvious element in rural society was the tenant farmer, of Irish or planter stock, occupying the level beneath the smallholder and above the cottier.

Petty was one landowner who developed his Irish estates in a deliberately experimental mode, and invested heavily (to little return), but this was not the norm. Land use remained unmodernized; enclosure was still rare, and 'booleying' remained frequent, as well as widely distributed holdings and complex open-field farming systems. At the same time, however, the landscape was undergoing alteration; the road system was being laid out as we know it; permanent hedgerows were growing. Deforestation created new fields; root vegetables were introduced. Planned villages were largely a post-1660 development, the square replacing the triangular pattern; so were landlord-built churches. Most of all, perhaps, the development of the countryside in Restoration Ireland is reflected by changes in architecture after 1660.

This is not particularly true of the housing of the poor, which was, as usual, much criticized by contemporaries for being un-English; the idea of its appositeness for Irish conditions was not entertained. The idea of hearth tax (which was doubled for houses with two chimneys) was on one level a crude attempt at graduated taxation, but its efficiency is debatable. The homes of the peasantry were much as they have survived – long, low, thick-walled cottages with thatched roofs, sometimes roped down. When a chimney was built, a new room, important for social purposes, was often added behind it: traditionally 'west of the hearth' in some localities, oriented differently in others. But for real innovation in Restoration Ireland, one has to look to the homes of the gentry.

This is not often realized. The noble architecture of the period is underrated, first because the storms of Irish history have carried it off (like the Earl of Orrery's Charleville, burned in 1690, or Buttevant, swept away the same year); and second, because the only known surveys of contemporary architecture are no longer in existence. A house like Beaulieu (1667) in County Louth is seen as unique – severe, beautiful, built by the Tichbornes on land purchased (not confiscated) from the Plunketts. But evidence is to be found elsewhere of a vital domestic tradition. Eyrecourt, County Galway (1660s), with its ambitious wood-carvings, massive doorcases and a famous baroque staircase, represented an artisan mannerism that was probably typical. Annesgrove, built by the royalist James Cotter in County Cork, was a remarkable and ambitious essay in the French manorial style, with pyramidal-roofed towers. This was on a considerable scale, like the classically strict and elegant Kilcreene House at Kilkenny, with its fine local marblework. But smaller houses, like Mosstown in Longford, Ballyarthur in Wicklow, or Shannongrove, built at the turn of the century, were as distinctive, if less well-known.

The development of this architecture was accompanied by the continuing adaptation of tower-houses. Many, like Ardfert Abbey in County Kerry, would be adapted yet again in the eighteenth century, thus concealing the previous innovations. A house like Assolas near Kanturk is a tower-house turned into a seventeenth-century manor house, with an eighteenth-century front added later; on a grander scale, Palladian *palazzetti* like Carton in Kildare swallowed up seventeenth-century houses. But specific developments within this period are still discernible. Significantly, fortifications were adapted. In the 1640s houses like Galgorm Castle in County Antrim or Coppinger Court in Cork featured important defence works. But when the architect of Richill (built in Armagh a few decades later) copied details from the Cork house, he substituted gables for battlements.

Did these decades of peace and episodic prosperity allow a native style to develop? There had always been elements of it, even in Wentworth's freakish palace at Jigginstown (1637), with its 380-foot frontage and endless brick-vaulting. In the cannibalistic way of Irish architecture, the interiors of Jigginstown ended up in Ormond's remodelled Kilkenny Castle. But it is more germane to look at the illustrations of houses in Dineley's *Tour*, which show the essentials of houses like Ballykitt, County Clare – simple rectangles with a projecting frontispiece, and wide-eaved platform, or hipped roof, on fashionable Dutch lines. Finnebrogue, County Down, retains the earlier H-block plan but with a steep roof, featuring dormer windows and decorated chimney-stacks as well as an elegant *piano nobile*. Interestingly, it also retains peat walls as internal partitions. Elsewhere, Boate describes lining damp Irish limestone with brick or panelling: Waringstown, a large classical house built in County Down about 1667, has walls of rammed earth.

By the end of the century, pediments and classical details were appearing; and though much seventeenth-century Irish decoration 'would pass unnoticed as Jacobean work in England',[5] there is already a trace of the 'bucolic baroque' that is so surprising in Irish Georgian houses. Many early eighteenth-century Irish houses could as well date from the Restoration period. Professional designers and 'artificers' were just beginning to appear; Continental architectural patternbooks were known; and Irish builders and carpenters had a better reputation than English ones. But the patron's taste was the important factor (Orrery learned his architecture in Geneva).

'Gentleman's seats were built or building everywhere,' wrote William King, remembering 1685; though his view was generally an idealized one, there seems some substance in it. As ever, this varied from one locality to another. Some landlords developed road networks and estate villages; planting and landscaping became notable, with tree-lined walks dissolving cleverly into the surrounding woodland. Gardens and arboretums had begun to be fashionable, though deerparks were still the norm. Fencing and orchards were encouraged, with fruit trees imported from Holland; the great tradition of studfarming was just beginning. But as in 1600 temporary and movable field partitions kept a fluid quality in the landscape; the rundale system continued well-established in Donegal, even if dying out in Tipperary.

The development of 'proprietorial geography' still remains striking. Powerful agents like Sir George Rawdon created the lay-outs of Lisburn and Portarlington; a single demesne wall at Hillsborough cost £2,000. It was a great age of brick-building. Towns had spread, rather uncertainly, with the plantations; there was still a tendency to centralize round the larger ports.

Though the viceregal residence was extended for Ormond, the age saw only one great Irish public building: William Robinson's Royal Hospital at Kilmainham, whose function – and, to a certain extent, style – were inspired by Les Invalides. It was built on ground taken from Phoenix Park, which at that point stretched south of the river. Though none of its other seventeenth-century buildings came near Robinson's masterpiece, Dublin at this time began to resemble the spacious city spread around the Liffey that was created in the eighteenth century, as well as attaining the status of Britain's second city. Some great town-houses went up that are no longer standing. There were large-scale extensions to Trinity College, originally modest enough, though on a scale previously unknown for non-military buildings in Ireland; the 1670s saw the erection of impressive French- and Flemish-influenced ranges, which would disappear in the College's great Georgian expansion. Dublin also acquired a celebrated, if rather *louche*, theatre in Smock Alley, which further enhanced its pre-eminence. The date of the city's great population growth is debatable, but there is a strong argument for seeing the phenomenon as part of its late seventeenth-century expansion – which may, in turn, have been founded on the capital's precocious development under the Cromwellian regime of the 1650s.

Outside Dublin, urban development was erratic and public buildings undistinguished. A tourist in 1683 described the new session house at Naas, 'advanced upon pillars which are yet so disproportioned and dwarfish that a mean artist might judge them set up in the darkest time of barbarism and before proportion or symmetry was thought on'. But this reflected the conventional English shudder at Irish 'incivility'. Foreigners were conscious of travelling through a country where settlement patterns were clearly visible, and 'frontier' areas concealed a sleeping tension. The self-consciously 'civil' planter culture was imposed on a world of woodkernes, Gaelic survivals and casual violence; though Dublin produced its scientific Philosophical Society, in the countryside the authority of hereditary physician families held sway.

But it is worth noting that the traveller was generally trying to seek out the most 'Irish' experiences possible; and that, as the seventeenth century wore on, these were harder and harder to find in unadulterated form. John Dunton[xiii] was determined to search out pure Gaelic society, but he had to wait until he penetrated Iar-Connacht (Connemara), 'a

---

[xiii] John Dunton (1659–1733): bookseller, traveller and political satirist; *The Dublin Scuffle* and *Conversation in Ireland*, 1699; intended to publish 'Teague-land, or A Merry Ramble to the Wild Irish', but it remained in manuscript form. Among the most illuminating commentators on everyday life in Ireland, despite a fondness for the prurient.

wild, mountainous country in which the old barbarities of the Irish are so many and so common'. Until then, he wrote disconsolately, 'I looked for Ireland in itself to no purpose'.[6] This idea of 'Ireland' is worth thinking about. What people consider recording is usually, by definition, what is exceptional. Restoration Ireland should be profiled through oblique sidelights and implicit assumptions, as much as through the highly coloured, primitive set-pieces recorded by observers who found what they determinedly set out to find. In Restoration Ireland the two worlds of planter culture and Irish life may have penetrated each other more than we know; and here, too, is an anticipation of the eighteenth century.

CHAPTER SEVEN

SHIPWRECK AND DELIVERANCE: THE FOUNDATIONS OF ASCENDANCY

I

PERHAPS ONE REASON why Restoration Ireland has seemed to some historians to be in stasis lies in the profession's preoccupation with government and politics. No parliament was summoned after 1666; government was centralized in Dublin, and the presidencies of Munster and Connacht allowed to lapse. Ormond, a sort of Irish Grand Vizier for the Stuarts, dominated politics as Viceroy from 1662 to 1669, and again from 1677 to 1685; but he, like all other Irish administrators, was trapped between the demands of English factions and the discontent of various Irish elements — land figuring largely in the calculations of both. The Restoration had left one side dissatisfied and the other insecure.

This instability is the important factor: the vital thing about the Restoration 'settlement' was its unsettled nature. This is notably true of land titles, but also affected the security of government. While the idea of a 'cabal' taking over English politics after Clarendon's fall is no longer believed in, Irish government did remain the puppet of English factionalism. This is most clearly seen in the fate of the provincial presidencies.

Restored in 1660, the presidencies were not developed as agencies of efficient legal and civil administration — a role they had come to fulfil before the upheavals of the 1640s. In Connacht the office declined into a sinecure. In Munster, by contrast, Orrery used his presidency positively, to take initiatives in legal and administrative matters; but the system as a whole was abolished in 1672, returning the south-west to its congenital state of unrest. Significantly, the reasons behind the abolition of the system did not have to do with criticism of the aristocracy, or with the rivalry between Presidential initiative and the institutions of common law; rather, the presidencies were doomed because of Charles's surreptitious diplomacy. His private priorities following the secret Treaty of Dover in 1670 necessitated the removal of Orrery, scourge of the Catholics, in 1671–2; and the personal nature of his presidency meant that the office went with him. Thus Irish administration was dictated, as under Wentworth, by English priorities.

It is true that the Restoration Viceroy occupied a position of different magnitude from that of the pre-Cromwellian Lord Deputy; but he still remained very vulnerable to court intrigue in London, as Ormond found out. And Irish opinion of a Viceroy depended on how far his influence at court was thought to reach. The other limiting factor involved money. The Crown experienced a continuing financial crisis in the 1660s and 1670s, which had immediate reverberations for the Irish administration. After 1660 there was an Irish revenue from quit-rents, while customs and excise and hearth tax were made over in return for giving up feudal claims. But there was no relaxation in money problems until the early 1680s, when improved administrative efficiency and a decrease in Crown expenditure coincided with an overt reversion of policy to traditional Stuart priorities.

Thus the Irish revenues had immediate political importance in England, and not only for their celebrated exploitation by Charles's mistresses. The idea of farming out revenues was taken to excess even by contemporary standards; this climaxed in the scandalous handing over of the entire exchequer to Lord Ranelagh and the Duchess of Portsmouth. New sources of income were pressed for all they were worth, notably the hearth tax from 1662; but the latter was to be of more profit to twentieth-century demographers than to seventeenth-century administrators. Revenue had to be supplemented by subsidies until the economy picked up towards the end of the reign, though Ormond's second period of supremacy from 1677 enabled an attempt at some kind of financial efficiency.

Once again there was a change of approach with James's accession in 1685; but the alteration that seized public attention was the new policy of Catholicization. James was not the extremist fanatic of Whig historiography; he wanted full acceptance rather than dominance for Catholicism. This, he felt, was the only necessary precondition for the true faith automatically to take over. Others, however, were less patiently prepared to await such a determinist process. Already Richard

Talbot,[i] favoured by James, had come to prominence as the champion of irredentist Catholic claims; of Old English background, he had acted as 'agent-general' for the Irish Catholics in land suits. Now he came to the forefront of politics in both islands, raised to the earldom of Tyrconnell. The novelty was not all it seemed. In his last years, Charles had in principle taken many of the decisions that would be implemented by James and Tyrconnell. And though Tyrconnell was kept out of the viceroyalty until 1687, and then awarded only the title of Lord Deputy, he was influential none the less.

The rise of Tyrconnell should not obscure the important fact that, to even the most devoutly Catholic king of England, Irish Catholics were 'different' – for reasons of strategy as much as property. Nor was James a papalist: as King of England and of Ireland, he insisted on his right to nominate to Catholic sees. Throughout the crisis of his brief reign, he recognized the conflict between English and Irish interests just as clearly as that between Protestant and Catholic. This policy was to allow Tyrconnell to proceed with, and take responsibility for, Catholicization, while the King himself could keep an eye on Protestant sensibilities. What happened was unsettling enough. Catholic judges provided one shock; army appointments another. The army in Ireland, effectively all-Protestant under Ormond, became the cutting edge of the policy of Catholicization. As so often in Ireland, a historical justification was invoked, spuriously or not: officers who had served the Commonwealth were to be 'investigated', which involved a remarkably speedy purge.

The law and the army were thus overtly 'Catholicized'; so was local government, the third prime instrument of Protestant influence. Some corporations were ready to embark upon an experiment in weighted power-sharing, with one bailiff Protestant and one Catholic. Dublin,

[i] Richard Talbot (1630–91): fought with Preston and then Ormond; escaped abroad, 1649; served under the Duke of York (the future James II); opposed Ormond as the Irish Catholics' chief agent at court, 1661–70; helped many of his co-religionists to their ancestral estates, while helping himself in the process; created Earl of Tyrconnell, 1685; became Commander-in-Chief and virtual governor of Ireland, supervising the re-entry of Catholics to public life; became actual Lord Deputy, 1687; sent 3,000 Irish soldiers to assist James in England but wavered as to his temporal allegiance; determined on the Jacobite cause only when assured of French assistance for the greater cause of Irish-Catholic ascendancy; created Duke, 1689; encouraged moves for the repeal of the Act of Settlement; fought at the Boyne, 1690; advised James to retire to France; followed him when his attempts to make terms with William were opposed by the Irish party; returned as Lord Lieutenant, 1691, to witness further defeats and die.

under its new charter (November 1687), retained a considerable Protestant representation on the corporation; Belfast managed to keep a composition of half and half. But the inevitable concomitant of these developments was still what every Irish Protestant expected and dreaded: a planned reorganization of the land settlement.

Here, too, the first steps were limited enough. As outlined under Clarendon, landowners in possession were to pay for confirmation of titles, and the proceeds were to be used to compensate Catholics. James's and Tyrconnell's intended development of this policy seems to have centred on disturbing the Cromwellians as little as possible, while trying to accommodate Catholic 'innocents' with a proportion of their holdings. Whether this would have been workable can only be inferred; it seems likely that the psychological displacement involved would have sparked off an open confrontation. As it was, the uneasy political stability was tipped over by a *deus ex machina* from another quarter.

This was the birth of a Catholic heir in June 1688, and the escalation of the political tempo caused by James's importation of Irish regiments in the autumn; memories of fifty years before were inescapable. William landed in November 1688; James left England the following month. By then the first confrontation had taken place in Ulster, symbolically involving the soon-to-be famous walls of Derry.[ii] The materials for conflagration were ready for ignition. What would follow was one of the greatest myth-inspiring confrontations in the continuing saga of Irish history.

The death-knell for the world described in the last chapter was struck when Ireland became a theatre of European war in 1689–90. Irish history has understandably tended to see the struggle between James and William as a battle over possession of Ireland (and, tangentially, England); but it should be remembered that William invaded England for reasons that were European, not English, and part of the 'revolution' he brought was a revolution in English foreign policy. It was as a part of this process that Ireland was brought on to the international stage. The impetus that led to James's last stand at the Boyne came from Louis XIV's encouragement rather than his own ambition. But French counsels were divided: the advocates of an expeditionary force to Ireland met with much opposition. The nature

---

[ii] Thirteen 'Apprentice Boys' refused to allow Antrim's Catholic army in the gates on 7 December; Tyrconnell backed down and allowed the city to keep its Protestant garrison.

of the planned intervention was also controversial; though soldiers and generals arrived, Tyrconnell's great need was money, not men, and this was never really met. Both sides, in fact, were handicapped throughout by disputations between allies of different nationalities.

But Ireland's peculiar conditions imposed an Irish configuration on the confrontation; in history and ballad, at least, the war of the three kings was the last stand of Catholic Ireland against Protestant Ascendancy, imparting the epic aura still immortalized in the naïve art of Belfast gable-ends. This reading begs many questions: from the beginning, for instance, the 'Catholic' side was deeply split, with traditional antipathies between Old English and Gaelic Irish coming sharply into focus. But this was blurred by the far more obvious dichotomy between the interests of Catholic Irish and Protestant settlers. The two traditions, locked in conflict, were commemorated in the iconography of the war: 'The Battle of the Boyne', 'Aughrim's Great Disaster', 'The City of the Broken Treaty', became subjects for historical novelists and painters as well as historians.[1] The Manichean duality inseparable from representations of Irish history set hard. What was symbolized as 'The Shipwreck' for the Gaelic Irish in Ó Bruadair's great poem was providential deliverance to the defenders of Derry.

II

The long perspective may put 1688 in terms of the continuing European war; but contemporary perceptions in England and Ireland saw it as a constitutional and political crisis for the British Isles. In Ireland, particularly, minds went back to 1641. Local Protestant militias were set up early on and, especially in Munster, there were signs of retreat into settler enclaves.

The Irish reaction to the 'Glorious Revolution' seemed predictable, given the commitments of the settler interest; but, in fact, the Protestant position was not entirely sure, and several of those who had opposed the Jacobite dispensation still could not immediately switch their allegiance to the usurper. It needed the brutally reductionist Lockian arguments of William King,[iii] published in 1691, to spell it out: ''Tis property that makes government necessary and the immediate end of government is to preserve property; where therefore a government,

iii For biography, see p. 118 above.

instead of preserving, entirely ruins the property of the subject, that government dissolves itself.'[2] It should be remembered that one of King's reasons for writing was to excuse those Protestants who had stayed in Jacobite areas from accusations of collaboration; there had been some fairweather clerics, like Anthony Dopping[iv] of Meath, who had even sat in James's Irish parliament in 1689. But by and large the Protestants' path was clear.

Irish Catholics, similarly, grasped at once not only the necessity of supporting James, but the advantage of emphasizing that this course was the constitutionally proper one. Tyrconnell's style was even-handed and impartial rather than triumphalist; he knew enough not to be as euphoric as some of his supporters. In fact, he was widely supposed to be ready to come to an agreement with William that would preserve the Irish-Catholic interest; it is possible that something like this could have been tried, had James not come to Ireland. But even before that event, a strong lobby of Irish-Protestant refugees had coalesced in England, suggesting to William the traditional way of levying an Irish army – by promising them confiscated rebel estates. By early 1689 Tyrconnell was urgently negotiating for French aid; by March all Ireland outside Ulster was under a Catholic administration. Those Protestants who had not fled were disarmed and uneasy, but had not yet been threatened. In Ulster, however, direct negotiations had begun between William and centres of resistance like Derry and Enniskillen.

Tyrconnell's chief concern was his army. Half of it had been rede-ployed in England by 1689; Tyrconnell immediately issued a flood of commissions. By the end of January he claimed to have raised 40,000 men. Predictably, they were enthusiastic but inexperienced; in addition they were ill-equipped and unpaid. Money and arms were Tyrconnell's chief need. The requisitioning of horses and weapons from the civilian population was interpreted as an anti-Protestant policy, but, in fact, it reflected strict necessity. French reinforcements came in April 1689, but they numbered only 3,000 men: money remained lacking. When the army was reorganized, and some blatantly unsuitable and inex-perienced elements weeded out, it reportedly stood at 35,000. Its

---

[iv] Anthony Dopping (1643–97): educated at Trinity College, Dublin; chaplain to Ormond, who secured his promotion to the see of Kildare, 1697; Bishop of Meath and Privy Councillor, 1682; resisted Tyrconnell, 1687–9; attended William III on his triumphal procession to St Patrick's Cathedral, July 1690; preached against the Treaty of Limerick as being too concessionary to Catholics, 1691; published *Modus Tenendi Parliamenta in Hibernia*, 1692.

weapons remained ineffective – unfortunately for Tyrconnell, armourers were generally Protestant – and there was much jealousy of the French. The uneven nature of Tyrconnell's army would be a vital factor influencing Catholic fortunes in the struggle ahead.

In March, James arrived at Kinsale. It is worth noting that he was presented to local Protestant dignitaries, and made conciliatory gestures to committed Williamites like the recalcitrant townspeople of Bandon. There is also a tradition that Quakers had considerable influence at his court (they certainly sat on Jacobite corporations). James's conciliation of Protestant elements was probably calculated with an eye to English opinion; from the outset he saw Ireland principally as a springboard to Scotland, and, though hailed enthusiastically by the Irish Catholics, he remained an unwilling avatar. This uneasy relationship with his Irish supporters and the misunderstandings on both sides were demonstrated by the tensions that characterized the so-called 'patriot' parliament of 1689.

The evidence for this convocation tends to be preserved in pamphlets, since its proceedings were afterwards negated; it was seen as the epitome of Catholic revanchism, made possible by Tyrconnell's reorganization of local administration. Certainly there were only six Protestants in the Commons, and many blanks in the representation of Ulster. There were, however, five Protestants in the Lords, and the bishops summoned were those of the Protestant Church, four of whom attended. This was a reflection, not only of the reality of Jacobite authority over much of Ireland, but also of the fact that for some Protestants, William's usurpation remained constitutionally dubious. The most important characteristic of the 1689 parliament, however, was its Old English complexion: its aim has been defined as creating 'an English dependency under a Catholic oligarchy'. Nationalist historians of the future would take this parliament as proof of the tolerance and pluralism of the Jacobite cause;[3] some contemporaries at least presented a similar case, though it may have originated in a desire to emphasize Old English elitism versus Gaelic extremism.

James's opening speech accordingly stressed liberty of conscience, and was conspicuously vague about intentions regarding the Act of Settlement; he continued to oppose legislation that would restore the Catholic Church to pre-Elizabethan status. The Acts of Supremacy and of Uniformity, prescribing use of the Book of Common Prayer and other Anglican practices, were left standing, and though the income of Protestant clergy was reduced to tithes paid by their own flocks, they were left in possession of Church lands. Much of this caution reflected the uncertain constitutional basis of the proceedings – not only because of James's expulsion from England, but also because the provisions of Poynings' Law necessitated that Irish legislation be first certified in England. This could not, obviously, be complied with; but it was argued that the actual presence of the King in parliament obviated such a step. To be on the safe side, the parliament tried to repeal the law, but eventually gave in to James's opposition. It did, however, pass an Act declaring that the English Parliament had no right to pass laws binding Ireland, and doing away with the English courts' right of appellate jurisdiction in Irish matters. Both issues would recur in 'patriot' politics over the next century.

These decisions overrode James's worries regarding the rights of the English Parliament, and his apprehension about general opinion across the Irish Sea. But a tougher battle was joined over the repeal of the Act of Settlement, partly because its defenders included many Catholics who had acquired land under its provisions. The Act was eventually repealed, though James encouraged its opponents. Those holding land in 1641 could now take steps for recovery of property lost under the Cromwellians, while those refugees who were held to have connived at rebellion against James stood to forfeit. This was seen as a traumatic reversal for Protestant interests, though perhaps it should also be seen in terms of a rhetorical tit for tat, since, thanks to the activities of Irish-Protestant refugees in England, Irish Jacobites already stood to forfeit estates if the war went against them. Of more immediate importance was the fact that, even though a court of claims was never set up, the Act led to upheavals within the army; many officers deserted their posts to find out their chances of reclaiming property. One comes back again to the ramshackle nature of Tyrconnell's war-machine.

Another reversal of traditional roles was epitomized by the Act of Attainder, identifying over 2,000 individuals as traitors to James. Again, this led to distractions over the explosive issue of landholding, as the estates of such traitors were sequestrated to compensate and reward Jacobites. This legislation, together with the Act of Settlement that was closely bound in with it, led to much recrimination at the time and afterwards. A great deal must rest, however, on how those Acts would, or could, have been carried out – which history was not destined to show. Lecky, judicious as usual, summed up the much-reviled Act of Attainder:

It was a conditional attainder launched in the midst of a civil war, against men who, having recently disregarded the summons of their sovereign, were beyond the range of law, in case they refused to appear during an assigned interval before the law courts for trial. The real aim of the Act was confiscation; and, in this respect at least, it was by no means unexampled.[4]

Parallel legislation was, in fact, introduced in England at this time.

If future land confiscation was in the minds of the 1689 legislators, a more immediate preoccupation was raising money for administration and war. The subsidy voted to James proved difficult to collect, and the Irish government resorted to devaluation in the form of minting the celebrated brass and copper coinage whose value fluctuated with the fortunes of war. In the short term, this was not unsuccessful; but it was a gift to Williamite propaganda for generations. The remaining legislation of the parliament is important only as an indication of the Irish Jacobite mentality. Their economic ideas show a certain commitment to protectionism, but also an assumption that Anglo-Irish trade would continue to form the axis of the economy. Here James's influence may have been important – as it certainly was in blocking efforts to legislate for a special relationship between Ireland and France. The approach overall was Old English, oligarchic, royalist and rather Anglocentric. If this was 'patriotic', the 1689 parliament deserves its sobriquet; but it was nothing like 'patriotism' in the sense understood by the nineteenth- and twentieth-century commentators who coined the term.

III
==

The deliberations and diversions of the 1689 parliament took place against the background of stiff resistance in Ulster, crystallized in the Protestant defence of Derry. This provided a story and a myth beloved of military historians of the time and ever since; the images of siege and delivery, treachery and self-reliance, would endure. The 30,000 Protestant refugees within the walls identified their Jacobite attackers, quite erroneously, as representatives of that Gaelic *émeute* they had been bred to fear; the city's strong English links ensured promises of supplies and support from Williamite forces, though by the time they arrived the Jacobites had occupied the surrounding territory, and they had to return. Derry was driven back on its own resources – another important component of the myth; so was the supposed 'treachery' of its pessimistic commander, Colonel Lundy[v] and the fiery Protestantism

---

[v] Robert Lundy (*fl.* 1688–9): entered Londonderry as Lieutenant Colonel in the service of James II, December 1688; bound himself to the Williamite cause and

of the Revd George Walker.[vi] Most of all, the siege of Derry would become a historiographical high point, building on heroic contemporary narratives, and eventually on Macaulay's pyrotechnical *tour de force*. A celebration of Derry's deliverance would become an annual ritual, though only following the centenary in 1790. Thus the invention of this tradition coincided, not only with the high point of Protestant Ireland's colonial nationalism, but also with a revival of sectarian tension, which would have a far longer life.

In the Derry myth, the weaknesses and inexperience of the besieging force are not often taken into account (though clearly recorded in dispatches back to France); it is also important that they allowed considerable numbers to leave the city. There were certainly epic scenes of tenacity and near-starvation before the eleventh-hour arrival of food supplies on 28 July enabled the defenders to outstay the Jacobites outside. Elsewhere in Ulster, equally successful, if less spectacular, resistance gave spokesmen from the province an important part to play in the Privy Council's Irish Committee. And in August, after much delay, Marshal Schomberg's army set off for Ireland.

This was a large and fairly professional force, though ill-equipped and, it later transpired, containing a considerable element of Jacobite fifth-columnists. With its arrival, tension escalated between Catholics and Protestants in Jacobite Ireland; at the same time James's advisors rediscovered some initiative, and the Jacobite army underwent some frantic reorganization. It remained better, however, at presenting a challenge than sustaining an attack. There was little military activity in the autumn, both forces suffering from bad weather and unhealthy camp conditions; Schomberg declined confrontation at Dundalk. In the spring of 1690 reinforcements for the Jacobites arrived from France,

appointed Governor, February 1689; advised an immediate surrender at the approach of James's army, April 1689; overruled but allowed to escape before the siege of the city began; accused of closet Jacobitism, his sole thought was probably self-preservation. Burned in effigy on every anniversary of the siege: his name became the Unionist synonym for 'traitor'.

[vi] George Walker (1618–90): born in County Tyrone; educated at Glasgow University; became Rector of Donoughmore, 1674; raised a regiment at Dungannon, 1688; forced to take refuge in Londonderry, April 1689; became joint Governor, with Major Henry Baker, on the deposition of Lundy; sent to London, after raising the siege, to petition the King for pecuniary relief; received as a hero; encouraged to publish his *True Account* of the siege; appointed to the see of Londonderry, 1690; killed at the battle of the Boyne before taking up his bishopric. His account of the siege provoked alternative versions, notably from the Presbyterian defenders of the city, who claimed he had deliberately devalued their role.

and a mercenary Danish force for William – whose own intervention was finally forced upon him, leading to the great emblematic confrontation at the Boyne on 1 July.

The most striking thing about this confused battle is the internationalism of both sides: Irish, French, Germans and Walloons versus Irish, English, Dutch, Germans and Danes. This was a two-way process; the first large-scale Irish contingents in French armies also date from this time. Accordingly, when the Williamites carried the day, the Boyne was seen as an international defeat for Louis XIV: welcomed, ironically, by the Pope, though *not*, as so often claimed, greeted with a Te Deum at Rome. But it is uncertain whether it was the decisive battle of the war, though Protestants celebrate it still. Jacobites saw it as an indecisive engagement, Aughrim a year later being 'the great disaster'. In the immediate Irish context, that may be true; but to contemporaries, the Boyne looked like William's victory over James, who fled to France three days later. And it gave Dublin, which James had throughout refused to burn, to William. As one Protestant wrote, 'we crept out of our houses and found ourselves as it were in a new world'. By the winter of 1690–91 a civil administration was set up, and the process of treason indictment and land confiscation got under way with regard to the areas under Williamite control.

Militarily speaking, the battle of the Boyne was technologically innovative, deploying foot and horse grenadiers as well as dragoons. It also created a necessary Irish hero in the dashing cavalry leader Patrick Sarsfield,[vii] who led the die-hard Jacobite faction that fell back on Limerick. He was celebrated for his bravery but was notoriously not very bright; jealousy aroused by the Sarsfield mystique exacerbated the indiscipline and dissensions that already rent the Jacobites. On the other hand, his inspirational leadership helped raise Irish morale, and William's Irish campaign ended on a diminuendo, with his failure to take Limerick. Contemporaries alleged that, if James had not commandeered a fleet of French frigates to take him safely across the Channel, they could have cut off William's supply lines. But the basic

---

[vii] Patrick Sarsfield (d. 1693): descended paternally of an old Anglo-Irish family, his mother was a daughter of Rory O'More; assisted Tyrconnell in remodelling the Irish army; commanded James II's Irish troops in England, 1688; returned to Ireland, March 1689; expelled the Williamites from Connacht; poorly utilized at the Boyne, but the popular hero of the defence of Limerick, 1690; appointed Governor of Connacht; created Earl of Lucan, 1691; left uninformed at Aughrim; attempted to defend Limerick a second time; treated with Ginkel, September 1691; sailed for France, December 1691; mortally wounded at the battle of Landen.

fact remained that once James's cause was gone, the Irish resistance, however brave, could no longer bring about the kind of success previously within their grasp. This was all the more true after Marlborough had taken Cork and Kinsale, the classic ports for communicating with France. By now the Irish were allegedly admitting: 'We are fighting not for King James or the popish religion but for our estates.'

Security of property was, however, impossible in the light of the commitments made by William to raise money for the war. Abortive negotiations over 1690–91 revolved almost entirely round the terms of land confiscation; those Catholics who had acquired land in the post-Cromwellian distribution were open to almost any offer that might enable them to salvage some of their estates. The 'new interest' of Galway landowners, for instance, had in many ways benefited from the mid-seventeenth-century upheavals, both by giving mortgages to impoverished owners and by buying up holdings assigned under the transplantation scheme. They had not supported the repeal of the Act of Settlement, and were ready to come to any terms with William that would secure their possessions. On this level, as on others, a split became apparent between compromising Old English and intransigent Gaelic Irish.

Equally symptomatic was the fact that the Jacobite side relied for much of its effectiveness on the activities of mobile and resourceful 'rapparees'[viii] within the Williamite areas, many of whom achieved fabled status, and remained locked in conflict with the newly formed local militias. Fearing this situation would continue indefinitely, the government poured resources into the army commanded by Ginkel[ix] from the spring of 1691. The Jacobites were also reinforced by French help under Saint-Ruth.[x] After a terrible struggle in late June, the Williamites gained control of Athlone, the gateway to the west; the

[viii] *Rapaire* was the Irish word for a half-pike.

[ix] Godert de Ginkel (1630–1703): born in Utrecht; accompanied William to England, 1688, and to Ireland, 1689; distinguished himself at the Boyne; took over the Irish command on William's departure, September 1690; captured Athlone, June 1691; offered terms to any Jacobite who would surrender; victorious at Aughrim, July 1691; took Limerick, October 1691; sailed for England, December 1691; created Baron of Aughrim and Earl of Athlone, before accompanying William to the Continent, 1692.

[x] Charles Chalmont, Marquis de Saint-Ruth (d. 1691): French general; commanded MacCarthy's brigade in Savoy; sent by Louis XIV to command Irish army, May 1691; driven by a loathing of Protestantism, he showed great energy but greater vanity; his haughty refusal to communicate with Sarsfield, his second-in-command, prevented the Irish from capitalizing upon the advantage he had won for them before his death at Aughrim.

last major battle was fought at Aughrim on 12 July 1691. By this point the Jacobites had recovered themselves yet again, further inspired by the element of religious crusade fostered by Saint-Ruth, famous as a scourge of the Huguenots. Plans were even canvassed for recrossing the Shannon, attacking the Williamites in the rear, and storming Dublin. But all hope went after Aughrim, where they lost the day in a welter of heroics, confusion and alleged treachery: 'the most disastrous battle in Irish history'.[5] The Irish cavalry, brilliant at the Boyne, here broke and turned, probably after Saint-Ruth's death, though the decisiveness of that event is still debated. The losses were enormous, in what was to be the last great pitched battle in Irish history.

Peace terms were already being speculated about when the Jacobites were driven back on Limerick as a last redoubt (Galway surrendered shortly after Aughrim). They could still muster above 20,000; but to the congenital faults of inexperience and a lack of equipment was now added a deep demoralization. On the other hand, it was late in the campaigning season, and their supplies were healthy; all sources agree that Limerick could have held out longer than it did, though not whether there was any point in so doing. French aid remained, as ever, the key variable; a convoy to relieve Limerick was arranged, but it was subject to the usual endless wrangling and procrastination. It arrived, in the event, more than a fortnight after the treaty was signed. Ultimately, it was the Jacobites who suggested treating for peace – to everyone's surprise, and with remarkable alacrity. Tactically, the decision may have been premature; but the reasons appear to have been dictated by morale rather than strategy.

Immediately after his victory at the Boyne, William had issued a declaration that he would not pardon the upper – in other words, landed – classes who had 'rebelled'. The corollary was obvious, and land confiscation remained the preoccupation. In the field, commanders were less intransigent; the terms that Ginkel wanted to offer in May 1691 (before Aughrim) involved pardon and restoration of their estates for all those in the army who surrendered, and freedom of religion to Catholics as enjoyed in the reign of Charles II. Even after Aughrim, the terms allowed to the citizens of Galway were similarly tolerant. But such ideas were always susceptible to limitation by intransigent Irish Protestants, who were responsible for pressing Ginkel to besiege Limerick rather than tempting its defenders by generous terms. Foreign commanders like Ginkel preferred to end things quickly by diplomacy; they thought the real issue had departed with James; they wanted to save money and bring their troops home;

and, in this case, taking Limerick was a much more thorny proposition than civilians realized.

As it was, the Jacobite overtures eased the situation for Ginkel. He rapidly agreed that Sarsfield's army could withdraw to France, which seems oddly generous; but it prevented large-scale guerrilla resistance, already a severe problem for the Williamite administration. This suited Sarsfield, who for personal as well as tactical reasons wanted to withdraw with his supporters to France; but it caused some dissension on the Jacobite side, while many Williamites were equally astonished that they ended up shipping a large army *gratis* to Louis XIV. In the event, 12,000 soldiers, with many followers and children, emigrated, and provided an important element in French military affairs even after the Treaty of Ryswick in 1697. But, besides setting up an important connection between Ireland and the Continent for the future, they bequeathed a dilemma affecting those they left behind them: could Irish Catholics ever be considered loyal to William, when they continued to be, in a sense, represented abroad by an army fighting for Louis?

Negotiations about the civil articles of the treaty were more complex, and involved the Catholic archbishops and Solicitor-General as well as the army leaders. The Jacobites started bidding high, demanding restoration of Irish Catholics to their pre-revolutionary estates, free liberty of worship, full civil rights and parochial organization. This was refused, but negotiations began in earnest from this base. There was, however, a fundamental point that needed clarification: whatever terms were agreed, whom did they affect? Simply the army remnant that negotiated them – *or* the Irish-Catholic community whom they represented? The latter interpretation was insisted upon by the Jacobites, and agreed by Ginkel; an English Williamite observer described the wider definition as 'the first thing insisted upon by them, and agreed to by us'. But as eventually published and put into practice, this wider interpretation was not included – the 'missing clause'. The war ended as it began, with a constitutional confusion.

As signed on 3 October, the Treaty of Limerick gave Catholics the same liberties of religion as enjoyed under Charles II or as were 'consistent with the laws of Ireland'. Free exercise of religion was not specifically promised, nor were any details of the position of priests made clear. If those still resisting William took the Oath of Allegiance, they would be pardoned and allowed to keep their property, practise professions and bear civilian arms. Those who opted for French service or had already surrendered were not included in these provisions. Nor were there any general safeguards for Catholic property; here, as elsewhere, an unfavourable reading of the treaty could construe it as affecting only those who had been directly party to it. No lawsuits were to be undertaken on the basis of acts committed in war, though various special cases were detailed.

The Williamite Lords Justices, though not involved in the negotiations, put their names to these terms, which were seen by many Protestants as dangerously lenient to Catholics. The Irish parliament never ratified the 'missing clause' which extended the agreed terms to all under the protection of the Jacobite army – effectively, in the counties of Limerick, Cork, Clare, Kerry and Mayo. It was omitted from the fair copy sent from Limerick to London and had to be reinserted by letters patent, leading to endless recriminations.[6] The contemporary argument that it was lost through hasty transcription at Limerick is unconvincingly disingenuous. What matters is that it gave the Irish parliament an opening, which it exploited, to restrict the terms of the treaty, though there were some who dissented, including William King. The ratification process also left out the clause regarding Catholic rights as in the reign of Charles II; bishops and clergy could be banished by edict from 1697. And though many Irish Jacobites retained their property under the treaty, the legislation of the early eighteenth century helped to destroy them.

The letter of the law could make out a case that this legislation did not 'break' a treaty that was drafted with questionable looseness, and never ratified by parliament. The question arises whether the terms struck by Ginkel at Limerick could ever have been 'kept', given the Continental situation and the contemporary denial of civil rights to Catholics in all Protestant-dominated countries. No amount of contextual argument or historical revisionism, however, can produce a moral defence.

The bitterness over the Treaty of Limerick epitomized the two cultures left confronting each other in Ireland amid the debris of William's war. One was Catholic, French-connected, romantically Jacobite (despite the Stuarts' dismal record in Ireland) and temperamentally Gaelic (despite the Old English leadership of the Jacobite cause). The great poet of this culture in adversity, Dáibhí Ó Bruadair,[xi] preserved in his poetry the sense of survival in a dark time and a

[xi] Dáibhí Ó Bruadair (c. 1625–98): perhaps the finest of Gaelic Irish poets; his verses supply clear evidence of the antipathy to English manners, law, religion and language felt by the Irish-speaking gentry of Munster in the late seventeenth century; specific subjects of his verse include panegyrics on Sarsfield and cries for a second Brian Boru; involved in both sieges of Limerick.

preoccupation that his own death would be the death of the culture that had bred him. He in fact died in 1698, railing against the new order. His most famous poem was called 'An Longbhriseadh' ('The Shipwreck').

> Níl tuisle ná taitneamh fá ar scamaladh sluagh an phuirt
> Re tuilleadh agus ceathrachadh sámhfhuinn nár fraigeasa
> Is mithid damh scaradh re senmaibh suaracha
> Is nach ionamhas eatha na eallaigh a luach dom thigh.
>
> Cine mo charad dá measa gur gua mo ghuth
> Eaid m'uilleanna is m'easna na dteastaibh le dua mo chruibh
> Tré thurrainn a ngradaim gé leath chiorruigh lua mo ruisc
> Ní shilfinn an dadamh dá rabhainn im chuanaire.
>
> Not a slip or success that hath shadowed our country's host
> For forty Novembers and more, have I failed to weave;
> It is time for me now to desist from such futile tunes,
> Whose reward brings no treasures of corn or herds home to me.
>
> If the tribe of my friends believe that my words are false,
> My elbows and ribs of my hand's toil give evidence;
> Though the strength of my eye is half spoiled by their fall from rank,
> I ne'er should have shed a tear, had I been a flatterer.[7]

But the defeat of Ó Bruadair's culture was the victory of triumphalist Protestantism and the governing caste that took as its watchword Protestant 'Ascendancy'. The issues that separated the two cultures in 1685–91 were sustained through the decades that followed. The traumatic events of James's short reign and its aftermath created the foundation of Ascendancy, with all its tensions and contradictions: a political and social ethos that must be seen as a function of these years, and not roped off into the 'Georgian' enclave of eighteenth-century Ireland.

IV

The foundations of Ascendancy rested on the penalization of Catholics; but to understand this operation it is necessary to note the position of Irish Catholics before the Protestant victory. Even before James's reign, local evidence from comfortable towns like Kilkenny and Wexford shows well-off Catholics living in accord with the Protestant Church and its institutions. Mixed marriages in Wexford, for instance, required a licence from the Protestant bishop but were entered in the Catholic register, and the children were baptized Catholics. Conditions varied locally, but, generally speaking, the higher the economic status of Catholics, the better their relations with Protestants. This being so, the important point about the pattern imposed after the war was that it attacked Catholic property as much as popish practices.

Though confiscation by outlawry continued through the 1690s, proceedings against Catholics for 'domestic treason' effectively ended with the war. But in 1695 the Irish parliament, which now began meeting every two years for financial reasons, passed legislation disarming papists and keeping them from foreign seats of learning – a direct reflection of current bad relations with France. The famous restriction on the value of horses owned by Catholics also dates from this time; and two years later all Catholic bishops and regular clergy were formally banished, and intermarriage made grounds for disinheritance. As yet, such edicts were not observed very strictly, and the letter of the law was more draconian in England, where Catholics were forbidden to buy or inherit real estate. The spirit of this legislation, however, was extended to Ireland in the 1704 Act 'to prevent the further growth of popery', which curtailed the position of Catholics far beyond even the most restricted interpretation of the Treaty of Limerick. Inheritance rights were done away with as between Catholics; purchase and leasing rights were restricted; exclusion from professions and public life followed. Sacramental tests and Oaths of Allegiance and Abjuration constituted further restrictions, for Dissenters as much as for Catholics. The election of 1713 saw a correspondingly large proportion of formal converts to Protestantism among the MPs; but by 1728 their power-base was cut away by an Act explicitly depriving Catholics, and even Protestants with Catholic views, of the right to vote.

Here again the emphasis was political rather than proselytizing: such mechanisms were contemporarily accepted practice against a politico-religious minority. But the point was that in Ireland those treated as a 'minority' were, in fact, a mathematical majority; and here, too, the volatile issue of land ownership played a special role. Through the 1690s the familiar complex of confiscation, forfeiture and regrant wound its way through the Irish courts. The Treaty of Limerick, in fact, protected and even restored a much larger proportion of Catholic land than often is realized, especially when compared with the misleading report published in 1699 by the commissioners inquiring into

Irish land. Even the spirit of the 'missing clause', omitted though it was, may have been tacitly observed in the counties to which it would have applied. The arrangements made by Ginkel with the inhabitants of Galway ensured the maintenance of Catholic landed influence in the county. Another moderating effect of confiscation was brought about by the parliamentary campaign against William's grants of Irish land to Dutch favourites; this led to the administration of Irish forfeitures by trustees who heard claims from Catholics as well as Protestants. It also provoked Jonathan Swift's[xii] first political pamphlet, *A Discourse of the Contests and Dissentions between the Nobles and the Commons in Athens and Rome* (1701). Laws against intermarriage, for instance, were gauged to restrict property-owning rather than to impose apartheid. By 1703 (and the final adjustments made to the Williamite land settlement), the Catholic share of Irish land ownership had fallen to 14 per cent; a half-century more would reduce it to 5 per cent. Technical ownership was not the same as possession; a Catholic gentry continued to exist in the west. And the list of Catholic laymen who stood surety for Catholic priests under the 1704 Act indicates a propertied Catholic class, especially in Clare and Connacht, though many of the names recur on later 'convert rolls' that indicate formal adherence to Protestantism for civil purposes. Elements like the O'Hara Boy family in Sligo or the Magans of Ummamore made the transition from Gaelic aristocracy to Georgian gentry. But they cannot be taken as typical.

A grey area is also discernible in the position of priests. The 1704 legislation recognized their existence *de facto*, as they could be registered

---

[xii] Jonathan Swift (1667–1745): born in Dublin; educated at Kilkenny and Trinity College, Dublin; ordained, 1694; entrusted with the mission to London to secure the 'first fruits' for the Church of Ireland, 1707–11; commenced the *Journal to Stella*, 1710; wrote the *Conduct of the Allies*, his first work for the Tories, 1711; became Dean of St Patrick's, Dublin, 1713; considered himself to be exiled in Ireland after the fall of the Tory ministry on the death of Queen Anne; wrote *Proposals for the Universal Use of Irish Manufactures*, 1720, and *The Drapier's Letters*, 1724; published *Gulliver's Travels*, 1726. His other Irish works included *A Short View of the State of Ireland*, 1727; *A Modest Proposal*, 1729; *The Legion Club*, 1736, and the posthumously published *Story of the Injured Lady*. His political philosophy was consistent support for the principles of the revolution, plus a belief in strong state support for the Church: necessarily, therefore, he gravitated to the Tories when it became evident that Whiggism meant latitude for Dissent, while Toryism no longer implied the necessity of alliance with Jacobitism. His Irish patriotism is the 'patriotism' epitomized in the fourth *Drapier's Letter*, owing nothing to nationality, everything to a universal sense that 'government without the consent of the governed' is slavery.

under law; but the terms of the Oath of Abjuration, denying the claims of the Stuarts, raised difficulties (they were, in fact, very largely prepared to take the Oath of Allegiance). The original design, however, was progressively to curtail registrations and thus ensure that all practising priests died out in a generation. This misfired, as did the encouragement of 'priest-catchers' who were rewarded for 'discovering' unregistered priests. This was an occupation despised by Protestant as well as Catholic public opinion, and was principally notable for causing a number of embarrassing riots. Mass-houses continued to exist, and priests still served in them; there is evidence of increased toleration from about 1730, though the legislation stayed on the statute book.

It is difficult to reconstruct the rationalization behind these policies; the circumstances of the European war and the values of the Glorious Revolution must be taken into account along with traditional Irish antipathies. Civil and moral liberties were carefully differentiated by contemporaries. Sir Richard Cox, Justice of Common Pleas, when opposing toleration for Dissenters, remarked: 'I was content every man should have liberty of going to heaven, but I desired nobody might have liberty of coming into government but those who would conform to it.' Archbishop King put it less brutally when he laid down that 'Papists should be debarred all public trust', but held it was wrong 'to take away men's estates, liberties or lives, merely because they differ in estimate of religion'.[8] The Protestant parliament was less ingenuous about the problem. And it all came down to the privileges of the minority Established Church and its members.

The Church of Ireland had survived the great crisis, and reaped its reward. Although Presbyterians retained their *regium donum* and even had it doubled, their position at law was not much more enviable than that of the Catholics; the Established Church remained the fountain of privilege in Ireland, more closely linked than ever to the Church of England and the possessors of land. In return, membership gave exclusive rights to political power. There were those within the Church who felt it had become too much an instrument of the civil power in the aftermath of the Williamite wars; a reforming movement developed with the aim of reclaiming some of its initiatives. But pluralism, sinecures and spectacular inequities of income remained – with the related habit of dependence upon the landlords. The Church was also reliant on state help even for what reforms took place. Whatever the wishes of reformers like Bishop Foy,[xiii] it was an arm of the estab-

[xiii] Nathaniel Foy (d. 1707): born in York; educated at Trinity College, Dublin; ordained and became Canon of Kildare, 1670; Doctor of Divinity, 1684; imprisoned

lishment, caught between the final authority of the government in London, the unreconstructed attitudes of local administration in Dublin Castle, and the legislators at College Green. Its convocation was no longer important; the influence of the episcopate, with its strong English complexion, was paramount.

Where Protestant vitality was to be found in post-war Ireland was in the world of Dissent, particularly in Ulster. Northern non-conformists set themselves firmly against the efforts of the Established Church to reconcile them to episcopacy; the early 1700s saw a number of celebrated confrontations. The distinctive Presbyterian culture of the north-east was reinforced by a flow of Scots settlers from the 1690s, an alleged 50,000 families by 1715; under Anne, the number of nonconformists supposedly equalled those of episcopalians in Ireland. The denial of their civil rights and the bitter antipathy felt for them by the Church of Ireland set them in a mould that was firmly anti-establishment in more senses than one. This antipathy went further than irritation at the Presbyterians' endless harping on the part they played in 1689–91. Swift's *Tale of a Tub* portrayed Dissent as a 'corruption of religion' that bore a basic affinity to popishness; and it was the Established Churchmen's anger at the English House of Lords' overruling the King's efforts to prevent the Irish Society leasing lands to Dissenters that inspired William Molyneux's *Case of Ireland*.[xiv] The newcomers from Scotland were not land speculators but energetic traders and farmers; within a generation, their wealth, especially that gained through the linen trade, would make them even more unpopular with the Protestants of the Established Church.

Though there was no Toleration Act for them in Ireland until 1719, they kept up an aggressive profile; Presbyterianism utilized a far more efficient social machinery than the Established Church. This may have been forced upon them by the technical anomalies of their position under Anne – denied validity for their marriage and burial ceremonies, and with their freedom of education and worship draconically limited. Much of this was not observed in practice; in a sense, the English government did its best to hold the ring between the Established Church and the Ulster Presbyterians. The exception was the brief Tory triumph at the close of Anne's reign, which boded ill for Dissenters.

with Archbishop King for preaching in favour of the Established Church and against a favoured preacher of King James, 1690; appointed Bishop of Waterford and Lismore, 1691; spent much of his own money improving his diocesan palace and endowing the free school at Grantstown.

[xiv] See below, pp. 161–2.

But the 'Test' clause in the 1704 Act, obliging holders of public office to take sacraments according to the usage of the Church of Ireland, gradually excluded Presbyterians from town corporations even in Ulster. Despite the *regium donum* and the Toleration Act, their equivocal relationship with the civil power remained, and would provide a key theme in the radicalization of the Irish political world after 1780, when the threat of Catholic disaffection apparently receded.

Up to then, the Established Church saw little need to meet the Presbyterian claims; if matters ever came to a head against insurgent Catholicism, they knew the Dissenters had no choice but to be on the Protestant side, whatever the internal divisions. But the Presbyterian argument against the Test Act was not in favour of general religious freedom; rather, that the Presbyterian Church was a legitimate national expression, in a way that the Society of Friends, for instance, and Roman Catholicism were not. The Presbyterian political culture was always ready to withdraw compliance from authority; their loyalty was conditional, believing that if the King had the power to set up Church government, it was only the power to set up the *right* Church government. This attitude was forged in the post-war years, as was the resentment felt by oppressed Catholics; and the forceful energy of Presbyterianism was perceived by the Established Church as a distinct threat to their own comfortable but passive position.

The Established Church's antagonism towards Dissent continued to be manifested – not only in the writings of Swift, but also in numerous sermons. Given the uncompromising basis of Presbyterian political culture, both bishops and landlords feared for their authority; the repeal of the Test Act became an election issue from this point on. In fact, after the influx of Scots round the turn of the century, immigration fell off and the number of Presbyterians actually decreased through emigration. But they made up the preponderant part of the population in the north-east, an area already demarcated as different; and they felt they accordingly deserved a right to dominate rather than simply to be tolerated. This helps account for the special odium in which Ulster Presbyterians were held; points could be stretched for Huguenots and Quakers, who occupied a much less threatening position. The threat of Dissenting radicalism remained in high relief, pointed up by doctrinal divisions over the supposed growth of rationalist and Arian beliefs denying the Trinity. The education of Ulster students for the ministry was usually received in Scotland, especially at Glasgow University; and contemporary controversies in Scotland tended to be reproduced in Ulster 'like fault lines in the geological structure'.[9] In 1726 the New

Light movement produced open schism. Again and again, traditional orthodoxy was challenged by an assertion of the right of private judgement. But in the Ulster context, fundamentalism, though attacked in every generation, tended to win out. 'No temporizing' in theology was joined with 'no surrender' in politics. Thus, despite their role in 1688–91, the Ulster Dissenters' interest remained against the government; there were even recurrent fears of a Presbyterian *coup d'état*. Meanwhile, the patronage of the Established Church was woven closely into the civil administration in early eighteenth-century Ireland, as part of the essential structure of that peculiar age; it was a pattern that evolved in the compromises and pressures of the post-revolutionary era from 1691 to 1714.

Politics in Dublin reflected this. A brief parliament was summoned in 1692, but many Irish MPs had already been extremely active in the convention of 1689–90 during their London exile; they continually emphasized the Protestant interest's worries about the government and court going soft on Catholics. Legislation regarding land and defence were the first priorities in 1692 rather than raising money, though this rapidly became the priority of the pragmatic Viceroy, Sidney.[xv] The Irish political nation remained deeply suspicious of him, and of the readiness of English law officers to invoke Poynings' Law when it suited them. An important element of discontented Irish lawyers in the 1692 parliament manipulated the upheavals that characterized its deliberations; through their London contacts the country opposition at Westminster joined forces with the Irish-Protestant interest to block court policy.

In some ways the 'court and country' interests that split English politics were replicated in Ireland, for Irish reasons – notably in the general attack on the initiatives claimed by the Privy Council in Ireland. Sidney interpreted the Irish opposition rhetoric as the language of separatism; but it really represented the usual ambitions of the Protestant elite, expressed in provocative actions like rejecting mutiny and militia bills prepared in England. And the temper of the 1692 parliament was more clearly indicated in their reasons for retaining the records of the 1689 parliament – it was for 'the honour of the Protestants

[xv] Henry Sidney (1641–1704): one of the earliest intriguers for the accession of William to the English throne; brought William to England, November 1688; created Viscount Sidney, 1690; accompanied William to Ireland and fought at the Boyne; made Lord Lieutenant of Ireland, 1692, but, alarmed by Protestant anger at the Treaty of Limerick, he dissolved the Irish parliament, which led to his withdrawal, 1693; became Earl of Romney, 1694.

of Ireland to preserve the records of the Irish barbarity' – and in their desire to extend habeas corpus to the Protestants of Ireland alone. Attacking Sidney's Money Bills was their way of bringing pressure to bear; given Poynings' Law, it was all they had.

Though parliamentary tactics against the government were blocked, the opposition succeeded in obtaining the result they wanted from the subsequent inquiry into the state of Ireland. This indicted the government since 1690, condemning their over-conciliatory attitude to Catholics as well as accusing them of corruption in the matter of forfeited estates. Such fears lasted; in the great parliamentary crisis of 1713, one of the Irish opposition's accusations against the Tory government was that it allowed widespread Catholic participation in the general election. The way was clear for the advancement of Protestant interests. This inquiry, and the ensuing lord deputy-ship of Capel,[xvi] laid the basis for the adroitly managed parliament of 1695, which brought in anti-Catholic legislation on a wide front and allowed the Irish Commons to initiate the heads of Money Bills before sending them to England for ratification. Thus the two chief insecurities of the post-war Protestant interest were pandered to: their fear of Catholic resurgence and their sensitivity about constitutional dependence.

All this indicated the need for a system of political manipulation, and formed the background to the practice of local grandees 'under-taking' the business of parliamentary management. But the system had its origins in the troubles of the 1690s, rather than emerging new-minted from the agitation of the mid-1720s. Irish politics assumed their peculiar form after 1692. By 1709 a slightly bemused observer of the Irish parliamentary scene at College Green remarked: 'upon the whole, from what I have been able to make of the people here, they are all politicians and deeply engaged on one side or the other, though the men of interest seem much superior in number to the men of conscience'.[10] There would be a brief 'rage of party' in the last days of Anne's reign, but the general trend of politics remained along these lines.

The point to be made is that 'patriot' politics have their origin

---

[xvi] Henry Capel (d. 1696): a fierce enemy of Catholicism in the English Commons, 1660–92; created Baron Capel of Tewkesbury, 1692; sent to Ireland as one of the three Lords Justices to replace Sidney, 1693; raised to the dignity of Lord Deputy, 1695, to ensure the passage of the King's desired laws through an Irish parliament; at the parliament he called, May 1695, the acts of the Parliament of James II were annulled and the Williamite settlement confirmed.

in the raucous tones of the post-war Protestant interest, not in the development of Grattan's oratory three-quarters of a century later. Sidney's impression of the 1692 parliament was alarming; the Commons talked 'of freeing themselves from the yoke of England, of taking away Poynings' Law, of making an address to have a habeas corpus bill, and twenty other extravagant discourses'. The reasons behind such rhetoric were disingenuous enough; but the contagion could spread. William Molyneux's celebrated critique, *The Case of Ireland's being Bound by Acts of Parliament in England Stated*, was one example; it parallels not only the activities of the parliamentary opposition but also the desire of reformers of the Church of Ireland for a certain measure of independent action in the period just after the war. Besides being 'the moving spirit behind Irish natural philosophy',[11] Molyneux had been member for Dublin University in the 1692 parliament and served on a commission for examining army accounts; he then turned his attention to analysing English legislation regarding Irish trade in the mid-1690s, which led to the celebrated but overrated Act forbidding the export of woollen goods in 1698–9.[12]

Molyneux's pamphlet appeared at the height of the controversy; it also reflected contemporary Irish resentment over English treatment of forfeited estates. Molyneux argued the case for Ireland's status as a separate kingdom and the logic of Irish members being represented at Westminster, if that was where Ireland was to be legislated for. The tract could be used by the lobby against trade regulation as well as by those pressing the pretensions of the Irish parliament. Molyneux derived his arguments from eclectic sources in political thought (Grotius, Pufendorf, Locke, Anglo-Saxon historical developments). Though many of the points had been made before, this was a new formulation since the Williamite regime had altered the position of the Privy Council in England: though Poynings' Law formally enjoined the referral of Irish legislation to the Privy Council, it was now really answerable to the English Parliament. Molyneux's argument entered murky waters when it came to 'origins': if there had been an ancient contract between the English Crown and the Irish nation, it was a nation that Molyneux's own ancestors had subsequently deprived of its property and civil rights. Molyneux's rather barefaced way of coming to terms with this point deserves quotation: 'The great Body of the present People of *Ireland* are the Progeny of the *English* and *Britains* [Britons], that from time to time have come over into this kingdom; and there remains but a mere handful of the Ancient *Irish* at this day, I may say, not one in a thousand.'[13] This was the central evasion of the 'patriot' position: it required identifying the Protestant Ascendancy as the only true Irish 'nation'.

Molyneux died, aged only forty-two, while the storm over his pamphlet was at its height; but his arguments had a long history. Swift wrote his *Story of the Injured Lady* less than a decade later, in 1707, though it was not published at the time. Here Ireland's claim to equality with England was advanced, along with the rights of the Irish parliament, the need for Irishmen in Irish jobs, the necessity of free trade and the iniquity of Poynings' Law. Swift combined these requirements with a vehement defence of the Church of Ireland's privileged position, and a total dedication against toleration for Dissenters. This was his great fear of a Whig government in office, though the robust Archbishop King pointed out that 'as to oppressing Ireland, a Whig and Tory parliament and ministry are much at one'. If Swift's views appear bigoted and inconsistent, in their day they seemed both representative and logical.

Swift also echoed Molyneux's description of Ireland's constitutional situation: 'Confusion and Uncertainty'. In contemporary terms, a measure like the Woollen Act demonstrated not so much an aggressive English government controlling Irish trade, but the use made by English factions of Irish issues; and the Irish colonial mentality further interpreted such legislation as weakening their position *vis-à-vis* that of Catholics and Dissenters. Such resentment, however, failed to prevent the passing in 1720 of the Declaratory Act known as the 'Sixth of George I': 'an Act for better securing the dependency of Ireland'. The outcome of the old controversy over the powers of the House of Lords, the Declaratory Act abolished the Irish Lords' right of appellate jurisdiction, thus defining Ireland's status as a dependent kingdom. By implication, it overrode the rights under common law claimed as the foundation of Ireland's 'independence' by colonial nationalists; they had to fall back on arguments of natural right, which raised the awkward question of the rights of Catholics.[14]

They, too, inhabited the 'dependent kingdom' of Ireland. But by then it was a kingdom containing a Protestant elite who had intermarried, established dynasties, stored up fortunes, built houses, colonized both the polite society and the political institutions of the capital, and defined themselves against the cultures of Catholicism and Dissent. By the early eighteenth century, for all the continuing equivocations and odd survivals, Irish society and politics had undergone a series of seismic shocks. Indigenous elites had been wiped out, along with the culture they represented. The descendants of settler gentry asserted their ascendancy in a polity that had the status of a dependent kingdom, but psychologically and pragmatically partook of attitudes best called colonial. The uniqueness of Irish development from that time to this owes everything to the fundamental and protracted revolution of the seventeenth century.

PART TWO

======

CHAPTER EIGHT

THE ASCENDANCY MIND
======

It would be well for all outsiders who would understand
Ireland and its tragic history, or indeed any phase of it,
always to keep before them the fact that the Ascendancy
mind is not the same thing as the English mind.
                        Daniel Corkery, *The Hidden Ireland*

I
======

The Irish eighteenth century arouses strong feelings. Those who lived
at the top of that gilded world, and lasted on into the early years of
the Union, never forgot the style and the savour of life before the fall;
but Victorian evangelicalism produced an intellectual, as well as an
aesthetic, reaction against the assured splendours of the Georgian ethos.
In the 1890s W. E. H. Lecky devoted a major section of his great work
on eighteenth-century history to a discussion of Georgian Ireland that
was ambivalent but inspirational; it remains one of the best sources.
The foundation of the first Irish Georgian Society in 1909, and its
publication of J. P. Mahaffy's[i] deliberately reactionary celebration of
Georgian style, brought reassessment into disrepute; by the 1930s there
was a dual tradition of interpretation, represented on the one hand by
Daniel Corkery's[ii] condemnatory *The Hidden Ireland* and on the other

---

[i] John Pentland Mahaffy (1839–1919): born in Switzerland of Irish parents; educated
at Trinity College, Dublin, becoming a Fellow, 1864, and first Professor of Ancient
History, 1869; his writings included scholarly histories of ancient Greece and Egypt,
an account of the foundation and fortunes of Trinity, 1903, and a monograph on his
special subject, *The Art of Conversation*, 1887. Provost of Trinity College, Dublin,
1914–19; knighted, 1918.

[ii] Daniel Corkery (1878–1964): born in Cork; writer of short stories, plays and a
novel, but remembered chiefly as a critic; *The Hidden Ireland*, 1924, encouraged his
countrymen to seek their cultural heritage in an exclusively Gaelic past, while *Synge*

by the commitment of W. B. Yeats[iii] and Elizabeth Bowen[iv] to the imagined world of their ancestors.

The great bold rooms, the high doors imposed an order on life. Sun blazed in at the windows, fires roared in the grates. There was a sweet, fresh-planed smell from the floors. Life still kept a touch of colonial vigour; at the same time, because of the glory of everything, it was bound up in the quality of a dream.[1]

Belief in the dream required a personal commitment to the history of the Ascendancy class. To the Catholic or Dissenting traditions, those values seemed at once oppressive and frivolous. 'Nothing but an insidious *bonhomie*,' wrote the Ulster poet Louis MacNeice,[v] 'an obsolete bravado, and a way with horses.' Certainly, analysis of the Georgian Ascendancy required deliberate selectivity; it attracted a kind of social historian not in much repute nowadays. The sources involved the inevitable Mrs Delany's[vi] memoirs and letters, the correspondence of

and Anglo-Irish Literature, 1931, was a stern critique of the idea that the writings of Anglo-Irishmen could be espoused as the national literature. Professor of English at University College, Cork, 1930; Senator, 1951–4; sat on the Irish Arts Council, 1952–6.

[iii] William Butler Yeats (1865–1939): born in Dublin; poet; influenced by John O'Leary and, later, Maud Gonne, he sought to stimulate a national literature; published *The Celtic Twilight*, 1893, and had his plays *The Countess Cathleen* and *Cathleen ni Houlihan* produced in Dublin, 1899 and 1902; helped establish the Abbey Theatre, Dublin, as Ireland's national theatre, 1904; gradually shook off nationalist alliances while remaining concerned with the national question and an idealized vision of his own Anglo-Irish heritage. Senator of the Irish Free State, 1922–8; awarded the Nobel Prize for Literature, 1923.

[iv] Elizabeth Bowen (1899–1973): born in Dublin; reflected on her Anglo-Irish ancestry in *Bowen's Court*, 1942, and on her Dublin childhood in *Seven Winters*, 1943, and on the Ireland of 'the Troubles' she observed in early adulthood in *The Last September*, 1949. Some of her other novels are also concerned with, or set in, Ireland, and many of her best short stories. CBE, 1948, and awarded honorary degrees by Trinity College, Dublin, 1948, and Oxford, 1956.

[v] Louis MacNeice (1907–63): born in Belfast; son of a Church of Ireland clergyman; educated at Marlborough and Oxford; first book of poems, *Blind Fireworks*, 1928; regarded as a junior associate of Auden, Spender and C. Day Lewis in the 1930s; went to Spain, 1936. Ireland appears in his early verse a country alienated from the real world, but emerged in his post-1945 work as a haven from what Yeats termed 'the filthy modern tide'. CBE, 1958.

[vi] Mary Delany (née Granville; 1700–1788): born in Wiltshire, into a highly connected family; first visited Ireland, 1731–3, and made the acquaintance of Swift and his circle, including the Revd Patrick Delany (d. 1768), the Dean's friend, executor and biographer, whom she married a decade later; lived over twenty years in Ireland, liking the country and its inhabitants; in widowhood, her sociability made her a favourite at the English court.

Emily, Duchess of Leinster[vii] and her sisters, the writings of the Earl of Orrery,[viii] some of Arthur Young's[ix] *Tour*, and most of Sir Jonah Barrington's[x] *Personal Sketches* (the last was responsible for ideas of eighteenth-century society cherished by Yeats, Joyce, Sheridan Le Fanu and probably Thackeray). It should be noted that, but for Barrington, and with Orrery as a partial exception, all these observers were of English origin.

This is not to say that such authorities are invalid: rather, that their perceptions come from a certain restricted angle. Nor should one generalize from the age of Swift to that of Grattan: in all areas of life there was a movement to a more finished and grand style in the last two decades of the century, as Lecky noted. But it remains legitimate to view the Georgian Anglo-Irish as possessing an elite culture, and to attempt some definition of how they saw their world, before embarking on analysis of the complex, vigorous society developing outside their parks, their drawing-rooms and their show-piece capital city.

For the atmosphere of Anglo-Ireland from the early eighteenth century cannot adequately be represented by the correspondence of the great ladies at houses like Carton, Castletown and Delville, reading *Candide*, building shell-houses, and even (in the Duchess of Leinster's case) considering Rousseau as a tutor for their children. It is important

[vii] Emily Fitzgerald, Duchess of Leinster (née Lennox; 1731–1814): daughter of Charles Lennox, second Duke of Richmond and a goddaughter of George II; married James Fitzgerald (d. 1773), Earl of Kildare, 1747; at the time of this marriage, Fitzgerald was created Viscount Leinster, and in 1766 he was made Duke of Leinster; married secondly her children's Scottish tutor, William Ogilvie, 1774. She had twenty children, of whom at least three were by Ogilvie.

[viii] John Boyle (1707–62): succeeded as fifth Earl of Orrery, 1731, and as fifth Earl of Cork, 1753; his grudging *Remarks on Swift*, 1751, his sometime friend, represented the first attempt at a character of the Dean after his death, but was quickly answered, and superseded, by Delany's *Observations*, 1754.

[ix] Arthur Young (1741–1820): agriculturalist and traveller; went to Ireland, 1776; became agent to Lord Kingsborough in County Cork, 1777–9; published his *Tour in Ireland*, 1780, which Maria Edgeworth claimed contained the most faithful portrait of the Irish peasantry ever to have appeared.

[x] Jonah Barrington (1760–1834): born in Abbeyleix; educated at Trinity College, Dublin; called to the Irish Bar, 1788; became a judge of the Irish Admiralty Court, 1798; in the Irish parliament he opposed the Union with his own vote but procured others for the government; knighted, 1807; published *Historic Memoirs of Ireland*, 1809, his disingenuous account of the corruption employed in the passing of the Act of Union; foreign residence relieved financial embarrassment, 1815; removed from the Bench for misappropriation of funds, 1830. Between 1827–32 he published further *Historic Memoirs* and the racy *Personal Sketches*, which confirmed him as the chief historian of 'the half-mounted gentlemen' of Ireland.

to recapture a more gamy flavour – an echo of colonial Virginia, or even the Kenya highlands in the 1920s. Marginalized if not isolated, the Anglo-Irish developed a ruthless but ironic pursuit of style. This incorporated the elements of classicism, discipline and restraint so much celebrated by posterity: the 'passion and precision' eulogized by Yeats, who saw Bishop Berkeley's[xi] attempt to distinguish Irish thought from that of other nations as 'an event as important as the battle of the Boyne'. Later philosophical authorities concur that Berkeley was very far from making any 'nationalist' effort; but, with his Georgian peers, he has come to stand for a cast of Irish mind that flourished in that rarefied air.

What *did* develop among the Anglo-Irish of the eighteenth century was more like a class consciousness, in the sense that this can form among an upper caste even in pre-capitalist society. The term 'Ascendancy' deserves examination. According to Barrington, the term 'Protestant Ascendancy' was coined late in the century by John Giffard, editor of the *Dublin Journal*, and 'became an epithet very fatal to the peace of Ireland'; a more stringent modern commentator finds the phrase first systematically used (as 'Protestant Ascendancy') in the early 1790s.[2] Membership of the Ascendancy in eighteenth-century Ireland was not, as one might assume, restricted to descendants of families who had acquired a noble patina through settlement of estates or military service; nor did the term comprehend the entire 25 per cent of the population who were Protestant. The definition revolved round *Anglicanism*: this defined a social elite, professional as well as landed, whose descent could be Norman, Old English, Cromwellian or even (in a very few cases) ancient Gaelic. Anglicanism conferred exclusivity, in Ireland as in contemporary England; and exclusivity defined the Ascendancy, not ethnic origin. They comprised an elite who monopolized law, politics and 'society', and whose aspirations were focused on the Irish House of Commons.

Within the charmed circle there was notable fluidity; from some points of view, it was an aristocracy of self-made men. The Ascendancy

[xi] George Berkeley (1685–1753): born in County Kilkenny; educated at Trinity College, Dublin; published his *Principles of Human Knowledge*, 1710; became Bishop of Cloyne, 1732; wrote a series of Irish tracts, of which the most remarkable was *The Querist*, 1735–7, posing many pertinent questions that never received a satisfactory answer. Other Irish works included a *Letter to the Roman Catholics*, 1745, *A Word to the Wise*, 1749, and the pithy *Maxims on Patriotism*, 1750. Although he saw it as his duty to seek their conversion, he was always tolerant and generous towards the Catholics of his poor diocese, whom he regarded as part of his charge.

could recruit to itself; as in England, careers were often open to men of talent prepared for formal religious conformity. Many of the great names of the Ascendancy world – Foster,[xii] Flood,[xiii] Hely-Hutchinson,[xiv] Grattan,[xv] Fitzgibbon,[xvi] Curran[xvii] – were from a pro-

[xii] John Foster (1740–1828): born in County Louth; educated at Trinity College, Dublin; MP for Dunleer, 1761, and County Louth, 1769–1821; Chancellor of the Irish Exchequer, 1784; Speaker of the Irish House of Commons, 1785–1800; opposed the Relief Bill of 1793, seeing in concession to Catholics the overthrow of the Protestant nation; an anti-Unionist, reading the Act of 1801 as a further strain upon the loveless marriage of necessity contracted between Anglo-Ireland and Westminster. Became Irish Chancellor of the Exchequer again, 1804; created a UK peer as Baron Oriel, 1821.

[xiii] Henry Flood (1732–91): natural son of a chief justice of Ireland; educated at Trinity College, Dublin, and Oxford; entered the Irish Commons, 1759; assumed the leadership of the opposition 'patriots'; secured the passage of the Octennial Bill, 1768, and the rejection of the Money Bill, 1769; much criticized for accepting office as Vice-Treasurer of Ireland, 1775; became a colonel of the Volunteers and spoke in favour of Irish free trade, 1779; returned to opposition, 1781, but eclipsed by Grattan; entered the English Parliament, 1783; opposed Catholic relief, supported parliamentary reform; left a grant to Trinity College, Dublin, for the establishment of a chair of Irish – for antiquarian purposes rather than from a desire to see the language revived.

[xiv] John Hely [-Hutchinson] (1724–94): born in County Cork; educated at Trinity College, Dublin; MP for Lanesborough, 1759, Cork, 1761–90, and Taghmon, 1790–94; began his parliamentary career in opposition but found government service more rewarding; became Provost of Trinity College, Dublin, 1774, and attempted to make the University constituency a family borough; favoured Catholic emancipation.

[xv] Henry Grattan (1746–1820): son of a recorder of, and MP for, the city of Dublin; educated at Trinity College, Dublin; associated with Flood in squibs against Townshend's viceroyalty (Baratariana, 1770); called to the Irish Bar, 1772; entered the Irish parliament, 1775; carried the amendment to the address in favour of Irish free trade, 1779; moved addresses in favour of Irish legislative independence, unsuccessfully 1780–81, successfully 1782; declined office but granted £50,000 by the Irish parliament as a token of gratitude; championed the cause of Catholic relief; seceded from the Irish Commons with other constitutional nationalists, 1797; returned to oppose the Union, 1800; sat in the imperial Parliament, 1805–20; refused the chancellorship of the Irish Exchequer, 1806, as he had refused all office.

[xvi] John Fitzgibbon (1749–1802): son of a convert from Catholicism; educated at Trinity College, Dublin, and Oxford; MP for Dublin University, 1778–83, appearing a moderate 'patriot', and for Kilmallock, 1783–9, inalienably a government man; supported Pitt's Regency policy, 1789, at which time the idea of a Union was already in his mind as the lesser of two evils; Lord Chancellor of Ireland, 1789–1801; created Baron Fitzgibbon, 1789, Viscount, 1793, Earl of Clare, 1795, and a UK peer, 1799; tempered his ruthless general policy during the 1798 rebellion with sympathy for individuals, notably Lord Edward Fitzgerald; the passing of the Act of Union was due mainly to his efforts; zealous legal reformer, more zealous opponent of Catholic relief.

[xvii] John Philpot Curran (1750–1817): educated at Trinity College, Dublin; called

fessional background, and achieved eminence through their own efforts. Nor did recent conversion, even from Catholicism, present any great problem, as Fitzgibbon's career demonstrates. Even poor Protestants could rise. The classic instance is William Conolly,[xviii] Speaker of the House, owner of Rathfarnham Castle and builder of the great Palladian mansion Castletown: he began life as the son of an obscure blacksmith (or publican) in Donegal. Luke Gardiner[xix] was another *arriviste* who founded an Ascendancy dynasty; while the Earl of Milltown, who built Russborough, the loveliest of Irish *palazzetti*, was grandson of a brewer and building speculator.

This gave the Ascendancy a certain vitality and a robust dislike of 'airs'; the correspondence of a grandee like Lord Shannon[xx] is unfailingly sardonic about 'greatness'. At the same time Shannon (great-great-great-grandson of Richard Boyle, the 'great' Earl of Cork) was a cool observer of the pushiness that attends the irresistible rise of new men. There were, inevitably, differentiated levels within the Irish aristocracy, and the very grand families tended to intermarry with the English aristocracy, to hold peerages of both creations, and sometimes to acquire, through marriage, a preponderance of landholdings in

to the Irish Bar, 1775; MP for Kilbeggan, 1783–6, Rathcormack, 1786–97, and Banagher, 1800; consistent supporter of Catholic relief and parliamentary reform; defended a number of the leading United Irishmen throughout the 1790s, including Hamilton Rowan, Napper Tandy and Wolfe Tone, but refused to become involved in unconstitutional nationalism; opposed the Union as 'the annihilation of Ireland'; treated his daughter, Sarah, severely on the discovery of her secret engagement to Robert Emmet, 1803; Master of the Irish Rolls and Privy Councillor, 1806–14; friend of Moore, Byron, Godwin and Sheridan.

[xviii] William Conolly (d. 1729): rose to power and wealth as Commissioner of Revenue and Lord Justice; MP for Donegal, 1692–9, and County Londonderry, 1703–29; Speaker of the Irish House of Commons, 1715–29; first of the great parliamentary managers of the 'Irish interest'. The custom of wearing linen scarves to encourage Irish industry was first observed at his funeral.

[xix] Luke Gardiner (1745–98): MP for County Dublin, 1773–89; introduced measures for Catholic relief into the Irish House of Commons, 1778 and 1782, which were partly carried; Irish Privy Councillor, 1780; created Baron Mountjoy, 1789, and Viscount, 1795.

[xx] Richard Boyle (1728–1807): son of Henry, first Earl of Shannon; educated at Trinity College, Dublin; MP for Dungarvan, 1749–60, and County Cork, 1761–4; became an Irish Privy Councillor, 1763, and no subsequent Irish administration felt easy without his support; succeeded as second Earl of Shannon, 1764; English Privy Councillor, 1782; Vice-Treasurer of Ireland, 1781–9; first Lord of the Treasury, 1793–1804; created a UK peer as Baron Carleton, 1786. Calculating placeman and pensioner, and probably the greatest borough-monger (in scale) of his borough-mongering age.

England. For our purposes, it is more profitable to look at society at its lower levels: the middling landowners, the clergymen, the lawyers. The mix within Ascendancy society was exemplified by that quintessential Ascendancy institution, Trinity College: defined by Anglicanism but containing sons of peers, of shoemakers, of distillers, of butchers, of surgeons, and of builders. Arthur Young could not understand why many of the students were receiving a useless and inappropriate higher education instead of being put to a trade. Institutions like Trinity, and the social fluidity within the Ascendancy dispensation, created an *esprit de corps* that gave the life of the privileged a particular and memorable flavour.

This was further amplified by their complex relationship to England – stemming from their position of conscious but resented dependence. Increasingly, the Ascendancy were prey to fears that England would let them down by breaking their monopoly: resentment of English pressure towards liberalizing the laws against Catholics and Dissenters remained a constant irritant, and would eventually work with other pressures to create polarization in the 1790s. Recurrent political crises were sparked off by the defensiveness and oversensitivity that remained the keynotes of the Ascendancy political consciousness: 'uneasy arrogance, suspicion of "destructive" British measures, and the claim to speak on behalf of "the country" characterized the political profile of the class'.[3] These are the attitudes most memorably expressed in Swift's campaigning pamphlets against the import of English manufactures (1720), and subsequently against the royal grant of a minting patent for halfpence to William Wood. This action was seen not only as debasing the Irish currency unnecessarily, but as doing it over the heads of the Irish Privy Council: hence Swift's deduction that 'government without the consent of the governed is the very definition of slavery', though public agitation concentrated more on the injustice of being palmed off yet again with 'brass money'.

In fact, Ireland did need more coin – if not halfpence – and Wood's money was up to mint standards. But the argument against 'tyranny', which Swift later built into Gulliver's third voyage as the rebellion of the Lindalinians, is important in that it was couched in terms of an appeal to natural as well as historical rights; principle was asserted rather than precedent. And this raised two implicit difficulties. One was that the argument from principle implied inclusiveness of *all* Irishmen, however much the theoreticians of colonial nationalism might strain at it. The other difficulty lay in questioning the royal prerogative to issue such a patent; for since the days of Patrick Darcy[xxi] royal prerogative was the ultimate basis of the colonists' argument that the Irish parliament had dual status with Westminster. These troublesome implications helped to keep economic criticisms as the front-line of the argument against Wood's patent; but the larger issues galvanized public opinion, to the extent that the patent was withdrawn, and the whole venture ignominiously scrapped.

Resentment over such issues was pointed up by a generalized anti-Englishness, and an annoyance at the way plum Irish jobs were monopolized by English mediocrities – and worse. English bishops in the Irish House of Lords came to form a specific political interest. Swift affected to believe that the English government always chose holy and godly Englishmen for Irish appointments, but they invariably happened to be murdered by bandits somewhere around Chester, who stole their letters of appointment and proceeded to Ireland in their stead.

The nature of Ireland's constitutional dependence upon England was itself a vexed question, complicated by the uneven nature of the relationship and uncertainty about the ultimate location of responsibility for the Irish executive. The Ascendancy attitude towards England was expressed, like many of its characteristics, most notably in architecture: it lies behind the extraordinary determination to embellish Dublin with public buildings that would be not only equal to, but *greater than*, those of London. Like the self-conscious pretentiousness of the government buildings unveiled at Stormont outside Belfast in 1932, this, in fact, indicated a realization that their status was not international but colonial, and a determination to compensate for it.

If antagonism towards England was exacerbated by the Hanoverian practice of appointing Englishmen to Irish jobs, it was necessarily moderated by traffic in the other direction too. Ascendancy careerism necessitated playing to an English audience. Many landowners, for instance, relied on office-holding to supplement their incomes: 37 per cent of the 150 Irish peers in 1783 were employed in the royal household, central government, the foreign and colonial service, or full-time service in the army. Edmund Burke,[xxii] who forms with Swift and

---

[xxi] See above, p. 84.

[xxii] Edmund Burke (1729–97): born in Dublin, of a Protestant father and a Catholic mother; educated at Trinity College, Dublin; became private secretary to the Marquess of Rockingham and entered Westminster, 1765, despite rumours of closet Catholicism and the attitude of the Whig oligarchs, who treated him as an 'Irish adventurer' and kept him from high office all his life; acknowledged as a first-rate orator, in spite of

Berkeley the great intellectual triumvirate of Ascendancy culture, is the supreme example of the career of talent, made in England; publication of his full correspondence has indicated how English experience expanded his view of Ireland. Seeing Ireland in a wide-ranging imperial context, as, indeed, did Theobald Wolfe Tone,[xxiii] he became both an integrationist and a Catholic emancipationist. The restricted and exclusive views of Swift, however, were more typical of Ascendancy attitudes; those who remained within the Irish context realized with brutal clarity on what limitations their power depended.

Ascendancy ambivalence between living in Ireland and hoping to expand a career in England remained a constant in Irish life; it was the *leitmotif* of much of Swift's career. The dependence and resentment of provincial ambitions are violently expressed in the lines written at Holyhead on 25 September 1727, when he had finally given up hope of an English preferment, and was waiting for a favourable wind to take him back to Ireland and the dying Stella:

> Lo here I sit at Holyhead
> With muddy ale and mouldy bread:
> All Christian victuals stink of fish,
> I'm where my enemies would wish.
> Convict of lies is every sign,
> The inn has not one drop of wine.
> I'm fastened both by wind and tide,
> I see the ship at anchor ride.
> The captain swears the sea's too rough,
> He has not passengers enough.
> And thus the Dean is forced to stay,
> Till others come to help the pay.

---

his Irish accent; invited to become MP for Bristol, 1774; rejected, 1780, for championing Irish free trade and Catholic relief; advocated economical reform, 1780–82; spent a decade conducting the unsuccessful impeachment of Warren Hastings, 1786–95; published *Reflections on the Revolution in France*, 1790; officially broke with the Whigs, 1792; wrote his letters to Sir Hercules Langrishe, 1792 and 1795, which reveal the extent of his concern for the Irish Catholics. Of all specific political questions, Irish ones moved him most in his last years.

[xxiii] Theobald Wolfe Tone (1763–98): born in Dublin; educated at Trinity College, Dublin; has been interpreted both as the founder of Irish nationalism and as a frustrated imperialist; his first nationalist pamphlet attracted the attention of the Whig Club, 1790, but his ideas were soon far in advance of theirs and he came to regard republicanism as a necessary adjunct to pure patriotism; spent his last three years in Paris; accompanied abortive French expeditions to Ireland in 1796 and 1798, when captured; committed suicide on being refused a soldier's death. His *Journals* reveal a mild humourist within the revolutionary, but the latter always held sway.

In Dublin they'd be glad to see
A packet though it brings in me.
They cannot say the winds are cross;
Your politicians at a loss
For want of matter swears and frets,
Are forced to read the old gazettes.
I never was in haste before
To reach that slavish hateful shore:
Before, I always found the wind
To me was most malicious kind,
But now the danger of a friend
On whom my hopes and fears depend,
Absent from whom all climes are cursed,
With whom I'm happy in the worst,
With rage impatient makes me wait
A passage to the land I hate.
Else, rather on this bleaky shore
Where loudest winds incessant roar,
Where neither herb nor tree will thrive,
Where nature hardly seems alive,
I'd go in freedom to my grave,
Than rule yon isle and be a slave.

The image of a 'land of slaves' recurs in Swift's Irish polemic, though the implication of how 'liberation' may be achieved is often necessarily fudged. The Dean's particular bitterness represents a personal, and physiological, catharsis, but also stands for something characteristic of the Ascendancy caste: a certain savagery of mind, amplified by a subconscious recognition of the fundamental insecurity of their political and social position.

Visitors noticed that the peculiar circumstances of Irish life created strange intimacies and explosive connections: a sense of hustling rootlessness was evident along with the air of Augustan ease. Most of all, Georgian Ireland was epitomized by a pervasive and characteristic addiction to violent resolutions, evidenced in endless tales of duels, abductions and litigations. Even in Barrington's hilarious tales of 'Bucks' and 'Tigers', the dominant tone was one of ferocity rather than fun. This was supposedly moderated by the later years of the century – a change of ethos rather improbably put down to Chesterfield's[xxiv] brief viceroyalty. The prodigious drinking bouts were less

[xxiv]Philip Dormer Stanhope (1694–1773): succeeded as fourth Earl of Chesterfield, 1726; an able diplomat who, as Irish Viceroy, 1745–6, employed tact and tolerance to keep Ireland quiet during the rising of 1745. Projected the planting of Phoenix

in evidence, though claret (known as 'Irish wine') continued to be far cheaper, if of worse quality, than in England. Lord Orrery wrote in 1736:

Drunkenness is the Touch Stone by which they try every man; and he that cannot or will not drink, has a mark set upon Him. He is abus'd behind his Back, he is hurt in his Property, and he is persecuted as far as the Power of Malice and Intemperance can go.[4]

Even when not seen through an alcoholic haze, however, Ascendancy attitudes tended to resolve themselves into violent statements; knocking a man down, Arthur Young observed, was spoken of so casually in Ireland as to make Englishmen stare. But it was 'spoken of' rather than necessarily carried out; and part of the objective *was* probably to make an Englishman stare. The diary of 'Copper-faced Jack Scott', otherwise known as Lord Clonmell, incomprehensibly released to the world by his family, reflects the life and attitudes of a particularly brutal timeserver (Solicitor-General, Attorney-General, Prime Serjeant, Lord Chief Justice, in ten years): at one point he reflected that 'a civilized state of war is the safest and most agreeable that any gentleman, especially in *station*, can suppose himself in'.[5] In this he spoke for many of his class.

But the reductionist brutality of much of the Ascendancy ethos reflected, at least in part, a baulked sense of differentiation and nationality. Thus, in 1723 the Duke of Grafton helplessly described Archbishop King, of all people, as 'to a ridiculous extravagance, national', though King was capable of using the English descent and identification of the Ascendancy as a reason for treating them better than the mere Irish. A sense of 'national' as well as anti-English identification is inseparable from Swiftian polemic:

> Remove me from this land of slaves,
> Where all are fools, and all are knaves;
> Where every knave and fool is bought,
> Yet kindly sells himself for naught;
> Where Whig and Tory fiercely fight
> Who's in the wrong, who in the right;
> And when their country lies at stake
> They only fight for fighting's sake,

Park. Claimed he wished to be remembered only as 'the Irish Lord Lieutenant', though it was his *Letters* to his son that immortalized him.

> While English sharpers take the pay,
> And then stand by to see fair play;
> Meanwhile the Whig is always winner
> And for his courage gets a dinner.

The confused but strongly felt identity of colonial nationalism is reflected in the use of the word 'Irish'. Berkeley, as a Trinity student of eighteen, referred to the Irish people as 'natives'; a few years later he had come to think in terms of 'we Irish'. Those who in the 1690s called themselves 'the Protestants of Ireland' or even 'the English of this kingdom' could see themselves as 'Irish gentlemen' by the 1720s. In between, there was some doubt as to whether they wanted to be *called* 'Irish'; but they increasingly felt that this was what they were, one way or another – a feeling solidified by various resentments. "Tis hardly possible for anyone (on your side),' wrote Bishop Evans of Meath to Archbishop Wake in 1718, 'to conceive the generall, unaccountable aversion these people (tho lately come from England and Scotland) have to the English name.'[6] And he was describing the Ascendancy.

Those of Anglo-Irish stock who lived largely in England tended to compensate by anti-Irishness. Thus Lord Orrery saw Ireland as 'Vulcan's forging-shop', enlivening to observe but death to live in. His expressed feelings, however, sum up the ambivalence of Anglo-Irishness.

It has been said of the Germans that they are a hundred years behind the rest of the world in knowledge and the elegancies of Life. I wish it is not an observation applicable to the Irish. However, I must confess their long intestine Wars, their constant and slavish dependence upon another Kingdom, and their just dread of popery, are some sort of excuses for the fire of their brains and the fury of their hearts. But till their Situation or their Manners are altered, I hope it will not be my ill fortune to live amongst them. At the same time I speak and think this, I solemnly declare that in every material point wherein I can serve this unhappy Kingdom, I will to the utmost of my power. I know the bread I eat must come from hence: I know my Ancestors have been very great and happy here, nor am I ungrateful to Heaven and to Ireland, for the blessing I enjoy in my Wife. All I entreat of fate is not to fix my dwelling here.[7]

Adoptive Irishness was another thing, giving rise to a curiously schizoid identification; Lady Louisa Conolly, an English Lennox by birth, wrote to her sister 'one cannot esteem and love the Irish, though one may like them; but yet it is right for *an Irish person* to live among them'. Her younger sister, Lady Sarah Lennox, writing artlessly about

living in Ireland, further indicates the contemporary morality about
residency:

My brother has left off teasing me about Ireland and Irish people. Mr Fox and
my sister put me in a passion more than anybody ... Lord Kildare, they said, had
rather live in London. That I allow. But I don't that he sent George to school
here that he might have a taste for England, and only go now and then to look
at his estate, but to live here. I never heard Lord Kildare say this or anything that
looked like it, but the contrary. For I have heard you, I am sure, and, I think,
Lord Kildare, say that it was wrong in Lord Hillsborough to live here when he
had an estate there ... My sister also says that you don't love Ireland at all, and
that you had rather a thousand times live here, but that you don't shew it because
Lord Kildare thinks it right you should. She allows you to be fond of Carton,
but that you would leave it all with very great pleasure to come with the children
and live here, and only go for a couple of months in four or five years – sure that
is not possible![8]

The contemporary perception of absenteeism as a problem is shown
by a number of angry pamphlets as well as ineffective legislation against
the practice. The general picture of absentee landlords living an easy
life off exorbitant rent-rolls needs qualification. Irish rents were always
low in relation to the capital value of land, and never really provided
an economic return; this, as much as careless practice, accounts for the
tiny proportion ploughed back into estate improvements. In defining
'absenteeism', it is also worth remembering the endlessly peripatetic
nature of eighteenth-century aristocratic existence; in a life of restless
movement, to spend six months out of every two years on an Irish
estate could be considered evidence of a fair commitment to residency.
There could also be special reasons for absenteeism: some Catholic
landlords found it necessary rather than convenient. Careers in the
army, the diplomatic corps and English politics provided further causes.
And some lived away from their estates not in order to spend money
but to save it.

A large proportion of absentees, moreover, had estates in both
England and Ireland, due to the ramifications of inheritance law and
marriage settlement; and though there were English absentees who
liked to live on their Irish estates, the preference usually went the other
way. But the highlighting of absenteeism by contemporaries and
historians should not draw too much attention away from the resident
gentry, whose public preserve was the parliament at College Green.
That robust Ascendancy enclave was representative of an element in
Irish life that, if exclusive, was still firmly centred on Ireland. Those

who lived away from their Irish property are, in a sense, a distraction, traditionally given much more attention than they deserve.

II

In attempting to define the ethos of Ascendancy culture, the figure of Swift recurs again and again: the immortality conferred by the extraordinary immediacy and personality of his writing is evidenced by his unexpected but powerful presence in Irish folklore, where there is a considerable oral tradition of stories about 'the Dean'. Certainly for the historian he remains the chief of those great writers produced by the eighteenth-century Ascendancy: Berkeley, Burke, Goldsmith[xxv] and Sheridan,[xxvi] none of them, it should be noted, of aristocratic origin. Though they are often claimed for the mainstream of the English literary tradition, their use of rhetoric, choice of material and verbal dexterity marked an 'Irish' style. Above all, these Irish writers adopt a characteristic and quizzical approach to argument, of which Berkeley's pamphlet *The Querist* is a distinguished example. Irish literature in English was stamped by preoccupation and perspective rather than an overtly 'national' content: it was distinctively Irish none the less.

Swift expresses this most clearly; one biographer has claimed that most of his apparently idiosyncratic and contradictory reactions are 'intelligible reflections' of his Irishness.[9] His distinctive brand of Tory values, which could lay claim both to Revolution principles and to the Hanoverian succession, certainly reflects local conditions; Irish Toryism combined these Whig tenets with pessimistic conservatism

[xxv] Oliver Goldsmith (1728–74): born near Ballymahon, County Longford; son of a poor Church of Ireland clergyman; educated at Trinity College, Dublin, Edinburgh and the Continent; returned to London, 1756, and became a literary, but never a political, hack; won fame as an essayist, *c*. 1759, but now remembered for *The Vicar of Wakefield*, 1766, *She Stoops to Conquer*, 1773, and his two long poems, *The Traveller*, 1764, and *The Deserted Village*,1770. Debate continues as to the Irishness of the last, but he remained primarily a 'citizen of the world': of an Irish 'nation' he left no proof that he had any conception.

[xxvi] Richard Brinsley Sheridan (1751–1815): born into a leading Irish literary family; educated at Harrow; wrote numerous comedies for the stage, 1775–9; entered Westminster, 1780; consistently supported all conciliatory policies towards Ireland, but only in opposing the Union did he admit his own Irish identification. Otherwise, unique in his ostensible ability to jettison Irishness.

and anti-Laudianism. In Swift's case, there are careerist reasons, too; from Irish middle-class origins, a good education at Kilkenny School and Trinity College, a fast ascent in the Church, chaplain to Lord Berkeley, 1699–1700, he inevitably gravitated to England, and was there disappointed. Only after his return to Ireland in 1713 did his real 'Irish' status develop; and he did not publish any Irish pamphlet until 1720. There is a sense of cutting his losses, but also a determinedly Irish identity that owes little to disappointment or resignation. Many of his arguments carry the authentic exclusiveness and brutality of colonial nationalism. But the apparently savage attacks on Irishness should be construed as exercises in despairing irony; his admiration of the achievement of 'gentlemen of Ireland' and his blaming Irish defects on 'the poverty and slavery they suffer from their inhuman neighbours' are equally important. He could equate 'patriotism' with 'virtue' in a sermon preached against Wood's halfpence:

> By the love of our country, I do not mean loyalty to our King, for that is a duty of another nature; and a man may be very loyal, in the common sense of the word, without one grain of public good at his heart. Witness this very kingdom we live in. I verily believe that, since the beginning of the world, no nation upon earth ever shewed (all circumstances considered) such high constant marks of loyalty in all their actions and behaviour, as we have done: And, at the same time, no people ever appeared more utterly devoid of what is called a Public Spirit. When I say the people, I mean the bulk or mass of the people, for I have nothing to do with those in power.[10]

Virtue must be carefully defined, in considering the thought of a man who described religious cant as flatulence, and charity as diffused lust; at times he comes near to dismissing religious zeal as rationalized passion. But an important aspect of Swift's patriotism involved England's role: she was there to be complained of.

Swift's restless desire to expose and his hatred of easy clichés mirror another important aspect of the Ascendancy mentality: its use of a particular and specialized social language, reflected in the code, the nicknames and the private words so evident in the letters and journals of Shannon, Tone and Swift himself. This was in part distinctly Irish: on the last page of Swift's *Journal to Stella* there is a word that could (just) be the Gaelic greeting *Sláinte*. Maria Edgeworth[xxvii] showed the

[xxvii] Maria Edgeworth (1767–1849): born in Oxfordshire; settled in Edgeworthstown, County Longford, 1782; wrote moral tales for children and assisted her father, Richard Lovell Edgeworth, with his work on *Practical Education*, 1798; published *Castle Rackrent*, 1800, the first Anglo-Irish novel and the earliest venture into

Irish use of language to be figurative, poetical and metaphorical rather than blundering; and the Ascendancy adopted this too. But it more accurately reflects the oddly intimate world of Ascendancy life (which possibly inspired Sheridan's *School for Scandal*, ostensibly set in London though it is). This world was small enough for everyone to know everyone else; Swift's correspondence with printers, clergymen, doctors, politicians and strong-minded women provides a profile. In a similar way half a century later, Barrington's memoirs show a closely related, varied world, where professional and landed society mixed closely and lived adjacent to each other, meeting on the same rather *louche* circuit and, through Barrington's eyes at least, subscribing to a certain cult of dilapidation.

Most of all there was a preoccupation with what was taken to be Ireland's *uniqueness*. Swift returns to this again and again; in his *Short View of the State of Ireland* (1728), dealing with Irish poverty, he defines it as a case in reverse of the norm. What would seem in another country evidence of riches is in Ireland a sign of poverty; the cost of living indicates not high wages but grasping landlords; the low interest rates represent not a healthy state of public finance but a decline in trade; building stands for a sign of depression, not of prosperity. 'There is not one Argument used to prove the riches of *Ireland*, which is not a logical Demonstration of its Poverty.' The economics of this are highly questionable, but the argument is characteristic of the Ascendancy approach. Accepted wisdom, which often means liberal wisdom, does not apply to the Irish case.

Eventually, Swift's notorious *Modest Proposal* consigned the whole country to cannibalism. Standing on its head the cliché that the country's wealth was its people, Swift suggested that the Irish should breed their children only for eating. It is a terrible *reductio ad absurdum* of the argument for domestic consumption of domestic products, which comes at the end of a life's work spent flaying panaceas:

I desire the Reader will observe, that I calculate my Remedy *for this one individual Kingdom of* I R E L A N D, *and for no other that ever was, is or I think ever can be upon Earth*. Therefore, let no man talk to me of other Expedients . . . til he

---

'local' fiction in English; her subsequent *Tales of Fashionable Life* included two Irish works, *Ennui*, 1809, and *The Absentee*, 1812; ended her life engaged in local famine relief. The *Essay on Irish Bulls*, a study of popular Irish humour that she wrote with her father, 1802, reveals the extent of their Irish nationality, as they perceived it: 'As we were neither *born nor bred* in Ireland, we cannot be supposed to possess [the] amor patriae in its full force: we profess to be attached to the country only for its merits.'

hath, at least, a Glimpse of Hope, that there will ever be some hearty and sincere Attempt to put *them in Practice*.

But, as to myself; having been wearied out for many Years with offering vain, idle, visionary Thoughts; and at length utterly despairing of Success, I fortunately fell upon this Proposal; which, as it is wholly new, so it hath something *solid* and *real*, of no Expence, and little Trouble, full in our own Power; and whereby we can incur no Danger in *disobliging* ENGLAND: For this Kind of Commodity will not bear Exportation; the Flesh being of too tender a Consistence, to admit a long Continuance in Salt; *although, perhaps, I could name a Country, which would be glad to eat up our whole Nation without it.*

The public opinion of Ascendancy Ireland can be prospected through less rarefied sources, too: notably the press. The development of Dublin newspapers was initially slow: at least a generation behind England, despite the absence of paper duties and Stamp Acts. But odd publications had sprung up from the mid-seventeenth century, and from mid-1703 to 1773 the first regular Irish newspaper appeared thrice weekly in the form of *Pue's Impartial Occurrences*, linked to a celebrated coffee-house of the same name. The *Dublin Gazette* followed in 1706 and then the *Dublin Journal*, which started in 1725 and saw out the century. These were joined by many others, including the long-lived *Freeman's Journal*; thirty-three newspapers were founded in the reign of George I, and by 1760 over 160 had begun life, more than a third of which lasted more than a year. This remained, up to about 1760, a Dublin phenomenon; compared to their English equivalent, Irish provincial towns produced little in the way of periodicals. Nor did they carry a great deal of Irish news, tending to refer to 'Ireland' as if they were not being written and printed there. In the early part of the century, 'constant comparison and identification with England was a *leitmotif*'. But the Wood's halfpence affair brought the press to a new level of political commentary; and from the time of the 1729 famine crisis, local economic issues became a staple too. From the 1730s, also, the tone of Irish newspapers becomes more 'literary' and more distinctively 'Irish'; the *Freeman's Journal* from 1763 would be the premier 'patriotic' paper for many years.

Despite this outburst of activity, and the inroads on the monopolies of the stationers' guild from the early eighteenth century, newspaper publishing remained a Protestant business. Though Catholics were largely employed in the publishing of chap-books, there would be no 'Catholic' press until the nineteenth century. This meant a limitation on the circulation possibilities of the newspapers, and tended to dictate an editorial content that stressed exclusivity and conservatism. It is still notable that the attitudes of the eighteenth-century press were tolerant of decent and 'honest' Catholics, including clerics, and even Pope Benedict XIV, who was praised for his agreeable manners and his modesty. This supposedly made him despise the doctrine of his own infallibility, 'as well as many of the absurdities taught and believed by the best Catholics'.[11] Much of the great newspaper expansion of the age was, in fact, based on advertising rather than on a public appetite for 'news'; it was the pamphlet literature that provided the real record of the day, and which linked oligarchic politics with a popular audience. None the less, the newspapers remain a repository of evidence indicating prevalent attitudes – some of them rather at variance with the traditional picture of the Ascendancy.

The same is true of the Dublin Society, founded in 1731 to promote agriculture, manufactures and the useful arts. Its members, besides professional men and the clergy, represented the tradition of experimental, improving landlordism, disapproving of absenteeism and Barringtonian braggadocio; from voluntary beginnings, the Society became patronized by parliament, and played a vital part in the development of distinctively Irish trends in architecture and associated crafts. There is a continuity, of a sort, with the ethos of the Philosophical Society[xxviii] in the membership of Sir Thomas Molyneux, at least. But the Dublin Society was firmly pragmatic and directed towards practical economics rather than theoretical science. Much of the eighteenth-century achievement can be traced to its influence, from the foundation of the Botanic Garden at Glasnevin (1795) to the professionalization of West's drawing-school, which the Society took over. Gradually, with its increasing reliance on government subsidies, the Society became more formalized, and was known for organizing large-scale projects and competitions rather than the innovations of its early days.

It still stands, however, for an encouragement of distinct Irish initiatives; as does the foundation of the Irish Academy in 1785 (the Royal Irish Academy from 1786). This capitalized on the interest in the Irish past, and in Irish achievements, which nearly a century of stability had allowed to develop. Its founders saw it as a decisively 'national' institution, in Ascendancy terms. But in the early nineteenth century, it would unintentionally help nurture an intellectual interest in native antiquity that would be put to the purposes of an ideology very different from that of 'colonial' nationalism.

In the eighteenth century, organizations like the Dublin Society and

[xxviii] See above, pp. 125–6.

the Royal Irish Academy show that the Ascendancy culture had two sides – and also indicate a development over the half-century between their foundation dates. What they both appealed to was the ethos also to be found among the 'improving' landlords, who similarly represented an urge to proselytize among their less enlightened neighbours. Landlord enterprise and investment were notably high in the 1740s and 1750s, reflecting the fact that rent-rolls had doubled from the mid-1740s; financially, mid-Georgian Ireland was an era of landlord prosperity. Their rising incomes narrowed the gap between nobles and middling gentry, in social as well as financial terms. Rents had been raised sharply in the period from 1710 to 1730, with the falling in of leases that had been set low in the post-war period. This development gave rise to many accusations of rapacity, but probably still left Irish land undercharged in terms of its capital value; the next notable rise, from the mid-1740s, aroused much less criticism, and seems to have been more easily afforded. The final period for a sustained boom in rent levels was the last quarter of a century. The economics of rural life will be considered elsewhere; but it should be stated here that some at least of the income that Ascendancy landlords reaped from their estates was deflected into an 'improving' and inquiring approach to Irish life. None the less, the image that endures is that of those described by Barrington as 'half-mounted gentlemen'; even his 'gentlemen every inch of them' and 'gentlemen to the backbone' are typified more by their expenditure than their investment. While this may be morally deserved, it derives in many cases from a highly questionable historiographical tradition.

III

The ethos of urban life carries a similar imprint: the Ascendancy created a civic culture, where charitable undertakings like Mosse's hospital at the celebrated Rotunda, begun in 1751, were ostentatiously connected to social ambition and aristocratic gaiety. The hospital was planned as the centre of a fashionable Vauxhall-type pleasure-ground, and featured an extraordinarily baroque chapel. Ascendancy life in Dublin was not notably 'cultured'; it was, for instance, largely undistinguished by musical achievements or serious patronage; Handel's celebrated première of *Messiah* on 13 April 1742 is, in fact, an outstanding exception to the general rule. Urban entertainment at a more visceral level was enjoyed with great gusto; so was the culture of dining out, marked by what Barrington remembered as 'that glow of well-bred, witty and cordial vinous conviviality which was, I believe, peculiar to high society in Ireland'. Much of this centred round the great 'characters' of the Irish Bar, a company of lawyers whose wit, ingenuity and slapdash brilliance became legendary; though this is, in real terms, less important than the Bar's real function as a gateway to politics. In social life as in topography, all Ascendancy Dublin that mattered revolved round the Parliament House at College Green.

The magnificence of that topography was, of course, the most lasting creation of the Ascendancy. Much of Georgian Dublin, miraculously preserved through decay until the 1960s, has since then vanished like Tyre and Sidon; but odd traces remain, along with much pictorial evidence of what has been lost. Contemporaries, especially Londoners, were amazed by the inappropriate grandeur of what they expected to be a provincial town; it struck one English observer like being 'at table with a man who gives me Burgundy, but whose attendant is a bailiff disguised in livery'.[12] The scale on which the city was laid out at this time owed much to Ormond's viceroyalty in the preceding century; he had saved the vast Phoenix Park from royal speculation, and contributed the idea of a city whose buildings faced on to the river, instead of treating the quays merely as back-alleys for loading. But it was not until the early eighteenth century that Ormond's ideas of grandeur were at last lived up to – not only in streets, squares and immense public buildings, but in a style of architecture that declared itself in adaptations like Thomas Ivory's new designs for the Blue-Coat School. And by the time of the Union in 1800, the Irish capital would be transformed out of all recognition.

This was true not only of individual buildings but of the urban lay-out as a whole. By the late seventeenth century, the vested interests of the Corporation, which had blocked plans for bridging the Liffey, had been overcome, though the river continued to constitute a marked north–south divide that would endure. With the succession of bridges, the city spread out through the suburbs planned on a grid-framework by Sir Humphrey Jervis, a private developer who later became Lord Mayor. The direction of expansion was north, east and south-east, generally for upper-class residential purposes, conditioned by 'private speculation, guided here and there by viceregal hints and municipal enactments'.[13] In the eighteenth century, expansion continued to the north-east and along the south bank; fashion ignored the more logical, and usual, line of extension to the west. By the end of the century, the patterning of the city was further regularized by the concentric ovals of the circular roads, North and South, and the corresponding canals, Royal and Grand.

Luke Gardiner and others laid out the grandest residential streets on the north side, like Henrietta Street: a broad hill of large houses, rising to what would be the King's Inns. Besides Gardiner himself, its residents included the Archbishop of Armagh and later the Earls of Kingston and Thomond, as well as the great politician John Ponsonby;[xxix] Richard Cassels[xxx] was responsible for some of the houses, which had staircase halls of great grandeur and which survived until early twentieth-century speculation. Dominick Street, with Robert West's stucco interiors, followed. The Gardiner estate was also responsible for the great scale of Sackville (now O'Connell) Street, planned as an elongated residential mall, but turned (to its detriment) into a thoroughfare with a bridge at the end (1790). The modern smart commercial centre, between Grafton Street and Merrion Square, was laid out as early as 1709; the private enterprise behind this undertaking was organized by Lord Molesworth and Joshua Dawson. The street commemorating the former retained many eclectic but beautiful features of the period until very recently.

Cassels's great cut-stone town-houses for Ascendancy nobles, which rose from about 1740, are far grander but somehow less impressive. Tyrone House, now part of the Department of Education, was one; Leinster House, now the seat of Dáil Éireann, another, which is traditionally credited with beginning the move of high fashion to the south side of the city. The second half of the century saw further extensions to the north, around Rutland (now Parnell) Square, featuring Lord Charlemont's house, now remodelled into the Hugh Lane Municipal Gallery of Modern Art. Great society polarized either round this area or round Leinster House, and remained thus until the early

---

[xxix] John Ponsonby (1713–89): second son of Brabazon, first Earl of Bessborough; educated at Trinity College, Dublin; MP for Newtownards, 1739–61, and County Kilkenny, 1761–83; became first Commissioner of the Revenue Board, 1744; Irish Privy Councillor, 1748; elected Speaker of the Irish House of Commons, 1756; resigned the speakership, and dismissed from the Revenue Board, 1771, when his authority was shaken by Viceroy Townshend; ceased to take an active part in politics after 1776, yielding the leadership of the family interest to his son, George, subsequently Irish Chancellor of the Exchequer; still retained enormous parliamentary influence.

[xxx] Richard Cassels (d. 1751): German architect invited to Ireland, c. 1720; built up an extensive practice designing 'Big Houses' for Ascendancy families; his major public buildings were the Rotunda and the Fishamble Street music-hall.

nineteenth century, when the social status of the north side began a decline, culminating in a steep plunge in the early twentieth century.

Evidence of other great houses remains: 86 St Stephen's Green, built for Richard Whaley and now part of University College; the dramatically tall Powerscourt House, with its granite façade; Belvedere House, looking down North Great George's Street, and concealing an opulent interior behind a puritanically plain front elevation. But more characteristic were the ubiquitous terrace-houses of early Georgian Dublin, with their long gardens, their lanes behind, and the rigorously generous proportions allowed to first-floor rooms and windows; while from the exterior, the characteristic 'patent reveal', a white-plaster lining round the window-recess, projecting just outside the brickwork, reflected light into the glass and emphasized the decisive proportions. Otherwise, though balconies, elaborate fanlights and semi-circular rear bows make their appearance after mid-century, exterior decoration remained at a minimum; regularity never becomes overpowering. Decorous aesthetic standards were often enforced by the details of Corporation leases. The idiosyncratically grand city that they created is one of the most memorable achievements of the Ascendancy style.

The public buildings of that city, connected mainly with the later eighteenth century, reflect the growing inclination of Ascendancy families to spend more time there, and the associated importance to them of parliamentary life. The Parliament House itself is the enduring symbol of this. Built at a cost of £95,000, it was deliberately far grander than Westminster, and achieved European primacy among buildings of the kind. It was designed by one Member of the Irish parliament, Sir Edward Lovett Pearce,[xxxi] and completed by another, Arthur Dobbs; later it would be adapted by James Gandon.[xxxii] Begun in 1729, the design embodied Burlingtonian ideas of classical propriety: Lovett Pearce was of Irish stock but had travelled widely in Italy as a soldier. Its monumental strength and clarity were extremely influential, inspiring, among much else, Smirke's façade for the British Museum a century later. The interiors were remodelled by Francis Johnston in

[xxxi] Edward Lovett Pearce (1699–1733): born probably in County Meath; MP for Ratoath, 1727; his design for the new Parliament House adopted, 1728; became Surveyor-General of Ireland, 1730; knighted, 1732.

[xxxii] James Gandon (1743–1820): born in London of Huguenot stock; resided in Ireland from 1781; built the Customs House, the Four Courts, the Military Hospital at Phoenix Park and the King's Inns; retired to London in anticipation of an Irish rebellion, 1797, but returned to live on his estate at Lucan, 1808. An original member of the Royal Irish Academy, 1786.

the early nineteenth century, and the old House of Commons disappeared when the building was taken over as the Bank of Ireland; but much of the original effect remains. The culmination of Georgian Dublin's public building comes at the end of the century, with Gandon's heroic Four Courts and his Customs House.[14] Though Gandon's early work remains mysterious, and his life was unsatisfactory before John Beresford[xxxiii] 'smuggled him over' to Dublin (instead of St Petersburg, where he was also tempted), he became the great figure of Dublin architecture. Pushed hard by the parliamentary group who manned the Wide Streets Commission and were bent on creating public splendour, he finished his controversial project of a new Customs House to the east in 1791; it is the great expression of Dublin's neoclassical age, surpassed only by the Four Courts. With the Parliament House, they form a great trinity of buildings, on an exceptional scale even for the second city of an empire.

The Wide Streets Commission, which masterminded much of this development, was set up in 1758, manned by a powerful group of MPs and the Lord Mayor. They managed both to spend money and to enforce aesthetic standards: by 1800 they were spending £25,000 a year and had created the lay-out of avenues that converge on the present-day O'Connell Bridge, while the city as a whole was characterized by classical terraces and wide streets, with vistas of mountains at the end.

This authoritarian and centralized tradition may, however, be dated earlier – probably back to Lovett Pearce's predecessor as Surveyor-General, Colonel Thomas Burgh.[xxxiv] His buildings establish the severity and rigorous planning of the best Dublin architecture, characteristics that survived the transition from Palladian to neo-classical idioms from the 1760s. Traces of the more artisanate and provincial tradition remain in buildings like Dr Steevens' Hospital (1719, but more like a seven-

---

[xxxiii] John Beresford (1738–1805): born in Dublin; educated at Trinity College, Dublin; MP for Waterford, 1760–1805; Irish Privy Councillor, 1768; Chief Commissioner of Revenue, 1780; Pitt's principal Irish adviser, he wielded immense, though unobtrusive, influence in Irish affairs; English Privy Councillor, 1786; dismissed from office during the concessionary viceroyalty of Lord Fitzwilliam, January to February 1795, he returned to help the government bring about the Union; retired from office, 1802.

[xxxiv] Thomas Burgh (1670–1730): son of Revd Ulysses Burgh (later Bishop of Ardagh); educated at Trinity College, Dublin; served in the Williamite army in Ireland and abroad; Surveyor-General of Ireland, 1700–1730. Designed the original Customs House, 1707, the Royal Barracks, Celbridge Collegiate School and Trinity College Library.

teenth-century composition); and Dublin church-building remained generally unremarkable except for St Werburgh's (Burgh again) and St Ann's, Dawson Street, though there is a fine 1774 cathedral in Waterford and five churches in Cork that date from the 1720s. Bearing out Yeats's gibe that the only evidence of religious veneration in the Irish Protestant mind was directed towards Trinity College, the rebuilding that went on in this quintessential Ascendancy institution during the 1750s is far more impressive: not only the west front, but the Burlingtonian stone mansion that still fulfils the function of Provost's House.

Much of the Burgh tradition was inherited by Francis Johnston, born in 1760; a native architect, he symbolically followed Gandon in adapting Lovett Pearce's Parliament House twice after the Union. Johnston was the great influence in domestic Irish architecture in the early nineteenth century, significantly in his classical rather than his experimental Gothic mode, for 'Georgian' lasted in Irish building down to the 1860s. This traditionalism is partly explained by the prevalence of amateur gentlemen-architects in the country; Gandon complained of the Irish landowners' propensity for designing houses themselves. Some produced distinguished work, like Nathaniel Clements's[xxxv] group of houses with characteristic pavilions, scattered through Down and Meath, or Agmondisham Vesey's Lucan House, a Palladian villa, now, appropriately, the Italian embassy.

By the middle of the eighteenth century, in fact, Irish country gentlemen were building obsessively. In 1737 Lord Orrery remarked:

Nature has been profusely beneficent to Ireland, and Art has been as much to England. Here, we are beholden to nothing but the Creation; There you are indebted to extensive Gardiners [sic] and costly Architects. Our nobility, like the old Patriarchs, live in cottages with hogs, sheep and oxen. Your Patricians sleep not but in Palaces and under splendid Rafters.

But this was elaborate satire; and he went on to remark that 'we are imitating you as fast as Poverty and native Simplicity of Manners will permit us'.[15] The great boom in country-house building had, in fact, already begun by the 1720s. Its continuation owed much to the amateur tradition; symbolically, the first work on architecture to be printed in Ireland was not by any of the master architects, but was a *General*

[xxxv] Nathaniel Clements (d. 1777): gentleman-architect; MP for Dunleck, Cavan and Leitrim successively, 1761–77; Deputy Vice Treasurer and Teller of the Irish Exchequer; built The Lodge, Phoenix Park. Father of Robert, first Earl of Leitrim.

Treatise (1734) by John Aheron, a builder of provincial country houses. Even the great Gandon had to make it clear to his patrons at Waterford (where he designed a courthouse) that he was an architect, not a building contractor: the line between them was still a hazy one. Three years later, gentlemen-architects were further aided by the publication of John Payne's *Twelve Designs of Country Houses*. The wealth of Georgian country houses, often built by new men on new lands, expresses Ascendancy values in an idiosyncratic way; a specifically Irish feature was their plaster decoration, the characteristic form of ornament that spread from immigrant craftsmen in Dublin like the Francini brothers to native masters like Robert West and later Michael Stapleton.

However, for the most spectacular expression of domestic architecture in the countryside, it was·at first usual to employ a foreign architect. Some, like Richard Cassels and later the Sardinian Davis Ducart, evolved a style that came to be considered unmistakably 'Irish': compact and restrained, relying on motifs like Venetian windows, a classic component of Irish country houses. But the Florentine Alessandro Galilei's Castletown, begun for William Conolly in 1722, created its own terms: a vast *palazzo* in County Kildare, with wings added by Lovett Pearce and an important contribution, in the Irish tradition, by Conolly himself. In some ways this limestone block, with its darker wings, remained unsurpassed: it was intended to be 'an epitome of the resources of Ireland'. Cassels's neighbouring Carton rather unsuccessfully followed the trend; but his collaboration with Francis Bindon, the County Clare painter and architect, produced a perfect house at Russborough near Blessington, with its theatrically long front in golden Wicklow granite. With the rise of neo-classicism from the 1760s, there came Thomas Cooley's massive country houses like Caledon and Rokeby; Wyatt's influence is notable in Mount Kennedy and Castle Coole. But the striking inheritance of the age is less grandiose: the countless classic, small Irish houses. Consistent, severe and stylish beneath their deceptive plainness, they constituted 'a totally pervasive vernacular, capable of a suitable response to almost any architectural problem'.[16] The classical idiom was used with almost intuitive correctness by innumerable country builders, as well as by tradesmen, guildsmen and those trained in the Dublin Society's architectural classes. There are very few architectural solecisms in the classic, tall, plain Irish house; but the architects of some of the best remain unknown.

As in Dublin, an intimate scale could be related to unashamed grandeur: thus the plasterwork of the modest Riverstown House, County Cork, could be transferred with perfect propriety to the ceilings of the Viceregal Lodge. The interiors of even the smallest houses carried through the classicism of their façades. At the same time, Irish adaptations were manifold: the projecting shallow bows softening the ends of a rectangular block, the surprising third storey accommodated at the rear of an ostensibly two-storey house, transforming the interior space. Palladio's idea of an 'economic' lay-out, integrating farm-buildings as adapted pavilions, is often found in the work of his many Irish followers, though it was hardly ever adopted in England. Even the smallest houses can accommodate pavilions linked by screen walls. But with this elegance, there remained an uncompromising and almost brutal severity, brought to a high level in Francis Johnston's classical masterpiece in County Louth, Townley Hall, which also epitomizes the Irish trick of a plain façade concealing a splendid interior. That same uncompromising decisiveness characterizes the little Georgian farmhouses of the later part of the century: two storeys over a basement, three-bay façades, a hipped roof, the front door an adapted Venetian window, with sometimes a modest portico. The beauty of Irish Georgian architecture is that it is never pretty.

It can, of course, be described simply as a local variant of the dominant European model; but it retains a special integrity. The Ascendancy also put their stamp on country towns, though their own houses were obviously the priority. The 'estate villages', whose geometric topography still strikes the traveller, date from this era, their characteristically wide streets reflecting not so much the demands of a pastoral economy as the ambition of a local landlord. That Ascendancy desire to build and to plan deserves some attention: it may indicate an obsession with putting their mark on a landscape only recently won and insecurely held. The idea might be extended to the development of a very competent school of landscape- and portrait-painting at the time; the Ascendancy patronized and subsidized memorials of land, houses and family rather than devotional sculpture or churches. The same obsession led them to encumber their land up to and beyond its real value rather than to sell it: land went with identity, and defined a name (the Richmonds of Castle Richmond or 'the MacDermots of Ballycloran'). Building cost them more than they could afford, but it was psychologically essential.

Ascendancy finances were complex; the marriage market (just beginning to be the subject of research) does not seem to have recruited much wealth from outside. In English alliances, the Irish gentry traded at a disadvantage and had to make correspondingly large payments. After mid-century, demographic trends led to the increased longevity of dowagers as well as large numbers of surviving children: both factors could put a great strain on the settlement of an estate. They also help explain the pattern of rental increases – exaggerated though these were – and the failure, or inability, to invest in improvements. Yet a rage for building continued to characterize the Ascendancy stereotype. Wyatt's palatially Grecian Castle Coole bankrupted the Earl of Belmore; Cooley's much smaller Rokeby Hall cost the Archbishop of Armagh £30,000; Emo Park was still unfinished in 1798 when the first Earl of Portarlington died, and nearly beggared his descendants. The great Cloncurry mansion at Lyons meant an outpouring of money, often to no avail (£850 was spent on transport alone for a cargo of Italian statuary, which was wrecked in Dalkey Bay). Finally, when the Ascendancy's political supremacy ended after the Union in 1800, they continued to build, in some ways more energetically than before. Contrary to popular impression, they spent more time at their country houses after the loss of their parliament. Increasingly, however, the larger Irish houses were treated to castellation and gothicizing, though small-scale houses kept to classical sobriety for decades. Previously, this style had largely been the preserve of the Old Catholic gentry who had held on to ancestral lands (Malahide, Dunsany, Gormanston). Maurice Craig has speculated that the Ascendancy followed suit after 1800 for reasons that lay deeper than mere fashionability; by now, 'they sought – at the subconscious level no doubt – to convince themselves and others that they had been there a long time and that their homes, like so many in England, reflected the vicissitudes of centuries'.[17] W. B. Yeats and Elizabeth Bowen, quintessential commentators on the Ascendancy psychology, were equally preoccupied with the houses of the era, which are almost personalized in their writing and which are seen as in constant danger of destruction.[xxxvi]

[xxxvi] Yeats's lines, inspired by Coole Park, in *Purgatory* provide just one illustration:

> Great people lived and died in this house;
> Magistrates, colonels, members of Parliament,
> Captains and Governors, and long ago
> Men that had fought at Aughrim and the Boyne.
> Some that had gone on Government work
> To London or to India came home to die,
> Or came from London every spring
> To look at the may-blossom in the park ...
> But he killed the house; to kill a house
> Where great men grew up, married, died,
> I here declare a capital offence.

The Ascendancy built in order to convince themselves not only that they had arrived, but that they would remain. Insecurity and the England-complex remained with them to the end.

So did the culture of exaggeration, and of the exaggerated attitude, as evident in the Ascendancy rebels of the 1790s as in Barrington's squireens. Their defensiveness led them to claim a spuriously long connection with the country, rather as the Church of Ireland claimed to be 'the Church of St Patrick'. They evolved an idea of the 'Irish nation' that was as visionary as the twentieth-century 'Rock of the Republic'. The fact that it depended on a sectarian definition of citizenship as mercilessly reductionist as the purest classical façade was taken for granted: so much so that the Ascendancy easily ignored the exclusive and oppressive basis of their power. And they were celebrated, first by nineteenth-century historical novelists and then by twentieth-century intellectuals, for the wrong reasons. Yeats reinvented Georgian Ireland as 'that one Irish century that escaped from darkness and confusion';[18] Elizabeth Bowen remarked, with equal inaccuracy, that, at the last resort, the Ascendancy 'lived at their own expense'. In a very Anglo-Irish mode, this judgement reverses economic fact to express something not far from the psychological truth.

CHAPTER NINE

===

ECONOMY, SOCIETY AND THE 'HIDDEN' IRELANDS

I

===

THE 'ALTERNATIVE' IRELAND of the eighteenth century has its own historiography and breeds its own controversies. The terms were dictated by Daniel Corkery's *The Hidden Ireland*, ostensibly a study of eighteenth-century Munster poets. Corkery's study brilliantly broadened out to present the portrait of 'a land dark, scorned, and secretly romantic', insisting that 'Irish Ireland' was a peasant nation, with no urban existence and no middle class, oppressed by an alien gentry and its hangers-on. Only in occasional Big Houses that remained in Gaelic hands was the old practice of poet and patron kept alive. There Corkery discerned a great regional poetry, 'unique as historical memorial of a hidden people'; mediated through local 'courts' of poetry descended from the ancient bardic schools. The figures who dominated this world were not eccentrics but academics; and the poetic literature was an explicitly historical source, reflecting an escalation of misery throughout the century.

Corkery's pioneering and powerfully written work created an image of eighteenth-century Ireland that endured, implicitly reinforced by studies of 'Georgian' Ireland that emphasized the other, removed world of Ascendancy culture. But the mentality analysed in Corkery's *Hidden Ireland* is purely that of the Gaelic aristocracy as expressed through their bards: and where they declare resentment at, for instance, rents and leases, they are complaining about developments that worked to the advantage of ordinary men and women, no less Gaelic, or Catholic, than they were. L. M. Cullen has gone so far as to claim that the 'hard-drinking, idle life' eulogized by the Munster poets is, in fact, that enjoyed by the obnoxiously parasitic 'middleman' class in the dairying lands of Cork and Kerry — the sample area from which too many generalizations have been drawn, from the days of Froude onwards.

The fact remains that Gaelic literature provides a perception of Ireland at this time that cannot be derived from the observations of English travellers and Ascendancy memoirs, and often conflicts with them. Territorial, ethnic and family loyalties are expressed in Irish; the English language was used for concerns like law, leases and formal politics. But poetry in Irish remained a living presence, transmitted with extraordinary speed. The Frenchman Charles Étienne Coquebert de Montbret, travelling in Kerry in 1790, found the people permeated with poetry and characterized by 'a strange preoccupation with things of the mind'. He also knew all about Eileen ní Conaill's great Gaelic lament for Art O'Leary, even though he had been killed less than twenty years before. Elsewhere he noted: 'a great deal of Irish is spoken, but nowhere does one see *notices* in Irish, as no one knows how to read it'. The demands of literacy and modernization inevitably favoured the English language; but the older world was memorialized in the poetry.

Poets like Aodhagán Ó Rathaille,[i] Seán Clárach Mac Domhnaill[ii] and, later on, Eoghan Ruadh Ó Suílleabháin[iii] preserved a continuity of underground culture, often casting their poetry in a newer, freer and more musical metre; they produced public verse, often elegiac in character, which expressed conventionally Jacobite politics in terms that by mid-century were necessarily visionary. Such poets came from, or existed at, a social level that was less privileged than their predecessors', and they bemoaned the fact; their position was *parti pris*, and this affects the value of their work when seen as historical evidence.

The reaction of historians like L. M. Cullen has been an astringent refusal to rely on the 'prejudices and myopia of contemporaries'. They

---

[i] Aodhagán Ó Rathaille [Egán O'Rahilly] (1670–1726): born in County Cork; elegist of the decay of the Gaelic order as accelerated by the Jacobite defeats of 1690–91; satirist of the boorish 'upstart' planters. He gave the *aisling* poem its distinctly Jacobite character, where a vision of Ireland appears as a beautiful but unhappy woman, appealing for deliverance to the still-potent idea of the Stuarts.

[ii] Seán Clárach Mac Domhnaill [John Clarach MacDonnell] (1691–1754): born in County Cork; trained for the priesthood; pioneered the idea of translating Homer into Gaelic; undisputed chief poet of Munster in his day, presiding over the courts of poetry; wrote harsh satire on the cruelty of a local landlord; forced to seek refuge abroad; wrote of the European wars, 1740–48.

[iii] Eoghan Ruadh Ó Suílleabháin [Owen Roe O'Sullivan] (1748–84): born in County Kerry; hedge-school master and poet; soldier, sailor, wastrel and rake; mortally wounded in a drunken brawl. Revisionist of the *aisling*, suggesting that by his time such verse and, by implication, the propsect of a Stuart restoration should not be taken too seriously.

prefer to analyse eighteenth-century society and economy in terms of statistical reconstruction, and written evidence that does not come from political pamphlets and surveys produced to prove a point. The supposed economic effects of partial constitutional independence in the 1780s, and then of the Act of Union after 1800, skewed the evidence; economic nationalism created its own retrospective truths. Recent historiography, rather than quoting the picture of cottier squalor in Arthur Young's *Tour* yet again, prefers to concentrate on the Ireland glimpsed in accounts like that of Philip Luckombe, who, visiting supposedly primitive Kerry in 1780, found energetic plans afoot to industrialize Killorglin, develop mines near Killarney, and increase the navigation capacities of the River Laune. What comes across is a great degree of variation, both regionally and temporally, in the pattern of poverty. Cycles, hitherto unallowed for, are now an established part of the picture; and so is regional differentiation. As another Frenchman, Crèvecœur, noted, 'the Irish themselves, from different parts of the kingdom, are very different. It is difficult to account for this surprising localization. One would think, on so small an island, an Irishman would be an Irishman: yet it is not so.'[1]

But what cannot be rationalized away is the general unanimity of contemporary impressions: that where Ireland was poor and backward, it was astoundingly so. Eighteenth-century observers were by no means all from identically biased backgrounds; but they all agreed on this. Revisionist historiography has established that Irish prosperity was growing; but this was relative. And where the prosperity struck foreign observers, it often struck them as a surprise.

The complexity of the picture reflects lurches in the graphs of economic growth and subsistence patterns. The 1720s were a crisis decade for Irish agriculture, with fearful problems of dearth; but a marked recovery followed in the early 1730s, largely boosted by the widely distributed linen industry and the injection it provided to domestic incomes. Agricultural prices remained uncertain, apart from beef. Contemporary polemics, especially from the late 1730s, present a picture of tillage giving way to anti-social grazier farming; but this syndrome was exaggerated in order to provide extra arguments for extending leases to Catholics, who, it was held, raised beef only in order to capitalize on the punitively short leases allowed to them by law.

The fluctuations in Irish farming, however, did not depend as much on legislative restrictions as upon the developments in agriculture across the Irish Sea. The great expansion in sheep and wheat farming in eastern England inevitably shifted Irish preoccupations towards beef production; the English wool industry affected Irish priorities, too, and not only in encouraging the Irish linen boom. There was an increasing tendency, first to spin woollen yarn on a domestic basis in Ireland itself, and then to replace lowland sheep-grazing with beef or grain: a movement that would help provoke rural crisis at the end of the century. The textiles that provided a steady basis of growth were linen and cotton. Through the Linen Board, founded at Dublin in 1711, some attempts were made at central regulation and management, though this institution is probably more important as a paradigm of the close-knit ethos of Dublin life, and as an example of the interlocking memberships of political and administrative bodies there, than for any direct influence it may have had in encouraging the industry. Cotton production developed more episodically; its production was increasingly mixed in with that of linen, and domestic spinning was widespread across the south by the 1770s. Over the next two decades new manufacturing techniques were rapidly adopted: there was considerable official aid as well as landlord initiatives (Balbriggan, Malahide and Prosperous were all famous cotton villages). By the 1790s several large-scale enterprises had developed, though the pattern of growth remained very unstable; the industry in the south-west declined from about 1800, giving way to Dublin and Belfast, though isolated provincial centres remained important.

Textiles and the provisioning trade, both agriculturally based, remained vital areas of production; the same was true for brewing and sugar refining. Where other industries existed, they tended to be decentralized and domestically located. Glassworks and metal factories were developing in some port towns, reliant as they were on imported material. Other factories and mills followed water-power; this was true for linen and paper as well as grain. However, steam-power was in use on the Leinster coalfields by 1740, and in Ulster by the 1790s. If the scale of Irish industry was small, its dispersal was impressive; and some industries, like brewing and glass, made the vital transition to large-scale production processes by the late eighteenth century. The size and style of countless late eighteenth-century flour mills in rural towns still amazes the traveller, as they amazed Arthur Young.

But the basis of Irish wealth was agriculture itself: particularly cattle-raising, which provided the only consistent growth-area of agricultural export throughout the century. By mid-century butter prices had recovered; and dairying around Dublin became important, with an accompanying improvement in livestock and the importation of foreign strains. By the time of the French wars, beef and butter were established as the basis of the great boom in agricultural production, joined by grain at the end of the century.

Yet this picture must be seen against the succession of crop failures and famines (1728–9, 1740–41, 1744–5, 1756–7) that paralleled shortages in Europe as a whole, but could lead in Ireland to horrifying local crises. Where imports could be sustained, harvest failure did not necessarily mean famine; but evidence like the letters of Charles O'Conor[iv] of Belanagare shows fearful conditions in remote areas like Roscommon during 1756 and 1757. Indeed, the crises of the 1750s led to the policy of bounties to encourage grain production, after an important government investigation of tillage in Ireland during 1757. By 1780, nine Acts were passed to encourage tillage; the conditions enjoined were often highly unrealistic, though O'Conor's letters show a preoccupation with reclaiming and 'subduing' unprofitable heath, which was probably widespread. Potatoes were often grown on marginal land to prepare it for corn. Several experts criticized the policy of extending grain cultivation as inappropriate for Irish conditions. But mills spread across the midlands; transport bounties encouraged the export of locally produced grain to the metropolis; and by the last quarter of the century, Dublin markets were dominated by Irish wheat, a development reflected in the national diet.

Pasturage none the less remained dominant up to the 1780s, if exaggerated by contemporary authorities like Samuel Madden[v] and Thomas Newenham.[vi] It was favoured by the practice of not charging tithes on pastureland, as well as by the adaptability, flexibility and quick returns characteristic of this kind of farming. But from 1780,

[iv] Charles O'Conor (1710–90): born in County Sligo; succeeded to Belanagare, 1750; published tracts on the state of Irish Catholics, so moderate that they were thought to be the work of a liberal Protestant; edited Castlehaven's *Memoirs* and published *Dissertations on the Ancient History of Ireland*, 1753; founded the first Catholic Association, with John Curry and Thomas Wyse, 1756; edited O'Flaherty's *Ogygia Vindicated*, 1775; published two essays in Vallancey's *Collectanea*, 1783; MRIA, 1785.

[v] Samuel Madden (1686–1765): born in Dublin; educated at Trinity College, Dublin; ordained 1721; established premiums for the encouragement of learning, at Trinity College, and of Irish agriculture, manufacture and trade, under the auspices of the Dublin Society, which he helped Thomas Prior to found, 1731; his chief printed work was *Reflections and Resolutions Proper for the Gentlemen of Ireland*, 1738. Nephew of William Molyneux; friend of Swift and Dr Johnson.

[vi] Thomas Newenham (1762–1831): born in County Cork; educated at Trinity College, Dublin; MP for Clonmel, 1798; opposed the Union; wrote on the natural and economic resources of Ireland; a consistent advocate of Catholic emancipation.

Year ending 25 March	Exports	Imports
	£	£
31 December 1700	814,746	792,473
1710	712,497	554,248
1720	1,038,382	891,678
1730	992,832	929,896
1740	1,259,853	849,678
1750	1,862,834	1,531,654
1760	2,139,388	1,647,592
1770	3,159,587	2,566,845
1780	3,012,179	2,127,579
1790	4,855,319	3,829,914
5 January 1801	3,714,779	5,584,599
5 January 1811	6,099,337	6,564,578
5 January 1816	7,076,123	6,106,878

Table 1: *Exports and imports of Ireland 1700–1816.*
Source: L. M. Cullen, *An Economic History of Ireland since 1660.*

interacting with rapid population expansion, all observers noted the extension of tillage. Export figures are available in an unbroken run from 1772–1819, and show wheat exports increasing twentyfold, oats tenfold and barley sixfold over the period. And this evidence for tillage extension leaves out the phenomenal expansion in flax growing, which will be considered elsewhere.

Agricultural production provides the background to the great growth of Anglo-Irish trade in the eighteenth century; for in this period, the English industrial revolution did not threaten or constrict Irish economic development, but worked to complement it. Claims that the Irish trading economy was restricted by English legislation, especially regarding textiles, are incompatible with the picture of incontrovertible growth. The classic answer, that smuggling provided a way round, no longer appears adequate. A smuggling 'culture' was immortalized in traditions of families like the O'Connells of Derrynane, and contraband was certainly encouraged by legal difficulties and inefficiency, though the comparative laxness of Irish laws beside those of English might well mean that it was less of a threat.

Those who postulated a massive illegal trade in exporting wool to France had a political and constitutional case to make; French import figures show a modest input of Irish wool, rising at certain times and in certain circumstances, but the great trade in Irish woollen yarn remained centred on Liverpool and Bristol. Powerful Quaker interests in the worsted yarn trade, like the Grubbs of Clonmel, the Newenhams of Cork, the Pims of Dublin, and the Jacobs and Strangmans of Waterford, set up an energetic network of links with co-religionists in England. And from the mid-1740s Anglo-Irish trade in textiles and agriculture entered a quarter-century of boom that Cullen has called an 'economic miracle'.

This was boosted by the ramifying linen trade, and the lucrative provision trade created by war conditions abroad: the British navy was Ireland's best beef customer. Like butter, beef was really a colonial (or imperial) trade; both exports fluctuated in European terms but were solidly based on colonial demand. Ireland was, after all, a key component of the imperial system, in which American Irishmen were already making their mark; careerist ex-Catholics were to be found setting up family networks in a surprising number of imperial outposts. Imperial wars meant that the lucrative Irish trade in provisioning European armies was embargoed (as was to be the case during the American Revolution): but under these circumstances, ample compensation was provided by supplying the squadrons that docked at Cork. The demands of this trade pushed prices up to levels that necessitated government control after violent demonstrations in the streets of seaport towns.

Despite the claims of Lecky and other historians, embargoes did not fundamentally damage the provision trade. The important development was that by 1800 the great weight of Irish food exports were utterly dependent on the English market. The causes are associated as much with changes in European production patterns as with deliberate English policy. But the salient facts are that in the last three decades of the eighteenth century, beef exports to Britain quadrupled; butter doubled (a trade that was carefully organized and demarcated, with a strict survey of weights and measures); pork increased eightfold. And those imports from England that grew at a corresponding rate are significant: sugar, tea, drapery and most of all coal. Though the west still depended on peat for energy, and tourists like Coquebert de Montbret found local mining ventures all over the midlands and south, coal imports remain a vital index of economic, and demographic, growth. And they soared in the last decades of the eighteenth century.

This picture of Irish trade indicates an important merchant culture, characterized not only by traditional *émigré* networks like those between Galway and Spain, or Waterford and Bordeaux, but also by the Quaker interests already mentioned, whose ramifications stretched from Cork to Pennsylvania. From 1730 to 1780 Irish merchants built up the American connection. The produce of the middle colonies (flax seed, wheat, rum) was shipped to Ireland, to a disproportionate degree. Indigo, tobacco and sugar came to Ireland as well, through English entrepôts. American manufactured imports also came through Britain, often arranged by bills of credit drawn on Irish merchants for goods received. This kind of trade was more to the advantage of America's development than Ireland's; Irish agricultural exports to America declined as America became more self-sufficient, though the complexity of trading patterns between America, other colonies, Britain and Ireland may well mean that the volume of such trade has been underestimated. But here, too, networks of energetic Irish entrepreneurs were of considerable importance.

Such merchants were central but underrated figures in eighteenth-century Irish life. Functional and commodity specialization, as well as the rise of organized banking facilities and the centralized organization of the industries like linen, reduced their importance. But up to the 1780s, despite the modest scale of their enterprises and a recurrent problem of under-capitalization, merchants were the key figures of the Irish trading economy. Great figures like the Huguenot David La Touche began as merchants and progressed to being bankers; many combined the two offices. A private bank could provide remarkably large returns on capital, though the risk, and frequency, of failures was high. Though there was no Irish mint, there was until 1826 a separate Irish currency; banking arrangements were independent, and credit uncertain in economic fluctuations. Through bills of exchange, the movement of capital was arranged within Ireland and abroad. By the 1750s banking was centred in Dublin and Cork, but local banking activity was still to be found in towns like Waterford, Clonmel, Athlone, Belfast and Galway. Merchants were an important component of this mechanism, providing short-term banking functions, though attempts were made to limit their ambitions. They were vulnerable to bad harvests and trade contraction, circumstances that could trigger a percussion of credit squeezes. This kind of uneven development, rather than the traditional picture of steady stagnation, is what characterized the eighteenth-century Irish economy.

Thus the dislocation of the 1770s, especially in the linen industry, created a banking crisis, and in turn helped set off the rise of the Volunteer movement, demanding relaxation of import and export regulations in 1779.[vii] But, contrary to contemporary assertions about adverse balances of payments, the supply of specie in Ireland actually trebled from 1776 to 1779. Again, such assertions have more to do with constitutional campaigns against English legislative claims than with any realistic analysis of the economy. And British investment in Ireland was actually encouraged by high Irish interest rates on public funds, as well as by lotteries and tontines: export and import deals were often financed from the English side. With the development of industrial and capital investment, financial arrangements became more refined; between the 1720s and the 1790s cash supply increased tenfold. A Bank of Ireland was actually founded in 1783, but it did not yet transform the situation, though it provided extra flexibility. The backwardness of banking, in fact, is one area where the Navigation Acts *can* be seen as restricting Irish development, since they inhibited a direct colonial trade and complicated the mechanisms of re-export. But even here their effect was secondary and diffused rather than directly constricting.

II

Given this background, it is not surprising that eighteenth-century Ireland was an increasingly urbanized society. Towns still accounted for a small proportion of the population, but a handful of small towns had developed into market-centres by the end of the century (Mullingar, Maryborough and Ballinasloe were essentially created by eighteenth-century markets). There were fifty-eight borough towns with 300 houses or more, and eighty with 150 or more; Dublin's population rose to over 180,000 and Cork's to 80,000. Cork, indeed, was at its peak as an Atlantic trading port: Coquebert de Montbret, visiting it in 1790, noted that it was transformed since Smith's description of it in 1750. Wesley preached there in April 1778 on 'abstaining from fleshly desires: a necessary lesson in every place and nowhere more so than in Cork'.

But the real growth was in Ulster – Newry, Belfast and Derry all expanded beyond recognition. By 1783 Belfast had a Chamber of

[vii] See below, pp. 245–7.

Commerce, by 1785 a Harbour Corporation and a White Linen Hall. The Linen Hall would eventually also house the 'Belfast Society for Promoting Knowledge' and its comprehensive library, bringing together commerce and study in a typically Belfast conjunction. By the end of the decade a vigorous banking structure had developed. In the French wars the city would increase its grip on the linen trade with Britain, while Newry's and Dublin's share declined. Belfast was still a commercial rather than a manufacturing centre. But by the 1790s it had recognizably become a regional capital; it would wax as Dublin waned in the nineteenth century.

The collection of hearth tax shows that port towns were wealthier than those inland (except Kilkenny), but there were many prosperous small towns, often laid out by landlords; Mitchelstown in Cork is a classic example of a numerous genre. Increasing mobility was facilitated by a network of roads (whose quality travellers disagreed about) as well as the celebrated canals. (The Newry navigation, 1731–42, was the earliest man-made canal in the British Isles.) There was a wave of roadbuilding by turnpike trusts in the early eighteenth century: from the 1760s local grand juries could levy a rate for roadbuilding. Stage-coach routes radiated out from Dublin to the north, south and west (though western Connacht was not easily accessible until the early nineteenth century), adding mobility to the list of factors that facilitated economic growth.

The wool trade was one activity that used the improved network, moving from fairs in sheep districts to the combing and spinning centres of Leinster and Munster, and thence to the ports. Dairying areas sent their produce out through four great harbours: Cork, Waterford, Limerick and Dublin. Coal was carried down the inland waterway system. Overall, however, the transport network was more sophisticated than the level of economic activity required: one result of initiatives taken by a colonial parliament. Official involvement in the economy was evident elsewhere, too: not only in the Linen Board, but in state-backed canal ventures and colliery schemes; in the bounties offered on grain export and tillage; and most notably in backing individual ventures into cotton production. By the end of the century Ireland's industrial and commercial potential was perceived as a distinct threat by English mercantile opinion. Nor were Ireland's obvious advantages restricted to cheap and plentiful labour, though this contributed to them. The economy as a whole presented an impressive capacity for development.

This at once raises the question of who made money in eighteenth-century Ireland: and here one encounters that important, if unexpected, element, the middle-class Catholics of the towns. From about 1750 their economic power becomes a prime preoccupation in political calculations. Some Catholic fortunes had been made through traditional Continental connections; far more came from native developments and were established early on. The Catholic merchants of Cork constituted a powerful interest by 1708. The Penal Laws succeeded by mid-century in decimating the Catholic landowning classes, but even strictures like the prohibition upon holding mortgages did not prevent sizeable fortunes being made by Catholics as moneylenders. By the time the Bank of Ireland was set up in 1783, Irish Catholics were in a position to subscribe 10 per cent of the total capital. The idea of a powerful Catholic middle class sits oddly with Corkery's view of a 'hidden Ireland'; but it indubitably existed, and its social influence increased with economic and professional success. Ascendancy monopolies meant that the Catholic profile was low, and their political activities took highly specific forms; but in the political education of this important class lay the dynamics of sensational developments in the late eighteenth and early nineteenth centuries.

What, then, did the Penal Laws mean in actuality? This raises important questions of evidence, since everyday practice is much harder to record than the letter of the law; and the attitude behind both can only be inferred. Certainly, as early as 1718 the arrest of the Catholic Archbishop of Dublin by a bounty-hunting ex-priest was seen simply as an embarrassment by the government. Though intolerance survived much longer in some areas than others, by the 1730s the worst was over. But de facto toleration could not be taken for granted; several causes célèbres indicate there were always those ready to use legal formalities. Though by the end of the century Catholic clerics could be highly respected as pillars of local society, here as elsewhere the events of the 1790s would show the reality beneath.

Even at the height of their oppressiveness, little use was made of provisions like the Protestant right to claim land from a Catholic by 'discovery'. Many of the recorded cases were in fact collusive 'discoveries' by friendly Protestants who returned the land secretly to its Catholic owners. The Penal Laws should be related to the anti-Jacobite paranoia of the early eighteenth century, which helps explain their relaxation after the failure of 1745. How far the original ideologues of the Penal Laws really believed that laws could alter people is an interesting question; certainly belief that Catholics could be converted to Protestantism by policies repressing Catholic practices was soon moderated. Conversions actually *increased* after the laws were moderated in the 1770s. But in the early years of the eighteenth century the laws provided a key mechanism for the reinforcement of Ascendancy. Though the British government tried to moderate them from time to time, the Irish parliament – fiercely conscious of the forfeitures on which their property was based – insisted that the laws remain on the statute book, no matter how loosely enforced. Civil disabilities were linked with religious restrictions. Arms-bearing, a vital symbol of social standing, education and most of all property-owning were hedged by limits. In 1728 the franchise had formally been removed from Catholics; it was already constricted by the intro-duction of an elaborate Oath of Abjuration, yet another contravention of the Treaty of Limerick, which had guaranteed that no Oath except that of Allegiance would be expected from Catholics. Up to 1728 many Catholics had none the less managed to cast votes; there were still many Catholic freeholders, especially in the west. When the vote was formally removed, an initiative of the Irish House of Commons rather than the British government, it meant – given the nature of eighteenth-century political culture – the loss of a valuable possession, which in itself had conferred a certain security, especially in terms of relations with a landlord or a Protestant neighbour.

From mid-century, relaxations coincided with general develop-ments, like the moderation of papal claims in the temporal sphere. In 1761 Charles O'Conor wrote to his friend John Curry: 'former gover-nors punished us more as Irishmen than latter governors have punished us as Papists, and the present governors do not punish us at all. Our afflictions proceed entirely from the laws, not from them.'[2] O'Conor was himself a landed Roscommon Catholic gentleman; in some other areas, like Tipperary, such an element was strong enough to form a political interest aligned against local Protestants. It was by now real-ized that the code could not convert Catholics in large numbers – at least, not in any meaningful way. Stories abounded, like that of the newly Protestant owner of Oranmore who, when asked by the rector what had led him to the light, answered: 'Oranmore'. And numerous observers noted that such utilitarian motives were understood and even respected by contemporaries; those old Irish families who turned Protestant still retained a special relationship with their Catholic neigh-bours.

In 1776, shortly before the process of repealing the laws began, Arthur Young expressed to Anthony Foster, Lord Chief Baron of the Irish Exchequer, his surprise at their severity. 'He said they were severe in the letter, but were never executed ... This ... brought to my mind an admirable expression of Mr Burke's, in the English House of Commons, "Connivance is the relaxation of slavery, not the definition of liberty." ' Moreover, even if observance was patchy, punitive bills for registering priests were still being introduced by Irish M Ps after 1750, even if they were not reaching the statute book. Out of all proportion to their actual effect, the Penal Laws reflected Protestant fears and affected Irish mentality, creating a tension of resentment born of enforced deference as well as necessitating the elaborate concealments and stratagems of Catholic political activity. Here, at least, the concept of a 'hidden' Ireland has a real meaning.

When significant relief came in 1778, and full property rights were granted contingent upon, an Oath of Allegiance, it was the result of English pressure and political crisis, as well as the unquantifiable but effective pressure from Catholic commercial and financial interests (there had been a severe banking crisis earlier that year). The case was made, from both sides, on the grounds of pragmatism rather than justice: removal of restrictions would encourage stability and commitment to the status quo. Above all, as the ironic Charles O'Conor remarked in 1786, 'we are all become *good Protestants in politics*'.[3]

But they had conspicuously not become good Protestants in religion. The eighteenth-century Catholic Church was handicapped by an impoverished clergy and a hierarchy whose authority was often shaky; yet it retained its vitality. It was still beset by the traditional problems of Irish Catholicism: internal indiscipline, vague and latitudinarian bishops, factional squabbles, often with a family orientation. But its peculiar nature was also manifested in the evolution of those practices that defined rural Catholicism and brought worshippers together. The difficulty of centralizing congregations, as well as the poverty of the priests, encouraged habits like the 'stations', whereby the priest heard confessions by moving round selected households at Easter and Christmas; the importance of marriage and baptism fees has a similar origin. The close integration of the priest into local society occasioned some resentment: wakes could involve satiric parodies of sacramental services, and the figure of 'the greedy priest' recurs in eighteenth-century poetry. The Whiteboy agitations[viii] are evidence that anti-clerical resentment could be organized into resistance. But this was a minority phenomenon, and it coexisted with the rooted piety that enabled the Church to survive. To exaggerate it is to miss the point.

[viii] See below, pp. 223–5.

Evidence like Hugh MacMahon's report on the Ulster diocese in 1714 shows a strength of devotion that remained constant. It should also be pointed out that the rich and varied rural lore of fairies, charms, banshees, superstitions, 'special days', rituals, sympathetic magic and amulets could and did live alongside the particularly Irish Christianity of the countryside, and could even be assimilated into it. The celebrated Croagh Patrick pilgrimage originated in the pre-Christian feast of Lughnasa; and the ancient magic of pieces of cloth tied to bushes became attached to mass-rocks and holy wells.

Rural Catholic society also bred a similarly idiosyncratic educational system in the celebrated, and mythologized, 'hedge schools', stressing the classics and Gaelic culture, which in the early eighteenth century gave the basis of their education to many future priests. But from a comparatively early date there was also a more established educational network: by mid-century all parishes were supplied with schools. Even the 1731 'Report on the State of Popery' shows numerous discreet mass-houses; by 1750 a full parochial structure is indicated by the records of visitations, and this was accompanied by educational initiatives at all levels. From mid-century, too, pressure was brought from Rome to cut down on the number of friars and to tighten up ordination procedures, with the unintended result that the numbers of clergy dropped in relation to the soaring population. In 1747 a Jesuit reported: 'never was a city better provided with learned and zealous instructors than Dublin is at present; we now begin to have vespers sung and sermons preached in the afternoons. You see hereby how peaceable times we enjoy.'[4]

The Jesuits, in fact, were very influential in emphasizing the importance of religious organization. They were operating in a milieu where the increasing acceptability of open Catholicism is indicated by the proliferating number of Catholic booksellers, catering for a middle-class reading public, and by the numerous respectful references to Catholics in the press.[5] A valuable cache of papers exists in the survey compiled by Father John Fottrell, who toured Dominican convents and monasteries in 1734–5 (he was arrested in 1739); the record shows forty Dominican houses, even at this early date, many well stocked. It is not surprising that by mid-century the authorities had perforce to connive at Catholicism in many places.

This was especially true in the west. Galway and Mayo were still dominated by a Catholic gentry, often, like the Moores and the Bellews, possessing considerable commercial interests in Spain, chanelling an invisible income from the Continent to all levels of society.

Even here, some large landowners had to conform, like the Brownes in Mayo and the Martins in Galway; but many of those who did, like Lord Athenry, maintained close relations with the titular Catholic dignitaries of their locality, and even continued to exercise their right of presentation to local parishes. The prominent Catholics who did not conform kept a low profile at first, but the foundation of the Catholic Association in 1759, unaggressive though it was, gave them a public identity. Even before this, in 1751, Charles O'Conor advised his son in Dublin that the system could be used:

> You live now in a busy, elbowing scene; if you have any sagacity, you will make reflections on every incident and reap instruction and, whatever it be, strive to adapt it to the rank you are to fill hereafter: that of a Roman Catholic in a Protestant country, that of one in a low way, obnoxious to the laws. A wise man will derive advantages even from that situation in which bounds are set to all hopes and fears. It is, indeed, a condition of life more eligible than our dull brethren can imagine or benefit by.[6]

But even O'Conor's last years were darkened by a 'discovery' suit for his lands brought by a converted relative, threatening his last 800 acres, 'the plank on which we came ashore after our great shipwreck'. Ó Bruadair's metaphor persisted.

The distribution of population in Connacht in 1749 is conveniently profiled by a census taken in the diocese of Elphin; it shows large households, swelled by servants as much as children, and a great preponderance of Catholics. Protestants were restricted, more or less, to the Big Houses, a syndrome which did not apply to areas like Wexford or Carlow in the east. Tithes in Connacht were levied only on corn and sheep (in Munster they extended to potatoes, milk, eggs and chickens). Relations between the two communities in the west were generally good; when unrest broke out, it often originated in attempts to Protestantize (by the introduction of imported tenants rather than by proselytizing). This was the background to the life of the marginalized Catholic country gentleman – intellectual, as recorded by the papers of Charles O'Conor of Belanagare; a patron of poets like the great Carolan[ix] as well as a friend of the local gentry. (Similarly, the collected letters of the O'Connells at Derrynane show a Catholic

---

[ix] Turlough Carolan (1670–1738): born in County Meath; blinded by smallpox at fourteen; trained as a harper; welcomed at the houses of the Catholic gentry, whom he celebrated in his songs as fallen Milesians, 1692–1738; had twenty tunes published in the first collection of Irish secular music, 1724; regarded as the chief musician of Gaelic Ireland at his death.

Big House preserving the old traditions in another western fastness.) O'Conor is a symbolic figure in his determination to compile materials of an Irish history that would clarify events rather than fight old battles over again; at the same time, he was eagerly prepared to believe anything that would, like Vallancey's[x] theories, 'beyond contradiction show the early use of letters in Ireland' and assert the civil nature of early Irish society.

O'Conor and his friends epitomize not only the preoccupations of the Catholic gentry and intellectuals, but also the obsession with Gaelic antiquity that would spread to Protestant society also by the 1780s. Late eighteenth-century tours like Luckombe's give close attention to antiquarian survivals, and to the living remnants of the ancient Gaelic nobility – deferred to, Luckombe thought, with 'a secret pleasure'. In the upper classes of both traditions, an intellectual fascination with the Irish past had taken hold, which would have diverse and far-reaching results.

But to comprehend the general Catholic experience of the eighteenth century, it is essential once more to stress the existence of a commercial middle class. Their life is less recorded than that of the remnant gentry; discretion argued against the itemization of property. But it is impossible to disregard contemporary claims, on both sides, that the bulk of the country's trade was carried on by Catholics. There are logical reasons – not only their own exclusion from acquiring landed property but also the Ascendancy's contempt for trade. Outside the Church, the medical profession and the Continental armies, there were few alternatives. Irish Catholics did not embrace the spirit of capitalism by reversing the spirit of Max Weber's celebrated thesis: they referred to 'entering a mercantile career' rather than 'trade', they readily claimed grand Milesian descent and noble birthrights, they continued to send their sons into romantic but unprofitable foreign service. But they built on and extended a seventeenth-century tradition, making fortunes and gaining influence in the process.

Thus as early as 1708 Cork Catholic merchants could exert pressure on the Council to rescind by-laws aimed at Catholic commercial success; while in cities like Cork and Limerick the intention of exclud-

---

[x] Charles Vallancey (1721–1812): born in Windsor, of Huguenot descent; as a military engineer in Ireland, 1762, became interested in Gaelic antiquity but never learned the language; Secretary of the Society of Irish Antiquaries, 1773; F R S, 1784; his valuable work was the publication of *Collectanea de Rebus Hibernicis*, 1770–1804, to which other antiquarians contributed; his own works sought to prove the antiquity of the Irish tongue by tracing its evolution from Punic, or similarly extravagant, origins.

ing them by statute was turned on its head, and Catholics became the dominant element. There were vituperative Protestant reactions to this development: a significant campaign was waged to enforce statutory anti-Catholic taxes like quarterage, but this was (even more significantly) unsuccessful. Despite contemporary claims, Catholic businessmen were not numerically dominant; they were still a minority of Dublin merchants (about one-third) in 1780. But their clannishness, their wealth and their organization against discrimination maximized their influence; it could also be translated into effective political lobbying.

However, the effect of the Penal Laws was intended to fall most decisively on land ownership, and it did. Catholics were confined to 31-year leases, though under certain conditions rent movements could make short leases appear desirable for the tenant. Catholic rents were supposed to be pegged above a certain level, but this was unenforceable. Such restrictions were removed in 1778 (by which time short leases had become the norm), along with rights such as that of a Protestant son to dispossess his Catholic father. But by then the Penal Laws had done all they could. Catholics were about 75 per cent of the total population, and over 90 per cent in certain ecclesiastical provinces; yet, Arthur Young calculated in 1776, they held only 5 per cent of the land. This, however, ignores the considerable number who held profitable leases. Relaxations of property restrictions really came only when this pattern had been solidly established.

Thus in the 1780s and 1790s Catholics gained the right to purchase and bequeath land, though not in parliamentary boroughs. Priests were formally allowed to live in the country, though still on restricted terms (including the prohibition of steeples and bells on their churches). Educational restrictions were repealed; by the 1790s the government was encouraging the foundation of Catholic colleges like St Patrick's, Carlow, and St Patrick's, Maynooth, and there was much support for the idea of state payment of priests. Intermarriage, the right to practise at the Bar and finally the franchise followed in 1792–3.

By then the French Revolution and a general radicalization and polarization in Irish life had changed matters beyond recognition – for Catholics, Episcopalians and Presbyterians. By the later eighteenth century, Protestants might contribute to Catholic Church building-funds; Protestants and Catholics might attend each other's funerals. But as Burke had pointed out, practical freedom of action was not the same as toleration, much less integration. Confessional identities were still the primary fact of Irish life, and would remain so.

III

If the Catholic world represented one Ireland outside the Ascendancy Pale, Ulster epitomized another. 'No sooner did we enter Ulster,' wrote Wesley in 1756, 'than we observed the difference. The ground was cultivated just as in England, and the cottages not only neat, but with doors, chimneys and windows. Newry, the first town we came to, (allowing for its size) is built much after the manner of Liverpool.' The difference from the rest of the island was in part a matter of settlement and tradition; but by now it had been reinforced by economic development. For Ulster had become characterized by linen production.

Though Huguenots are popularly given the credit for eighteenth-century linen expansion, this reflects the career of Samuel Crommelin[xi] rather than a general syndrome; Quakers were just as prominent, and in some linen areas like Armagh there was a preponderance of Catholics. Though marketing and financing were centred on Dublin, the growth of the industry was most notable in the north-east – Antrim, Armagh, Down, Derry and the periphery. Flax cultivation spread into Connacht and Leinster; government and landlords encouraged the development of local weaving projects. After the linen slump of the 1770s, the industry revived, at cottage level, throughout Ireland – not just in Ulster. Part-time weaving added to farming incomes in many areas. But the large-scale trade remained established principally in the north-east and round Dublin. Active linen towns like Dungannon, Banbridge, Armagh, Londonderry, Strabane, Dundalk and Enniskillen prospered through commerce as well as manufacture; the hearth tax returns indicate well-off communities. The mid to late eighteenth century was the heyday of the local linen markets, with their independent weavers, and an organization centred on the Linen Halls; by the end of the century large-scale operators had taken over who

---

[xi] Samuel-Louis Crommelin (1652–1727): born in Picardy, France; compelled to emigrate upon the revocation of the Edict of Nantes, 1685; became 'overseer of the royal linen manufacture of Ireland' on William III's invitation, 1700; settled in the Huguenot colony at Lisburn; published his *Essay on Linen Manufacture in Ireland*, 1705; received a parliamentary vote of thanks for his invaluable services, 1707; extended his work to encourage the manufacture of hempen sailcloth in the south, 1717–25.

bypassed local networks and dealt directly with Dublin. Eventually, they would bypass Dublin too.

But before that, linen production created an intricate and inter-dependent domestic economy that characterized relationships in Ulster. Annual sales by independent weavers were estimated at £2,170,000 *in cash* as late as 1803. The importance of linen earnings permeated society. Domestic labour kept large families on the land, encouraged subdivision and pushed up rents. Travellers always noted the intensive cultivation of the weaver districts. At the end of the century, the shift to cotton production would help bring about a corresponding economic dislocation in the traditional yarn-spinning areas.

Thus to Ulster's peculiar religious, tenurial and settlement charac-teristics was added a potent new source of differentiation. How far the pre-existing differences conditioned the adoption of the linen culture is uncertain; but contemporaries certainly noted that bleaching enter-prises were nearly entirely monopolized by Protestants. And overall, an ethos emerged where colonial tradition, idiosyncratic landholding patterns and the prosperity of the linen industry reaffirmed the separatist egalitarianism of Ulster Protestant culture.

One vital result of Ulster's productive ability and comparative prosperity in this period was that the Ulster economy could interact with the effects of industrial revolution in Britain. Thus Belfast became a channel for the import of manufactured goods and a focus of econ-omic activity. While towns like Newry remained linen centres, Belfast also took in cotton; by the mid-1780s large quantities of cotton-wool were being imported. By the 1790s the weaving industry was so active that they were importing supplementary yarn as well. The great leap in growth would occur in the early nineteenth century; but the poten-tial was already there, founded on the textile industry and a vital commercial vantage.

While linen-yarn exports, and then linen cloth, dominated the western part of the province, north-east Ulster had begun the process of building a varied and powerful economic base. Even its agricultural economy was, in a sense, idiosyncratic – continuing to be founded on the less profitable export of live cattle rather than beef and butter. Though there were disadvantages, and the province missed out on the great profits of the Atlantic commodity trade, this had the effect of encouraging diversification into marginal areas like rush-weaving, rabbit-warrening, illicit distillation and fishing. There, too, a broad-based and flexible local economy was in the making.

Economic variation was matched by cultural and political differentiation. Under the dispensation of an episcopalian Ascendancy, Presbyterianism maintained a heightened sense of persecution – rather like that of the Catholics, if with less material cause. Politics and religion intertwined; a provincial sense of elitism and independence separated the Presbyterian consciousness from both Catholics and Church of Ireland. The 1704 'Act to Prevent the Further Growth of Popery' had excluded Dissenters from public office, and they remained barred from bodies like town corporations, even in Ulster, until 1780. This, in turn, effectively cut them off from influence in borough politics, just as their non-landed base excluded them from county politics. The gentry monopolized local politics; to compensate, a small tenant farmer-weaver class took an aggressive line in out-of-doors agitation. And the professional men and merchants of Belfast would emerge in an even more radical guise towards the end of the century: a possible connection back to the libertarianism and radical social values of the 'New Light' secession from mainstream Presbyterianism in the 1720s, whose influence was to be found on the radical wing of the Volunteering movement in the 1780s.

Volunteering (which will be dealt with in the next chapter) was more directly connected with another Presbyterian political identification in the 1770s, and one which furnished them with a range of aggressive tactics: explicit sympathy with American discontents. Their own catalogue of tax grievances and political exclusions formed the basis of recurrent Presbyterian political activity. After 1768 the imposition of regular elections under the Octennial Act created the conditions for more regular political involvement. But they remained galvanically affected by the contractual emphasis in Presbyterian political thought, powerfully preached by the Ulsterman Francis Hutcheson[xii] as Professor of Law at Glasgow. And given the conditions of Ulster society, this was a contractual idea that would not necessarily move on to embrace a belief in popular sovereignty – since popular sovereignty would swamp the cause of the righteous.

The ways in which eighteenth-century Ulster society was defined have already been indicated. It had lively urban centres in Belfast, Newry and Londonderry; in Belfast, chambers of commerce, libraries

[xii] Francis Hutcheson (1694–1746): born in County Down, of Scottish Presbyterian descent; educated at Glasgow University; published his *Inquiry into Our Ideas of Beauty and Virtue*, 1725, which won him the friendship of Archbishop King and Viscount Molesworth; elected to the chair of Moral Philosophy at Glasgow, without solicitation, 1729; taught Adam Smith; although he coined the phrase 'the greatest happiness of the greatest number', his path led directly to Jefferson rather than to Bentham.

like that of the Linen Hall, clubs and even theatres brought together people of different persuasions. Private schools flourished, individual newspapers appeared, like the *News Letter* and the *Mercury*. Belfast merchants and manufacturers were an articulate, cosmopolitan-minded class. Armagh, less celebrated, has been usefully profiled by a 1770 census: this shows deep divisions, spatially and culturally, between the religions. Protestants were located round the thriving commercial centre, Catholics at the periphery. Members of the Church of Ireland monopolized the professions; Catholics did labouring work; Presbyterians were occupied in manufacturing and trade. There was not much overt sectarian conflict; Ulstermen and Ulsterwomen shared some common values, as well as living carefully demarcated lives, and there were even some cross-denominational connections. The analyst of this census has concluded that all Armagh enjoyed a definite sense of community: the kind of apparent contradiction that would characterize Ulster society for the future.[7]

Ulstermen were increasingly active politicians, on a national as well as a local level. They may not have been the automatic radicals often claimed, but they were radical enough to create an identifiable tradition. Even before the foundation of the United Irishmen in 1791, the Northern Whigs embraced democratic rhetoric; ideas of republicanism were floated early on, as well as a radical language that Presbyterian local politicians adapted in the nineteenth century. But even the superficial radicalization of some elements in Ulster society had gone along with a hardened and aggressive sectarian polarization in mid-Ulster: where competition for land, and the economic fluctuations of the weaver's life, were already producing violent confrontations. By the 1790s this was already driving out Catholic families from north Armagh, the most densely populated county in Ireland, and south Derry.

That same economic uncertainty was also reflected in a much greater kind of emigration: the flow of Ulster families to North America. In Ulster, rents rose as linen prosperity increased; whenever the linen profits faltered, a crisis threatened. This pattern sharpened as the agricultural economy became less mixed; and when leases fell in from the 1770s, there were Catholics ready to bid for them. The traditional view that grasping Ulster landlords created the emigrant drain has not borne detailed examination – though there may be something to contemporary fears that draconian measures against rural violence (the 'Steelboys') created a rush to the ships. But the reasons lay deep in the structure of Ulster society, where a readiness to move and settle and subdue land was traditional. So was a religious and cultural apartness that enabled communities to emigrate and stay together.

The very nature of Ulster trade facilitated it: the ships that brought flax seed from America often returned with emigrants. North America remained the majority destination for Ulster, though the West Indies attracted many from the south. Up to 1720 New England had been the most favoured landfall; it was followed by Pennsylvania, Delaware, New York and South Carolina. Cheapness of land was as important a consideration as religious freedom; and perhaps more important than either was the origin of the ships that came to Ulster ports. The rate of emigration, though often exaggerated by contemporary impressions, gathered speed from 1720; probably several thousand Irish people emigrated to America in the late 1720s. The prosperity of the 1730s led to a decline, but the rate picked up again by the 1760s, when about 20,000 took ship from the Ulster ports, climaxing in the early 1770s: at least 30,000 left between 1770 and 1774.

Ulster continued to dominate the picture. Two-fifths of the total of American emigrants in the colonial period came from Ulster – up to 250,000 souls. They appear to have been much less exclusively Protestant than popularly supposed, and included many Anglicans as well as Presbyterians: the predominant 'Ulster Scot' stereotype does not stand up to the statistics, since about 100,000, mostly Catholic, probably came from the south in the same period. The Ulster Scots, however, stood out: possibly because, even in the New World, they remained ostentatiously separate. Even more importantly, distinctive Ulster Scot communities could evolve because Ulster *women* emigrated, too – a development not replicated elsewhere in Ireland, except Dublin, until the nineteenth century.

Once emigration was an established fact, it set up its own self-perpetuating rhythm. Those who went were mostly indentured labour, travelling free; very few were either convicts or independent investors. The claims that they were farmers of substance generally stem from propaganda of one kind or another. Government attitudes were not yet in favour of the phenomenon, especially when it meant losing Protestants; but an interventionist line was never taken (plans in the mid-1770s to curb emigration were overtaken by events). The whole business of emigration was tightly organized even before the Famine exodus of 1740–41. By 1790 Doyle estimates the number of the United States population of Irish stock at 447,000 – two-thirds of them originating from Ulster.

Immigration into eighteenth-century Ireland was far less considerable. Generally purpose-directed, it included Protestant refugees like the celebrated Huguenots who settled at Portarlington and elsewhere; there were also German Palatines and Moravians (the word 'Palatine' is still memorialized in some village place-names). There were some bizarre attempts at social engineering, like the projected 'New Geneva' settlement near Waterford in the 1780s, where colonies of Genevese were expected to implant democratic values, watch-making skills and the Protestant work ethic. A university was to be built, and a land reclamation scheme begun. But they never arrived, and the place became a barracks. More successful, but almost entirely unrecorded, are the unofficial immigrants. In 1790 Coquebert de Montbret found a surprisingly large number of Frenchmen who had stayed on after internment as prisoners in the Seven Years War. It is unlikely that they ever went back to France. Elements like these make up a more varied and less predictable society than the traditional generalizations allow, while active patterns of internal migration added to the general picture of mobility and vitality.

IV

If population movement preoccupied contemporaries, what strikes historians most forcibly is population growth. Demographic expansion is the basic fact of the eighteenth-century Irish experience, most of all for those living on the land. As Cullen has put it, 'historians have wrongly seen accelerated population growth as something imposed on an existing land system, whereas it was in fact something which altered the original system almost beyond recognition'.[8] The population doubled over the century, reaching between 4,500,000 and 5,000,000 in 1800. This was by then apparent to contemporaries: members of the Royal Irish Academy began writing articles about it in the 1790s. But when and how this began to happen is less certain.

The *doyen* of Irish population studies, Kenneth Connell, believed that the key period was 1780–1830, the fundamental cause being increased marital fertility, with early marriage enabled by the potato diet and facilitated by the ease of acquiring small tenancies. But the nature of the evidence for eighteenth-century population figures has recently come under stringent examination, which enforces some reconsideration. The figures are dominated by the hearth tax returns, up to 1793 giving the number of inhabited houses. After that year, a large proportion of single-hearth households were relieved, making the tax returns far less useful to historians. Connell believed the hearth tax figures were drastic underestimates, but they have now been judged more reliable than he allowed, as well as indicating a much greater regional variation than might be expected – population density decreasing dramatically in grazing and sheep-walk areas or in localities with a strong tradition of emigration. Mortality rates also appear to have varied considerably in times of agricultural crisis. Reassessments of the tax evidence for the early eighteenth century, once dismissed as hopelessly corrupt, give a population growth rate that rises early on, in a pattern of 'sharp but insecure growth', and average family sizes appreciably larger than contemporary Britain, though the invariably teeming cabins conjured up by late eighteenth-century travellers owed a good deal to Malthusian preconceptions.[9]

The great spurt in population appears to have come at the end of the period. But theories about the pattern of growth, beginning early on, are bedevilled by ambiguous evidence. The accepted idea of very early marriages has been queried: there is much disparity and selectivity in figures from the pre-registration age.[xiii] Nor is there a self-evident connection between early marriages and the potato diet; in Ulster, rural domestic industry could as easily have been a cause. And early marriage might also be seen as the continuation of a practice evident from the seventeenth century.

The social complexion of population increase is also an open question; but it seems likely that it was the labouring population that grew most dramatically from this point – a process probably compounded by the growth of the farming class forcing younger sons a rung down the social ladder. In this area, trends have to be inferred: as is the case with family and sexual history. There is a single known reference to contraception in eighteenth-century Irish literature: predictably occurring in Brian Merriman's[xiv] bawdy poem *Cúirt an Mheáin Oidhche* (*The Midnight Court*). But illegitimacy was low, and prostitutes were rare (outside Dublin, where they thrived). The birth of children was generally and traditionally seen as desirable; their additional cost was

[xiii] Even later on, the 1841 census can be taken to demonstrate a different pattern from the oral evidence collected by the inquiry into the state of the poor in 1836, though the reliability of the census itself is a matter of controversy.

[xiv] Brian Merriman (*c.* 1747–1805): born in County Clare; schoolmaster and farmer; settled in County Limerick; won Dublin Society prizes for his flax crop, 1797. Wrote *Cúirt an Mheáin Oidhche* (*The Midnight Court*) in 1780 (published 1800), a satire on Irish sexual life written in the style of, but also mocking, the romantic *aisling*.

negligible, bearing in mind the subsistence economy, cheap energy and cheap food. But such attitudes are impossible to quantify into growth-inducing factors. Nor can it be conclusively stated when the potato diet became a staple; it certainly did not explain the great density of population in Ulster, which was the province least dependent on it. It seems most likely that, as a determinant of population growth, it was important but not crucial.

What can be said is that population increase in the later eighteenth century was very rapid even by contemporary European standards; and that it slowed from the 1820s, accompanied by a pressure on living standards and a rise in the marriage age as well as a great increase in emigration. All are often thought of as distinctively post-Famine, but they begin about twenty years before the horrors of 1846. The vital point is that a country that showed a fair, if uneven, degree of dynamism and development potential in the eighteenth century failed to participate in the kind of nineteenth-century industrialization that could sustain it. Thus we are presented with a picture of population growth within an economy structurally unable, in the long run, to cope with it.

This makes the question of eighteenth-century diet an absorbing one. In the earlier period potatoes were important but not as yet staple; Madden in the 1730s saw them as a substitute food for 'one fourth part of the year'. In Munster, however, they took hold; by mid-century they were the main winter diet of the cottier class (traditionally consumed up to 17 March, St Patrick's Day), except in Ulster. By 1780 they were a year-long staple and were being exported in dried form to America. The age of the potato had arrived.

The agricultural advantages were self-evident. It was a good crop for reclaiming marginal land. One acre could support a family of six, even though the recorded quantities consumed were impressive.[xv] The eighteenth-century potato was better than the watery, if heavy-cropping, 'lumper' that took over in the early nineteenth century, especially when supplemented with milk or buttermilk, fish and vegetables. What else was eaten varied up the social scale. Beef and poultry were for the farming class; the Ulster Scots favoured porridge and root vegetables. Though fishing was still widespread, it was increasingly an export industry; it is noticeable that late eighteenth-century poetry

---

[xv] An average of ten pounds per person per day, though the practice of peeling the boiled potato probably reduced intake to a less astounding level. The peelings, naturally, went to feed the pig.

takes a shellfish diet as the nadir of poverty. This is evidence of commercialization: food that was bought rather than foraged had become the desideratum. Thus imported bacon was preferred, and domestic cheese-making lapsed. Milk and butter, while still important, no longer played the ubiquitous part in diet that was so often recorded a hundred years before.

The adoption of the potato was accompanied by that of the pig, an increasingly necessary part of peasant life, though the pork trade begins to be commercialized only from about 1770, and a single cow was still a more prized possession. This process helped reduce the milk diet of the labouring poor and elevated still further the importance of the potato. The other rural staple, strong tea, was only becoming general at the end of the century, except in prosperous northern weaving communities. In poor rural areas it remained something of an exotic until the nineteenth century – a status indicated by the fact that the beverage's name continued to be pronounced in the French manner ('tay').

While the physique of the peasantry was famously good, the Irish poor were subject to classic illnesses like smallpox and post-famine typhus. Remedies tended to be as questionable as Bishop Berkeley's famous tar-water. There were urban workhouses for the afflicted but no parochial Poor Law: dispensaries and town hospitals were organized as charities, often administered by local grand juries that were, by definition, Protestant. Though Irish medicine had its notable successes, like the avant-garde maternity care at the Rotunda hospital, the approach was haphazard. The Penal Laws had left a medical calling, alone among the professions, open to Catholics, so there was some vitality in it. But rural districts still depended greatly on traditional remedies, wise women, herbalists and faith healers.

The land that sustained this population was let and farmed in a complex manner, not adequately described by Lecky's classic account of absentee owners, middlemen administrators and exploited cottiers. Middlemen, for one thing, often farmed the land themselves as well as leasing it out: they were not parasites pure and simple. The term, and many of the generalizations accompanying it, were given currency by Arthur Young and used too freely by his successors. In dairying areas, the middleman structure was a necessary means of capitalizing the tenants, as middlemen provided stock for the farms they relet. Middleman functions were performed by different types at different times, and their position was altered by the development of stock farming, and by demographic pressure. The system as a whole was being phased out in favour of direct tenancies by the late eighteenth century.

Similarly, absenteeism, as already discussed,[xvi] was much exaggerated: landlords contributed more to local investment and involvement in the rural economy than used to be accepted. The whole question of letting land was a complex one, as one land agent explained to his employer:

> You are to observe that tenants will not hold land in Ireland from year to year as in England but expect leases of 21 years, sometimes 40 years or 3 lives. For in Ireland the tenants make all repairs and improvements at their own charge, consequently lands there must be leased out or lie waste.[10]

Leases became a kind of currency, given the historical fragmentation and discontinuity of landholding and the pattern of absenteeism. In poorer areas of Ulster during the earlier eighteenth century, rents were often low and leases very favourable, due to agricultural price crises and a high level of emigration. This, however, militated against landowners making improvements; while elsewhere in Ireland, uncertainty of renewal discouraged tenants from similar activity.

> A farm is always left by the retreating tenant in the most impoverished state; the drains are choaked; the ditches and fences destroyed, the land exhausted and overrun with weeds; the house and offices fallen, or greatly out of repair, so that the farm is in reality of less value from five to ten shillings an acre than it was a few years before.[11]

Little research has been carried out on rents actually paid, but a survey of several Ulster estates in the eighteenth century concludes that 'the *overall average* level of rents of determinable holdings was well below, and in some cases catastrophically below, the current market price for leased property'.[12] Long leases were not always an advantage in times of uncertain prices; but periods of consistent agricultural prosperity, especially later in the century, made a long lease at a fixed rent attractive to tenants, so landlords became less and less ready to grant them. It was this development that squeezed out the middleman system.

Agriculture was dominated by tenant farmers, holding small farms for tillage, larger for grazing. There is plenty of evidence that this afforded a decent way of life in areas like Meath, the midlands or north Waterford, though foreign observers concentrated upon the landless labourers and cottiers with their miserable homes, scanty livings and migratory work patterns. This was the obvious picture in the west

---

[xvi] See above, pp. 179–80.

and south-west, already highly differentiated areas. But there were a number of important regional markets, and where the market dominated, there was a tendency to larger farms, and less subdivision.

Where subdivision was rife, it was encouraged by the survival of the rundale system, especially in peripheral areas of Ulster; but from the later eighteenth century landlords mounted a concerted campaign to eradicate it. Also in this period, rising agricultural prices brought great hardship to the cottiers, tied as they were to cash rents and without enough land to supplement their incomes by agricultural production for the market. In the dairying areas of the south and west they could eke out some employment; and here observers like Young saw them existing on their potato patches, which were all that kept subsistence a possibility. But the strength and stability of tenant farming in other areas was less noticed, though it perhaps goes some way to explain the lack of agitation for security of tenure or compensation for improvements.

Underneath it all an invisible network of settlement frontiers persisted, inherited from the colonization of the previous century. Certain areas in the east and south retained concentrations of Protestant farmers (Carlow, Wicklow, north Wexford, parts of Cork); in other regions, ancient Gaelic family identifications survived. Implicit tension, often sectarian, was a feature of the eighteenth-century countryside, breaking out into crisis at certain points like the 1760s. Such movements were sometimes focused on a Jacobite scare, in the earlier part of the century. But the cattle-maiming outbreak in Connacht in 1711–12, known as the 'Hougher' movement, represented a different syndrome, one that would recur: resentment at the extension of pasture farming, which disadvantaged small occupiers. The agitators issued proclamations that declared in favour of a traditional economy and called for an end to dairy farming ('selling of milk, like huxters'). Those charged included some gentry, reflecting Galway's special composition, but also the general nature of the resentment. This was amplified by the fact that pastureland was effectively exempt from tithe – which put the burden of Church support on to the poorer members of society. Potatoes were tithable in Munster and elsewhere, and taxed at a high rate, which helps explain the geography of economic disaffection.

This unrest was expressed by the varied, energetic and complex structure of agrarian 'secret societies' that dominated eighteenth-century peasant life and throws some light on Irish rural society as seen from 'below'. Generally, the causes of violence were localized. In 1763 the 'Oakboy' movement in the north sprang up against taxes levied for road-building, especially when used to private advantage by land-lords. It mobilized Catholics as well as lower-class Presbyterians and Anglicans, and represented the small farmer/weaver class at their most aggressive. Demonstrations were spectacular and carnivalesque, as was the case with the more widespread 'Whiteboy' movement in the south. This developed in the 1760s in north County Waterford and Tipperary, and mobilized a wide range of grievances – even extending to anger at excessive exactions by Catholic priests, as well as at the more predictable potato tithe. Resentment against conacre rents and the enclosure movement helped mobilize labourers, cottiers and small farmers: deer-parks and orchards were special objects of attack, as well as the doubled, and even trebled, rents of the 1760s. Eventually, the movement brought in urban craftsmen, too, reflecting the part-time rural identification of many tradesmen. Observers like O'Conor and Luckombe were clear that the movement was economic, rather than political or sectarian; Catholic bishops spoke against it; and although a celebrated priest, Father Sheehy, was executed as a Whiteboy under the 'Whiteboy Act' of 1765, this was a manifest injustice.

Yet another local movement in the next decade was the 'Steelboy' agitation in south Antrim: a rebellion against the much exaggerated renewal fines on Lord Donegall's estates. The Steelboys declared their principles of Presbyterian egalitarianism and loyalism, and their resent-ment at land being given to papists prepared to pay high rents. Their organization was sophisticated, forcing the gentry to barricade their houses; their cause spread into a generalized protest against cess, tithes and high rents. But even on the Donegall estate, the Steelboys reflected the depressed condition of the smaller tenants rather than expressing conscious resentment of landlord rapacity. They also represented a popular notion of fair rent levels and standards of equity, which could be applied to cess as well, and a wish to regulate potato and meal prices – something, indeed, like an acceptable 'moral economy'.

These attitudes come through all the protest movements. Tithes were the great common cause of resentment, especially where, as in Munster, grassland was exempt but potatoes taxed. Enclosure, tax, rent and wage levels were attacked in illegal, highly mobile nocturnal gatherings and raids, proclaiming ideas of redress and restoration rather than revolution. Their iconography appealed to 'captains', chiefs, kings and queens of Irish rural tradition; the Tipperary Whiteboys called on 'Queen Sive', occasionally coupling her improbably with King George. If not revolutionary, they were capable of secret oath-bound organ-ization on a parochial basis; they were part of an underground that had learned not only to separate the formal law from popular notions of legitimacy, but also how to impose an alternative discipline through intimidation. Their proclamations parodied the legal documents of the day; sometimes an enemy's horse or cow was symbolically tried, found guilty and executed. The language of these economic movements was at least potentially political.

In the 1780s economic discontent in Cork and Kerry produced the 'Rightboy' movement, whose name indicated yet again a claim on traditional 'rights'. They condemned the auctioning of leases ('canting') as a perversion of justice (English justice); they called for levies to be made commensurate with different tenants' ability to pay, reflecting the decline in wages of the cottier class, while their smallholdings were being undermined by inflated taxation as well as more effective tax collection. At the same time, the Rightboys (like the Houghers, though not the Whiteboys) brought in farmers and gentry to their number, the latter possibly for reasons of local politics; Protestants joined as well as Catholics. The level of actual violence was low, and the pageantry and ritual highly elaborate. Tithe was a great grievance, as a tax extorted by 'pampered theologians, whose God was their belly and whose religion was a hogshead of wine'; enclosure was also resented. The Rightboys cleverly utilized the system to make the claiming of tithes a practical impossibility; they also attacked Catholic priests' dues, wanting them pegged at a maximum level, and they claimed that domestic entertainments for the clergy imposed unnecessary expense on the poor. Priests accordingly opposed the movement, and excommunicated known Rightboys, who retaliated by boycotting mass and attending Protestant churches.

The Rightboys were powerful enough to make the government tread warily; though draconian changes in the law were introduced, they were utilized only with great caution. As with other movements, there was a component of millenarian prophecy and popular passion; the government had great difficulty with sympathetic juries. While the Steelboys can be seen as reacting to the widespread agricultural crisis of the early 1770s (crop deficiencies, low cattle prices, high food prices), both the Whiteboy and the Rightboy movements flared up at moments of prosperity rather than dearth. In fact, it may have been the crisis brought about by drought in 1781 that defused Whiteboyism.

These movements reflect special conditions rather than a governing syndrome throughout the century. But they happened; they became part of rural tradition; they were connived at ('the Boys' can be seen as an affectionate and exonerating term); they helped identify rural violence as part of the popular tradition. At the end of the century, with sectarian polarization and political crisis, these traditions would form the vital basis for the power of the Defenders.

All this was linked closely to the economic picture already drawn. In the last decades of the eighteenth century, there were structural weaknesses beneath the apparent prosperity. A population explosion had increased the landless classes. The domestic textile industry was insecurely based – woollen workers were already hard hit by the 1780s. The domestic decline of cotton and linen was about to become apparent. This decline would interact with rural overpopulation, as a supplementary income source for the rural workforce dried up. Local grievances of the tithe, cess, rent and enclosure had episodically mobilized networks of resistance. And from all this, the political crisis of late eighteenth-century Ireland cannot be separated.

CHAPTER TEN

THE STRUCTURE
OF POLITICS

I

FOR THE SMALL and exclusive 'political nation' in eighteenth-century Ireland, politics were an affirmation of status. Thus political activity achieved a high rhetorical importance. By the later eighteenth century this had fused with the anti-English language of 'patriotism', and the anti-government ethos of opposition from the 1750s, to produce developments that were later interpreted as nascent nationalism. Before examining the appearance of politics, however, it is worth recalling the structure that lay beneath them.

Though ostensibly replicating the English system, the Irish parliament was manipulated far more directly by the executive; and the circumscribed political position of the Ascendancy gentry who sat at College Green ensured that they invariably gave in. But some accommodation had to be made. The Irish government, against which political activity was defined, possessed restricted powers and operated a small civil establishment. Yet it had to manage a lively parliamentary political culture, aided from Queen Anne's reign by the co-operation of local Irish politicians. These extracted a certain say in policy-making, and a more decisive share of patronage, in return for ensuring the passage of essential government business through the Irish House of Commons. Such 'friends' of the administration were known as 'undertakers': a phrase used from the 1740s, but a system whose essential characteristics could be observed long before then.

Thus expressed, the Irish system appears closely to reflect the Namier version of contemporary English politics; certainly, after the brief 'rage of party' under Anne, political groupings reflected an Irish version of 'court and country' or 'outs' versus 'ins', and the reasons why men went into parliament represented a world of visceral interests rather than ideological principles. But Irish conditions led to important local adaptations. Suspicion of the executive often provided a ready-made 'cause' for opposition in the Dublin parliament, where the idea of a continual opposition to the King's government was considered much less constitutionally questionable than in contemporary England, since the Irish Viceroy, though representing the Crown, was essentially a party nominee. Another important Irish variation arose from the fact that the Irish political culture was one where state interference, in the economy and elsewhere, was common practice: grants, tariffs, bounties and centralization were accepted along with the cultivated individualism of the eighteenth-century ethos. Government had, in this sense, a higher profile than across the Irish Sea. Institutions like the Dublin 'House of Industry', set up to cope with the poor, were by the end of the century administered as government departments rather than by rate-aided corporations; and the creation of an embryonic constabulary in disturbed counties during 1786–7, though it could be seen by contemporary opinion as a style of government 'suitable to the meridian of Turkey', went ahead none the less. If the resources of Irish government were limited, its powers, and its precedents, stretched surprisingly far.

This was the kind of paradox that new governors had to confront. The Viceroy found himself in an odd position: possessing many Crown powers but occupying a highly political appointment, and subject to being overridden by a British Prime Minister or Home Secretary. For instance, he was theoretically in charge of Irish defence, but in practice he came up against an Irish Commander-in-Chief. Early in the century the appointment was seen as a banishment; later it still carried the aura of a consolation prize. But it rapidly became a preserve of heavyweight grandee politicians, often holding a seat in Cabinet. This is one of the contrasts that makes analogies with the American colonies every bit as misleading as they are enlightening. Though the salary seemed generous, occupants had to be rich: by 1782 they were earning £20,000 a year but still failing to break even. Those who tried to entertain economically had their reputations mercilessly destroyed by Dublin 'wits'. This development reflected the fact that Viceroys came to spend far more time in Ireland than had been the case when they frequently handed over to Deputy Lords Justices and turned up only for rare parliamentary sessions. The viceregal establishment required a steward, a comptroller, a chamberlain, aides-de-camp and all the trimmings of a little court: it was a curious mixture of grandeur and gimcrack, arousing much ridicule throughout the institution's lifetime. It remained the centre of the 'fashionable' world, a function reflected in the extremely grand staterooms of Dublin Castle. From 1782 there was a far more satisfactory residence in Phoenix Park as well.

An effective Viceroy provided the semblance of a figurehead but an inept one rapidly demonstrated that the post required real qualities. 'I must confess,' wrote Lord Northington sadly to Charles James Fox,

> that it is a very wrong Measure of English Government to make this country the first step in Politics, as it usually has been; as I am sure Men of Abilities, Knowledge of Business, and Experience ought to be employed here, both in the Capacity of Lord Lieutenant and Secretary; and not gentlemen taken *wild* from *Brookes* [Club] to make their Denonuement [*sic*] in public life. I feel very forcibly the Truth of this Observation in my own instance, and wish heartily it was better supplied.[1]

But the ironic and highly talented Lord Chesterfield felt that there was much that could be done with the office, apart from the trivial preoccupations that it enforced.

> I am sensitive I shall be reckoned a very shallow Politican from my attention to such trifling objects, as the improvement of your lands, the extension of your Manufactures, and the Increase of your Trade . . . whereas an able Lord-Lieutenant ought to employ his thoughts in greater matters. We should think of jobs for favourites, sops for enemies, managing Parties, and engaging Parliament to vote away their own and their fellow subjects' Liberties and Properties.[2]

The Townshend viceroyalty[i] is usually taken as the traditional point when Irish politics received a sharp jerk from the administration's reins: a resident Viceroy faced up to the over-mighty undertakers and resumed political control for the government. But it is questionable whether any Viceroy could exert such pressure, at least on a lasting basis; and undertaker power should be seen as a sign of the strength of the local politicians, rather than of the 'shackled and spiritless' position attributed to them by traditional historians.

The whole question of Irish government and politics demonstrates the centrality of Ireland to British government deliberations – again, 'colonial' parallels notwithstanding. (At the Cabinet meeting in February 1765 that decided upon the necessity of a resident Viceroy, four out of the nine men present had themselves served in the Irish government.) The Irish political crises of the 1760s reflect the dislocations of metropolitan politics in the early years of George III's

---

[i] George Townshend (1724–1807): succeeded as fourth Viscount Townshend, 1764; Lord Lieutenant of Ireland, 1767; commissioned to counter the power of the undertakers and establish a ruling party dependent upon the Crown; found this could be achieved only by recourse to the patronage system he had been sent to stem; took to drink; recalled, 1772; created Marquess, 1786.

reign; they also indicate the kind of government thinking that was attempting to cope with administrative and legislative problems in Massachusetts, Virginia and Jamaica. But Irish proximity, Irish political culture and most of all Irish history exerted a different kind of pressure.[3]

The official who had most to do with Irish politics was the Chief Secretary – a post created in vital apposition to the Viceroy, to whom he was almost a junior partner. Besides being effective departmental head of the Castle administration, he sat in the House of Commons to present and defend government policy; like the Viceroy, he resided regularly in Ireland from the 1760s. The job was famous for exerting an almost unbearable degree of pressure: from Castlereagh[ii] to Balfour, it would be a proving-ground of reputations. Below the Chief Secretary were various government departments on a miniature scale, dealing with questions like finance, the army, the militia and barracks. The Wide Streets Commission and the Linen Board, already encountered, were also technically branches of the Irish government. The whole corpus was generally referred to as 'The Castle'. As an accumulation of offices and administrative mechanisms that had piled up since medieval times, the structure included many anomalies and sinecures. It provided a favourite target for Radical sniping in England as well as Ireland, and was increasingly called to account to Commissions of Inquiry, but it had developed its own peculiar identity and sustained an oddly resilient life. And the pinchbeck court, the questions of precedent, the ancient computations of fees and remuneration, the patronage, the Byzantine intricacies of jobbery – all these would endure, more or less, until 1922.

It also provided Dublin opinion with a continuous spectacle and a fund of stories.

Lord Townshend, seeing [Hely-Hutchinson, Provost of Trinity College] one day toddling up the drawing-room of the Castle in some apparent impatience, exclaimed to Sir John Blaquiere[iii] 'See, see, here comes the Prime Serjeant: is there

---

[ii] Robert Stewart (1769–1822): born in County Down; entered the Irish parliament, 1790; became Viscount Castlereagh, 1796; as acting Chief Secretary of Ireland, 1797–8, forestalled rebellion by arresting leading United Irishmen and procuring English troops to replace the Irish militia; as official Chief Secretary, 1799–1801, secured the Union; pressed for the introduction of a Catholic relief bill; resigned on the King's refusal to grant one; took charge of Irish affairs in Addington's 1801 ministry; prepared plans for Irish tithe commutation and for the state payment of Catholic priests; Secretary for War and the Colonies, 1805; Foreign Secretary, 1812–22; became Marquess of Londonderry, 1821; committed suicide.

[iii] John Blaquiere (1732–1812): born in London of Huguenot descent; went to

anything vacant?' 'Nothing that I know of,' replied Sir John, 'but a majority in a cavalry regiment.' 'Oh well, give it to him – give it to him at once, to stop his mouth.' The Provost actually departed a major of dragoons, and sold out next morning!⁴

True or not, such stories indicate the intimacy, accountability and interdependence that characterized the world of Ascendancy politics.

This is also demonstrated by the position of the 'undertakers': – the great aristocratic power-brokers whose 'interests' managed borough politics up to the 1760s in an uneasy arrangement with the government. In England they could be seen as an 'aristocratical', reactionary and potentially unconstitutional 'opposition' to the King. They were certainly 'powerful, independent men whose expectations and desires a Viceroy slighted at his peril'.⁵ But within the trammelled Irish system, their powers were necessarily limited, and their relationship with government symbiotic (an 'undertaking' implies a contract binding on *both* sides). To take Townshend's *démarche* of 1767 as marking the end of a system is too cut and dried. For one thing, the position of the great borough-mongers had been much circumscribed since the political crises of the 1750s, which had identified them so closely with the Castle that they could no longer carry many independent members and 'patriots'; for another, their collusive relationship with the administration lasted on. Even after 1767 the undertakers retained powers of patronage outside the ambit of the Viceroy's influence; if he could appoint to the Revenue Board, they could still control the structures of local politics. Ten years after the magic date of 1767, one undertaker alone, Lord Shannon, still had a solid following of at least seventeen in the Irish House of Commons.

Thus Viceroys like Townshend by no means exerted unquestioned control: his anxiety to make full use of the powers of patronage comes as no surprise, though the government in England remained cautious. The wheels still had to be greased. Linking structures between the government and parliament remained of great importance: groups like the 'friends' of the administration led by John Beresford in the 1770s, who corresponded closely with English politicians as well as with the Castle. A necessary continuity was preserved by contacts with the

Ireland as Chief Secretary, 1772; entered the Irish parliament, 1773; advocated a tax on absentees; Irish Privy Councillor, 1774; as Commissioner of the Paving Board, supervised great improvements in Dublin in the late eighteenth century; Baronet, 1784; raised to the Irish peerage as Baron De Blaquiere, 1800. Probably the only Chief Secretary to reside in Ireland beyond the term of his office.

lesser Castle officials, like the Under-Secretaries, who stayed longer, and often knew more, than their more visible chiefs (there were only three of these throughout the period from 1747 to 1761). The Irish system of government had to manage the Irish parliament, and this required intuition, manipulativeness, control of patronage and knowledge of the local terrain, which could not be provided by the Castle alone.

II

Since the management of parliament was a large part of government's *raison d'être*, the nature of that parliament requires definition. From the 1720s the Irish House of Commons was a Namierite paradise: factions, families, interests, connections, 'friends of government' (inconstant) and independent 'patriots' (not always consistent). The political ethos at College Green was so tightly constrained by 1688 principles that little room was left for ideological distinctions. Whereas in England the revolution meant the victory of Parliament, in Ireland it represented the final guarantee of colonial ascendancy. Under William and Anne, 'Whig' and 'Tory' traditions had persisted, but the reality rapidly became that of court interest versus country (or 'patriot') opposition. After the brief 'rage of party' dissipated from 1715, anyone called 'Tory' lost all political credibility; and the factional nature of Irish parliamentary politics simplified the government's task of parliamentary control.

The government had to get its business through parliament; and, given the nature of eighteenth-century government in Ireland, many important areas of public policy came under parliamentary scrutiny. The impressive Public Accounts Committee system at College Green has been used by historians to reconstruct the complex financial administration of the age. The government played on the deferential and traditional relationship of MPs to the Castle, but it also wielded patronage through the civil service, legal posts, pensions, and (more subtly) the Church and the army. A new Lord Lieutenant was rudely introduced to this system by an overwhelming avalanche of demands, often couched in aggressively importunate terms. And with the establishment of factional politics came the age of the great individual who could monopolize 'undertaking' a successful parliamentary passage for government business, in return.

In Irish politics, Lord Charlemont[iv] remarked, 'personal friendships are as strong and binding as public principle is weak'. Family relationships were vital, as is demonstrated by the use to which a successful public man like 'Speaker' Foster put his own patronage in bureaucracy and politics. Family alliances from the early eighteenth century often provide the subtext to political associations in later generations – as is the case with the Ponsonby family's connections to Boyles in Ireland, and Burlingtons and Cavendishes in England. The great 'undertaker' of the 1720s was William Conolly,[v] who had been Speaker, a Lord Justice and First Commissioner of the Revenue, thus engrossing parliamentary weight, constitutional kudos and tremendous powers of patronage. His undertaker functions were inherited by Henry Boyle, first Earl of Shannon;[vi] but he left a family connection headed by Thomas Conolly,[vii] related by marriage to English Richmonds and Foxes as well as Irish Leinsters. Through such great families (as well as by means of political churchmen like Primate Stone[viii]) manipulation

[iv] James Caulfeild (1728–99): born in Dublin; succeeded as Viscount Charlemont, 1734; travelled in Europe, 1746–54; successfully employed as a mediator between Henry Boyle and Primate Stone in the mid-1750s; served gallantly against the French at Carrickfergus, 1760; created Earl of Charlemont, 1763; resided in London, frequenting the literary coteries, 1764–73; returned to Dublin, regarding Irish residence as the first patriotic duty; made Commander-in-Chief of the Volunteers, 1780; supported Grattan on the Regency question; founded the Whig Club, 1790; opposed Catholic emancipation and the Union.

[v] See above, p. 172.

[vi] Henry Boyle (1682–1764): born in County Cork; entered the Irish parliament, 1707; regarded as the leader of the Whigs in Ireland, 1729; one of the greatest placemen of his age, he became Irish Commissioner of Revenue, Privy Councillor, Chancellor of the Exchequer and Speaker by 1733; acquired national popularity, 1753, for opposing the government's attempt to appropriate a surplus in the Irish Exchequer; created Earl of Shannon, 1756; frequently a Lord Justice.

[vii] Thomas Conolly (1738–1803): entered the Irish parliament, 1760; Irish Lord of the Treasury, Commissioner of Trade and Privy Councillor by 1784; as the commoner with the 'largest connection' he was one of the ten 'chief persons' in Ireland with whom Cornwallis first broached the idea of the Union, 1798; supported the Union, under the influence of his kinsman Castlereagh, although the measure extinguished his political importance.

[viii] George Stone (c. 1708–64): born in London; educated at Westminster and Oxford; went to Ireland as chaplain to Dorset as Lord Lieutenant, 1730; became Dean of Ferns, 1733, and of Derry, 1734; Bishop of Ferns and Leighlin, 1740, of Kildare, 1743, and of Derry, 1745; Archbishop of Armagh, an Irish Privy Councillor and Lord Justice, 1747; the most determined opponent of the Irish interest, he engaged in a power struggle with Henry Boyle, which was only settled when they agreed to a power-sharing pact, 1758; a 'second Wolsey'.

was possible but necessarily dense and complicated. Through the 1750s family groupings like those centred on the Ponsonbys or the Kildares were matched and balanced against the great undertaker interests of Stone and Shannon; but a new generation begins to appear in politics from the 1760s, coinciding with the new dispensation of George III's reign. And this includes not only great political fixers in the old mould like John Hely-Hutchinson, but new voices of political opposition like Henry Flood.

In the same period, the rapid succession of Viceroys was ended by Townshend's residency, and his ensuing attack on 'faction', paralleling political catch-cries in Westminster. The Irish government's attempt to control parliament was also strengthened by a stable English government under Lord North from 1770. This is the background to the Irish government's attempts to plant out a 'Castle' group of politicians to maintain majorities at College Green, organized by the Chief Secretary. Inevitably this led to clashes with the traditional undertaker groupings, as well as with the nascent 'patriot' opposition. But, as before, the government still had to conciliate the great borough-owners for their support. And Townshend's original plan, to create a Castle interest out of men unconnected with the previous undertakers, was doomed from the start. By the late 1780s a group of Irish politicians known, confusingly, as 'the Irish Cabinet' had emerged: they advised the Irish government, helped them to confound the 'patriot' opposition and took the cream of the jobs. They included men like Foster, Fitzgibbon, Beresford, Parnell[ix] and Archbishop Agar[x]. Their function was similar to the old undertakers; in some ways they were just as recalcitrant; and the position of the Viceroy did not become noticeably easier.

The make-up of the House of Commons that they dominated reflected the history of Ascendancy. As profiled for the reign of George

---

[ix] John Parnell (1744–1801): entered the Irish parliament, 1776; became a Commissioner of the Irish Revenue, 1780; succeeded to his father's baronetcy, 1782; became Chancellor of the Irish Exchequer, 1785; a British Privy Councillor, 1786; a conservative who followed the government line in a liberal direction when it paid to do so; his opposition to the Union was on constitutional rather than patriotic grounds. Great-grandfather of Charles Stewart Parnell.

[x] Charles Agar (1736–1826): born in Dublin; educated at Westminster and Oxford; returned to Ireland as chaplain to Northumberland when Lord Lieutenant, 1763; became Dean of Kilmore, 1765; Bishop of Cloyne, 1768; Archbishop of Cashel, 1779; Archbishop of Dublin, 1801–9. He also amassed great wealth and temporal influence; an Irish Privy Councillor, 1779; created Baron Somerton, 1795; Viscount, 1800, and Earl of Normanton, 1806; having opposed the Union in 1799, he agreed to support it in return for a permanent seat in the House of Lords.

II, before the regular elections introduced by the 1768 Octennial Act, 50 per cent of the MPs were of Stuart or Cromwellian families and 75 per cent were of planter stock. Over 50 per cent were primarily landlords, reflected in the parliament's predisposition to identify Catholicism principally as a threat to property. This leaves a large segment of professionals – lawyers and army men were nearly as important as country gentry, though commercial and industrial interests were, for obvious reasons, underrepresented. Trinity College was a strong common factor, as well as being directly represented as a constituency. The Commons was vastly more important than the Irish House of Lords, which was thinly attended and largely ceremonial: the government lost its grip on the upper house only at moments of high political crisis, despite the presence there of energetic opposition grandees like Charlemont. Political vitality was restricted to the Commons. At the same time as Irishmen in London provided the contemporary stage with an injection of life, the House at College Green supplied political theatre for a Dublin audience.

This was not only a question of dramatic performances and the illusion of influence. The high Irish style of parliamentary rhetoric was celebrated: a language of baroque metaphor and personification, punctuated by brutal rejoinders. The most businesslike debates were far less well-attended than those which permitted lofty attitudinizing. But along with the high premium placed on entertainment value, it is necessary to remember something harder to recapture: the political morality of the age. The standards even of a great placeman like the second Earl of Shannon are clearly indicated by his correspondence: and, amid all the dealings and bargains, there is a preoccupation with what contemporaries saw as decency and consistency within the norms of 'gentlemanlike' behaviour. Latter-day denunciations of 'corruption' are not much help in understanding this.

This should be borne in mind when considering the ramshackle electoral system on which the Dublin parliament rested. One hundred and fifty constituencies each returned two members. Thirty-two of these were county constituencies, based on a forty-shilling freeholder franchise that could be very variably assessed: various attempts were made to regulate them exactly, to tie down registration procedure and to examine qualifications. In fact, few county elections were contested. Generally speaking, straightforward 'influence' politics ruled; but 'influence' itself was less straightforward than often assumed and operated within the norms of expected political behaviour. Moreover, even a local landlord or his nominee could be opposed by an 'independent' interest, often using the 'patriot' cry: in such cases, elaborate and expensive contests developed. Electoral contests could, moreover, be moderated by the arcane mechanisms of duelling. The whole process was subtler and more complicated than it appears: even when a Duke of Leinster or an Earl Fitzwilliam had the power to return both county members, he usually was careful to choose them from local families who would otherwise oppose him. Career politicians jealously guarded their independence. The power of a few individuals can be exaggerated: no one borough-owner actually returned more than nine members to the Irish parliament between 1777 and 1800.

There were 117 boroughs (plus Trinity College), and membership for these was less prestigious. As in contemporary England, a borough could be anything from a deserted field to a populous town; and freedom to vote could be claimed by birth, apprenticeship, marriage or a variety of esoteric qualifications. Also as in England, borough freeholders could be entitled to vote in counties. Boroughs were administered, rather erratically, by governing bodies. Some were more 'open' than others as regards representation; Dublin had a strong and liberal opposition press that weighed in against the interests of the Castle and the aldermen.

Open boroughs, being more desirable to sit for, produced ardent and expensive contests, with the usual difficulties regarding qualification and impersonation. (One Cork voter in 1783 was heard to complain 'I'm tired polling'.) They indicate a local political structure that was not as moribund as traditional accounts have it. The residual local institutions of vestries and borough corporations engaged in varying levels of activity: grand juries, nominated by sheriffs, not only conducted judicial assizes but also fixed the county rate and handled roads, bridges, gaols, courthouses and infirmaries. For all the importance of central government, local bodies retained wide powers of taxation and patronage: the inevitable concomitant was a lively political existence. And municipal power-structures created the terms of borough representation in parliamentary affairs. Those records that survived the destruction of the Public Record Office in 1922 show that violent conflicts occurred at local government elections in boroughs whose *parliamentary* profile remained placid and uncontested. The fighting had already taken place, and the terms of influence been decided.

In Irish representative politics at all levels, Protestantism and Ascendancy held the reins; the hereditary and exclusivist nature of the ruling class was much in evidence, though, for Anglicans, the avenues to self-advancement remained open. Politics at local levels show a strong sense of obligation on both sides, as between electors and patron; though the nature of eighteenth-century political morality is hard to recapture, there were standards that should not be breached. Members had to demonstrate a certain responsiveness to the electorate: at moments of high political interest like the passing of the Octennial Act, constituents issued instructions. The traditional picture of Irish voters who were very poor, and therefore dependent, may not be accurate. There was certainly a great prevalence of freehold tenures, which included leases for 'lives'. But the Protestant nature of the electorate, the fact that tenants downgraded their status for fear of rent rises (preferring to register as forty-shilling freeholders than ten-pound qualifiers), the breadth of definition that took in 'forty-shilling freeholders', the electorally invisible supplementary incomes provided by domestic linen industry – all this indicates a voting class more affluent, and therefore more independent, than the usual view. The enfranchisement of Catholics in 1793 changed this; and it should be noted that it was the class complexion of the new electorate, rather than its religious affiliation, that preoccupied many contemporaries above all.

The other characteristic traditionally attributed to the eighteenth-century political system in Ireland is the prevalence of 'political agronomy': the letting of land in quantities, and on terms, dictated by conferring franchise rights rather than achieving economic efficiency. This, however, was not as widespread as once thought; and local studies of areas as politically different as Louth and Down show that deference was as influential as dependence. 'Geography, tradition, kinship, gratitude, self-interest of various kinds – all contributed to an interest such as Lord Shannon's in County Cork.'[6] And the personal fiefs built up by men like John Foster in Louth depended on personal popularity as much as economic power.

III
===

When all is said and done, however, the varied, colourful and highly personalized world of Irish politics sustained a superstructure that was essentially limited and dependent. For the actions of College Green were restricted by the fact that, under the 1720 Declaratory Act ('the sixth of George I'), the Westminster Parliament could legislate for Ireland, and under Poynings' Law they had to transmit heads of bills for approbation in England. Moreover, imperial and foreign concerns were kept at Westminster. And it was imperial and foreign concerns that raised the pressure of politics from mid-century: a development that was capitalized upon by 'popular' political opposition and open division between ruling groups within Parliament. This was as true for Ireland as for Great Britain. The parallel that may come most readily to mind is with America: by the end of the Seven Years War, Ireland was causing more trouble than the thirteen colonies. The desire for budgetary control and frequent parliaments, and the difficulties of patronage, underlay much political demonstration, and set up a current running towards confrontation. Besides constituting part of the metropolitan polity, affected by dislocations in government and politics that were in themselves responses to the imperial crisis, Ireland presented its own colonial aspect.

From mid-century the Irish parliament reflected an increasing and acrimonious debate about issues like pensions, army finance, the duration of parliaments and taxation of absentee landowners – all of which were guaranteed to bring into focus the relationship of Irish affairs to English authority. Finance bills provided a special area of dissension, exacerbating local sensitivities about Ireland's 'distinct and separate executive'. Increasing scrutiny of expenditure and reference to committees climaxed in the celebrated dispute over the 1753 Money Bill. In fact, this was a Supply Bill granting additional duties to make up the revenue, which in that year went into a surplus; the Irish Commons delayed their right to a say in its disposal. Remarkably, this crisis placed the Speaker, Henry Boyle, alongside the 'patriot' opposition and much out-of-doors opinion and against the Castle administration; this alliance, armed with a combination of weapons described by Horace Walpole as 'satires and claret', created considerable embarrassment. In 1753–4, as so often, political instability coincided with a credit and banking crisis; this set off rumbles about English discrimination against Irish trade, and English exploitation of the Irish establishment (in terms of jobs and sinecures); threats of non-importation boycotts followed. The question of revenue surpluses was an extremely delicate one from this time on; the Irish House of Commons ostentatiously voted to use them to reflate the domestic economy and fund public works. More importantly, the question of colonial dependency, and the reaction to it, had been raised; and with Boyle's defection the system operating had been demonstrably incapable of handling such a crisis. Neither the Speaker nor the 'patriots' had intended a rebellion: rather, a show of strength and a statement of principle. But it alarmed the government no less for that.

A resident Viceroy was seen as one answer; subsequent Cabinet discussions revolved round the avoidance of 'drawing in question the nature of the connection between Great Britain and Ireland'. Whether or not Townshend personally expected to have to reside in Ireland is debatable, but the idea was in the air by the early 1760s and his position enforced it. Crises continued; the Commons actually rejected a Money Bill in 1769, leading to prorogation of parliament by Townshend and an implicitly constitutional confrontation with the undertakers. Further dislocation followed. By 1774 an absentee tax had been defeated, after much behind-the-scenes lobbying; and Townshend had rearranged his support-system by such strategic blows as establishing control over the Irish Revenue Board. But he carried out his policy with far less recourse to blatant jobbery than has traditionally been claimed: a deliberate and successful manipulation of 'opinion' seems equally important, which in itself tells us something about the nature of contemporary politics.

Townshend's successor, Harcourt,[xi] compounded his success; but when the government had to organize an appropriate parliamentary response to the American crisis in 1776, it still cost them twenty-two Irish peerages and £11,000 a year in pensions. In many ways, even Townshend's success showed up the rickety structure beneath the system. If the government was controlling the legislature more directly, those questions of constitutional dependence that were traditionally avoided were necessarily thrown into sharper relief: the relationship was no longer obscured by the undertakers, and in essence it remained a visible problem until removed by the radical surgery of the Union in 1800.

These questions of constitutional dependence also served to bring into public focus a sort of local Irish radicalism, evident from mid-century. In many cases this shades into 'patriotism', which will be considered elsewhere; but the figure of Dr Charles Lucas,[xii] a Whiggish apothecary prominent from the 1740s, is more easily seen as a native

---

[xi] Simon Harcourt (1714–77): succeeded as Viscount Harcourt, 1727; created Earl, 1749; Privy Councillor, 1751; Lord Lieutenant of Ireland, 1772–7.

[xii] Charles Lucas (1713–71): born in County Clare; elected to the Common Council of the City of Dublin, 1741; published numerous tracts advocating municipal reform; riotous behaviour during his candidature for the parliamentary representation of Dublin, 1748, led to his imprisonment; escaped to London; studied medicine at Paris, Rheims and Leyden; MD, 1752; MP for Dublin, 1761–71.

Wilkes. Lucas attacked oligarchy in local politics, and constitutional dependence on England in the national sphere; by 1749 he had been declared a public enemy and forced into exile, but he returned to parliament in 1760, and was voted a salary by the Commons of Dublin in 1766 (vetoed by the outraged aldermen). Lucas reminds us that there was a Dublin 'mob' that could actually storm parliament in 1759, inflamed by rumours of a union: this was politicization at a fairly basic level. But independent opposition tended to be gentlemanly, 'patriotic' and ambiguous, the great example being Flood, who violently opposed Townshend and then took office as Vice-Treasurer for Ireland under Harcourt. This miscalculation left the field of 'patriotic' opposition to the unparalleled Henry Grattan, barrister, polemicist, failed poet and opera fanatic, who produced the ultimate in florid rhetoric and cleverly never undertook any duties more pragmatic than oratory.

Politics outside parliament will be treated in a later chapter; but when considering the world that surrounded College Green, prominent local radicals like the egregious Napper Tandy[xiii] should not be forgotten. Nor should the world of journalism. Up to 1784 there was little effort to trammel the freedom of the press; Pue's and Faulkner's Dublin Journal were succeeded by more recognizably modern journals, and newspapers became increasingly political. Lucas's early career and his struggles with the Aldermen of Dublin had in essence been made by the press; he founded the Freeman's Journal with Henry Brooke in 1763, though it was bought by the administration for a secret service pension of fifty pounds in 1786. The Castle had itself backed papers against Lucas in the 1740s; the increasingly popular complexion of the Irish press is demonstrated by reports of parliamentary debates (Westminster as well as College Green), character assassinations and much playing to the gallery.

From mid-century, observers noted the increasing responsiveness of parliament to public opinion and the growing influence of the press.

[xiii] James Napper Tandy (1740–1803): born in Dublin; son of a small tradesman; earned immense popularity for his attacks on municipal corruption; an enthusiastic Volunteer; helped Tone and Russell found the United Irish Society; became Secretary of the Dublin branch; raised a 'national guard', 1792, on the rejection of the Catholic petition; forced to flee to America; went to Paris, 1798; given command of a body of soldiers who landed at Donegal; issued a proclamation and became insensibly drunk; carried back to his ship; captured in Hamburg; avoided the death penalty because the manner of his arrest was thought to have contravened international law; liberated through the representations of Napoleon at Amiens, 1802; eulogized in nationalist folklore.

The *Freeman* took up both America and Wilkes, and reprinted Thomas Paine's *Common Sense*; John Magee's *Dublin Evening Post*, founded in 1778, was ready to suggest attractive improbabilities like the illegitimate relationship of Lord North to George III. The *Post* claimed a circulation of 3,000 in 1781, and was a vital conduit for the Dungannon resolutions in 1782, though it was also capable of refreshing sarcasm about Grattan. The *Volunteer Journal* (1782) was influential and radical enough for the government to back the *Volunteer Evening Post* against it: 'the press is the principal operative power in the government of this kingdom', remarked a Chief Secretary. Eventually, by calling for complete severance from England, the *Volunteer Journal* provoked the government into legislation against it in 1784. Up to this, a wide interpretation of the libel laws had been the preferred method of press censorship, giving the Dublin radicals a ready-made cry of 'the freedom of the press'.

By 1779 Buckinghamshire[xiv] found the Irish press more terrifying than 10,000 soldiers. Dublin newspapers were circulated through the country; 'a labouring man now hardly goes to work until he has read the news'.[7] The publicity given to Volunteer conventions and manifestos had a potent publicizing effect, naming participants and creating reputations. But this took place against the radicalization of Irish political life, which must be considered as part of one great theme from the 1770s: the impact of America.

[xiv] John Hobart (1723–93): succeeded as second Earl of Buckinghamshire, 1756; as Irish Viceroy, 1777–80, he was forced to concede free trade and the first measures of relief for Catholics and Dissenters; viewed the rise of the Volunteers with 'impotent dismay'; described himself in 1780 as 'a man whose mind has been ulcerated with a variety of embarrassments for 30 weary months'. (Not to be confused with George Nugent-Temple-Grenville, the first Marquess of Buckingham, who was Irish Viceroy twice in the 1780s.)

CHAPTER ELEVEN

===

AMERICANS, VOLUNTEERS AND THE POLITICS OF 'PATRIOTISM'

I

===

REVERBERATIONS SET OFF by the American explosion of the 1770s dominated politics in Dublin as in London, but the effect was less straightforward than might be supposed. Irish political opinion identified with the American cause on more than one level. There were the strong connections established by emigration, mentioned already; there was also Irish resentment at the trade restrictions of the imperial system. This should not be seen as symptomatic of a desire for 'independence': it represents rather the wish to engage more profitably in imperial trade. Certainly, the ideology of 'independence' in America owed much to 'Scotch–Irish' (in other words, Presbyterian) political tenets; but this is not the place to analyse the complex Irish dimension within revolutionary America.[1] On the Irish front, it might seem obvious that parallels with the constitutional position of the American colonies highlighted constrictions imposed on the Irish parliament: and this was an argument pressed hard in public. 'We are in water-colour what they are in fresco,' declared one Irish MP.

But the Irish campaign for parliamentary 'independence' was in essence a call for the restoration of lost rights, not the granting of new ones. They saw themselves as fellow-sufferers at the hands of English policy. It was the 'unconstitutional proceedings against America' that most galvanized Irish opinion, as much as any specific sense that the American and Irish causes were the same. When Charlemont and Leinster led a 'patriot' group in the Irish House of Lords who claimed that the pretensions of the British Parliament had raised an unjust war, they were preoccupied just as much by financial questions – as well as the desire to seize an issue that provided instant 'radical' credibility.

Early 'Americanism' in Ireland often defined itself by negatives. It reflected a robust anti-Englishness; and it was linked with anti-Catholic declarations, especially after the Quebec Act.[i] Irish Catholics, therefore, tended at first to stress their loyalty. But American issues were not irrelevant to them; even the assimilationist, cautious, middle-class Catholics within the system could eventually adopt their cause. More predictably, a strong pro-American lobby developed in Belfast, balancing the Americanism that Benjamin Franklin found pronounced among Dublin 'patriots' as early as 1771.

For their part, the Americans used an ideological frame of reference that apparently shared much with the 'colonial nationalism' of late seventeenth-century and early eighteenth-century Ireland; Swift's arguments could be deployed for American purposes, while Lucas and Flood were rhetorically hailed as brothers-in-arms. But in Ireland, matters proceeded more cautiously. Initial reactions to colonial extremism tended to be muted: there was a fear of disrupting the imperial system wholesale. What really precipitated matters was not any blinding recognition of a common cause: it was the fact that the Whigs at Westminster used the American crisis to link with the 'patriot' opposition in Dublin in a campaign to embarrass the government.

This alliance utilized immediate issues, like the removal of troops from Ireland to fight in America, and the embargo on the export of foodstuffs declared in February 1776. In fact, commercial resentment at these measures, which were taken to enable the government to victual the fleet, and at the suspension of vital trades like linen and timber, accomplished more than any lofty feelings of brotherhood could have done: and it was commercial resentment that North's government listened to.

By early 1778 government plans were moving to an adaptation of the entire imperial economic system, giving Ireland access to direct import and export trade with the colonies. Any dramatic rearrangements were short-circuited by protectionist petitions from industrial pressure-groups in England; the eventual concessions were so hedged as to be deeply disappointing. The right to import direct from the colonies was withdrawn, and though export rights remained, woollens and glass stayed on the prohibited index.

The backlash in Ireland eventually produced the non-importation

[i] The Quebec Act, passed on 22 June 1774, established a permanent government for Canada, extended Quebec's territory south to the Ohio River, and provided for religious tolerance for Catholics.

agreements, the boycotts of English goods and the 'Buy Irish' campaigns that mobilized anti-government opinion. Though the tradition of Swift was invoked, the 'nationalist' content of such activity needs careful definition: it represented not only radicals like Napper Tandy and opposition politicians like Ponsonby, but also the impeccably establishment opinion of grand juries throughout the country at large. The line taken was not separatism but, once again, imperial reorganization in Irish interests; it took bank failures, deficits in government revenues and a threatened crisis over defence requirements to bring the campaign within striking-point. And external pressures created the conditions in which so-called 'free trade' was granted in 1779: war with France, the formation of Volunteer corps and the escalation of publicly expressed discontent.

The dilatory style of North's government meant that commercial restrictions were not lifted until military demonstrations by armed Volunteers in College Green implied a resort to unconstitutional action, and a 'patriot' ramp within the House threatened to withhold assent to finance bills until 'free trade' was granted. But the government had been taking soundings from politicians since the early summer, and the idea had been in the air for a year before that. In the Irish context, the 'free trade' thus achieved meant 'equality in trading rights' not *laisser-faire* economics: full access to colonial commerce and a repeal of restrictions on glass and wool. The economic importance of this is disputed; what was undeniable was the apparent victory of out-of-doors pressure. At the high point of crisis in 1779–80 (a British crisis, not just an Irish one), the whole system of government was inevitably called into question; Buckinghamshire's position was made nearly impossible. Administration quidnuncs saw him as reaping the results of trying to govern on the cheap; opposition rhetoric presented a picture of tyranny finally confounded. Significantly, support for the Americans slackened after Irish 'colonial nationalism' won this famous victory: it had, in a sense, served its purpose.

But the American crisis and the loss of the transatlantic colonies precipitated the kind of reconsideration on both sides of the Irish Sea that inevitably led to further confrontations. Issues of economic policy, commerce, imperialism, led to queries about the basis of representation: the next great issue in Irish politics would be political and constitutional reform. And in the Irish context, reform meant facing the question of Catholics – always the limiting factor on any constitutional speculations.

Catholic opinion by now had its own organization, in the Catholic

Committee founded by Curry,[ii] O'Conor and Wyse[iii] by 1760. Though generally identified with emollient Catholic peers like Lords Kenmare, Trimleston, Fingall and Gormanston, it had access to sympathetic political figures like Anthony Malone.[iv] While the initial Catholic line on America was ostentatiously to emphasize their own loyalty, the imperial crisis raised a vital question: were Irish Catholics reliable enough for the defence of the country not to be at risk?

The Irish military establishment was made up of regiments and battalions stationed in the country for short rotas. Up to 1770 they numbered 12,000; they had expanded to 60,000 by 1800. In time of peace the army carried out policing and even some bureaucratic functions: they were a constant presence in local Irish life. Recruitment, however, was always restricted; the atavistic fear of arming Catholics remained, and the ideal, if not the invariable practice, was for non-Irishmen to serve in Ireland. This, too, moderated from 1770; by 1775 recruitment was practised at large throughout the country. The position of Catholics was left formally uncertain; but they were increasingly taken into the troops. By the Napoleonic era, besides the celebrated Anglo-Irish influence in British officer corps, Catholic Irishmen would form a very large proportion, possibly a third, of the regular army's rank and file.

This development was associated with the British government's increasingly relaxed attitude towards Catholics in general. The 1774

[ii] John Curry (d. 1780): born in Dublin; educated at Paris and Rheims; returned to Dublin and rose to eminence as a physician; a founder of the Catholic Committee, 1756; published *Observations on the Popery Laws*, with Charles O'Conor, 1771, and *Historical and Critical Review of the Civil Wars in Ireland*, 1775, which sought to counter the Protestant account of the massacres of 1641.

[iii] Thomas Wyse (*fl. c.* 1700–1770): of the Manor of St John, County Waterford; his descendant and namesake, Sir Thomas Wyse, suggested in his history of the Catholic Association that while O'Conor and Curry looked to the aristocracy and clergy for support for the first Catholic Committee, it was his ancestor who attempted to embrace the people in the movement, and who conceived the idea of a Catholic representative body, which was the precursor of the 'Catholic parliaments' of O'Connell's day.

[iv] Anthony Malone (1700–1776): born in Dublin; educated at Oxford; called to the Irish Bar, 1726; entered the Irish parliament, 1727; became Prime Serjeant, 1740; Irish Chancellor of the Exchequer, 1757; dismissed from office, 1761, for maintaining the rights of the Irish parliament; soon recalled; sympathized with the Whiteboys of Munster, whom he tried in 1762; ascribed their outrages to local grievance rather than national or international conspiracy; a liberal-minded 'patriot', but perhaps a timid one, for whom the lure of office was often too great; praised by Grattan for his oratory and intellect.

Act allowing Irish Catholics to take an Oath of Allegiance should be seen in the same context as the Quebec Act of the same year. In 1777–8 Whig pressures within the Parliament at Westminster worked towards further concessions; it was intervention from Britain, after the entry into war with France, which brought about the Catholic Relief Act of 1778. This cautiously removed restrictions on Catholics' holding land: but its first draft had been far more sweeping, removing all disabilities except parliamentary representation and the holding of Crown office. The limited nature of the eventual legislation is one indication that it did not originate in any generous impulse of the Ascendancy; further evidence is to be found in the parliamentary debates. Grattan affected to believe the government was trying to create a Catholic interest against the Protestants of Ireland; he wanted to keep the enforced 'gavelling' of Catholic estates and reserve freeholds for Protestants. By the time broader freedoms for Catholic property-holders were laid down in Gardiner's bill of 1782,[v] Grattan had become a Catholic champion: but by then, he had political reasons for aligning himself against the redoubtably anti-Catholic 'patriot' Flood.

This had come about as a result of the other great response to the imperial crisis of 1778–9, which focused on the vital questions of defence and the Catholics: the Volunteering movement. Irish defences were notoriously open (a celebrated French expedition under Thurot had actually captured Carrickfergus in 1760); there were strong arguments after 1778 for reviving a militia to strengthen the depleted Irish army. In 1779, the government was receiving intelligence reports of large-scale French invasion plans directed at Cork and Galway, which would supposedly galvanize local discontents into a national resistance. But, in the usual fashion of North's government, a procrastinated decision was pre-empted: this time by the gentry's initiative of raising local Volunteer corps. This had already been done to combat rural disturbances in the early 1770s; from early 1778, starting in Ulster, the movement spread. Its loyalist complexion was stressed, and militia discipline ostentatiously adopted. Rural Volunteer corps were organized by local landowners or co-operative associations of gentry; in the towns they were raised by occupational corps like lawyers or, by 1781, hairdressers. Given contemporary legislation, it had to be a formally Protestant movement, but from early on Catholics were admitted to Volunteer ranks in several places including Kerry, Cork and, less

[v] Rights regarding education, marriage and property were liberalized for Catholics, but they were still forbidden, for obvious reasons, to buy land in parliamentary boroughs.

predictably, Armagh. The numbers enrolled are hard to specify, since the evidence is restricted to subjective claims and newspaper reports, but by 1780 they probably numbered between 30,000 and 40,000. The government had no choice but to co-opt them into defence plans, and even provide them with artillery.

What did the Volunteers represent? If the initiative came from the gentry, in many corps the membership went down to tradesmen and artisans. They shared expenses, much of which went on elaborate uniforms and the banners that a century later still adorned the halls of country houses, including that of the gentleman 'patriot', Charles Stewart Parnell. They would probably not have been a very effective military force, but they provided competent policing functions. Their joint manoeuvres and, most of all, their reviews were occasions of great local importance. Principally, Volunteering was a great psychological affirmation: of citizenship, of 'patriotism', of exclusive identity. A corps took on the political complexion of the local grandee: Lord Shannon's Cork Volunteers were called 'The True Blue Legion'. And in terms of county organization, they rapidly represented an important political dimension, analogous to Wyvill's contemporary movement in Great Britain.

This point was rapidly seized by opposition politicians: Hussey Burgh's[vi] famous metaphor represented the government sowing serpent's teeth that sprang up as armed men. The Volunteers were very far from radicalism: they showed great alacrity in breaking up demonstrations by journeymen claiming the right to form combinations. But they were anti-government, and ready to refer to the necessity of preserving the Constitution of 1688 against 'evil counsellors'. As already seen, they took a forward part in demonstrations in favour of 'free trade'; subsequently, orchestrated by opposition politicians like Grattan, Yelverton[vii] and Burgh, they mounted a campaign to repeal Poynings' Law and the 1720 Declaratory Act. After this had been

[vi] William Hussey [Burgh] (1742–83): called to the Irish Bar, 1769; entered the Irish parliament, 1769; became Prime Serjeant, 1777; advocated free trade for Ireland, and its attainment owed as much to his efforts as to Grattan's; Chief Baron of the Irish Exchequer, 1782; long remembered for his political and legal oratory.

[vii] Barry Yelverton (1736–1805): born in County Cork of poor parents; educated at Trinity College, Dublin, as a sizar; his early career was as a teacher; called to the Irish Bar, 1764; King's Counsel, 1772; entered the Irish parliament, 1774; became a Volunteer, 1780; very influential in pressing the constitutional legislation of 1782; Attorney-General, 1782; Chief Baron of the Irish Exchequer, 1783; raised to the Irish peerage as Baron Avonmore, 1795; created an Irish Viscount and a Baron of the UK, 1800, for his support of the Union.

achieved in 1782, some Volunteer conventions moved on to the language of political reform and accountability to constituents; but by then the movement was splitting fast. Its political influence was inseparable from the crisis conditions of 1779–82.

Volunteer resolutions of 1779–80 tended to adopt high-flown constitutional declarations of 'independence', reflecting the language of their leaders in parliament. But this in itself was a limited development; the 'patriots' in parliament were meeting reverses in 1781, and the great Volunteer convention of Dungannon in 1782, which adopted resolutions calling for the repeal of constitutionally limiting legislation, can be seen as a risky bid for out-of-doors support. It is significant how quickly some grandee leaders of Volunteer corps, like the Duke of Leinster, began to break with their more radical elements; this has been interpreted as an implicit conflict between the interests of borough-owning aristocrats and middle-class agitators after 1782. But such fissures are exaggerated; the Volunteers cannot be analysed in such reductionist terms. They represented the values of 'patriotism', finding an out-of-doors voice. And 'patriotism' has to be understood in terms of contemporary Irish politics.

II

What was 'patriotism'? A political journal called the *Patriot* had existed in the 1750s, and outlined many nascent 'patriot' attitudes. Much of the old 'country' identification in politics is there; but it became a political ethos that would also mobilize middle-class and Presbyterian support if the occasion demanded. The rights of Irish Protestants provided one catch-cry; under the leadership of Charlemont and Flood in the 1760s, so did constitutional 'redress'. Legislative independence became part of the package; by 1779 one 'patriot' was calling for 'the right of personal freedom, or of regulating our own motions without any foreign control, so long as they do not infringe upon the rights of others'.[2] But a figure like John Foster, who shared none of these attitudes, was a 'patriot' in the economic sense: Foster's Corn Law, instituting export subsidies when prices were low and prohibiting export when prices were high, was a classic 'patriot' measure. Men like Foster could be called 'ministerial patriots'; but more archetypical 'patriots' like Burgh and Yelverton were orators rather than men of business (Yelverton became Attorney-General but gave it up as soon as possible). Flood, of course, had compromised himself by becoming Vice-Treasurer; other 'patriots' were careful to avoid the same mistake.

'Patriotism' was never 'popular'; Yelverton and other 'patriots' took a conspicuously pro-landlord and anti-people line on issues like the Tenantry Bill in 1780. 'Patriotism' might loosely be called 'gentry nationalism': it also had strong affinities with *colonial* nationalism. The word was used as early as 1721, by Philip Yorke.[viii] 'The subjects of Ireland were to be considered in two respects, as English and Irish ... the Irish were a conquered people and the English a colony transplanted hither, and are a colony subject to the law of the mother country'.[3] Half a century later, the Ascendancy did not see themselves as 'colonial' in a literal, American sense: they were Irishmen with English civil rights. Lucas said Ireland was 'a free and perfect state or common-wealth, annexed to the Crown of England but under a *separate and distinct* government, upon the like foundation, and after the same model, as that of England.' Most 'patriots' would have agreed; but their political psychology was colonial by heredity, in a distinctive and complex way.

They were able, in fact, to take a high line with England *because* they were exclusive in Ireland: had 'patriotism' represented the excluded three-quarters of the Irish nation, they could not have afforded to press so radically for constitutional 'liberty'. As it was, Poynings' Law and the Declaratory Act were identified as defining Ireland's shackles; Grattan and his supporters wanted the British Par-liament to make explicit their lack of legislative rights over Ireland. But the Crown connection was frequently extolled, and 'patriotism' in parliament betrayed a tendency to back off at key points. In 1780 Burgh introduced an *annual* Irish Mutiny Bill, intended to precipitate a basic constitutional confrontation; but when it was returned from England as a *permanent* measure, it was accepted in this form at College Green. The hyperbolic language of Grattan and the 'patriot' use of the press created high expectations among contemporaries, as well as encouraging wishful thinking among later nationalist historians. Thus Grattan in 1780:

Never was there a parliament in Ireland so possessed of the confidence of the people; you are the greatest political assembly now sitting in the world; you are

---

[viii] Philip Yorke (1690–1764): returned to Westminster, 1719; his first recorded speech on the supremacy of the Westminster to the Irish parliament established his reputation as a constitutionalist, and he was made Solicitor-General and a baronet, 1720; he rose through the legal ranks to become Lord Chancellor, 1737; created Baron Hardwicke, 1733, and Earl, 1754.

at the head of an immense army; nor do we only possess an unconquerable force, but a certain unquenchable public fire, which has touched all ranks of men like a visitation.

Turn to the growth and spring of your country, and behold and admire it; where do you find a nation who, upon whatever concerns the rights of mankind, expresses herself with more truth or force, perspicuity or justice? not the set phrase of scholastic men, not the tame unreality of court addresses, not the vulgar raving of a rabble, but the genuine speech of liberty, and the unsophisticated oratory of a free nation ...

Sir, we may hope to dazzle with illumination, and we may sicken with addresses, but the public imagination will never rest, nor will her heart be well at ease – never! so long as the Parliament of England exercises or claims a legislation over this country: so long as this shall be the case, that very free trade, otherwise a perpetual attachment, will be the cause of new discontent; it will create a pride to feel the indignity of bondage; it will furnish a strength to bite your chain, and the liberty withheld will poison the good communicated.

The British minister mistakes the Irish character: had he intended to make Ireland a slave, he should have kept her a beggar; there is no middle policy; win her heart by the restoration of her right, or cut off the nation's right hand; greatly emancipate, or fundamentally destroy. We may talk plausibly to England, but so long as she exercises a power to bind this country, so long are the nations in a state of war; the claims of the one go against the liberty of the other, and the sentiments of the latter go to oppose those claims to the last drop of her blood. The English opposition, therefore, are right; mere trade will not satisfy Ireland – they judge of us by other great nations, by the nation whose political life has been a struggle for liberty; they judge of us with a true knowledge of, and just deference for, our character – that a country enlightened as Ireland, chartered as Ireland, armed as Ireland, and injured as Ireland, will be satisfied with nothing less than liberty.[4]

But Grattan was a quintessential 'patriot' in being a good House of Commons man, with moderately conservative instincts, who knew his limitations, kept his hands free from office and produced Irish rhetoric for Irish purposes.

The golden moment for 'patriotism' came in the legislation of 1782 that amended Poynings' Law and repealed the Declaratory Act; but it was finally facilitated by drastic political shifts in England. The process was begun by Yelverton's Act amending the practice whereby the Irish parliament had to 'confirm statutes made in England'; the tempo was speeded up by the Volunteer convention at Dungannon in February 1782 that asserted Ireland's right to legislative independence, limited Money Bills and an independent judiciary, as a slate to be presented to MPs at election time. But the situation was transformed by the fall of North's government in March, and its replacement by the Rockingham Whigs. For they had given hostages to fortune, with generous Irish promises, in their opposition days: a classic out-of-office tactic, not usually called to account. The links forged between oppositions in the two countries over the upheavals of the sixties and seventies, and sporadically kept up, now had dramatic importance.

Further pressure in London was applied by William Eden, a politician of wide Irish experience, recalled from Dublin in some pique and determined to embarrass the government; within the Rockingham party both Fox and Burke wanted to bring off an Irish coup with something like a general treaty. Given all this, Grattan's amendment to the address on the opening of the Dublin parliament falls into place as a step in a process, not a sudden *démarche*. Behind the bravura of his great peroration calling for legislative independence lie some intriguing pointers towards the limitations of the 'patriot' position. His indefensible claim that Ireland was 'a country in which every living man has a share in the government' shows the 'patriot' conception of the political nation; his emphasis that the Volunteers must now disband and his deliberate playing down of their part in the expected victory reflect the riskiness of the whole Dungannon tactic, and the doubts felt by parliamentarians about the principle. By July the Declaratory Act was repealed and Poynings' Law amended: Irish bills could no longer be altered in England. Flood's ensuing campaign for a Renunciation Act, renouncing England's power to revive such legislation, was eventually successful; it also led to an irrevocable political separation between him and Grattan. The great struggle was apparently over.

What remained of Ireland's constitutional dependence on Great Britain? The English Privy Council was still a superior authority but generally kept its rights in reserve. Royal assent to Irish bills was conferred under the Great Seal of Great Britain (though again, it was only once withheld). It was generally assumed that foreign and imperial affairs remained reserved to Westminster, though, in fact, this was not so: Ireland could technically have sent ambassadors abroad, and could have claimed the right to found a navy. There remained a large and uncertain constitutional area to argue about.

Constitutional argument was, however, generally short-circuited by the same traditional mechanisms that enabled English government to get on with Irish politics: informal structures of parliamentary management. Much of this was *ad hoc*, and any real conflict would generally come up against the old impasse: a change of government in Ireland was generally dependent on events at Westminster. Matters had to be arranged through the mis-called 'Irish Cabinet' of expert politicians like Fitzgibbon, Beresford and Foster. A circle was being continually squared. In the 1790s Irish radicals turned their attention, logically enough, to the position of the Lord Lieutenant, and the fact that ultimate authority for public expenditure lay, at the last resort, out of the hands of the Irish parliament. But they got nowhere. The desire for a sort of proto-dominion status was essentially anachronistic, at least until a time after the monarch was no longer a figure in politics; at a more visceral level, the politics of the imperial economy forbade it. Irish parliamentary management continued to enable Castle government to get its business done – after 1782 as much as before. The reality of 1782 was largely cosmetic: an effect created by Grattan's speeches, which were carefully adjusted long after the event, and by the retrospective idealizations of nineteenth-century nationalists.

Yet the years from 1782 to 1800 are known as those of 'Grattan's parliament', rather than Rutland's or Buckingham's government. A cynic might conclude that this was because Grattan symbolized the pretentiousness and impotence of so-called parliamentary 'independence'. Certainly, 1782 changed little that was not already in the process of alteration. J. C. Beckett has concluded: 'even if the Declaratory Act had remained in force the British Parliament would have refrained from legislating for Ireland in defiance of the House of Commons ... [and] a study of the operation of Poynings' Law before and after 1782 suggests a conclusion of the same general character'.[5] None the less, especially when the major divisive issues were out of the way, after 1785 Irish public life seemed to epitomize a golden age for the Ascendancy *haute bourgeoisie* at play. These were also the years of the parliament's increasing alienation from the politically conscious propertied classes, and of recurring rural protest movements: it is easy to see College Green as existing in its own Georgian never-never land until pulled rudely to earth at the end of the century. But 'Grattan's parliament' did represent, albeit rhetorically, the odd sense of Irishness felt by the Ascendancy, which helps explain why it was so easily co-opted into later nationalist tradition. And it also epitomized the intensity of conviction that lay behind those who were not necessarily straightforward 'patriots', like Foster and Fitzgibbon, for whom the British connection was seen as political life or death.

It is, in fact, the British connection that should be stressed: for Irish parliamentary politics continued to react to changes in England, and English politicians continued to see Ireland as an appropriate area for intervention. Thus the Foxite Whigs hoped 'to reap a harvest in Ireland' that would confer party advantage in England; and they spoke of 'engrafting a few slips of Whiggism' into Irish politics.[6] If this was never quite possible, it remained a continuing effort. From the Dublin side, much attention was directed towards English models; the continued derivativeness of much Irish metropolitan culture, the obsession with refining the Irish accent, the provincial snobberies so characteristic of Dublin life, should be seen in this context. The political class continually emphasized their community of culture and tradition with England; the Gaelic revivalism of O'Conor, O'Halloran[ix] and Curry was never really adopted by the 'patriot' culture, though figures like Flood had developed antiquarian interests by the late eighteenth century, and country gentlemen competed with each other in their archaeological finds. 'Patriot' nationalism remained exclusive: the rule of an enlightened elite, rather than the broadening of national interests that was so important to the self-image of the American revolutionaries. And this, too, remained as true after 1782 as before.

Thus the Catholic question, while raised out of doors in 1783–4 and impinging on House of Commons politics, was left to one side; Flood's parliamentary 'reform' formula, presented by Volunteer pressure, conspicuously bypassed them. With the ascendancy of Pitt in British politics, the advantage in Ireland went to the hard men who emphasized the profitability of the British connection, like Foster, Fitzgibbon and Beresford. Pitt, initially interested in parliamentary reform for Ireland, was persuaded from Dublin Castle by Rutland[x] and Orde[xi] to leave the Irish system alone: it answered the special circumstances of

[ix] Sylvester O'Halloran (1728–1807): born in Limerick; educated in Paris and Leyden; practised medicine in Limerick, where he founded the Infirmary, 1760; wrote on surgical subjects before turning his attention to antiquarian research; wrote *Insula Sacra*, 1770, a plea for the preservation of the ancient Irish annals; *Ierne Defended*, on the validity of ancient Irish history, and his *General History of Ireland* to the close of the twelfth century, both 1774. Became an honorary member of the Royal College of Surgeons in Ireland, 1786.

[x] Charles Manners (1754–87): succeeded as fourth Duke of Rutland, 1779; became Lord Lieutenant of Ireland, 1784; advocated a union as the only alternative to separation; gave magnificent entertainment at Dublin Castle and made a grand tour of the Big Houses of the country, 1787; his talent for conviviality ensured the popularity of his viceroyalty.

[xi] Thomas Orde [-Powlett] (1745–1807): became Chief Secretary and entered the Irish parliament, 1784; introduced propositions for a commercial union of England and Ireland that were rejected by the Irish parliament after they had been materially altered, to Ireland's disadvantage, in the English Commons, 1785–6; proposed an innovatory scheme for education in Ireland, 1787, but recalled before it was put into effect.

the country. Significantly, he turned instead to the politics of the economy.

Pitt always saw England's Irish question as a problem of economic relations; and he was not alone. Camden told Castlereagh in 1796 that the most important concern of Irish politics that could be handled from Dublin was 'the consideration of its internal economy and its aptitude to various improvements'. Foster's biographer has shown that his politics were dominated by economic considerations, to the extent of divining economic solutions for ostensibly political problems; the same may have been true for many combatants in the Irish political arena. In the Irish context, a forward line on economic 'freedoms' helped to define political liberalism; the country gentry remained obsessive about British interference in markets and production patterns. It is notable how Grattan's great orations of the early 1780s emphasized the economy. Significantly, the issues that brought popular agitation into line with decisive parliamentary action and raised basic questions of British authority tended to deal with ostensibly mundane issues like the importation of refined British sugar.

This remained true after 1782. Celebrated economic initiatives of 'Grattan's parliament', like Foster's Corn Law of 1784, were often the outcome of campaigns that had begun long before (Jenkinson and Foster had been canvassing plans to favour Irish corn exports since the 1770s). Moreover, Ireland's position in imperial trade was in some ways rather disadvantaged after 1782 – since Britain now negotiated commercial regulations without reference to Ireland, and Ireland had little bargaining power on her own account. From 1783 to 1784 a strong movement gained momentum in favour of a tariff barrier to protect southern textile industries; another 'Buy Irish' campaign got under way. Significantly, Ulster refused to join in; Belfast opposed protectionism, and northern witnesses at investigatory commissions blamed the industrial crisis of the south on its own fecklessness. The peculiar economic nature of Ulster was by now emphatically apparent.

When prominent Dublin M Ps headed a campaign to restrict imports from Britain, especially woollen goods, the government saw it as the thin end of a wedge that would lead to separation: economic discontents, as usual, were expected to produce a political outcome. Foster and Fitzgibbon shared these preoccupations. Though 'Grattan's parliament' never enacted directly protective measures, limitations like the restrictions on re-exporting colonial goods to Great Britain seemed to point up their implicitly inferior status: this being so, it may seem surprising that Pitt's plans for reconstructing Anglo-Irish commercial relations in

1784 came to nothing. But he wished to remove and rationalize duties and commerce in a manner that would produce an eventual free trade: in a sense, economic union. And, given the political implications of economic legislation for Ireland, this could be taken to presage a constitutional union too. North, for one, thought it did, and should.

At first, however, 'patriots' like Grattan supported Pitt's ideas, except the clause that imposed a charge on Irish revenue to pay for imperial defence, where a compromise was effected. Initial opposition was strongly expressed among British commercial and industrial interests, where a petitioning and lobbying campaign was organized by influential entrepreneurs like Wedgwood and Peel. The question also mobilized opinion along party divisions at Westminster, capitalizing upon the groundswell of public opinion against Pitt's excise tax on cotton. Fears were expressed of a great drain to Ireland of skilled trainees – and of the Irish parliament deliberately setting itself to crush certain English industries by preferential legislation. Burke, significantly, opposed Pitt on imperial grounds. Inevitably, Pitt's original proposals were adapted.

The changes made were not substantial. But adaptations enforced at Westminster aroused the usual 'patriot' rhetoric about England trying to legislate for Ireland yet again. Fox rather belatedly adopted the line of opposing Pitt's economic proposals in order to defend Ireland's constitutional independence; Grattan followed the same argument, preferring constitutional rhetoric to economic advantage. Fitzgibbon wondered sarcastically when it would be realized that 'the recollection of Mr Grattan's splendid periods is but a slender compensation for poverty and the most absolute dependence on Great Britain'; but those who, like him and Foster, supported Pitt's proposals were accused of seeking a union without the name. The opposition line was curiously reductionist: 'Nothing that is subtle and intricate,' said Flood, 'can ever be the foundation of settlement and concord.' Constitutional insecurity ruled out political imagination: another enduring theme in Anglo-Irish relations.

In fact, commercial legislation of the late 1780s, like the Irish Navigation Act (which helped confer advantages on Irish trade with France and the United States), really replicated the aborted British legislation in a constitutionally tactful way. In the 1790s Ireland was allowed into the East India Company monopoly and permitted to re-export colonial goods to Great Britain. Much of the essence contained in Pitt's commercial propositions eventually came about. But their importance lies in the directly political reverberations that such ideas set off – and the uncertainty about Ireland's status that was betrayed on both sides of the Irish Sea.

III

It may not, then, be an illegitimate exercise of hindsight to infer the inevitability of a union looming behind the golden years of 'Grattan's parliament'. The political system made it possible; constitutional uncertainty, brought into high relief by recurring crises over commercial relations, brought it into men's minds. It had been North's recipe for defusing the Irish crisis of 1779. Moreover, once party politics in both countries became intermingled – even, in the case of the 'patriot' alliance with the Foxite Whigs, interdependent – there was a constant danger of Irish influence overturning the political balance in England. And the image of the College Green parliament as a destabilizing factor in the political system of both countries was strengthened after 1782 by its flirtations with ideas of political reform.

Though Grattan maintained the idea that MPs were the servants of their electorates, it was not a generally held opinion. But the 1780s saw a number of hotly contested elections in previously close boroughs, and the idea of accountability began to be heard. 'Political reform' in Ireland evolved as ideas of franchise reform and reconstruction, the counteracting of borough influence, the abolition of rotten boroughs and the secret ballot. Through the medium of the political press, there was an overspill from the contemporary reforming rhetoric in Great Britain: the Volunteer convention at Lisburn in July 1783 addressed inquiries to Cartwright, Jebb, Price, Wyvill and other prominent British reformers. But there was also a strong and cynical public recognition of the way Irish votes, and Irish MPs, were tied to patronage: Volunteer conventions raised such issues again and again.

And there remained the special condition of Irish politics: could reform accommodate Catholics? If British liberals felt that the Catholic franchise must be part of any reform package, such an idea tended to defuse reforming zeal in many Irish quarters. Irish reform always had its own ethos; one plan, cheerfully accepting that political power was a material possession, floated the idea of democratic joint-stock companies of subscribers who would buy as many seats as possible, and then hire accountable MPs to fill them. Some Volunteer conventions aired schemes for a Catholic franchise; some resorted to the language of French aid and alternative assemblies; others produced plans for voting and procedural reform that applied to the Protestant nation only. And it was the latter approach that carried through to the reform petition presented by Flood to the Irish House of Commons in 1783: a plan for three-year parliaments, franchise and procedural reform, and tighter strictures on pensions, within a political system defined, as before, by religious ascendancy.

The plan was rejected, not only by the exertions of conservatives like Foster and Fitzgibbon, but also by 'patriot' parliamentarians like Grattan and Charlemont who disapproved of the crudity with which the Volunteers now tried to exert direct political pressure. By 1784 Grattan was referring to them as 'the armed beggary of the nation'. However, the 'giddiness' apparent in Irish politics at this time was a function of the instability of Westminster politics during the temporary ascendancy of the Fox–North coalition. Further efforts at Irish reform agitation in 1784 also sputtered out; attempts to start up country meetings in the autumn were met by apathy, and in some quarters open antagonism. Above all, the Catholic question sabotaged attempts at free discussion of the general principle; and the very nature of 'Grattan's parliament' made out-of-doors agitation irrelevant, since it did not possess the machinery to respond to such tactics without corresponding pressure from across the Irish Sea. In a sense, neither the Irish parliament nor the majority of the Volunteers could accommodate radicalism.

The Regency crisis of 1788–9, moreover, pointed up the fundamental issue of unsettled relations with Great Britain. During the King's incapacity, the Irish government favoured proceeding by a bill to create a Regency, as argued by Pitt; the Irish opposition supported the Foxite tactic of asking the Prince of Wales to assume power on his own account. They were swayed in this direction not only because of traditional Foxite connections, but also because it seemed a procedure that would emphasize the Irish parliament as a separate and coequal power under the Crown. Even Shannon, Ponsonby and Leinster left the government side over this; Ponsonby, for one, apparently expected that the Regent would hand back the powers of the undertakers to local great men. The Irish parliament moved to address the Regent according to Fox's plan; but the Viceroy refused to transmit the address, and the King rescued the situation by recovering.

One result was a residual 'Irish Whig' group, opposing the government, calling for the 'freedom of this kingdom' as an indispensable guarantee of the connection with Great Britain, and attacking Crown influence in parliament. The language of 'patriotism' could be adapted to many purposes. More importantly, parliamentary rhetoric was outflanked by radical Whiggery outside it – notably the Belfast Whig Club, founded in 1790. If the obvious ideological prelude to this radicalization is the fall of the Bastille, it should not be forgotten that the same year saw the Regency crisis highlighting yet again the anomalous, unresolved constitutional position of Ireland in relation to England. It also raised fears of ministerial interference, as much a danger after 1782 as before it. On both political and ideological grounds, the break with past security falls in 1789, when unwelcome realities began to come sharply home. Historians nowadays find it easy to be anachronistically uncharitable about the pretensions of 'Grattan's parliament'; by the same token, they have come to appreciate the much-reviled Fitzgibbon, if only because he put the actual position with such brutal clarity. And 1789 gave him the opportunity for a classic statement of the reality behind Ascendancy politics: when he reminded

the gentlemen of Ireland that the only security by which they hold their property, the only security they have for the present Constitution in Church and State, is the connexion of the Irish Crown with, and its dependence upon, the Crown of England ... If they are not duped into idle and fantastical speculations under the pretence of asserting national dignity and independence, they will feel the effects to their sorrow. For give me leave to say, sir, that when we speak of the people of Ireland, it is a melancholy truth that we do not speak of the great body of the people. This is a subject on which it is painful to me to be obliged to touch in this assembly; but when I see the right honourable member [Grattan] driving the gentlemen of Ireland to the verge of a precipice, it is time to speak out ... Sir, the ancient nobility of this kingdom have been hardly treated. The Act by which most of us hold our estates was an Act of violence – an Act subverting the first principles of the Common Law in England and Ireland. I speak of the Act of Settlement; and that gentlemen may know the extent ... I will tell them that every acre of land which pays quitrent to the Crown is held by title derived under the Act of Settlement. So I trust gentlemen ... will deem it worthy of consideration how far it may be prudent to pursue the successive claims of dignified and unequivocal independence made for Ireland by the right honourable gentleman ... If the address of both Houses can invest the Prince of Wales with Royal power in this country, the same address could convey the same power to Louis XVI, or to his Holiness the Pope, or to the right honourable mover of this resolution ... We are committing ourselves against the law and against the Constitution, and in such a contest Ireland must fall.[7]

'Ireland' here had the limited meaning that Irish politicians – 'patriots', placemen and all – understood. But the crisis of the 1790s would be precipitated by elements and influences outside that gilded world, breaking in suddenly after those brief decades that saw what Barrington defined with unconscious irony as the 'rise and fall of the Irish nation'.

CHAPTER TWELVE

'ENTHUSIASM DEFYING PUNISHMENT': REVOLUTION, REPUBLICANISM AND REACTION

I

IN IRELAND AS IN other European countries, the tempo of events during the 1790s was frenetically speeded up: the themes of revolution and republicanism predominated, and, by the end of the decade, reaction had set hard. The nature of Ireland's peculiar crisis was strongly rooted in the social tensions already described; the final catharsis focused all the contradictions of eighteenth-century conditions. But it was precipitated by an international dislocation: the French wars from 1793, too often divorced by historians from the Irish scene.

In several ways, the pressures of war brought Irish discontent to a head. The Irish budget, in balance before 1793, ran at an increasing deficit, ineffectually met by haphazard taxes and snowballing loans. Expenditure quadrupled from 1792 to 1800, and the constant danger of financial instability heightened the sense of crisis. In politics, another important development was that the Irish radicals became disillusioned with the performance of constitutional opposition at College Green, since *soi-disant* 'patriot' politicians fell in with the government line.

At the opening of this session [of 1793] every man thought ... that the Catholics must be completely emancipated, and a radical reform in Parliament effectuated, but the delusion was soon removed. It was suddenly discovered that it was necessary to have a *strong* government in Ireland; ... the War had [*sic*] been approved by Parliament, 36,000 men have been voted ... the gunpowder bill is passed; the volunteers of Dublin have been insulted, their artillery has been seized; soldiers hourly are seen with a Police Magistrate at their head parading the streets, entering and searching the houses of citizens for arms; and finally the officers of the only society which had the spirit to observe on those proceedings, are seized and thrown into prison.[1]

That 'society' was the United Irishmen, and their history reflects the inspiration, radicalization and disillusionment that the events of the 1790s brought to Irish society at much wider levels.

Behind the French wars lay, of course, the French Revolution. The articulate and reflective William Drennan[i] wrote that the events of 1789 had 'all the fascination of a novel, attended with the conviction that it is reality'. 'Reality' in Ireland, as usual, meant the Catholic position; and one of the first reactions of the government to international insecurity involved reconciling the Irish Catholics. The imperial example, notably in Canada, and the fashion for the nostrums of tolerance, already made further steps in their emancipation desirable; then, from 1789, pro-Catholicism became part of the respectable anti-Revolutionary package. Irish Catholics already possessed an organized pressure-group in the Catholic Committee: this responded to the change in establishment attitudes by becoming radicalized from 1791. A new complexion was evident in its leading spirits – notably the organizing secretary, Theobald Wolfe Tone.[ii] Six of the subcommittee of thirteen appointed to draft new demands in early 1791 (notably for a limited enfranchisement) went on to become United Irishmen; twenty-five members of the Catholic Committee elected in 1792 were already members of the organization. At the same time, the Committee adopted a high public profile. Though not socially radical, they wanted equality for Catholics, within the system, without delay; Edmund Burke provided the intelligent conservative rationale for such a step, and contemporary conditions demanded it.

Inevitably, this attitude was adopted at a time when the government was already moving cautiously towards emancipatory measures, and

[i] William Drennan (1754–1820): born in Belfast; educated at Glasgow and Edinburgh; *Letters of Orellana, an Irish Helot*, 1784; wrote the original prospectus of the United Irishmen, 1791, and many of their addresses while Chairman of the Society, 1792–3; tried for sedition but acquitted, 1794; withdrew from politics but continued to express his national feeling in poetry inspired by romanticism. Considered himself an 'aristocratical democrat'.

[ii] See above, p. 175.

bringing strong pressure to bear on Dublin Castle. As far as Pitt and his advisers were concerned, enfranchisement of Catholics was a necessary first step for a more regulated and satisfactory connection with Ireland: by which some already meant a constitutional union. Sensing a little on offer, the Catholic Committee promptly demanded a lot; the Castle was worried enough by their *rapprochement* with equally discontented Dissenters to accept that movement was necessary. The situation was complicated by divisions within the Catholic Committee itself; these have been interpreted in an Estates-General analogy, where the Second Estate was being challenged by the Third, while the First, divided among itself, hung back.[2] But more importantly, the Committee's spokesmen readily disavowed traditional bogies like papal infallibility or the irrelevance of keeping faith with heretics: liberals on both sides were encouraged to feel that religious sects were converging in all essentials, and that divisions were a thing of the past. The Committee adroitly balanced its radical firebrands with the more traditional elements of propertied Catholic conservatism. Tone was particularly astute at this, to the annoyance of his more naïve radical friends.

Catholic politicking should be seen against the background of a volatile situation, where fears of a Protestant backlash leading to a sort of UDI were frequently voiced, and where the powerful influence of the 'Irish Cabinet' was implacably anti-enfranchisement. Given this, the legislation of 1792–3 was impressive enough. One limited measure was introduced in 1792, which advanced the important issues into the arena of discussion; the 1793 Act, backed by an aggressive Catholic convention on the model of the Volunteers (or, indeed, the early days of the French Revolution) finally brought real gains. Enfranchisement was granted, though not right of representation; posts conferring political power were still debarred. But inevitably, deferment had meant that more was granted than originally intended. It happened against a background of much opposition: Grattan, for instance, affirming that he was a friend to Catholic liberty only as far as it was consistent with Protestant Ascendancy. Significantly, it was French military advances in late 1792 that shifted Irish-Protestant opinion to conciliating Catholics in the interests of national unity as a war loomed. And there was still a severe backlash from invincibly Protestant bodies like the Dublin Corporation and many grand juries.

No less significantly, the Catholic Committee had in the end bypassed the Viceroy and presented a petition directly to London, thus tacitly threatening to withold support from the system of Irish government as established in 1782. The 1793 Act, as the debates made clear, was granted in order to retain that support. 'England,' as Sir John Parnell put it, 'thinks the connection can be better preserved by a change of system.'

Whether this related to any change of attitude at more basic levels is much less certain. The Dublin United Irishman W. P. Carey adopted as the masthead device for his *National Evening Star* an Episcopalian, a Presbyterian and a Roman Catholic shaking hands; but even this modest hope laid him open to attack. (He later turned informer, and died a respectable citizen.) There were some radical provincial papers, such as Denis Driscoll's *Cork Gazette*, that celebrated the dawn of a new era. Irish Catholics had become dramatically better off than those in England, who were not enfranchised until 1829; but the practical results of 1793 were less sweeping. Some Catholics appeared on grand juries and in army offices; others were called to the Bar, Daniel O'Connell among them. But the local base of politics continued to follow the old patterns – especially on town corporations, where the Protestants closed ranks. Brakes and restrictions continued to limit Catholic advances within the system. Meanwhile, the goal of representation in parliament ('emancipation') became more clearly defined; while Pitt's government, already thinking of a union as the ultimate desideratum, was reluctant to grant emancipation prematurely, as it would remove one of the primary inducements towards such a measure.

For the moment, energies continued to be directed towards reforming the existing system. Political reform, the unfinished business of the Volunteer movement, was a cause adopted by the radicals of the Catholic Committee, and thus taken up by the United Irishmen from 1793 to 1794, as well as by the 'Friends of the Constitution' group within the parliamentary opposition, who had obvious links with the Foxite 'Friends of the People' across the water. This did not necessarily denote radicalism; 'reformers' like Ponsonby and Grattan were primarily concerned to strengthen landed representation, and entrench the aristocratic element within the College Green parliament.[3] And, like the Foxites, they would eventually secede from parliament and leave the way clear for reaction. The government might respond by accepting several opposition bills regarding the civil list, placemen, pensions and so on in 1793; but reform was short-circuited, like so much else, by the declaration of war, as well as by the intrinsic conservatism of gentry politics.

The limitations of the situation, as well as the polarization of Irish politics after 1793, must be remembered when considering the fiasco of the Fitzwilliam viceroyalty in 1795. The appointment of Lord Fitzwilliam[iii] was the result of the advance of the Portland Whig group to Pitt's government; given the traditional links of Rockingham Whigs with the Irish opposition, it was seen as conferring an important advantage upon Grattan and his friends. But Fitzwilliam's extraordinarily crude and hasty tactics in office negated the advantage. He went far beyond contemporary practice, as well as outside his instructions, in dismissing from office the adherents of 'Irish Cabinet' views; once seen as a martyr in the cause of Catholic emancipation, his behaviour now appears both ignorant and silly. It probably reflected general attitudes among the Portland Whigs, who seem to have taken Ireland as their brief, and became annoyed when Pitt tried to impose restrictions on Fitzwilliam in advance.

Certainly, the new Viceroy had a very different, and constitutionally unprecedented, notion of his powers and function; things got out of hand early on. He took too seriously the inevitable letters of advice from Irish politicians, and assumed he could do all he was advised to. Within two days of arrival, he had instituted a series of peremptory dismissals: The First Commissioner of the Revenue, the Solicitor-General, the Attorney-General, the heads of the departments at the Castle, many of them in office for twenty years or more. It was a *putsch* that ignored the practice of Irish government, and was followed by a breakdown of communication with the increasingly dismayed London government. Fitzwilliam then presented an outline for total Catholic emancipation, which was impossibly premature and impolitic as far as the government was concerned; Grattan, working closely with the Viceroy, promptly introduced such a bill; at this point, after seven weeks in Ireland, Fitzwilliam was dismissed. Grattan's bill went on to be debated in May 1795, and was defeated by 155 votes to 84.

The effects were destabilizing. Once again, as in the Regency affair,[iv] a crisis of Irish government had highlighted the inherent uncertainty about the nature of the connection. Furthermore, the electric issue of

[iii] William [Wentworth-] Fitzwilliam (1748–1833): succeeded as Earl Fitzwilliam, 1756; succeeded to the Marquess of Rockingham's vast estates in Yorkshire and Wicklow, 1782; Lord President of the Council, 1794 and 1806; Lord Lieutenant of Ireland, December 1794–March 1795. His political mentor Burke advised him 'to begin the arrangement of Ireland as if it had been but this day thought of': uncharacteristic advice he took too literally.

[iv] See above, pp. 256–7.

Catholic emancipation had been aired in a way that made it impossible to deliver; and popular alienation had been created to a degree that government overtures, like support for Catholic colleges, could not compensate. The pattern of political polarization already evident outside the charmed circle of high politics became inevitable. The Fitzwilliam affair ended a three-year crisis over Catholic emancipation, threw into sharp relief the limitations of constitutional Protestant 'nationalism', and heightened sectarian identifications in Irish life. The political establishment withdrew into increasingly conservative attitudes, proclaiming their close links with the government and reaffirming the Protestantism of their local power-bases; while officials subsequently sent from London, like Camden[v] and Castlereagh, remembered Lord Fitzwilliam's fifty days as an awful warning. All this was of great importance for politics outside the establishment, increasingly dominated by the United Irishmen.

II
===

This movement, the vital germ of Irish radicalism, cannot be separated from the general Irish reaction to the French Revolution. Fashionable Irish people had always tended to Francophilia; there was accordingly a wide circulation of literature to do with the early Revolution, and much favourable comment in the newspapers. Trinity College took its characteristic adversarial role, conferring an honorary degree on Burke a few weeks after the publication of his *Reflections*. As the Revolution gathered momentum, so did celebration of its great occasions. And so did political argument: vehement pamphlets came from the conservative side, to counter republican salvoes. The level of informed opinion was remarkably high on both sides: this discourse indicates a politically literate society, exasperated by the incompetence of landlord government. Here we can discern some of the impetus behind the early United Irishmen Clubs.

[v] John Jeffreys [Pratt] (1759–1840): succeeded as second Earl Camden, 1794; unpopular successor to Fitzwilliam as Lord Lieutenant of Ireland, 1795; against Catholic relief; sought to promote state-aided education in Ireland to reduce the influence of the priests; laid the foundation-stone of Maynooth College, 1796; panicked at the outbreak of the 1798 rebellion; replaced as Lord Lieutenant, June 1798; Secretary of State for War and the Colonies, 1805; Lord President of the Council, 1805; created Marquess Camden, 1812.

The origins of the Belfast Club may lie in the 1791 celebrations of Bastille Day; the Club was formed the following October. Belfast was notably 'French', Dublin less so. But there, too, was an educated middle-class element, and an initial desire to see the men of small property represented in politics – which could, with the radicalization of events in France and the rise to influence of men like Thomas Addis Emmet,[vi] move on to ideas of universal male suffrage and complete Catholic emancipation, as well as the secret ballot, payment of MPs and a general range of radical nostrums.

But how and when did the United Irishmen move from being parliamentary reformers to constitutional revolutionaries? Eventually, their oaths and catechisms would posit a linear historical development. 'What have you got in your hand? A green bough. Where did it first grow? In America. Where did it bud? In France. Where are you going to plant it? In the crown of Great Britain.' But what should be borne in mind is not only the percussion of events in Ireland from the early 1790s, but also the Presbyterian tradition of libertarian republicanism that long antedated 1775 or 1789. Dissenting ideology is there from the beginning: far more apparent, and far more galvanic, than the vague and shadowy Gaelic nationalism that was taken on board in the late 1790s. The traditions of Enlightenment debate were diffused through Belfast 'society' (notably via education in Glasgow); this encouraged the fashion for Paine (seven Irish editions of the *Rights of Man* between 1791 and 1792) and the full newspaper reports of Convention debates. But deism was never popular, even among the most advanced Belfast United Irishmen. And northern radicals retained a basic dislike of Catholicism, not only because of its counter-revolutionary implications. Despite the belief that the age of religion was over, ancient identifications ran through radical Irish discourse; 'the Catholics' were always referred to as a distinct group, if only a political one. Even when they were allies, they tended to be seen as irritatingly obsessive. Consciousness of Catholics *qua* Catholics remained evident

---

[vi] Thomas Addis Emmet (1764–1827): born in Cork; educated at Trinity College, Dublin, Edinburgh and the Continent; called to the Irish Bar, 1790; leading counsel for the United Irishmen; took their oath in open court to prove its legality; Secretary to the Society's Supreme Council, 1795; arrested, 1798; exiled, 1799; attempted to interest Napoleon in an invasion of Ireland, 1802, but came to regret the connection of Irish and French politics; sailed for the USA, 1804; joined the New York Bar; built up a large practice, specializing in pleading for the liberty of escaped slaves. Characterized by Drennan as 'possessing more eloquence than energy, more caution than action'.

in the discussions even of advanced United Irishmen like Drennan, Russell,[vii] McCracken[viii] and Neilson.[ix]

Neilson's paper, the *Northern Star*, appeared from January 1792 and reflects some of the attitudes of Belfast United Irishmen. It could always be relied upon to explain and rationalize the reverses and convulsions of events in Paris through the early nineties – supporting the execution of the King, as did Tone and Drennan. On domestic issues it trod a more careful path, beginning by advancing political reform and criticizing the violent methods of 'those infatuated people called Defenders'. It was, inevitably, prosecuted all the same; but its ability to reappear made it a focus of radical energy until it went down for the last time in 1797.

The *Star* and Tone's enthusiastic views have coloured the reputation of Ulster radicalism. But the old siege mentality was still much in evidence in most of the province. Antrim and Down, with very few Catholics and a strong New Light Presbyterian tradition, were radical; the rest of Ulster was not. And though 1792–3 saw a great revival of Volunteering in Ulster, and the summoning of reform conventions supported by many gentry, this should not be simplistically interpreted. Francis Hutcheson's ideas of armed militias to protect civil rights may have been returned to Ulster with interest. But many within the movement specifically declared against republicanism, and aired deeply held worries about Catholic emancipation. Pro-Catholic United Irishmen might argue that Catholics had been 'educated to liberty' by association with Protestants, but this was not entirely convincing. Even Drennan, one of the most generously minded, was fatalistic rather

---

[vii] Thomas Russell (1767–1803): born in County Cork; joined the British army, 1782; an original member of the United Irishmen, 1791; contributed to the *Northern Star*; imprisoned, 1796–1802; met Robert Emmet in Paris and given the task of raising Ulster, 1803; arrested in Dublin; tried and hanged at Downpatrick for high treason.

[viii] Henry Joy McCracken (1767–98): born in Belfast of Huguenot descent and into a leading family in the linen trade; an early but not original member of the United Irishmen, 1791; arrested, 1796; took a leading part in planning the 1798 rebellion in the north, while on bail; commanded the County Antrim insurgents; captured on the eve of a projected escape to America, after some weeks in hiding; tried and hanged.

[ix] Samuel Neilson (1761–1803): born in County Down, son of a Presbyterian minister; had made his fortune as a draper by 1790; abandoned business for politics; editor of the *Northern Star*, 1792; arrested, 1796; released on bail and played a part in preparing the 1798 rising; rearrested and gave 'honourable information'; imprisoned and exiled, 1799: favoured Union; died in the USA.

than enthusiastic about the process of Catholic *rapprochement*. 'It is churlish soil, but it is the soil of Ireland, and must be cultivated, or we must emigrate.'[4]

Belfast radicalism also tended to be cynical about the sister movement in Dublin, which got under way slightly later. By the end of 1792 a renewed and radicalized Volunteering movement seemed about to take off, using tactics and iconography borrowed from the French Revolution; but it was short-circuited after some near-confrontations with the government. Northern Volunteers tended to sneer at the outspoken radical paper sponsored by Emmet and Arthur O'Connor, the *Press* ('vulgar for the vulgar', according to Drennan). However, in Ulster also Volunteers backed off from confrontation over reform; the revival collapsed slowly from early 1793. Again, the vital development of war with France was instrumental. But even without such an issue, it is doubtful whether infiltration by United Irishmen could ever have succeeded in radicalizing gentry Volunteers to the point of open defiance. Subsequent developments would be accelerated by counter-revolutionary measures brought in by Pitt's wartime administration; from early 1794, no longer restrained by their Volunteer allies, clear-sighted United Irishmen saw that conspiracy and elitist organization were the only weapons open to them.

This was as true in Dublin as in Belfast. The Dublin United Irishmen, formed a month after the Belfast Society, began by capitalizing on the current of political feeling that worked to bring Catholics and radicals into a reforming coalition; their rapid polarization is well documented, an advantage to the government of the day as well as to historians of the future. From early on their membership included ex-Volunteers like the irrepressible Napper Tandy and Hamilton Rowan,[x] as well as members of the politically marginalized professional and business classes, including many textile manufacturers, who stressed the advantages of campaigning for protectionist measures. The working classes were conspicuously absent from the rolls of the Dublin United Irishmen. The aristocratic mavericks came later, though the movement as a whole is inevitably identified with their reputations.

After the United Irishmen's reconstruction in 1794 and the arrest of

[x] Archibald Hamilton Rowan (1751–1834): born in London; settled in County Kildare, 1784; a founding member of the Northern Whig Club, 1790; joined the United Irishmen, 1791; tried and sentenced for sedition, 1794; escaped to France; the memory of atrocities witnessed during the Reign of Terror made it impossible for him to join any Irish revolutionary enterprise; pardoned, 1803; settled in County Down.

many of its members, the liberal Francophile middle class were much less prominent in the Society. Their place was taken by glamorous figures like Lord Edward Fitzgerald,[xi] the epitome of radical chic, and Arthur O'Connor,[xii] who translated the ideas of Swift and Molyneux into the rhetoric of the 1790s. Such men had links, personal as well as political, with English radical Whiggery – Fox, and those to the left of him. They were also closely connected to the provincial network of United Irishmen in Ireland itself: as early as 1793 there were at least nine Clubs in towns like Armagh, Lisburn, Clonmel and Limerick. The influence of men like Fitzgerald stressed the French connection (he had romantically married a supposed daughter of Philippe Égalité) and 'breaking the connection' with England – though it was tacitly admitted that geographical and, by now, cultural propinquity would always necessitate some kind of association. Notions of federalism were being floated even in the late 1790s. Contradictions of this kind within the movement are best expressed by its most famous member, Wolfe Tone.

Tone was brilliantly articulate, and his cleverness, humour and personality have been passed down to posterity through his extraordinarily immediate and entertaining journals.[5] The secret language, self-mockery and in-jokes apparently convey a jocular and lightweight character: 'a flimsy man', remarked one contemporary. Certainly his inconsistency and self-advancement have been much stressed, as well as his inability to recognize the sectarian underpinning of all political activity in Ireland, outside the small Francophile intelligentsia. Even in his days as spokesman of the Catholic Committee, he held to the

[xi] Lord Edward Fitzgerald (1763–98): born in Carton House, County Kildare; son of the first Duke of Leinster and Emily, daughter of the Duke of Richmond; joined the Sussex militia and served in America, 1779; MP for Athy, 1781; rejoined the army in Canada, 1788; MP for County Kildare, 1790; attracted by revolutionary thought; visited Paris, staying with Tom Paine, 1792; cashiered from the army for toasting the abolition of all hereditary titles; associated with the United Irishmen from their early days but did not formally join the Society until 1796; led a military committee of the United Irishmen, 1798; captured and mortally wounded in a skirmish in a house in Thomas Street, Dublin.

[xii] Arthur [O']Connor (1763–1852): born in Mitchelstown; educated at Trinity College, Dublin; called to the Irish Bar, 1788; MP for Philipstown, 1791; did not oppose government until 1795; determined to abandon Irish politics and seek an English parliamentary seat, 1796; persuaded to act otherwise by Lord Edward Fitzgerald; joined the United Irishmen; edited the *Press*; arrested in England, 1798; released, 1803; went to France; appointed a general by Napoleon and married the daughter of Condorcet; grew fiercely anti-clerical, to the extent of deriding the O'Connellite movement for Catholic relief as priest-ridden. Eccentric, churlish, megalomaniac.

fundamental Irish-Protestant belief that Catholicism was a dying superstition – though this did not prevent his *Argument on Behalf of the Catholics* (September 1791) from being a brilliant pamphlet that persuaded many Dissenters that it would be dangerous *not* to join the emancipation cause.

But Tone's really important quality was his ability to become a dedicated and ruthless revolutionary. From his early days at the Irish Bar, satirically nicknamed 'Marat' and mocking his own radical pretensions, he actually came to live out the reality of international conspiracy. Like Irish radical politics as a whole, Tone must be seen as undergoing a fundamental change in 1793–4. The United Irishmen were suppressed in May 1794. While Tone had been quite capable in the early 1790s of casting a line towards the government, praising Grattan and cultivating Irish Whigs, by April 1794 he could produce memoranda for French agents that were radical in a reductionist way.

In Ireland, a conquered and oppressed and insulted country, the name of England and her power is universally odious, save with those who have an interest in maintaining it, such as the Government and its connexions, the Church and its dependencies, the great landed property, etc.; but the power of these people, being founded on property, the first convulsion would level it with the dust. On the contrary, the great bulk of the people would probably throw off the yoke, if they saw any force in the country sufficiently strong to resort to for defence. It seems idle to suppose that the prejudices of England against France spring merely from the republicanism of the French; they proceed rather from a spirit of rivalship, encouraged by continued wars. In Ireland the Dissenters are enemies to the English power from reason and reflection; the Catholics, from hatred to the English name. In a word, the prejudices of the one country are directly favourable, and those of the other directly adverse, to an invasion. The Government of Ireland is to be looked upon as a Government of force; the moment a superior force appears it would tumble at once as being neither founded in the interests nor in the affections of the people.[6]

This was the kind of activity that sent him into exile in June 1795, after the government had incriminated a number of United Irishmen in treasonable activity. By then, there was no turning back. Most importantly, in Ireland radical identifications had begun to fuse with nationalism, in the sense that the establishment was defined as *English*. All ills, in Tone's view, could be traced to the English connection. The idea of *native* oppressors was not much entertained; they were written off as an oligarchy of collaborators.

'Nationalism' as such had not been part of the original United Irish package. They were internationalist liberals, anti-government rather than anti-English. Even when anti-Englishness took over, they had little time for 'ethnic' considerations; recent fashions for traditional music and poetry, and archaeological divinations of the 'Celtic' past, seemed to middle-class radicals at best silly and at worst savage. The United Irishmen were modernizers: they appealed, as they themselves put it, to posterity, not ancestors. (Given the way that the ancestors of Belfast radicals had treated the Gaelic Irish, this was just as well.) They looked to Hutcheson, to Locke, to America, and most of all to France.

III

The connections between Ireland and France during the Revolutionary era have been brought only recently into focus by historians.[7] For the French, Ireland was the traditional backdoor to England, as it had been for Spanish strategy in the sixteenth century; the ideas mooted by the radical wing of the United Irishmen also fitted in with the Revolutionary tactic of puppet republics. For the Irish, especially the Belfast radicals, admiration of the French army and French military achievements was axiomatic, apparently overwhelming all local divisions: at the 1792 Bastille celebration dinner in Belfast, Tone noted Dissenters and Catholics 'chequered at the head of the table'.

From 1793 the conditions of war added a new dimension to everything. 'What injury have the French done to *us*?' was a common reaction – along with the subversive idea of Ireland making a separate peace. Nor were the issues strategic alone. In the later 1790s the idea that a French invasion would bring about radical changes in landholding was much canvassed by agrarian agitators, and was seen as a way of persuading the rural classes to support them, though such a development was expected to follow a French landing as a natural sequence, rather than being put into operation by the French as an engineered policy. Much more coherently, from the early 1790s a complex pattern of French–Irish contacts can be traced. This built upon the traditional connection with institutions like the Irish College, as well as upon the new ideological community of interest between radicals in both countries, and the personal connections of political leaders like Fitzgerald and O'Connor. From 1792 schemes for French aid, and hypothetical offers from Paris, were the currency of radical conspiracy. And more effectively, from late 1793 the French leadership was interested in Ireland as a base for destabilizing England.

This was no less true for being a point constantly emphasized by Pitt's government. The arrest and trial of French agents in 1794–5, and the subsequent implication of United Irishmen like Tone and Rowan, was less of a publicity coup than the government had hoped; but it helped bring about a closer *rapprochement* between exiled United Irishmen and the French government. Extreme reactions were further encouraged by Fitzwilliam's recall and the refusal of Catholic emancipation. Most of all, the resort to international conspiracy on the part of radicals was encouraged by the hope that domestic discontent was reaching a level where it would predispose 'the people' to a mass rising.

The likelihood of this in the mid-1790s is arguable. Taxation certainly provided a diffused discontent throughout the *menu peuple*; during the 1790s Irish taxes, hitherto kept at a low level, began to rise. The much-publicized exemption of single-hearth houses from the hearth tax in 1795 was more than offset by the exigencies of war, a financial crisis in 1797, new taxes on leather and salt, and most of all the elimination of transport subsidies on the internal grain trade. The year 1797 has, indeed, been pinpointed as 'a turning-point in Irish fiscal history'.[8] The malt trade and the milling economy of the south-east were much affected, leading to violent resistance to attempted tithe collection in the region during late 1797. Even if tax increases were small in proportion to the general expenses of rural inhabitants, they had to be settled in cash, and so were doubly resented. Combined with the Protestant–Catholic tension latent in most country areas, notably those where a settlement 'frontier' or a deliberate immigration policy can be discerned, the stage was set for emotional resistance to the highly charged issue of tithes; and, eventually, for the sectarian *grand peur* that swept the countryside at all levels and facilitated rural mobilization in 1798.

Moreover, a form of rural agitation was already in existence that could utilize this framework: 'Defenderism'. From 1792 arms-raids had been carried out on isolated houses around the Cavan–Monaghan border, and evidence of oath-taking was being brought to the attention of the perplexed and alarmed authorities. The disturbances spread out to east and west, and it became evident that this rural movement was based on a more coherent and threatening ideology than earlier agitations. It involved some claims for land redistribution as well as historical memories of the Stuart cause; archaic and conservative elements were mingled with a new subversiveness. The ideas and oaths of the Defenders were transmitted by the highly mobile rural workforce, and some rural schoolmasters were involved in the mid-

1790s. Taxation and tithes were perceived as grievances; low rents were demanded for potato patches. Though the roots of the movement in some areas went back to sectarian feuding in the 1780s, and it would eventually take a strongly Catholic line, dues to the Catholic Church were resented as well.

Moreover, Defenderism was not definitively a 'peasant' movement: it was strong in towns and centres of rural industry, and was sophisticated enough 'to, for instance, send arms-buying delegations to London. It also managed to absorb French ideology even without the help of the United Irishmen – though Defenderism tended to identify the French cause as Catholic and anti-English rather than 'republican'. And the sectarian tinge characteristic of the movement in the north gradually took it over.

This was closely related to the rural economy of Armagh, with the land hunger attendant upon the linen industry, and a competitive balance of religious elements. The Armagh linen culture has been used as an explanation why Protestant tenants there became Orangemen rather than United Irishmen:[9] an alliance with landlords was necessary to maintain perceived economic status as much as Protestant Ascendancy. Further, the Volunteering movement, with its dislocation of automatic Protestant support for the government, had brought about a reaction at lower levels of society. From the 1780s a percussion of sectarian incidents and local boycotts was set off: the government was evidently incapable of disciplining the Protestant 'Peep O'Day Boys', who claimed they were simply enforcing the Penal Laws reneged upon by the gentry. Especially in Armagh, the chosen method of disciplining this reaction involved enrolling such discontented elements into the Volunteers. And, as the living standards among weaving communities were seen to decline from the mid-1790s, Protestant aggression became more and more clearly articulated.

Defenderism was in one sense a 'defence' against this. By the mid-1790s, local *causes célèbres* like the battle of the Diamond near Loughgall, County Armagh, on 21 September 1795, which inaugurated the Orange Order, had taken a definitively sectarian tinge. Protestants wanted to ban Catholics from the local linen industry; Protestants were colonizing traditionally Catholic areas in the Ulster borderlands; and, most importantly, local Protestant gentry from the mid-1790s abandoned what one of them called 'the farce of impartiality between the parties' and openly supported the Orangemen. In these conditions, Defenderism rapidly became an 'anti-Protestant, anti-state ideology';[10] it was also anti-English and capable of spectacular violence.

How did this movement relate to the United Irishmen? Arthur O'Connor described the Defenders as 'an unthinking oppressed people, entirely without national views'. This was not strictly accurate; but the United Irishmen took on the job of directing Defender energies against the government rather than against local authority-structures. And when the Defenders coalesced with the reconstructed and radicalized United Irishmen after 1794, native sectarian animosity soon swamped imported secularism. The French, to them, were Catholics at war with Protestants; they looked to a deliverance of the Irish Israelites at the hands of the Revolution.

At the same time, Defenderism can be claimed to have been 'republican' in a national, anti-monarchical sense before the input of United Irish influence. A catechism found upon a man hanged at Carrick-on-Shannon read:

'Are you concern'd?'
'I am.'
'To what?'
'To the National Convention.'
'What do you design by that cause?'
'To quell all nations, dethrone all kings, and to plant the true religion that was lost at the Reformation.'
'Who sent you?'
'Simon Peter, the head of the Church.'[11]

De Latocnaye, travelling through Ulster in 1796, was surprised to encounter the language of 'equality, fraternity and oppression' among cabin-dwellers, and noted that it was linked directly to complaints of over-taxation. There is much local evidence to the same effect. Defenders were organized and articulate in a way that the Whiteboys, for instance, had never been. They took oaths, stressing egalitarianism and 'consecrations' to the National Convention and the Liberty Tree. But their iconography was not inspired only by the French Revolution (and the language of Freemasonry); it went back to the Limerick Treaty and the Battle of the Boyne, in a way that divided them from their radical Presbyterian allies. And their commitment was passionate. 'Defenderism puzzles me more and more,' remarked the Under-Secretary at Dublin Castle in September 1795; 'there is an enthusiasm defying punishment.'[12]

IV
==

From the middle of the decade, events set towards a crisis. The United Irishmen drifted into radicalism after 1793–4; the celebrated trials for seditious activity gave a rostrum to men like Rowan and Drennan, and created Curran's reputation as their advocate. Once the taint of treason attached firmly to Tone and Rowan, the government could suppress the Society itself, which it did in May 1794. The movement was subsequently reconstructed, especially in the north, as an oath-bound secret society, dominated by middle-class extremists. Small local 'societies' (almost cells) swore in a maximum of thirty-six and were linked nationally (they borrowed a good deal from Presbyterian organization). A tight structure was one result; but another was an unwise profusion of written records. The pattern was military. Three 'societies' formed a 'company', more a battalion, and officers had military titles. In many areas, the new organization subsumed Defenderism, which helped to spread it. There were supposedly 6,000 sworn in County Antrim by mid-1796; the United Irishmen themselves reckoned 117,000 in Ulster and Louth by early 1797, and 121,000 by June.

By 1797 the reorganized United Irishmen were powerfully established in Leinster; then Munster, and by 1798 Connacht. Here, though, the Defender influence predominated; even in the towns, Defender oaths were sworn by urban radicals from 1795. The 90,000 'United Irishmen' in Cork in 1798 may have been largely indistinguishable from Defenders. Middle-class radicalism was by now in close alliance with rural agitation.

None the less, the United Irishmen retained middle-class strengths. They represented members of the army, the law, medical science, the Church (Dissenting and Catholic) and the gentry, as well as booksellers, brewers and tradesmen. An influential number infiltrated the navy, planning to mutiny and commandeer their ships for the cause: seventy men from four ships of the line were court-martialled for this in 1797. Weaponry was stockpiled and 'revolutionary committees' drafted for several areas; finance was provided by levies, subscriptions and lotteries.

Ideologically speaking, 'French ideas' continued to be combined with the old commonwealthman doctrines of resistance to tyranny. They tended to hang back from direct incitement to immediate revolution: much of their rhetoric cautiously awaited the hour, in traditional Irish fashion. This may have been deliberately disingenuous; but it is more likely a reflection, yet again, of tension between middle-class radicalism and Defender 'enthusiasm'. Much still depended on whether France invaded, and on what line was taken by the Irish government in the face of escalating tension at local level.

For at the same time, Orangeism was similarly becoming a national organization with a tightly defined and hierarchical structure; in its reliance on marches and the display of traditional icons, it drew on the club movement of the post-1690 generation, and mobilized popular Protestant emotions. The word 'Orange' became a bogy for Catholics in areas as far south as Cork, irrespective of whether they actually contained any Orange Lodges. Wexford was a notable example, as would later become apparent.

The original oath of the Orange Order enjoined members 'to support the King and his heirs as long as he or they support the Protestant Ascendancy': the vital Ulster theme of conditional loyalty recurs. Their zealotry and provincialism made the governing classes shudder. But given the local importance of the organization, and the conditions of the late 1790s, the influence of the Order gained inexorably – especially through their membership of the Militia and, from 1796, of the newly founded Yeomanry.

The Militia had been founded in 1793, a 'respectable' force under officers possessing landed property. Formally, men served by ballot; effectively, they volunteered. The force gained greatly in importance as more and more troops left Ireland to serve abroad. Discipline was uncertain, and tension in-built: in most areas officers were Protestant and men Catholic. Certainly, there were many Defenders within the ranks, as contemporary trials show.

A Yeomanry corps under officers commissioned by the Crown was set up in late 1796; by 1798 it mustered about 40,000. Largely Protestant, it was perceived by radicals as an armed expression of conservative domination; it was especially unpopular in Presbyterian Ulster, though Belfast eventually raised two companies. Essentially, it embodied many of the old Volunteering values. As a part-time and rather lax force, it was open to United Irishmen infiltration; again, much-publicized trials raised the fear of potential disloyalty in Crown forces to an obsession. In fact, detailed examination indicates that indiscipline rather than disaffection was the norm.[13] But soaring desertion rates, the invasion scares of the late 1790s, financial crises and unrest in the navy built up tension.

From 1795 the government was deluged with draconian advice

from local magistrates. The Indemnity Act of that year gave them considerable latitude; the next year, an Insurrection Act conferred sweeping powers, making oath-administration a capital offence. Prosecutions under the Whiteboy Act had already ramified, but the nature of the evidence remained problematic. In 1797 one-seventh of the prosecutions at assizes were for 'political' offences (oaths, conspiracies, assassination), but the conviction rate varied between 20 and 30 per cent. Reluctance of juries and intimidation of witnesses were generally blamed. The conviction rate rose in 1798; but legal difficulties led inevitably to reliance upon martial intimidation.

In late October 1796 habeas corpus was partially suspended. Constitutional opposition was at a discount. Grattan had seceded from parliament; others joined the government side; opposition Whigs lost all radical credibility. A move to hold public meetings and raise petitions in 1797 was short-circuited. The flow of 'information' reaching the government stressed gossip, fears, predictions and innuendo; some of their informers, significantly, were ex-United Irishmen who had become offended by the movement's 'popish' tendency. Demonstrations in solidarity with those arrested and interned became more violent from late 1796. In April 1797 the authorities came down strongly on the Belfast radicals; McDowell estimates 500–600 'political' arrests in Ulster in the year up to September 1797. This was accompanied by a drive to bring in arms. By March 1797 Chief Secretary Pelham was telling General Lake[xiii] to use his discretion freely and forget the 'delicacy' that affected magistrates. Illegal house-burning, on suspicion of United Irish membership, was used as a limited tactic; so was the billeting of troops on suspects. By 1798 every contemporary correspondence conveys a general mentality of fear. Sedition was seen everywhere; whole villages fled to sleep out of doors on nights of supposed massacres; civil war à la Vendée was threatened. The language of political extremism held sway, and with it the reassertion of older identifications. A letter to Lord Charlemont in May 1797 told him: 'your old Ballymascanlan Volunteers, who six months ago were all United Irishmen, are now complete Orangemen, which

[xiii] Gerard Lake (1744–1808): rose steadily in the British army; MP for Aylesbury, 1790–1802; Governor of Limerick, 1794; Commander of the Forces in Ulster, 1796; Lieutenant-General, 1797; Commander-in-Chief, April 1798; routed the Wexford rebels at Vinegar Hill, June; reverted to being second-in-command; Humbert surrendered to him at Ballinamuck, September; installed as MP for Armagh to vote for the Union; resigned, 1799; ended his career as Commander-in-Chief in India. Created Baron, 1804; raised to a viscountcy, 1807.

is more congenial with their feelings.'[14] And to his informant, the most amazing thing about 'this astonishing increase of Orangemen' was that 'immense numbers of them are in Belfast'. By a similar process, though actively revolutionary priests seem to have been 'a deviant minority', the United Irish oaths by May 1798 enjoined members 'to be true to the Catholic religion, and to assist the French should they land in this kingdom'.[15]

By 1798 the response of officers commanding the Militia and Yeomanry was expressed by one of them: 'to excite terror, and by that means obtain our end speedily'. But to lance the infection required a controllable soldiery, and this was not in evidence. The authority of magistrates was at a discount; and even allowing for misrepresentation, the draconian attempts of the military to impose order were counterproductive. This was dramatically expressed by Sir Ralph Abercromby, who took over the command at the end of 1797. After attempting to tighten up discipline, in February 1798 he issued his famous general order describing the army as 'in a state of licentiousness which must render it formidable to everyone but the enemy'. Though politicians and administrators had been saying so incessantly in private correspondence, this was considered an unforgivably impolitic statement; it led to his resignation (not particularly wished for by Pitt's government) and the reversion of command to Lake, who set to 'disarming' Ulster.

This escalation of crisis becomes more comprehensible in the light of what had happened at the end of 1796, when a French expedition had come within a hair's breadth of successfully landing in west Cork. This had been the culmination of United Irish diplomatic activity in Paris; long obsessed with the mechanics of French invasion, they had finally overcome the ambivalence of French attitudes towards intervention. This was essentially the achievement of Wolfe Tone. He believed in 'open war' against England, and repudiated the 'system of private assassination'; but this was a principle that only made sense if French aid on a large scale could be involved. Arriving in France in 1796, he acted, with considerable panache, as the accredited national representative of a foreign power. French tacticians were already canvassing ideas of *chouan* expeditions to Britain; Tone made the vital connection with Carnot and the generals, and raised the bidding. His memoranda to Carnot show an adroit exaggeration of public discontent in Ireland, and an impressive command of military arguments. In Lazare Hoche he discovered a kindred spirit – an energetic enthusiast out to make his reputation. Thus the invasion of Ireland became absorbed into the Hoche–Bonaparte rivalry: it could have played the part in Hoche's career that Italy did in Bonaparte's. And Hoche's premature death in 1797 closed a chapter for Ireland as it opened one for Napoleon.

By then, Tone had accompanied a 43-ship fleet and 15,000 men to Ireland in December 1796, only to see the force split up by storms, disagree about landing and return home. Directory enthusiasm for the venture was limited, as peace negotiations with Britain were just beginning. But Bantry Bay remains a great might-have-been in Irish history.[xiv] With only 11,000 troops in the area, the effect of a landing is incalculable: official opinion at the time thought that Ireland could not have been saved. The potential reaction of the local populace is doubtful, though a rather Machiavellian United Irishmen argument claimed that they would rise, if only to guard against becoming too dependent on the French. But the mere fact of such a large expedition increased the likelihood of local support for a subsequent venture – which was still considered by the French. Tone had won out against the many competing *émigré* revolutionaries in Paris, in advancing the United Irishmen's cause on to the agenda of grand strategy, though it was eventually stymied by the intense politicking between extremists and moderates in the French government and army. Meanwhile, the authorities in Ireland had been precipitated further into the prevalent condition of paranoia.

V
=

Lake's brutal but ultimately effective measures in Ulster were one result; another was the arrest and internment of many United Irish leaders, including the Leinster Directory. Though Drennan remarked 'it is a perfect asparagus bed, and bears cutting', the initiative moved to the energetic, who were often the incompetent. Co-operation with the underground in Britain was short-circuited by a simultaneous swoop on the United Englishmen, whose growth, and inspiration from Ireland, were a preoccupation of Pitt's secret service. Thus when the crisis came, in Marianne Elliott's words, 'the rebellion was not a United Irish one as it would have been a year earlier, but a protective popular uprising which a spent United Irishman leadership failed to harness'.[16]

[xiv] John Stuart Mill's *Ireland and England*, 1868, contains an urbane fantasy about the development of an Irish republic under Hoche's dictatorship.

Nor was it the 'war' Tone wanted. It broke out around Dublin from 23 May 1798, and owed little to the plans for co-ordinated attack on the centres of government power that had been canvassed over the previous year. What *did* happen rapidly adopted a sectarian rationale, and reflected the hysteria of local gentry and Orange recruits as much as supposedly deliberate provocation by the government. What did *not* happen in the north is as important as what did in the south; the geographical index of intensity runs from Wexford and Wicklow in the east to Sligo and Mayo in the west, while Ulster and the south-west were hardly affected – outside some action in Antrim and Down, still adhering to the cause of radical Presbyterianism. The organization was not sophisticated in military terms, tending to revolve round bands of pikemen with local leaders; local pressures rather than ideological attitudes seem to have brought about enlistment. Defender arguments were articulated (the Stuarts, and the French as Catholic deliverers); economic grievances were not. In a curiously contingent and haphazard way, some unlikely figures became involved in leading local rebellions; this was probably due to the defeatist mentality brought about by government policy in the previous two years, as well as by the traditional patronage exercised by the gentry over local 'fleets', or gangs.

There may have been United Irishmen plans for a June rising; certainly, an air of improvisation hangs over the events of May. The Dublin outbreak was controlled in a week, but Wexford was a different matter. This may owe much to a tradition of 'frontier settlement' and a highly politicized, assertive and active Catholic gentry. The county had reacted strongly to the Insurrection Act, which had been proclaimed in late 1797; but local antipathies probably accounted for a good deal. Protestant–Catholic relations were truculent, at the artisanate level as well as among the gentry: in north Wexford, the proportion of Protestant settlement was exceptionally high. The arrival of notably Orange Militia companies (North Cork and Donegal) increased the tension.

The insurgents' success owed a good deal to the speed of events: they took Enniscorthy and attempted to spread out the rebellion into Wicklow, but, despite some effective generalship, they failed. A campaign marked by horrific and unforgotten atrocities on both sides – already described as 'Protestant' and 'Catholic' – ended in the rout on Vinegar Hill, 21 June 1798, and left an inheritance of heightened sectarian animosity. When the Wexford pattern was known in Ulster, many insurgents defected, or even became Yeomen. Castlereagh remarked: 'The religious complexities of the Rebellions in the South gradually separated the Protestants from the Treason, and precisely in the same degree, appeared to embark the Catholics in it.'[17] And when the new Viceroy, Cornwallis,[xv] arrived, he was surprised that the reductionist Catholic–Protestant interpretation was held by everyone.

The 1798 rising was probably the most concentrated episode of violence in Irish history. Mass atrocities were perpetrated in circumstances of chaos and confusion, symbolized by the oddly assorted icons of the rosary and the 'cap of liberty'. By the end of the summer, the death-roll on both sides, from various causes, has been estimated at 30,000. It is not surprising that when a French expedition finally arrived, at Killala in August 1798, it came to little; it was, in any case, really a rushed commando raid, representing only a fragment of the projected force. The strange episode of the Republic of Connacht is a footnote to Irish history. Mayo had never been a United Irish stronghold, though the local response on behalf of 'France and the Blessed Virgin' was impressive and French professionalism brought off some striking coups, including the famous 'Races' of Castlebar. But the rebels were slaughtered at Ballinamuck, County Longford, by the Downshire, Armagh and Kerry Militias. The final diminuendo to the year of the French came when Bompard's fragmentary expedition was intercepted off Donegal, and Tone was captured; he subsequently committed suicide while awaiting execution.

He had been, in a sense, outpaced by events, and his contemporary reputation was, ironically, much less than that of the ludicrous Napper Tandy. But the revelations of the extent of the French connection in United Irish trials stunned contemporaries, and this was seen as Tone's achievement. His reputation also gained from the great forensic tradition of Irish nationalism epitomized in Curran's speeches, which established the United Irish martyrology and invoked an historical continuum of resistance that had not necessarily occurred to the people he was defending.

The legal mopping-up operations continued through to 1801.

[xv] Charles Cornwallis (1738–1805): succeeded as second Earl Cornwallis, 1762; gained military experience in America, 1775–81, and administrative experience as Governor-General of India, 1786–92; created Marquess, 1792; Viceroy and Commander-in-Chief in Ireland, May 1798; introduced clemency into army strategy; regarded abolition of the Irish parliament and Catholic emancipation as the dual means to pacify the country; loathed jobbery but ensured that promises made in return for Union votes were kept; declined a Union dukedom; resigned when Catholic relief failed to succeed Union, 1801; joy at leaving Ireland alloyed by the sense that he left the country dangerously half reformed; returned to India but died before resuming the governorship.

| | May to November 1798 | | March to December 1799 |
	Ulster	Rest of Ireland	All Ireland
Death	72	264	231
Imprisonment	14	2	12
Corporal Punishment	67	15	24
Transportation	186	241	240
Securities or Acquitted	75	83	152
Total	414	605	659

Table 2: *Sentences May to November 1798 and March to December 1799.*
Source: R. B. McDowell, *Ireland in the Age of Imperialism and Revolution.*

Courts martial operated summary but quite closely supervised proceedings. Leaders tended to be punished, while followers received amnesty; a few aristocratic figures, like Fitzgerald and the Wexford gentleman Beauchamp Bagenal Harvey,[xvi] were attainted. Banishment rather than execution was the eventual fate of many – or detention abroad until the end of the war with France, that vital catalyst of so many recent events. Stringent inquiries into the origins of the rebellion obstinately vindicated the case advanced by the state prisoners: moderates had been forced into extremism by repression, and carried on the tide of events. Conspiracy theories about French organization on the grand scale could not be substantiated. Eventually, the official line tended to clemency: local authorities were less merciful, though there were Galway magistrates who captured rebel leaders and then acted as their defence counsel. Generally, conviction rates at sample assizes from 1798 to 1799 average from 16 to 22 per cent, and sentences were often mitigated. About a quarter of the death sentences in 1798 were commuted (see Table 2).

But statistics will never show exactly how many lives were lost in casualties inflicted by troops during and after the rebellion, which

[xvi] Beauchamp Bagenal Harvey (1762–98): born in Bargy Castle, County Wexford; educated at Trinity College, Dublin; called to the Irish Bar, 1782; joined the United Irishmen, 1792, and presided at their meetings, 1793; as their leading country gentleman, an instinctive and politic choice as Commander-in-Chief of the Wexford insurgents, 1798; prohibited all excesses on penalty of death; relieved of his command after the defeat at New Ross; took refuge on Great Saltee Island; discovered and tried; hanged on Wexford Bridge.

certainly reached many thousands. And the process of detention and sentencing dominated public life as the decade came to an end. It is a poignant symbol of the era that the abandoned 'New Geneva' settlement in County Waterford, conceived as an ideal community,[xvii] became instead a barracks for rebel prisoners awaiting transportation – and as 'Geneva Barracks' it is still known.

VI

The subsequent step of a constitutional union between Ireland and England seems a logical consequence of the 1798 rebellion: a structural answer to the Irish problem, with overtones of 'moral assimilation' and expectations that an infusion of English manners would moderate sectarianism. But it had long been canvassed in England – though it came about more hastily than the planned measure of liberalization, modernization and emancipation often posited. Though Irish receptivity to French ideas was emphasized, the strategy had as much to do with fear of the intractability of the Irish parliament over joint issues: in a sense, when planning a union, the 1780s were as much in the government's mind as the 1790s.

The new system abolished the Irish parliament, while retaining the Castle government. The representation of Irish constituencies was to be transferred to Westminster, with the representatives carefully restricted to one hundred. The number of boroughs was cut down, with compensation to patrons; the counties remained as two-member constituencies; the Irish peers elected twenty-eight of their body to sit in the Lords, along with four Irish bishops. Any idea of a devolved Dublin assembly for purely Irish affairs was dropped early on. The economic theory behind the Act visualized the British Isles as a single economic unit and a single trade area. But the inequities in the two national debts effectively decreed that public finances remain separate (the Irish Exchequer was not amalgamated until 1816). General United Kingdom expenses were to be met in the ratio of fifteen to two. Duties were to be abolished except for that on Irish grain entering Great Britain.

There is a vast pamphlet literature covering the arguments for and against (though the press remained curiously muted). The Unionist

---

[xvii] See above, p. 217.

side tended to brutal truths, and to borrowing the Whig line by deprecating the colonial and elitist nature of the College Green assembly as no great loss: logic demanded a union as the only alternative to separation. The argument relied on the concept of constitutional union as an integrative force, which experience would disprove; even at the time, there were large questions raised by the contradictions inherent in the mechanisms of union, well put by Grattan:

It is not an identification of people, as it excludes the Catholic from the parliament and the state; it is not an identification of government, for it retains the Lord-Lieutenant and his court; it is not an identification of establishments; it is not an identification of revenue; it is not an identification of commerce, for you have still relative duties, and countervailing duties; it is not an identification of interest, because England relieves herself as she increases the proportion of Irish taxation, and diminishes her burdens, by communicating them to Ireland. The present constitution may be said to be nearly an equal trade and an equal liberty, and the Union to be a tax and a drawback upon that equal trade and upon that equal liberty; for so much a diminution of that identification of interests, if it be not an identification of interests, still less is it an identification of feeling and of sympathy. The Union, then, is not an identification of the two nations; it is merely a merger of the parliament of one nation in that of the other; one nation, namely England, retains her full proportion; Ireland strikes off two-thirds; she does so, without any regard either to her present number, or to comparative physical strength; she is more than one-third in population, in territory, and less than one-sixth in representation. Thus there is no identification in any thing, save only in legislature, in which there is a complete and absolute absorption.

It follows, that the two nations are not identified, though the Irish legislature be absorbed, and, by that act of absorption, the feeling of one of the nations is not identified but alienated.[18]

As this may indicate, the Union was violently opposed by Ascendancy politicians: ministry men like Foster, Parnell and Ponsonby joined with opposition 'patriots' like Grattan in defence of their parliament – not in attack upon the British connection, though Grattan accused the government of adopting 'the novel and barbaric phraseology of empire'. There was some readiness to adapt the 1782 arrangements; 'colonial nationalism' had to be careful of its language after 1798. And after 1800 the nature of Ireland's colonial dependency had changed. The colonial elite were absorbed into the metropolitan system; Ireland was excluded from sharing in the nineteenth-century constitutional developments of colonies elsewhere.

Nor was the Ascendancy prepared to make common cause with Catholics. The latter hoped for emancipation under the Union, and constituted an important Unionist lobby. These provided unlikely allies for Fitzgibbon, the great Irish advocate of the measure, which separated out those who, like him, were ultimately committed to Britain rather than to the Anglo-Irish Ascendancy. This line is not, however, as easy to draw as it might appear. Lawyers and commercial interests were generally antipathetic. Cork was in favour, and so was the Ulster linen interest; but there was a strong Orange lobby against. Disillusioned radical intellectuals like Drennan were dismissive about what was at issue ('the old, corrupt, incoherent connection which is called by Grattan and Giffard "the Irish constitution" '[19]). And, significantly, the anti-Unionist side was fundamentally split between those who supported Catholic emancipation and those who did not.

On its first introduction in January 1799, the bill was narrowly defeated; but it continued to be pressed from London, and the anti-Unionists weakened their position by relying on general appeals to public opinion rather than mounting a broad front of alternative measures. Pressure was brought to bear within the Irish parliament in the accepted way. Castlereagh put it clearly to Camden:

> Those who thrive by the game of Parliament are in general in their hearts against it, and unless connected with their own aggrandizement in some shape will either oppose it or give it but a languid support which encourages opposition in others.[20]

Therefore the government side must fight the weapons of 'the favour and patronage of the Crown'. Jobs, places and peerages were created with an energy that brought the mechanisms for executive control of the legislature to their *reductio ad absurdum*. Contemporary conventions were observed more punctiliously than is sometimes allowed: there was much agonizing over what was, and was not, correct practice in purchasing support. But in the end, the operation tended to degenerate into a trade in 'borough stock'.

By January 1800 when parliament met, Castlereagh was fairly sure of a majority in favour. In its way, the Union was a crude political Reform Act, disenfranchising eighty boroughs, and reducing thirty-two to one member. What it did *not* do was cause economic decline, as so often subsequently stated. Certain protective legislation was retained; and though the Irish national debt did rise steeply, this was the continuation of the process whereby war had destabilized Irish finance from 1793. By 1798 the Irish government had owed its solvency only to credit from London. And the British economy was entering a revolutionary expansion, against which Ireland could never have competed.

The other thing the Union did not do was emancipate the Catholics. An impressive range of heavyweight political influence, including Pitt's and Castlereagh's, was behind such a measure; but it was short-circuited by local Ascendancy pressure (notably Fitzgibbon), and Portland's readiness to defer to it. This put paid to the British notion of diluting Irish Catholicism into the Union, rendering it a harmless minority within a united nation. But that idea in itself assumed that Ireland could, by this stage, have been absorbed – which the events and inheritance of the 1790s left a very open question.

What was that inheritance? For one thing, an organized peasant underground. Defenderism lasted in Ireland, while the United Irishmen became merely a diplomatic presence in Hamburg and Paris. And the sectarian rationale had triumphed; five Militia soldiers, sworn into the Defenders in 1799, drank a toast 'that the skin of an Orangeman might make a *parapluie* to the tree of liberty'.[21] Similarly, the Yeomanry had become Protestantized and Orange; 'loyal' meant 'Protestant'.

And subversion continued. Invasion schemes and plans for general uprisings still appeared in government reports; there was much United Irish activity in England during 1798–9, especially in London. In the summer of 1800 two United Irish emissaries visited Hamburg and Holland with a remarkably businesslike and well-informed memorandum that detailed requirements for a French invasion. Characteristically, the First Consul simulated interest while merely using the incident as a tactic in peace negotiations with Britain.

One of the emissaries was Robert Emmet,[xviii] who surfaces periodically on the international revolutionary circuit at this time; there are strong connections between his activities and the English conspiracy of Colonel Despard. The old United Irish network continued to work, if not the fully centralized conspiracies conjured up by the government (and some historians). Old 1798 men turn up as late as the underground activities of the 1820s, working through the Spenceans and other channels. In the end, Emmet mounted what seemed like his own

[xviii] Robert Emmet (1778–1803): born in Dublin; educated at Trinity College, Dublin, where he was a leader of the United Irishmen and a distinguished orator in the Historical Society; discussed Irish independence with Napoleon and Talleyrand; returned to Dublin and pressed ahead with plans for a rising, 1802; fled to the Dublin mountains; arrested by Major Sirr; eloquent in the dock, but more so in the silence of his unpronounced epitaph; hanged. Sarah, daughter of John Philpot Curran, provided the love interest in his short, romantic history.

operation in Dublin in 1803; but this was only after detailed overtures and negotiations with the French and others. The secrecy and professionalism of his preparations, and the extent of the organization among tradesmen and artisans in Dublin and provincial towns, are striking. Several of the reasons for his failure were purely contingent – shortage of artillery, unreliability of *matériel*, failure of communications with the French – and there appears to have been the potential for a decisive response in Ulster and Wicklow at least. But it fizzled out in confusion, and is remembered mainly for Emmet's attitudinizing in the dock.

His ideas were those of elite separatism; neither social idealism nor religious equality appear to have figured. He may not even have declared that no man should write his epitaph until 'my country takes her place among the nations of the earth'.[22] But he is inaccurately remembered as a noble and sacrificial dreamer, a powerful inspiration for early nineteenth-century romantics, the Little Englander Robert Southey as well as the Irish literary *émigré*, Thomas Moore.[xix] And he would take his place in the martyrology of a retrospective nationalism, whose interpretation of the late eighteenth century invariably played down the importance of the French connection, and elevated inchoate domestic failures into clear-cut moral victories.

[xix] Thomas Moore (1779–1852): born in Dublin, son of a grocer; educated at Trinity College, Dublin; friend of Robert Emmet but shunned the United Irishmen; came to England in 1800, which was to remain his home thereafter; studied law and wooed 'society'; while the *Irish Melodies*, 1807–34, appealed to a sentimental idea of Ireland that could be translated into the homeland of every guilt-ridden voluntary exile, *Captain Rock*, 1824, revealed his awareness of, and concern for, the plight of Catholics of a real rural Ireland with which he could have had little personal contact. Biographer of Sheridan, Byron and Lord Edward Fitzgerald. Later contenders for the title of 'national poet' refused to acknowledge a debt to him often revealed by their work.

PART THREE

PART THREE

CHAPTER THIRTEEN

THE MOBILIZATION OF POPULAR POLITICS

I

THE FACT OF the Union was to set the rhetorical terms of nationalist politics over the next century: and this has led to some reluctance to confront the question of how much difference it actually made. Apart from the absence of the College Green assembly, changes were ostensibly minimal – which may be a reflection of the limited nature of that assembly itself. The government of Ireland, far from being integrated with that of Britain, remained a special case. The institution of the Viceroy and his court, much criticized by radicals as an anomaly, continued. The balance of power between Viceroy and Chief Secretary remained variable, dependent upon residency, Cabinet membership and ability – though the growing power of the chief secretaryship was recognized by its status as a prime ministerial appointment, not a viceregal one. Above all, the Castle continued; with its complex machinery of patronage and contacts, manipulated politically by the Chief Secretary and administratively by the Under-Secretary, to the despair of incoming Lords Lieutenant. 'You will become very familiar before you leave Ireland,' Peel[i] caustically warned De Grey[ii] in 1841,

[i] Robert Peel (1788–1850): representation of Cashel bought for him by his father, 1809; Chief Secretary for Ireland, 1812–18; prudent in the distribution of patronage and vigorous in all aspects of his work; invited to become MP for Oxford University, 1817, in recognition of his services to Protestantism; Home Secretary 1822–7 and 1828–30; Prime Minister, November 1834–April 1835; sought to offer constructive criticism of the Whigs' Irish policy, and all aspects of government legislation while in opposition, 1835–41; Prime Minister for the second time, 1841–6; determined upon sending out 'a message of peace to Ireland', 1845; increased the Maynooth grant; established the Queen's Colleges for non-sectarian higher education; enabled to repeal the Corn Laws in consequence of the Irish Famine, 1846; resigned upon the defeat of an Irish coercion bill; fell from power before his Irish policy had matured, therefore leaving the legacy of the land question, which he saw as 'the monstrous evil' of Ireland, to his chief disciple, Gladstone.

[ii] Thomas Philip de Grey (1781–1859): first Lord of the Admiralty and Privy

'with the expression: "My father over and over again refused a peerage." '

The most notable post-Union development, in fact, built upon the established tradition of state involvement in areas like education, public health and emergency public works, where intervention became both more decisive and more extensive in Ireland than in contemporary Britain. The idea of a centralized and impartial administrative ethos was applied early on, reflecting the inefficiency of Irish local government, the inadequacy of the gentry and the poverty of the parishes. The Irish, even those who made it to Westminster as MPs, were rather left out of this. Ireland came to be seen as an appropriate area for administrative energy, and even experiment: but this was without reference to the small proportion of Irish MPs, or to any larger constituency of opinion in Ireland at large. The process could be read as evidence that, whatever the Union was doing, it was not making Ireland a little England.

But along with the pre-Union dispensation, the Protestant Ascendancy lasted on; and the Union was identified as their guarantee of protection. It imposed a constitutional brake; it would have to be undone before anything could be done. It formed the rhetorical issue of Irish politics: the thing to be for or against, the simple reason for everything. It also came to symbolize the confessional divide that remained the structural reality of Irish politics.

Intellectual life in the early nineteenth century reflected this – notably in the retailing of history, which was becoming an Irish obsession. The subtext of books like Denis Taafe's *Impartial History of Ireland* (1809–11) or Francis Plowden's *Historical Review of the State of Ireland* (1803) was really – respectively – the invalidity or the necessity of Union.[1] The Irish past, even the pre-Christian era, was enlisted into the argument; throughout, the same events were read in diametrically opposite terms by Unionists and by nationalists. And an Irish habit of historical–political argument became quickly evident: the effort to negate an opposing case by claiming that an event (1641, 1691, 1798, 1801) *should not* have happened, was thus in a sense illegitimate – and could therefore be discounted.

Political energy in the age of the Union was also manifested in less rarefied terms: what is most striking is the mobilization of Irish politics at local and national level, a process linked with modernization and,

Councillor, 1834; Lord Lieutenant of Ireland, 1841–4; impartial, but often at odds with his Chief Secretary, Lord Eliot; noted for his hospitality and encouragement of native manufacture.

ironically, Anglicization, in terms of language at least. But most of all it was closely connected with the recognition by the Catholic majority that, as the political game came to be played in terms of democratic numbers, they must be the inevitable winners.

Against this, Protestants adhered to their monopoly of offices and influence. If the Union *had* been complete, Catholics could have been given access to the spoils system of the political nation, and constituted a safely diluted minority within the United Kingdom. As it was not, they could not; and they found another route. Meanwhile, the composition of local governing bodies like grand juries and town corporations remained invincibly Protestant; though inefficiencies were tackled in the reforms of the 1830s, the composition of the ruling class was left undisturbed. The Unionist mentality transcended the many differences that stratified Protestant society; no matter how many levels of status and degrees of resentment existed between grand aristocrats, minor gentry, strong farmers, Dublin professionals and urban trades-men, if they were Protestants they were, perforce, Unionists. National-ist Ireland, largely Catholic, formed its own identity (including the exploitation of an Irish stereotype for English consumption, an oddly collusive process often reflected in the vast literature of nineteenth-century 'travels in Ireland'). In this, as in other spheres, the key figure is Daniel O'Connell.[iii]

[iii] Daniel O'Connell (1775–1847): born in Carhen, County Kerry; educated at St Omer; called to the Irish Bar, 1798; protested against the Union in his first public speech, 1800; joined the Catholic Committee; called for constant agitation, not dignified silence; opposed the vetoist policy; set up the Catholic Board, 1811; founded the Catholic Association, 1823; elected M P for County Clare, 1828, causing the crisis that led to the granting of Catholic emancipation; re-elected for County Clare, 1829; subsequently sat for Waterford, Kerry, Dublin and Cork; initiated radical legislation throughout the 1830s, believing reform a necessary prologue to repeal; ratified this policy by negotiating the 'Lichfield House Compact' with the Whigs, 1835; founded the Repeal Association, upon the prospect of Peel's return to office, 1840; first Lord Mayor of Dublin in the reformed Corporation, 1841; called off the Clontarf 'monster meeting', October 1843; prosecuted nevertheless; tried, January 1844; sentenced to a year's imprisonment, May; sentence quashed by the House of Lords, September; quarrelled with Young Ireland over education and the possibility of armed insur-rection, 1845–6; made a last appeal to the Commons that they save Ireland, February 1847; set off on a pilgrimage to Rome; died at Genoa. The greatest leader of Catholic Ireland.

II

Before considering his achievement, it is vital to stress a more visceral kind of politics; for another sphere in which the Union brought little change was that of agrarian violence. The early nineteenth century saw the proliferation of rural protest movements, the 'banditti' or 'Whiteboys' of contemporary accounts, who can be categorized, often according to locality, as Whitefeet, Threshers, Terry Alts, Rockites, Carders, Caravats, Shanavests or Ribbonmen – the last term applicable to an organization with a more generalized political view than many of the others. All, however, adhered to an alternative conception of law and government – a phenomenon invariably stressed by foreign observers, struck by their own immunity from gangs of malcontents who saw travellers as not involved in their local struggles. The political dimension was never far away, often focused in the figure of a mythic leader – like 'Captain Rock', whom Thomas Moore used for his *Memoirs of Captain Rock* (1824), satirizing the literary form of pious family biography in order to delineate the reasons for Irish disaffection.

Agrarian violence escalated in the 1830s, with what amounted to episodic warfare over the payment of Church tithes; though methods of collection had been adapted by a Composition Act in 1823, the system still burdened non-Church of Ireland members in a spectacularly inequitable way, and mobilized a wide cross-section of resentful opinion. Coercive legislation reached its apogee in the 1830s. But the geographical pattern was interesting. Clare, Tipperary and Limerick remained the epicentre, for no very obvious reason, except to bear out the classic contemporary diagnosis by George Cornewall Lewis: where soil was fertile, the population dense, and the peasantry 'one degree removed above the lowest level of poverty', violence would recur. Recent aerial surveys show a notable concentration of deserted villages in this area, which were certainly populous centres in the early nineteenth century.

Where an area became known for rural violence, a self-perpetuating dynamic was probably created; there were also structural reasons in the tensions of the Irish agrarian economy, which will be considered more fully in the next chapter. These could vary. Some secret societies seem to have been formed from small-scale consumers and labourers marginalized by the wartime boom, bereft of leases and facing inflated rents and prices. Others may have been the victims of economic dislocation following 1815. To judge by the demands articulated, many organizations reflected changing patterns of agriculture: 'the struggle of the peasant to remain on the land in the face of pressures to turn him into an agricultural or industrial labourer'.[2]

This was the background to the Whiteboy revival, especially in Munster; inference from transportation figures and imperfect court records implies the existence of several thousand Whiteboys active over the first half of the nineteenth century, across several counties. The lower (but not lowest) levels of the peasantry, with some urban artisans, seem to have predominated; the classic picture of hedge schoolmasters as conduits of subversion is also borne out by court records. Structures of recruitment and involvement could be quite formal, stressing the importance of local reputation and respectable family connections. What is not generally apparent is evidence of a nationalist or crusading motivation: the exception being Ribbonism, a movement that was anti-Protestant, with nationalist and sectarian overtones inherited from eighteenth-century Defenderism. It was strongly based among the Dublin artisans, as well as forming contacts with the agrarian Whiteboys and Rockites in the early 1820s. Active in protectionism and intimidation, with links to the nascent trade union movement, it inculcated the vital aspect of all the secret societies: solidarity. 'I was a very experienced Ribbonman,' recalled one informer regretfully in 1841, 'and delighted in that business; it was the pleasantest that could be found, for there was more real friendship in it than in any other society in the world; was in it when a boy, and like it in my heart still'.[3]

In all the societies traditionalism was stressed, in the rituals of masks, white shirts worn over clothes while out on a raid, the formal appointment of 'captains', the association with the high point of rural festivals, the symbolic transvestism. Tactics were equally traditional: the arms-raid, the threatening letter, the disguised visit at midnight, the mutilation of animals as well as people. Most of all, there was a commitment to a traditional notion of custom, and of solidarity: 'the cause', which did not need to be defined. A consciousness of conflicting interests, and of invasion of rights, can be discerned, if not of 'class' conflict per se. The eighteenth-century Whiteboy's supposition that a right relationship between landlord and tenant was possible is less obvious. It was this sense of solidarity and readiness for confrontation that O'Connellism would later tap.

Eventually, trapped in the rising spiral of agrarian violence, the Whig government in the 1830s would first try to intervene in tithe collection, then increasingly withdraw their support, and eventually, in 1838, cancel arrears and convert tithes to a rent charge. But the issue did not always appear so identifiable: before 1815, there were persistent rumours of Bonapartism among the peasantry, and after the war allegations of close connections with contemporary radical movements in Britain persisted. The state of the law in Ireland rapidly became one of the pressing issues of the day.

British political opinion interpreted this, in Peel's words, as 'the Irishman's natural predilection for outrage and a lawless life which I believe nothing can control'. The failure of rural authority, with magistrates both partial and pusillanimous, was compounded by an incomprehensible preference for lawbreaking and acceptance of outlawry. Cornewall Lewis was more perceptive; a realization of the legitimization concept lies behind his famous description of the secret societies as 'a vast trades union for the protection of the Irish peasantry'. The official mind, however, was more receptive to a solution by means of police reform, one of the key areas where Irish innovation outpaced English developments.

The existent arrangement of magistrates and constables, reinforced by the military, was obviously insufficient; the crisis of public order in 1812–13 prompted unsuccessful experiments in the role of both magistrates and militia. From 1814, Peel as Chief Secretary was drafting plans for a new 'Peace Preservation Force' involving a resident chief magistrate with an 'extraordinary establishment' of police for proclaimed districts – a system that was later developed into an all-Ireland county constabulary. Even in the comparatively calm years from 1826 to 1830, 84 people were killed and 112 wounded in clashes with the police, who were attacked bitterly by Catholic politicians. By 1831, 183 disablement pensions were being paid out. From 1829 Peel, fresh from organizing the London Metropolitan Police, turned his mind to reorganizing the Irish police, visualizing a strictly neutral force, nominated by central government, and removed from the authority of the magistracy. Though his plans were abandoned after opposition in Parliament, they were later given legislative form by the Whigs in 1836. This happened only after the involvement of the constabulary in tithe collection had been bitterly resented, and after the general inefficiency of the magistracy had forced the government to circumvent them by a severe Peace Preservation Act (1833) and the institution of courts martial for the agrarian offenders.

Under the regime of Thomas Drummond[iv] the inspectorate was reorganized; magistrates lost the right to appoint constabulary; and attempts to ensure impartiality were made by forbidding the police to enrol in 'political or secret societies', or, indeed, to vote. The system that had emerged, named the Royal Irish Constabulary from 1867, was a centralized, paramilitary force, with officers who also acted as stipendiary magistrates. It would be the blueprint for later colonial police forces throughout the British Empire.

This response, however efficient, shows little recognition of the psychological reality behind rural unrest. Generally, the rationale of the secret societies was strictly logical; but tension, and the fear of dearth, ran at a high enough level in the 1820s to produce the kind of millennial expectations classic in a marginalized rural society exposed to such pressures. These were often focused around the phenomenally popular *Prophecies* of Pastorini, promising a delivery from bondage and the destruction of Protestantism, in the year 1825. Possibly by using the networks of Ribbonmen printers, the *Prophecies* were disseminated with extraordinary speed, especially in County Limerick. The sense of crisis and impending apocalypse was not peculiar to rural Catholicism; Protestant pamphlets and even fiction of the time indicate a similar intensity of feeling. And it has been claimed that millennialism was *less* characteristic of the Irish peasant consciousness than might be expected, since Anglophobia provided a secular substitute (though in the case of Pastorini, the two worked together). But in agitations like the Rockite movement of the early 1820s, millennial expectations acted as a kind of cement, binding landless labourers and small farmers together. The Rockites, alone among secret societies, burned down Protestant churches, expressing a reaction to Protestant proselytism, the Orange Yeomanry and the new constabulary.

Significantly, anti-Protestant millennialism was as much of an embarrassment to O'Connell's Catholic emancipation movement as were the Rockites; O'Connell stigmatized the Pastorini craze as an

---

[iv] Thomas Drummond (1797–1840): born and educated in Edinburgh; entered the Royal Engineers, 1815; joined the Ordnance Survey for Scotland, 1815, and Ireland, 1824; headed the Boundary Commission in connection with the 1832 Reform Act; Under-Secretary for Ireland, 1835–40; ensured that the spirit of the reforms of the early 1830s was realized; stressed that 'Property had duties as well as rights'; mainspring of the Irish Railway Commission, 1836; buried in Ireland, his home by adoption. The success of the government of Ireland during his era reflects much personal credit, but also the fact that he worked well in a good administrative team, headed by Lords Mulgrave and Morpeth.

ultra-Protestant plot. But the relationship between the so-called 'banditti' and the O'Connellite Catholic Association that dominated Irish public life for the second half of the 1820s is of great interest. In this period, secret societies were notably quiescent. Were they following a new, universal leader, as the Castle authorities characteristically alleged? Or, by a less clear-cut process, was the Catholic Association providing the kind of identity previously affirmed by joining the Caravats, Shanavests or Terry Alts?

Certainly, there is some local evidence of traditionally opposed factions uniting in support of O'Connell. Yet several of the targets of peasant assassination were, in political life, important lieutenants of O'Connell's movement; and O'Connell's followers sometimes formed *ad hoc* vigilante organizations against Whiteboyism. The objective interests of middle-class Catholic organizers and the marginal rural classes were certainly not the same. But this did not mean that O'Connellism, which had its own millenarian dimension, did not answer some of the same needs. Above all, the shape of Irish party politics would owe much to the underground tradition of local agitation. Political mobilization in Ireland anticipated industrial and commercial modernization; in such a context, peasant loyalties and power-structures would last on.

III

The more obvious face of democratic mobilization was the Catholic movement – which was formally opposed to the world of the secret societies. Middle-class Catholics rapidly became part of the unofficial establishment; in 1835 Gustave de Beaumont would note that this class 'seems almost dazzled by its own splendour. It scarcely believes in so magnificent an elevation succeeding so rapidly to so great degradation.' But this process had antedated Catholic emancipation. From the early nineteenth century, Church discipline and organization had been strengthened to cope with the inexorable rise in population; a cadre of leaders evolved, trained at Carlow or Maynooth. On the one hand, this aroused the predictable atavistic paranoia among Protestants; on the other, there is the spectacle of George IV visiting Ireland in 1821 and respectfully meeting the Catholic hierarchy in full panoply. The King was noticeably drunk; but he would still have had to make the gesture stone-cold sober.

In 1821 the granting of 'emancipation' – full rights of political representation and civil office-holding – was still on the agenda; a limited measure had just been passed by the Commons and rejected by the Lords. Another bill in 1825 seemed so sure of passing that O'Connell unwisely accepted the attached restrictions (government payment of clergy and disenfranchisement of the forty-shilling free-holder vote); but it too failed in the Lords. From the mid-1820s, however, his manipulation of a new style of popular politics would make such scruples irrelevant. By then, the principle of emancipation was the priority – not the restrictions supposed necessary for Irish conditions.

The background to O'Connellism did not comprise only, or even principally, the dispossessed rural classes. By the 1820s the Catholic gentry and large commercial interests of towns like Waterford had evolved a 'liberal Catholic' politics, using, oddly but effectively, Whig constitutional traditions and some Radical nostrums to claim access to democratic institutions: the Catholic middle class forged in the eighteenth century was coming into its own. As usual, Irish history was also enlisted – notably the broken treaty of Limerick. And contemporary precedents in Spain were instanced (much as Poles, Czechs and Slavs would later use O'Connell for *their* own purposes).

Nationalism, or even anti-Unionism, was not a necessary part of this; Catholic emancipationists could be liberal Unionists, as were Thomas Wyse,[v] Thomas Moore and Bishop James Doyle of Kildare and Leighlin.[vi] But the language and implications of Catholic organization were inescapably radical and could threaten separation. Doyle could warn the government in a public letter of May 1824 that 'if a

[v] Thomas Wyse (1791–1862): born on the manor of St John, County Waterford; educated at Stonyhurst and Trinity College, Dublin; married Letitia Bonaparte, 1821; separated 1828; strategist of the return of a liberal Protestant in County Waterford, 1826; his tactics in marshalling the forty-shilling freeholders adopted by O'Connell at Clare, 1828; historian of the Catholic Association, 1829; MP for County Tipperary, 1830–32, and Waterford, 1835–47; a minister under the Whigs, 1839–41 and 1846–9; British Minister at Athens, 1849; knighted, 1856. An architect of the national education and provincial college schemes. Never a Repealer, but an instinctive federalist.

[vi] James Warren Doyle (1786–1834): born in New Ross; educated Coimbra; fought for the Spaniards and acted as an interpreter for the British in the Peninsular Wars; ordained, 1809; Professor at Carlow College, 1813; Bishop of Kildare and Leighlin, 1819; published his *Vindication of the Irish Catholics*, 1824, and *Letters on the State of Ireland*, 1824–5, under the initials 'JKL'; gave valuable evidence to various parliamentary commissions on Ireland, 1825–32; a respected pastoral reformer. The first influential prelate to join the Catholic Association, but universally regarded as an ecclesiastical statesman rather than a political priest.

rebellion were raging from Carrickfergus to Cape Clear, no sentence of excommunication would ever be fulminated by a Catholic prelate'. This was almost certainly untrue, but it showed that Catholicism could now afford offensive tactics.

What changed from the early 1820s was the relationship of Catholic leadership to the masses. Up to then, pressure-groups working for Catholic interests had always been inhibited by the necessity of accepting government involvement in Church administration as a *quid pro quo*: they were reliant on support from English allies who saw no reason not to acquiesce. This was altered when Daniel O'Connell harnessed the masses in his Catholic Association, founded in 1823 and subsequently reconstituted to avoid prosecution. Support was overwhelming across Munster and Leinster (Connacht, oddly, never became a stronghold). It was an open, accountable mass movement, funded by the 'Catholic Rent' subscribed at a small rate by hundreds of thousands: a penny a month rapidly created a vast income (£20,000 was funded in nine months). Less tangibly, the principle of subscription provided the masses with a sense of commitment, and gave the leaders a barometer of support.

What did the Association do in return? It worked for tenants, for the Church, for the whole Catholic community. It was often accused of planning to become an alternative parliament; in fact, it specifically denied such an ambition, but it became a potent threat when the Association started taking over electoral influence in the later 1820s, after the fiasco of the 1825 Bill. The central organization began to vet new parliamentary candidates; pledges were required; a safe return could effectively be ensured, given the importance of the forty-shilling freeholder Catholic vote (a privilege not possessed by their co-religionists in England). The local agents, almost invariably priests, relayed information about rights like petitioning parliament: a political education was put in process. From early on, O'Connell adroitly cast a line towards the Reform party in England – a policy ingeniously combined with the enlistment of priests as free members, exhorted to exercise their civil rights of political organization, to the trepidation of some of his colleagues. The politicizing process was fired by a sense of a crusade: 'There is a moral electricity,' said O'Connell, 'in the continuous expression of public opinion concentrated on a single point.'

This had to be backed up by the implicit threat of mass disobedience, of a unilateral withdrawal of allegiance, even of a refusal to recognize the legitimacy of the state. O'Connell's achievement was to indicate this while maintaining a commitment to pacific principles: but it is unlikely that it could have been as effective without the ominous precedent of Whiteboyism and Ribbonism.

There is a further paradox here, when the actual composition of O'Connell's lieutenants is analysed. Lawyers were noticeably prominent: barristers on circuit, like O'Connell himself, spread the organization of the Association, another reason for its geographical distribution. Prosperous farmers, businessmen, the urban merchant community and newspaper editors were also much in evidence. They were adept at playing the numbers game in terms of electoral pressure. One notable example was Thomas Wyse, a politically minded Waterford gentleman; and Waterford was where, in 1826, Protestant influence at the polls was decisively challenged, and beaten. Populism and clerical influence had arrived openly in Irish politics.

Confrontation escalated with the accession to power of Wellington and Peel — not themselves ultra-Protestants, but supposedly representative of ultra opinion. O'Connell tapped the potential of the county elections — often uncontested after 1800, and hitherto treated as sewn-up cases. Unlike the boroughs, however, votes were widely dispersed among Catholics, notably tenants holding land on the term of a life, which qualified as a freehold. Landlords had retained the rights of such potential voters in case of a contest; O'Connell liberated them. Even before the confrontation tactics embarked upon after 1825, this was clear; as Goulbourn reported to Peel in 1824, 'it is not concealed that whenever an election shall take place the people will be placed in opposition to their landlords and such members only returned as shall please the Association'.[4]

The famous Waterford election of 1826 was steered by propertied local Catholics (Wyses, Gallweys, Meaghers, Hayeses) and backed by liberal Protestants, who feared further destabilization. This element also provided the candidate. The organization involved salaried agents, registration books, travel facilities for outlying voters, and a controversially high profile taken by priests, even if it was exaggerated by the defeated Beresford interest. The funds of the Catholic Association were used to provide alternative employment, or even housing, to those harassed by the Beresfords for deserting them. In 1828, the year when Catholic churchwardens took over collecting the Catholic rent for O'Connell, the fund raised was £22,700. The result was a great reversal for the Ascendancy, and it was followed by others. Tactics varied, as did local conditions; but the overall message was the same. Half the county constituencies in 1826 were the scenes of a new kind of political struggle; in most of them the landlord interest was clearly vanquished. Peel put the issue clearly, in his terms:

The old question still remains: Are these things the mere effect of artificial distinctions and disqualifying laws, or is there a deeper cause for them in the spirit of popery, in a state of society in which the land belongs to one religion, and the physical strength to another, and in a bigoted priesthood so independent of all authority that it would be almost better they should be dependent on the Pope?[5]

O'Connell was now the focal figure of Irish politics, and had also achieved an international reputation. His protean energy embraced a number of overlapping, and in a sense conflicting, reputations. He could be seen as a European radical – educated in France, like many sons of the Catholic gentry, he had imbibed 'French ideas' of the liberal Catholic variety (and his career was to be a considerable influence on Lamennais). He declared allegiance to the theories of Bentham and Godwin, though not very clearly. He was a passionate anti-slaver – not only in the British imperial context, but also in the United States, which did not endear him to Irish America or to some of his more Carlylean colleagues in the Young Ireland movement. He was also a great legal performer, endlessly skilled in the vagaries of English and Irish law, and built a legendary reputation (and income) as a barrister, celebrated and preserved in Irish folklore.

But perhaps most importantly, his background blended Gaelic clansmen and local Catholic gentry. Ignorant of Ulster, having rarely if ever been north of Monaghan, his roots were deep in the Irish-speaking family fief of Kerry where he was reared, the scion of rich, adaptable survivors, the O'Connells of Derrynane. Fostered out to a local family, his first language was Irish, but he was not the 'man of the people' that his European admirers often supposed. His Kerry persona was naturally seigniorial, and enabled him to dismiss the Irish language robustly as a drawback in the modern world, which earned him the disapproval of later nationalists. It also gave him a genuine feeling for popular politics, and an ability to identify with the people. Though O'Connell had youthfully flirted with the United Irishmen in the 1790s, the contrast with Tone's condescension towards 'Poor Pat' could not be greater. In private life he was an indulgent landlord, and in his opinions generally antipathetic to factory reform and to many trade unions (though not all); he believed the state should readjust the economic balance between landlord and tenant, but that industrial workers should be waged out of profits and rewarded according to performance.

Rather than a Benthamite economist, he was really a liberal Catholic moralist.

O'Connell's self-presentation in his letters[6] bears examination: grandiose and self-mocking at once. He loved organizations, bands, public show, emotion, uniforms; the newly fashionable iconography of wolf-dogs, round towers, twining shamrocks, and classic poses suited him perfectly.[vii] He was above all a Catholic leader, playing the Catholic card. From early on, in his speeches against the Union, he insisted on the unreality of sectarian divisions, declaring a rhetorical preference for Penal Laws under an Irish Protestant regime rather than liberty beneath English government; but later comments in public and private are less conciliatory, though he never lost sight of the importance of Protestant support.

From 1826 Catholic emancipation was inevitably on the agenda: apart from upheavals in Ireland, it was a powerful card in the Whig game after Liverpool's death. Though individual members were anti-Catholic, the Whig Party was pro-emancipation, and Whig politicians began exchanging collusive letters with O'Connell early on. The emancipation *coup* was in the end delivered by the threat posed when O'Connell himself was elected at Clare (ruthlessly pillorying a decent pro-Catholic opponent in the process). It was a vast demonstration of populist political organization, and clerical power: 'a solemn and religious ceremony', according to O'Connell. Priestly influence had managed to dent that of the landlords. And it presented the possibility of a secessionist parliament constituted of mandated but unlawful Catholic MPs, returned by well-drilled Catholic freeholders.

Government opinion now felt the Irish forty-shilling freeholders must be got rid of, even at the price of Catholic emancipation. As Peel put it, 'the instrument of deference and supremacy had been converted into a weapon fatal to the authority of the landlord'. In the legislation of 1829 a general Oath of Allegiance, unexceptionable for Catholics, was introduced, and state offices, apart from a few very grand exceptions, opened to them. At the same time, a string of minor restrictions about modes of worship and tithes were instituted; the Catholic Association was dissolved; against all O'Connell's public efforts, though in line with some of his private prejudices, the forty-shilling freeholders were disenfranchised by raising the threshold of county voting qualifications to ten pounds. The boroughs were left untouched; though spectacularly corrupt, they were corrupt in the Protestant interest.

[vii] It is preserved to bravura effect in the monumental silverwork of the period.

Thus liberation for Catholics was accompanied by a drastic reduction in the county voters, from 216,000 down to 37,000.[7] This measure was supported by English Whigs, and many Irish-Catholic activists – including urban chambers of commerce – were not particularly sorry. The passing of the forty-shillingers, always easily dragooned whether by their landlords or their priests, was not greatly noted at the time. Far more important was the fact that Catholic emancipation had been passed, and the manner of its passing. The results might be negligible in most areas; many areas of public life remained a Protestant monopoly, though, for instance, this did not apply to legal offices under Drummond's under-secretaryship, when O'Connell's influence was at its height in government circles. A Catholic middle-class 'ascendancy', already in the making, was given a vital psychological boost. Wellington (who from December 1825 had been looking for a conciliatory settlement) described the Catholic clergy, nobility, lawyers and gentry as 'a sort of *theocracy*', governing Ireland with the backing of Rome. As he went on to point out, the exclusion of Catholics from formal power had not succeeded in restricting their social power – or, as it happened, their political influence. In 1829 their claims, made manifest, created a formal constitutional revolution.

IV

By the 1830s the confessional basis of Irish political identification had become highly accentuated. The first few decades of the Union saw 'the creation of a distinctly Protestant political culture'[8] – and one that contained its own conflicts between Whiggish Ascendancy values and the openly sectarian attitudes of the urban bourgeoisie. This was amplified by the effects of the Reform Act, introducing a residency qualification, excluding non-resident freemen, and increasing the freeholder vote: the result was a concentration of political organization within boroughs, and the formalizing of existent sectarian feeling. Popular Protestantism became a coherent force in urban politics. This was in turn reinforced by the boom in Protestant evangelicalism from the early nineteenth century, epitomized by the Hibernian Bible Society (1806), the Religious Tract and Book Society (1810), and the countless smaller organizations gathered under the umbrella of the Irish Evangelical Society. The 'Second Reformation' was hailed in a torrent of pamphlets, and in sermons; from 1819 to 1833 the Religious

Tract and Book Society claimed to have distributed over a million tracts. The actual state of the Church of Ireland bore little relation to the fervent ideal of a civilizing mission in the steps of St Patrick (who was appropriated by Protestant antiquarians as an avatar of the Reformed Irish Church). As with Protestant politics, the psychology was that of a minority on the defensive.

Ulster, as usual, was different. Presbyterianism in this period was splitting between the fundamentalism of Henry Cooke[viii] and the 'New Light' doctrines of Henry Montgomery;[ix] significantly, Cooke (in some ways a Protestant analogue of O'Connell) became the dominant figure, closely connected with New Reformation ideology. Cooke's ascendancy indicated that Ulster had little use for political and theological liberalism by the 1820s; there, economic prosperity was already identified with the Union. 'Look at Belfast and be a Repealer if you can', demanded Cooke. 'When I was a youth I remember it almost a village. But what a glorious sight does it now present − the masted grove within our harbour − our mighty Warehouses teeming with the wealth of every climate . . . all this we owe to the Union.'[9]

At the same time the Orange Order had changed its composition and gone through several vicissitudes before becoming both strengthened and radicalized in the 1820s; the question of Orange demonstrations and public order was a permanent headache for the administration. The character of the movement remained continuously adaptable − at some times a political lobby, at others a social club. Baron Smith in 1813 described the attitudes of northern Orangemen as

a spurious and illiberal loyalty which grows up amongst the vulgar classes, and which is very turbulent, bigoted, riotous and affronting, very saucy, and overbearing, almost proud of transgression, necessarily producing exasperation, and often leading to the effusion of blood. It is a rebellious and insurrectionary propensity gone astray, and running contradictorily in the channel of Allegiance.[10]

[viii] Henry Cooke (1788–1865): born in Londonderry; educated at Glasgow; ordained, 1808; settled, for life, at the church built especially for him in May Street, Belfast, 1829; drove the Unitarians from the Synod of Ulster, 1829; opposed the national education system, 1831, and secured state aid for the Synod's own scheme, 1840; architect of Protestant union, proclaiming the 'banns' of a political *mariage de convenance* between Episcopalians and Presbyterians, 1834; challenged O'Connell to debate Repeal in Belfast, 1841.

[ix] Henry Montgomery (1788–1865): born in County Antrim; educated at Glasgow; advocate of Catholic emancipation; founder of the remonstrant Synod of Ulster, 1829; remained liberal in politics. As the father of non-subscribing Presbyterianism, his religious radicalism weakened him against Cooke.

After O'Connell's electoral success, the growth of local ultra-Tory 'Brunswick Clubs' escalated: more than just a continuation of Orange-ism by other means, they mobilized many who would not otherwise have become active. Forming Clubs might be seen as potentially subversive in England, but was considered a reasonable an.l necessary response in Ireland – especially Ulster. Irish Brunswickism was evan-gelical, anti-Catholic, aristocratic in leadership, but dominated at the lieutenant level by lawyers and clergymen, and lower down by work-ing-class cohorts; there were nearly 200 Clubs throughout Ireland by 1828.

Attempts to coax liberal Protestants into a countering assertion produced nothing like the same commitment. Hard-line Protestantism was able, however, to commandeer the state-founded 'Kildare Place Society', intended to subsidize non-denominational elementary edu-cation, but soon heavily tainted with proselytism. When the Whig administration of the 1830s tried to set up a National Board of Edu-cation that represented a religious cross-section, it was similarly doomed. The Board subsidized teachers' salaries and set up 'model schools', teaching a utilitarian diet of values that might be seen as a rather crude attempt at social control, but were at least secular. They therefore pleased nobody. The Church of Ireland founded its own Church Education Society: the Presbyterians used the scheme to fund its own denominational schools; the Catholic hierarchy eventually withdrew support too.

Here, as elsewhere, the identification with Protestantism was seen as the *sine qua non* of Unionist survival. Catholic emancipation, which had been favoured by many Protestants, was only part of the motiv-ation; Whig legislation, and O'Connell's campaign for the Repeal of the Union, were equally important. The language of the apo-calyptically anti-Catholic Dublin Protestant Operative Association, led by the Revd Tresham Gregg,[x] responded to Repeal with a violent rhetoric that dominated working-class Protestant politics. In towns like Cork, which had its own Protestant Operative Association, Protestant

[x] Tresham Dames Gregg (*c.* 1800–1881): born Dublin; educated at Trinity College, Dublin; ordained, 1826; a powerful controversialist in the extreme Protestant cause; deprived of his official appointments on this account by Archbishop Whately, 1832; remained chaplain of the suffragan parish of St Nicholas-Within until death; popular leader of the Dublin Protestant democracy in the 1830s and 1840s, ensuring it remained an anti-Whiggish, anti-O'Connellite but also anti-Peelite force: author of *Protestant Ascendancy Vindicated*, 1840, *Free Thoughts on Protestant Matters*, 1846, and innumerable other tracts, pamphlets and plays.

political energy was mobilized against the influence of new Catholic money as well as the landed Ascendancy interest. The figure of the insecure 'commercial' or *petit bourgeois* urban Protestant is too often forgotten (as is that of the chronically underpaid Protestant curate, whose income was put on the line by the tithe agitation).

The political proving-grounds of this class were the unreformed town corporations. The events of 1800 to 1832 freed them from aristocratic domination; from being automatic mechanisms for returning MPs to parliament, they became battlegrounds for patronage and local power in which the moneyed Catholic interest played a part. From the 1820s the language of sectarian division dominated corporation politics. Orangeism had a role to play; though legislation against unlawful societies had threatened it since the 1820s, and the Order was formally dissolved in 1836, this was caused as much by conspiratorial allegations in Britain as by events in Ireland. There, the movement maintained a lively existence at local levels, forming, like the Masonic Order, part of the social cement of Protestantism in the new era.

From 1830 such reactions were aggravated by Whig policy. In 1833 the Irish Church Temporalities Act indicated that the government was prepared to use the state to reform the Church, suppressing ten bishoprics and intervening in the administration of sparsely populated parishes. The Irish Church became the key cause for English Tories, too: 'the field of battle,' said John Wilson Croker,[xi] 'in which we are to fight for all our property and all our institutions'. At the same time, the sense of Protestant beleaguerment was heightened by crisis in the textile trades, and by measures like the 1840 Municipal Reform Act, opening the corporation electorates to ten-pound householders. One of the noted orators against the 'popish ascendancy' threatened by municipal reform was Isaac Butt:[xii] a figure representative of the young

[xi] John Wilson Croker (1780–1857): born in Galway; educated at Trinity College, Dublin; called to the Irish Bar, 1802; satirized Irish society in his *Intercepted Letter from Canton*, 1804; *State of Ireland Past and Present*, 1808, an important pro-Catholic pamphlet history; MP for Downpatrick, 1807–12, and Athlone, 1812–18; represented various English constituencies, 1818–27 and 1830–32; unsuccessfully contested the prized Dublin University seat, 1818, which he was to hold only from 1827–30; Secretary to the Admiralty, 1809–30; associated with the *Quarterly* from its foundation, 1809; retired from Westminster upon the passing of the Reform Bill, 1832. First to apply the term 'conservative' to the Tories, 1830, for which 'cant' he was pilloried by Macaulay and Disraeli.

[xii] Isaac Butt (1813–70): born in County Donegal; co-founder of the *Dublin University Magazine*, 1833, the organ of intellectual Irish Toryism; Professor of Political

lawyers, academics and journalists grouped round the *Dublin University Magazine*, who determined from the 1830s to assert an identity that was Protestant, Unionist and Irish. The ideology of this group was based on making the Union work, and also on asserting their Irishness; they included many names later prominent in Irish politics and litera- ture. But their emphasis on the validity of Protestant Irishness was in effect divisive, since it amounted to a Protestant claim on traditions also claimed by Catholics. And by 1840 the two were divided into mutually exclusive political camps.

Most of all, Ulster defined itself as separate – for economic as well as religious reasons.[xiii] O'Connellism implicitly admitted this, and spoke of 'invading' the province to rescue 'our Persecuted Brethren in the North' – though in the event, he tended to leave Ulster strictly alone. A Catholic 'mission' to spread the word of Catholic emancipation in County Monaghan during September 1828 brought about a con- frontation with incensed Protestants that nearly resulted in a massacre. And from 1829, in the complex chequerboard of Irish political allegiance, the north was generally the electoral preserve of the con- servatives.

Irish politics after 'emancipation' would set hard into a sectarian mould, though O'Connell tried hard to deny the process. 'There is no longer a Catholic party opposed to a Protestant party,' he declared in 1833. 'The fading remnant of the Ascendancy is at one side, the Universal People at the other.' But a Wicklow land agent recorded a different local reality only the year before: 'Our politics are a curious commodity. They are mere county politics and have little or nothing to do with any general principle or feeling save that of Catholic versus Protestant.'[11] Certainly, what did *not* happen was the 'great moral and political change' anticipated by O'Connell's activist lieutenants like

Economy, Trinity College, Dublin, 1836–40; called to the Irish Bar, 1838; brilliantly, but hopelessly, defended the exclusively Protestant Dublin Corporation at the Bar of the House of Lords, 1840; O'Connell's leading opponent in the debates on Repeal in the reformed Corporation, 1843; QC, 1844; allowed himself to express the depths of his national feeling, in the early 1840s, in economic tracts and prose fiction, while remaining an Orange Tory in party politics; defended Smith O'Brien and T. F. Meagher, 1848, and the Fenians, 1865–8; Conservative MP for Youghal, 1852–65; President of the Amnesty Association, 1869; founder of the Home Government Association, 1870; Home Rule MP for Limerick, 1871–9; his decease marked the end of the law-respecting tradition of constitutional nationalism. Great and flawed in private as in public life: a beatific sinner.

[xiii] See below, pp. 321, 342, 388–9.

Sheil.[xiv] Protestant monopolies continued in spheres like the civil service, the police and legal appointments – as every observer pointed out through the 1830s and 1840s. At the same time, urban and local police acquired a sectarian edge; so did agrarian grievances. What mattered about Catholic emancipation's significance lay in the expectations held out of the measure, and the method of its passing, rather than the direct effects of the Act itself.

V

Thomas Wyse found rural Ireland less interested in passionate discussion of ideas than the towns, but often more vehemently sectarian; the emotional dynamic that sustained O'Connellism was rurally based. County elections certainly became increasingly aggressive from the 1830s, boisterousness turning to violence. But in the immediate post-emancipation period, what is most striking is the inheritance of a spreading structure of urban 'Liberal Clubs', which had capitalized on the political energies released by the 1826 general election campaign and continued in existence. Again, Waterford provides an example, with Thomas Wyse the key influence. From the late 1820s Liberal Clubs spread through Leinster and east Munster – effectively, local political machines for the Catholic Association, but with an appeal that outlasted the issue.

How far were these clubs 'liberal' and how far Catholic? Wyse, who early on had an eye to Waterford municipal government, emphasized that the local Club 'abhorred exclusions, monopolies and oppressions of all kinds, but none more than those created or continued by religion, ignorance and intolerance ... whether Catholic or Protestant'. There was even some Catholic clerical opposition in County Waterford. The outlines for organization were wide-ranging and ambitious; in Cork, the proto-socialist philosopher William Thompson[xv] was prominent.

[xiv] Richard Lalor Sheil (1791–1851): born in County Kilkenny; educated at Stony-hurst and Trinity College, Dublin; called to the Irish Bar, 1814; wrote, with some success, for the Dublin and London stage, 1814–20; O'Connell's chief opponent on the veto question, seeking to conciliate liberal Protestant opinion; further distanced himself from O'Connell after 1829; MP for various Irish constituencies, 1831–51; Vice-President of the Board of Trade, 1839; defended John O'Connell, 1844; Master of the Mint, 1846; British Minister at Tuscany, 1851.

[xv] William Thompson (1775–1833): born in County Cork; wealthy landowner and critical student of Bentham, Godwin and Owen; published *An Inquiry into the*

Subcommittees were formed on issues of local grievance; the leadership cadres were drawn from the well-off merchant and professional classes, with strong links to local chambers of commerce. A few liberal Protestants took office, though they tended to worry about the close association of the Clubs with the collection of Catholic Rent.

The Clubs provided, in short, a political education. After 1829 they continued as 'News Rooms', 'Reading Clubs' or 'Independent Clubs', and, though many lapsed or were commandeered by landlord interference, some helped to perpetuate the radical element that emerged within the Catholic Association, speaking the language of separation and republicanism in accents unwelcome to O'Connell and Wyse. They were the portent of difficulties to come.

Much of the political energy transmitted by the Club movement was directed into the movement for Repeal of the Union. This is usually portrayed as the logical continuation of O'Connell's early career; in fact, it really represented a contradiction. For one thing, those who attacked the Union refused to admit that Catholic emancipation would hardly have been possible without it. And if 'Repeal' meant a return to the *status quo ante* 1800, this was a nonsense; since the constitutional revolution of 1829–32, such a step would mean a Catholic, nationalist assembly, which would be utterly incompatible with the traditional Castle scenario. The trick was never to define what Repeal meant – or did not mean. Later, in the Home Rule era, Repeal came to be shorthand for the unacceptable face of nationalism; 'We all declare against Repeal,' remarked one moderate, 'and then put whatever meaning we like upon the declaration.'

By 'Repeal' O'Connell probably meant, first, a recognition of the illegitimacy of the Union; and then negotiation of an alternative mechanism of government. He was still, however, conscious of the need of some connection:

A parliament inferior to the British parliament I would accept as an instalment ... if it were offered me by a competent authority. It must first be offered to me – mark that – I will never seek it ... I will never ask for or work for any other, save an independent legislative [*sic*], but if others offer me a sub-

---

Distribution of Wealth, 1824, and an *Appeal* for the equality of the sexes, 1825; his property, which he willed to the co-operative movement, was later wrested back by his family. A pioneering socialist, he was quoted by Marx, whom the Webbs called 'Thompson's disciple'. Added atheism and vegetarianism to his sins against convention.

ordinate parliament, I will close with any such authorized offer and accept that offer.[12]

Pushed to it, he would indicate a conservative measure of self-government: 'one King, two legislatures'. But the parliament would logically be Catholic and native Irish.

The caution with which political reform was applied to Ireland strengthened his resolve.[xvi] But 'Repeal' remained an emotional claim, shaded into the broad spectrum of Radicalism. O'Connell's invocations of the spirit of 1782, not to mention loyalty to the Queen, indicated that the demand was limited as well as unspecific: 'an invitation to treat', in Oliver MacDonagh's words. The ideal was to force the British into offering *something*, and negotiate from there.

Much of this was necessitated by immediate political difficulties. The English opposition, with whom O'Connell and his parliamentary followers had to collaborate, were uninterested in Repeal, an issue contemptuously dismissed even by most Radicals. Irish Protestants were, of course, invincibly opposed. While O'Connell was strengthened by good results in the 1832–3 election, and enabled to engage in balance-holding experiments at Westminster that produced favourable legislative results, these tactics were not electorally effective in Ireland. There, a great campaign mobilized much more dramatic support – and appealed more obviously to O'Connell's fragmented and near-indefinable electoral base. The structure of traditional patterns of local 'influence' continued in many areas: a matter of competing threats. Thus from the mid-1830s O'Connell had to combine an uneasy alliance with the Whigs, with tightrope-walking over the legality of his ultimate objectives. The tactics were in a sense interdependent; with the Whigs out of power after 1841, the Repeal campaign was renewed with tremendous éclat, 1843 being boldly nominated 'Repeal Year' – which brought the whole issue uncomfortably near definition at last.

There were other pressures, too: notably the background of agrarian violence that was focused on the tithe issue, since this was an O'Connellite cause as well. The 'Tithe War' escalated violently in the 1830s, partly due to hysterical overreaction by police and clergy, before the eventual resolution that tithed income should be converted to a once-

---

[xvi] The Representation of the People (Ireland) Act of 1832 added only five seats to the existing one hundred, and introduced a ten-pound franchise in the boroughs; the electorate now numbered 92,141 (1.2 per cent of the population). For the terms of the 1850 Franchise Act, see p. 343 below.

for-all rent charge creating a general fund for clerical costs. It was this development, and the debate over the state's right to 'appropriate' the surplus of the revenues of the Irish Church, which gave O'Connell and the Whigs the basis of an open alliance: the 'Lichfield House Compact' of 1835, which lasted until Peel's triumph in 1841. An Irish element in the House of Commons had achieved the position of holding a balance that could put one of the major parties into power on a *quid pro quo* basis; and this was a significant development for the future.

It also led to limited and much criticized reforms in the area of Poor Law and Municipal Corporations;[xvii] and to co-operation between O'Connell and Thomas Drummond, the Under-Secretary in Dublin. There was a change in Castle style, long remembered as a brief golden age. Orange magistrates who 'encouraged violation of the law' were to be deprived of the commission of the peace; three Catholics were made judges; the Attorney-General and Solicitor-General were invariably Catholics. Less inspiringly, the new deal in politics also provided places and patronage for Irish MPs, which weakened their position in some quarters at home. In a sense, this was what O'Connellite politics had to show for ten years of activity: scant though it was, it made more difference to the status quo than the chimera of Repeal. The question was whether such limited payment on account was enough to answer the expectations raised by the political mobilization that had originated in the 1820s. The 'Young Ireland' movement indicated that it was not.

VI

Young Ireland was a splinter of the Repeal movement, grouped round the young journalists and publicists who started the *Nation* newspaper:

[xvii] The Poor Relief (Ireland) Act of 1838 extended the English system to Ireland against the advice of a previous Commission of Inquiry. It divided Ireland into 130 Unions, with workhouses run by Boards of Guardians consisting of representative ratepayers, administering indoor relief only. The Famine provided horrific proof of the system's irrelevance to Irish conditions; see below, pp. 327–8.

The Irish Municipal Reform Act (1840) dissolved fifty-eight Municipal Corporations and reconstituted ten; towns that had a valuation of less than one hundred pounds were administered by the Poor Law Guardians.

principally Thomas Davis,[xviii] John Blake Dillon[xix] and Charles Gavan Duffy.[xx] It also indicated what the Repeal movement, with its middle-class backing, gentry–merchant M Ps and deliberate ambiguities, was *not* appealing to. The strength of this alternative tradition is indicated by the runaway success of the *Nation*: the readership was possibly 250,000 by 1843 (though the circulation may have been much less, as there was a strong tradition of communal readings). Young Ireland's ideology bore a superficial resemblance to European romantic national-ism; but if it imbibed the cultural sense of nationality inculcated by German philosophy, this was via Carlyle rather than Herder, and, contrary to rumour, there is no evidence that Davis ever visited Germany. In many ways, the spirit of the *Nation* was as modernist and utilitarian as O'Connell. Irish circumstances made adoption of European-style nationalism impossible: for one thing, Young Ireland

[xviii] Thomas Osborne Davis (1814–45): born in Mallow, County Cork; educated at Trinity College, Dublin; called to the Irish Bar, 1838; joined the Repeal Association, 1840; contributor to the Dublin liberal press; co-founded the *Nation*, 1842; unofficial, but unchallenged, leader of the Young Irelanders, 1842-5; stood up to O'Connell over the issue of non-denominational education. Author of some of the most popular Irish ballads of his own and later ages, notably 'A Nation Once Again'. Undoubtedly the single greatest influence upon his contemporaries, in literary and political life; while he sent Ferguson in search of the Irish past, he inspired the nationalism of Mitchel and secularized that of Duffy. Remembered as the purest Irish patriot of his own or any age, which has perhaps clouded the fact that his reputation in his lifetime was the result of ceaseless labour on the committees of all the societies of which he was a member, both those sponsoring political nationalism and those, like the Royal Irish Academy, concerned with defining the parameters of nationality.

[xix] John Blake Dillon (1816–66): born in County Mayo; educated at Maynooth and Trinity College, Dublin; joined the Repeal Association, 1840; called to the Irish Bar, 1841; co-founded the *Nation*; active in the 1848 rising; escaped to France; settled in America; practised at the New York Bar; returned to Ireland after the 1855 amnesty; became M P for County Tipperary and first Secretary of the National Association, 1865, having eschewed politics for a decade; denounced Fenianism.

[xx] Charles Gavan Duffy (1816–1903): born in Monaghan; largely self-educated; Editor of the *Vindicator*, a weekly established to promote the interests of northern Catholics, 1839; entered King's Inns, Dublin, 1841; co-founded the *Nation* and became its first Editor; joined the Irish Confederation at its inception, January 1847; arrested, July 1848; released, April 1849; 'chaperoned' Carlyle around Ireland, 1849; joined the Tenant League; M P for New Ross, 1852-5; emigrated to Australia, 1855; Prime Minister of Victoria, 1871–2, and Speaker, 1876; knighted, 1873; returned to Europe, 1880; published his reminiscences of the 1840s and early 1850s as *Young Ireland* (1880–83) and *The League of North and South*, 1886. A biography of Davis, 1890, and an autobiography, 1898, followed to ensure that succeeding generations viewed mid-century Ireland through his *fin de siècle* prism. President of the Irish Literary Society, London, 1892; died in Nice; buried in Dublin.

could not define their Irishness linguistically, though Davis tried. This was one reason why Mazzini dismissed their cause as bogus. None the less, the ideology of a spiritual rebirth through nationhood struck strong Irish echoes; so did the idea of the nation's history as the shared story of a racial community struggling against foreign domination. The Young Irelanders' inability to proselytize through the Irish language might remain a theoretical stumbling-block; but their ideas received all the wider dissemination for being retailed in English.

Young Ireland's series of popular histories, published in 'The Library of Ireland', stressed the romance of violent resistance to English oppression, so long as it was safely in the past. Along with the example of William Tell and the 'men of '82', 'The Sword' was deified in Davis's ballads and the rhetoric of T. F. Meagher:[xxi]

Be it for the defence, or be it for the assertion of a nation's liberty, I look upon the sword as a sacred weapon. And if, my lord, it has sometimes reddened the shroud of the oppressor like the annointed rod of the high priest, it has at other times blossomed into flowers to deck the freeman's brow. Abhor the sword and stigmatize the sword? No, no, my lord, for in the cragged passes of the Tyrol it cut in pieces the banner of the Bavarian, and won an immortality for the peasant of Innspruck [sic]. Abhor the sword and stigmatize the sword? No, no, my lord, for at its blow a giant nation sprang from the waters of the Atlantic, and by its redeeming magic the fettered Colony became a daring free Republic. Abhor the sword and stigmatize the sword? No, my lord, for it scoured the Dutch marauders out of the fine old towns of Belgium, back into their own phlegmatic swamps, and knocked their flag, and laws and sceptre, and bayonets into the sluggish waters of the Scheldt.[13]

The banality and doggerel of *Nation* publicity helped to spread the message. Part of the thesis emphasized the inclusiveness of the Irish tradition: Davis, a Protestant, adopted the necessarily pluralist ideology of the Irish-Protestant nationalist, which was in his interest as well as in his tradition. Thus, rather illogically, he emphasized the contribution of Norman blood and Westminster values to the Irish cause, while attacking 'sullen Saxonism' and glorifying the racial virtues of the Celt.

[xxi] Thomas Francis Meagher (1823–67): born in Waterford; educated at Clongowes and Stonyhurst; studied law, but grew more interested in the politics of Repeal; a founder of the Irish Confederation; unsuccessfully contested Waterford, 1848; arrested after the abortive rising, July; sentenced to penal servitude for life; escaped to America, 1852; joined the New York Bar; helped Mitchel found the *Citizen*, 1854; founder of the *Irish News*, 1856; organizer and Brigadier-General of the Irish Brigade, fighting for the Union in the American Civil War, 1862; Secretary of Montana State, 1865; accidentally drowned soon after being appointed temporary Governor.

In the end, though, his celebration of Irish history necessitated backing Catholic nationalism against alien Protestantism. Many of the other Young Irelanders arrived at the same destination more briskly; and the roots of the movement were culturally separatist, essentially Anglophobic and increasingly sectarian. They cherished a certain cult of Carlyle, reading *Sartor Resartus* while undertaking rapt tours of the Irish landscape. Young Ireland took to logical extremes the feelings that O'Connell alternately pandered to, and conjured away again.

As with O'Connell, Young Ireland adopted more realistic goals when pushed to it, on occasion postulating something like a Commonwealth before its time. More usually, however, they preached purist political tactics and criticized O'Connell's style — the blandishment, wheedling and bullying of the Irish Bar — along with what Davis's journalist friend Daniel Madden called 'the Donnybrook Fair school of Irish patriotism'. From O'Connell's adoption of 1843 as 'Repeal Year', Young Ireland campaigned aggressively for 'Simple Repeal'. From this year, too, O'Connellism adopted the 'monster meeting', adding the techniques of the revivalist gathering to the ethos of an Irish fair. This was part of the brinkmanship of Repeal, stressing threats of parliamentary secession, alternative courts and a 'Repeal police'. It was a defence against outbidding from the Young Ireland wing, but increasingly forced upon O'Connell the one thing the Repeal movement had always avoided: a specific programme.

This orchestration of rising expectations was interrupted by Peel, who relied on O'Connell to back down at the threat of an open confrontation — which he did at Clontarf in October 1843, when O'Connell postponed a 'monster meeting' after the government prohibited it, backing the threat with military force. As a political decision, O'Connell's choice was correct: had he pressed ahead with the summoning of an alternative parliament, promised for Clontarf, the government had plans ready to suppress it. Nor did Clontarf end the momentum of Repeal, as often claimed. But O'Connell's image was badly dented among a public nurtured on extremist rhetoric; the government saved his credibility only by sending him to prison on a trumped-up conspiracy charge early the next year.

By the early 1840s, then, Irish public life was characterized by a lively culture of political engagement: evidenced by the Repeal Clubs, the *Nation*, new divisions in local politics, a moderate federalist movement to which O'Connell made characteristically contradictory overtures in 1844, and the exhortations of the *Dublin University Magazine*. Increasingly, the ideological tone was set by Young Ireland, now attracting influential moderates like William Smith O'Brien.[xxii] They were not social radicals; John Mitchel,[xxiii] their most extreme orator, would become a well-known American slaver. But as a purist elite, they appeared prepared, in their rhetoric if not in immediate political tactics, to welcome a nationalist revolution.

What kind of revolution? In the age of Fourier, Saint-Simon and the Spenceans, there was little utopian or radical social theory in Ireland, though William Thompson should not be forgotten. Nor should Fintan Lalor,[xxiv] theoretician of a peasant revolution linked to nationalist consciousness, though his lack of direct contact with the peasantry was evident even to his sceptical Young Ireland colleagues.

[xxii] William Smith O'Brien (1803–64): born in County Clare; educated at Harrow and Cambridge; supported the ministerial interest as M P for Ennis, 1826–31; avowed himself a member of the Catholic Association in his first important speech, July 1828, but continued to oppose O'Connell's radical politics; M P for County Limerick, 1835–48; formally joined the Repeal Association, January 1844; led the Association during O'Connell's confinement; quitted it upon the prospect of O'Connell treating with a Whig ministry, 1846; co-founded the Irish Confederation; stressed the need to employ 'the force of opinion' against Mitchel's more violent counsels, but felt circumstances had changed by March 1848, and urged the formation of a National Guard; arrested and tried but released, May; planned a rebellion for August; wanted his name omitted from the War Directory of 21 July, but agreed to lead an immediate insurrection upon the suspension of habeas corpus, 23 July; arrested; sentence of death commuted to transportation for life; *Principles of Government, or Meditations in Exile*, 1856; unconditionally pardoned, 1856; henceforth abstained from politics.

[xxiii] John Mitchel (1815–75): born in County Londonderry; son of a Presbyterian minister; educated at Trinity College, Dublin; a solicitor at Banbridge until 1845; joined the Repeal Association, 1843; wrote for the *Nation*, 1845; *Life of Aodh O'Neil*, 1846; established the Irish Confederation; withdrew from the *Nation* and Irish Confederation, December 1847; established the *United Irishman*, in which he advocated a 'holy war' to sweep English influence from Ireland; arrested, March 1848; sentenced to fourteen years' transportation; escaped, 1853; settled in America; edited collections of the poetry of Mangan and Davis; *The Last Conquest of Ireland (Perhaps)*, 1860; Fenian agent in Paris, 1866, but declined to become Chief Executive of the Fenian Brotherhood in America, 1867; returned to Ireland upon being returned unopposed as M P for County Tipperary, February 1875; re-lected in March, a new writ having been issued upon the charge that he was a convicted felon, but died eight days later. *Jail Journal*, 1854, a classic of nationalist invective rather than prison literature (perhaps).

[xxiv] James Fintan Lalor (1807–49): born in Queen's County; son of Patrick Lalor, Radical M P for the county, 1832–5; crippled from birth; educated at Carlow College; wrote to Peel, urging land nationalization as a means of suppressing the Repeal agitation, 1845, but subsequently supported the physical-force movement for Irish independence; wrote for the *Nation*, 1846–7; founded a Tenant League in Tipperary, 1845; took charge of the *Irish Felon*, June 1848; arrested, July; released in poor health, November; continued to urge a rising, which amounted to an attack upon a County Waterford police barracks, September 1849.

None the less, they had their own illusions about the class basis of their movement: 'O'Brien and the national gentry,' enthused Duffy, 'with Ferguson[xxv] and the national middle class'.[14]

The Peel government's programme of Irish conciliation from 1841 was not unconnected with these developments. The Irish land system was investigated by an influential commission under the Earl of Devon, which began the slow process of interpreting the Irish land situation as different in kind from England. Legislation aimed at wooing the Catholic Church, protecting the status of their charities and putting Maynooth on a permanently viable financial basis, followed – a Rubicon for Peel personally, and for his most important follower, Gladstone. Peel's Irish experience was certainly influential; but so was his readiness to follow up the initiatives of his colleagues, and his consciousness that the younger clergy had become alienated because of their Repeal commitment. So, also, were the increasingly close contacts between the government and the Catholic hierarchy. But this did not prevent him running on the rocks over his government's efforts to construct university provision that would be acceptable to Catholics. The scheme was undermined, not only by ultra-Protestants in Britain, but by irreconcilables among the Irish hierarchy. And this was the element that O'Connell generally supported, as he had done by opposing the Charitable Donations Bill. Anti-Peelism was always tactically attractive, as his hopes remained directed towards a Whig return. It was the kind of issue that also brought to the surface the tensions within the Repeal movement at large.

Many Young Irelanders, notably Davis, welcomed the government's idea of non-denominational colleges; as would be the case again in Irish history, a split over religion and education broke politics wide open. The disagreement presaged a wider rift over violence; though the Young Irelanders had agreed with O'Connell over the Clontarf cancellation, they concealed the fact in later controversies. By the

---

[xxv] Samuel Ferguson (1810–86): born in Belfast; educated at Trinity College, Dublin; contributed to *Blackwoods*, 1832; and to the *Dublin University Magazine*, 1833, defining its philosophy as national and Unionist without contradiction; called to the Irish Bar, 1838; Secretary of the inter-party Irish Council, 1847; spoke at the Protestant Repeal Association, 1848; abandoned public politics upon marriage to a Guinness heiress, 1848; QC, 1859; did not publish a volume until *Lays of the Western Gael*, 1865, but had already inspired, and been inspired by, an important generation of Irish writers, as acknowledged in his 'Lament for Thomas Davis', 1845; first Deputy Keeper of the Public Records of Ireland, 1867; *Congal*, 1872; knighted for archival work, 1878; President of the RIA, 1882; *Ogham Inscriptions*, 1887. A bridge between the flowering of national studies in the 1830s and the literary renaissance of the 1890s.

mid-1840s the Young Irelanders were, rather like O'Connell, being pressed towards the realization of their rhetoric. The catalyst was provided by the great natural disaster of the Famine that struck in 1846.

This will be considered in the next chapter, but the Young Irelanders' revolutionary gesture should be noted here. Extremist Young Irelanders, reconstructed into the 'Irish Confederation' and grouped round Mitchel's *United Irishman* (1848), set the tone of Francophilia, 1798 revivalism, and separation. The rhetoric was militaristic and republican; an insurrectionary ethic founded in an almost psychotic Anglophobia. The Famine provided the rationale for accusing the British government of genocide, but the roots went deeper than that.

So Britain's '1848 revolution' happened in Ireland, with an incoherent conspiracy followed by a rising inescapably connected with a 'cabbage patch' in Tipperary, led by Smith O'Brien. Mitchel and Meagher had already been arrested; Mitchel was sentenced to transportation, and enabled to follow a career of frenetic Carlylean attitudinizing. The influence of works like his *Jail Journal*, as well as the draconian measures of public order that followed 1848, indicated the essential importance of Young Ireland: that it was far more influential in how it was interpreted than in what it did. And the rhetoric of Young Irelanders eventually flowed into the general stream of Repeal nationalism – even if the events of 1848 indicate a very different approach to political realities.

It is ironic that Catholic emancipation appears in British terms as an important step in secularizing the state, but in Ireland laid the foundation of politics as interpreted in terms of confessional identification. The priests had arrived in politics – not, according to them, because they wanted to, but because, given the designs of a Protestant government upon a Catholic people, they had to. This argument was not negated by episodes of 'Catholic' government like Peel's 1841 administration; the clerical function was to explain politics to their people. 'Clearly as much the leaders of a Party as the representatives of a Church,' remarked de Tocqueville after dining with assorted clerics in 1835. And the clerical party had taken its place in the broad spectrum of nationalist politics.

Occasional dicta issued by the episcopate enjoining their priests to avoid 'politics' do not contradict this; nor does the generally conservative and anti-revolutionary line adopted by the Catholic Church. Ostensibly unpolitical 'charitable organizations' or even instructions to their flocks to abstain from certain political commitments, could be used for objectively political ends. And interference from Rome, often instigated by British diplomacy, was cleverly circumvented.

O'Connell, dying at Genoa in May 1847, might go down in Young Ireland historiography as 'next to the British Government, the worst enemy that Ireland ever had': Mitchel, Duffy and Doheny[xxvi] all wrote autobiographical 'histories' that traduced him mercilessly. But he became the centre of a Catholic cult, celebrated as the 'Liberator' of Catholics rather than of Irishmen. Protestant nationalists always called for pluralism – as they had to. But they were never representative of a consistent strain, rather representing a series of reactions against a governing syndrome. Such ideologues used the nineteenth-century myth of 'Grattan's parliament' to articulate a theoretically non-sectarian nationalism, defined by living in Ireland rather than by being Gaelic or Catholic. But the formulation that 'we cannot give up a single Irishman' ignored the considerable minority of Irishmen who saw their primary identity as British. This myopia could only be reinforced by the clericalist politics that were formed in the 1820s and 1830s, where parties were based on religious, cultural and historical identities rather than on class interests. The picture was not to change. O'Connell himself may have been a 'primitive liberal' rather than a confessional politician; and he treasured his few Protestant Repealers. But he never succeeded in evoking much support from the British radicals whose cause he espoused (except the Chartists, of whom he was deeply suspicious). Despite its inconclusive and pluralist rhetoric, Repeal was as closely identified with clerical organization as Catholic emancipation had been. Tension might remain between priest and politician: clerical suspicion of liberalism and nationalism continued; so did disapproval from Rome. But by the 1840s Catholicism had been securely identified as the national experience. Young Ireland might preach secular European romanticism, but in Ireland nationalism was almost entirely Catholic; and Unionism was principally, if less exclusively, Protestant.

[xxvi] Michael Doheny (1805–63): born in County Tipperary; son of a small farmer; self-educated; became a successful barrister; joined the Repeal Association, 1842, and the Irish Confederation, 1847; wrote for the *Nation* as 'Eiranach'; fled to the USA after the 1848 rising, where he helped found the Fenian Brotherhood. *The Felon's Track: History of the Attempted Outbreak in Ireland*, 1849.

CHAPTER FOURTEEN

═══

THE FAMINE:
BEFORE AND AFTER

I

═══

THE GREAT POTATO Famine of 1845–9 opened an abyss that swallowed up many hundreds of thousands of impoverished Irish people: the poverty-stricken conditions of rural life in the west and southwest, a set-piece for astounded travel books in the early nineteenth century, apparently climaxed in a Malthusian apocalypse. Traditionally, historians used to interpret the effects of the Famine as equally cataclysmic: it was seen as a watershed in Irish history, creating new conditions of demographic decline, large-scale emigration, altered farming structures and new economic policies, not to mention an institutionalized Anglophobia among the Irish at home and abroad.

As a literal analysis, this does not stand up to examination: at least as far as the supposed economic effects are concerned, all the processes just mentioned can be traced to well before the Famine, even if the disaster accelerated them to a level where they became qualitatively different. If there is a watershed year in nineteenth-century Irish social and economic history it is not 1846 but 1815, with the agricultural disruption following the end of the French wars. Some contemporaries at least recognized this: as one witness to a parliamentary commission on Irish poverty sighed, 'it would have been better for the Irish farmer if Bonaparte never lived or never died'.[1] What is less clear is, in terms of economic history, what the Famine actually brought about. 'Discussion about whether the Famine constituted a watershed often seems to take for granted that we know what happened during the Famine,' a senior economic historian has remarked; 'we don't.'[2]

This pithy statement deserves some examination. We know the terrible story of the events that took place, especially in areas that attracted national attention like Skibbereen, or those Poor Law Unions whose Relief Committees engaged in lengthy correspondence with the central administration. But we may not know what the direct economic results of these events were. We know what the administrators of 'relief' and the civil servants thought they were doing.[3] But we constantly come up against lacunae in statistical evidence, notably regarding the basis on which figures were gathered, as well as the standard difficulty with evidence from contemporary witnesses, put memorably by Thackeray in his *Irish Sketch Book* of 1842. ' "To have an opinion about Ireland", one must begin by getting at the truth; and where is it to be had in the country? Or rather, there are two truths, the Catholic truth and the Protestant truth ... Belief is made a party business.'

We remain unsure about the background to Irish poverty, the spectacular agrarian problem of the pre-Famine decades, and its relation to subsistence crises; even the patterns of the Irish agricultural economy before the Famine have been analysed in widely differing terms and by widely differing methods.[4] Certainly Ireland struggled through crop failures and subsistence crises throughout the early nineteenth century. But was the country becoming richer or poorer? And was poverty the result of overpopulation? Contemporaries automatically assumed so, and worked out their remedies accordingly. But economic historians are no longer so sure, and one econometric study finds little relation between income per capita and areas of population density; nor do income levels seem to have varied with patterns of fertility and marriage. The overpowering horrors of starvation and mass mortality obviously outweigh these speculations, but do not make them any the less necessary.

What can be stated unequivocally is that the potato was a dietary staple by the 1840s; with the question of its relation to population increase, we again encounter controversy, though the established view that it was by then a primary pre-condition (if not the necessary one) has not been convincingly refuted. It enabled subsistence on a tiny holding, providing food for nine months of the year; it sustained early and fecund marriages. It was also miraculously prolific and nutritious: the only single cheap food that can support life as a sole diet, according to recent nutritive research. However, even good potatoes are deficient in vitamin A, and the supplements of milk and fish (necessary for a fully balanced diet) were becoming rare among the very poor by the 1830s. By then, too, 'cups' and 'lumpers' were replacing the less prolific but better 'apples' and 'minions'. Nor could it be stored for more than a year (the period between the exhaustion of stores and the reaping of harvest was increasingly precarious). It was expensive to transport, so trade was limited (only 20 per cent of the crop was exported). The main method of 'conversion' was by raising pigs, an important part of the potato ecology. Otherwise the crop was consumed on the farm. At the very period when commercialization in other types of food was developing rapidly and extensively, the potato imposed its own constrictions. It has always aroused strong feelings, not least among its devoted historians; Cobbett's letters from Ireland (1834) depict it as an immorality, whereas the eccentric American traveller Asenath Nicolson was loud in its praises (she was a food faddist; and actually stayed in the poorest cabins of the west). Both were writing, in any case, of the period before the apocalypse.

There had been fourteen partial or complete potato famines in Ireland between 1816 and 1842, and some catastrophic crises in the eighteenth century, notably 1740–41. From the autumn of 1845 a new fungus disease – *phytophthora infestans* – struck the Irish potato, operating with cruel rapidity and unpredictability in moist, mild conditions, and reducing the crop to rottenness. It would not be correctly accepted as a fungal infection for over half a century; the bewildering variety of analyses offered and panaceas suggested came nowhere near effectiveness. The blight redoubled in 1846, preventing a new crop being sown. In 1847 incidence of the disease declined, but it returned in 1848–9. The result, in areas where the labouring population was dependent on a potato diet, was a subsistence crisis that was beyond the powers either of the existing state apparatus or the prevalent conceptions of social responsibility – in Ireland at least.

There were what amounted to contemporary potato famines in Scotland and Belgium as well, but with nothing like the Irish results. Part of the analysis must concern itself with government policy; but equally important is the condition of the Irish economy in the years before the Famine.

II

One fundamental fact is that the economy was, in terms of structure and development, extraordinarily uneven; the other concerns the effect of post-war conditions on agriculture. The movement of prices, which remained high from 1790 to 1814, benefited tenants, especially those on long leases. But from 1814 to 1815 prices fell, while rents, in real terms, rose: a process amplified by population expansion putting further pressure on land. The same period saw the accelerating decline of local cottage industry engaged in textile production (Bandon had 2,000 weavers in 1825, but less than a hundred by the 1840s); wages fell commensurately. The picture is a complex one, bearing in mind the variation of conditions mentioned already. The idea of a 'dual' economy, neatly split down a north–south axis into retarded agrarian west and commercialized, urban east, does not really hold up; modernization, diversification and money usage varied all over the island, while commercialization had penetrated, if unevenly, to many areas of the west. A major study of County Cork indicates considerable variations in the pre-Famine age, and also shows that both population increase and subdivision of holdings were less intense than claimed for elsewhere; it also indicates a wide variety of employment patterns, and staggering levels of seasonal unemployment in the less developed south-west.

Most of all, Ulster must be seen as a special case. As the domestic cotton industry declined from the early nineteenth century, capital was not redeployed into mechanized cotton mills; instead the linen industry was converted to power looms and became the foundation of tremendous profits. By 1839 thirty-five linen mills in Ulster employed nearly 8,000 workers; the subsequent adoption of steam-power boosted potential even more. Though the market for linen was permanently disadvantaged by cheap cotton, the industry expanded throughout the Famine era, creating economic conditions that could cope with local crop failure. Yet textile industries elsewhere in Ireland declined, and local economies did not diversify; in the twenty years or so before the Famine, actual de-industrialization took place in many areas. Dublin, whose population reached nearly a quarter of a million before the Famine, and Belfast expanded; so did agricultural market centres like Mallow, Tullamore and Navan. But many smaller towns stagnated or declined, especially ports and textile centres (Dingle, Lismore, Bandon, Portarlington, Athboy). Why did Ireland, outside Ulster, fail to industrialize?

The answers may seem obvious: absence of energy-sources, a backward agricultural economy, a lack of capital accumulation. But many of these issues raise chicken-and-egg queries, or provoke comparisons that raise further questions. Ulster, for instance, had insufficient useful coal but managed to import it; neither the logistics nor the expense would have presented insurmountable problems elsewhere either. Where isolated enterprises were set up, they often flourished. There was evidence of entrepreneurial activity, but it very often chose to invest profits in land and the appurtenances of gentility: Charles Bianconi, whose 'long cars' revolutionized coach transport, is a notable example. Perhaps above all, Ireland's reputation dissuaded potential investors; George Cornewall Lewis remarked in 1836 that 'the insecurity of property in Ireland, whether real or supposed ... prevents the English or Scotch capitalist from transmitting materials to be manufactured in Ireland'.

Contemporaries noted another kind of psychological block, too, probably connected with the seasonal, low-wage nature of Irish employment patterns, and the notably low productivity rate of work. It was often alleged that the Irish embodied a resistance to long-term strategies, which created a 'poverty trap'. A certain strain of contemporary critic invariably added injunctions about the power of 'combinations', or trade unions in the artisan trades, but this seems to have been a secondary factor at most, though skilled labour was certainly dearer than in England. Another, and possibly very important, barrier was imposed by the emigration of so many of the young, the strong, the enterprising and the hardworking, which was taking place well before the Famine. Irish emigrants worked hard and often advanced themselves[i] in exactly the ways enjoined unsuccessfully upon the Irish who stayed at home.

What matters more than counterfactual speculation is that Ireland *did* remain dependent on agriculture, and that this agriculture was in many areas (not all) conducted at a fairly backward and unproductive level. The rural community was by no means universally impoverished – the small farmer on, for instance, a holding of six to fifteen acres could employ a labourer and maintain cattle. But he was not frequently encountered in the west. Where the Famine struck hardest reflects fairly accurately the prevalence of subsistence farming on tiny holdings: the west and south-west, upland parts of Tipperary, Cavan. Death rate figures show that areas like east Leinster and north and north-east Ulster were not hard hit by comparison[5] – Ulster least of all, with its diversified economy. Local evidence is available from a surprising number of well-run estates in east County Wicklow, and this generally indicates that the population was maintained above the level of destitution; the picture in the invaluable diaries of the Scottish Elizabeth Smith of Baltiboys, in the west of the county, is more harrowing, though here, too, starvation was kept at bay. It is apparent (and logical) that more modernized, commercialized areas, with developed transport links and higher per capita income were less

[i] See Chapter 15 below.

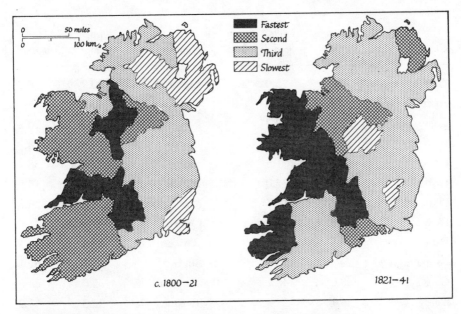

Map 6: *Population growth in Ireland c. 1800–1821 and 1821–41.*
Source: C. Ó Gráda, 'Demographic Adjustment and Seasonal Migration in Nineteenth-century Ireland' in L. M. Cullen and F. Furet (editors), *Irlande et France X V I I^e–X Xe siècles: pour une histoire rurale comparée.*

devastated. The relationship between urbanization and actual mortality levels is more questionable, probably because fever, a more frequent killer than starvation, could spread more quickly in congested areas. There is a strong statistical correlation, unsurprisingly, between low income and excess mortality; but this did not mean that potato dependence alone characterized the worst-hit areas. Mokyr finds 'the actual average devoted to potatoes was statistically insignificant in explaining excess mortality; far more important were general economic variables such as income, literacy and capital-labour ratios'.[6]

What is incontestable is that the labourer class was hardest hit, followed by the smallest farmers, even though these classes, already accustomed to seasonal migration, were in some ways better equipped to survive Famine conditions. The results would be social readjustment as well as population decline. This last was dramatic: it has been computed at 2,225,000 over 1845–51, through disease, starvation and emigration. (The population, 8,200,000 in the early 1840s, would sink to 4,400,000 by 1911.) Here, however, the figures need examination in terms of what the Famine meant. Large-scale emigration pre-dated

County	Upper bound	Lower bound	County	Upper bound	Lower bound
Antrim	20.3	15.0	Limerick	20.9	10.0
Armagh	22.2	15.3	Londonderry	10.1	5.7
Carlow	8.8	2.7	Longford	26.7	20.2
Cavan	51.8	42.7	Louth	14.6	8.2
Clare	46.5	31.5	Mayo	72.0	58.4
Cork	41.8	32.0	Meath	21.2	15.8
Donegal	18.7	10.7	Monaghan	36.0	28.6
Down	12.5	6.7	Queen's	29.1	21.6
Dublin	0.7	−2.1	Roscommon	57.4	49.5
Fermanagh	39.1	29.2	Sligo	61.1	52.1
Galway	58.0	46.1	Tipperary	35.0	23.8
Kerry	36.1	22.4	Tyrone	22.3	15.2
Kildare	12.0	73.4	Waterford	30.8	20.8
Kilkenny	18.1	12.5	Westmeath	26.3	20.0
King's	24.9	18.0	Wexford	6.6	1.7
Leitrim	50.2	42.9	Wicklow	14.6	10.8

Table 3: *Average annual excess death rates 1846–51, by county (per 1,000).*
Source: Joel Mokyr, *Why Ireland Starved: A Quantitative and Analytical History of the Irish Economy 1800–1850.*

the potato blight; in the first half of 1841 it was running at a rate that, if sustained, would have meant 130,000 emigrants a year. The figure of about 1,500,000 who emigrated in the Famine years should be set against this background – though the rate certainly reached undreamt-of levels, with the peak rate, in 1851, 250,000.

The figures for Famine deaths are equally stunning, and equally they raise problems. At least 775,000 died, mostly through disease, including cholera in the latter stages of the catastrophe. Here again the authorities disagree. A recent sophisticated computation estimates excess deaths from 1846 to 1851 as between 1,000,000 and 1,500,000, varying widely from county to county, as usual; after a careful critique of this, other statisticians arrive at a figure of 1,000,000.[7] The projection of decline in terms of 'excess' raises the question of what rate the population would have gone on increasing at *without* the Famine, and whether it was still increasing when the Famine struck – which has become a contested question. But no amount of disagreement can conceal the devastating extent of depopulation or the horrific conditions in which lives were lost. And the question that has preoccupied historians, far more than attempting to arrive at how many died, is: what could the government have done to stop it?

III

In the Belgian famine of 1867, the government unwillingly purchased food for distribution, as well as organizing public works and removing tariffs. The initial British reaction in 1845–6 was not much different, though policies fluctuated more, and the time-lag in putting them into effect was potentially fatal. The idea that food produced in the country should not be exported was not adopted anywhere, and would have been considered an economic irrelevance at the time. It would also have required the assumption of powers that no contemporary government possessed, and inevitably caused violent resistance among the farmer classes; in any case, from 1847 Ireland was importing five times as much grain as she was exporting. Large-scale livestock slaughter and redistribution, while a technical possibility, raised similar difficulties – though a number of landlords adopted this strategy, in Wicklow at least. Fundamentally, however, relief was up to government initiative; and this, in the long run, was not up to the challenge.

Peel's policies in 1846 were more effective than sometimes allowed. The government co-ordinated relief measures through public works and price control: both strategies were based on the experience of previous famines. Half of the public works were financed from local rates, at a high cost (nearly £500,000 in the first year). The mechanism for this existed since 1817; the impressive harbour at Kingstown (now Dun Laoghaire) originated thus. A central loan fund financed public works, and a reorganized Board of Works was in existence from 1831. But government machinery embodied the usual *ad hoc* response to Irish differences; it was not capable of bearing the unprecedentedly huge weight. Within both the government and the Treasury, humanitarian impulses came up against a violent disapproval of subsidized improve-ment schemes; there was also an attitude, often unconcealed, that Irish fecklessness and lack of economy were bringing a retribution that would work out for the best in the end.

Under the Peel dispensation, food depots were set up and prices

kept down by the distribution of Indian meal. This was not an unfamiliar food to the Irish, as so often claimed; it had been imported in
considerable quantities over the last fifty years, and was regularly
resorted to in times of famine. Perhaps because of this, it was certainly
unpopular. Prices were fixed on a scale that went down to fourpence
a stone for the poorest. However, obsessive contemporary theories
about keeping private traders in business and only distributing food to
the unemployable interfered with the system's effectiveness.

So, in a sense, did the Board of Works that oversaw everything. Its
public works schemes were doggedly adhered to amid conditions
whose severity made such expedients irrelevant; the celebrated (and
often mythical) piers where no boats could land, walls round nothing,
roads to nowhere, are poignant metaphors for a policy that was neither
consistent nor effective, but which expressed economic beliefs held by
the governing classes in both countries. Demands from some localities
for a 'dole' to keep people working on their farms were defined by
Sir Charles Trevelyan[ii] as 'the masterpiece of that system of social
economy according to which the machine of society should be worked
backwards, and the government should be made to support the people,
instead of the people the government'.[8]

Much retrospective condemnation has been heaped on Trevelyan's
shoulders as permanent Head of the Treasury and final arbiter of
Famine relief policy; in fact, he simply epitomizes the Whig view of
economic theory, as did Wood[iii] and Russell.[iv] They monitored Irish

[ii] Charles Edward Trevelyan (1807–86): born in Taunton; joined the Indian Civil
Service; Assistant Secretary to the Treasury, 1838; oversaw and virtually shaped Irish
relief during the Famine; defended the export of food from Ireland in *The Irish Crisis*
(1848), in which he also intimated that the Famine was the design of a benign
Malthusian God who sought to relieve overpopulation by natural disaster; knighted,
1848; Chairman, with Sir Stafford Northcote, of the Commission whose Report of
1853 shaped the British civil service for the succeeding century and beyond; returned
to Indian office.

[iii] Charles Wood (1800–1885): Chancellor of the Exchequer, 1846–52; insisted that
Irish poor rates should be paid at the normal rate, autumn 1847, a policy overruled
by the Lord Lieutenant, Clarendon; President of the Board of Control, 1852; first
Lord of the Admiralty, 1855; GCB, 1856; Secretary of State for India, 1859–66;
created Viscount Halifax of Monk Bretton, 1866; Lord Privy Seal, 1870–74.

[iv] Lord John Russell (1792–1878): third son of the sixth Duke of Bedford; represented Bandon, 1826–30; leader of Whigs in the Commons and principal advocate
of parliamentary reform in the Cabinet, 1831–2; visited Ireland and opposed demands
of Irish executive for coercion, 1832; advocated abolition of tithe, and other radical
Irish Church reforms, 1833; introduced first Irish Poor Law, 1837; Colonial Secretary,
1839; supported Peel's Irish policy and his repeal of the Corn Laws, 1845–6; Prime

affairs after Peel fell from power in 1846; only Russell knew Ireland at first-hand. Under the new dispensation, government intervention was to be strictly limited; private initiative must be relied on to provide food wherever possible, with the result that prices soared to levels that the wages paid by the public works could not meet. Government policies were by no means passive, and certainly not careless; but they were generally ill-founded. Public works *did* continue; so did advances to landowners under the terms of the 1847 Land Improvements Act, totalling £3,000,000 in all. But sweeping plans for railway construction were not adopted; nor were ideas of land reclamation schemes, recurrently advanced as the panacea for the Irish problem. The Devon Commission had identified 3,775,000 'improvable' acres, which attracted much attention; but even if they had been reclaimed, it is unlikely that they would have been used for tillage. Arguments about the cost of schemes and sensitivity about the responsibilities of the Board of Works tended to stymie any plans that were advanced. The railway question was already controversial since a commission of 1837, commandeered by Drummond, had pressed for a greater degree of state control than was considered acceptable, and offended the private enterprise lobby; despite some imaginative suggestions, the great age of the Irish railway was to come after the Famine.

Most of all, the question of payment became an obsession. If this burden fell on local rates, it was expected to produce a more widespread commitment to 'efficiency'. The twin obsession was with the dangers of 'pauperization' on the supposed scale of the old Poor Law in England. Public works were not abandoned in favour of direct relief until 1847. Soup kitchens, based on the organization of the Poor Law Unions, distributed food, mostly gratis, to millions by late 1847. But they were unable to cope with the conditions of a bitter winter and ravaging disease – from 1847, the great threat. It has been claimed that 'if one takes policy and structure as the criteria, Ireland had one of the most advanced health services in Europe in the early nineteenth century'.[9] But 600-odd country dispensaries and a system of centrally controlled county fever hospitals could hardly cope with the conditions of 1847–8, when skeletal armies milled at their doors and in the west whole families walled themselves into their cabins and died.

Minister, 1846–52; replaced public works schemes with outdoor relief, 1847; introduced Coercion, 1848, and Encumbered Estates Acts, 1848–9; reacted to 'papal aggression' with the Ecclesiastical Titles Bill, 1851; Foreign Secretary, 1852; edited Moore's *Memoirs, Journal and Correspondence*, 1853–6; created earl, 1861; Prime Minister, 1865–6; retired from public life.

In the 1830s even the most dedicated proponent of a Poor Law for Ireland had written: 'The occurrence of a famine, if general, seems to be a contingency altogether above the powers of a Poor Law to provide for.'[10] But the Poor Law became, in the final stages of the Famine, the last resort. Relief climbed to unforeseen levels, outdoors and indoors; the Irish poor-houses had 135,000 inmates by February 1848, 215,000 by June 1849. The burden on the rates was unenforceable, given the limited resources of Irish property. Government loans and special levies had to be brought into play; central government was locked in a permanent struggle with local Boards of Guardians. The situation was exacerbated by the fact that Irish Poor Law Unions were already far larger units than those in Britain, containing 63,000 people on average, instead of 27,000: overcrowding was horrific. The Poor Law Extension Act of 1847 restricted admittance and incorporated the Gregory[v] clause, which denied relief to anyone possessing more than a quarter-acre of land; this boosted the landlord desiderata of land clearance and emigration, and has been credited with 'disintegrating the fabric of rural society'.[11]

In a sense it simply reflects contemporary analysis of the Irish poverty problem that was assumed to form the background to the Famine crisis; 'the two great deficiencies in Ireland are *want of capital*, and *want of industry*. By destroying small tenancies you would obtain both.'[12] A dislike of what was seen as the Irish habit of allowing excess population to 'loiter about upon the land' was accompanied by an equally simplistic desire to divert them into 'great and flourishing towns'. Most analysts ignored the position that Ireland now occupied, for good or ill, *vis-à-vis* industrialized Britain; the concomitant of protection for Irish industry was a strategy rejected by nearly everyone (the unconventional Isaac Butt, who had been Professor of Political Economy at Trinity College until 1840 and published *Protection of Home Industry* in 1846, was an exception).

What part did private relief schemes play? In Scotland, which also saw widespread crop failure, the principal difference in what subsequently happened was that landlords were able to help feed their tenants and generally did so. For the most part, the same was not true

[v] William Henry Gregory (1817–92): Conservative M P for Dublin, 1842–7; actively supported Russell's outdoor relief measure, 1847; Liberal-Conservative M P for Galway, 1857–71; supported the Land Acts of 1870 and 1881, having introduced a bill in 1866 that anticipated some elements of them; Irish Privy Councillor, 1871; Governor of Ceylon, 1871–7; knighted, 1876; retired to Coole Park, County Galway. His autobiography published by his widow, Augusta Gregory, 1894.

in Ireland. More reliance was put on the local Relief Committees set up by Act of Parliament in 1847, comprising magistrates, clergy of both denominations and large ratepayers. Technically voluntary, they reported to the government. The government lent money to them for local schemes, and equalled the sums subscribed locally. They produced some real effect; the evidence from Cork in early 1847 shows huge grain imports (threatening to glut the market), lowered Indian meal prices and Relief Committees distributing food in every Poor Law Union. But the length of the crisis, and the unevenness of supplies, altered the picture. Moreover, close Whig supervision of Relief Committees continually checked to see that they were not exceeding their brief.

Voluntary religious organizations were less trammelled; the great reputation of the Society of Friends (Quakers) in Famine relief during the visitation has never been forgotten. Other Protestant groups and individuals played a prominent part, some of whom at least were guilty of proselytism – if not on the epic scale often attributed to them.[vi] The government by and large adhered to their belief that private enterprise should provide the bulk of the food supply; hardly anyone supported the idea that the government *itself* should enter the market except, once again, the indomitable Butt.

An absorbing local study of the Famine years in Killaloe, County Clare, itemized the reasons why distress was limited in the parish: 'the

---

[vi] See D. Bowen, *Souperism: Myth or Reality* (Cork, 1970). But its existence cannot be explained away; it was bitterly remembered by the Quaker Alfred Webb in his unpublished autobiography:

> Upon the Famine arose a widespread system of proselytism, now happily almost at an end. In their despair and misery, our poor naturally caught at any sources of relief, and a network of well-intentioned Protestant associations spread over the poorer parts of the country, which in return for soup and other help endeavoured to gather the people into their churches and schools, really believing that masses of our people wished to abandon Catholicism. A society for which we printed, with Archbishop Whately as President – the Society for Protecting the Rights of Conscience – gave fishing boats and otherwise assisted those whom they supposed to be persecuted for making the change. As distress mitigated, the baseness of these assumptions was shown. Those who really became Protestants were few and far between. The movement left seeds of bitterness that have not yet died out, and Protestants, not altogether excluding Friends, sacrificed much of the influence for good they would have had if they had been satisfied to leave the belief of the people alone. In matters of conversion in these countries, Protestants are blunderingly and ineffectually above-board, whilst Catholics are more effective and persistent, and, from their own point of view, wise. Others may rejoice in their positive beliefs; I more and more rejoice and prize my conviction that none will be judged because of their belief or nonbelief. (I, 120–22)

indulgence of certain landlords, the availability of local grain, the employment works on the Shannon, the partial success of the Government relief schemes, and above all the tremendous efforts of the local Relief Committees and of the Society of Friends'.[13] The records of the Killaloe Committee show a constant struggle with a niggardly and dilatory central administration, eventually forced to acquiesce in gratuitous food distribution by January 1847. There were no deaths from starvation in the parish. Here, as shown by other local studies, some local landlords behaved well; a survey of Cork similarly shows the Earl of Kingston spending half his annual rental in relieving distress, and the Earl of Shannon borrowing enormous sums to create employment and distribute charity. The Colthursts spent more than their rental on relief works; the Devonshire and Middleton estates had as good a record as those of the Fitzwilliams and Grattans in Wicklow. Mrs Smith's diary records stock cattle being slaughtered and distributed, and soup kitchens operating from the end of 1846. But she also makes clear that the landlords who exerted themselves were not typical: 'It's nonsense to talk of good landlords as the rule, they are no such thing, they are only the exception. In my walks about this little locality have I not found evidence against them that would fit me for a witness before the Committee of the House, on the causes of Irish misery?'[14] Landlords did not, by and large, apply for large sums from the Board of Works for relief schemes: possibly because of the spectacular debts that they were already financing from the supposedly solid collateral of land (the Marquess of Downshire borrowed £186,500 between 1810 and 1840). Large debts still accrued to the Board under the loans scheme, which had to be written off in 1853. But, by and large, the class who possessed most did least. Store cattle were not slaughtered on a large scale; indeed, the number of most types of livestock increased during the Famine years, a statistic partially explained by the fact that those sectors hardest hit by the Famine possessed comparatively few cattle (pigs, by contrast, declined in number). There is also an argument that in times of dearth, dairy cattle were, like poultry, more valuable for what they could produce alive than dead.

The scrappy evidence recording how people experienced the Famine brings sharply home the importance of commercialized food distribution; and, within the system, of who had the resources to claim entitlement to what food there was. Michael Doheny, a Young Irelander recording his experiences on the run in stricken west Cork and Kerry in 1848, only occasionally mentions the Famine. Eggs and potatoes are regular fare in cabins; bacon, bread, tea and whiskey are purchased; in 'the most filthy' cabin above Killarney, where 'the dung of the cattle had not been removed for days, and half-naked children squatted in it as joyously as if they rolled on richest carpets', the fugitives are treated to 'the finest trout I ever saw', with 'boiled new milk, slightly curdled, a delicacy little known in the circle of fashion, but never surpassed either in that or any other'; the next morning they ate 'excellent new potatoes, butter, new milk, and a slice of the flesh of fried badger'.[15] Again and again, the variation is striking; and inability to recognize the severity of the visitation was not confined to the Dublin administrative classes. Eastern Ulster violently opposed paying the special rate-in-aid levied from 1849 to alleviate distress elsewhere. The government was capable of admitting that the south-west and west had special difficulties. There, from early on, government meal was sold direct to the people; but once again, many starved through bureaucracy. Overall, local differentiation partly explains why the government so much underestimated what faced them from 1846.

IV

What long-term effects did the Famine leave behind it? It is now established that it did not instigate the process of population decline. Though the population of Ireland had passed 8,000,000, probably reaching 8,200,000 by 1846, its growth rate had peaked some decades before. There is a lively controversy about the respective importance of fertility and mortality in the process, but the argument for an exceptional degree of fertility seems strongest. The figures themselves raise further questions; the 1851 census has many shortcomings, and criticism has also been levelled at those of 1831 and 1841. The picture of drastic population decline during the 1840s remains, though it varied widely – nearly 30 per cent in Connacht, half of that in Leinster. However, if one takes the figures gathered in 1851, the growth rate had been slackening since 1821. At that point it was running at 17 per cent; in the 1820s it fell to 14.9 per cent; by 1841, it was 5.25 per cent. Population patterns may have been responding to the increased difficulty in gaining access to land in the agrarian dislocations after 1815; they may also reflect the changed age and sex distributions as more and more young men emigrated. A case can be made that the percentage of women marrying at very young ages dropped dramatically over the 1830s in rural districts.[16] In fact, statistical surveys and econometric reconstructions never bear out the contemporary impression that the Irish married exceptionally young; here, as elsewhere, the new economic history is markedly at odds with the older variety that relied heavily on literary evidence.

The actual marriage rate was falling, and emigration was already statistically significant, long before the potatoes failed. The population *total* still rose, with the momentum of previous growth; but the patterns that produced that growth were already changing. And the conditions of early nineteenth-century Irish life – the vastly increased rural proletariat, sustained on marginal scraps of land – were the result of birth rate and marriage patterns that developed in the late eighteenth century, in response to the possibility of marriage without capital resources (a rare scenario in rural societies, except those newly industrialized). Both local and national studies show that the Irish population was stabilizing (and conceivably even falling) well before the Famine. In this as in the agrarian economy, for a more illuminating picture of what the Famine did, we have to examine the trends of the pre-Famine era.

To conceive of Irish rural society in the early nineteenth century as made up of 'landlord and tenant' creates a dangerously simple impression. It was a complex, layered structure, embracing many levels of society, representing an agriculture that was responding fast but unevenly to altering market forces. The element of middling farmers was increasingly important; beneath them came the smallholders of one to fifteen acres; and then the ranks of the 'cottiers'. Cottier society, especially in the west, represented a different ethos from the diversified farms of the north and the commercialization of the midlands and east: labourers, receiving their wages in land, dependent on potato farming carried out on scraps of land held by terms of conacre for less than a year at a time. By the Famine the number of smallholders and cottiers outnumbered the farmers two to one, a balance that would change dramatically.

The smallholding and cottier economy was what contemporaries perceived as the Irish problem – often cast in terms of overpopulation, though the panaceas advocated rarely tackled this question directly. Ideas of competition, free trade and landlord reform were endlessly mooted instead. Not until long after the Famine was a circumstantial, relativist approach to the problem of Irish rural poverty taken – and then only in terms of tenure and ownership, whose relevance was, in fact, arguable. Rents may have been high in relation to the productivity of the land; but this did not affect the cottiers and agricultural labourers as much as the better-off farmers. Moreover, the experience of the latter showed a picture of agricultural 'improvement'; yet the 'condition of the people' emphatically did not. In the pre-Famine decades a vast quantity of theoretical (and partial) evidence was collected about the Irish agricultural economy; but it should be set against the conditions that dictated Irish agricultural production after 1815.

From this point, the sustained fall in agricultural prices had destabilized the basis of the agrarian economy. In wartime, profitable tillage and a booming population had been sustained by high profits. After the war, economic logic dictated a reversion to pasture farming, less labour-intensive and easier to manage on narrowing cost margins as the value of agricultural profits fell. To consolidate farms and put them out to grass seemed an obvious answer, as cattle and sheep held their value better than tillage products, now competing once more with European produce for the British market – a market that also wanted more and more livestock products.

This may have been the logical direction for Irish agricultural production to take, but there is some disagreement about how far and how soon it actually did so. Though livestock production and export climbed from the 1820s, grain export to Britain more than trebled too. This period saw the adoption of the iron swing plough, new drainage schemes, the long-handled scythe, improved stock-breeding and the reclamation of much land (though statistics for this are notoriously unreliable[17]). But such innovations cannot reconcile the improved cereal production *with* a swing to pasturage. It seems likely that the constrictions of Irish rural conditions prevented a wholesale shift to profitable pasturage; there were too many people to redeploy, with a labour supply increasing as the opportunities for it declined. The process was slower than economics dictated. Moreover, one concomitant of a switch to livestock was that access to land now depended upon possession of capital (in its oldest form – animal stock), whereas during the tillage boom even the poorest smallholder could make a bid. And meanwhile the population continued to rise.

Tillage expansion, less and less profitable though it was, continued at least up to 1830, and possibly up to the Famine, reflecting both population density and a lack of capital. Some local studies, as in County Down, show pasturage actually declining through the 1830s, with pigs, potatoes and cereals increasing. But stock-rearing encroached from about 1830. As long eighteenth-century leases fell in, renewals were made on short and insecure tenancies; land clearance, and maximization of profit, became the priority. By the 1830s rent arrears were mounting up, and so were evictions – though the evidence seems to be against this being as regular an occurrence as often claimed (or as much as the landlords would have liked). By and large, people stayed on the land to an extent unjustifiable economically; Raymond Crotty sees an economically redundant labour-force of about 1,500,000 (including dependants) by 1845.

This must be related to agrarian unrest. Definition of what was at issue tends to be influenced by the work of Cornewall Lewis, who understandably saw the situation too much *vis-à-vis* that in England, and shared the contemporary obsession with the landlord system. Conflict seems to have broken out far more often between the organized rural poor and more advantaged farmers and graziers; but local variations in class composition are reflected by the involvement of quite well-off farmers in Whiteboyism, especially after the agricultural slump hit counties like Wexford. Agitation against tithes may often have been simply displacement activity; though the system always provided potential for resentment, the issue was often reduction or regulation rather than abolition. Regulation of clerical fees could mobilize a wide range of support; so could attempts to reduce food prices, or a concerted resistance to distraint for recovery of rent due. Evictions, which increased after the fall in grain prices from 1813, and varied with the commercialization of agriculture, were another important variable. Overall, the chief mobilizing factor concerned the availability of, and entitlement to, land: agrarian organization responded to the pressures attendant on land clearance, resistance to subdivision, and a decline in long-term leasing: small landlords and strong farmers were the obvious targets.

The traditional picture of insecurity of tenure as a basic cause both of agrarian unrest and of poverty needs modification; Mokyr finds that only a quarter of land under cultivation was let without lease[18] (though this may have been the land that was sustaining – or not sustaining – that element in the population most 'at risk'). Other econometric historians have alleged that pre-Famine productivity was more impressive than is usually allowed: evidence is adduced from livestock values, savings-bank deposits, and the surprisingly high proportion of the population (23 per cent) in housing defined as first or second class by the census of 1841. Here again, though, one must query the relevance of this to the cottiers and smallholders of the west.

What changes, then, did the Famine make? Holdings of very small farms declined drastically, if one takes the contemporary figures at face value: these show farms from one to five acres to have declined by two-thirds: from 44.9 per cent of Irish land in 1831 to 15.5 per cent in

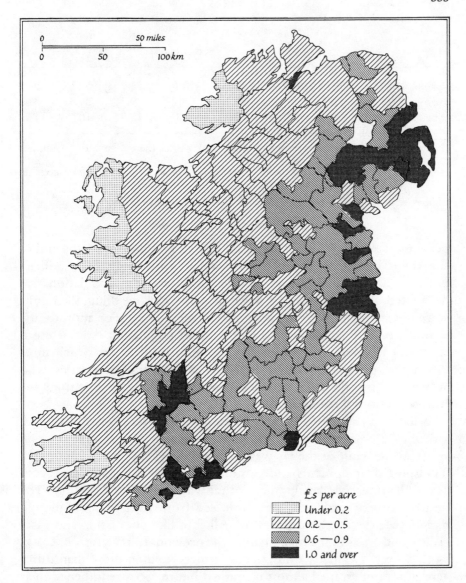

Map 7: *Valuation of rural areas c. 1850.*
Source: J. H. Johnson, 'The Two "Irelands" at the Beginning of the Nineteenth Century'
in N. Stephens and R. E. Glasscock (editors), *Irish Geographical Studies in Honour of E.
Estyn Evans.*

£s per acre
Under 0.2
0.2 — 0.5
0.6 — 0.9
1.0 and over

1851. The actual picture was probably less dramatic, but even revised
statistics show a decline of one-half.[19] At the other extreme, holdings
of above thirty acres register a sharp increase, from 17 per cent to 26

Acres	1841	1844*	1851	1861 (percentages)	1871	1881	1891
Above 15	—	36.0	50.9	52.6	54.7	56.1	57.4
Above 30	17.3	—	26.1	27.7	29.3	30.3	31.5
Above 50	—	9.2	13.8	15.0	15.9	16.6	17.2

* The 1844 data relate to 'persons holding land' rather than 'farms' or 'holdings'.

Table 4: *Proportion of all Irish farms of more than one acre (a) above fifteen acres (b) above thirty acres (c) above fifty acres, 1841–91.*
Source: K. T. Hoppen, *Elections, Politics and Society in Ireland 1832–85.*

per cent. Taken with the staggering drop in population, by the end of the 1840s Ricardian theorists were apparently seeing their policies put in train: small tenancies had decreased and the population was decimated. And yet the magic failed to work. For one thing, the results were not uniform; the west continued a special case. For another, the removal of tiny farms and the reduction of population did not mean that Irish farming approximated to English models, on which most theoretical postulations were based. The few contemporaries who argued that consolidation and clearance might *not* be the best thing for Irish conditions were never listened to.

What was happening before the Famine now accelerated: livestock farming on medium-sized (by Irish standards) farms took over in many areas, while in the far west subsistence-level poverty continued. Transport developments and commercialization boosted the process, as did the intensive development of railways later in the century. The number of dry cattle may have doubled from 1841 to 1851, though dairy cattle stayed about the same. All this, like population and marriage trends, was in the making over the previous thirty years. In Cork, as elsewhere, Donnelly finds, 'large farmers holding more than thirty acres not only escaped almost unscathed but in fact strengthened their position during the Famine years'.[20]

The large landlords, however, did not. They were seen as to blame for the catastrophe by many – illogically, but understandably. Their rents declined and their rates soared. Many (at least 10 per cent) went bankrupt; the Encumbered Estates Act of 1849, freeing landed property from legal encumbrances that prevented its sale, epitomized what had become of them. Irish estates worth £20,000,000 changed hands in the 1850s. But they were not broken up by native tenants raising themselves to the level of proprietors, nor did English capitalists enter the market on a large scale. The purchasers were local speculators, and solvent members of the landlord class: as usual, Irish capital was available when the object in question was the purchase of land. In February 1847 Elizabeth Smith, reduced to her husband's half-pay pension and her own earnings from journalism, had noted that:

the large farmer is doing well, his produce selling for three times the price of an ordinary year, his consumption though more costly still very fairly proportioned to his profits ... The large proprietors must be content with half their usual income and it must be spent share and share upon their people, very little on themselves; the lesser proprietors will suffer more as they have fewer luxuries to dispense with.

By the end of the year she acidly described the auction of Kilbride Manor and contents, where there were no gentry to bid, but farmers from two-roomed cabins came to pay sky-high prices for pretentious but inappropriate furniture.[21]

V

In *The Kellys and the O'Kellys* (1848) Anthony Trollope, who lived in Ireland and knew it well, delineated the social geography of a small Irish town just before the Famine:

The village of Dunmore has nothing about it which can especially recommend it to the reader. It has none of those beauties of nature which have taught Irishmen to consider their country as the 'first flower of the earth and first gem of the sea'. It is a dirty, ragged little town, standing in a very poor part of the country, with nothing about it to induce the traveller to go out of his beaten track. It is on no high road, and is blessed with no adventitious circumstances to add to its prosperity.

It was once the property of the O'Kellys; but, in those times the landed proprietors thought but little of the towns; and now it is parcelled out among different owners, some of whom would think it folly to throw away a penny on the place, and others of whom have not a penny to throw away. It consists of a big street, two little streets, and a few very little lanes. There is a Court-house, where the barrister sits twice a year; a Barrack, once inhabited by soldiers, but now given up to the police; a large slated chapel, not quite finished; a few shops for soft goods; half a dozen shebeen-houses, ruined by Father Mathew; a score of dirty cabins offering 'lodging and entertainment', as announced on the window-shutters; Mrs Kelly's inn and grocery-shop; and, last though not least, Simeon

Lynch's new, staring house, built just at the edge of the town, on the road to Roscommon, which is dignified with the name of Dunmore House. The people of most influence in the village are Mrs Kelly of the inn, and her two sworn friends, the parish priest and his curate.

The 'large slated chapel, not quite finished' and the influence of the parish priest indicate the importance of the Catholic Church, and this was another trend that the events of the 1840s accentuated. The practice of devotion in Catholic Ireland certainly intensified in the post-Famine age, a process sometimes attributed to the influence of Archbishop (later Cardinal) Paul Cullen,[vii] and sometimes to the psychological trauma following 1845–9. The evidence for a 'devotional revolution' tends to be impressionistic rather than quantitative; but certainly the ratio of priests to people altered dramatically. About 1840 it has been computed as one priest per 3,000 of the population, and one nun per 6,500. As early as 1850 the balance had altered to 1:2,100 and 1:3,400 respectively; by 1871 it was 1:1,560 and 1:1,100. Not only was the population decreasing; the number of priests increased by 20 per cent, and of nuns by 50 per cent, over the decade.

The implications for both religious and social discipline are obvious. Moreover, the priests' increasing control over their flocks had been preceded (from about 1830) by the bishops' increasing control over their priests. The complaints and controversies over clerical avarice, drunkenness and immorality decreased as religious practices became more formalized; the eighteenth-century practice of 'the stations' (devotions held in houses around the parish) was replaced by ritual in newly built churches. The status and character of the priesthood may have changed too. The common contemporary generalizations about Maynooth replacing urbane French-educated priests with rough-hewn peasant nationalists do not stand up to examination: seminarists came from the middle ranks of farming and shopkeeping society.

[vii] Paul Cullen (1803–78): born in County Kildare; educated at Shackleton's Quaker school, Ballitore, Carlow College and the Urban College of the Propaganda, Rome; ordained, 1829; as rector of the Irish College and the Propaganda College, sought to counter British influence at the Vatican; Archbishop of Armagh, 1849–52; summoned the first synod of the Irish Catholic clergy to be held since the twelfth century, the Synod of Thurles, 1850; Archbishop of Dublin, 1852; apostolic delegate for the foundation of the Catholic University; promoted an Irish Brigade to assist papal troops against Garibaldi, 1859; opposed Fenianism and all political movements that did not primarily promote the interests of his Church, but attempted to institutionalize the bond he believed should subsist between Catholicism and nationalism in founding the National Association, 1864; first Irishman to become a Cardinal, 1866.

Priests' incomes had already increased considerably, probably averaging £150 *per annum* in 1825, compared to £65 in 1800. The social and political authority of the priest had been established in the age of Catholic emancipation, though his effectiveness probably relied at least in part on the fact that he articulated sentiments and prejudices already accepted by his flock.

Whether the post-Famine 'devotional revolution' constitutes a change in basic attitudes may be questioned. The rate of mass attendance trebled, but the previous low attendance need not signify a lack of devotion. It should probably be related to the lack of churches at the beginning of the nineteenth century (many of those that did exist did double-duty as schools or even threshing-floors). By the Famine, the deficiency in numbers was mostly remedied: the great wave of church-building in the later nineteenth century tended to be for replacement purposes. But the inadequacy of places for worship in pre-Famine Ireland certainly went with a less organized, less canonical and less 'Roman' religion than that which took over from the 1850s.

This is not to say that 'modernizing' tendencies were not evident before then. The effect of Father Mathew's[viii] great temperance crusade might be instanced here: as Trollope noted, it was highly effective in the short term. Production of whiskey more than halved in the early 1840s. Many of the travel-writers of that age (Asenath Nicolson as well as Mr and Mrs S. C. Hall) were equally concerned to spread the temperance word, and were convinced that the battle was being won. Though the Catholic Church looked slightly askance at the Protestant aura of the movement, it roused strong adherence among a population who appear to have been open to enthusiasms; the Missioners awoke an excited response as well (and there was also a contemporary religious revival among Protestants). Such reactions do not fall neatly into pre-Famine and post-Famine schemes. Revivalism, like modernized religious practice, seems to have taken root in the more Anglicized, prosperous areas early on; church attendance in pre-Famine Wexford, for instance, had already reached far higher levels than in remote Galway, and it was always high in urban areas. Moreover, it was the

[viii] Theobald Mathew (1790–1856): born in County Tipperary; joined the Capuchins; ordained, 1814; worked tirelessly for the welfare of the poor of Cork; induced by Protestant friends to pledge himself to temperance reform, 1838; transformed a local concern into a national movement, although professing no proselytizing or political purpose; civil list pension, 1847; overworked in Famine relief, 1848; extended mission to America, 1849–51; declined a bishopric, having fallen into ill health, 1851; never recovered.

same 'respectable' farming and shopkeeping classes who survived the Famine where the less regularly devout cottier classes did not. Before the Famine, farmers were outnumbered two to five by smallholders and cottiers; by 1881 they were equal in number. Thus the Famine may have promoted rural *embourgeoisement*; but self-conscious Irish respectability was already in existence before the Famine (an ethos memorably characterized by Thackeray as 'wild, dismal and *genteel*').

From the 1850s religious societies proliferated; devotional aids and new devotions became the norm: 'the rosary, forty hours, perpetual adoration, novenas, blessed altars, *Via Crucis,* benediction, vespers, devotion to the Sacred Heart and to the Immaculate Conception, jubilees, triduums, pilgrimages, shrines, processions and retreats'.[22] These tended to replace holy wells, bonfires, 'patterns', wakes, protective charms, effigies and the ancient celebration of high points in the agricultural calendar. Contemporaries noticed the abandonment of magical practices in rural life from the late 1840s. It is possible that the trauma of the Famine helped destroy the psychological reliance on magical practices to 'control' patterns of crop yields, subsistence and disease, though it is impossible to arrive at a mechanical theory about it. Nor should one underestimate the personal influence of Cullen – authoritarian, Romanist, obsessed with conspiracies, constitutionally nationalist, indefatigably planting out like-minded nominees among the hierarchy. None the less, the process of devotional readjustment (if not revolution) was in train before the Famine. There is much local evidence of reforms, such as the consecration of Dublin's Pro-Cathedral in 1825 with magnificent liturgical ceremonies. What was important after the Famine was the drastic readjustment of population in terms of class as well as numbers.

Catholicism in the post-Famine age provided a highly organized, coherent identity that helped Irish society cope with the psychological impact of disruption. The Gaelic language was increasingly abandoned: a large proportion of emigrants came from Irish-speaking areas, and those left behind were not anxious to preserve it. Its eradication was the achievement of ambitious parents as much as of English-speaking schoolteachers. Even more fundamentally, habits of marriage apparently altered. The average age of marriage rose, as did the number of those staying unmarried. This has been associated with the decline of very small land units, and the practice of one son taking over the family farm (often after an interminable wait). It seems likely that here again the picture is skewed by emigration and the alteration of rural class-structure: rather than people changing their habits, those who had always behaved like this may simply have become predominant. Increased longevity of parents also accentuated the process.

Similarly, the mercenary rural marriage, carefully negotiated, is usually taken as the *leitmotif* of post-Famine life. The substantial dowries offered with farmers' daughters always surprised outsiders; and more attention was paid to the land than to any other part of the bargain (there is a vivid picture of a prospective bride's father and uncles arriving to check this out, 'turning over the soil in field after field'[23]). In fact, this approach had long been characteristic of the small-farmer class, as was the low illegitimacy rate (though it varied regionally), implying sexual restraint. But the Famine decimated precisely the class that traditionally favoured improvident early marriages. The small-farmer ethos took over, postponing fertility, avoiding subdivision, and insisting on a firm material basis for marriage (which often resulted in the wife achieving a higher economic status than in other rural societies). Sexual puritanism was seen as part of the package; traditional Irish preoccupations with obligations to family and kin militated against irregular sexual connections, and social disapproval of illegitimacy was marked in remote rural areas (where, incidentally, the Church was least influential).

Here, as elsewhere, modern Ireland was in the making. Education was an important part of the process; there was already a high level of literacy by the 1840s, and the proportion continued to rise. Just before the Famine, the National Board of Education was spending £100,000 *per annum,* and there were 12,000 teachers registered in Ireland; by 1849, 500,000 pupils were being taught in 4,321 schools. Attendance levels were high; contemporaries noted the priority placed upon education, whatever about the quality of the education received. This was accentuated by the Famine and by the Church's ability to manipulate the educational system. Cullen's viscerally realistic views about the National system deserve quotation: 'very dangerous when considered in general, because its aim is to introduce a mingling of Protestants and Catholics, but in the places where in fact there are no Protestants this mingling cannot be achieved'.

Post-Famine Ireland, then, entered upon a complex process of social readjustment. But the problem of rural poverty still remained, if in diluted form. The Poor Law had been demonstrated as inadequate; after the Famine, panaceas emphasized interference with land tenure, and public investment. In fact, insecurity of tenure was not necessarily a structural reason for poverty, and nor were levels of rent; conacre farmers on the margin of subsistence were not really affected by tenurial considerations. In the wider sphere, underinvestment was perceived as a primary problem, but again, the relationship to security of tenure is problematic. Most of all, the favourite 'answer' of economic theorists remained irrelevant: for this was industrialization.

Belfast and eastern Ulster remained the only area of large-scale industrialization. The special nature of the region was emphasized by the fact that so much of the industrial wealth was in Protestant hands (one 1820 estimate put the ratio of Protestant to Catholic capital in Belfast as forty to one). Skilled and semi-skilled jobs also became a Protestant preserve. But though the northern propensity to indus-trialize was regularly linked with Protestant virtues, this was not the same thing. The basic pre-condition appears to have been the diversified farming pattern that embraced cottage industry from an early stage, and continued to sustain a dense population in comparative comfort. The decline in Irish population through the later nineteenth century was overwhelmingly accounted for by the decline in rural areas of the twenty-six counties outside the unit of what is now Northern Ireland; emigration from northern and eastern Ulster remained very low, and Belfast grew from 75,000 in 1841 to 387,000 in 1911.

In Ulster, industrial villages based on linen mills had proliferated from the 1830s; there was very little such development in the rest of Ireland, though the great Malcolmson cotton empire at Portlaw, County Waterford, would continue until the 1860s. Otherwise, vision-ary plans for industrializing Ireland through textile factories had little effect. Even where a cottage industry based on producing linen yarn did take hold, as in Mayo up to about 1830, machine production tended to make it redundant. Outside Ulster, manufacturing industry tended to go into decline from about 1820, possibly amounting to a process of actual deindustrialization.

Finally, what happened to political attitudes and structures after the Famine? Obviously, an abiding resentment of 'England' was one result. Whether an Irish parliament and government would have articulated a different approach to the Famine is an open question; but they would certainly have behaved more efficiently. Moreover, English governmental attitudes exposed the illogic and double-think of Union: when a rate-in-aid was finally imposed in 1850 to distribute the burden, it was imposed on Ireland alone, not throughout Britain. Where the terms of Union might unduly disadvantage Britain, they were tacitly ignored. (Again, Butt characteristically pointed this out in his *Letter on the Rate in Aid,* 1849.)

Locally, too, bitterness was not forgotten. Social relations and attitudes were affected by the preservation of 'bad' landlords in the long Irish memory. By 1850 a priest in County Clare could tell his congregation: 'my advice to you is to throw over altogether the legal rights of the landlords and seek for your just rights and not your legal rights. I would not give anything for the landlords' legal rights but to tell you to throw them over altogether.'[24] Ironically, much of the evidence shows that it was farmers, not landlords, who treated the needy worst – bringing cases to petty sessions against the starving who stole turnips from their fields, and loudly objecting when the compassionate magistrate dismissed the cases. Local antipathies were sharpened by resistance; a study of Cork contradicts the usual assumption of 'apathy', showing many cattle-raids and food riots in 1846–7, and there were rent strikes and intimidatory tactics in Clare and elsewhere. But generally, violent reactions were more characteristic of the areas least drastically affected.

Political violence in post-Famine Ireland continued, though its rationale may have changed; the language of politics (especially as reflected in street ballads) became modernized and Anglicized as the values of the farming class took over, and with them a certain self-consciousness. Elections remained arenas of much furious vehemence and broken heads. A sharpened edge of antagonism is discernible in relations between farmers and landlords: the latter felt the former had benefited at their expense, resenting the way that labourers had been offloaded on to the rates, and accusing the farming class of using the conditions of the 1840s to their own profit. Landlords' efforts to claim increased rent were often beaten off by armed crowds; by 1849 many inefficient landlords had given up, accepting rent abatement or taking advantage of the Encumbered Estates Act. The age of the strong farmer was to hand.

This was accompanied by changes in political structure after the Famine. The unpredictable, haphazardly defined political nation, based on franchise valuation that differed in effect from county to county, proofs of 'possession' and bizarre registration procedures, was shaken up by the demographic contraction. The nominal county electorate probably fell from 60,597 to 15,000–18,000 (while the total electorate dropped from 121,194 to about 45,000). The 1850 Franchise Act finally overhauled the registration system, and simplified the franchise to an occupation qualification, based on systematic (but rather restrictive) Poor Law valuations of twelve pounds in the counties and eight pounds in the boroughs. This tended to exclude many of the poor and marginal who would have qualified before, whereas prosperous farmers were now sure of inclusion. 'The changing pattern of farm holdings after the Famine, the ability to acquire more land, and the consequent growth in the presence of twelve-pound-and-over farmers within the total farmer community steadily increased the proportion of that community able to claim the vote.'[25] In the same era, the country shopkeeping interest achieved a political weight of its own, capitalizing on rising prosperity from the mid-1850s and the inexorable spread of retailing. Urbanization accompanied the process, with several boroughs increasing their population in the post-Famine years. The values of the railway-station bookstall were replacing those of the street ballad.

In these developments lay the seeds not only of post-Famine trends within the agrarian economy, but of political confrontation within the rural world. The small-scale but solvent farmer of, say, twenty to thirty acres and fifteen-pound valuation would underpin the mass movements that challenged landlordism. They were secure in no longer being outnumbered and threatened by a labourer and cottier class that had entered a precipitate decline – except in areas of the west, where the economic problems of pre-Famine Ireland continued in concentrated form. The values, beliefs and influence of the farming class in post-Famine Ireland entered their own ascendancy, mediated through Church, social institutions and, eventually, politics.

CHAPTER FIFTEEN

IRELAND
ABROAD

I

EMIGRATION IS THE great fact of Irish social history from the early nineteenth century. It cannot simply be seen as part of the disruptions attendant upon the Famine; a large-scale exodus began long before it, and continued long afterwards. Moreover, the results of the phenomenon altered Irish domestic history as well as affecting the countries that received the emigrating Irish; the outflow enabled the continuance of patterns of Irish rural life that were essentially archaic, and created a particular social composition among the people who stayed.

The tradition of leaving Ireland, for economic or political reasons, goes back a long way[i] – not only to the great Ulster migrations to colonial America, but also to the eighteenth-century Irish settlements in towns all over Britain. In the nineteenth century, however, the stream became a flood. Statistics are notoriously unreliable. But between 1815 and 1845, at least 1,000,000 and possibly 1,500,000 emigrated;[1] between 1845 and 1870 at least 3,000,000 left. By 1890 there were 3,000,000 Irish-born people living overseas – 39 per cent of all those alive who had been born in Ireland. There was, in a very real sense, an Ireland abroad.

It is slowly being realized how important this was for the social and economic history of nineteenth-century Britain. Well before the Famine, for instance, 100,000 Irish-born people were living in Manchester; the large-scale (and very useful) Royal Commission on 'the state of the Irish Poor in Great Britain' dates from 1836. The census reports indicate 419,256 Irish-born people in Britain in 1841 (52 per cent of them male) and 733,866 in 1851. Breakdowns indicate that

[i] See above, pp. 44, 133, 151, 202, 215–16.

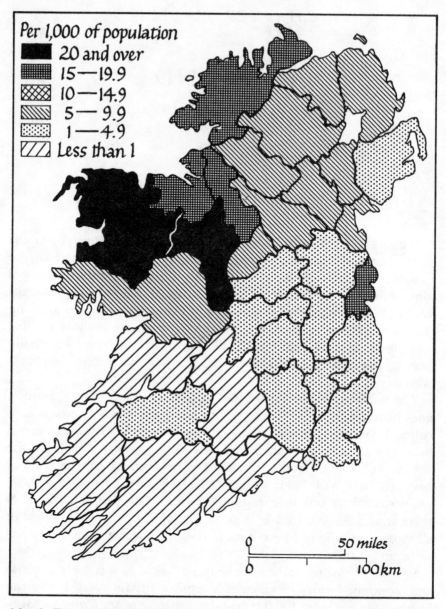

Map 8: *Temporary emigrants 1841, by counties.*

Source: J. H. Johnson, 'Harvest Migration from Nineteenth-century Ireland', *Transactions of the Institute of British Geographers*, no. 41 (June 1967). (Statistics from 1841 census of Ireland XXXVI–XXXVII.)

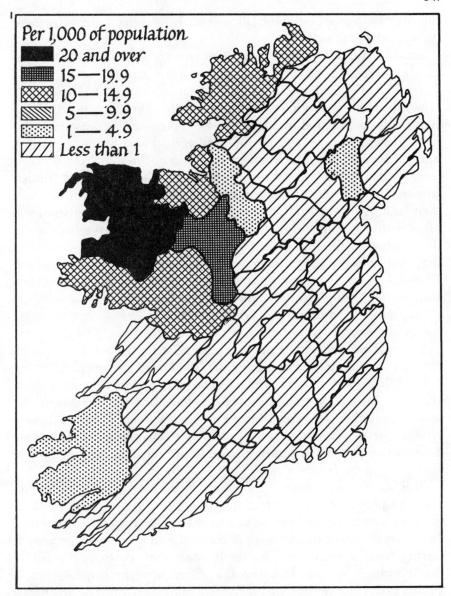

Map 9: *Migratory agricultural labourers 1900, by counties.*
Source: J. H. Johnson, 'Harvest Migration from Nineteenth-century Ireland', *Transactions of the Institute of British Geographers*, no. 41 (June 1967). (Statistics from 'Report on Migratory Irish Agricultural Labourers', Cd 341, Dublin, 1900.)

Irish women and children formed a high proportion of emigrants to Britain. The result was the formation of a self-sustaining Irish community, and an influx of labour that helped shape the growth of British industrial society.

Seasonal migration from Ireland, often very far afield, was a long-standing practice: in the eighteenth century Arthur Young found 3,000 to 5,000 men going annually from south-east Ireland to the Newfoundland fisheries, and returning. More typically, nearly 3 per cent of the population of Mayo in 1841 embarked on seasonal work in England. The *spailpín*, or migrant agricultural labourer, was an integral part of the agricultural economy in north-west Ireland. They were generally the owners of tiny farms (or their sons), not landless labourers; the profits of temporary migration enabled them to retain their land. After the Famine, the problem shifted. The destination was often northern England or the midlands, rather than the harvests of the south-east; the flow from Donegal to Scotland became notable; the time spent in Britain lengthened; and the type of work altered. Changes in transport and communications affected them; steamship competition brought the Belfast–Glasgow fare down as low as three-pence, and the Midland and Great Western railways even provided special services for harvesters.

Seasonal migration did not really decline until about 1900, with changes in farming techniques, and the fall in relative wage possibilities. It may, however, have continued a concealed existence, since what began as seasonal migration must often have become permanent. An autobiography like Michael MacGowan's *The Hard Road to Klondike* (*Rotha Mór An tSaoil*) shows the process whereby the annual Donegal–Scotland migration led almost insensibly further afield, ending up – in his case – on the frozen Yukon.

Nor was seasonal migration the only incentive to large-scale movement in pre-Famine Ireland; emigration from the north and north-west has convincingly been linked to changes in the textile industry.[2] In the great days of the complex domestic farming-weaving economy, during the late eighteenth and early nineteenth century, the family could support various additions that fitted into the general plan of production. The decline of linen-yarn spinning from the 1820s disrupted this, and made many family members redundant, except where the transition to weaving machine-spun yarn could be made, as around the Lagan valley. Thus, long before the crisis of the 1840s, the north-west was becoming economically marginalized, and even the north-central counties were unable to sustain the density of population that had grown up around the domestic linen industry. The traditional route for seasonal migration from Drogheda to Dundee lay to hand;

a more permanent exodus started to take place, destined for the textile industry in that part of Scotland.

This kind of emigration by easy stages should be remembered, especially considering the apocalyptic aura of tragic exile that developed around the transatlantic outflow of later decades. Many Irish people came to view emigration as a necessary evil. They were, of course, encouraged to see it like this by theoretical social engineers and improving landlords, who presented it as a humane answer to the perceived problems of poverty and overpopulation (though not all saw it as a cost-effective solution: James Mill, Malthus, Ricardo and McCulloch were all unenthusiastic about emigration, for various reasons). Plans for state assistance fluctuated, dependent upon domestic conditions. During harvest crises in the late 1840s, and again in 1879, large amounts of money were made available to 'special category' emigrants, which assisted many to otherwise unattainable destinations, like Australia. Similarly, certain landlords involved themselves on a large scale, such as the Fitzwilliams in Wicklow and Colonel Wyndham in Clare, who actually purchased land in America and settled Irish tenants on it. But imposed emigration tended to remain in the realm of theory. What really made the practice take off, and continue, was its autonomous endorsement by the Irish people.

This could, at particularly low points, be directed towards the state schemes; at Mallow, in 1849, the Poor Law Guardians had to suspend a state-aided scheme because its announcement caused a great flood into the poor-house of people claiming to qualify. More characteristic was the development of an expectation among certain sectors of the Irish rural population that emigration was an inevitability (again, the casual way in which Michael MacGowan first went to Scotland, without discussing the matter at home, is striking). It was no less harrowing for that, and nationalist Ireland, especially after the Famine, interpreted emigration as an obscene result of British malevolence – though some patriots, like William Smith O'Brien, advocated it for economic reasons. It remains difficult to see how the Irish economy, under any feasible management, could have sustained all those who left. Despite the attempts of economic historians to uncouple the connection between overpopulation and poverty, it seems evident that from the early nineteenth century bad seasons, poor harvests and failures in the potato crop produced an inevitable rise in emigration; and that the cottier and labourer classes were, as ever, most liable to provide the 'at risk' surplus.

The horrific conditions of Famine emigration tend to impose a picture that is not relevant to the whole process of nineteenth- and twentieth-century emigration. With commercialization and improved communications, the perceived and desired standards of living became far higher than the actual possibilities at home – a process that would endure.[ii] The importance of those who had gone before, in setting up a 'chain', is closely linked with this. The established routes were followed: Conrad Arensberg, investigating County Clare in the 1930s, tells of a boy's golden opportunity to emigrate to Australia being rejected because those of the family already established in Boston would not hear of it. Between 1848 and 1867 an estimated £34,000,000 was sent back from America to the United Kingdom, 40 per cent of it in the form of pre-paid tickets. Much of this went to Ireland. The 'chains' of those imported by forerunners have been analysed by David Fitzpatrick: they show, among other patterns, that so-called Ulster 'Scotch–Irish' brought their parents out, while southern Catholics tended to opt for siblings and friends of the same generation. Encouragement was provided by advertisements, stories of magical opportunities in a promised land, and that favourite set-piece for genre painters: the reading aloud of the 'emigrant letter'.

Throughout the nineteenth century the mechanisms of emigration became more efficient: brokers, entrepreneurs and subagents entered the traffic, manipulating increasingly professionalized propaganda. The conditions of the actual voyage were thrown into sharp relief by the horrors of 'coffin ships' during the Famine, when, for instance, 20 per cent of emigrants from Cork to Quebec died, either on board or after landing. The testimony of those who survived (including investigators who actually took a steerage passage and then exposed the nightmare conditions of starving and overcrowding) took effect; regulations to mitigate this were in force by the later nineteenth century. Some landlords saw the arrangement of a reliable passage, and the equipment of their emigrating tenants, as part of their duty; many more (notoriously Lord Palmerston[iii]) did not. Even those who did could not expect

---

[ii] In 1967 the per capita GNP in Ireland was half that of the average of fourteen countries in north-west Europe, and a quarter that of the USA.

[iii] Henry John Temple (1784–1865): succeeded as third Viscount Palmerston in the Irish peerage, 1802; entered parliament as a Tory, 1807; Secretary for War, 1809–28; Whig Foreign Secretary, 1830–34, 1835–41, 1846–51; Home Secretary, 1853; Prime Minister, 1855–8 and 1859–65. His family had acquired Irish lands, appointments and titles since 1609 but remained bound to Broadlands, Hampshire; a fairly exemplary, if absentee, Irish landlord; visited his great estates at Palmerston, County Dublin, and in County Sligo to oversee major improvements, including the building of a harbour.

to be thanked for it. The horrors of the fever-ridden Atlantic crossing in the 1840s were inextricably linked with the destitution that had brought so many to their deaths in Ireland, on board ship, or at the notorious points of disembarkation. The monuments to dead immigrants at Quebec and Montreal tell their own story, while one at Grosse Isle gives the version as recorded by the Ancient Order of Hibernians in 1909: 'Thousands of the children of the Gael were lost on this island while fleeing from foreign tyrannical laws and an artificial famine in the years 1847–8. God bless them. God save Ireland!'

As the mechanisms for emigration became smoother, and the practice established on a large scale, the idea of forced expulsion became less and less relevant. The Catholic Church, for instance, emerged as an important agency of emigration, especially religious orders in search of new recruits. By the late nineteenth century American-based houses of the Sisters of the Holy Cross, the Dominicans and the Sisters of Mercy were competitively 'gleaning the country'. The spread of Catholicism abroad was frequently perceived as one of the advantages of the emigrant flood. None the less, the Irish 'Catholic' world view – that philosophical acceptance of stasis noted by so many nineteenth-century travellers – was not conducive to enterprising emigration. Nor was the tendency to defer to established authority and the low tolerance for individual deviation that were part of the same syndrome. Even when emigration had become established as an almost automatic part of rural life, it conflicted sharply with the high value that Irish country people put upon communalism, kinship and a sense of place. To leave home meant a psychic disruption. 'The depressing and harassing nature of the frightful, restless life I have here has made a mush of my mind,' complained one Irish-speaking emigrant of the 1820s (who had nevertheless made enough money to buy his own farm at Utica, New York).[3]

What created the powerful pressure to emigrate, especially after the Famine, was an equally intrinsic part of the Irish rural mentality: the need to preserve the family farm. Emigration after the Famine did *not* release land for consolidation into larger units, as the theoreticians had hoped; farm owners were not emigrating. Their 'assisting relatives' were, and those who were encouraged by the family, at home and abroad, to clear the way for an undivided inheritance by leaving. Subdivision and partible inheritance had long given way to the 'stem family' method of descent, where one inheritor took over, often late in life. This is closely connected with the type of person who emigrated from Ireland. In contrast to other migrant nationalities, women made

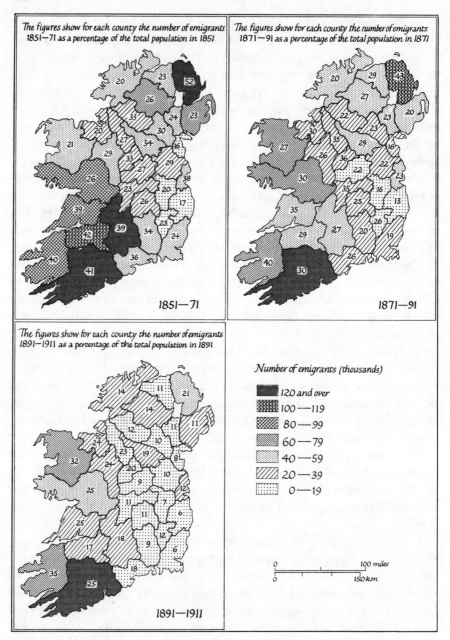

The figures show for each county the number of emigrants 1851–71 as a percentage of the total population in 1851

1851–71

The figures show for each county the number of emigrants 1871–91 as a percentage of the total population in 1871

1871–91

The figures show for each county the number of emigrants 1891–1911 as a percentage of the total population in 1891

1891–1911

Number of emigrants (thousands)

- 120 and over
- 100—119
- 80—99
- 60—79
- 40—59
- 20—39
- 0—19

0   100 miles
0   150 km

Map 10: *Emigration 1851–1911, by counties.*

Source: T. W. Moody, F. X. Martin and F. J. Byrne (editors), *A New History of Ireland.
Vol. IX: Maps, Genealogies, Lists, A Companion to Irish History, Part II.*

up as large a proportion as men, at some points even outnumbering them. Irish emigrants were also likely to be unattached, rather than family groups (except at the height of the Famine). Young adults, especially in their early twenties, preponderated. Emigration was often seen as a stage in life, *en route* to marriage or full employment. The finances of emigration were important here: the cost of a single ticket could be more easily raised, and the earnings of one representative emigrant could be channelled back to bring out other members of the family later on. (Though the formal cost of a passage varied little, prices were affected by discounts and fluctuations in demand, as well as trading patterns that created empty ships needing to be filled.) Before and during the Famine, the landless rural poor often found the cost of an Atlantic voyage prohibitive; later on, price reductions and remittances from relations altered this. But throughout the nineteenth century, emigration was the resort of the young, the single and those who lacked access to a farm or to textile skills.

Where did they come from? Before the Famine, the north predominated: first through the great eighteenth-century Ulster exodus to North America (a much more diverse process than the 'Scotch–Irish' myth allows), and then because of dislocations in the textile industry. After the Famine, Connacht played an increasing role, as relative costs lowered and remittances accumulated. The poorer and less industrialized areas always preponderated; the eastern coast and north-eastern counties (where alone there were towns of a size worth migrating to) figured much less dramatically. But the general pattern was widely diffused: those under the age of twenty-four were leached away from nearly every Irish county during the 1850s, at two and a half times the rate of depletion in English counties. During this period those emigrating as a result of the consolidation of holdings were a higher proportion than later on; they accounted for a heavy migration to Australia from the south midlands. During the Famine period, areas with a high proportion of landless labourers, like west Cork, had a surprisingly low emigration rate; when to emigrate with a family cost a year's wages, few of this class could afford to leave. The contemporary impression that 'the more substantial class of peasants' were going is borne out by detailed research.[4] But after the 1850s Cork shows a larger and larger proportion of landless labourers leaving, achieving an emigrant total of 425,000 by 1891, which was proportionately higher than from any other county. Emigration from Connacht, by contrast, where tiny holdings continued, fluctuated with crop yields; poverty still restricted the readiness to emigrate; population increase in the poorest districts continued, as the changed patterns of marriage and fertility took longer to penetrate than in the east. Only from the 1880s did Connacht emigration become a distinct syndrome, probably because the harvest crises at last coincided with a sufficient level of remittances and state aid at a more realistic level than before.[iv]

Traditionally, those who left the west went to the United States (and sometimes to New Zealand); those from the north and north-east preferred Canada, though they often moved on to the United States. The south-west and the north midlands had connections with Australia. Munster channelled its emigrants to the USA through Queenstown. The Donegal–Scotland axis has been mentioned; and all areas sent emigrants to Britain through Liverpool, where arcane patterns of discrimination appeared amongst them, the Ulster and Leinster Liverpool-Irish looking down upon the Connacht harvesters passing through. Emigration to Britain was at least considered reversible, and was sometimes so in practice. But despite the folklore of 'The Returned Yank', very few came back from America to live in Ireland, far less than returned to Italy, Sweden or Greece.

Hiccoughs in the host economy could dictate alterations of pattern, for, generally, the emigrants went where the jobs were. Bristol, for instance, was nearby, and had a large pre-Famine tradition of Irish settlement, especially from Cork; but since it was in economic decline, the post-Famine influx was correspondingly small. The textile towns of Lancashire were a more logical destination; the early life of Michael Davitt[v] provides a classic and harrowing example of eviction in Mayo

[iv] From 1881 to 1910 Leinster's, Ulster's and Munster's proportions of emigrants fell by 53 per cent, 47 per cent and 41 per cent respectively compared to the period 1851–80; but Connacht's increased by 8 per cent.

[v] Michael Davitt (1846–1906): born in County Mayo; emigrated to Lancashire, 1851; lost his right arm in a mill accident at eleven; joined the Fenians, 1865; organizing secretary of the IRB, 1868; sentenced to fifteen years' penal servitude, 1870; released, 1877; went to America; worked with John Devoy upon a 'new departure' for the nationalist movement, combining agitation for self-government and land reform; formed the Land League of Mayo, 1878, and the National Land League, 1879; helped organize the American and Ladies' Land Leagues, 1880; met Henry George; impressed by his land schemes; elected MP for County Meath while in prison, 1882; persuaded Parnell to found the National League upon suppression of the Land League; gave evidence to the Parnell Commission, 1889; edited Labour World, 1890–91; anti-Parnellite MP for North Meath, 1892, and South Mayo, 1895–9; co-founded United Irish League, 1898; sought to reconcile constitutional and revolutionary nationalism, and to democratize each; symbolized his growing concern for the cause of international labour by visiting the leaders of the Russian revolutionary party, 1903–5; published The Fall of Feudalism in Ireland, 1904.

Thousand per annum

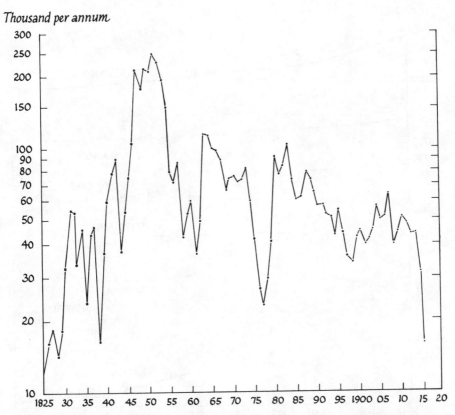

Figure 1: *Irish overseas emigration 1825–1915. Number leaving the United Kingdom per annum. Statistics refer to Irish-born passengers leaving United Kingdom ports for destinations outside Europe and the Mediterranean. Precise criteria were altered several times, and the graph is most useful as a guide to short-term and cyclical fluctuations.*
Source: David Fitzpatrick, *Irish Emigration 1801–1921*, Studies in Irish Economic and Social History No. 1. (Statistics from Commission on Emigration Reports, 1955, 314–16, with correction of erroneous returns up to 1842.)

leading to employment, and mutilation, in the mills of Haslingden. In York, large numbers of Irish flooded the city after the Famine, though many may have worked up to twenty miles out in the country as field-hands – a pattern established long before.[5] All over, Irish wives and children entered the workforce, too, though in an irregular and episodic way that may not have been captured in statistics.

Destinations altered with time. In the late nineteenth and early twentieth centuries, the great emphasis was on emigration to the United States; from 1876 to 1921 this was the destination of 84 per cent of Irish emigrants, compared to 7 per cent for Australia and

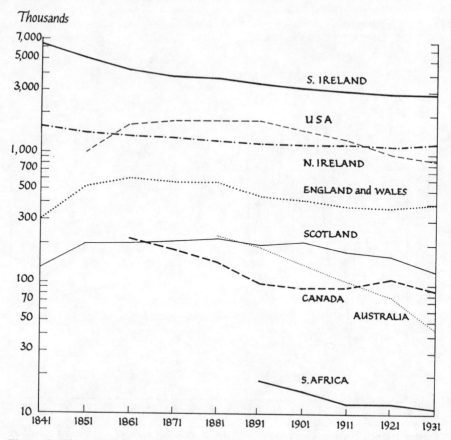

Figure 2: *The Irish-born population in selected countries 1841–1931. The figures are in thousands and are plotted on a logarithmic scale.*

Source: R. Lawton, 'Irish Immigration to England and Wales in the Mid-nineteenth Century', *Irish Geography*, vol. iv (1959). (Statistics based on the birthplace tables in the 1841–1936 census of Ireland, the 1841–1851 census of Great Britain, the 1861–1931 census of England and Wales, and the 1861–1931 census of Scotland.)

Canada and 8 per cent for the United Kingdom. This last computation reflects not only industrial depression and world war, but also a probable statistical underestimation. From about 1914, however, America's change of attitude towards immigrants took effect, though the quota laid down for the Irish was never, in fact, filled, and remittances declined; Britain took over once more. By the low point in Anglo-Irish diplomatic relations during the 1930s, the high rate of emigration was reflected in biased and hysterical assertions made about the likelihood of repatriating the Irish; by 1946–51 over 80 per cent of Irish emigrants were headed for the United Kingdom. By this stage, though, it was not only a matter of how many left; at least as important was the long-standing establishment of communities, born and resident in Britain or America, but indisputably Irish.

II

Evelyn Waugh once remarked, apropos his 'immigrant' friend Cyril Connolly, that to the Irishman there were only two final realities: Hell and the United States. To many in the nineteenth century, they seemed presented as alternatives; and there was little hesitation in choosing. The long tradition of a new start in America embraced not only Presbyterian pioneers, but also a flood of post-1798 refugees, many of whom rose to social and political prominence. The Jeffersonian notion of a land of political liberty (and later the Jacksonian idea of a lusty democratic free-for-all) became part of the Irish-American dream; so did a pronounced note of anti-Englishness. As the post-1800 Protestant emigration centred on Canada, by mid-century Irish Catholics were concentrating upon the United States.

From 1820 the scale of transatlantic migration increased dramatically. Lower passage cost and new rates (especially via Liverpool) interacted with the flight from the land of those whom it could not sustain: casualties of the post-war farming dislocation, or 'children of circumstance', as one emigrant put it. Those from the small farmer classes stressed their desire to achieve 'independence', a quality supposed, often unrealistically, to flourish in America. At this stage they were prepared to attempt a rural life; their post-Famine successors generally turned away from the land, and headed for American railways, factories and mines. The traditional syndrome of Irish America presents an ex-rural population firmly located in towns and cities: though this, like so much else about the subject, has been exaggerated.

Rural America was, of course, so vast and unpopulated that it bore no resemblance to the intimate and gregarious nature of country life at home. But if immigrants preferred city life, the choice was largely economic, not psychological. It was easier for the unpropertied to find quick work in towns and factories, or on canal and railway projects; Irish women could become domestic servants, or in some cases textile workers. They were 'a model industrial proletariat'.[6] They were also, or could be, unruly and easily criminalized in urban conditions; as much as a quarter to one-third of the Famine immigrants may have been Irish-speaking; they easily became the targets for American nativist and anti-Catholic prejudice. A 'savage' stereotype was created and in some ways remained.

The progress of Irish America was a complex business. Immigrants continued to flood in, at a rate of about 100,000 a year in the 1860s. From about 1870 Irish immigrants were more literate and more modernized; though they remained excluded from the upper bourgeoisie, they had created by the end of the century a privileged immigrant sector. Many of them had left the mines and the factories for the police force, the nursing profession and the civil service. They purchased property more easily than other immigrant groups; they invested heavily in the Catholic Church; in the twentieth century they made good use of the Catholic educational system and of the GI Bill. By the end of the nineteenth century a series of influential Irish-American bishops had brought the Catholic Church, with its strong Irish identification, into the mainstream of American life. The Aliens laws did not affect them. Irish-American millionaires were a recognized element in big business, if not in 'society'. Yet the subculture remained.

This was partly due to the geography of settlement, and the areas they had made their own. The notorious cellars of Boston, colonized in the 1840s, and the wooden tenements (called 'barracks') run up for Irish immigrants in New York had been the nucleus of an immigrant culture where solidarity, defensiveness and Hibernocentricity were notable. They were not impermeable 'ghettos'; settlement could spread out; intermarriage did occur. But the rhetoric, especially the political rhetoric, stressed their separateness.

This was expressed by the continuing Irish-American commitment to politics 'at home'. The identification with the Repeal movement is notable; it is tempting to see in it evidence of psychological displacement, and a failure to accustom themselves to actually being in America. The image of 'bondsmen made free' was less strong than that of Exodus: a people wandering the world, bereft of their holy land.

The fact that this was unrealistic, and that those who organized such displacement politics were probably merely a vocal minority, is not really relevant; the emotional identification is. As a pressure-group, the Irish in America continued to use their ethnic identification to influence foreign policy. The kind of Irish nationalism that flourished in America repudiated O'Connellite pragmatics in favour of a purist, racialist notion based on hatred of Britain; it was the culture of *Speeches from the Dock*, and the ideal of rural Ireland propagandized in novels like Charles J. Kickham's[vi] *Knocknagow*.

Within the American culture, such beliefs could help to affirm a respectable identity, as well as reinforcing resentment of the British power that had supposedly denied the emigrant 'respectability' at home. By the 1870s Irish-American societies like Clan na Gael[vii] were providing well-drilled sister movements to nationalist organizations at home. The National League of America in the 1880s tapped great sources of funds for the constitutional Home Rule movement in Ireland, though the rhetoric had to be tailored into an extremist shape for the purpose; the half-American descent of Charles Stewart Parnell[viii] may have been more important than often realized.

Moreover, a vital part of the Irish-American political culture revolved around the belief that emigration was – in Alexander Sullivan's[ix] words – 'not a social necessity but a political oppression'. The

[vi] Charles Joseph Kickham (1828–82): born in County Tipperary; son of a prosperous shopkeeper; rendered partially blind and deaf by a gunpowder accident in his early teens; a leader of his local Confederate Club, 1848; joined the Fenians, 1860; appointed to their Supreme Executive; co-editor of the *Irish People*, 1863; sentenced to fourteen years' penal servitude, 1865; released in poor health, 1869; subsequently published *Poems, Sketches and Narratives, Illustrative of Irish Life*, 1870, and three novels, of which the most popular was *Knocknagow*, 1879. Confessed that much of Irish literature of his age was propaganda rather than art, and turned to Shakespeare, Burns and George Eliot for his 'intellectual food'.

[vii] Founded in New York in 1867: an oath-bound organization recognizing the Supreme Council of the IRB as the legitimate 'government' of Ireland. Closely connected with radical Irish nationalism up to the 1930s, and the arena for a series of violent power-struggles between Irish-American nationalist leaders.

[viii] Charles Stewart Parnell (1846–91): born in Avondale, County Wicklow; Home Rule MP for Meath, 1875; a leader of the parliamentary 'obstructionists', 1877–8; first President of the Land League, 1879; leader of the Irish Parliamentary Party, 1880; imprisoned, October 1881; released under the 'Kilmainham Treaty', May 1882; played the Liberals off against the Tories to secure Gladstone's conversion to Home Rule, December 1885; accused by *The Times* of complicity in the Phoenix Park murders, 1887; vindicated, February 1889; cited as co-respondent in the O'Shea divorce petition, December 1889; deserted by English nonconformist opinion, the Irish-Catholic hierarchy, the Liberal Party leadership and, ultimately, the majority of the Irish Party, December 1890; married Katharine O'Shea, June 1891; died in her arms fourteen weeks later.

[ix] Alexander Sullivan (1847–1913): born in Maine, USA, of Irish parents; became a lawyer in Chicago, 1872; National Chairman of Clan na Gael, encouraging it to act independently of the IRB, 1881–5; first President of the Irish National League of America, 1883–4; virtual dictator of 'the Triangle' that financed the dynamiting

technically voluntary nature of most emigration was irrelevant; it was seen as caused directly by the Famine, and the Famine itself was increasingly perceived as the epitome of British oppression. This was vital, not only in calling forth great donations from the American urban working class to the Land League in 1879–82, but also in raising $10,000,000 for de Valera's American Association for the Recognition of the Irish Republic between 1919 and 1921. Similar support continues to this day.

Almost equally notable was the part played by Irish Americans in domestic politics. Though up to 1870 the Democratic Party generally excluded Irishmen from elective posts, the Irish machine in local politics became formidable. The Tammany syndrome[x] pre-dated infiltration of the Democratic Party at national level. The Irish-American political style, with its aggressively democratic Jacksonian identification, and its ethos of Catholic pragmatism and tribal organization, became a byword. The technicalities varied from place to place. Organization was not always as tight as Tammany; in Boston and Chicago, Irish urban politics represented a loose association of fiefs rather than a centralized machine. But they remained much criticized for sacrificing opportunities to create urban welfare schemes in favour of handing out a self-perpetuating round of jobs for the boys.

In fact, by the twentieth century there was a strong strain of Irish-American politics that was not antipathetic to collectivized welfare measures; and more radical Irish-American labour organizers some-times went against Democratic Party caucuses and tried to overthrow them from the inside. They, in their turn, aroused the antagonism of the Catholic hierarchy and organizations like the Ancient Order of Hibernians, who played the Irish nationalist card against them. It is probably correct to say that the Democratic Party represented more relevant issues, to a larger number of Irish Americans, than organizations like Clan na Gael or the A O H. It is a cliché that by 1963 the President of the United States, the Speaker of the House of Representatives, the Majority Leader of the Senate and the Chairman of

campaign of the 1880s, against the more cautious counsels of Devoy; discredited when implicated in the murder of a fellow-Fenian, 1889.

[x] 'Tammany' was the name of the headquarters of the New York county branch of the Democratic Party (originating in the Society of St Tammany, a club founded in 1789). Under 'Bosses' like Croker and Tweed in the later nineteenth century, it became a synonym for machine politics and the procurement of jobs, especially for immigrants, in return for bribes.

the National Committee were all Irish-American Catholic Democrats; but it is a revealing cliché all the same.

The language of Irish-American politics remained, however, as much Irish as American; and it is easy to generalize about the stereotype of Irish-American culture. This appeared philistine (Synge's *Playboy of the Western World* was vituperatively attacked by Irish-American audiences), hardworking and materialist. It was not Republican in the American sense, but it was right-wing – embracing Father Coughlin[xi] as well as Senator McCarthy.[xii] It was influential but conservative in labour politics, despite the importation of 'Molly Maguire' tactics to the Pennsylvania coalfields. It was anti-WASP; and even after social and economic success had conspicuously been achieved, what one historian calls 'a self-indulgent communal morbidity'[7] remained – much traduced by Irish-American novelists. It was capable of self-mockery, notably in the great journalism of Finley Peter Dunne,[xiii] whose 'Mr Dooley' constitutes the best guide to later nineteenth-century Irish-American attitudes.

The Irish-American experience, however, is far more varied than this. The Protestant strain, for instance, persisted, emphasizing integration and self-advancement, and making the break far more easily. And Catholic Irish America embraced far more than Boston, New

[xi] Charles Edward Coughlin (1891–1979): born in Ontario, Canada, of American parents of Irish descent; ordained, 1916; in radio sermons and journalism, moved from supporting the New Deal to violent attacks; removed from CBS's airwaves, 1934; launched his own radio network, the National Union for Social Justice, and a journal, *Social Justice*; association with the quasi-fascist Christian Front led the American Catholic hierarchy to forbid his broadcasting, 1941; dissolved the National Union for Social Justice, 1944; performed parochial duties until 1966.

[xii] Joseph Raymond McCarthy (1908–57): born on an 'Irish settlement', Wisconsin, USA; admitted to the Wisconsin Bar; circuit judge, 1939; First Lieutenant (Marines), serving in Intelligence, 1942–4; elected to the Senate, backed by the conservative Republican Voluntary Committee, 1946; re-elected, 1952; charged the State Department with allowing communists to shape foreign policy; Chairman of Senate Committee on Government Operations and Permanent Subcommittee on Investigations, 1953; excited the wrath of the military hierarchy by alleging communist subversion of the army, thereby contributing to his swift political demise; censured by the Senate for contempt and obstruction of the legislative process, 1953; fell into relative obscurity. Last years marked by illness and heavy drinking.

[xiii] [Finley] Peter Dunne (1867–1936): born in Chicago of Irish parents; City Editor of the *Chicago Times*, 1888; Managing Editor of the *Chicago Journal*, 1897; began writing Irish dialect stories, 1892; reflected on American politics in those comprising the observations of 'Mr Dooley', 1893–1919; moved to New York, 1900; retired from journalism, 1919; remained on the periphery of national politics.

York and Chicago, on which too many of the generalizations are based. In fact, Catholic diocesan organization began in the deep South during the early nineteenth century, due to the pronounced Irish-Catholic presence there, while less than 20 per cent of the Irish-American community were in New England by 1900, and 30 per cent were in the Mid-West. The regionalization of Irish America is just beginning to be analysed;[8] the monolithic generalizations will be correspondingly broken down. But enough verisimilitude remains in the general picture to be worth stating.

III
==

The great step of emigrating to America, marked by agonizing rituals like the mock wake, appeared more apocalyptic than the decision to go to England: much nearer, and infinitely cheaper to reach. The Cork–London passage dropped to a halfpenny a head in the 1840s. The long-standing Irish communities in places like London's St Giles added familiarity; and there seemed to be a possibility of returning. Statistically, the number of Irish-born in the British population by 1861 was low enough: 3.5 per cent at most. But this concealed the fact that the Irish *community* contained many born in Britain; and this 'community' may have included as many as 1,500,000 by the later nineteenth century.[9] Moreover, the density of settlement varied dramatically, concentrated on south-west Scotland, north-west England and London, which had an Irish community of 178,000 by 1861 and 350,000 by 1900.[10] From 1841 to 1851 the number of Irish in England and Wales increased by 79 per cent; nearly 25 per cent of Liverpool was 'Irish' by 1851.

The concept of an 'Irish community', taking in the second generation at least, is vital. It reflects the tightly bound community ethos, expressed in the solidarity among Irish travelling labourers described by Patrick MacGill,[xiv] as well as in the familial and community sense of the Irish

---

[xiv] Patrick MacGill (1891–1963): born in County Donegal; emigrated to Scotland at fourteen; worked on the railways; published, at his own expense, *Gleanings of a Navvy*, 1911; the semi-autobiographical novels, *Children of the Dead End* and *The Rat Pit*, 1914, proved huge successes in England, but failed in Ireland under criticism of being anti-clerical; recorded his experiences at the Front, as a private with the London Irish Rifles, in *The Amateur Army*, 1915, and *The Great Push*, 1916; forgotten by the late 1920s; retired to America. Not primarily concerned with nationality, but those novels relating the experiences of the Irish poor in Scotland are his most powerful.

settlements. Despite the fact that, in London at least, Irish family sizes were quite small, and the demographic pattern approximated to English rather than Irish patterns, they retained the strong kinship claims and obligations of the Irish countryside. These were reinforced by the wall of anti-Irish prejudice, conveniently articulated by Carlyle, Kingsley and Elizabeth Gaskell, and exacerbated in the workplace by popular obsessions that the Irish influx meant blacklegging, strike-breaking and undercutting wages, as well as by the fears that they would impose a crippling weight on English charity.

Local studies (which are proliferating)[11] indicate that this was not actually the case. There is some substance to the belief that the Irish invariably took over the poorest areas of cities, monopolized unskilled and menial jobs, and contributed to the ethos of squalor, rowdiness, drunkenness, violence and vagrancy recorded by many observers. 'Irish' slums were graphically illustrated in the *Builder*; typhus was known as the 'Irish fever'. Prostitution was one of the few vices they were *not* automatically connected with, though the incidence of illegitimacy among the Irish in Britain was higher than at home. And though the levels of anti-Irish violence outside Lancashire and Glasgow were low, the presence of the Irish gave a powerful boost to organized (if pre-existing) anti-Catholicism, especially in the north-west.

There were ironies here. In fact, the Irish could make common cause on many issues with radical Nonconformists; and the Irish in Britain were not noticeably devout, while much care was taken by the Catholic hierarchy to prevent the Church accentuating national apartness. The Irish in Britain had several identifications, which could lead to several kinds of anti-Irish discrimination, but which also produced a curiously mixed picture. Attitudes to the Irish, as well as attitudes among the Irish, were a complex matter: young Michael Davitt, after losing an arm in an industrial accident, was sent to a Lancashire Wesleyan school with the aid of the local Methodist cotton manufacturer, encouraged by his Catholic parish priest – who believed 'in different denominations all mingling together in social harmony and brotherly love – no distinction between Protestants and Catholics, English and Irish, but all blending together in one social brotherhood'.[12]

On the other hand, there are Tenniel's *Punch* cartoons of ape-like Paddies, which have been taken to indicate a racial typography. But Victorian attitudes were more complex than this; as has been pointed out in the lively debate that has grown around the subject,[13] 'Hibernia' was represented equally often as a model of Grecian purity. The prejudice was one of class as much as of race: particularly as part of the British notion of superiority involved self-congratulation on the Celtic component within their supposedly unique composition. A little of it, of course; not too much. The phrenological characterization of the Irish – 'Generous, Careless, Hasty, Laborious, and Brave'[14] – carries a condescension and an imputation of untrustworthiness that recall the 'savage' views of the seventeenth century, as well as the jokes about 'Irish Bulls' icily exposed by Maria Edgeworth.

The 'Irish' stereotype – contributed to, as with the Jewish stereotype, by the victims themselves – included the idea of a people too clever for their own good (or England's), but educable all the same. This attitude was not conducive to giving the Irish self-government, but it did not prevent the middle-class Irishman from making his way through accepted career structures. Prejudice there certainly was, but it is hard, overall, to feel that 'racialist' is the correct term. Similarly, the Irish were not segregated on the basis of race, which is why the word 'ghetto' is too loosely used; segregation, like discrimination, was based at least as much on class. Settlement was dictated by area of origin, by kin and by neighbourhood links – as with all immigrants (including those from elsewhere in England).

In some ways, the Irish in Britain did remain obviously separate: largely through religion and politics. The fundamental identity with Catholicism remained, despite considerable falling off in observance among the second and third generations. Detailed investigation of Irish Catholics in nineteenth-century Manchester has found them only 'marginally more faithful in church attendance than working-class people of other denominations'.[15] Catholic schools, however, remained the mechanisms whereby faith and cultural identity were reinforced; and they proliferated and were passionately supported. The hierarchy in Britain was not particularly anxious to place Irish priests among Irish settlements, but they could not avoid it; and this helped reinforce the sense of identity.

Geographical identification was also important. The evidence is that where there *was* a distinct Irish area much intermarriage took place within it; local studies of York and Bristol show that dispersal led to 'marrying out'. Even in towns without a distinct Irish settlement, there was a tendency to congregate in 'lodging houses' run and patronized almost exclusively by the Irish; and work patterns also became sharply demarcated, notably in Liverpool. All this helped sustain a sense of apartness that many contemporaries expected would express itself in political action.

Did it? Marx, Engels and others optimistically discerned in the Irish alienation and propensity to violence a potential for revolution. This never appeared, but high claims have been made for the Irish influence in radical movements from the 1820s on. Labour leaders like John Doherty[xv] were prominent from the 1820s, followed by Feargus O'Connor[xvi] and Bronterre O'Brien[xvii] in Chartism. More substantially, Chartist ideology shows a strong influence: the heavy emphasis on land ownership as the basis of inequity echoed Irish radical ideas, and the very name of the *Northern Star* was a direct reference to the Irish radical tradition. The 1842 Chartist petition called for Repeal of the Act of Union; however, Irish claims had been an automatic part of the English radical slate since 1815, for their embarrassment value as much as anything else. What is harder to discern is rank-and-

[xv] John Doherty (*c.* 1798–1854): born in County Donegal; emigrated to Manchester; imprisoned after a strike, 1818–21; elected Secretary of Manchester Spinners' Union, despite his Irish-Catholic background, 1828; founded *The Conciliator, or Cotton Spinners' Weekly Journal*; Secretary of the Society for the Enforcement of the Factory Act and of the National Association for the Protection of Labour, 1830; allied the National Association for the Protection of Labour to the Owenite Co-operative movement; transferred his *Voice of the People* from Manchester to London to symbolize new attempts at national organization; founded the *Poor Man's Advocate*, 1832; returned to Manchester, becoming Secretary of its Spinners' Union again, 1834–6, and their advocate before a parliamentary Select Committee, 1838; withdrew from public life.

[xvi] Feargus O'Connor (1794–1855): born in Connorville, County Cork; nephew of Arthur O'Connor, and like him inordinately proud of his imagined descent from the High Kings of Ireland; educated Portarlington Grammar School and Trinity College, Dublin; called to the Irish Bar; Repeal MP for County Cork, 1832–5; quarrelled with O'Connell over policy; founded the Marylebone Radical Association, 1835; Honorary Member of the London Working Men's Association, 1836, but lost patience with Lovett, who in turn was contemptuous of all 'Irish braggadocio'; founded the *Northern Star*, 1837; imprisoned after the abortive Newport 'rising', 1839, although not personally involved in it; rebutted middle-class support for Chartism, 1840; as MP for Nottingham, 1847–52, concentrated upon Irish questions and the promotion of his land schemes; oversaw the last Chartist petition of Parliament, 1848; irrationality gave way to insanity, 1852.

[xvii] James [Bronterre] O'Brien (1804–64): born in County Longford; educated at R. L. Edgeworth's school and Trinity College, Dublin; studied law in Dublin and London; wrote on Repeal and the state of the working class for Carpenter's *Political Letters*, 1831; edited the *Poor Man's Guardian*, 1832; differed with O'Connor in the London Working Men's Association, of which they were Honorary Members, over Irish and trade union policy, 1836; launched *Bronterre's National Reformer*, 1837; joined the *Northern Star*, 1838; imprisoned, 1840; condemned O'Connor as 'the dictator'; propounded Babeufian schemes for land nationalization; became a lecturer in adult education; died in poverty. Regarded as the 'schoolmaster' of Chartism; came closer than any of his peers to formulating a coherent social policy.

file alliance between Irish nationalists and English radicals, for all O'Connor's efforts. Daniel O'Connell's powerful influence was cast diametrically against it; his eclipse and death, and the radicalization of Young Ireland, helped the process and in 1847–8 the Irish Confederates formed close links with extremist Chartism. *Causes célèbres* like the sentencing of John Mitchel in May 1848 led to great demonstrations in Lancashire – the only area in England where Irish Confederate Clubs were organized, with a rather incoherent commitment to violent methods and a propensity to combine tactically with Chartism. Here the key figure was Terence Bellew MacManus:[xviii] a link forward to the Fenian movement, if only because his funeral occasioned the movement's first great public demonstration in Ireland.

The Fenians in Britain will be considered again. But it is worth noting that they numbered an alleged 80,000 in the United Kingdom by 1865, and the allied organization, the National Brotherhood of St Patrick, was publishing a successful newspaper, the *Irish Liberator*, and running fifteen branches. This was the culture that produced Michael Davitt, and many others. By the end of the century, cultural and other revivalist movements in Ireland almost automatically created sister organizations in Britain. The need was there, if only for symbolic activity: for the Irish in Britain, 'freeing Ireland' stood in as a metaphor for liberation from their own daily round.

This commitment meant more than direct engagement in the cause of British radicalism. Great claims were often made for the importance of the Irish as a voting bloc, but their dispersal, and their liability to move in search of jobs, make this hard to discern – with odd exceptions like T. P. O'Connor's[xix] fief in the Scotland division of Liverpool. They seem to have remained readier to mobilize for Irish issues than British ones – a process that was at last focused and 'legitimized', in

---

[xviii] Terence Bellew MacManus (1823–60); born in County Fermanagh; became a successful shipping agent in Liverpool; joined Young Ireland, 1844; with Smith O'Brien at Ballingarry, July 1848; arrested in attempting to flee to America; a death sentence commuted to exile; escaped Van Diemen's Land, 1852; settled in San Francisco; failed to re-establish himself in shipping; died in poverty.

[xix] Thomas Power O'Connor (1848–1929): born in Athlone; joined *Saunders's Newsletter*, and subsequently the *Daily Telegraph* and the London office of the *New York Herald*; wrote a searing *Life of Beaconsfield*, 1879; Home Rule MP for Galway, 1880, and for the Scotland Division, Liverpool, 1885–1929; founded the *Star*, 1887, thereby inaugurating the 'new journalism' – radicalism and a dash of the 'human touch'; the latter remained without the politics in his literary paper *T. P.'s Weekly*, 1902; first British film censor, 1917; Privy Councillor, 1924; father of the Commons for many years. Published *Memories of an Old Parliamentarian*, 1929.

Gearóid O Tuathaigh's phrase, when Gladstone adopted Irish Home
Rule in 1886. This kept the Irish a Liberal vote until the 1920s, despite
the prominent activity of individual Irish people in the trade union
movement (notably the 1889 dock strike). The mere presence of the
Irish in a community was supposed to boost an antagonistic Tory vote,
but this is hard to demonstrate. Politically, the Irish in Britain remain
enigmatic. A vocal minority became highly politicized, especially
within labour organizations; but moderate Home Rule mobilized far
more of the Irish in Britain than anything else, including Fenianism.
And though the 'union of hearts' between Liberals and Irish in the
1880s integrated an Irish element into the fabric of British politics, the
issues – as with the Land League offshoots that took root in Scotland –
were inescapably Irish.

What of the Irish outside the traditional supposed 'ghetto' picture?
They made up a high proportion of the army and navy, peaking at
55,000 in 1861. As artisans, they became noted for stonemasonry and
shoemaking, though the skilled trades generally kept them out, and
even in chosen callings like tailoring they rarely achieved mastership.
There was also a migrant Irish middle class, which should not be
forgotten: notably active in journalism and politics, reflected fict-
itiously by the milieu of Thackeray's *Pendennis* and actually by the
careers of T. P. O'Connor, Justin MacCarthy[xx] and Frank Hugh
O'Donnell.[xxi] The Irish presence in London literary life was not, of
course, just a post-Famine phenomenon. The complex structures of
literary nationalism need delineation; so does the middle-brow
clubman culture epitomized by so many Home Ruler MPs (at least
twenty-three of Parnell's MPs in 1880 were primarily English resi-

---

[xx] Justin MacCarthy (1830–1912): born in County Cork; joined the *Cork Examiner*,
1847, and the Liverpool-based *Northern Daily Times*, 1859; contributed to the
Westminster Review; edited the *Morning Star*, 1864–8; considered settling in America,
but returned to serve the new Irish Parliamentary Party, 1871; Home Rule MP for
County Longford and Vice-Chairman of the Irish Parliamentary Party, 1879; led the
majority faction after the 1890 split, but remained on friendly terms with Parnell;
retired, 1900; civil list pension, 1903. A leading popular novelist, biographer and
historian of his day.

[xxi] Frank Hugh O'Donnell (1848–1916): born in County Donegal; educated Queen's
College, Galway; joined the *Morning Post*; became Foreign Editor; Home Rule MP
for Dungarvan, 1877–85; his renomination refused by Parnell, 1885; unsuccessful in
an ill-judged libel action against *The Times*, 1888, which led to the setting up of the
Parnell Commission; retired abroad, 1888; attacked Yeats's national theatre company
in *Souls for Gold*, 1903, and *The Stage-Irishman of the Pseudo-Celtic Revival*, 1904;
jaundiced historian of the Irish Parliamentary Party, 1910.

dents). This was part of the Irish emigrant world, as were Irish doctors and publicans, Irish businessmen (less common), Irish lawyers at the Bar, and aspirant Irish painters and musicians in London's bohemia.

The Irish *menu peuple* were climbing up from the slums by the later nineteenth century. Crime levels among the Irish in York, for instance, fall off from about 1870; some social mobility is evident, though markedly less than in many other immigrant communities, and the old occupational structures remained extraordinarily dominant. They had by then their own recruitment chains and closed shops. The theory that Irish immigrants were less concerned with 'getting on' than other immigrant subcultures apparently holds up. Closely connected with this was an implicit reluctance to identify with Britain, in the way that Irish Americans identified with the United States. 'Home' remained Ireland, where they automatically returned for Christmas and during holidays.

The Irish emigration to Scotland had its own colouration. The long tradition of seasonal migration set up a connection that rapidly became permanent; by 1851, 6.7 per cent of the entire Scots population was Irish-born, a percentage that rose to over 18 per cent in Dundee and Glasgow. Here, too, the Irish found prejudice to contend with; anti-Irishness and anti-Catholicism took special colouring where Presbyterian values saw the very existence of destitute Irish Catholics as an outrage. The Irish provided navvies for the Union Canal and labourers for Edinburgh's New Town; their reputation for work went before them, as well as for enterprise: the notorious so-called 'bodysnatcher', William Burke, has been hilariously interpreted in this light.[16] The traditional connection between Belfast and Glasgow became increasingly important, with the growth of the shipbuilding industry in both cities; shipyard workers could operate between the two, especially after the Belfast-based Harland & Wolff set up a new shipyard on the Clyde in 1912.

The Belfast influence might also be discerned in the growth of popular factionalism, epitomized by the ritualized Green–Orange opposition of the football matches between Rangers and Celtic. Though confrontations were less violent than in Liverpool, issues like Orangeism, the inspection of convents and 'No Popery' continued part of the Scottish political fabric; and Catholics remained a disadvantaged minority there until the 1920s.

In Edinburgh, an Irish proletariat predominated in the Old Town from the early nineteenth century, though their numbers receded from about 1860. A vigorous local Catholic culture reinforced their identity, and helped, paradoxically, to bring about a degree of social assimilation. Other Scottish centres of Irish settlement included Dundee, whose linen mills offered employment to women and girls as well as men, Paisley and Greenock – where they monopolized the sugar refineries. Here and elsewhere, group identity was strong, and intermarriage rare. But overall, the Irish in Scotland appear less alienated and less exiled than in England; possibly because, no matter how irrationally, the consciousness of present exploitation was not exacerbated by the cultivated memory of past oppression.

IV

The Irish exodus was not restricted to America and Britain, though these were the destinations of the vast majority. To go to Australia, for instance, required assistance; the passage cost was four times that across the Atlantic (except, of course, for immigrants to the penal colonies). There was, however, a marked attraction to New Zealand, especially during the late nineteenth-century gold rush, and a strong Irish settlement developed along the west coast. Here, as in other areas where the overall population was small and the Irish influx large, there were fewer obstacles to social mobility and intermarriage. There was a strong Irish-Catholic flavour to politics, and the influence of Cardinal Cullen stretched to appointments in the New Zealand hierarchy. But even here, the question of restricting Irish immigration became a political issue, and Ulster Protestants were tacitly preferred to southern Catholics.

The same themes declared themselves in North America, Australia and Britain: Catholicism, schooling issues, the initial prejudice against rural immigrants living in urban conditions, their climb to political influence, often through labour organizations. By the twentieth century the relationship between Ireland and Irish communities all over the world had become symbiotic. Conrad Arensberg found that the Clare village of Cross in the 1930s 'is said locally to be supported by the Shanghai police force; the first man to go is now Chief of Police in the International Settlement there, and many places in the Force have gone to men of Cross'.[17] 'If there wasn't America,' Robin Flower was told on the Blaskets a decade later, 'the Island wouldn't stand a week.'

But necessity and future advantage did not blunt the psychological impact of leaving Ireland. Kerby Miller has pointed out that in Irish the words denoting emigration carry the implication of placelessness and a sense of banishment. The close, vital and passionate relationship of the Irish with land meant a traumatic wrench when it was left; hence the importance of mechanisms that kept the sense of connection alive, like the Irish pub in Manchester or Chicago. In 1881 the priest at St Patrick's in Soho recorded his readings to the women of St Bridget's Confraternity: the stories of William Carleton,[xxii] A. M. Sullivan's *New Ireland*, even the much traduced Samuel Lover.[xxiii] Memories were kept vividly alive; it is notable how Mayhew's Irish informants in the London slums could give him details of their parents' origins. Signs were conveyed by the pictures in an emigrant kitchen or parlour: the Saviour, the Pope, Robert Emmet, St Patrick, later John F. Kennedy. Stories of Patrick Sarsfield, 1798, and later 1919–21, fulfilled the same function. And the cultural revivalism of the later nineteenth century performed a special function for those abroad. A contemporary observer noted of the Gaelic League of London in 1906:

> In the League there were dozens of folk ordinarily in revolt against the whole trend of life around them. In the League they were at home, they were themselves upholding an unpopular standard in a strange land, and they seemed necessarily more intense in their faith, more zealous in their work, than the folk in Ireland at home would be.[18]

Catholic nationalist culture continued to emphasize a coherent, communalistic, self-sufficient nation; emigration was not interpreted as a rational, individualist alternative, but as evidence of British disruption of the Irish way of life. A race-memory of exploitation, oppression and banishment flourished long after these concepts had become ana-

---

[xxii] William Carleton (1794–1869): born in County Tyrone; youngest of fourteen; educated hedge school; 'failed priest' and 'poor scholar'; discovered by the Revd Caesar Otway, who commissioned him to write for the *Christian Examiner*, 1829; *Traits and Stories of the Irish Peasantry*, 1830; wrote three propagandist novels for the Young Irelanders' 'Library of Ireland', 1845, but these fell far below the achievement of *Fardorougha the Miser*, 1839, *Valentine McClutchy, the Irish Agent*, 1845, and *The Black Prophet*, 1847. Perhaps the finest-ever delineator of Irish rural life and, as such, a precursor of the literary renaissance.

[xxiii] Samuel Lover (1797–1868): born in Dublin; painter and musician; elected to the Royal Hibernian Academy, 1828; *Legends and Stories of Ireland*, 1831; settled in London, succeeding Moore as the Englishman's favourite Irishman; Lady Morgan persuaded him to expand one of his popular ballads into *Rory O'More: A National Tale*, but he remained more comfortable with the stage-Irishry of *Handy Andy*, 1842; toured England with his one-man show 'Irish Evenings'; civil list pension, 1856; died in St Helier, Jersey.

chronistic; the memory of 'home' was preserved in the imagination as it had been when the emigrants (or their parents) had left.

'Home' was, in fact, both preserved and altered by the very fact of emigration. As hundreds of thousands of young Irish people emigrated in every generation, what was left behind was – in a chilling phrase – 'a residual population'. Emigration, even before the Famine, was removing the most biologically reproductive; it affected population growth indirectly as well as directly, and may help explain the decline in marriage rates before the Famine as well as after. It also acted as a 'safety valve', draining off an element that might have created political and social disruption at home (and sometimes *did*, at times of low emigration due to foreign recession or domestic war). The few who returned, interestingly, sometimes provided that disruptive element, notably in anti-clerical Gaelic League politics at the end of the nineteenth century.

More characteristic was the consolidation of rural conservatism; emigration accentuated postponement of marriage and enabled the development of the strong-farmer class, as well as sustaining uneconomic western farms. Though underemployment continued in some areas, by the 1860s there was an emphatic shortage of labour in places like County Cork, and an ensuing rise in agricultural wages. These doubled between 1850 and 1870, though given the increased cost of living, and an economy increasingly based on cash, this need not have conferred much advantage. Much more important were the emigrant remittances, which had reached £1,404,000 by 1852. These often enabled a fairly comfortable old age for parents; they also provided a bulwark against the need to modernize the agricultural economy, invisibly supporting smallholdings and sustaining the shift to labour-extensive pasture farming (in County Cork, an area of high emigration, the acreage under tillage halved between 1851 to 1891). In the west the invisible income from abroad enabled the continued rearing of large families, who took their part in the emigration chain.

For all the breast-beating by politicians and clerics about the tragedy of emigration, it enabled the retention of 'the family farm' and the rural ethos that gave both politics and the Church their particular influence. It also reinforced conservatism and even, in the north, sectarianism – since emigration accentuated the process whereby areas with Catholic minorities became more strongly Protestant as Catholics left, and Protestants left Catholic-dominated areas with equal alacrity.[19] And Ireland's failure to industrialize is certainly connected with the removal of exactly the sector of the population that would otherwise have constituted an ex-rural workforce looking for relocation. It *was* relocated: but in the textile factories of Scotland and England, and the mines and railroads of North America. Cheap emigration enabled labour to move where capital was; without it, the opposite process might have taken place. Finally, one returns to the question of psychology. Both at home and abroad, the extraordinary exodus of Irish people created the sense of being part of an international community, centred on a small island that still claimed a fiercely and unrealistically obsessive identification from its emigrants. In its way, the process was one of the most influential developments in the Irish mentality over the period dealt with in this book.

CHAPTER SIXTEEN

LAND, POLITICS AND NATIONALISM

I

THE PERIOD FROM 1848 to the mid-1870s is too often glossed over as a lull between the Famine and Parnell. In fact, it was then that the themes were established that dominated Irish life and politics for the rest of the century: the altered social balance in the countryside, the development of expatriate nationalism, the settlement of Ulster's economy and politics into their modern mould, and the emergence of a disciplined nationalist parliamentary party.

Much of this followed on the psychological adjustment to post-Famine conditions. R. V. Comerford's intriguing thesis deserves examination: 'the dominant feeling left behind by the Famine was not a desire for self-government but a sense of embarrassment and inadequacy', along with heightened disunity among the farming classes.[1] Certainly the post-Famine years demonstrate something like a failure of political authority, or at least an uncertainty as to where it was located. The assertion of rearguard landlord influence, the rise to political prominence of a new clerical generation, and the development of various political organizations trying to capitalize on the post-Famine dispensation are all reflections of this; so is the lively and varied local political culture of 'influence' and elections. The traditional view of the period separates out two strands of political activity, 'constitutional' and 'revolutionary', and sees political initiative oscillating between Young Irelanders and Tenant Leaguers, Fenians and Home Rulers. But it may be more enlightening to infer an overall, continuous effort to reorganize political expression in a way that would reflect the new realities of post-Famine Ireland – north and south. The eventual monolith of organized parliamentary nationalism from the late 1870s is not so much a replacement of this confused picture as a development of it.

II

==

The structure of social and political power in nineteenth-century Ireland revolves around the fortunes of the landed classes; since landed power became the crucial issue in 1879, it is important to look at what happened to the landlord class after the Famine. Generally, they continued to emphasize profit-extraction rather than investment. Debts and encumbrances continued, too, even among those who had managed to retain their estates after 1849. The idea of an outflow of Irish capital in the form of rents to absentees does not stand up. But a great deal of money, in the form of rental income, was pledged in debts, often abroad. Even when an estate's income was not mortgaged, it tended to be lodged in Irish banks 'whose gaze was firmly fixed on the London money market'.[2] Proportionately speaking, smaller estates carried a heavier debt burden, and found it harder to service the interest charges; the largest estates were, as before, often the best run.

How does this relate to the classical picture of rackrents and evictions? The terrible clearances of the late 1840s and early 1850s were not sustained throughout the period; of the 90,000 evictions apparently recorded from 1847 to 1880, 50,000 took place between 1847 and 1850. From 1854 to 1880 the annual rate of actual eviction dropped to 1.36 per 1,000 holdings; the annual number of houses levelled usually stayed below one hundred. Statistics were always problematic, raising difficulties of definition as well as actual occurrence; even where an eviction took place, as opposed to a notice merely being served, the tenant was often reinstalled as caretaker. Statisticians also misleadingly included the subtenants of an evicted tenant among those ejected, though they actually stayed *in situ*. There were individual *causes célèbres*, like the Derryveagh evictions of forty-seven families in 1861, which probably reflected particular local conditions;[3] in the Derryveagh case, both the police and officialdom tried to find a way to block the landlord's intention, but the laws of property prevented them. The image of the ruthlessly clearing landlord remained in the mind of the public; the sensational publicity that accompanied evictions was one reason why landlords preferred to avoid them. But where they did occur, the decisions were as often taken by large leaseholding farmers, who were farming an estimated 75 per cent of Irish land by 1854. This is the picture given, for instance, in the fiction of the Fenian novelist Charles Kickham.

By 1870 there was a wide variety of landlords. The 'typical' landlord owned about 2,000 acres; but by 1876 less than 800 landlords owned half the country. 302 (1.5 per cent of the total) owned 33.7 per cent of Irish land; 15,527 (80.5 per cent) owned 19.3 per cent. 13.3 per cent, owning 23 per cent of the land, were resident outside the country; 36.6 per cent resided in Ireland, but not on their own estates. The picture of 'cormorant vampires' (Davitt) or 'coroneted ghouls' (Fanny Parnell[i]) has long been disproved; if the post-Famine Irish landlords were vampires, they were not very good at it. Certainly, income was stressed above investment; though it can be argued that the 'investment' priority is less relevant to Irish pastoral farming than the English model implies, and J. Donnelly's survey of Cork finds landlords putting more money in after 1850, with demesne farming becoming profitable along with new stock, drainage techniques, model housing and railway expansion. A few did embark upon imaginative estate management and experiments with non-pastoral resources, including Charles Stewart Parnell, who was nearly bankrupted by it.

How did they treat their tenants? Farms were generally held on yearly arrangements; post-Famine legislation allowed a wide freedom in making terms, but the law considered these leases as practically renewable and continuous, except by legal action consequent upon failure to pay rent. As to actual rent levels, it is very difficult to generalize. As a rule, rent probably absorbed 25–40 per cent of tenants' gross incomes. But on a subsistence-level holding in Connemara, any rent at all was too high; while on a large farm in the midlands, rent fell far behind price levels, to the great advantage of the tenant. Despite the myth of the rackrent, rents could be raised only at lease expiration, and most landlords preferred a regular income to the risk of default. Some rents were high, and some landlords evicted ruthlessly when they were not paid. But when the crisis of the late 1870s came, many landlords were already receiving an inadequate income for solvency – just at the point when farmers wanted to pay less.

Analysis of individual estate records shows that rent increases between the Famine and the Land War ran at a low rate, and varied widely even on the same estate. Surveying fifty estates between 1851

[i] Frances [Fanny] Parnell (1845–82): born in Avondale, County Wicklow; assimilated the romantic nationalism of their mother to a greater extent than her brother Charles; emigrated to America, 1874; wrote for the *Boston Pilot* and the *Nation*, 1879; launched the Ladies' Land League in New York, October 1880.

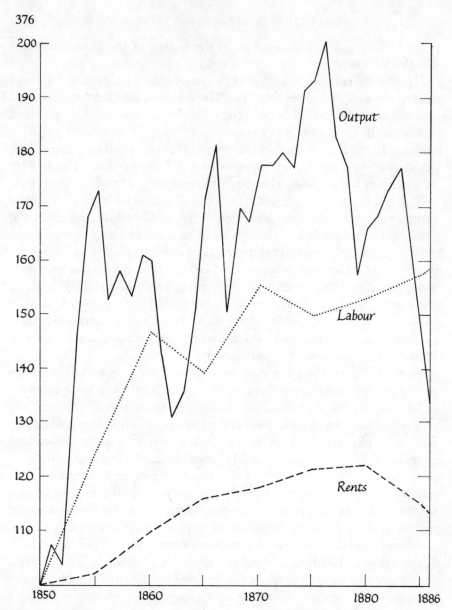

Figure 3: *Agricultural output, labour costs and rents 1850–86. These curves show fluctuations at current prices from a base of one hundred in 1850, when output was £25,000,000, labour costs £11,500,000 and rents £10,400,000.*

Source: W. E. Vaughan, *Landlords and Tenants in Ireland 1848–1904*, Studies in Irish Economic and Social History No. 2.

and 1881, W. E. Vaughan has found an average rise of 20 per cent – half what would have been necessary to give landlords a proportionate share in the increased profits of agriculture. Sporadic rent increases maximized ill-feeling, while remaining unconnected to price levels; no policy of index-linking was generally adopted. Donnelly's picture of Cork bears the general picture out: the few determined attempts to force rents up to ruthlessly commercial levels attracted violent and counter-productive publicity.

Collectively and statistically, post-Famine landlords constituted a rich and powerful interest; individually, their economic position left a lot to be desired. Unlike their English counterparts, they did not benefit from mineral deposits or urban growth. Taxation, recurrent charges, debt servicing, family encumbrances and wages were all fixed, and vulnerable to fluctuations in rents. 'An Irish estate is like a sponge,' wrote Lord Dufferin, having decided to sell up in 1874, 'and an Irish landlord is never so rich as when he is rid of his property.' Farming conditions from the 1850s benefited their demesne farms, but benefited their tenants still more. Why they did not achieve solvency by reconstructing their economic position is an unanswered question. Bad estate management is part of the reason; so is defeatism, faced with the limitations of Irish conditions. Those who did reorganize their estates were resented as introducing 'English' ideas of interference. 'It is a very curious thing,' said a witness at the Bessborough Commission in 1880, 'that what the people call a good landlord is a man who lets them alone.'

Letting the tenants alone on their farms was one thing; interfering with them in terms of social and political control was another. The landlord class still monopolized local government as JPs, Poor Law Guardians and grand jurors, though the number of those qualifying for grandee status was declining, and the law-enforcement system had long passed from their control. In the county elections of the 1850s and 1860s they exerted a powerful influence, having in a sense recovered authority since the days of O'Connell. In Parliament, two-thirds of the 105 Irish MPs at Westminster in 1852 were from landed families; in 1859, 87 were landowners, 65 possessing more than 2,000 acres. The county electorate had been quadrupled by the 1850 Reform Act,[ii] but the electorate remained dominated by middling and strong farmers over whom the landlords exerted their 'fair and legitimate influence' – which depended not only upon possession of property but also upon residency.

[ii] See above, p. 343.

For local landlords, *esprit de corps* took in the hunting-field, the marriage market, the grand jury and Dublin clubs. Catholic gentry subscribed to this social tribalism, rather than to solidarity with pleb-eians of their own religion. The identity of the Irish landlord class was fortified by contemporary criticism from the kill-joy English establishment, especially pious young Whigs, who saw the Irish gentry as hopeless, feckless Bourbons. From their side, the Irish landlords believed no one English understood them; their correspondence is full of resentment at English politicians 'without a foot of land in the country' who presumed to tell them their business. 'Knowing the country' became, in many cases, shorthand for aggressive pessimism, and a bedrock determination that no common ground was possible between their interests and those of the increasingly prosperous and organized rural bourgeoisie outside the demesne wall.

Though an Irish Whig tradition was maintained up to the 1870s, much of the landlord political culture subscribed to an idiosyncratic Toryism. In local politics, they found themselves increasingly ranged against priests as rival brokers of influence, and they relied on traditional weapons. 'Notices to quit' might be threatened on recalcitrant electors, but there were next to no political evictions in post-Famine Ireland; tactics were more likely to involve early demands for payment, with-drawal of benefits, a straightforward rent abatement for those who voted right, or reliance on deference and paternalism – which *did* exist in the Irish context, as any perusal of estate memoranda will show.[4]

Thus there was much exertion of 'improving' influence, many visitations of farmhouses and cabins (to the profound irritation of the inhabitants), lavish dinners for an heir's coming of age or marriage – and the ensuing expectation that tenants would come up to the mark in elections. Landed domination of politics remained longest where ownership was most concentrated; agents of the larger estates exercised a great degree of autonomous political control. The politics of *quid pro quo* lasted on; Ascendancy memoirs betray a constantly shifting perception of when the good old days of deference collapsed. To the mid-nineteenth-century mind, it was in the Catholic emancipation campaign or the Tithe War; later perspectives put it at the first Home Rule elections or the Land War; finally, the golden age was seen as before the rise of Sinn Féin. In fact, political deference probably lapsed beyond control in the 1870s.

This relates to the position of the stronger tenants in the post-Famine age, already sketched above.[iii] The movement to pasture continued,

[iii] See above, pp. 334–7, 344.

with the cattle population escalating from the end of the Famine, and tillage spectacularly declining. In 1851, 400,000 acres had been under wheat; by 1910 this had fallen to less than 48,000. Flax, root crops and greens held their own until the 1860s. But hay and meadow inexorably took over, while the acreage of pasture increased by nearly 2,000,000 acres between 1851 and 1901. Railway links and steamships boosted store cattle, while dairying stabilized. The decimation of the vulnerable agricultural proletariat accompanied the triumph of labour-extensive agriculture outside the west.

Thus financial prosperity increased in the grazing areas, along with the desire to consolidate and extend holdings – reinforced by the emigration patterns described in the last chapters. There was one severe agricultural depression, from 1859 to 1864; otherwise prices rose, and agricultural profits with them (by an estimated 78 per cent between the 1850s and the 1870s[5]). By 1854, 60 per cent of Irish land was being farmed by 90,000 farmers holding above fifty acres. The large farmer-grazier tenant could achieve near-gentry status; many of them were, effectively, landlords, if not landowners. Differences of interest within the 'tenant' sector followed. There were differences between those who reared cattle, and those who fattened them; and far greater differences between those integrated into this kind of farming, and the small mixed farm in marginal areas. The smaller farmers' share of the increased output is more questionable than the graziers' profit, and their position was less secure. And the tenant renting a scrap of land in the west was operating on a different level yet again.

Meanwhile, industrial output, outside the Lagan valley, remained negligible. Export produce was primarily foodstuffs, based on agricultural products: biscuitmaking, distilling and brewing (dominated by the legendary Arthur Guinness & Sons by the later nineteenth century). Ireland outside the north-east was characterized by a farming economy, largely dependent on the British market; contrary to so many generalizations there *was* an Irish urban middle class, but it was largely comprised of people in service or distribution industries in provincial towns, whose occupations were rurally derived or 'professional'. It should not then be surprising that the dominating political issue had to do with the land: notably the idea of 'Tenant Right', which began appearing on political platforms in the 1830s, and came to general attention after 1850.

When this happened, it tended to reflect a fluctuation in the stability of agricultural profit; but tenurial considerations are by no means automatically connected with the recurrent rural crises of nineteenth-century Ireland. Security of tenure, as time would show, would not turn Irish farmers into efficient investors. But, as so often before, what people thought to be important achieved a rhetorical, and therefore political, importance of its own.

Tenant Right was defined in a number of ways: by Lord Palmerston as 'Landlord Wrong', and by others as 'the 3 F's': free sale, fair rent and fixity of tenure. Paul Bew has cogently pointed out that even this specific definition meant different things in different places; the economic importance of 'free sale' of one's interest in a holding might be irrelevant in Connemara, but worth hundreds of pounds in Meath. The notion of 'free sale' relates to the supposed 'Ulster' custom of selling the 'interest' in a holding to an incoming tenant; customary rights of this kind, in fact, occurred all over Ireland, and were apparently coming under threat in 1850 as a result of post-Famine dislocations and the crisis in grain prices. Connected with the sale of 'interest' in a rented holding was another intrinsic Tenant Right: the right to compensation for improvements made to the property. But in Ireland most attention was paid to the sale of interest.

This carried two implications, one moral and one economic. The moral implication was that the tenant had a certain *right* in the property, above and beyond the right conveyed by paying rent – since it outlasted the period for which rent was paid. This was often held to reflect the general Irish historical sense that the land was the people's before it was the landlords'. The economic implication is equally significant: if payments were made by incoming tenants, often at a surprisingly high level, in order to occupy a holding for which they would then pay rent, it must have been worth their while to do so. In other words, the formal rent must have been pegged at a lower level than the land could have borne: the incoming payment (like 'key-money' for a rent-controlled flat nowadays) making up the difference.

This leads on to the second 'F', fair rent, which was impossible to define. 'Griffith's valuation', often taken by the tenants as the standard, was known to be pitched well below a realistic economic level; it was calculated when prices were abnormally low, and had never been intended as a rental guide. Rents where 'Ulster custom' money was paid were obviously low enough to make the saleable interest an attractive proposition; in fact, in areas where the practice prevailed, even those without leases could expect incoming payments (which could reach eight to ten pounds per acre in east Ulster). Thus they had effective security of tenure, which might otherwise be held to mean simply unbreakable leases. The logical meaning of 'fair rent' was rents fixed by tribunal; and it would come to this in the end, with Gladstone's Land Act of 1881. By then, 'fixity of tenure' was following on hard, in the shape of state-aided land purchase by the occupying tenantry, which would make 'free sale' an irrelevance.

In the 1850s, however, Tenant Right technically meant an amalgam of these claims, on behalf of the farming classes, demanded of the landlords. But the rhetorical flavour conveyed by Tenant Right was more extreme: it could also mobilize feeling against clearances and 'conquest'; and could on occasion postulate a movement to reorganize agrarian production, lowering the grazing ratio and reverting to labour-intensive tillage. Some Tenant Righters called for the breaking up of grazing farms, though more were themselves graziers. Like other agrarian issues of nineteenth-century Irish politics, it knitted together a number of incompatible grievances by identifying the landlord as enemy.

III

Land issues came up in Irish politics from the 1840s. To take the most radical (and least representative) formulation first, the cogent broadsides of James Fintan Lalor in the late 1840s set the tone for most later land agitators. Beginning with unrealistic and grandiloquent appeals to the landlord class to join the neo-Young Irelanders in 1848, he rapidly moved on (in his *Irish Felon* letters) to demonstrating that the Irish land question was an issue between 'a people and a class'. For the purposes of rhetoric he treated the tenantry as one, though elsewhere – and more accurately – he remarked that farmers would never acquire pikes for rebellion, simply because they grudged the two shillings' expenditure. His ideas are interesting because they are a direct reaction to the Famine (and possibly to theories imbibed on a mysterious visit he may have made to France in 1827), rather than the debased Germanicist romanticism of average Young Ireland. The Famine, Lalor held, had 'dissolved society' and exposed landlordism both morally and economically. Independence for the farming class must be the basis of national independence, and must precede it: in a memorable metaphor, it would be the engine that would drag national independence in its train.

Whether or not Lalor was correct, his tactics were prescient: the rent strike and the boycott, advocated by ideologues for a tenantry who were, however, less anxious to push things to any conclusion that threatened their livelihoods. Lalor's own rising in 1849 was a mere hiccough. But his ideas, which cast agrarian agitation in the form of guerrilla war, influenced extremists among the Confederate Clubs, and would be revived by radicals in the early 1880s and by socialists in the early twentieth century. What was important in the short term was that they did *not* express the real demands of the farming classes.

These were epitomized by the more moderate claims of the Tenant Protection societies, formed locally from 1849–50, campaigning for rents fixed by independent valuation and solidarity among tenants who were prepared to abide by such valuations. The leadership of such societies represented 'respectable farmers', affected by the price crisis in tillage crops, and emerging into 'a critical level of prominence *vis-à-vis* landlords on the one hand and the landless or near landless on the other';[6] it was also connected with a movement in Ulster to defend the customary practice of sale of interest. The question was how far it could translate itself into an influential political pressure-group.

Post-Repeal Irish politics had reverted to polarization between Irish Liberals (a shadowy and cautious reflection of English Whigs, electorally organized by sympathetic administrations in Dublin Castle) and Tories – a livelier and more 'native' growth. Irish Liberalism would become increasingly marginalized with the rise of Home Rule; Irish Toryism, ideologically flinty and hotly Protestant, would in many ways anticipate Unionism. In the 1850s and 1860s the Tories created a central organization (1853), and built up a strong urban base among the sectarian artisanate, the Trinity College professional bourgeoisie and – inevitably – the people of Ulster. The Disraelian Conservative Party had an eye to Irish talent, especially lawyers; Tory Viceroys like Eglinton[iv] and Marlborough[v] were more adept at playing the Irish popularity game than the Whigs. Both Irish Liberal and Tory MPs were overwhelmingly from the landed classes. The challenge facing

[iv] Archibald William Montgomerie (1812–61): succeeded as thirteenth Earl of Eglinton, 1819; entered the Lords, 1834; Protectionist Whip, 1846; Privy Councillor, 1852; Lord Lieutenant of Ireland, 1852 and 1858–9; proved 'princely' and thus popular; inaugurated a Select Committee to inquire into national education, 1854; created first Earl of Winton, 1859; patron of the 'Eglinton tournament', 1839.

[v] John Winston Spencer Churchill (1822–83): styled Marquess of Blandford, 1840; Conservative MP for Woodstock, 1844–5 and 1847–57; succeeded as seventh Duke of Marlborough, 1857; Privy Councillor, 1866; Lord President of the Council, 1867; KG, 1868; declined the Irish viceroyalty, 1874; accepted it, November 1876; endeavoured to promote Irish trade, while his Duchess, Frances, eldest daughter of the third Marquess of Londonderry, instituted a famine relief fund, 1879; left office, 1880.

the Tenant Protection movement was how to break into the enclosed subculture of Irish politics.

This was apparently facilitated by the fact that the MP William Sharman Crawford[vi] had already embarked upon a campaign to legalize customary Ulster tenant rights; publicists like Gavan Duffy and Frederick Lucas[vii] were equally predisposed to work through Parliament, the result being an all-Ireland Tenant League that emerged as the first Irish political organization with a social, rather than a political, platform. It was, however, far from being a 'League of North and South', as Duffy grandiosely christened it. Whether it represented the interest of 'tenants' as normally conceived is also questionable; John George Adair, the evicting landlord of Derryveagh, offered himself as a Tenant Right candidate in 1857. In voting terms, tradesmen and the declining artisanate saw it as irrelevant; some shopkeepers, merchants and strong farmers supported it, but the towns more or less ignored it. (The authentic tone of the out-of-touch radical schoolmaster may be heard in Tenant League addresses like the one that dealt with the morality of leasehold tenure by references to Cicero and Epictetus, delivered from the balcony of Cronin's Hotel, Limerick.[7])

The Tenant Right movement briefly spawned an Independent Irish Party in the early 1850s, but never really threatened the old moulds of Irish political representation. Besides leadership difficulties, and the incompatibility of interests between Ulster and the south, there was a characteristic religious difficulty. The Independent Irish Party was based on an alliance between Tenant Righters and the so-called 'Irish Brigade' – Irish MPs who had come together against the anti-popery

[vi] William Sharman [Crawford] (1781–1861): born in County Down; staunch Protestant in faith, but political advocate of Catholic relief; MP for Dundalk, 1835–7; moved for the conversion of the Tenant Right custom into law; declined to join the Repeal Association; rejected O'Connell's influence, 1837; denounced the Tithe Bill as a sacrifice of the tenant to the O'Connellite–Whig alliance, 1838; on the Chartist committee that drafted bills embodying the six points, 1838; MP for Rochdale, 1841–52; advocated federalism for the redress of Irish grievances, 1843; founded the Ulster Tenant Right Association, 1847; retired to Crawfordsburn, 1852.

[vii] Frederick Lucas (1812–55): educated at a Quaker school, Darlington; espoused Roman Catholic emancipation; grew interested in Irish politics; converted to Roman Catholicism and published his *Reasons*, 1839; contributed to the *Dublin Review*; founded the *Tablet*, 1840; advocated advanced ultramontane views; removed the *Tablet* from London to Dublin, 1850; aligned the Tenant League with the Irish Brigade to form the Irish Parliamentary Party, 1851; MP for County Meath, 1852; denounced Cullen's prohibition of clerical interference in Tenant Right politics; visited Rome to seek papal support for his policy, which proved unforthcoming, 1854.

campaign that dominated English politics in 1850–51. The alliance – never really a 'party' – suffered demoralization when two prominent members accepted government posts from the Peelites, and ran into further trouble when Archbishop Cullen demonstrated reluctance about allowing priests to canvass openly for the Independents in elections. It finally split up in the late 1850s over the question of independent opposition to the 1859 Reform Bill.

The Independent Party was a rather incoherent response to short-term crises, made to bear a heavier weight than it deserves by historians with an eye to retrospective continuities. Though in no way an ancestor of Parnell's Home Rulers, its spirit was continued in the Farmers' Clubs of the mid-1860s, articulating the interests of the larger farmers. Meanwhile, county politics settled back into the landlord-dominated mould, and tenants returned to following the party odysseys of local gentry, as delineated by Theo Hoppen. The Conservative Registration Society made inroads into the county electorate; in the 1859 election, 55 out of 105 Irish seats were Tory-occupied.

In fact, the fate of the Independent Irish Party should be taken as evidence of the residual strength of the Irish political system as it operated in mid-century. The county electorate was dominated by middling farmers, the boroughs by shopkeeping interests. Localized, diffuse personal interests predominated above national issues. Powerful local brokers emerged, like the Galway parish priest who was Chairman of the Corporation, of the Gas Company, of the Mechanics' Institute, and of the Commercial Society, and owned the Lough Corrib Steam Company: whose political activities had nothing to do with Tenant Right, and everything to do with getting a steam-packet service to America. Similarly, the chance of a railway galvanized the electorate where land issues did not: in 1852 half the Cashel electorate agreed to support *anyone* who could provide a rail link to the town.

Certainly, the impression of a fragmented, venal, localized political culture in mid-century is exaggerated by bringing the historian's microscope too close to the subject; but many contemporary observers noted it too. 'The very whisper of a dissolution sent a visible thrill through the town, and the prospect of common gain swallowed up amid the people all other passions, religious and political, and united ordinarily discordant forces in amity and brotherhood.'[8] Corruption, violence and intimidation reached epic levels; investigations into elections in the 1850s constantly refer to 'savagery', 'rage', towns 'in a blaze' and 'in a state of siege'. Injuries and deaths filled columns;

gunboats and marines were stationed off coastal boroughs in 1868 and 1872. The spice of sectarianism was present in 1852, but was not essential; the rural mob, as well as urban factions, constantly reiterated that they were ready to *die* in the cause, and often did.

All this coexisted with a political nation increasingly urbanized, modernized and educated. Between 1841 and 1861 the proportion of people living in settlements of 500 and upward increased from 17.8 per cent to 23.7 per cent; towns became centres of exchange and dispersal of goods as Ireland's transport revolution proceeded in default of an industrial revolution. Railways proliferated (nearly 3,500 miles of track by 1900); the 'market' invaded the rural economy along with advertising, foreign goods, credit and, eventually, the bicycle. The rate of internal migration doubled between 1841 and 1881; the Post-Office quadrupled the number of letters carried and extended its network, (providing unforeseen opportunities for future guerrilla strategists in 1919–21).

Though secondary education was a slow growth, bedevilled by violent denominational politicking, primary education was making great inroads on illiteracy; much attention has been paid to the altered ratio of priests to people after the Famine, but not enough to that of teachers to pupils. The number of National Schools doubled between 1850 and 1900, and illiteracy among those above five years decreased from 47 per cent in 1851 to 12 per cent in 1911. Those who could both read and write had risen from 33 per cent to 84 per cent. A varied and lively provincial press had developed; despite the declining population, the number of newspapers doubled in the second half of the century. These usually adopted a high political profile (often idiosyncratically Tory), thus emphasizing localist political cultures rather than imposing national issues. 'Modernization' had undoubted political effects – some more indisputable than others, as with the pawnbrokers and bank managers who could influence indebted borough electorates. At the end of the 1870s the impressive mobilization of the Land League would drive the message home. But for the 1850s estate identifications, and family and kinship, continued to be electorally influential; and so, inevitably, did religion.

I V

'Whatever public spirit exists in Ireland just now,' wrote W. J. O'Neill Daunt[viii] in his journal for 14 August 1859, 'is rather religious than political.' The high profile of organized Catholicism in the elections of the 1850s, and the political importance of the Irish Brigade, bore him out. But the political attitudes of the Catholic Church in Ireland are not clear-cut. The leadership of the Church often represented the strong-farmer class, but as an institution the Church was equally suspicious of gentrified graziers and dangerous labourers: it put its faith in the values of the small farmer. In political matters, the hierarchy preferred to keep their influence in the background, except over Church-in-danger issues, or at high points like the 'Disestablishment' election of 1868 – a matter that aligned them incongruously with the Liberal Party. One reason why the hierarchy had to tread carefully was that individual priests were passionately involved in local politics, right across the spectrum; Cardinal Cullen, who until his death in 1878 dominated Irish Catholicism, had to exercise his authority over the priesthood with great care.

Cullen achieved a more complex and subtle synthesis than he is often given credit for; the interpretation of his priorities as purely ultramontane, ignoring the trafficking of nationalist politics, is based unrealistically on his vast correspondence with Rome. The broader picture shows his constant efforts to sustain Irish Roman Catholicism as a national Church while tirelessly monitoring 'nationalism' for signs of secular impropriety. Never a 'nationalist' in the sense of his rival MacHale,[ix] he was still a nationalist *faute de mieux*, given his anti-

---

[viii] William Joseph O'Neill Daunt (1807–94): born in County Offaly; became a Catholic, 1827; M P for Mallow, 1832–3; a founding member of the Repeal Association, 1840; secretary to O'Connell as Lord Mayor of Dublin, 1841; *Personal Recollections of Daniel O'Connell*, 1848; inaugurated the ultimately successful phase in anti-state Church agitation, 1856; Secretary of Home Government Association, 1870. Having written historical novels in early life, in retirement he reflected on his age in a series of recollections posthumously published as *A Life Spent for Ireland*, 1896.

[ix] John MacHale (1791–1881): born in County Mayo; ordained, 1814; Lecturer and Professor at Maynooth, 1814–25; *Letters of Hierophilos*, 1820–25; *Evidences and Doctrines of the Catholic Church*, 1825; Coadjutor to Bishop of Killala, 1825; proposed denominational education, tithe abolition, Tenant Right and Repeal for Ireland in a letter to Lord Grey, 1831; Archbishop of Tuam, despite government opposition, 1834; opposed

English, anti-Protestant proclivities and the temper of the times. His political campaigns were 'religious' in the sense that they revolved around denominational education; he believed Fenianism was the result of mixed education, which was not the least of the reasons why he anathematized it. And he was preoccupied with the dangers of revolutionary anarchism and nihilism: Continental examples were inescapably vivid to a hierarchy so closely linked to Rome. But anti-Fenianism did not imply anti-nationalism. Cullen simply took a different path.

This is obscured by the attitudes taken up by radical nationalist priests like Father Patrick Lavelle,[x] and by the cult of Terence Bellew MacManus among Maynooth students. Cullen saw most seminaries as hotbeds of revolution (except his own College of the Holy Cross at Clonliffe); he presided over a Church that was violently *engagé* in local politics, controlling, for instance, a quarter of the votes at Kinsale, working with the drink interest at Waterford, defying the hierarchy by celebrating mass for a dead Fenian in one place, or by backing a Tory candidate in another. Clerical intimidation was the common denominator of most election petitions. Priests and people were often locked in conflict, but the priest's political role was generally accepted: a sign of the confessional nature of Irish life. The passionate commitment of Catholic Ireland to the papal cause in 1859–60, when an Irish Brigade of St Patrick travelled out to the Papal States to fight for the Pope, was a further indication. Irish Catholicism, like Cullen himself, was propelled into a political stance.

So, of course, was Irish Protestantism. With the development of organized Catholic politics, the differences between Anglicans and Presbyterians in Ulster became less important: the evangelical fervour of the 1850s, and the Catholic triumphalism of the same decade,

---

Newman's appointment to the Catholic University, 1851; influence declined as Cullen's grew; opposed papal infallibility at Vatican Council I, 1870; opposed the Land League. Published translations and original work in idiomatic Connacht Irish. The first Irish bishop since the sixteenth century to be educated solely in Ireland.

[x] Patrick Lavelle (1825–86): born in County Mayo; educated at Maynooth and the Irish College, Paris, where he also lectured; parish priest of Mount Partry, 1858; led MacHale's crusade against the 'new reformation'; attacked the Bishop of Tuam's treatment of his tenants in 'The War in Partry', 1860; Vice-President of the National Brotherhood of St Patrick, 1861; delivered the oration at the grave of T. B. MacManus, 1861; lectured on 'The Catholic Doctrine of the Right of Revolution', 1862; Cullen sought his suspension; pleaded his case in Rome, January 1864; parish priest of Cong, 1869; *The Irish Landlords since the Revolution*, 1870; denounced for clerical intimidation at the Galway election, 1872.

reinforced their common Protestantism. So did the economic conditions of Ulster life. The great industries focused into the Lagan valley complex – textiles, shipbuilding, engineering, foundrywork – were closely linked to imperial markets and to a British identity: the brilliant entrepreneurs of the Belfast shipping industry, William and John Ritchie,[xi] Edward Harland,[xii] G. W. Wolff[xiii] and George Clark,[xiv] generally came from Britain (W. J. Pirrie[xv] is the only exception).

[xi] William Ritchie (1755–1834): born in Ayrshire; built ships on the Clyde; settled in Belfast with a team of skilled labourers, July 1791; launched *Hibernia*, 1792; constructed Belfast's first graving dock, 1800; used Irish oak to build vessels that he boasted to be unrivalled. The firm of Ritchie & MacLaine built Belfast's first steamboat, *Rob Roy*, 1820, the engine being made in a Lagan foundry. Pioneer of modern Belfast shipbuilding; prominent Presbyterian and general philanthropist. John Ritchie was his brother's sometime partner, before setting himself up as a shipbuilder on his own account, 1807.

[xii] Edward James Harland (1831–95): born in Scarborough, Yorkshire; apprenticed in Newcastle; worked in Glasgow and on Tyneside; moved to the Belfast shipyard of Robert Hickson & Co., 1854; bought up the firm with the assistance of G. C. Schwabe; took Schwabe's nephew, G. W. Wolff, into partnership, 1858; the innovator of the firm, inventing the 'Belfast bottom'; withdrew from active involvement, *c.* 1880; alderman, 1884; Lord Mayor, 1885 and 1886; Baronet, 1885; Conservative M P for North Belfast, 1889–95. A Unitarian.

[xiii] Gustav Wilhelm Wolff (1834–1913): born in Hamburg, educated in Liverpool; apprenticed in Manchester; joined Hickson's; became Harland's private assistant and virtual partner, 1858; Conservative M P for East Belfast, 1892–1910; given freedom of the city, 1911; patron of local Orangeism; born a Jew but became an Anglican. Formally involved in Harland & Wolff until 1906, but took a back seat much earlier: 'Sir Edward builds the ships, Mr Pirrie makes the speeches, and, as for me, I smoke the cigars.'

[xiv] George Smith Clark (1861–1935): born in Paisley; trained at Harland & Wolff's; entered into partnership with Frank Workman, 1880; established Workman, Clark & Co. with the support of a relative, whose family owned the Allen Line, 1891; Baronet, 1917; overextending after the war, he suffered near bankruptcy; accusations of breach of trust and contract forced the company into temporary liquidation, 1927–8; taken over, 1935. A staunch Orangeman; M P for North Belfast, 1907–10; organized the Unionist gun-smuggling committee, 1912; donated considerable sums to the Ulster Volunteer Force; Senator in the Northern Ireland parliament, 1922–35. With employees of Workman, Clark led the move to expel Catholics from the shipyards and other industries, 1920.

[xv] William James Pirrie (1847–1924): born in Quebec of Ulster parents; apprenticed at Harland & Wolff's, 1862; became a partner, 1874; Chairman, 1895; promoted the 'big ship' and innovations in marine engineering; overstretched the company after 1918, refusing to accept that the boom had ended. In politics: Honorary Treasurer of the Ulster Defence Union, 1893; Lord Mayor of Belfast, 1896–7; first Freeman of the City, 1898; rejected by the Conservative establishment as candidate for South Belfast, 1902; financed the Liberal Party in Ulster in the 1905 general election; barony, 1906;

Liverpool was a vital factor in their expansion. By 1849 the steam-power needs of the linen industry accounted for 250,000 tons of coal imported to Belfast every year, which would quadruple by the end of the century; a constant trade of colliers plied between Britain and the north-west. The factory culture that came with the development of mechanized flax spinning spread to the shirtmaking centre of Derry, and provided opportunities for female labour; but generally, northern industry contracted round the Lagan valley, instead of spreading out from it. And with this concentration of industry there developed an intensely sectional and disputatious workforce.

Labour divisions along sectarian lines were paralleled by settlement frontiers within the growing urban sprawl of Belfast. The 1861 census showed the city one-third Catholic. By 1857 the 'Pound' area, taking in Divis Street, Barrack Street, Albert Street and part of the Falls Road, was exclusively Catholic; Sandy Row and the Shankill Road had affirmed their own Protestant identity. Urban sectarian riots around the 12th of July were recurrent from the 1850s – in 1857, 1864 and 1872 the carnival turned rapidly to carnage. And Ulster politics became accordingly polarized.

By the 1860s the Orangeism of the local police was being generally noted. The tradition of Ulster Liberalism, Presbyterian-led and Reformist, capitalized on some Catholic support over Church Dis-establishment in the 1860s; it enjoyed one last hurrah when Orange populist elements supported them in the early 1870s, and another, briefly, when land issues brought Catholics and Protestants together in the early 1880s. The land issue might contain the potential for interdenominational voting; but in Belfast the Presbyterian vote was inexorably turning Tory. By 1880 Ulster Liberalism had become a rural party. Conservatism had a strong urban base in Belfast, where the shipping and engineering empires subscribed to Tory politics; the 'protestant operative' tradition found expression in Orange values and craft exclusiveness. Popular Protestantism made occasional assertions against Conservative hegemony, but the process of polarization is not contradicted by the diverting career of the Protestant folk hero and Orange radical William Johnston of Ballykilbeg:[xvi] once at Westmins-

chaired a Belfast meeting at which Redmond spoke on Home Rule, 1912; returned to the Unionist fold, becoming a Senator in the Northern Irish parliament, 1922; Viscount, 1921; died on business in South America, buried in Belfast. The greatest Irish businessman of his generation.

[xvi] William Johnston (1829–1902): born in Ballykilbeg, County Down; educated at Trinity College, Dublin; entered the Orange Order, 1848; imprisoned under Party

ter he reverted to recognizable Toryism. From 1851 to 1870, though the Order declined in the countryside, the membership of Belfast Orange Lodges trebled; the number of halls increased; the marches grew larger; and a middle-class leadership evolved. Orangeism did not involve itself directly in formal politics at this stage; it did not have to. For all the British Conservative suspicion of it, it was a self-sustaining native growth. So, in its way, was Irish Toryism, which, with the polarization of the 1880s, would be subsumed along with Orange values intó Unionism.

V

The final component in the evolution of mid-nineteenth-century Irish politics was Fenianism. The name is appositely vague for a movement that emerged, rather than being founded. Though formally constituted as the Irish Republican Brotherhood (IRB) in 1858, the Gaelicist label of Fenians (a reference to the Fianna army in the medieval saga of Fionn Mac Cumhail) was the identification that stuck. It brought together the remnants of Anglophobic Young Ireland like John O'Mahony[xvii] and James Stephens,[xviii] organizers of local nationalist

Processions Act, 1868; MP for Belfast, 1868–78; Inspector of Fisheries, 1878; dismissed for violent speeches against the Land League and Home Rule party; MP for South Belfast, 1885–1902; advocate of security of tenure, temperance reform and women's suffrage. His novels, *Nightshade*, 1870, which denounced 'prowling Jesuits' and 'Liberal Protestants', and *Under Which King?*, 1873, reflected his political opinions.

[xvii] John O'Mahony (1816–77): born in County Limerick; educated at Trinity College, Dublin; joined the Repeal Association, then Young Ireland, 1845; joined the Irish Confederation with Smith O'Brien, 1848; escaped to France; moved to New York, 1852; wrote for the Irish-American press; co-founded the Emmet Monument Association, 1855; translated Geoffrey Keating's *Foras Feasa ar Éirinn*, 1857; proposed to Stephens a new republican organization, thereby inaugurating Fenianism, 1858; organized a Fenian regiment, of which he was colonel, in the American civil war, 1861–5; ceased to be Head Centre of American Fenianism with the rise of the 'Senate' wing, 1865; an attempt at reassertion in 1866 failing, he lost political influence; died in New York, buried in Glasnevin.

[xviii] James Stephens (1825–1901): born in Kilkenny; became a civil engineer; joined Young Ireland; aide-de-camp to Smith O'Brien, 1848; fled to Paris; toured Ireland, 1856–7; convinced himself of the feasibility of revolution; founded the IRB, 1858; visited the USA to promote funds; blamed O'Mahony for the delay of revolution, 1861; *On the Future of Ireland*, 1862; founded the *Irish People*, 1863; revisited USA, 1864; stimulated funds by promising a rising in 1865; fixed upon the anniversary of

clubs like O'Donovan Rossa,[xix] and expatriate nationalists who formed societies with code names like 'The Emmet Monument Association'. Technically, the IRB was the conspiratorial, pledge-bound secret society based in Ireland, while the Fenian Brotherhood was a support organization, largely based in America, intended to provide the sinews of war: but the word 'Fenian' did duty for both. In fact, the IRB in its early days avoided naming itself altogether: 'the organization', 'the brotherhood', 'the firm', served as identification. As Charles Townshend has pointed out, this signified that from its inception 'the group occupied a more or less natural place in Irish political life'.[9]

In many ways the Fenian ideology was equally familiar: in some areas it merged with existent Ribbon societies and adopted their ethos. But its central motivation revolved round the view of England as a satanic power upon earth, a mystic commitment to Ireland, and a belief that an independent Irish republic, 'virtually' established in the hearts of men, possessed a superior moral authority. This was amplified by Blanquist and Mazzinian influences from Europe, and a preoccupation with the revolutionary opportunities generated in the event of Britain entering a foreign war. This found strong support from the compensatory nationalism-in-exile among Irish Americans, as well as in the revolutionary underground of post-1848 Paris.

The personnel and organization of early Fenianism has recently been the subject of much study (which has established, among other things, that Stephens's founding the movement was *not* contingent upon a 3,000-mile walk around Ireland to take the pulse of the patriotic nation[10]). Stephens, the inspirational megalomaniac, Kickham the puritan rural-

---

Emmet's execution, 20 September; the plan was discovered and the offices of the *Irish People* raided, 15 September 1865; escaped to Paris, and thence to New York, April 1866; received rapturously upon proclaiming his intention of promoting another rising; denounced for having taken no action, 1867; returned to Paris, retired to Ireland, 1891; lived at Blackrock in comfortable obscurity until death.

[xix] Jeremiah O'Donovan [Rossa] (1831–1915): born in County Cork; started a grocery business; founded the Phoenix Society at Skibbereen, 1856; joined the IRB, 1858; imprisoned, 1859; Business Manager of the *Irish People*, 1863; arrested, 1865; released on condition of exile, 1871; went to the USA; edited the *United Irishman*; published *Prison Life*, 1874; organized the Skirmishing Fund, 1875, which later financed the Dynamiters; Head Centre of American Fenianism, 1877; alienated colleagues by personal attacks and drunkenness; *Recollections*, 1898; died in New York; buried in Glasnevin, where Pearse, in a re-enactment of the MacManus funeral, spoke of him as the personification of the Fenian dead who would inspire Ireland to freedom.

ist, and Luby,[xx] the *déclassé* Protestant nationalist, were all representative of different strains within it. The 'secret' organizational basis, revolving around 'circles' based on the revolutionary cell, did not confer the discretion intended – partly because of the nature of the leadership. Many of those prominent in the organization were from well-off strong-farming or shopkeeping backgrounds; 'the alienated sons of commercial prosperity',[11] dedicated to romantic nationalism and the profession of journalism. They were, therefore, most scathing about the ambitious farming classes, and put their faith in what they saw as 'the people'. Their followers tended to be 'the class above the masses', according to Lord Strathnairn in 1869; a sample of those under investigation by Dublin Castle from 1866 to 1871 shows nearly 50 per cent skilled workers, and only 5 per cent farmers or farmers' sons. Schoolteachers, the marginal agricultural classes and the *petit bourgeois* of the small towns were also drawn to the movement. Its social ideals were fuzzy, though Stephens at least joined the First International, and foreign socialists had hopes of the movement. Most importantly, some Fenian cadres were ready to see land issues – even the question of land redistribution – used as a mobilizing mechanism towards independence, *à la* Lalor. But the leadership, especially Kickham and O'Leary,[xxi] held to the purist view of nationalism first.

The transatlantic connection reflected these tensions and differences. In its early days, Fenianism looked to America for military afforcement – particularly from demobilized Irish-American soldiers after

[xx] Thomas Clarke Luby (1821–1901): born in Dublin, son of an episcopal clergyman; educated at Trinity College, Dublin; abandoned ideas of the Church upon joining Young Ireland; contributed to the *Nation*; joined the Irish Confederation with Smith O'Brien, 1848; imprisoned, 1849; went to Australia; accompanied Stephens on Irish tour, 1856–7; co-edited the *Tribune*; formulated the Oath of the IRB, 1858; led the movement during Stephens's absences; edited the *Irish People*, 1863; arrested, 1865; released on condition of exile, 1871; settled in New York; wrote on Fenianism for the *Irish Nation*, 1882; O'Leary's *Recollections* are dedicated to him in acknowledgement of his assistance in their composition.

[xxi] John O'Leary (1830–1907): born in Tipperary; educated at Erasmus Smith and Carlow schools and Trinity College, Dublin; attended Irish Confederation meetings; briefly imprisoned for involvement in 'the Wilderness affair', 1848; studied medicine at Queen's College, Cork and Queen's College, Galway; hesitantly undertook an American mission for the IRB and contributed to the first avowedly Fenian organ, the *Phoenix*, 1859; watched Fenian progress from London, 1861–3; co-edited the *Irish People*, 1863; arrested, September 1865; released 1874; retired to Paris; enabled to return to Dublin by the Amnesty Act, 1885; *Recollections of Fenians and Fenianism*, 1896; prominent in the literary revival and sometime mentor of W. B. Yeats and Maud Gonne.

the civil war. This expectation faded, after a number of exploits had led to the realization that American foreign policy was not amenable to the idea of war with Britain. What replaced it was more important: money and ideological support from a powerful sister organization, Clan na Gael, affiliated to the IRB from 1877; and the completely dedicated support of John Devoy, in many ways the Lenin of the movement.[xxii]

Above all, Fenianism created a mentality. It captured the imagination of many of the children of the strong farmers, and even of some landlords: Fanny Parnell brought her first poems to the Fenian paper the *Irish People*. It developed a genius for publicity and for conducting 'secret' affairs in public. Literary Fenianism was a vital development; the Fenians were incurably verbal, producing endless memoirs and a vast corpus of emotional fiction, of which Kickham's novels are the only apparent residue. (Much of the *Irish People* consisted of John O'Leary's acid ripostes to the great influx of unsolicited verse.) The funeral of Terence Bellew MacManus, organized by the National Brotherhood of St Patrick (a sister organization later commandeered by the IRB), showed the Fenian gift for public occasion; in a sense their attempted invasions of Canada in 1866 and 1870, and the Irish 'insurrection' of 1867, were equally well-managed publicity coups. The subsequent arrests, trials, speeches from the dock, imprisonments, sufferings and occasional daring rescues constituted the real effect. Even the infiltrators and informers who sabotaged Fenian policy contributed to the mystique: they wrote their memoirs too.

Thus Fenianism could bring about the formation of an open 'Amnesty' movement on behalf of the Irish political prisoners – enlisting the support of moderate politicians who could not endorse Fenianism itself. It could organize public meetings in support of, for instance, the gaoled O'Donovan Rossa's embarrassingly successful candidature in the 1869 Tipperary by-election. It could engage the services of Isaac Butt in the highly influential state trials. Locally, it could enlist not

[xxii] John Devoy (1842–1928): born in County Kildare; joined the Fenians; served in the Foreign Legion in Algeria, 1861–2; in charge of Fenian infiltration of the British army, 1862; arrested, 1866; released on condition of exile, 1871; went to America; became prominent in Clan na Gael; secretly visited France and Ireland, 1879; founded the *Irish Nation*, 1882, and the *Gaelic American*, 1903, which he edited until death. The force behind the financing of many Irish projects from the 1870s to the eve of independence, when relations with de Valera grew strained, 1919; visited the Irish Free State, 1924; *Recollections of an Irish Rebel*, 1929; died in Atlantic City; buried in Glasnevin.

only sympathetic priests, but also a wide variety of previously disparate and incoherent political identities, often by mobilizing resentment against the larger farmers. And in the wider sphere it could give politicians and intellectuals (Matthew Arnold as well as Gladstone) an opening for positive initiatives – in theory at least. This did not require carrying the 'war' into Britain itself, though O'Donovan Rossa and others subscribed to the theory. The deaths caused by the violent attack on a Manchester police van in 1867, and the fatal explosion at Clerkenwell prison the same year, were not assassinations but unintended results of attempts at yet more sensational 'rescues'.

Fenianism abroad bore some resemblance to a serious and well-equipped revolutionary cadre. At home, it would be employed as a useful paper tiger by the hierarchy; Cullen affected to believe that the Fenians were Freemasons, and thus covertly encouraged by the government. But many priests made the sacraments available to Fenians, and Archbishop MacHale officiated at a high mass for the executed 'martyrs' after the Manchester débâcle. Fenianism provided a sphere of anti-British, anti-establishment and anti-clerical politics, articulated by bourgeois Catholics like Kickham and O'Leary who reiterated that their religious commitment was unaffected on the spiritual level. 'We saw from the start that ecclesiastical authority in temporal affairs should be shivered to atoms before we could advance a single step towards the liberation of our suffering country'. 'Bishops and priests may be bad politicians and worse Irishmen':[12] the point was that Fenian commitment was, in a sense, religious too.

Led by Cullen, the hierarchy responded – by backing an O'Connellite 'National Association', founded in 1864 and pressing for action on Disestablishment, the land question and education. It was seen correctly by the Fenians as an attempt to cut them out, and had considerable political potential. But the National Association has been paid more attention by historians than by contemporaries; its aims were too diffuse, and it never captured the imagination in the way that Fenianism did. By that date, Fenians were claiming 80,000 supporters (though 50,000 seems more likely); autonomous branches all over Ireland had formed a lively recreational culture of picnics and fake cricket matches where they could meet and drill; the movement provided a social outlet as well as a political identity.

In all this, secrecy rather went by the board. The high point of 'Fenian fever' was the late 1860s. The movement was reconstructed with a new constitution in 1873, when it declared that it would await the promised war against England until it was endorsed by a majority

of the Irish nation; meanwhile, it occupied the sphere of moral intransigence, and interacted with the politicized Farmers' Clubs, spreading
from the 1870s. Thus 'Fenianism', in its generalized sense, responded
to the well-meaning abstractions of armchair nationalists like Cardinal
Newman: 'If I were an Irishman I should be (in heart) a rebel.' The
real terrorist outrages of the 1880s would be carried out by far more
ruthless and unrepresentative offshoots like the Invincibles – at whom
Fenians threw up their hands in horror. Their strength remained
moral and passive: the kind of distinction missed by Marx and other
enthusiasts of the International, who saw Fenianism as a destabilizing
mechanism within the British system. Its importance was to sustain
republican separatism as part of the political language of mid-nineteenth century Ireland; and, in a sense, to make it respectable.

VI

The climax of the period may conveniently be taken as the end of the
1860s, when Irish matters arrived on the agenda of British politics. The
textbook view emphasizes Gladstone[xxiii] individually taking up his
mission to pacify Ireland; but, in fact, the Irish Church, Irish education,
Irish land and Irish disaffection were already established issues. (What
might Disraeli's mission have been if he had been returned to power
in 1868?) Gladstone's consciousness of Irish problems, while not new
and strongly influenced by his Churchmanship, had previously been
affected by the cold light of Peelite finance; as a reformist leader of the
Liberal congeries in the 1860s, his vantage had to be different. Not that
his terms were necessarily democratic. 'In my opinion this Empire has
but one danger: it is the danger by the combination of the three names,
Ireland, United States and Canada.'[13] But he was, as he devastatingly

xxiii William Ewart Gladstone (1809–98): Conservative MP for Newark, 1832;
opposed the appropriation clause of the Irish Church Temporalities Bill, 1833; *The
State in Its Relations with the Church*, 1838; hoped for Cabinet office as Chief Secretary
for Ireland, 1841; resigned from the Cabinet over the Maynooth grant issue, 1845;
Colonial Secretary, 1845–6; Chancellor of the Exchequer, 1852–5, 1859–66, 1873–4
and 1880–82; Liberal Prime Minister, 1868–74, 1880–85, 1886 and 1892–4; dis-
established the Church of Ireland, 1869; passed two Irish Land Acts, 1870 and 1881;
passed Compensation, Arrears and Coercion Acts, 1880–82; split his party and lost
the 1886 election over his conversion to Home Rule; dropped a Land Purchase Bill,
1886, and failed to pass Home Rule Bills, 1886 and 1893; retired to Hawarden, 1894.

admitted, propelled towards positive measures by the activity of Fenians – a remark that the organization savoured for years.

He remained preoccupied by the rejuvenation of the 'natural' leaders of Irish society, landlords and Protestants, in whom he put his faith. However, the ground he chose was that indicated by Cullen's National Association. Tenant Right remained smouldering, and a Catholic university had been the object of much negotiation between the hierarchy and Derby's government: but Gladstone moved first to disestablish the Church of Ireland (now representing only a fifth of the Irish population) – a potent gesture to his Nonconformist allies in Britain. It has been remarked that, for his part, Cullen was put into the piquant position of supporting 'a free church in a free state', which went against all his principles: but this is to assume that he saw the Church of Ireland as a Church worthy of the name, which he emphatically did not ('effete and bearing all the marks of the decrepitude of age and of approaching inevitable dissolution'[14]). The Church of Ireland itself was appalled at the bizarre alliance between papists and Dissenters, and deeply traumatized by the change in status brought about by Gladstone's Act of 1869. In fact, the terms were extremely generous: though technically expropriated, it was generously re-endowed, the surplus going to various charitable purposes.[xxiv] The Church was probably enabled to preserve far more than if it had entered an independent Ireland still in its Established state fifty years later; but an important principle had been declared. It was followed by an equally astute, but insubstantial, measure, the Land Act of 1870.

This cautiously introduced some principles of tenant protection – about one and a half of the '3 F's'. The 'Ulster Custom', of recognizing the outgoing occupant's investment in his holding, was legalized where it existed. Tenants were to be compensated for improvements they had made, if they were evicted. However, since improving tenants were *not* the kind of tenants who were evicted, this hardly met the case. The same criticism can be levelled at a further provision, which was that those evicted for reasons other than non-payment of rent were to be compensated. Theoretical arrangements were also made for land purchase by occupying tenants (a principle also introduced into

---

[xxiv] The Church was to become a voluntary body from 1871, with its holdings and property (not in use) vested in a body of Commissioners. A large proportion of the estimated value (possibly £10,000,000) was paid out in compensation; the rest (about £13,000,000) went to poor relief, education and agriculture. Capital sums were also made over to the Presbyterian and Catholic Churches, to replace the *regium donum* and the Maynooth College grant.

the Disestablishment Act), but on terms that could apply to very few.

There was no central provisión for rent control (though a minor clause opened the way for it, by introducing the concept of a rent judged by the courts 'exorbitant' under certain conditions). Those who had to vacate on the expiry of a lease were not protected; at the time of the Act, 77.2 per cent of agricultural holdings were held 'at will', 5.1 per cent in fee or on leases renewable for ever, and only 17.7 per cent on terminable leases. But many landlords responded by forcing tenants to accept restrictive leases, putting them beyond the Act's provisions; the reactions of many tenants to the 1870 Act was to interpret the acquisition of leases as 'not a lengthening of the legal yearly tenancy, but a shortening of the continuous traditional tenancy'.[15] Little was changed in practice. Tenants grumbled, and landlords were outraged. But the reasons for their outrage were significant. However tentatively, Gladstone had interfered with property rights; his theoretical principles of compensation implicitly admitted the Irish tenant's *moral* property in his holding. Drafting the Act, he had consulted (contrary to many claims since) with tenant spokesmen; he accepted, to the dismay of many Cabinet colleagues, the Irish historical sense of a certain vested right in the land that had allegedly been expropriated from their ancestors. When, after an abortive attempt to seize the nettle of Irish university education, Gladstone left office in 1874, he had made, at least, a decisive gesture. Perhaps because of this, he turned with relief to anti-Romanist polemic in the controversy over the Vatican decrees.

Moreover, if Fenianism in its broadest sense is inseparable from Gladstone's adoption of a positive Irish policy, it is also influential in the final political development of these years: yet another attempt at a coherent grouping of Irish MPs to advance Irish issues at Westminster. This time, however, the group led by the idiosyncratic Irish Tory Isaac Butt adopted the language of 'Home Government' or 'Home Rule' – phrases that can be found as early as 1857 in the leader-columns of Fenian-influenced literary journals like the *Celt*, and which in Butt's formulation meant a developed parliament at Dublin, for Irish affairs, emphatically within the Empire, and compatible with a federalized arrangement for United Kingdom government. Butt, always open to ideas and down on his political luck, was capitalizing on the political energy released by the Amnesty Association; as this implies, 'safe' Fenianism was looming in the background. Other planks in the platform included denominational education and land reform; also, given the fury of the Ascendancy after Gladstone's initiatives, there was a strong backing from disillusioned Protestants, ready to consider Butt's notion of federalism, though it was too constitutionally sophisticated for British opinion, and remained evasive on the vital question of representation regarding imperial affairs.

This Protestant support tailed off as Catholic issues came to the fore, though initially the hierarchy remained suspicious of Butt and preferred Catholic Whiggery to quasi-Protestant Home Rule. However, the secession of several bishops from the National Association to the new grouping by 1873 was a hopeful sign; and vitally, the secret ballot introduced in 1872 gave political organization in the localities a new direction. In 1873 the movement, hitherto merely a strategy, became a party. The aura of establishment constitutionalism remained; but there were rumours that the IRB had been squared to give Butt's organization three years to deliver what it could, and the new party's organization in England (the Home Rule Confederation of Great Britain) rapidly came to resemble a Fenian front organization. This should be remembered along with the traditional picture of Butt's Home Rulers as gentlemanly opportunists.

In the results of the 1874 elections, Home Rule was subscribed to by a spectacular fifty-nine MPs. The new movement had apparently subsumed Irish Liberalism. Though its personnel remained dominated by land, the new intake from 1874 showed an increase in bourgeois–professional interests – notably journalism and the law – and even two tenant farmers. With Fenian rhetoric in the background, and an impatient Young Turk element within the party, the Home Rulers were ready to respond to crisis in Ireland and insensitivity from the government. Both conditions would be met in full measure by the end of the decade, when the sudden decline in agricultural prices became a vital factor for Irish political history.

What followed was the politics of Parnellism. Home Rule was converted under a charismatic leader to an aggressive political campaign of threat and bluff, based on what had eluded every other Irish parliamentary initiative: a disciplined, pledge-bound, dictatorially organized party machine. It came about after the rapid displacement of Butt and his circle by impatient politicians like Biggar[xxv] and

---

[xxv] Joseph Gillis Biggar (1828–90): born in Belfast; became head of the family firm; joined the Home Government Association, 1870; MP for County Cavan, 1874–90; inaugurated 'obstructionism', 1875; elected to the Supreme Council of the IRB, 1875; expelled for refusing to break with constitutionalism, 1877; elected Treasurer of the Land League, 1879; temporarily suspended from the Commons twice in 1881; warrants issued for his arrest, 1881, but never imprisoned; once 'obstruction' was

O'Connor Power,[xxvi] both closely connected with Fenianism in their local bases – though purist Fenians in the Paris and New York conclaves were deeply suspicious of constitutional flirtations. The way Fenianism altered its nature from the early 1870s, looking more kindly on constitutional initiatives, was closely connected with corresponding adaptations within Home Rule. The Home Rulers would institutionalize Anglophobia, play publicity politics by demonstrating ostentatious 'independence' on foreign policy issues, and emphasize the rhetoric of separatism when it suited them. But they would also retain a strand of Buttite imperialism; and they capitalized on an electorate that had become, by the 1870s, 'compact, politically aware, shorn (at least in the counties) of the most bribable, the most fickle and the most subservient, slowly expanding but still a recognizable elite'.[16] A generation of upheaval in land ownership, religious ascendancy and nationalist politics logically culminated in the emergence of an Irish Home Rule party at Westminster.

crippled by procedural legislation, 1881–2, he treated the House with great respect; conducted his own case before the Parnell Commission, 1889. Born a Presbyterian; received into the Catholic Church, 1877, allegedly to annoy his sister.

[xxvi] John O'Connor Power (1848–1919): born in County Galway; emigrated to Rochdale; joined the IRB; involved in the Chester Castle raid and in rescuing two Fenians from Manchester, 1867; detained six months without trial, 1868; studied for the priesthood at St Jarlath's, Tuam; joined the Home Rule League, 1873, encouraging other Fenians to give constitutionalism a trial; MP for Mayo, 1874; prominent obstructionist; expelled from the IRB for refusing to leave the Home Rule party, 1877; considered as a successor to Butt as its leader; claimed to have anticipated the 'new departure' by a decade; first MP to join the Land League of Mayo, 1879; stood as a Liberal in the 1885 election; lost and retired from politics. While a Home Ruler, let it be known he considered Butt a 'traitor' and Parnell a 'mediocrity'.

CHAPTER SEVENTEEN

THE POLITICS OF PARNELLISM

I

WRITING TO A radical feminist associate in 1910 about her unpublished memoir of the Land War, Anna Parnell[i] outlined her approach to the interpretation of history.

> I avoided personalities as much as possible, as I consider the actions of particular individuals are unimportant in history, while the actions of groups, classes, etc. of persons are most important, because the former are not met with again, and the latter are.[1]

It is an ironic reflection, because Irish history in the 1880s and 1890s is inescapably linked with the personality of one man, Anna's brother Charles Stewart. He not only dominated politics in Britain and Ireland, but gave his name to a political system, or more accurately a political ethos, that became known as 'Parnellism'.

What was Parnellism? In its smear campaign of 1887 that attempted to link the Irish MPs with political assassination, *The Times* postulated the conjunction of 'Parnellism and Crime'; by then Parnell had achieved unchallenged supremacy, having presided over a successful campaign for land reform in Ireland, controlled extremism while benefiting politically from it, and forced Home Rule on to the agenda of the Liberal Party. Parnellism meant all of this. Yet in 1879 he had still been a rebel within the Irish Parliamentary Party, focus of a small advanced group, ridiculed by rivals like O'Donnell and O'Connor Power as a dim and limited 'gintleman' chosen as a front man. In some

---

[i] Anna Catherine Parnell (1852–1911): educated at the Metropolitan School of Art; organized a famine relief fund, 1879; prompted by her sister, Fanny, to establish the Ladies' Land League in Ireland; set up its Committee, January 1881; distrusted by her brother, who doubted her political acumen and suppressed her organization; retired to England, 1882; drowned at Ilfracombe.

ways he was limited; but he was a completely dominating figure. And, more than is often recognized, he was also a representative one.

Parnell possessed the political charisma of a handsome, arrogant aristocrat. But he was also an encumbered landlord, far into debt well before he entered politics. He was half American, inheriting on his mother's side anti-Britishness, as well as instability. He had been exposed, along with his sister Fanny, to the romance of Fenianism from the 1860s. He had experienced at Cambridge, to his irritation, the condescension of the English middle classes towards Irishness: though, with representative Anglo-Irish ambivalence, he was happiest in secret uxorious bliss with an Englishwoman, living under assumed names at genteel watering-places along the Sussex coast. In all this, he reflected more general aspects of the Irish experience. He was equivocal by nature – especially in his rhetorical relationship with extremism. Parnell's supposed Fenian connection was really a triumph of language, especially on American platforms; at home he achieved a highly political use of silence. While his record as leader was ostensibly restrained, except at times of crisis, a personality cult developed round him greater than that around any other Irish leader.

Inevitably, there was a hollowness at the centre. 'We created Parnell,' insisted Tim Healy,[ii] speaking for the party, 'and Parnell created us. We seized very early in the movement the idea of this man with his superb silences, his historic name, his determination, his self-control, his aloofness – we seized that as the canvas of a great national hero.'[2] Another later opponent, Michael Davitt, saw Parnellism as the replacement of nationalism by 'the investing of the fortunes and guidance of the agitation, both for national self-government and land reform, in a leader's nominal dictatorship'.[3] And Conor Cruise O'Brien, in what remains the classic analysis of Parnell's system and ethos, defined

[ii] Timothy Michael Healy (1855–1931): born in County Cork; educated at Christian Brothers school, Fermoy; railway clerk at Newcastle-upon-Tyne, 1871; Parliamentary Correspondent of the Nation, 1878; secretary to Parnell in America, 1880; MP for various Irish constituencies, 1880–1910; secured the 'Healy Clause' in the 1881 Land Act, ensuring that tenant improvements did not result in rent increases; called to the Irish Bar, 1884; supported the Plan of Campaign, 1886; co-leader of the anti-Parnellite Irish National Federation, 1891; expelled, 1895; founded the clericalist People's Rights Association, 1897; rejoined the Irish Parliamentary Party, 1900; expelled for refusing to disband the People's Rights Association, 1902; joined the All for Ireland League, 1910; KC, 1910; counsel for W. M. Murphy during the inquiry into the 1913 lockout, but also a noted advocate of the suffragettes; sympathized with Sinn Féin and stood down at the 1918 election; first Governor-General of the Irish Free State, 1922–8.

Parnellism (after Pareto) as 'a system in which the emotional "residues" of historical tradition and suppressed rebellion could be enlisted in the service of parliamentary "combinations" of a strictly rational and realistic character': adding that, for this to work, 'the ambiguity of the system must be crystallized in terms of personality'.[4]

There were two major ambiguities in Parnellism: the relationship between Home Rule and separatism, and the relationship between land agitation and nationalism. It was the land issue that supplied, in 1879, the politically mobilizing factor that made Parnell: the Fintan Lalor analysis adapted. But it had always been seen by purist nationalists as a 'sectional interest', rather like Catholic education: both should be avoided in the short term, first because they exposed the divisions within the Irish 'nation', and second (more importantly) because, if settled, they might remove the impetus towards separatism. Old-style Fenians were prepared to see 'Home Rule' advanced in constitutional terms, but were suspicious about the adoption by nationalists of bread-and-butter issues. However, what happened in 1879 gave them no choice.

The background to the agricultural crisis of the late 1870s is one of rising expectations, suddenly checked – though there is disagreement about the seriousness of the check. Agricultural production and profits expanded until 1876, as well as other indications of an improving standard of living. Though the landlord's share of the improved output may have been greater than the revisionists allow,[5] these years were remembered by tenants as prosperous. With a disastrous harvest in 1877 and an inadequate recovery in 1878, a very different picture was presented by 1879. Potato yields suffered particularly; blight reappeared in the south-west. Freak rain and cold throughout the summer and another hopeless harvest were accompanied by a drastic fuel shortage in the west. This coincided with falling prices brought about by the entry of American grain, and even beef, on to the British market.

Much has been made of the fact that the 1859–64 depression presented just as grim a picture; but no single year of that crisis was as bad as 1879. Potato production had fallen by three-quarters, and starvation loomed in the west, where, significantly, earnings from migrant labour also plummeted disastrously because of contemporary recession in Britain. The fall in income and cattle prices desperately affected the small farmers who supplied graziers with stock; credit, easily available from joint-stock banks and shops throughout the 1870s, began to be called in.

This was the background to the political organization of tenant resistance. It does not 'explain' that phenomenon; but the combination of economic crises came at a time when a modernized, and to a certain extent, politicized tenantry had become accustomed to making a good living. They had something to hold on to. Shopkeepers, large tenant farmers and traders were threatened as well as those on the edge of potato subsistence. Unlike the 1840s, a broad front existed, however precariously; and a political leadership was ready to utilize the crisis, backed by followers able to operate the complex associational mechanisms of a popular agrarian movement that would, unlike its predecessors, look forward rather than back, and set itself specific goals. The uniqueness of the land agitation of 1879–82 formed the crucible of Parnellism.

The emergence of the land issue also incorporated another vital element of the new political combination: Fenianism. Persistent rumours that the Supreme Council of the IRB had given Butt's Home Rulers a three-year term from 1873 seem borne out by its decision in 1876 to withdraw 'the countenance which we have hitherto shown to the Home Rule movement'. But many Fenians wished to go further, and land agitation provided the basis of an alliance with the constitutionalists. This situation, which provoked a crisis of authority within the ruling circles of the IRB, was the background to the association of Davitt, Parnell and, from America, John Devoy, in the so-called 'New Departure' of co-operation between Fenians, parliamentarians and 'advanced' nationalists. It was a fortuitous and uneven process, setting up many crossed lines between Clan na Gael in America, the IRB in Paris and the parliamentarians in Dublin. What emerged was an evolving strategy, never formally accepted by the purist IRB leadership, and from which Parnell kept himself technically detached. The final outcome, in October 1879, would subsume Fenian support into Davitt's and Parnell's Land League.[6]

From early 1878 the Lalorist notion of an attack on landlordism as a political campaign, backed by popular organization, was being floated: but not by the Home Rulers, and not in the specific terms later claimed by Davitt (who did not read Lalor until 1880). The vital first steps were taken in 1879; and for the first time, a popular movement took hold in the west. The vital seedbed of what looked to many like revolution was County Mayo.

Mayo had a history of tenant organization; it had a strong local tradition of Fenian influence mediated through politics by people like O'Connor Power and Matt Harris;[iii] it also contained a cadre of

[iii] Matthew Harris (1825–90): born in County Galway; became a successful building contractor; supported Repeal, Young Ireland, the Tenant League and Fenianism;

agrarian organizers, often returned emigrants conditioned by industrial Lancashire. It was also remarkable, as a detailed local study shows, for the rise in importance and prosperity of its shopkeeper–trader interest through the 1860s and 1870s.[7] Increased politicization and a very active local press lay behind the famous meeting at Irishtown on 20 April 1879 – an autonomous Mayo initiative planned by James Daly,[iv] one of the few involved who was not a Fenian, and therefore written out of subsequent history. O'Connor Power was co-opted as a 'name', and Davitt as an organizer, though he stayed in the background. Besides the current crisis, the specific Mayo issues of resentment against large-scale graziers, and calls to break up their land, surfaced from time to time; but against this, the Land League that subsequently emerged set its face.

Davitt, who had left prison with a reputation ready-made by the Amnesty campaign, and an instant gift for the lecture circuit, became the patron saint of Mayo radicalism; the co-option of Fenians (as individuals) gave the declaration of war against landlords an extra edge. At Westport on 1 June 1879, Parnell came to the fore, telling tenants to pay only those rents that were 'according to the times': 'keep a firm grip of your homesteads and lands'. The National Land League of Mayo was formed in August, and an all-Ireland organization followed in the autumn, with Parnell as President. By the next year, he was leader of the Irish Parliamentary Party as well. He was still only thirty-four, and Parnellism was in the making.

The concordat with some Fenians was part of an alliance between the land movement and the Home Rulers to use the tenant question as the basis for a general forward policy: it was not a separatist plot between the IRB and the Parliamentary Party. But it was inevitably open to such an interpretation, especially as the disingenuous Devoy would always insist there had been a 'compact'. Moreover, Fenianism was entrenched in the original executive of the Land League, four

agreed to support constitutionalism for a trial period, 1873; campaign manager for O'Connor Power in the 1874 Mayo election; founded the Ballinasloe Tenants' Defence Association, 1876; enlisted Davitt's support for the Mayo land reformers, 1879; MP for East Galway, 1885–90; led opposition to the papal rescript against the Plan of Campaign, 1888.

[iv] James Daly (c. 1835–1910): born in County Mayo; edited the *Connaught Telegraph*; secretary of the Mayo Tenants' Defence Association, 1878; organized Irishtown meeting which led to the formation of the Land League of Mayo; gave influential evidence to the Bessborough Commission, 1880; personality differences and his opposition to Davitt's land nationalization policy led to a breach with the Land League, of which he was the putative, conservative father.

members at least being Fenians. *The Times* Commission report of 1888 was not inaccurate: 'the object aimed at by Mr Davitt and the founder members of the Land League with regard to the revolutionary party was not to put an end to, or restrain its actions, by merging it with the new movement, but to point out to those holding Fenian opinions that the two parties did not clash'.

For a parliamentarian like Parnell, his involvement in the Land League meant riding a tiger. But it also provided him with the base he needed to overcome the moderate majority in the party; the ascendancy of Parnellism was confirmed by the 1880 election, by which time the campaign to reduce or even withold rents had spread over much of Ireland. Land League rhetoric was echoed by the politicians: the John Stuart Mill view of Irish landlordism as unprincipled in historicist terms, and indefensible in terms of current practice, was wholeheartedly adopted, with no allowance made for variations. Parnell's wildly successful tour of America in 1880 established him as the greatest political leader of nationalist Ireland since O'Connell. The land campaign destabilized rural Ireland, and climaxed with Gladstone's government adopting special coercive powers along with sweeping land law reform in 1881. The enthronement of Parnellism was accomplished by the subsequent proclamation of the League as unlawful, the arrest of Parnell in October 1881, the threatened takeover of rural lawlessness, its defusing from early 1882 as the tenants voted with their feet in the new rent tribunals set up by Gladstone's Act, and the eventual emergence of Parnell from Kilmainham in May 1882, to a tacit working arrangement with the Liberals.

II

An outline of the sequence of events, however, does little to explain their significance. One of the most important things about the Land League, and what it meant for Parnellism, was not what it did, but how it worked. It was a mass movement for tenant defence, aimed at establishing an eventual peasant proprietary, though this was not articulated anywhere and the idea of 'Griffith's valuation' as a fair basis for rent was general. It was technically legal and non-violent; its chief weapons were supposedly publicity and moral intimidation. The government's attempts to prosecute for seditious speeches were riven with problems; the League's official slogans were brilliant, economical and unactionable, like Fanny Parnell's 'Hold the Harvest!' But it was indissolubly linked with more violent rhetoric aired in the local speeches so painstakingly gathered by *The Times* Commission; and with the long tradition of rural crime.

Agrarian outrage had run at a low level from 1850 to 1880: the annual number of crimes thus defined rarely rose above 500. It was, in any case, an odd definition, taking in everything from murder to 'threatening letters', – the latter by far the most common offence. It is hard to find a close statistical correlation with evictions, or even with landlord behaviour; in one random sample of a hundred murders, family disputes and intra-tenant feuds account for two-thirds.[8] During the Land War of 1879–82, occasional agrarian murders like that of Lord Mountmorres in September 1880 drew great publicity; but the aggregate of homicides was low – sixty-seven for 1879–82, very few involving landlords or agents. The horrific Phoenix Park murders of May 1882, when the Chief Secretary and Under-Secretary were assassinated, had nothing to do with the Land War: and the formation of violent agrarian secret societies like the 'Royal Irish Republicans', active in north County Cork in 1881, were unconnected with the Land League.

What the League largely relied on was implicit violence. Tactics included the threatening letter, now a weapon of some antiquity, following almost a prescribed form and structure; the breaking up of tenants' celebrations for a landlord's marriage or coming of age; the institution of Land League courts to impose the moral law, which dangerously implied an alternative government, but which – according to some government thinking – were by 1881 actually restraining anarchic elements. Above all, rent was witheld, evicted farms were kept empty, and landlords ostracized by the traditional weapon of excluding the transgressor from all transactions within the community – now called, after its most celebrated victim, the 'boycott'.[v]

All this, however, relied on a substratum of intimidation and real violence, though it was hard to quantify or apprehend. Attending a court hearing during the next burst of land agitation in 1887, the self-

---

[v] Charles Cunningham Boycott (1832–97): born in Norfolk; retired from the army as a Captain and became Lord Erne's Mayo agent, 1873; prominent victim of the 'moral Coventry' policy to which his name was subsequently given, autumn 1880; crops harvested by fifty Cavan Orangemen, who worked under the protection of 1,000 members of the Royal Irish Constabulary, at a cost of £10,000 to the government, November 1880; left Ireland permanently, 1886; gave evidence to the Parnell Commission, 1888.

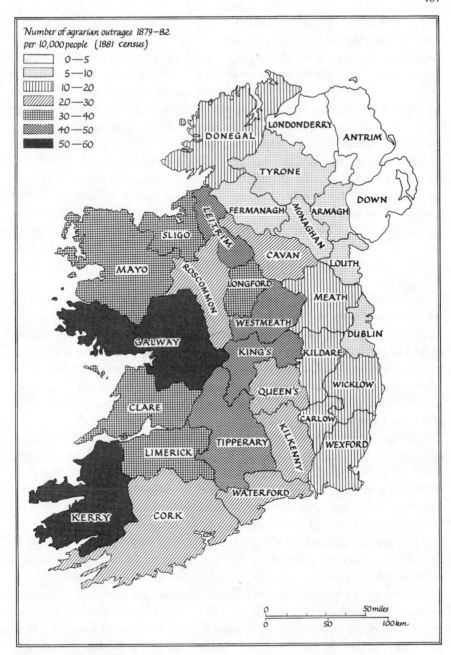

Map 11: *Agrarian outrages 1879–82.*

Source: David Fitzpatrick, 'The Geography of Irish Nationalism 1910–21', *Past and Present*, no. 78 (February 1978).

important fellow-traveller Wilfrid Scawen Blunt noted gleefully: 'The best of the joke is that the prisoners were all really guilty of a great deal more violence than could be proved, and everybody in the Court knew it, except the magistrates and the Crown people.'[9] The same was true in 1879–82. Assassinations did happen, as well as 'warning' shots into people's houses, and mutilations like ear-clipping. Animals were horribly tortured. Bands of young men imposed a kind of gang rule in certain areas. Land League activity can be correlated with the large numbers of frustrated single men in rural Ireland: the 1870s had seen a pause in the population drain, while the age of marriage remained late. Certainly, violent nocturnal group behaviour seems linked to *machismo* and sexual frustration. (There were those who thought agrarian agitation led to a more direct release: a parish priest urged the outlawing of the National League in 1887 because 'where there was one case of fornication [before the League], there are now 50'.)[10]

Whatever about this, Samuel Clarke's survey shows that levels of violence not only were 'vastly greater than can be explained by the degree of hardship'; they also varied in proportion with non-violent political activity, not with levels of distress. Thus violence was being employed as a political weapon. As the confrontation with the land-lords escalated, so did evictions: the highest peak was in the spring of 1882. From 1879 to 1883, 14,600 tenants were evicted – more than over the previous thirty years.

The government's response was always problematic. Mass meetings, civil disobedience, the refusal to pay rents or to quit holdings, raised their own problems; but 'coercion' was in many ways counter-pro-ductive, not least because of the crises it caused within the Liberal government. Ministers remained obsessed until a late stage by the idea of a criminal conspiracy started by a few 'village ruffians' who needed only to be put behind bars for tranquillity to be restored. The use of special magistrates, reinforced by detachments of troops, created a number of celebrated confrontations; the dilemma of the Liberal government faced by uncontrollable 'outrages' has been classically delineated by Charles Townshend.[11] Martial law passed through mini-sters' minds, but could never seriously be entertained. Parnell's arrest, and the outlawing of the Land League in October 1881, certainly released a kind of anarchy, apparently amplified by the Phoenix Park murders; the eventual course taken was by means of criminal law amendment techniques, including provision for special non-jury courts and full-scale surveillance of secret societies. Here, as in other areas,

Irish conditions enforced on British government the adoption of expedients that would have great future importance.

The reaction of the landlords also began incoherently, but evolved into organizations like the 'Property Defence Association' and the 'Emergency Committee' staffed by the Orange Lodges. They also reacted by adopting more ruthless practices of eviction, faced with non-payment of rent: in a sense, many chose to live up to their stereotype. Local studies show that determined landlords were able, even in the west, to find people ready to take on the farms of evicted tenants. But organized landlord resistance really developed only in the episodic revival of the Land War during 1886–7, when William O'Brien[vi] and John Dillon[vii] mounted a 'Plan of Campaign' to impose specific rent levels on selected estates. And by then even a Conservative government was not invariably prepared to back the landlord case to the hilt.

Landlord reaction raises the question: tactically speaking, what did

[vi] William O'Brien (1852–1928): born in County Cork; joined *Freeman's Journal*, 1875; accepted Parnell's offer of the editorship of *United Ireland*, 1881; imprisoned, 1881; author of the 'No Rent Manifesto', October 1881; Secretary of the National League, 1882; MP for Mallow, North-east Cork and Cork City, 1883–1918; organized the Kingston estate rent strike, which led to his reimprisonment, 1887; won Parnell's support for the Tenants' Defence Association, 1889; attempted to negotiate between Parnell and the anti-Parnellites, December 1890; founded the United Irish League, 1898; edited the *Irish People*, 1899; promoted Irish Parliamentary Party reunification 1900; active in the Land Conference, 1902; broke with the Irish Parliamentary Party upon their refusal to call a conference on self-government; supported the Irish Relief Association, 1904; rejoined the Irish Parliamentary Party, 1908, after failing to negotiate with Sinn Féin; resigned, 1909; launched the All for Ireland League, 1910; voted against the third Home Rule Bill in opposition to Partition, 1914; spoke on recruiting platforms, 1914–15; did not contest the 1918 election; declined nomination to the Senate, 1922; wrote two historical novels and many commentaries.

[vii] John Dillon (1851–1927): born in Blackrock, County Dublin; son of J. B. Dillon; supported Mitchel's campaign for election in County Tipperary, 1875; accompanied Parnell to America, 1879; MP for County Tipperary, 1880–83, and Mayo East, 1885–1918; imprisoned, 1881; signatory to the 'No Rent Manifesto', 1881; supported the Plan of Campaign, 1886; opposed Parnell, 1891; succeeded MacCarthy as anti-Parnellite leader, 1896; supported the United Irish League and Redmond as leader of the reunited Irish Parliamentary Party, 1900; opposed Wyndham's Land Bill, 1903, and the Irish Council Bill, 1907; supported the third Home Rule Bill; present at the Buckingham Palace Conference, 1914; leader of the Irish Parliamentary Party, 1918; led their withdrawal from the Commons upon the passing of the Military Service Bill, April 1918; defeated at East Mayo by de Valera, December 1918, and withdrew from public life.

the Land League want? Radicals on the executive wanted as many evictions as possible, to provoke a major crisis: therefore they tried to withold relief funds until *after* tenants had been evicted, in case they were tempted to use subventions to pay the rent. This strategy was pressed hard from 1880, when the harvest was good; it was the policy inherited by Anna Parnell and her radical 'Ladies' Land League', when they took over the direction of policy late in 1881. Many of the tenants, especially the strong farmers, were less uncompromising. Paul Bew has discerned, in the spreading of the Land War to the prosperous farmers of the east and south, an *embourgeoisement* of Land League strategy epitomized by the adoption of paying rent 'at the point of a bayonet' – maximizing procrastination and legal expenses, but mini-mizing the risk of actual eviction. This provokes the question: whose interests did the Land League ultimately represent?

The agricultural crisis of the late 1870s was a different crisis in different places. In Ulster, the crux was the fall in tillage prices; in the 'congested' west, the recurrence of famine conditions; in Tipperary and Cork, the 60 per cent drop in butter prices; in the small mixed farming of the south-west, a combination of all three. Thus different people were affected in different ways. Graziers in the midlands and east, for instance, were initially able to ride out the difficulty. However, if the desperate smallholders of Mayo provided the footsoldiery of the early Land War, 'there were many hundreds on horseback at the Irishtown meeting'.[12] The increasingly forward part played by the strong-farming interest has been carefully and convincingly traced by Bew, and was noted by contemporary observers like Bernard Becker: 'To show how completely the members of what ought to be a middle class, I mean the large tenant farmers, are identified with the peasant class, I may add that many of them, working with a capital of many thousands of pounds, are subscribers to the Land League, and that many are not paying their rent.'[13] Donald Jordan's exhaustive study of Mayo discerns 'two struggles' in the Land War: 'one carried out by the large grazing farmers with an eye to securing complete control over the land and advancing their political and agrarian status in an agrarian capitalist society, and a second carried out by the small farmers anxious to protect their small farm economy by rent reductions and an end to evictions in a time of economic crisis.'[14]

Another vital element was the shopkeeping interest – over-represented in most forms of rural political mobilization. Between 1881 and 1911, while the rural population declined, the number of grocers and publicans actually rose. This group was incorporated with the large-farming interest by kinship and commercial ties; activity in the Land War presaged their importance in local politics over the next decade. The urban trade interests, however, were less committed to land agitation; while the agricultural labourers eventually discovered they had little enough to thank the Land League for. In some areas, like Cork and Wexford, they made their feelings clear.[viii]

Yet the broad front of the tenantry fought under the banner of rent reduction, with the ultimate implication of resort to a rent strike and – vaguely – 'the land for the people'. Even if this was an economic irrelevance, it was a powerful moral engine. The solidarity experienced, however, was more as citizens than as tenants: Land League branches were based on townlands or parishes, not on estates. And the rank and file never took kindly to the all-out rent strike postulated by some radical leaders after the 'coercion' legislation of 1881. Anna Parnell, hoping for total resistance, was appalled to be told by a Land League member 'there's not a single tenant in Ireland who would not pay the rent if he could'. She asked: 'Then what was the Land League for? And what were we all supposed to be doing? And how was it that the Land League was still going on? In short, what did it all mean?' And answered herself bitterly: 'The Land League policy was invented to please the people and did please them. The head and the tail matched each other.'[15] Historians have asked the same question, and not arrived at a very different answer.

Davitt's idea of land nationalization, though it chimed in with notions of communal ownership under Brehon law (then fashionable in English academe as well as in Irish rhetoric), was perceived as equally irrelevant to the tenants' interests. In such a coalition, those interests were inevitably at variance; old agrarian radicals like Matt Harris in Mayo saw the union of graziers and farmers as a 'union of the shark and the prey'. Fast as it grew, the Land League remained a rather shaky structure, combining tight political organization with slovenly clerical administration and loose rhetoric. In a sense, the hectic conditions under which it operated made this inevitable. But it must be borne in mind in order to understand why Anna Parnell saw the League as 'a great sham', and why her brother wrote apprehensively to Katharine O'Shea[ix] from prison in 1881: 'I cannot describe to you the disgust I

[viii] The Labourers Act of 1883, providing housing schemes, required twelve further amending statutes over the next thirty-six years before it had much effect.

[ix] Katharine O'Shea (née Wood; 1845–1921): born in Essex; married Captain O'Shea, 1867; neglect and financial circumstances led her to live with her aunt, Mrs

always felt with those meetings, knowing as I did how hollow and wanting in solidarity everything connected with the movement was.'[16] Certainly the League could never define how far 'rooting the people in the soil' meant expropriation, or redistribution, or compulsory reallocation of fee simple. Parnell himself demonstrated a curious lack of realism in his recurring notion that landlords might, through land reform, join the cause of Home Rule. He may have been correct in seeing the establishment of a state-aided peasant proprietary as in the landlords' best interests (given the condition of his estate, it was certainly to his own advantage). But the idea of reconciliation turned out as chimerical as his dream of mining gold from his own Wicklow hills. He was the only landlord to come to the fore in the Land League, and almost the only Protestant.

With the leadership in gaol from autumn 1881, local factions and private feuds tended to run riot in many branches; the Ladies' Land League, stepping into the breach, found most of their business was expected to be the disbursement of relief payments and court expenses for tenants fighting ejectment notices, while the drift of cases to adjudication in the new land courts set an unmistakable trend. In the spring of 1882 they relinquished the uncongenial task with relief. But perhaps one of the most important, and least recognized, achievements of the Land League is that it provided a political baptism for a generation of radical Irishwomen who spoke on platforms, organized tactics, were denounced by the clergy and got arrested. Many of them would later be involved in the suffragette movement and Sinn Féin.

The more obvious outcome of the Land War was Gladstone's Land Act of 1881, which granted the tenants the right of free sale and introduced a complex mechanism for arbitrating disputed increases in rent. It also introduced the concept of 'statutory tenure', which essentially meant security of occupation as long as certain conditions obtained. In this it followed the recommendation of the Bessborough Commission, which in January 1881 squarely identified the remedy for the agrarian crisis as the '3 F's'. But Gladstone's initial ideas were extremely limited; influenced though he was by the historicist ideas about 'a living tradition of possessory right' on the part of the Irish occupier, he was also worried about 'robbing the landlords'. In any

Benjamin Wood, from 1875; supported her husband in his political career; met Parnell, July 1880, and shortly afterwards became his mistress; communicated with Gladstone in the Kilmainham Treaty negotiations, 1882; divorced, 1890; married Parnell, June 1891; published *Charles Stewart Parnell: His Love Story and Political Life*, 1914.

event, though the '3 F's' might confer tranquillity, the Bessborough Commission was quite aware that they would be irrelevant to marginal tenants in the west; for such, the majority recommendations of the Richmond Commission (investment and economic education) might have made more sense. In fact, contemporary arguments that fixed rents and security of tenure would perpetrate uneconomic small-holdings, subdivision and bad farming were largely borne out. A further criticism, from the tenants' side, was that those in arrears could not apply to the arbitration courts; by the 'Kilmainham Treaty' between Gladstone and Parnell, this important and discontented element was conciliated, their arrears being effectively written off.

This demonstrates that the 1881 Act was, as Barbara Solow puts it, 'less an economic policy than a political stroke': a complex method of lowering rents, overwhelmingly in the tenants' short-term interests. Parnell's response was equally 'political': he took a high line about the Act's inadequacy, but instructed tenants to 'test' it by bringing specific cases to its tribunals. Simultaneously, he adopted an attitude of rhetorical intransigence by issuing the ineffective 'No Rent Manifesto' while in Kilmainham gaol, from whence he emerged six months later to a rapidly calming landscape.

What were the long-term results? Through the 1880s, agricultural prices and profits continued to fall; rents similarly declined, or were simply not paid. In the next crisis, during 1886–7 (when the slump hit the dry cattle industry), a rent strike was mooted once more, under the 'Plan of Campaign' advocated by some of Parnell's lieutenants, but icily repudiated by their chief. Though this did bring rents sharply down in some areas, the Campaigners tended to concentrate their attention on estates already nearly bankrupt. The threat of rural anarchy was combated by the hard line imposed from Dublin Castle by Arthur Balfour,[x] with resident magistrates receiving summary powers in pro-claimed districts, and the criminalization of 'political' prisoners: the lessons of 1879–82 had been absorbed on both sides, but the conflict was on an infinitely smaller and more localized scale. The 1887 Land Act allowed excluded leaseholders into the rent arbitration system, and

---

[x] Arthur James Balfour (1848–1930): entered Parliament, 1874; his stern handling of the Scottish Land League, as Secretary for Scotland, 1886, was thought to augur well for his ability to deal with the Irish; became Chief Secretary for Ireland, 1887; met the Plan of Campaign with 'resolute government'; suppressed the National League while introducing such constructive measures as the Congested Districts Board, 1890, and the Land Purchase Scheme, 1891; became Conservative leader in the Commons, 1891; Prime Minister, 1902–5; O M, 1916; Earl of Balfour, 1922.

shortened the terms of fixed rents to five years; while the temporary agricultural price recovery of 1889–90 helped to wind down the agitation. By the 1890s rents had fallen to the level of 'Griffith's valuation', set nearly half a century before. They had also fallen roughly in proportion to falls in agricultural income.

For the landlords, the outlook was grimmer. Their costs were fixed; the legislative and economic results of the 1880s left their incomes drastically reduced. For many of them, the Land League ideal of a peasant proprietary by means of land purchase was their only way out – provided it could be financed generously enough by the state. This process began with the Ashbourne Act passed by the Conservatives in 1885, and climaxed in the Wyndham Act of 1903, and its adaptation in 1909. By this stage the landlords were more anxious for it than the tenants, who had to be tempted into the arrangement by interest payments pitched lower than rents. Most landlords retained their demesnes, which they could profitably 'sell' to the state and 'repurchase' on the same low mortgage rates as their tenants. Land purchase finally became compulsory in the new dispensation of the 1920s, when many of the Ascendancy families left, for political as well as economic reasons. It was a process that began, as so much else, in the upheavals of 1879–82.

Agricultural improvement was another question, and an unanswered one. It can be convincingly claimed that land purchase at such ostentatiously favourable terms, accompanied by the continued adherence to labour-extensive pasturage, sustained the unadventurous and uncompetitive format of Irish farming, with its attendant syndromes of high emigration and low investment. The enormous efficiency gap between good and bad farming remained. Tracts of uninhabited pasture were let on an annual basis, outside the new legislation; by 1900 ranching was prevalent in north and east Leinster, north Munster, east Connacht, west Connacht and Donegal – a style of farming that required large acquisitions of land, working capital and minimal labour, and seemed to negate the opportunities of land purchase made available to small farmers. The *haute bourgeoisie* thus created (often townsmen) were much resented, and anti-grazier hostility became endemic over the next decades.

International market conditions kept Ireland locked into this framework, later attempts to introduce Danish dairy-farming models notwithstanding. Raymond Crotty sees 'a profound long-term equilibrium' setting in from 1900, with 'a new freedom to farmers not to invest', and an uneconomic allocation of land.[17] This hard-headed approach tends to leave out the psychological, and historicist, significance of land ownership for the Irish farming classes. But certainly, the many contemporary accusations that the Land League's ideals were 'socialistic' or even 'communistic' merely carry a pungent irony; the only real exponent of land nationalization, Michael Davitt, was driven by 1889 to the periphery of Irish politics, denouncing the idea of land purchase as 'a gigantic swindle of public funds as well as an anti-home rule enterprise'. But neither argument meant much to the Irish nationalist audience.

III

How far did the Land League raise nationalist consciousness? According to a modern authority 'the League fostered, where it did not articulate, the identification of basic local demands with wider political issues, which in themselves lacked much meaning for the peasantry'.[18] It certainly reinforced the politicization of rural Catholic nationalist Ireland, partly by defining that identity against urbanization, landlordism, Englishness and – implicitly – Protestantism. It expressed non-deferential politics, neatly symbolized in the Land League practice of 'stopping' local hunt meetings. But how far these developments were consciously experienced is another matter. Bernard Becker, again, in November 1880:

> The more that is seen of the people of far Western Connaught the more distinct becomes the conviction that the present difficulty is rather social and economic than political. It is far more a question, apparently, of stomach than of brain. The complaints which are poured out on every side refer not in the least to politics. Very few in Mayo, and hardly anybody at all in Connemara, seem to take any account of Home Rule, or of any other rule except that of the Land League. The possibility of a Parliament on College-green affects the people of the West far less than the remotest chance of securing some share of the land. If ever popular disaffection were purely agrarian, it is now, so far as this part of Ireland is concerned.[19]

If land was the priority for the farmers, for the Fenians and the Irish Parliamentary Party it patently was not. Though landlords could be represented as congruent with the foreign oppressor, it was an argument hard to sustain except in the fly-blown 'historical' rhetoric to which all nationalist politicians resorted (including Parnell, descendant of ex-Cromwellian *arrivistes*). What mattered was that the Land War created the Irish Parliamentary Party as accredited national leaders; and Parnell, with his unerring instinct, swung political energy back to the parliamentary field from 1882. The Parliamentary Party could now deliver. The cross–class alliance of the early Land War was maintained, with the newly enfranchised small farmers and labourers voting Parnellite in 1885. Playing to the American gallery necessitated a high rhetorical line: 'None of us ... wherever we may be, will be satisfied until we have destroyed the last link which keeps Ireland bound to England,' Parnell allegedly said at Cincinnati in 1880. The next decade amply demonstrated how untrue this was.

At several key points in Parnell's career the old secessionist idea revived, of withdrawing from Westminster and setting up an assembly in Dublin. This presented itself in May 1878, during the crisis over obstructionist tactics in Parliament; in October of the same year, with Devoy's telegram and newspaper article announcing the supposed *rapprochement* between Fenians and constitutionalists; in October 1881, with the proclamation of the League and arrest of the leaders. In every case, Parnell opted to continue working within the system. Similarly, the high public drama of the Land War resolved itself into mundane political pragmatics. The mobilization of the shopkeeping element, the high-flown pyrotechnics of William O'Brien's *United Ireland*, the catering to rural Catholic interests, all found their place within the political framework of Parnellism. But the effectiveness of that framework itself relied on developments in English politics: the 1883 Corrupt Practices Act, reorganizing electoral practice, and the 1884–5 Franchise and Redistribution Acts. The latter added over half a million voters to the register – mostly small farmers and agricultural labourers – and, just as significantly, led to the absorption of most Irish boroughs into the new county constituencies. Both processes might almost have been designed to facilitate the mobilization of Parnellite politics.

The machine was organized through the National League, which attached local political structures closely to the highly talented and noticeably young band of lieutenants at the centre of the party. The new men came from the backgrounds of farming, trading, journalism, the law; they represented the interests who were simultaneously capturing the elective seats on boards of Poor Law Guardians, and who would take over local government after 1898. Many Parnellite MPs were paid salaries from party funds; they took a pledge to vote together even before they stood for election. They were planted out in constituencies by the national organization; the 1885 general election produced eighty-five Irish Home Rule MPs, and one in Liverpool,

T. P. O'Connor. Irish Liberals disappeared altogether, and Irish Conservatives were practically restricted to the north-east and the Trinity College representation. The Parnellite party retained a few 'gentlemen' and *littérateurs* of the old 1870s intake, but they were anything but typical. One was Parnell himself; another, ominously, was the incongruous Captain O'Shea.[xi]

Parnell's 'National League' for getting out the vote was ostentatiously referred to by some Tories as the 'Land League': in a way, they had a point. Though purely a political machine, it inherited the moral authority of the earlier organization. The county conventions that chose candidates acted under direction from above; Parnell monopolized the power of choosing candidates, only delegating as suited him. Significantly, the only occasion when the process broke down was the terrible Galway election of 1886, when Parnell forced the unwilling local party to take on Captain O'Shea – with whose wife he was by now inextricably involved.

Otherwise, local interests (like Tim Healy's 'Bantry Band') were reconciled firmly to the national structure. The necessity to pay the new type of MP meant that funds from American sympathizers and local subscriptions were carefully controlled. By January 1886 the National League had 1,262 branches; it was most active in the midland counties, not the west, thus contrasting sharply with the Land League. One political scientist's analysis shows a correlation of membership with the strong-farming classes, though not an overwhelming one.[20] It was a powerful structure, built into rural society, reflecting the perceived successes of the Land War: Parnellism incarnate. In all this it would provide a formidable weapon against its creator at the stormy end of his career.

The way it did so is connected with a vital fact about the National League's county conventions: they co-opted the Catholic clergy from early on, and priests comprised an average one-third of the conventions' membership. Initially the Church hierarchy had been extremely cau-

---

[xi] William O'Shea (1840–1905): born in Dublin; educated at Oscott and Trinity College, Dublin; retired from the army, 1862; unsuccessful businessman; nominal Home Rule MP for Clare, 1880; challenged Parnell to a duel, 1881, but subsequently acquiesced in his affair; acknowledged three children born of his wife by Parnell, 1882–4; intermediary negotiator of the Kilmainham Treaty, 1882; co-founded the unsuccessful Irish Land Purchase and Settlement Co. with Parnell, 1883; pressed Parnell to find him parliamentary seats, 1884–6; did not vote on the Home Rule Bill and resigned, June 1886; testified against Parnell at the 1888 Special Commission; sued for divorce, December 1889; granted a decree nisi, November 1890.

tious about the Land League: only five out of twenty-eight bishops supported its claims in the 1880 election. Priests were another matter, however: fourteen of the sixty foundation members of the League were clerics. And, as on other occasions in Irish history, the Church adroitly changed its footing to follow the way its flock was going. Priests appeared frequently on Land League platforms, and Archbishop Croke of Cashel[xii] became its most outspoken champion. His emotional endorsement of the Land League as in the direct line of the national resistance tradition (May 1880) gave it a tremendous boost; though prelates like MacHale worried about rural anarchy led by 'godless nobodies', and MacCabe[xiii] about the 'immodesty' of the Ladies' Land League, the Church lined up on the side of the Land League. The question was whether this necessarily transferred to its successor, and, indeed, to Parnellism at large.

The Church was always suspicious of Home Rule's Protestant origins, though Parnell's ill-concealed agnosticism was preferable to the wrong kind of devoutness. There was also the danger of a parliament in Dublin that might include a largely Protestant House of Lords, and – even worse – decide to reconcile Ulster by special weighting for Protestants and excessive caution regarding denominational education. This was, however, the issue upon which Parnell chose to reassure the bishops, a tactic already adopted by those Conservatives who looked for an imaginative Irish policy, grouped round Lord Randolph Churchill.[xiv] From 1884 Parnell took a forward line in condemning the

[xii] Thomas William Croke (1824–1902): born in County Cork; educated at the Irish Colleges of Paris and Rome; Doctor of Divinity, 1847; ordained, 1849; President of St Colman's College, Fermoy, 1858; attended the Vatican Council as a theologian, 1870; Bishop of Auckland, 1870; Archbishop of Cashel, 1875; supported the land agitation of 1879–80, but not the 'No Rent Manifesto', 1881; advised to take a less active role in politics by Leo XIII; author of the 'No Tax Manifesto', 1887; opposed Parnell, 1890. Advocate of temperance and Gaelic games, being first patron of the Gaelic Athletic Association.

[xiii] Edward McCabe (1816–85): born in Dublin; educated at Maynooth; ordained, 1839; Bishop of Gadara and assistant to Cullen, 1877; Archbishop of Dublin, 1879; issued a circular calling attention to the Roman Catholic University question, 1879; Cardinal, 1882. A townsman without sympathy for agrarian agitation; threatened by extremists.

[xiv] Lord Randolph Henry Spencer-Churchill (1849–95): third son of seventh Duke of Marlborough and Frances, daughter of third Marquess of Londonderry; MP for Woodstock, 1874; acting secretary for his father as Lord Lieutenant of Ireland, 1877–80; adopted the causes of Dublin Toryism; advocated conciliation as the policy that made sense of the Union, while opposing Liberal concessions; cultivated relations with leading Parnellites, 1884; advocated extension of the Irish franchise, 1884; Indian

'godless' Queen's Colleges and calling for full provision for Catholic educational control at all levels; thus a 'concordat' was established between Church and party, whereby the party was committed to the Catholic line on issues like education, and the Church formally backed the National League.[xv]

The testing time came in 1886–7, when a section of the party revived agrarian agitation, and the government prevailed upon the Pope to issue a rescript against it. The Irish hierarchy, however, tactfully but unmistakably indicated that neither priest nor flock need take any notice. Some Irish MPs were given the opportunity to reformulate a no-priests-in-politics line, with Rome a less sensitive target than Maynooth; otherwise things went on as before. By then the Catholic clergy had lined up with the national movement more or less unequivocally, making, publicly, the assumption that the 'whole nation' was Catholic and that their wisdom could as readily be political as well as spiritual. Thoughtful clerics saw that this implicitly awkward position involved more imponderables than merely the party's spectacularly un-Catholic leader; the in-built tension was noted well before the crash of 1890–91.

What was not often noted was the probable, even inevitable, effect of this *rapprochement* in the north. Ulster's forms of sectarian and Unionist politics, already in existence, were set hard by the dynamic political events of the 1880s. Politicization formalized the old divides; rural violence called up the ancient reactions of local vigilante groups; landlords organized frontier patrols and proclaimed their right to 'drill'. Despite a tradition of Tenant Right agitation, and an early commitment to the Land League programme in several Ulster counties (which helped bring about a modest Liberal revival in the 1880 election), the Land League was rapidly perceived as a nationalist front and the Orange Order took a violently adversarial line. The notion of Parnellism 'invading' Ulster was particularly potent, and significant, exploding into violent incidents in Monaghan and Fermanagh during 1883. From Belfast, the reaction to Home Rule added an economic rationale to religious and racial reactions – especially given Parnell's

Secretary, 1885; instrumental in the Tory–Home Rule entente of 1885; played 'the Orange card' when Gladstone announced conversion to Home Rule, February 1886; Chancellor of the Exchequer and Leader of the Commons, June 1886; promised an inquiry into Irish affairs; resigned, December 1886.

[xv] In fact, a Catholic university (technically non-denominational) did not emerge until 1908, when the Queen's Colleges at Cork and Galway were linked to a new University College in Dublin, based on Newman's old Catholic University.

public commitment to protective tariffs for Ireland, only abandoned at a very late stage of the game. The whole combination could hardly have been better designed to offend Ulster's most hysterical sensibilities.

As a Home Rule initiative from London moved into focus in 1885–6, the Ulster Unionist coalition brought together Orange Lodges and elite Conservative Party leadership – briefly encouraged by visits from slightly appalled English Tories, who were used by the Unionists rather than the other way round. A few years afterwards Lord Randolph Churchill, the most celebrated but least typical of these political guest artists, was asked what he would do about Ulster when the inevitable Home Rule *démarche* arrived. His reply, 'We shall tell Ulster to go to the devil', was not practical politics: largely because Ulster believed in the devil, and identified him with Dublin.

In 1885 the election results that destroyed Irish Liberalism were interpreted for Lord Salisbury by an Ulster grandee: 'it is not the farmers who hold Ulster for the Queen, but the labourers and artisans, officered by the landlords'.[21] The events of 1886 solidified the confrontational nature of Ulster politics and the marginalization of rural Liberalism. A Tyrone flax-spinner, once an 'ardent Gladstonian', is recorded attacking the 'uncultivated ignorant people' of the Catholic south, and declaring his determination to employ only Protestants at his mill:[22] this would be the authentic voice of Ulster Unionism.

Though Belfast exploded in sectarian riots in 1886, they had nothing to do with Churchill's celebrated visit: they began with a battle in the shipyards that arose from an allegedly triumphalist remark made by a Catholic to a Protestant, to the effect that the day of Protestant Ascendancy was dead. The Ulster Convention of 17 June 1892 symbolized the determination of that Ascendancy to retain its place in Ulster (though it reflected a wider variation of political identification than sometimes allowed); it constituted a class alliance that was underestimated by Irish nationalists and British politicians alike. So was the obsessive narrowness of Ulster's political vision, shuttered between historical blinkers. 'Loyalism' was self-defining; its conditional nature meant that Ulster could logically fight against the Crown to preserve the connection. And 'Home Rule' similarly defined itself as Catholicism enthroned and rapacious: not for Ulster the flexible speculations and definitions indulged in by British politicians on both sides when the issue was up for auction in 1885–6. When the contest was over, Conservative politicians turned to reinforcing Ulster's views; thus Balfour at Belfast in 1893:

Home Rule means to you that you are to be put under the heel of a majority which, if greater than you in numbers, is most undoubtedly inferior to you in political knowledge and experience. It means that the whole patronage of Ulster is to be handed over to a hostile majority in Dublin. You, the wealthy, the orderly, the industrious, the enterprising portion of Ireland are to supply the money for that part of Ireland which is less orderly, less industrious, less enterprising and less law-abiding . . .[23]

They hardly needed to be told. From the mid-1880s a powerful and integrated party machine was developed by Ulster Unionism, reinforced by organizations like the 'Ulster Defence Union' from the 1890s. The Home Rulers of 1886 and 1893 demonstrated an extraordinary insouciance about Ulster's intentions. The fact that they assumed that 'Ulsterizing' (Balfour's phrase) was largely bluff leads one to wonder how much their own commitment was rhetorical as well.

IV

Parnellism at Westminster defined itself first by obstructive tactics, then by a concentrated independence. The case has been made, not convincingly, that the Irish Parliamentary Party in the early 1880s should be seen as part of the Liberal–Radical coalition; and it is true that many of their declarations about lack of interest in British issues should not be taken at face value. Nor should the imperial identification that adhered to many of them be underestimated. But the principal importance of these factors lay in the fact that it made them open to tactical alliances with Tories as well as Liberals, an element of great importance with the approach of the 1885 election under the new conditions of franchise extension and redistribution.

The Liberal adoption of Home Rule had been prefaced by devolution schemes like those of Joseph Chamberlain,[xvi] and may seem

[xvi] Joseph Chamberlain (1836–1914): represented family business interests in Birmingham from 1854; MP for Birmingham, 1876; uneasy supporter of Irish coercion, 1880; acted as an intermediary over the Kilmainham Treaty, 1882; opposed Home Rule as a breach of the Empire, but never wavered from a belief in the necessity of strong local government for Ireland; worked out the Central Board scheme, 1884–5, which O'Shea led him to believe Parnell would accept; joined the Liberal Unionists in alliance with the Conservatives, 1886; contemplated a federal solution to the Irish question after 1886.

logical in retrospect. But the correspondence of politicians, and the newspaper speculation of the time, provide a salutary reminder that there was a strong current within Conservative thought that was prepared to consider a Home Rule initiative if political conditions required it. In the summer of 1885 both the Viceroy, Lord Carnarvon,[xvii] and the irrepressible Churchill were ready for an imaginative policy; the memory of Buttite Toryism lingered and Salisbury's brief government of 1885 entered office by grace of the Parnellites and provided the useful *douceurs* of a Land Purchase Act and an Intermediate Education Act. In the visceral terms of political bidding, however, once the Conservatives had flirted with the Parnellites, a Gladstonian counter-bid was inevitable. As early as June 1885 Gladstone forecasted privately that at the next election the Parnellite majority would 'at once shift the centre of gravity in the relations between the two countries'. The arithmetic of the polls left 335 Liberal seats, 249 Conservative and 86 Home Rulers: the exact balance. It also meant that Parnell could put only the Liberals in. They were tied to each other.

The Home Rule crisis produced a Gladstonian conversion to Home Rule, and a Conservative Party driven back on die-hard rhetoric. Diplomatically, Gladstone's *démarche* could not have been worse handled – especially in his treatment of Chamberlain. Chamberlain himself was maladroit (and devious) enough; but, if he was later credited as the 'Judas' who 'killed Home Rule', it should be remembered that he at least tried to extract a logical definition of what Home Rule meant, compared to devolution, and took his stand on that.

Others were less anxious to be specific. Politics were polarized round Ireland, conveniently for both Gladstone and Salisbury; the Liberals were reconstructed, losing Whigs and Chamberlain but regaining many Radicals and building a strong base on the Celtic fringe. Those who left Gladstone over 'Ireland' were those already worried by his interference with property, by his inclination towards extra-parliamentary agitation, by his anti-imperialism and by his sentimentality. Ireland had focused all these elements: the spectacle of the country under Land League law seemed to bear out the anti-Liberal dictum that government there should rely on force rather than opinion. Spec-

[xvii] Henry Howard Molyneux Herbert (1831–90): succeeded as fourth Earl of Carnarvon, 1849; Conservative Colonial Secretary, 1866–8 and 1874–8; supported Disestablishment and the Land Acts of 1870 and 1881; joined the Imperial Federal League, 1884; Lord Lieutenant of Ireland, 1885; committed to limited self-government for Ireland, but refuted Parnell's statement that he had said, privately, he was prepared to accept Home Rule, June 1886.

ific 'anti-Irishness' is less discernible, except in the sense that many actually adopted Home Rule because they longed to see the end of the Irish at Westminster – an attitude concealed by the treacly rhetoric of a 'union of hearts'. In fact, British and Irish hearts were as disunited as at any other point in their relationship. Home Rule was unwinkingly seen by English politicians in terms of English priorities and English opportunities – a perspective Parnell never lost. For 'public opinion' as constituted by journalists and academics, it was an ideological issue – largely because it was seen as separatism and anti-imperialism. But the mechanics of Home Rule as posed in 1886 hardly bore this out; here, the ambiguities of Parnellism came home to roost.

The bill was a non-starter, if an important marker. The Irish parliament was to have limited power, London retaining imperial, fiscal and security powers (not to mention control over foreign relations, currency, treason and the Post Office). Uncertainty prevailed until a late stage about whether Irish representation would be maintained at Westminster. It was known from the start that the Lords must reject it, even if the Commons passed it – which they did not. It was none the less Gladstone's finest hour: in full moral cry, he projected a rather unconvincing retrospective continuity, presenting his 'mission to pacify Ireland' as consistent since the 1860s. In fact, he had moved through a series of energetic but short-term reactions to immediate political problems; it was Disraeli who had put Ireland on the political agenda for the 1880 election. Gladstone had thought about Irish local government reform and some administrative devolution since the late 1870s, but he had always disliked the name 'Home Rule', preferring 'local autonomy'. Though he discovered the moral iniquity of the Act of Union from 1885–6, he still saw his Irish policy as reconciliatory: not separatist, and not even experimental. He stressed the Canadian example of 1867, though others gloomily looked to India and South Africa as more accurate imperial analogies.

What of Parnellism? After 1886 Parnell (like the Conservatives) lost the advantage of flexibility. He was committed to the Liberal alliance; he had done wonders within the Westminster framework; he had to ignore Irish land agitation (and even Irish political appearances); he became, incredibly, a popular figure in Britain, established as a hero by the exposure of the *Times* letters, linking him with the Phoenix Park murders, as forgeries. Though the investigative Commission delivered an unfavourable report about the links of the Land League with violence and extremism, this was not the public issue. His position was, in a sense, circumscribed, and his control over his party less assured than it had been, when the time-bomb of his private life blew up in 1890 – with the disastrous divorce case that revealed (in inaccurately lurid detail) his ten-year liaison with Mrs O'Shea.

The ensuing political crisis came over the reaction of English Non-conformists, not Irish Catholics; it was Gladstone's statement that the Liberal alliance was endangered by Parnell's continued leadership that precipitated the once-monolithic Parliamentary Party into schism. Gladstone had little strategic choice in his response to party pressure, but he showed curious unhelpfulness towards delegations from the Parliamentary Party during the internecine horrors of the split. Parnell, followed by a minority of his party, played for very high stakes by remaining intransigent, falling back on radical Fenian rhetoric, and barnstorming Irish platforms; but he was essentially a defeated man when he died suddenly at Brighton on 6 October 1891. His immediate legacy was a shattered party, split along a complex of old cleavages and resentments. Dublin had remained Parnellite, as had Roscommon and other assorted strongholds, usually urban. It is hard to discern a common denominator ('individualism' is the best that the political scientists can do): except, inevitably, for Fenianism, which adopted the Parnellite side at once. Clerical influence against Parnell, while pronounced, was not quite monolithic (there were occasional Parnellite priests). But the general line was unequivocal. 'You cannot remain Parnellite and remain Catholic,' a Meath priest told his flock in 1892.

Electorally, however, Parnellism was already a lost cause: in 1892 nine Parnellites were returned, against seventy-one anti-Parnellites. The great machine had deserted its creator. What is significant is how far the majority decided to stay with the Liberal alliance rather than follow Parnell back into the Anglophobia and intransigence of the pre-1886 rhetoric that he hastily adopted. The introduction of another Liberal Home Rule Bill in 1893, passing the Commons but being thrown out by the Lords, might seem a vindication of their stance but it left matters unchanged.[xviii] The Union would see out the century, Parnellism notwithstanding.

[xviii] Both the 1886 and 1893 Home Rule Bills provided for a two-order legislative body, with an upper house composed partly of peers in 1886, and entirely elective in 1893. A Lord Lieutenant would remain. Matters witheld from the Irish assembly's consideration included the Crown, peace or war, defence, treaties, titles or honours, treason, alienation or naturalization, trade, navigation, quarantine, beacons, light-houses, coinage, weights, copyright, establishment or endowment of religion, and non-denominational control of national schools. In the original 1886 draft no rep-resentatives were to remain at Westminster; 1893 allowed for eighty. The erection of

What can be seen as a result of Parnellism is the changed approach of Conservative (now 'Unionist') government in subsequent years, along with alterations in Irish local politics. Local government reform in 1898 replaced the grand juries with elected county councils, on a wide franchise (including women); the rural trading interest continued to hegemonize politics. By 1905, 40 per cent of county council officers were townsmen. (Moreover, 10 per cent of county councillors and 5 per cent of district councillors had IRB links.) This unexpectedly radical legislation has been interpreted as an example of 'constructive Unionism'. But it seems to have been decided upon rather suddenly in response to an unexpected crisis, and through the new obsession of legislators with the idea of 'simultaneity' and 'equalization' between England and Ireland — whereas if the previous one hundred years demonstrated anything, it was the need to accept differences.

The progressive economic policies of Chief Secretaries like Gerald Balfour[xix] and George Wyndham[xx] did not represent a sustained Machiavellian conspiracy to cut out nationalist demands; light railways, state-aided cottage industries, road-building, internal migration

forts and dockyards was reserved to the imperial Parliament in 1886, and landlord–tenant relations (for three years) in 1893. Taxation, apart from customs and excise, passed under Irish control by the 1886 terms, but was reserved for six years in 1893. Ireland's contribution to the imperial Exchequer was fixed at a maximum of £3,242,000 in 1886 (too much, in Parnell's view): in 1893, Ireland was to pay one-third of true revenue raised in Ireland. Judges were to be appointed by the Irish government, and police control to remain with the imperial authorities over a phased term.

The 1912 Bill was very close to that of 1893, retaining forty-two Irish MPs in the imperial Parliament. Reservations to the imperial Parliament (for an interim period) included old-age pensions, national insurance, labour exchanges, the Post Office, savings banks and friendly societies; tax collection and land purchase were reserved in perpetuity. The arrangements for taxation included the power to vary imperial taxes and impose new taxes, and the power to impose custom duties on articles subject to imperial customs duty.

[xix] Gerald Balfour (1853–1945): Conservative MP for Leeds Central, 1885; private secretary to his brother, Arthur, 1885–6; Chief Secretary for Ireland, 1895; carried the 1896 Land Act, which extended his brother's 1891 Act, and the Irish Local Government Act; President of the Board of Trade, 1900; retired from politics to pursue business interests and psychical research, 1906; succeeded as second Earl of Balfour, 1930.

[xx] George Wyndham (1863–1913): great-grandson of Lord Edward Fitzgerald and relative of the fourth Earl of Dunraven; private secretary to A.J. Balfour, 1887; Conservative MP for Dover, 1889; Chief Secretary for Ireland, 1900; encouraged the 1902 Land Conference, adopting some of its proposals in his 1903 Land Act, which clarified the Balfours' Acts; failed to solve the Irish university question, 1904; resigned over devolution scheme, 1905.

schemes and the foundation of a Congested Districts Board to deal with the problems of the west represented responses to political conditions and local initiatives by a new breed of politician and civil servant. They also demonstrated the economic problems left unsolved by the Land War.

Unionist legislation created the environment within which Horace Plunkett[xxi] and others attempted a 'non-political' initiative from the 1890s, introducing co-operative dairying and labour-intensive rural industry, along with agricultural credit arrangements and experimental farming. But here again, despite the steady growth of the movement, the inheritance of the Land War was too much for them. Irish farmers preferred to adhere to grazing (what Plunkett despairingly called 'their lotus-eating occupation of opening and shutting gates'); cattle-fattening and sheep-runs added surplus value to the land in a more attractive way than more labour-intensive forms of dairying. Moreover, the cynical reactions of the peasantry addressed by Plunkett's Ascendancy disciples were similarly discouraging ('Her ladyship has us *desthroyed* with goats'). Eventually, such initiatives ran hard against the reductionist nationalism and determined opposition of the rural shopkeepers and graziers who had done well out of the Land War. 'Who are the largest subscribers [to the parliamentary fund]?' asked a Macroom shopkeeper in a vituperative attack on the co-operativists' application for a Treasury grant. 'Why the shopkeepers of course, who as you know have always been the backbone of nationality in Ireland.'[24] In a sense this was the inheritance of Parnellism, and its epitaph.

V
==

The Parnellite era achieved epic status; it was mythologized into 'history' as early as *The Times* Commission. Parnell's lieutenants (Dillon,

---

[xxi] Horace Curzon Plunkett (1854–1932): son of sixth Lord Dunsany; launched his co-operative campaign, 1889; Unionist MP for South Dublin, 1889–1900; first president of the Irish Agricultural Organization Society, 1894; organized the Recess Committee, 1895; Vice-President of the resulting Department of Agriculture, 1899–1907; knighted, 1903; regarded himself as a Home Ruler by 1911; influential in the Irish Convention, 1917–18; founded the Irish Dominion League, 1919; member of the Senate, 1922, but left Ireland in 1923, after the burning of his home. Practical visionary. Published *Ireland in the New Century*, 1904, and *Noblesse Oblige*, 1908, among other works.

O'Brien, Healy) were not only endowed with talent but with youth: they outlived their era, and contributed to its memorials. As the 1890s showed, they had brought Irish priorities into English government in a new way; and the Irish Parliamentary Party, reunited from 1900, stood ready to play the balance-holding card again. Politically speaking, expectations had been raised all round. In the 1870s even the sympathetic Bright and Bradlaugh had thought any kind of separatism too much to countenance; by the end of the century, a large sector of the British governing classes were prepared to accept Irish Home Rule as an unwelcome inevitability. Even Balfour, talking to Wilfrid Scawen Blunt in September 1887, agreed that it was an eventual 'certainty', though it would 'break two or three parliaments. "After all," he said, "when it comes I shall not be sorry. Only let us have separation as well as Home Rule; England cannot afford to go on with the Irishmen in her Parliament." '[25] Few saw things as far. But Irish politicians had achieved far more than did the terrorist bombings occasionally attempted by splinter groups in the early 1880s.

The other side of the coin was the heightened consciousness of the irreconcilable elements left out of the Parnellite equation. In the late 1890s the western smallholders who had not profited from the Land War were welded into such a formidable organization by William O'Brien's United Irish League that they threatened the hegemony of the Irish Parliamentary Party itself, and enforced its reunification. On another level, in the post-Land War age the tradition of Protestant Home Rulers, looking on the measure as an efficiency strategy, dwindled to a tiny minority; far more typical was the obsessive, hierarchical subculture of the Protestant gentry and bourgeoisie anatomized by the novelists Somerville and Ross in *The Real Charlotte* (1894). Their world of social paralysis and stiff-necked exclusiveness would long outlast 'independence' and the drastic decline of their numbers in the twentieth century.

Most of all, the Ulster consciousness contemptuously repudiated anything Parnellism had to offer, and their reaction points up the hollowness in the whole construction. Could Parnell ever have kept his promise, made during the debate in 1886, that 'the Irish people' accepted Home Rule as a final settlement? Ulster Unionists were unconvinced; and Parnell's description of them as 'a miserable gang who trade upon the name of religion', and could be subdued by a thousand members of the Royal Irish Constabulary, was both triumphalist and obtuse. The reality of the matter was better expressed by one of Randolph Churchill's Dublin Unionist friends, writing mordantly in 1889 that even moderate devolution, however desirable, was now made impossible by Ulster.

> It cannot be made a subdivision of united Ireland, without depriving all the congenial inhabitants of the rest of the island of their only hope and support, and at the same time exposing the 'masses' living in Ulster to the most unbending and to them repugnant rule of the extreme Ulster party, and sacrificing all the 'loyalists' everywhere else. On the other hand it can't be kept as an England in Ireland without raising a frontier question of the most utterly insoluble character, and it can't be forced under the hateful yoke of home rule without destruction of its prosperity, if not without actual force.[26]

Dazzling as the political structure of Parnellism had been, it had never really defined what Home Rule meant. Was it an imperial cause (in which case Ulster might be kept) or closet separatism, which implied, at very least, Partition? The Home Rulers, it has been neatly said, were 'not a party with a policy, but a movement with an ultimate objective'.[27] The ultimate objective was, loosely, 'self-government', which for many meant an ultimate aspiration to separatism. As with the post-1921 ideal of 'unity', this could be comfortably relegated to an aspiration in perpetuity; but it was there just the same. Perhaps it was fortunate for the Home Rule party that the English political system never put it to the test.

It was easier to harp on the inheritance of 'literary Parnellism' as adopted by Yeats and Joyce: the powerfully emotional image of Ireland's 'uncrowned king' torn down by base followers; a prophet outcast with the Promised Land in sight. In the next generation, however, literary rhetoric would threaten to take on a mobilizing force all its own.

PART FOUR

CHAPTER EIGHTEEN

===

THE 'NEW' NATIONALISM

I

===

THERE IS A TENDENCY to see the twenty-five years between Parnell's death in 1891 and the Easter rising of 1916 as a vacuum in politics: political 'energy' being diverted mystically (and mechanically) into the channels of 'culture'. It is a theory put forward by W. B. Yeats in a famous passage, used as the epigraph to numerous later studies:

The modern literature of Ireland, and indeed all that stir of thought which prepared for the Anglo-Irish war, began when Parnell fell from power in 1891. A disillusioned and embittered Ireland turned from parliamentary politics; an event was conceived; and the race began, as I think, to be troubled by that event's long gestation.[1]

The same theme was used by the ill-fated Liberal Chief Secretary, Augustine Birrell,[i] in self-exculpation after the cataclysm: Irish culture in the early twentieth century was so exciting that Irish politics were perforce ignored. There was 'a leap to the front rank of thought and feeling altogether novel ... Irish literature and drama, and Messrs Maunsells' list of new Irish publications, and the programme of the Abbey Theatre, became to me of far more real significance than the monthly reports of the RIC'.[2]

Writing in the 1930s, Birrell may have felt that history was on his side; other memoirs emphasized the same priority, and many historians have followed them. But it may be asked whether, given the cir-

---

[i] Augustine Birrell (1850–1933): President of the Board of Education, 1906; Chief Secretary for Ireland, 1907; introduced the Irish Council Bill, 1907; established the National University of Ireland and Queen's University, Belfast, 1908; secured the 1909 Land Act; hardly involved with the Home Rule question at Westminster, nor the Buckingham Palace Conference of 1914; failed to counter the growth of Sinn Féin; resigned, Easter 1916.

cumstances of the time, the activities of the intelligentsia were really more significant than the actions of the politicians and 'agitators'. It is certain that Irish culture from the 1890s represented what Isaiah Berlin has called, in the context of 1920s Russia, 'a tremendous upward curve in European civilization'. (The parallels might be extended to a later stage of events as well.) But to see this activity as an alternative to 'politics' is more questionable: it might as logically be seen as another facet of a maturing and sophisticated society. There was, to borrow another Russian parallel, a clash of *generations*: Fathers of the old parliamentary era were confronted by Sons (and Daughters) who were affected by other, less compromising commitments. But whether this led inevitably to the 'long gestation' of Yeats's 'event' – the Easter rising of 1916 – is another matter.

The radical avant-garde of cultural nationalism were a small minority round the turn of the century, especially in contrast to the numbers affiliated to, for instance, the United Irish League (100,000 members and 1,000 branches by August 1901). The UIL's highly developed organization, first centred round the land purchase issue (and thus pushing at a half-open door), and expressing a strong predisposition against 'land grabbers', used the new county council elections to great effect. The fact that the United Irish League was subsumed into the reunited Irish Parliamentary Party from 1900, and the varied political fortunes of its leader William O'Brien, has condemned it to being written out of history; but the United Irish League represents the degree of political dynamism still mobilized by the 'old' political forms in the late 1890s, and O'Brien's historiographical stock has been steadily rising – not least because he was early on preoccupied by the need for Irish nationalism realistically to incorporate the sensibilities of Ulster Unionists.

To the contemporary observer in the period from 1892 to about 1906, there was far more 'political energy' displayed by this kind of activity than by the irreconcilably separatist 'underground'. Cultural and revolutionary Fenianism was operating at a very low level; splinter groups were active in the 1890s, wearily monitored by Dublin Castle, but they amounted to very little. IRB membership was remembered by contemporaries as largely 'passive and nominal' up to about 1912.[3] Many of the same needs were catered to by the Ancient Order of Hibernians, an aggressively Catholic organization, derived from Ribbon traditions but forming a sort of analogue to Orangeism. From the 1880s the Ancient Order of Hibernians became more and more important in Ulster, developing its own patronage structures and closely integrated into the electoral patterns of local government. From 1904, with the lifting of a clerical ban on its organization (as a 'secret society'), the Ancient Order of Hibernians began to spread over Ireland. By 1912 it was a force to be reckoned with in the south, where it was related closely to a contemporary wave of Catholic triumphalism, reflected in mass movements like the Sacred Heart devotion and the temperance Pioneers, though clerical opinion was always equivocal about what Cardinal Logue[ii] described as 'an organized system of blackguardism'. The Ancient Order of Hibernians was one powerful conduit of political 'energy' in the early twentieth century; the United Irish League another; from 1907, labour organization looked set to constitute a third.[iii] If any kind of a new dispensation was to displace the old Irish Parliamentary Party, it might be expected to focus round organizations such as these, rather than the minority rhetoric of cultural revivalism and revolutionary separatism.

The picture was changed by the involvement of Britain in two major wars – the scenario that every 'advanced' Irish nationalist had been praying for since the 1850s. The Boer War at the beginning of the century focused much moderate Irish opinion into an anti-imperial mould, and provided a mobilizing 'cause' against the government; the European war of 1914–18 altered the conditions of Irish politics beyond recognition. The radicalization of Irish politics (and, to a certain extent, of Irish society) took place between these two events, and largely because of them. But the connection between this process and the 'cultural' movement is not to be easily inferred. Because of the high standard of literature produced during the period, the emotional attitudes connected with Gaelic revivalism, and the articulacy of the survivors, the notion of a transferral of political energy into revivalist culture and separatist beliefs after 1891 is superficially attractive. But it did not appear so inevitable at the time.

[ii] Michael Logue (1840–1924): born in County Donegal; educated at hedge school and Maynooth; ordained, 1866; Professor of Theology, Irish College, Paris, 1866; Dean of Maynooth, 1876, Bishop of Raphoe, 1879; Archbishop of Armagh, 1888; denounced Parnell, 1890, and remained suspicious of the Irish Parliamentary Party thereafter; Cardinal, 1893; supported the Gaelic League but shunned Sinn Féin when it resorted to physical force; accepted the 1921 Treaty while protesting against Partition.
[iii] See below, pp. 438–44.

II

It is undeniable that the condition of established politics in the 1890s presented, on many levels, an unalluring picture. The Irish Parliamentary Party was in schism – the Parnellite minority, led by John Redmond,[iv] opposing the main body of the party under Dillon, further complicated by a splinter group under Healy. Further weaknesses were expressed in the way that the party at Westminster became increasingly 'imperial'; and in its reputation as a patronage machine, enmeshed in local politicking. There was a failure, on many levels, of political inspiration and direction. But the formidable machine remained, and the hegemony over electoral organization outside north-east Ulster and parts of Dublin. Nationalist and Unionist Ireland confronted each other, politically speaking, from positions of monolithic security; competition was unnecessary. In this strange stasis, local revolts, engineered by those with restless imaginations like William O'Brien, could take over an organization with surprising completeness. But if the Irish Parliamentary Party looks in retrospect as if it was waiting to be replaced, it retained both power and the potential for change – as well as its 'vampirist' capacity to take over whatever organization would ostensibly replace it.

For the moment it was the initiatives of 'constructive Unionism', notably the Land Acts of 1903 and 1909, and the attempt to deal with conditions at a local level in the west, which produced real results: by 1923 the Congested Districts Board had purchased and redistributed over 2,000,000 acres. Associated with this were the 'conciliationist' initiatives of those like Horace Plunkett and William O'Brien, whose formula of 'conference plus business' is more realistic and more impressive when viewed in the light of contemporary conditions than through the distorting prism of 1916. In the late 1890s the conciliationists

<hr/>

[iv] John Redmond (1856–1918): born in County Wexford; Clerk of the House of Commons, 1880; MP for New Ross, 1881, North Wexford, 1885, and Waterford, 1891–1918; raised £30,000 for the Irish Parliamentary Party on a mission to Australia and America, 1882–4; called to the Irish Bar, 1886; imprisoned, 1888; led the Parnellite minority of the Irish Parliamentary Party, 1891, and the reunited Irish Parliamentary Party, 1900; represented the tenants in the 1902 Land Conference; secured the introduction of the third Home Rule Bill, 1912; shattered, personally and politically, by the Easter rising and subsequent events.

actually convened committees on Irish affairs that not only brought
Redmond and Healy together, but even the Ulster Unionist Colonel
Saunderson;[v] the Irish Land Conference of 1902, probably inspired
from Dublin Castle but working through enlightened and ostensibly
'unpolitical' landlords, was the high point of this approach.[vi] As a
political initiative, 'conference plus business' was dealt an irreparable
blow by the devolution crisis of 1904, when the eccentric Under-
Secretary Sir Antony MacDonnell[vii] pressed too far ahead in an initiative that aroused Unionist paranoia and ended the career of George
Wyndham. The real reason for the breakdown, however, was that
none of the 'conciliationists' involved – Plunkett, Wyndham, O'Brien,
Dunraven[viii] – was representative of feeling within the groups from
whence they sprang.

From the nationalist side, the old suspicion of 'sectionalism' regard-

[v] Edward James Saunderson (1837–1906): born in County Fermangh; Royal Irish
Fusiliers, 1862; rose to the rank of Colonel; Liberal MP for Cavan, 1865; broke with
Gladstone over Disestablishment and sat as a Conservative, 1869; joined the Orange
Order, 1882; Deputy Grand Master of Ireland, 1884; *Two Irelands: Or Loyalty versus
Treason*, 1884; MP for North Armagh, 1885–1906; organized Ulster resistance to
Home Rule, bringing Lord Randolph Churchill to Belfast, 1886; leader of the
Parliamentary Unionists, 1888, and the Irish Unionist Alliance, 1891; refused to sit
on the 1895 Recess Committee or the 1902 Land Conference; member of the All-
Ireland Committee, 1897.

[vi] This produced the 'Wyndham Act' of 1903, which arranged for the sale of entire
estates to the occupying tenantry (when three-quarters of the tenants on any one
estate acquiesced), engineered by money advanced by the state on low terms (repaid
over $68\frac{1}{2}$ years at $3\frac{1}{4}$ per cent): the landlord was further tempted by a special 'bonus'
payment from the state on each sale. The principle of compulsion followed in an
amending Act of 1909.

[vii] Antony Patrick MacDonnell (1844–1925): born in County Mayo; educated at
Queen's College, Galway; Indian Civil Service, 1865; secured the Bengal Tenancy
Act, 1885; knighted, 1893; Lieutenant Governor of Agra and Oudh, 1895; Under-
Secretary for Ireland, 1902; largely drafted the Land Act, 1903, and the Irish Council
Bill, 1907; supported a devolution scheme that angered all major Irish interests, and
led to Wyndham's resignation, 1905; resigned over the Government's rejection of his
call for greater suppressionary powers, 1908; barony, 1908. Advocated Home Rule
in principle, while suggesting Ireland was not ready for self-government.

[viii] Windham Thomas Wyndham-Quin (1841–1926): born in Adare, County Limerick; 1st Life Guards, 1862; war correspondent in the Franco-Prussian war, 1870;
succeeded as fourth Earl of Dunraven, 1871; *The Irish Question*, 1880; Colonial Under-
Secretary, 1885–7; *The Outlook in Ireland: The Case for Devolution and Conciliation*,
1897; prominent in the 1902 Land Conference; President of the Irish Reform Association, 1904; proposed a federalist solution at the Irish Convention, 1917; Senator of
the Irish Free State, 1922.

ing any offer less than Home Rule remained; while the Unionists feared the smuggling in of Home Rule by the door of devolution. Dillon and his supporters preferred a sterile 'impossibilism' to 'conference plus business'; Plunkett's even-handed poking fun at pieties on both sides endeared him to few (though it makes *Ireland in the New Century*, 1904, an invigorating text). The conciliationist lobby was most effective in matters of agrarian economy, where the initiatives of Plunkett's Department of Agriculture and Technical Instruction in matters like afforestation and fisheries lasted on. But at a more basic level Plunkett's attempt to redirect the preoccupations of cattle farmers was doomed by structural conditions; modernized methods would be adopted only as and when they suited. Meanwhile, where there were glaring social problems to be tackled, they tended to be ignored by establishment political interests. And these problems were most evident in the towns.

The labour question in Ireland reflected the nature of Irish urbanization and Irish industry. The latter was largely a question of servicing, processing and transporting agricultural commodities; industrial development as normally conceived remained in an arrested state, as the urban population more or less stabilized in the late nineteenth century. Skilled and semi-skilled trades provided organizations like the Dublin United Trades Association (1863), but there was no parallel to the 'New Unionism' generated in Britain by large-scale industrial growth. Irish trade unions were generally rather inactive offshoots of British organizations. Attempts at overall labour organization usually failed; though the Irish Trades Union Congress was founded in 1894, it still represented mostly craft unions, and incorporated only about 60,000 workers by 1900.

The non-industrial base of Dublin was one of the main reasons for the precarious and extremely impoverished condition of its proletariat by the late nineteenth century. Their dependence on casual labour was reflected by the very high proportion of so-called 'general labourers'; appalled contemporaries record a bizarre and essentially pre-industrial profile of life in the lower depths. Slum Dublin was 'Georgian' in more than its architecture (many great terraces of Ascendancy townhouses having become warrens of indescribably squalid tenements). The centre of the city was a byword for spectacularly destitute living conditions, exacerbated by the increasingly sharp division between the spacious bourgeois suburbs to the south and the central concentration of slum dwellings, especially on the north side of the Liffey: a grim picture is shown by contemporary photographs as well as a growing historiography.[4] Dublin only enters the picture as a 'political' issue at certain high points, like 1913 and 1916. But at the same time as Plunkett's agrarian experiments, and the *narodnik* search by urban intellectuals for pure Gaelic values in the far west, life went on in eighteenth-century tenements bereft of water or sanitation; Dublin retained the worst urban adult mortality rate in the British Isles; the death rate did not decline until the early twentieth century, by which time it was the fifth highest in the world, beaten only by cities like Trieste and Rio de Janeiro. Living conditions were horrific by *contemporary* standards; the surveys before 1914 show 25 per cent of Dublin families living in one-room tenements occupied by more than four people, with at least 16,000 families living below the poverty line.

Yet Dublin politics remained orchestrated by the increasingly nationalist Corporation, dominated by small manufacturers, grocers and publicans, and fixed on the iniquity of British rule rather than the shortcomings of social organization in the city (the latter being rather vaguely seen, when it was thought about at all, as a function of the former). The government of the city never applied successfully for special grants from central funds; no 'civic gospel' suggested that a programme of urban renewal would constitute an appropriate activity for the Corporation. When Labour candidates stood for seats, they were usually unsuccessful (there were only nine Labour representatives by 1913). 'Scully [the High Sheriff of Dublin] is running in the interests of the United Irish League', wrote James Connolly[ix] sardonically in 1914, 'and high rents, slum tenements, rotten staircases, stinking yards, high death rates, low wages, Corporation jobbery, and margarine wrapped in butter-paper.'[5] This was not fanciful rhetoric: a housing inquiry of 1913 showed that sixteen Corporation members owned eighty-nine tenements and second-class houses.

[ix]James Connolly (1868–1916): born in Edinburgh of Irish parents; self-educated; joined the army at fourteen; probably deserted, 1889; founded the Irish Socialist Republican Party, 1896, and the *Workers' Republic*, 1898; in America, 1902–10; founded the Irish Socialist Federation in New York, published the *Harp* and active in International Workers of the World; Ulster organizer of the Irish Transport and General Workers' Union, 1910; led the workers, after Larkin's imprisonment, in the 1913 lock-out; acting Secretary of the Irish Transport and General Workers' Union, 1914; organized the Irish Citizen Army, 1914; committed the Irish Labour movement against the Allies, 1914; military commander of the Republican forces in Dublin, 1916; signatory of the Proclamation of the Irish Republic, inspiring its more socialistic clauses; executed Kilmainham, 12 May 1916. Wrote *Erin's Hope*, 1897; *Labour in Irish History* and *Labour, Nationality and Religion*, 1910; *The Reconquest of Ireland*, 1915.

Vested interests meshed with political apathy: Catholic nationalism, in the form of bishops as well as politicians, was firmly dedicated against committing any future Home Rule state to burdens of social expenditure and secular welfarism. Energetic representations from pressure-groups could not enforce a commitment to tenement clearance or rebuilding; the fact that several of the pressure-groups were organized by Protestants did not help their case. A more widespread kind of organization was necessary before national attention was brought to bear on urban conditions.

The agricultural slump from the late 1870s affected the service industries in the towns; working-class protest movements emerged, rather incoherently, from about 1880, vociferously articulating resentment against the land agitators. As wages continued to fall through the 1880s, however, more coherent attempts at labour organization were hampered by the easy availability of non-union labour. Some change was brought by the wave of strikes among the unskilled during 1889–91 (possibly inspired by the London dock strike of 1889); a few wage rises were won, but activity tapered off from the turn of the century, with a series of disputes ending in victory for the employers. The picture was ostensibly changed by the dynamic leadership of James Larkin[x] in 1912–13, and the apparent coincidence of the mass mobilization of the Irish Transport and General Workers' Union with a peak in wage rises. But the lock-out of 1913 essentially failed for the usual reason: a surplus of non-union labour, and the inability of Dublin workers to bring any vital industry to a halt.

What 1913 did indicate, however, was that labour organization in Ireland had moved into a new phase. It is quite impossible not to see these developments in terms of personalities, since without Larkin and, still more, James Connolly, the picture would have been very different.

[x] James Larkin (1876–1947): born in Liverpool of Irish parentage; reared in County Down; returned to Liverpool, 1885; became a dock foreman; sacked for joining a strike; Organizer of the National Union of Dock Labourers; organized Belfast strike action and launched a Dublin branch of the National Union of Dock Labourers, 1907; reformed the Irish branch of the Independent Labour Party and founded the Irish Transport and General Workers' Union, 1908; President of the Irish Trades Union Congress, 1911; led the workers in the 1913 lock-out; imprisoned, 1913–14; active trade unionist in America, 1914–23; imprisoned for 'criminal syndicalism', 1920; denounced the Treaty, 1922; released, 1923; tumultuously received in Dublin, but expelled from the Irish Transport and General Workers' Union by its anti-socialist committee; founded the Workers' Union of Ireland, 1923; Independent Labour TD, 1926–32, 1937–8 and Labour TD, 1943–4; secured the Trade Union Act and opposed the Wages Standstill Order, 1941.

Connolly, another returned emigrant, contributed almost single-handed a radical critique of Irish labour and Irish history, closely bound together, and symbolized by his tiny party of Irish Socialist Republicans, founded during his first spell in Dublin as Organizer of the Dublin Socialist Society. In a sense, his theory recognized the inadequacy of Irish labour organization outside the north-east, since its dynamic had to be contributed by the emotional motor of nationalism.

Connolly's innovative synthesis of Irish history in Marxian terms attempted to reconcile nationalism and socialism, often with brilliance; but while he relied heavily on the moral superiority of suppressed Gaelic communal systems before the coming of Norman feudalism, his later analysis construed the Irish economy in determinedly urban and industrial terms, tending to ignore the rural *embourgeoisement* of his own lifetime. Ulster, which he knew at first hand, presented a different set of problems, industrialized and anti-nationalist as it was: Connolly fell back for explanations on 'atavism' and the 'devilish ingenuity of the master class'. His main contribution was to argue that a nation-state must be established in Ireland as a necessary pre-condition for social and economic progress, not merely as a rather vague end in itself. And in a political ambience where nationalism, and, still more, Catholicism were usually militantly anti-socialist, this was an innovation.

They ordered things differently in Belfast. Here, the necessary pre-conditions of labour organization did exist – along with the huge gap between exceptionally high skilled wage rates and abysmally low unskilled rates. One-third of all Ireland's trade unionists lived there; and an Independent Labour Party branch was set up in 1892. There was an articulate labour voice in Belfast politics, which – in advocates like William Walker[xi] – was combined with a firm commitment to Unionism. With the rising temperature of national politics, this could mean that the eventual destination of such men was Protestant populism rather than socialism; and it was Walker's endorsement of Protestant orthodoxy that split the working-class vote and lost him a parliamentary by-election in 1905. When it came to the point, he opted

[xi] William Walker (1870–1918): born in Belfast; worked at Harland & Wolff's, organizing its semi-skilled labourers; member of the Belfast Independent Labour Party, 1893; Secretary to the first Irish Trades Union Congress, 1894; as representative of the Textile Operatives Society, recognized as the most important labour leader in Ireland; feuded with Connolly over the national question; lost much of his influence upon being appointed a National Insurance Inspector; delivered the economic argument against Home Rule in *The Irish Question*, 1908.

for the inspection of convents rather than the redistribution of the means of production. But even if the tribal map imposed itself rather than class demography, it should not be too readily assumed that Unionism always remained a monolithic class alliance.

Cracks appeared in the façade with Thomas Sloan's[xii] Independent Orange Order in 1903, emphasizing the supposedly 'radical' origins of Orangeism and its struggle on behalf of the Protestant working class. From this base, politicians like Lindsay Crawford[xiii] appealed cautiously across the sectarian divide: and from the Catholic side, Joseph Devlin[xiv] of the Ancient Order of Hibernians made some overtures for reasons of electoral strategy. But his base remained that of intransigently sectarian nationalism; while 'official' Unionism would reabsorb the Independent Orangemen when the cry of the Union in danger was raised once more. Crawford's eventual destiny as a Home Ruler seemed to bear out the worst apprehensions of Ulsteria: any political truck with nationalists must eventually end in sell-out.

None the less, there were other lines of division. One was the social barrier between skilled and unskilled, always sharply felt. Belfast recruitment patterns being what they were, this could be presented as a Protestant–Catholic divide as well. But, if the skilled workforce

[xii] Thomas Henry Sloan (1870–1941): born in Belfast; worked in Harland & Wolff's; prominent trade unionist and Orangeman; expelled from the Orange Order for criticizing Saunderson; founded the strongly working-class Independent Orange Order, 1903; Protestant Association MP for Belfast, 1902–10.

[xiii] Robert Lindsay Crawford (1868–1945): born in County Antrim; founding Editor of the *Irish Protestant*, 1901; Grand Master of the Independent Orange Order; author of 'The Magheramore Manifesto', which attacked the Ulster Unionist Council, demanded land purchase and a national university, and called on Orangemen to befriend their fellow-countrymen, regardless of creed, 1905; edited the *Ulster Guardian* until expelled from the Independent Orange Order for advocacy of Home Rule, 1908; emigrated to Canada, 1910; Irish Free State trade representative in New York in the 1920s.

[xiv] Joseph Devlin (1871–1934): born in Belfast; joined the *Irish News*, Belfast's first nationalist newspaper; Secretary of the United Irish League, 1902; Irish Parliamentary Party MP for North Kilkenny, 1902, and West Belfast, 1906–18; re-established the Ancient Order of Hibernians, and its President, 1905–34; founder member of the Irish Volunteers, 1913; accepted the temporary exclusion of six Ulster counties from the third Home Rule Bill, 1914; encouraged Irishmen to join the British army, 1914; declined chairmanship of the Irish Parliamentary Party, 1918; MP for the Falls, Belfast, defeating de Valera, 1918; MP for West Belfast in the Northern Irish parliament, 1922, but did not sit until 1925; withdrew again, having won concessions for Roman Catholics in the 1930 Education Act, 1932; MP for Fermanagh and Tyrone at Westminster, 1929–34.

was effectively Protestant, an absolute majority of Protestants also dominated every broad category of unskilled labour, leading to sectarian conflict within these areas too. Tension was increased by the rising expectations of Catholics in the early 1900s, now attending their own technical college: exacerbated by the strong predisposition of Irish Trades Union Congress circles in Belfast to see trade unions as existing for the interests of the skilled, and Protestant. A brief fling with New Unionism in the 1890s had fizzled out; the achievement of Larkin in 1907 was to revive the idea of a labour cause that transcended occupational, and even sectarian, barriers.

Larkin's chosen arena was a great dock strike: significantly, earlier agitation among the dockers had been short-circuited by the smear of a supposed 'nationalist' connection through Michael Davitt. Larkin introduced the tactics of all-out confrontation, panicking employers into calling for intervention by the troops. His combination of bravura leadership and canny use of the 1906 Trades Disputes Act led to the considerable achievement of sidelining the inevitable sectarian issue. One of Larkin's Protestant followers declared: 'I would like to know ... what Orangeism or Protestantism has got to do with men fighting for their just rights, when the issue lies not in religion but is a question of bread and butter, and shorter hours and better conditions which we should have had twenty years ago.'[6] The note of rationalism seemed carried further when Lindsay Crawford's Independent Orangemen took up the cause; the authorities were subsequently faced with a major police mutiny, by both Catholic and Protestant constables, and the need for large-scale military intervention. In 1907 labour seemed ready to bring about a major crisis that would shatter the old moulds of confessional politics in Belfast.

However, Larkin's reliance on sympathetic strike tactics broke down under the pressure of sectionalism: after the police mutiny, the strike became inevitably polarized along nationalist-versus-Unionist lines (Devlin joining the cause for anti–British rather than anti-employer reasons). When riots developed in August 1907, they took on the old Orange-and-Green pigmentation, as well as the old territorial patterns; by the autumn, the dockers had been isolated. In 1908, the Independent Labour Party candidates were wiped out in the council elections; and Larkin had himself been marginalized within the Dockers' Union, going on to found the Irish Transport and General Workers' Union in 1908. *Pace* Connolly's influential views, and contrary to middle-class Unionist wisdom, labour consciousness and trade union militancy were *not* automatically linked to a development towards nationalism.

Such feelings were compatible with 'specific views on the "back-wardness" of southern Ireland, the reactionary views of the Catholic Church, and the necessity of the Union for securing progressive development'.[7]

Larkin's subsequent path took him to Dublin, where his tactics of confrontation and strike were exercised on behalf of the coal carriers and carters. The foundation of the Irish Transport and General Workers' Union in 1908 gave the amorphous 'general labourers' a voice, and introduced some of the tactics of militant syndicalism on the European model, though this is to oversimplify a highly specific and complicated situation. Larkin was not a 'nationalist' in the narrow sense and saw as his priority the extension of the Independent Labour Party in Dublin; his cavalier attitude to anti-British pieties annoyed many, and added to the tensions of his working relationship with Connolly, who returned from the United States in 1910. Connolly's tactics tended to be 'political', Larkin's 'industrial'; Connolly's association with extreme nationalism in the late 1890s remained important. However, both were adaptable, and successful industrial agitation was mounted among the Dublin dockers in 1911, followed by riots and lock-outs; a percussion of labour disputes in 1913 followed, affecting a wide variety of Dublin industries and apparently presaging full-scale disruption. From June to August, there were thirty separate disputes:

Involved in strikes, lock-outs and sympathetic strikes were agricultural labourers, bill posters, biscuit makers, bottle makers, box makers, brass finishers, bricklayers, builders' labourers, cabinet makers, canal loaders, carpenters, carriers, carters, coach makers, confectioners, dockers, electricians, engineers, farm workers, gas workers, glaziers, hairdressers, horse shoers, iron founders, linen workers, manure workers, market gardeners, match workers, millers, newsboys, painters, paviors, plasterers, plumbers, poplin workers, seamen and firemen, soap makers, stevedores, stone cutters, tobacco workers, tramway employees, van drivers, wood machinists – even schoolboys at the national schools in Rutland Street.[8]

The climax of this development, and Larkin's personal apotheosis, was provided by the great Dublin dock-labour reorganization in 1913. By now the Irish Transport and General Workers' Union seemed well on the way to becoming 'one big Union', taking in agricultural labourers as well; its tactics provoked an epic struggle with Dublin's premier capitalist, William Martin Murphy,[xv] which galvanized the city from

[xv] William Martin Murphy (1844–1919): born in County Cork; took over the family contracting business at nineteen; Home Rule MP for St Patrick's, Dublin,

1913. The refusal of Murphy's Dublin United Tramways Company to employ members of the Irish Transport and General Workers' Union was the flashpoint of what developed into a large-scale lockout, accompanied by violent riots and baton charges. The outcome was, essentially, defeat for the union – caused in part by the collapse of support from the trade union movement in Britain, always ambivalent about supporting Larkin's departures into extremism. But, seen in relation to the Belfast crisis of 1907, for a considerable time it appeared that the critical confrontation in early twentieth-century Ireland would take place not between the British government and Irish nationalists, but between Irish capital and Irish labour.

The fact that this did not happen, and that the nationalist issue subsumed the labour issue, has preoccupied Irish labour historians ever since – as it preoccupied labour theoreticians at the time. The Irish Parliamentary Party could claim to represent labour interests outside Ulster, cutting the ground from under the nascent Independent Labour Party; but they could not, naturally, be seen as appropriate representatives for labour interests in the north, where organizers like Walker believed that the establishment of an Irish parliament could only be a backward step socially and economically. In the Belfast docks and shipyards, the tradition of labour was imperial: 'Imperialism is but the transition stage to the international union of the proletariat,' remarked the Belfast *Labour Chronicle*, whereas nationalism was 'dead or dying'. A logical reaction was to call for a workers' internationalism that would embrace the cause of Dublin labour, too, and Connolly subscribed to this in the earlier stages of his career. Later, this was displaced by his view of the relationship between England and Ireland as colonial, and therefore to be broken as a preliminary to socialist development. The working class's commitment to the European war of 1914 was a further blow to his faith in international solidarity, but well before then his priority had become the building of an Irish socialist movement in an independent Irish state: Fintan Lalor and John Mitchel predominated over Karl Marx. The first manifesto of his Irish Socialist Republican Party emphasized the interdependence of

1885–92; founded the *Irish Catholic* and the *Irish Independent*, 1904; refused a knighthood, 1907; dominated the Committee of the Irish International Exhibition, 1907; President of the Dublin Chamber of Commerce, 1912–13; leader of Dublin Employers' Federation up to and through the lock-out of 1913; spoke on British recruiting platforms, 1914; sought to find a means whereby all able-bodied Irishmen who refused to enlist could be dismissed from their employment; opposed Partition at the Irish Convention and in *The Home Rule Act (1914) Exposed*, 1917.

nationalist and socialist struggles, though it was unclear which liberation would come first.

In this process, participation in the opposition to the Boer War effort had been an important catalyst – as it was for nationalist intellectuals too. At moments of crisis, the nationalist intelligentsia tended to form a broad front with labour as represented by Connolly, both sides emphasizing anti-Britishness for the purpose. Thus the labour cause tended to be blurred into a nationalist image. In the crisis of 1913, Larkin was joined not only by George William Russell (AE)[xvi] and Yeats (for general anti-bourgeois reasons) but by Joseph Plunkett,[xvii] Thomas MacDonagh,[xviii] Eamon Ceannt,[xix] Padraic Colum,[xx] Countess

[xvi] George William Russell ('AE'): born in Lurgan, Co. Armagh; educated Dublin; poet, painter, agrarian reformer. Joined Irish Agricultural Organization Society, 1897, and edited the *Irish Homestead*. Published *Homeward Songs by the Way* (1894) and *Collected Poems* (1913). Edited the combative *Irish Statesman*, 1923–30. A dedicated mystic. Friend and guru to many figures in the Irish literary 'renaissance'; a genuine pluralist who became disillusioned with the new Ireland and moved to England in 1932. Died at Bournemouth.

[xvii] Joseph Mary Plunkett (1887–1916): born in Dublin; son of George Noble Count Plunkett; *The Circle and the Sword* (verse), 1911; edited the *Irish Review*, 1913–14; joined the IRB; Director of Operations of the Irish Volunteers, 1913; co-founded the Irish Theatre, 1914; helped Casement in attempts to secure German aid for a rising and reported to Clan na Gael on the progress of revolutionary preparations, 1915; member of the IRB Supreme Council and its Military Committee, and signatory to the Proclamation, 1916; married Grace Gifford, the artist, in Kilmainham on the eve of his execution, 4 May 1916. *Collected Poems* were published posthumously.

[xviii] Thomas MacDonagh (1878–1916): born in County Tipperary; educated at Rockwell College and University College, Dublin; joined the Gaelic League, 1901, assisted Pearse in the foundation of St Enda's, 1908; *When the Dawn is Come*, produced at the Abbey, 1908, and *Metempsychosis*, by the Theatre of Ireland, 1912; Assistant Lecturer at University College, Dublin, 1911; co-founded the *Irish Review*, 1911, and the Irish Theatre, 1914; founder member of the Irish Volunteers, 1913, and its Director of Training, 1914; organized the O'Donovan Rossa funeral, 1915; joined the IRB, 1915, being co-opted on to its Military Committee, April 1916; signatory to the Proclamation; executed Kilmainham, 3 May 1916. *Poetical Works* and *Literature in Ireland* appeared posthumously, 1916.

[xix] Eamon Ceannt (1881–1916): born in County Galway; son of a Royal Irish Constabulary officer; Clerk of the Dublin Corporation; joined the Gaelic League, 1900, becoming a member of its governing body; led Irish athletes to Rome for the jubilee of Pius X; joined Sinn Féin, 1908; founded the Dublin Pipers' Club, 1910; joined the IRB and a founder member of the Irish Volunteers, 1913; involved in Howth gun-running, 1914; member of the IRB Supreme Council and its Military Committee, 1915; signatory to the Proclamation; executed Kilmainham, 8 May 1916.

[xx] Padraic Colum (1881–1972): born in Longford; educated locally; became a railway clerk; contributed poetry to the *United Irishman* and wrote *The Saxon Shillin'*

Markievicz[xxi] and many others who would take arms against British
government three years later. The revolt of the Dublin slums was seen
as a mobilizing issue by feminists like Helena Molony[xxii] and Hanna
Sheehy-Skeffington,[xxiii] and movements like Inghinidhe na hÉireann
(Daughters of Ireland). It was this kind of broad anti–establishment
front that highlighted the general sense of crisis during the years before
the First World War, and led contemporaries to see in 'Larkinism' a
movement that would shake the foundations of Irish society more
thoroughly than Parnellism. But Larkin himself was to find (like

for a Cumann na nGaedheal playwriting competition, 1902; *Broken Soil* (also known
as *The Fiddler's House*), 1903, and *The Land*, 1905; redefined 'the Abbey play' as one
concerned with peasant reality rather than Celtic mythology; *Thomas Muskerry*, 1910;
co-founded the *Irish Review*, 1911; settled in the USA, 1914; *Collected Poems*, 1953.

[xxi] Constance Markievicz (née Gore-Booth; 1868–1927): born in London; educated
privately, the Slade and Paris; married Count Casimir Markievicz, 1900; joined Sinn
Féin, although impatient of Griffith's pacifism; launched Fianna Éireann, 1909; joined
Inghinidhe na hÉireann, wrote *A Call to the Women of Ireland* and contributed to *Bean
na hÉireann*, 1909; became an officer of the Irish Citizen Army, prompting the
resignation of Sean O'Casey; active in the Easter rising, a death sentence being
commuted because of her sex; President of Cumann na mBan, 1917; converted to
Catholicism; Sinn Féin MP for St Patrick's, Dublin, 1918, thereby being the first
woman to be elected to the Commons, but did not take her seat; Minister for Labour
in the Cabinet of the first Dáil Éireann while imprisoned, 1919–21; Minister for
Labour in the second Dáil; denounced the Treaty as a capitalist ploy; supported the
republicans in the civil war, 1923–4; Sinn Féin abstentionist TD for South Dublin,
1923–7.

[xxii] Helena Molony (1884–1967): inspired by Maud Gonne to join Inghinidhe na
hÉireann, 1903; edited *Bean na hÉireann*, 1908; assisted Constance Markievicz in the
foundation of Fianna Éireann, 1909; joined the Abbey Theatre players, 1909–20;
arrested for taking part in Sinn Féin protests against the 1911 royal visit; Secretary of
the Irish Women Workers' Union, 1915; joined the Irish Citizen Army and took part
in the attack upon Dublin Castle, Easter 1916; imprisoned, May–December 1916;
opposed the Treaty, 1922; executive member of Saor Éire, 1931. As President of the
Irish Trades Union Congress, 1922–3, embodied the Connolly tradition that she had
played a part in creating.

[xxiii] Hanna Sheehy [-Skeffington] (1877–1946): born in County Tipperary; educated
Royal University; founded Women's Graduate Association, 1901; married Francis
Skeffington, who took her name as she took his, 1903, and co-founded the Irish
Women's Franchise League with him, 1908, becoming its first Secretary; joined the
Socialist Party of Ireland; imprisoned for rioting upon the exclusion of votes for
women from the 1912 Home Rule Bill; messenger to the GPO, Easter 1916; refused
£10,000 compensation upon the murder of her husband, 1916; visited the USA, and
interviewed President Wilson, 1916–18; imprisoned on her return, but released upon
commencing a hunger strike; rejected the Treaty; judge of the Dáil courts; member
of the first executive of Fianna Fáil, 1926; Assistant Editor of *An Phoblacht*, 1932;
imprisoned, 1933; founded the Women's Social and Progressive League, 1938.

Sean O'Casey[xxiv] and other Irish socialists) in the 1920s that the new dispensation of national independence would be very different from a socialist New Jerusalem: nationalism not only absorbed pre-war social radicalism, but apparently negated it.

III
===

The short-lived vitality of Irish labour organization, however, constitutes a sphere of Irish 'politics' that, like O'Brien's United Irish League, tends to be played down by the Yeatsian version of the 1890s and early 1900s as a grey political vacuum, while 'the stirring of the bones' of cultural nationalism happened at a different level. Certainly, the period was marked by cultural revivalism: but the political relevance of this, in contemporary terms, is less easy to establish. In 1901 Dublin Castle police reports recorded that the most active organizations in Dublin were the Celtic Literary Society, the Gaelic League and the Gaelic Athletic Association: a trinity later assumed to represent a cultural revolution. To assume this, however, is to underestimate both the rhetorical continuity of 'literary Fenianism' and the long tradition of Celtic antiquarianism.

If the 'rediscoveries' of late eighteenth- and early nineteenth-century enthusiasts seem rather irrelevant to *fin de siècle* nationalist fervour, they still provided its necessary antecedent – the connecting link being provided by works like Standish James O'Grady's[xxv] *History of Ireland:*

[xxiv] John Casey [Seán O'Casey] (1884–1964): born in Dublin; self-educated; labourer; joined the Gaelic League, Gaelic Athletic Association and the IRB and gaelicized his name, c. 1903; wrote for the Irish socialist press; joined the Irish Transport and General Workers' Union, 1911, and Irish Citizen Army, 1913; Secretary of its Strikers' Relief Committee, 1913, and Army Council, 1914; resigned upon its association with Countess Markievicz; wrote *The Story of the ICA*, an official, but anti-Connollyite, history, 1919; encouraged by Lady Gregory, wrote his Dublin trilogy for the Abbey Theatre: *The Shadow of a Gunman*, 1923, *Juno and the Paycock*, 1924, and *The Plough and the Stars*, 1926. Political and artistic disillusionment led him into English exile in 1926, and *The Silver Tassie* being rejected by the Abbey in 1928, all but one of his subsequent plays were produced outside Ireland. Six volumes of autobiography, 1939–54.

[xxv] Standish James O'Grady (1846–1928): born in County Cork; called to the Irish Bar, 1872; popularized the sagas, rediscovered by O'Donovan and O'Curry in the 1830s, in his *History of Ireland: Heroic Period*, 1878–81, *Early Bardic Literature of Ireland*, 1879, and *The Coming of Cuchulain*, 1894, and illuminated Elizabethan Ireland in *The*

Heroic Period (1878–81). Works like this, and collections of folk-tales like Lady Gregory's[xxvi] *Gods and Fighting Men*, meant more than the scientific study of early Irish history pioneered by Eoin MacNeill[xxvii] in the early 1900s; the origins of Gaelic society retained the romantic gloss endowed by zealots like Alice Stopford Green. And this was closely connected with the campaign to re-establish the Irish language, Irish pastimes, and an Irish ethos, which developed from the 1880s.

The establishment of the Gaelic Athletic Association in 1884 was the first landmark, emphasizing physical training in the manner of contemporary Czech gymnastic clubs, and constructing a powerful rural network. In 1893 the foundation of the Gaelic League by Eoin MacNeill and Douglas Hyde[xxviii] created a unique pressure group.

Bog of Stars, 1893, and *The Flight of the Eagle*, 1897; edited and wrote much of the *All-Ireland Review* in the cause of constructive unionism, 1900–1907. Also wrote *Toryism and Tory Democracy*, 1886, an idiosyncratic misreading of the non-existent political philosophy of Lord Randolph Churchill, adapted to the Irish situation. Father of the Irish literary revival, who spent the last decade of his life in frustrated exile on the Isle of Wight.

[xxvi] Isabella Augusta Gregory (née Persse; 1852–1932): born in County Galway; married Sir William Gregory, 1880; in widowhood took up residence at Coole Park, 1892; edited her late husband's *Autobiography*, 1894, her grandfather-in-law's letters, as *Mr Gregory's Letter-Box*, 1898, and *Ideals in Ireland*, 1901; wrote her first play, *The Pot of Broth*, in collaboration with Yeats, 1902; wrote her individual efforts in a local dialect she termed 'Kiltartanese'; co-founded the Irish Literary Theatre, 1898; active director of the succeeding Abbey Theatre Company (the Irish National Theatre Society), 1904–28; had almost forty plays produced at the Abbey, notably *Spreading the News*, 1904, and *The Rising of the Moon*, 1907. Wrote *Our Irish Theatre*, 1913.

[xxvii] John [Eoin] MacNeill (1867–1945): born in County Antrim; convenor and first Vice-President of the Gaelic League, 1893; edited *Irisleabhar na Gaedhilge* and founder of Feis Ceoil, 1894; edited *An Claidheamh Soluis*, 1899; first Professor of Early and Medieval Irish History at University College, Dublin, 1908; Chief of Staff of the Irish Volunteers; unaware of a secret Military Council within the IRB until Easter 1916, when he countermanded the orders given by Pearse; imprisoned, 1916–17; MP for National University of Ireland, 1918–22; Minister of Finance in the first Dáil, 1919, and Minister for Industries, 1919–21; supported the Treaty; Minister of Education in the first executive council of the Irish Free State, 1922–5; Irish Free State representative on the Boundary Commission, 1924–5, resigning when it became obvious it would sanction no significant changes; headed the Irish Manuscripts Commission, 1927, and first President of Irish Historical Society, 1936. Wrote *Phases of Irish History*, 1919, and *Celtic Ireland*, 1921.

[xxviii] Douglas Hyde (1860–1947): born in Sligo; educated at Trinity College, Dublin; co-founded the Irish Literary Society in London, 1891, and President of the National Literary Society, Dublin, 1892; co-founder and first President of the Gaelic League, 1893; wrote the first modern play in the Irish language, *Casadh an tSugáin*, 1901; sat on the Commissions for Irish Secondary and University Education, 1901 and 1906;

Hyde's famous lecture of November 1892, 'On the Necessity for De-Anglicizing the Irish People', is inevitably and correctly seen as a vital statement; though he was preoccupied by an Anglo-Irish rather than a Gaelic idea of 'Irish' literary tradition and his 'de-Anglicization' meant, most coherently, anti-materialism (or, as Joseph Lee would have it, anti-modernization). The League's objective was specifically to revive the use of the Irish language, and introduce it into the educational curriculum at all levels; it campaigned (often successfully) for bilingual street names and signposts – the sort of issue that *did* claim the attention of Dublin Corporation. The early membership, especially as preserved in the acerbic memories of Sean O'Casey and James Joyce,[xxix] was respectable, suburban and bourgeois. It was also tiny. Four years after the Gaelic League's foundation, the minutes cautiously record, 'the secretary was authorized to buy a regular minute book';[9] growth up to 1899 was commensurately slow. The ensuing boom in membership, and more efficient organization, owed a great deal to the galvanic effect of the Boer War – in this area as in others nearly as crucial an event for Irish nationalism as the death of Parnell.

The development of the Gaelic League also owed a good deal to the activity of returned emigrants, more prepared to confront established pieties than those reared at home. Through these and other influences, an idealization of the lifestyle of the west became the theme of Gaelic League zealots: where Balfour's administrators saw an economic disaster area, the League saw the remnants of a Celtic 'civilization' that implied a spiritual empire far greater than England's tawdry industrialized hegemony. Psychologically, this may have been an important counter to generations of West Briton condescension. But the chauvin-

Professor of Modern Irish at the National University of Ireland, 1908–32; resigned as President of the Gaelic League upon its politicization, 1915; Irish Free State Senator, 1925–6; President of the Irish Republic, 1938. Major works: *Love Songs of Connacht*, 1893, and *A Literary History of Ireland*, 1899. An autobiography, *Mise agus an Conradh*, 1931.

[xxix] James Augustine Aloysius Joyce (1882–1941): born in Dublin; educated at Clongowes, Belvedere and University College, Dublin; condemned the provincialism of Yeats's national drama and its audience in 'The Day of the Rabblement', 1902; settled in Trieste with Nora Barnacle, 1904; returned to Dublin to seek a publisher for *Dubliners* (written 1904; published 1914), 1911–12; settled in Zurich, 1915–19; pioneered the modern 'stream of consciousness' movement with *A Portrait of the Artist as a Young Man*, 1916 and *Ulysses*, 1922; settled in Paris, 1920, and began work on *Finnegans Wake*, published 1939; returned to Zurich on the outbreak of war. Also wrote *Exiles*, a play, 1918, and two volumes of poetry, *Chamber Music*, 1907, and *Pomes Penyeach*, 1927.

ism of some Gaelic League pronouncements struck even sympathetic observers as near-ridiculous (a typical reflection of Patrick Pearse's:[xxx] 'I often fancy that if some of the Old Masters had known rural Ireland, we should not have so many gross and merely earthly conceptions of the Madonna as we have'). And the identification of Catholicism with 'true' Gaelic culture became rapidly inevitable; Hyde's innocent regret at this development rather ignored the implications of his own frequent pronouncement about 'the piety of the Irish Gael' who 'sees the hand of God in every place, in everytime, in everything'.

The barefoot children, turf fires and unrelieved diet of the west were romantically approved by the Gaelicist intelligentsia (who felt accordingly let down by the Connacht people's propensity to emigrate). Anti-materialism was often a code for anti-Englishness (given a valuable boost by the unconvincing gimcrackery surrounding royal visits in 1900 and 1903). The small but influential Irish feminist movement used Gaelicist channels, too: through the journal *Shan Van Vocht* founded in Belfast by Alice Milligan[xxxi] and Anna Johnson[xxxii] as well as Maud Gonne's[xxxiii] organization Inghinidhe na hÉireann (1900),

[xxx] Patrick Henry Pearse (1879–1916): born in Dublin; educated at Christian Brothers school and Royal University; called to the Bar but did not practise; became convinced of the necessity of cultivating a nationalism inspired by the native language; prominent in the Gaelic League from 1896; edited *An Claidheamh Soluis*, 1903–9; founded St Enda's, 1908; edited Bulmer Hobson's *Irish Freedom*; founder member of the Irish Volunteers, and inducted into the IRB, 1913; undertook a fund-raising mission to the USA on behalf of St Enda's and the Irish Volunteers, 1914; leader of the secessionist Volunteers upon Redmond's call for support of the British war effort; IRB Director of Military Operations; delivered the oration at the funeral of O'Donovan Rossa, 1915; head of the Provisional Government of the Irish Republic, delivering the Proclamation of Independence, Easter 1916; surrendered, 19 April; executed 3 May. Wrote the plays *The Singer*, 1910, *An Rí*, 1911, and *Eoin*, 1915; and *Songs of the Irish Rebels*, 1914.

[xxxi] Alice Milligan (1866–1953): born in County Tyrone; educated at Methodist College, Belfast, and King's College, London; wrote the historical novel *A Royal Democrat*, 1892; a founding Editor of the *Northern Patriot* and *Shan Van Vocht*, 1896; Ulster organizing secretary of the Gaelic League and the 1798 centenary celebrations; *Life of Wolfe Tone*, 1898; contributed to the *United Irishman* and *Sinn Féin*; wrote one of the earliest Celtic Twilight plays, *The Last Feast of the Fianna*, for the Irish Literary Theatre, 1900. Also wrote *Hero Lays*, 1908, and other poems and plays.

[xxxii] Anna Johnson [Ethna Carberry] (1866–1902): born in County Antrim; promoted the Irish language revival in Belfast where she co-edited the *Northern Patriot* and *Shan Van Vocht*, 1896–9; a Vice-President of Inghinidhe na hÉireann, 1900. Her poems, *The Four Winds of Eireann*, 1902, and prose, *The Passionate Heart*, 1903, and *In the Celtic Past*, 1904, were published posthumously.

[xxxiii] Maud Gonne [MacBride] (1866–1953): born in Aldershot; daughter of a British

which was founded, like so much else, in the ferment of the anti–Boer War movement. The 'Daughters of Ireland', whose members had to be of Irish birth or descent, were dedicated to 'complete independence' and aimed 'to discourage the reading and circulation of low English literature, the singing of English songs, the attending of vulgar English entertainments at the theatre and music–hall, and to combat in every way English influence, which is doing so much injury to the artistic taste and refinement of the Irish people'.

The last phrase should be noted. For all their militant anti–Englishness, this and other movements on the broad Gaelicist front were cultural, not political. The Gaelic League argument that language revival came before politics, and made them in a sense irrelevant, was not only a result of Hyde's Protestant–rectory scruples; it was advocated even by Pearse until a very late stage. As with the supposed analogy of Hungary, language revival would inevitably bring political autonomy, in itself 'an accidental and an external thing'. The point at which the underground influence of the IRB took over the Gaelic League cannot be delineated; but it was certainly not until well into the first decade of the twentieth century. Even then, to see it as a nursery of revolutionaries is to stretch a point very far. It has been shown that 50 per cent of government ministers or senior civil servants in independent Ireland, for the half–century after 1921, were Gaelic Leaguers in their youth.[10] But rather than proving that 'the League educated an entire political class', this may merely indicate the kind of urban, educated middle–class membership of the League – as well as the fact that government servants in the new state had to possess the elements of competency in what would come to be defined as 'the first national language'.

The values of the Gaelic League were thrown into sharp relief by contemporary literary developments – in the form of a prodigiously talented avant–garde writing in English from the standpoint of Irish preoccupations. The discovery of Ireland's past and the Irish identity as a literary trope on the part of a group of Anglo–Irish writers had its

army officer of Irish descent; educated privately in France; assisted her lover Lucien Millevoye in editing *La Patrie* and published *L'Irlande Libre*, 1897; founded Inghinidhe na hÉireann, 1900, of which she was first President; became a Catholic; took the title part in Yeats's *Cathleen ni Houlihan*, 1902; married Major John MacBride in Paris, 1903; formally separated, 1905; contributed to *Bean na hÉireann*, 1908; returned to Ireland, 1917; interned in the 'German Plot' arrests, 1918; first secretary of the Women's Prisoners' Defence League, 1922; attacked O'Casey in a public debate over *The Plough and the Stars*, 1926. Autobiography, *A Servant of the Queen*, 1938.

parallels in the past. But several things marked out the achievement of George Moore,[xxxiv] Edward Martyn,[xxxv] Augusta Gregory, J. M. Synge[xxxvi] and the young W. B. Yeats: eccentricity, a slight air of the *déclassé*, and a formidable talent for publicity. Hyde, who shared some of these qualities, in a sense straddled the two movements of Gaelic revivalism and Anglo-Irish literary developments. But the direction taken by Yeats, Moore and Synge would be essentially different, and not only because they were greater artists.

Their preoccupations were wider than those of the revivalists – French literary realism, giving way to obsessive Wagnerianism, for Moore; Ibesen for Martyn; hermeticism and occultism for Yeats. Lady Gregory's preoccupation with folklore was superficially assimilable to Gaelic revivalism, but its results did not always satisfy that audience. Nor, *a fortiori*, did the extraordinary plays of Synge – though he was far closer to many elements of life in the west than was the Gaelic League. (In Belmullet he heard an old man lament: 'I don't know what way I'm going to go on living in this place that the Lord created last, I'm thinking, in the end of time; and it's often when I sit down and

[xxxiv] George Augustus Moore (1852–1933): born in Moore Hall, County Mayo; son of George H. Moore; studied art and literary life in Paris, 1873–9; satirized Irish society in *A Drama in Muslin*, 1886, and the essays *Parnell and His Island*, 1887; *Esther Waters*, 1894; returned to Ireland, 1901; seeking to create a native drama in the English language, he collaborated with Martyn on *The Bending of the Bough*, 1900, and with Yeats on *Diarmuid and Grania*, 1901; joined the Church of Ireland; *The Untilled Field*, 1903; *The Lake*, 1905; left Ireland, 1911, reflecting on his experiences in *Hail and Farewell*, 1911–13.

[xxxv] Edward Martyn (1859–1923): born in County Galway; educated at Belvedere College, Dublin and Oxford; supported the Gaelic League; co-founded the Irish Literary Theatre, 1898, its early productions including his plays *The Heather Field* and *Maeve*, 1899; a fervent Roman Catholic, he threatened to resign from the Irish Literary Theatre when *The Countess Cathleen* was criticized on moral grounds; severed connection with the Abbey over its 'peasant play' policy; led the National Council to protest against the visit of Edward VII, 1903, which later merged with Sinn Féin, of which he was President, 1906–8; co-founded the Irish Theatre, 1914.

[xxxvi] John Millington Synge (1871–1909): born in Dublin; educated at Trinity College, Dublin, and the Royal Irish Academy of Music; travelled in Italy and France before settling in Paris, planning to undertake a career in art or music; encouraged to abandon such plans and seek Irish literary themes by Yeats; spent the summers of 1899–1902 among the Aran Islanders; appointed a Director of the Abbey Theatre, 1904, which produced all his plays: *In the Shadow of the Glen*, 1903; *Riders to the Sea*, 1904; *The Well of the Saints*, 1905; *The Playboy of the Western World*, 1907, and posthumously *The Tinker's Wedding*, 1909. His last work, *Deirdre of the Sorrows*, remained unfinished at his death from cancer. Also wrote *The Aran Islands*, 1907; *Poems and Translations*, 1910, and *In Kerry, West Kerry and Connemara*, 1911.

look around on it I do begin cursing and damning, and asking myself how poor people can go on executing their religion at all.')

Naturally, Synge, Yeats and Lady Gregory used and interpreted 'Ireland' for their own purposes just as cavalierly as did the Gaelic League; Yeats's identification of peasant mysticism with occult spirituality was every bit as unrealistic as Pearse's puritan vision. The ambition of the Yeats circle to found an Irish National Theatre was vitiated by their particular commitment to realism and modernism (which imposed its own distortions). In the process, they discovered a new 'language' in the cadences, rhythms and speech patterns of the inexhaustible west: a language made for drama and poetry.

From the late 1890s the foundation of the Irish Literary Theatre focused this. Though strongly influenced by contemporary European developments, its manifesto showed that its aims were ostensibly not far from those of the Gaelic League:

> We propose to have performed in Dublin in the spring of every year certain Celtic and Irish plays, which whatever be their degree of excellence will be written with a high ambition, and so build up a Celtic and Irish school of dramatic literature. We hope to find in Ireland an uncorrupted and imaginative audience trained to listen by its passion for oratory, and believe that our desire to bring upon the stage the deeper thoughts and emotions of Ireland will ensure for us a tolerant welcome, and that freedom to experiment which is not found in theatres of England, and without which no new movement in art or literature can succeed. We will show that Ireland is not the home of buffoonery and of easy sentiment, as it has been represented, but the home of an ancient idealism. We are confident of the support of the Irish people, who are weary of misrepresentation, in carrying out a work that is outside all the political questions that divide us.[11]

Yeats was at this time strongly drawn to extreme nationalist circles, and the play which he and Lady Gregory wrote as *Cathleen ni Houlihan* received tremendous acclaim from patriotic audiences in 1902: it was safe literary Fenianism, inspired by the centenary of the 1798 rising. But far more significant in the evolution of what had by now become the Abbey Theatre was the controversial reception in 1907 of Synge's *In the Shadow of the Glen* and *The Playboy of the Western World*. It should be remembered that the numbers who saw these plays were tiny, compared to those who flocked to 'light opera' and London-derived farces, let alone the music-hall. But the symbolic confrontation between the modernists at the Abbey and the outraged 'Irish Irelanders' has been seen as the drawing up of armies in a 'battle of two civilizations', since the unacceptable views of Yeats and Synge were identified by their opponents as the result of their Anglo-Irish background.

Synge gave as good as he got, at least in private: referring to the Gaelic League as 'senile and slobbering . . . sending snivelling booklets through Ireland like the scab on sheep'.[12]

Thus the emotions focused by cultural revivalism around the turn of the century were fundamentally sectarian and even racialist. To a strong element within the Gaelic League, literature in English was Protestant as well as anti-national; patriotism was Gaelicist and spiritually Catholic. This enforced a complex censorship, ironically defined by G. B. Shaw:[xxxvii] 'to satirize the follies of humanity is to insult the Irish nation, because the Irish nation is, in fact, the human race, and has no follies and stands there pure and beautiful and saintly to be eternally oppressed by England and collected for by the Clan [na Gael]'. The formation in 1902 of a Catholic Association of Ireland indicates the ascendancy of a sectarian frame of reference: its declared object was to destroy the Protestant influences 'which form a powerful network of hostile influence, always operating in restraint of the Catholic, Celtic and therefore genuinely native element in our country'.

In a sense this was the logical response to generations of English and Anglo-Irish condescension towards 'priest-ridden', 'backward' Ireland; it is similarly reflected in the Gaelic Athletic Association's adoption of the weapons of cultural boycott, forbidding its members to play 'English games'. There was something very invigorating in the name-calling by vituperative Dublin journalists, who from this period vied with each other in traducing the aspirants of 'West Briton' or 'Shoneen'[xxxviii] society, hanging on to the fringes of Dublin Castle. But although their target was, in Conor Cruise O'Brien's phrase, some symbolic dentist's wife who collected crests, the actual and undeserving victims were the luminaries of the Irish National Theatre; or the acute

[xxxvii] George Bernard Shaw (1856–1950): born in Dublin; moved to London, 1876; unsuccessful novelist; joined the Fabian Society, 1884; pioneered a new criticism that was subjective and inspirational; wrote *John Bull's Other Island* for the Irish Literary Theatre; a satire on Anglo-Irish manners, it was out of tune with the requirements of that school and was produced by Granville-Barker, London, 1904; sympathized with the 'martyrs' of the 1916 rising and campaigned to prevent the execution of Roger Casement; wrote *How to Settle the Irish Question*, 1917, and *War Issues for Irishmen*, 1918; Nobel Prize for Literature, 1925; co-founded the Irish Academy of Letters, 1932. The great post-war plays, notably *Heartbreak House*, 1920, and *St Joan*, 1923, staged the intellectual debates of the day, the Shavian protagonist being a teacher rather than a hero.

[xxxviii] 'Shoneen': Seóinín or Little Johnny, with overtones of Johnny-come-lately as well as John Bull.

Shavian novelist 'George Birmingham',[xxxix] triumphantly unmasked as a Church of Ireland clergyman in 1906 and repudiated by his colleagues in the Gaelic League. On every front the unpalatable truth was evident as spelt out by D. P. Moran:[xl] 'the Irish nation is *de facto* a Catholic nation' and the Protestant Ascendancy, no matter how much they learnt, spoke and wrote Irish, or repudiated the ethos of their class and caste, would be considered fundamentally un-Irish. The nationalist opinions of the young Yeats did not count, when the 'un-Irish' pedigree of his suspect artistic productions was so evident.

How far did this escalation of exclusivist attitudes indicate an increased commitment to nationalist extremism? The connection is not as self-evident as might be thought. Gaelic League rhetoric dealt heavily in Fenian-inspired rhetoric: the apolitical Hyde declared that 'every speech we make throughout this country makes bullets to fire at the enemy' and spoke of James Stephens's great example in breathing national spirit back into the land. Movements like the Gaelic Athletic Association traditionally had a large Fenian overlap; the commemoration ceremonies for the 1798 centenary were largely commandeered by IRB members. But it is worth remembering the recreational nature of much Fenian activity and the moribund nature of the organization at the time. Not only Arthur Griffith but even allegedly John Redmond could retain Fenian links while adhering to constitutional devolutionary beliefs in the real world of political strategy. Anglophobia was extremely important, but was not necessarily the same as separatism. Though D. P. Moran mercilessly pilloried the

[xxxix] James Owen Hannay [George A. Birmingham] (1865–1950): born in Belfast; educated at Haileybury and Trinity College, Dublin; ordained, 1889; member of the Grand Synod of the Church of Ireland, 1905–15; protested against its expression of attachment to the Union, 1912; army chaplain in France, 1916–17; chaplain to Lord Lieutenant of Ireland, 1920–22; settled in England. His more serious novels include *Benedict Kavanagh*, a plea for the Gaelic League and religious toleration, 1907; *The Northern Iron*, an historical romance of 1798, 1907, and *The Red Hand of Ulster*, an exploration of the spirit of northern defiance, 1912. Also wrote *An Irishman Looks at His World*, 1919, and many religious works.

[xl] Denis Patrick Moran (1872–1936): born in Waterford; moved to London, 1888, where he became active in the Gaelic League and Irish Literary Society; returned to Ireland to edit the *New Ireland Review*, 1898, in which he revealed his disillusionment with all facets of Irish nationalism; founded the *Leader*, 1900, advocating a 'thorough' political, cultural and economic nationalism, which he further elaborated in *The Philosophy of Irish Ireland*, 1905; organized a 'Buy Irish' campaign; criticized every section of the nationalist movement, but reserved his harshest criticism for the Yeatsian ideals espoused in the Anglo-Irish literary revival; member of the Steering Committee of the Irish Volunteers, 1913; lost influence from 1916.

Anglo-Irish literary movement in 'The Philosophy of Irish Ireland', he vituperatively attacked the pieties of Fenianism as well: 'prating mock-rebels', whining on about 'England stealing our woollen industries some hundreds of years ago'.

A great many people in Ireland, unfortunately, live from hand to mouth; most of them, apparently, think after that fashion also. They not only think in that unsatisfactory way, but they impose arbitrary limits on their thinking. There are certain things which the average Irish mind will never allow as debatable. The spirit of nationality is eternal – that is a fine-flowing Irish maxim. No one ever thinks of asking himself – is it? We nearly won in '98; we may win another time. Another undisputed view. No one ever dares to ask himself – Can we? ... We can never beat England, can't even remain long in a fight with her, on her own terms. All we can do, and it should be enough for us, is remain Irish in spite of her, and work out our own destiny in the very many fields in which we are free to do so.[13]

Like Hyde and Pearse, Moran saw political independence as secondary to cultural autonomy. Separatism did not necessarily enter into it. A great deal of the 'rediscovery of Irish identity' was a reaction by urban intellectuals against bourgeois Ireland: the grazier-shopkeeper-publican culture was attacked with equal contempt by Moran and by Synge.

There are sides of all that western life, the groggy-patriot-publican general-shop-man who is married to the priest's half-sister and is second cousin once-removed of the dispensary doctor, that are horrible and awful. This is the type that is running the present United Irish League anti-grazier campaign, while they're swindling the people themselves in a dozen ways and then buying out their holdings and packing off whole families to America. The subject is too big to go into here, but at best it's beastly ... In a way it is all heart rending, in one place the people are starving but wonderfully attractive and charming, and in another place where things are going well, one has a rampant double-chinned vulgarity I haven't seen the like of.[14]

This is the authentic shudder at the material world that characterized Gaelic revivalism. But in the early 1900s the majority Irish culture was not that of the cultural ginger-groups, Irish-Irelander and Anglo-Irish. It was that of respectable, provincial Victorian Ireland: reared, so far as things 'Irish' went, on Kickham's *Knocknagow*, the Young Ireland tradition of popular hagiographical 'history' and A. M. Sullivan's *Story of Ireland*: all written in florid English, all nationalist, but certainly not 'new'.

The revivalists attempted to impose a different language, in more senses than one. Many identified with the sense of a coming apocalypse, shared by so many *fin de siècle* European contemporaries. The fall of Parnell – to Yeats a 'Great Tragedian', whereas O'Connell was a Great Comedian – could be taken as a portent. But in the real world they supported, more often than not, the devolutionary strategies of the Irish Parliamentary Party; and they were more preoccupied by the educational policies of various governments than the opportunities for Irish 'independence'. The cultural revival of the 1890s answered the need of the Irish intelligentsia for self-definition and provided a rationale for cultural Anglophobia; is also helped the modernist avant-garde in their search for a theme; later it would provide an appropriate inspirational language for revolutionaries. But the direct political importance of these developments can be overstressed, and so can the decline in effectiveness of the old parliamentary political forms. Eoin MacNeill, one of the most influential proponents of Gaelic revivalism, wrote in 1904: 'In theory I suppose I am a separatist, in practice I would accept any settlement that would enable Irishmen to freely control their own affairs. If the truth were known, I think that this represents the political views of ninety-nine out of every hundred nationalists.'[15] It is hard not to feel that he was right.

IV
=

The radicalization of Irish politics in the early twentieth century arose out of the opposition to the Boer War around 1900, and was further encouraged by the outbreak of European war in 1914. The Boer War boosted membership of the Gaelic League (107 branches in 1899, nearly 400 by 1902); in Belfast, Catholic gangs took the names of Boer generals; the new county councils revelled in voting addresses of congratulation to Kruger; and the war also focused the energies of the political combination that would become known as Sinn Féin. Arthur Griffith's[xli] organization opposing the war developed into a movement

[xli] Arthur Griffith (1871–1922): born in Dublin; educated at Christian Brothers school; apprenticed as a printer; founder member of the Celtic Literary Society, 1893; active in the Gaelic League and I R B, 1893–1910; fought for the Boers, 1897–9; edited the *United Irishman*, 1899; founded the Irish Transvaal Society and Cumann na nGaedheal, 1900; *The Resurrection of Hungary: A Parallel for Ireland*, 1904; stressed the necessity of economic self-sufficiency for a self-governing Ireland; launched *Sinn Féin*, 1906; opposed 1912 Home Rule Bill; joined the Irish Volunteers, 1913; took part in Howth gun-running; imprisoned, although not a party to the rising, 1916; released,

that stressed autonomy under the Crown, while appealing to the radical nationalist tradition and incorporating a Fenian connection. Cumann na nGaedheal, as it was initially called, acted as a broad front forwarding cultural and economic nationalism, as well as feminism and pacifism.

Griffith was influenced not only by his interpretation of how Hungary had won dual-nationality status, but also by the ideas of economic autarcky pioneered by List. In October 1900 the declared objectives of Cumann na nGaedheal were

to advance the cause of Ireland's national independence by (1) cultivating a fraternal spirit among Irishmen; (2) diffusing knowledge of Ireland's resources and supporting Irish industries; (3) the study and teaching of Irish history, literature, language, music and art; (4) the assiduous cultivation and encouragement of Irish games, pastimes and characteristics; (5) the discountenancing of anything tending towards the anglicization of Ireland; (6) the physical and intellectual training of the young; (7) the development of an Irish foreign policy; (8) extending to each other friendly advice and aid, socially and politically; (9) the nationalization of public boards.[16]

None of this was very specific or very new; nor was the restriction of membership to 'all persons of Irish birth or descent undertaking to obey its rules, carry out its constitution, and pledging themselves to aid to the best of their ability in restoring Ireland to her former position of sovereign independence'. The last phrase meant nothing more than Griffith's idea of Grattan's parliament.

What was important was Griffith's advocacy of abstentionist tactics. The Irish *Ausgleich* would come about through withdrawal of support for British institutions, from Parliament down. The corollary, that such a policy would have to be backed up by violence and intimidation, was ignored; meanwhile Cumann na nGaedheal, reconstructed in 1905–8 as Sinn Féin ('Ourselves' or 'Our Own Thing'), provided a broad front that could incorporate Inghinidhe na hÉireann, the tiny Dungannon Clubs of extreme nationalists in Ulster (numbering forty to fifty members in Belfast by 1905), adherents of the Gaelic League and many others.

Several of these elements brought with them a predisposition to violent separatism, but there was also room for disaffected Irish Parliamentary Party members; there was an unsuccessful incursion into

1917; Vice-President of Sinn Féin; interned under the German Plot arrests, 1918; Sinn Féin MP for East Cavan; acting President of the Dáil, 1919; arrested, 1920; released under the July truce, 1921; headed the Irish delegation in Treaty negotiations, October–December, 1921; elected President of the Dáil, 1922; died from cerebral haemorrhage.

establishment politics, at the North Leitrim by-election in 1908; a few representatives on Dublin Corporation waved the Sinn Féin flag, but they had more or less disappeared by 1914. With the loss of anti-imperialist impetus after the early 1900s, the movement seemed to have shot its bolt. The importance of Sinn Féin was that it continued, providing a haven for various fringe movements, publishing yet another declamatory newspaper, advocating its vague and purist nostrums for theoretical 'independence': and it would be there after 1916, establishing an ostensible continuity between turn-of-the-century cultural revivalism and the new revolution. But by then it would be a different organization, operating on different terms. And this development, like so much else, was utterly unpredictable in the conditions of Irish politics before the crisis of 1910–14, and the catalyst of the war.

In 1906 the Irish Parliamentary Party still exercised hegemony over Irish politics; the advent of a Liberal government that year gave them some potential leverage, though the Liberals kept Home Rule very low down on their agenda. The fiasco of an inadequate measure to bring in a devolved Irish Council Bill in 1907 pointed up the fact that the Parnellite generation of politicians were old, increasingly out of touch with both the new elements of labour politics and fringe extremists. A sense was growing, reflected in much political correspondence, that the young were no longer subscribing to the Irish Parliamentary Party. Some Irish Parliamentary Party members, and not the most extreme, had flirted with Sinn Féin as the kind of movement that might attract the youth vote: but they tried this approach not because they were disillusioned with constitutionalism, but because they thought Sinn Féin might be the new vogue of constitutional politics. As ever, the Irish Parliamentary Party used extreme rhetoric when it suited them – notably in eulogies of the men of 1798 during the centenary celebrations. 'We today are in heart as great rebels as they were,' remarked John Dillon, disingenuously, and Tim Harrington actually suggested that young men should be ready to 'sacrifice life in the vindication of the sacred cause of national freedom' – if, of course, contemporary conditions demanded it, as they ostentatiously did not.

It might be questioned whether this kind of literary Fenianism was so very different from the language adopted in Patrick Pearse's experimental schools at Cullenswood House and The Hermitage, just outside Dublin. Here the theories of William Morris and fashionable European ideals of active, open-air education were mingled with Pearse's obsessional Celtic motifs: notably the mythical hero Cuchulainn, pictured by him as a slim, beautiful boy dying happily for Ireland. (A pupil at St Enda's later remembered visualizing Cuchulainn as an unseen but powerful member of the staff.) With the move to The Hermitage, an obsession with Robert Emmet took over (along with imminent bankruptcy). The Gaelicist intelligentsia sent their children to St Enda's, and received in return manifestos that informed them (in 1909) that the school sought 'to re-create and perpetuate in Eire, the knightly tradition of the macradh of Emhain Macha', dead at the Ford 'in the beauty of their boyhood'; the high tradition of Cuchulainn, 'better is short life with honour than long life with dishonour' and 'I care not though I were to live but one day and one night, if only my fame and my deeds live after me.'[17]

The rhetoric was aimed at ardent Gaelicists rather than worried parents, and it found its mark. The language of sacrificial politics was still theoretical; though Gaelicism was the vogue, realism still ruled. Michael MacGowan, whom we have encountered as an emigrant from Donegal to the Klondike,[xlii] returned in this period with money in his pocket. He was surprised and delighted to find the Gaelic League at work, Irish-speakers highly respected, and his native village visited by scholars, including MacNeill and Pearse. But he was equally pleased to find the railway from Letterkenny to Burtonport, the grants paid to fishermen, the improvements in roads and bridges, the housing grants, and the weaving industries – the work of the Congested Districts Board and 'a man named Balfour'.[18] The tradition of rural Irish realism was happy to accept the advantages of both.

The Irish nationalism that had developed by this date was Anglophobic and anti-Protestant, subscribing to a theory of the 'Celtic Race' that denied the 'true' Irishness of Irish Protestants and Ulster Unionists, but was prepared to incorporate them into a vision of 'independent Ireland' whether they wanted it or not. Though much of its ethos was provided by Gaelic League circulars, it was still the kind of nationalism founded on the ringing rhymes of Davis and the denunciations of Mitchel, rather than the scholarship of Hyde or the mysticism of Yeats. The little societies and the gestures of disaffection that flared up in the 1890s and early 1900s have been carefully monitored, and much significance has been set on them by historians working back from later events. But the upheavals of Irish politics from 1910, and still more from 1914, would bring about seismic changes; before then, the landscape was not so very different from what it had been for decades.

[xlii] See above, p. 348.

Pearse, making a speech in Tourmakeady, County Mayo, before 1914 'intimated that a day might come when they would strike a blow for Irish freedom ... a red-faced "fighting Irishman" shouted from the back of the crowd, "The likes of you wouldn't strike many blows!" '[19] In the event, the schoolmaster was right, and the heckler was wrong. But his supposition was reasonable enough for the time.

CHAPTER NINETEEN

=====

WAR AND REVOLUTION

I

=====

THE GROWTH OF THE 'new' nationalism just surveyed has traditionally been seen as the necessary prelude to the separatist struggle that began with the 1916 rising and continued until the Treaty of 1921; but the extraordinary upheavals of 1912–22 are more logically interpreted as contingent upon a series of social, political and military crises contained within that decade. The formation of private 'volunteer' armies, north and south, in defiance of the government, was sparked off by the impasse over Ulster's rejection of a Home Rule Bill in 1912; and this reflects the fact that public political life in Ireland up to 1914 continued to be hegemonized by the old Irish Parliamentary Party and its adjunct the United Irish League. Both organizations still managed to subsume movements like the anti-grazier agitations, evident yet again just before the war broke out; nationalist discourse still presented the stolid and unassuming figure of John Redmond as 'Leader of the Irish Race'.

In retrospect, the vitality of fringe movements in Dublin may appear more significant, and the diminishing subscriptions to United Irish League branches from about 1906 have an ominous inevitability. But the upheavals that presaged 1916 had their origins in extraneous crises, exacerbated by the inadequate and pusillanimous reaction of Liberal governments as much as by the miscalculations of constitutional nationalists. It should be noted that the cultural revolutionaries – Pearse as well as MacNeill – remained tactical moderates until quite late in the day. And the scenario for 1916 was created almost entirely by another extraneous event: the First World War, which set off within IRB circles a reaction almost Pavlovian in its dogmatism. An external war created the necessary conditions for a rebellion against the British government, even one that had put a Home Rule Bill on the statute book.

II

The way that this had come about, however, must excuse some cynicism about British intentions. From their accession to power in 1906, the Liberals subscribed to a conveniently vague 'step by step' approach to the Home Rule pledge; a drastically inadequate Irish Council Bill in 1907 had been rejected by a National Convention, and had given a temporary boost to the more intransigent claims of Sinn Féin. None the less, public attention was not greatly exercised; up to 1910 the main threat to public order, and the cause of fluctuations in political temperature, was the matter of cattle-driving in the western counties. What put Home Rule at the top of the agenda was, as before, the balance of the parties within British politics – brought about by the 1909 budget crisis, following the Conservatives' use of blocking tactics in the House of Lords.

The end of the Lords' veto, and a lessened majority for the Liberals, dealt the Irish Parliamentary Party a leading hand (though, ironically, Irish opinion was firmly opposed to Lloyd George's controversial budget). The election of January 1910 gave Redmond the balance, with Liberal and Conservative representation almost equally matched; the December election confirmed it. Efforts to show that the Liberals were not dependent upon the Irish do not convince; the latter profited moreover by being grossly overrepresented in terms of population, since under redistribution they stood to lose up to forty seats.

Redmond could not, however, play Parnell's part. He was already committed to the Liberals, besides being plagued by splinter groups on his own flank; he was also distracted by attempts on the part of British politicians to remove the Irish issue by a compromise conceived to their own satisfaction. The Liberals only grudgingly and indecisively accepted the logic of the Irish alliance;[1] but finally, the Parliament Act of 1911 reduced the Lords' veto to a delaying power, and in April 1912 a Home Rule Bill was introduced.[i] The Leader of the Irish Race could sit back and bask in hyperbole.

What was to matter more than the Liberals' payment of the Home Rule account, however, was the Conservatives' reaction. To under-

[i] For terms, see p. 425 above.

stand the violence of language used, and the speed with which they adopted extra-parliamentary (and unconstitutional) tactics, two things need to be remembered. First, the Tory belief that Liberal policy and tactics amounted to illegitimate use of a parliamentary majority was by now well established; and second, this conviction went with an equally intense belief that the government was not deeply committed to Home Rule, but had been hijacked into a corrupt bargain with Redmond. Hence – this argument went – the introduction of a bill was an insincere bluff that many Liberals would be glad to see called. Taken together, these beliefs provided the rationale for Conservative politicians to endorse a programme of direct action that led further than many expected: particularly in Ulster, where words were taken to mean what they said.

For the Liberals, the Ulster dimension remained in the background until a curiously late stage. This reflected a general lack of realism, or perhaps of interest; a strong element within the Liberal Party had tried to enforce a federalist arrangement rather than the Gladstonian framework that was eventually adopted. Liberal consideration of the difficulty tended to remain at the level of derisive comment through 1911; the intended strategy was apparently to pass the Home Rule Bill and then see what was needed to reconcile Ulster. As a tactic, this left the government vulnerable; and it gave up the initiative to those ready to seize it. In the north as well as the south, the way was open for extremists to follow the Lalorist technique advocated by Bulmer Hobson[ii] and other IRB tacticians, well defined by Charles Townshend: 'to force the English garrison into an aggressive posture, whereupon the military as well as moral advantage would pass to the Irish'.[2]

From 1912 to 1914, however, what is most striking is how far the government allowed the extremist initiatives to develop: particularly

[ii] Bulmer Hobson (1883–1969): born in Belfast; educated at a Quaker school, Lisburn; joined the Gaelic League, 1901; Secretary of the first Antrim Gaelic Athletic Association, 1901; founded the Protestant National Society and Fianna Éireann in Belfast, 1903; joined the IRB, 1904, co-founded the Dungannon Clubs, to promote nationalism in the north, and the Ulster Literary Theatre, 1905; Vice-President of Sinn Féin, 1907; introduced Sinn Féin to America, strengthening the Clan na Gael–IRB alliance; oversaw the national expansion of the Fianna, 1909; left Sinn Féin, 1910; edited Irish Freedom, 1910; Secretary of the Irish Volunteers, 1913; organized Howth gun-running, 1914; supported Redmond's demand for half the seats on the Irish Volunteer Force controlling body, and subsequently resigned from Irish Freedom and the IRB Supreme Council; became a civil servant in the Irish Free State. Wrote a history of the Irish Volunteer Force, 1918; a life of Wolfe Tone, 1919, and an autobiography, Ireland Yesterday and Tomorrow, 1968.

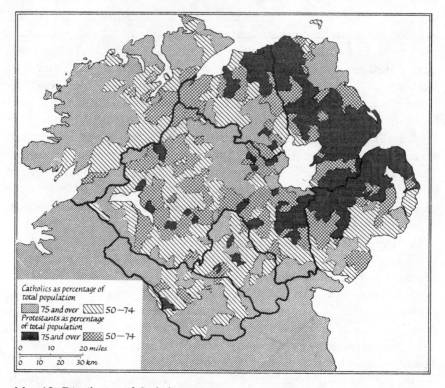

Map 12: *Distribution of Catholics and Protestants in Ulster 1911.*
Source: T. W. Moody, F. X. Martin and F. J. Byrne (editors), *A New History of Ireland.*
Vol. I X: Maps, Genealogies, Lists, A Companion to Irish History, Part II.

in Ulster. The private armies and civil disobedience that came into
prominence did not just appear from thin air in 1912, conjured into
being by Tory demonologists. The years 1886 and 1907 had shown that
the old sectarian moulds predominated over other political alignments;
election results since the early 1880s had demonstrated the inexorable
decimation of Ulster Liberalism (though from the 1890s the nationalist
vote held up well, exacerbating difficulties within the province). The
devolution crisis of 1904–5 produced a tightly organized Ulster Unionist Council, representing local Unionist Associations, the Orange Order
and parliamentary representatives; in 1911 it provided a convenient
berth for extremist Unionist Clubs and the Derry Apprentice Boys,
preaching imperial Unionism and the necessity of preserving close
links with the Conservative Party. The conditions of political crisis in
Britain reinforced a powerful network of support for Ulster Unionism
in the House of Lords, the army and the judicial bench; the contrast

between the new Ulster leader Carson[iii] and his bucolic-baroque predecessor Saunderson is symptomatic. Carson (who remained a Liberal
Unionist) was a brilliant Dublin lawyer, emotionally committed to
the Union, having made his career through the avenues of advancement
open to a clever Irish Protestant: he contributed to the high profile of
the movement, though it relied equally upon the organizing ability of
the Ulsterman James Craig,[iv] unimaginative but devout.

The removal of the Lords' veto in 1911, and the subsequent Home
Rule Bill, were presented in Ulster as issues that could not legitimately
be decided by party votes at Westminster; support for this argument
came from a wide spectrum of opinion, ranging from the respectable
to the great, including George V. The 'British Covenant' in March
1914 was endorsed by Astors, Bedfords and Rothschilds, pledging tens
of thousands; the Ulster question arrived in British politics as the issue
upon which the landed and plutocratic interests decided to confront
Lloyd George's welfare politics. Feelings among Unionists in the
south of Ireland provided even more vehement reinforcement; a Clare
landowner's instructions to his solicitor in early 1913 nicely encapsulate

[iii] Edward Henry Carson (1854–1935): educated at Portarlington School and Trinity
College, Dublin; Irish Bar, 1889; represented the government in its prosecution of
the Plan of Campaign, 1889–91; Irish Solicitor-General, 1892; Unionist MP for
Dublin University, 1892–1918; prominent advocate in many famous cases, including
Oscar Wilde's, 1895; knighted, 1900; Solicitor-General, 1900–1906; opposed devol-
ution, 1907; supported the Irish Universities Act, 1908; leader of the Irish Unionist
Party, 1910; declined to stand for the Tory Party leadership, 1911; supported an
amendment to exclude four Ulster counties from the 1912 Home Rule Bill; signed
the Ulster Covenant, 28 September 1912; moved for the exclusion of the whole of
Ulster from the Home Rule Bill, 1913; subscribed £10,000 to the Ulster Volunteer
Force, 1913; claimed responsibility for Larne gun-running in the Commons, April
1914; represented Ulster at the Buckingham Palace Conference, July 1914; Attorney-
General, 1915; resigned, October 1916; first Lord of the Admiralty, December 1916;
joined the Cabinet, July 1917; resigned upon finding Lloyd George was drafting a
Home Rule Bill for All-Ireland, January 1918. MP for Belfast Duncairn, 1918–21;
resigned as Unionist leader, 1921; Lord of Appeal, 1921–9; created a life peer as Baron
Carson of Duncairn, 1921.

[iv] James Craig (1871–1940): born in Belfast; stockbroker; Captain of Royal Irish
Rifles in South Africa, 1900–1901; Unionist MP for East Down, 1906, and Mid-
Down, 1918, and Northern Ireland MP for County Down, 1921–7; Grand Master
of County Down Orangemen; Quartermaster General of 36th Ulster Division, 1914–
16; knighted, 1918; Secretary to the Ministry of Pensions, 1919, and to the Admiralty,
1920–21; became leader of the Ulster Unionist Party, February 1921, and first Prime
Minister of Northern Ireland, June 1921, and held both positions for life; created
Viscount Craigavon, 1927.

the sense of impending apocalypse. All investments were to be withdrawn from

British Railways, British Industrials, or any Indian stock or enterprise ... In view of my probable early departure with my family to settle in a foreign country, of the possibility of my death in the Ulster War, and of the national break-up which I regard as inevitable in the near future, you will appreciate why I don't want a host of trust funds when the house of cards falls.[3]

For many Conservatives in Britain, Ulster was an appropriate area for exerting political energy, given the conditions of Liberal hegemony and reckless reform. An assault on property and Empire had been conspiratorially planned by a minority interest: this legitimized separatist threats on the part of Unionist Ireland. And 'Unionist Ireland' increasingly meant Protestant Ulster, ostentatiously left unmentioned in Asquith's bill. The question of whether Ireland was one nation or two hung in the air.

Already, behind the scenes, ideas of Partition had been floated: initially (in August 1911) based on the four counties of Antrim, Armagh, Londonderry and Down. Carson was talking in terms of the traditional nine-county province, for tactical reasons; a six-county unit was being discussed by British politicians in 1913–14. Churchill's and Lloyd George's formal submission of the exclusion idea to the Cabinet in February 1912 had not been generally assented to; but the 1912 debates highlighted the Ulster question, and by October 1913 the issue was threatening yet another general election. Asquith was belatedly pressed towards an implicit acceptance of Partition, for all his disingenuous statements to the contrary.

The nationalist reaction as presented by Redmond remained a formal *non possumus,* backed by repeated assurances to the Liberals that Ulster was bluffing. But by 1913 this had a hollow ring, given the formation of a disciplined, trained and armed force of Ulster Volunteers.

This was the background to Redmond's eventual acquiescence that Ulster counties be allowed to opt out of Home Rule on an individual basis, for six years – a concession that pleased nobody. The stakes Ulster was playing for were higher – indicated by the signing of a Solemn League and Covenant by nearly 250,000 people in September 1912,[v] and still more by the Ulster Unionist Council's rapid develop-

[v] The language is suggestive:
    Being convinced in our consciences that Home Rule would be disastrous to the material well-being of Ulster as well as the whole of Ireland, subversive of our civil and religious freedom, destructive of our citizenship, and perilous to

ment of an Ulster Volunteer Force from January 1913. Advice came from supporters in high army circles; by September 1913, the outline of a provisional government was organized. Along with this went a strictly military hierarchy, and contingency plans for the organization of a coup.

How did the legitimate government react? The legal position about drilling was curiously uncertain and tentative – a supposition prevailed that such paramilitary activity could be authorized by two JPs, but this was challenged by the end of 1913. None the less, the Ulster Volunteer Force went on drilling – and not with dummy weapons. Efficient networks for arms importation were developed, ignoring the government's proclamation against it in December.[4] This activity culminated in the landing of large quantities of armaments in April 1914 – both a brilliant publicity coup and an open challenge to the government. The Ulster Volunteer Force brought in about 25,000 firearms and three million rounds of ammunition, to add to the large (though varied and often impracticable) stocks already in hand. They now constituted a formidable military challenge.

Just as striking as the British government's inaction is the southern nationalist reaction: a curious blend of approval and wishful thinking. Pearse's article in *Irish Freedom* applauded the sight of Irishmen with rifles, and remarked:

Negotiations with the Orangemen might be opened on these lines: You are creating a Provisional Government of Ulster – make it a Provisional Government of Ireland and we will recognize and obey it ... Hitherto England has governed Ireland through the Orange Lodges: she now proposes to govern Ireland through the AOH. You object; so do we. Why not unite and get rid of the English? They are the real difficulty; their presence here the real incongruity.

Eoin MacNeill followed the same line ('the more genuine and successful the local Volunteer movement in Ulster becomes, the more completely does it establish the principle that Irishmen have the right to decide and govern their own national affairs'); George Birmingham wrote a satirical novel, *The Red Hand of Ulster*, arguing a similar case.

But the argument was specious and self-deluding, not least because it ignored the rationale behind Ulster's resort to arms. In order to

the unity of the Empire [we] do hereby pledge ourselves ... to stand by one another in defending for ourselves and our children our cherished position of equal citizenship in the United Kingdom and in using all means which may be found necessary to defeat the present conspiracy to set up a Home Rule Parliament.

sustain the view of the Ulster Volunteer Force as the prelude to Ulstermen joining the nationalists, a considerable degree of double-think was necessary (MacNeill, for one, privately feared that Ulster Volunteer Force tactics might include pogroms against isolated Catholic communities in the north-east). But there was also another, more comprehensible, reaction to the Ulster Volunteer Force: if parliamentary government was being threatened by a private army in the north, there could be no logical objection to the formation of a rival force to the south, ostensibly to protect the rule of law. And this was the genesis of the National Volunteers.

This force was supposedly inspired by a magazine article of Mac-Neill's; in fact, local Volunteering movements had already been evolving in imitation of Ulster, but dedicated to fighting the Home Rule cause. The Irish Parliamentary Party was at first opposed; but after lengthy and acrimonious negotiations Redmond secured a preponderance of his nominees on the Provisional Council, paralleling a process already taking place at local levels. This illustrates what David Fitzpatrick has christened the 'vampirizing' tendency of the Irish Parliamentary Party: 'The almost mechanical reaction of Home Rule organizers when confronted by an energetic popular movement claiming to be without politics was to infiltrate it, reorganize it, and add it to the cluster of party auxiliaries'.[5] When the National Volunteers apparently yielded to the blood-sucking embrace of the constitutionalists, the reaction of nationalist fringe groups like Sinn Féin was vituperative: *Irish Freedom* now referred to the Irish Parliamentary Party as 'after the British government ... the most evil force in Ireland' (which was just how Young Ireland used to describe O'Connell). But the I R B continued to be well-represented in Volunteer councils, and to use the movement for their own ends.

At the same time, the public profile of Volunteering stressed memories of the eighteenth century; local studies show pronounced patronage by the gentry. (In Meath, Lord Gormanston, the Marquess Conyngham and Lord Trimleston expressed support, and the Earl of Fingall became Inspector-General.) This element tended to disappear with the politicization of the Volunteer movement in autumn 1914. But even after reconstruction, local Volunteer officers tended to be chosen for kudos, such as their standing within the Gaelic Athletic Association, rather than military efficiency.

Indeed, when the National Volunteers imported arms on the Ulster model, the venture was organized in a manner more reminiscent of a John Buchan novel than of intransigent Gaelic republicanism: it was a gesture on the part of Home Rule sympathizers among the Anglo-Irish gentry, producing only 1,500 obsolete Mausers and 25,000 rounds of ammunition. The contrast with the Ulster operation could not have been more marked. But the Ulster Volunteer Force venture had been organized secretly; the Irish Volunteers were deliberately creating a provocative gesture. So it was this gun-running to Howth on 26 July 1914, not the Ulster Volunteer Force's action at Larne, which called out the troops; and their unsuccessful intervention ended in a fracas with an unarmed crowd, producing three civilian deaths at Bachelor's Walk in Dublin. This was the result of panic on the spot, much disapproved of by the Irish administration: the Chief Secretary, Augustine Birrell, promptly suspended the Assistant Commissioner of the Dublin Metropolitan Police, to local Unionist fury. However, taken with the government's inept handling of threatened army insubordination some months before, the radical nationalist case against the government seemed proved.

The army crisis had taken the form of the *soi-disant* 'Curragh Mutiny' in March. Officers stationed at the Curragh camp were, after a series of blunders and misunderstandings, given the option by their hysterical commanding officer of resigning rather than 'coercing Ulster'. In fact, all that was at issue was reinforcing depots in Ulster, rather belatedly, in order to keep the peace: there was no government plan to suppress the Ulster Volunteer Force. Moreover, the idea of exempting officers with Ulster backgrounds from service in the province would have applied to only five of the fifty-seven officers concerned. But the political assumptions and prejudices of a few high-ranking officers had enforced on an inept War Secretary a potentially disastrous admission: that the army would not, in any event, be used to 'coerce' Ulster into Home Rule. Several Cabinet members covertly subscribed to this view, and continued to do so. The 'force' option was now effectively ruled out. It was clear by mid-1914 that Ulster would have to be coerced into Home Rule, but that the British army could not be relied upon to do it.

The conditions of public order were by now under serious threat. The percussion of labour crises in Dublin, culminating in the great dispute and lock-out of 1913, was a further sign that Irish conditions were precipitating anarchy (cautious British trade unions were increasingly unwilling to bankroll Irish extremist activities). In November 1913 the locked-out workers had been drilled into yet another private army – a small force of about 200 called the 'Citizen Army', whose existence continued after the lock-out ended. Essentially controlled by

James Connolly, they were officially a socialist vanguard dedicated to public ownership: they rapidly incorporated revolutionaries from other fringe movements, like Countess Markievicz. But for the moment, their apocalyptic vision seemed far less near at hand than that of the Ulster Protestants.

The Ulster Volunteer Force had planned with military precision a *coup d'état* and declaration of practical independence; plans were finalized down to patterns of civilian evacuation and the design of a currency. By spring 1914 they could mobilize 23,000 men against the 1,000 soldiers in the province, and the increasingly demoralized police. The Ulster perception of Home Rule may seem ludicrously extreme in retrospect, but the mood was one of exaltation. Thus Major F. H. Crawford, organizer of the Larne gun-running, recalling his thoughts when lying off Kiel, with the whole venture in jeopardy:

I walked up and down the deck tormented by the thought of all those men waiting for me to bring them the weapons with which to fight for their religion, their liberty and all that was dear to them ... I went into my cabin and threw myself on my knees, and in simple language told God all about it: what this meant to Ulster, that there was nothing sordid in what we desired, that we wanted nothing selfishly. I pointed out all this to God, and thought of the old Psalm 'O God our help in ages past, our hope for years to come'.[6]

At the same time, by mid-1914, the Ulster leaders (Carson apart) had moved perceptibly towards demanding a way out for Ulster rather than an end to Home Rule for all Ireland. Politicians on both sides are on record as thinking even by late 1913 that county option, especially for the intricate cases of Fermanagh and Tyrone, would be so reasonable a solution that they would not dare to oppose it; therefore, they hoped the other side would continue to indulge in extravagant demands. Saving political face often appeared more important than hammering out a solution on its merits. By 1914 Bonar Law was still considering using the House of Lords to amend the Army Bill to save Ulster from 'coercion', and then provoke a first-rate constitutional crisis. But on more realistic levels, a six-county Ulster excluded from Home Rule was more and more clearly envisaged – though even this included areas of knife-edge majorities.

The Home Rule Bill as passed in May 1914 allowed opting out on a county basis for six years only; the Lords amended it to the exclusion of nine counties, for ever. A conference at Buckingham Palace, convened in July to work out an exclusion formula, brought the impasse no nearer resolution. The bill was placed on the statute book with the exclusion amendment left in suspension; while Asquith was seen by Unionist opinion as utterly unprincipled, for having forced through any measure of Home Rule at all. 'He has behaved like a cardsharper and should never be received into a gentleman's house again.'[7] None the less, Partition had been, in principle, secured. As Michael Laffan has percipiently remarked, 'if war had not broken out and if Carson had led a rebellion in August or September 1914 his aim would not have been to preserve Antrim, Down, Derry and Armagh, for their exclusion had already been conceded. It would have been to impose exclusion on Fermanagh, Tyrone and Derry City where Home Rule was desired by small but clear majorities' – a much less tenable endeavour.[8] Like Asquith, he was saved from the logic of his position by the guns of August.

III

The First World War should be seen as one of the most decisive events in modern Irish history. Politically speaking, it temporarily defused the Ulster situation; it put Home Rule on ice; it altered the conditions of military crisis in Ireland at a stroke; and it created the rationale for an IRB rebellion. Economically, it created a spectacular boom in agricultural prices, and high profits in agriculturally derived industries: though urban workers were less advantaged, and there was much resentment at the imposition of production quotas and the enforcement of tillage rather than pasture farming.

The war also accounted for a great outflow of recruits; about 150,000 were in active service by April 1916, and over 200,000 had enlisted by the end. Town labourers predominated over agricultural labourers, often encouraged by unemployment at home, and the prospect of a generous separation allowance for their families; Belfast provided a high proportion, for reasons of proletarianization as much as Protestantism. Overall, the Unionist community committed themselves to the war effort on an overwhelming scale: the time was ripe for a demonstration of commitment to imperial values. Constitutional nationalists often took a similar line. But the elements represented by Sinn Féin took the view that it was a British War (without many sharing the overt pro-Germanism of Sir Roger Casement[vi]); and inde-

[vi] Roger Casement (1864–1916): born in County Dublin; entered the British consular service, 1892; joined the Gaelic League, 1904; contributed to the nationalist press

pendent Ireland would later adopt a policy of intentional amnesia about the extent of Irish commitment to the war effort before 1916, symbolized by the deliberate and mean-spirited ruination of Lutyens's war-memorial park at Islandbridge.

At the time, Irish nationalists followed a more complex strategy. In a sense, the war clarified the position of the Irish Parliamentary Party. It could take the opportunity to demonstrate lofty independence, or it could prove that Home Rule was fully compatible with loyalty to Crown and Empire. Redmond chose to bet heavily on the latter strategy, and given that he had extracted a Home Rule Bill from Asquith he may not have felt that he had much choice. He offered full Irish support for the war effort, and suggested that all troops be withdrawn for active service, leaving Ireland to be guarded by the Volunteers, north and south.

In retrospect this may be judged quixotic, silly and overspontaneous; but it is of a piece with his earlier attempt to commandeer the Volunteers for Home Rule, and with the general nationalist obsession that joint action with the Ulster Volunteers was not only desirable but feasible. MacNeill interpreted Redmond's offer in this light. Redmond believed that joint action against Germany would weld Irishmen together, and said so repeatedly; there is some evidence that southern Unionist reactions bore him out. (The conciliationist William O'Brien argued along similar lines.) It is probable that Redmond subscribed to a 'dominions' approach more characteristic of Butt than Parnell, and drastically out of temper with the times. Where he miscalculated most disastrously was in his further offer, made more or less off the cuff in a speech at Woodenbridge, County Wicklow, on 20 September: here he pledged the Irish Volunteers to support the war effort *wherever needed*. Rather than defending Ireland alongside the northern brethren, they were to be consigned to Flanders as British cannon-fodder.

If Irish history has turning-points, Redmond's misjudgement at Woodenbridge may reasonably be seen as one: for it led directly to a

as 'Sean Bhean Bhocht'; earned an international reputation for his reports on human rights violations in Africa and South America; knighted, 1911; retired and joined the Irish Volunteers, 1913; attempted to secure German aid for the Irish struggle and to raise an Irish Brigade from prisoners of war in Berlin, 1914; captured upon returning to Ireland to deter the rising, 21 April 1916; sentenced to death, 29 June 1916; a reprieve being sought, the government allowed the 'Black Diaries', revealing his homosexuality, to be circulated, thereby turning opinion against him. Hanged, having been received into the Roman Catholic Church, 3 August 1916. His remains were returned to Ireland and reinterred at Glasnevin, 1965.

split between moderate and advanced nationalists in the Volunteer ranks. A large majority, possibly 150,000, supported Redmond's line, taking the name 'National Volunteers'; he may have felt well rid of the minority, estimated at anything between 3,000 and 10,000, who called themselves the 'Irish Volunteers', and essentially represented the radical, militant IRB-influenced element, with a central executive dominated by MacNeill, Hobson, O'Rahilly,[vii] Thomas MacDonagh and Joseph Plunkett. But as the war dragged on, the National Volunteers declined through enlistment and demoralization; the anti-war Irish Volunteers, on the other hand, flourished. They became closely identified with Sinn Féin's anti-recruitment campaign and the broad front of Anglophobia that merged inevitably into pro-Germanism. The recruiting campaign ran fairly quickly out of steam; a slow take-up was noted in rural areas by 1915. By 1917 figures prepared for the Cabinet showed that the percentage of male population represented by enlistment was down to 4.96 per cent in Ireland, compared to 17 per cent in England, Scotland and Wales. Redmond's bet had been placed on the wrong side.

The Irish Volunteers, on the other hand, represented a current of opinion that could only be strengthened with the continuation of the war. The divide between MacNeill's separatist Volunteers and Redmond's constitutionalists tended to break along the lines of the old radical agrarian tradition versus the parliamentarians; commitment to the nationalist line weakened in more Anglicized, urban working-class communities. A West Cork branch of the Irish Volunteers was interestingly profiled by a police inspector in 1915:

They are active propagandists, bitterly disloyal, and if only for their negative effect on recruiting, are potential dangers. They are almost entirely composed of farmers' sons, of military age, who before the war were followers of Mr [William] O'Brien, MP, but who are now in opposition to his war policy. Their organizers are known suspects, and their cry against conscription and war taxes appeals to the O'Brienite farming classes.[9]

[vii] Michael Joseph Rahilly [The O'Rahilly] (1875–1916): born in County Kerry; country gentleman and JP; settled in Dublin; wrote for the Sinn Féin press; joined the Gaelic League, becoming a member of its central executive, 1912; Managing Director of *An Claidheamh Soluis,* 1913; co-founder and Director of Arms of the Irish Volunteers, November 1913; prominent in Howth gun-running, 1914; opposed to the rising, he took the countermanding orders to Limerick on Easter Sunday, 1916, before joining the GPO garrison the next day; shot in the evacuation of the GPO the following Friday.

They also capitalized upon rural resentment at government regulation of profitable wartime agriculture. Most of all, they benefited from the looming threat of conscription. Though Ireland was exempted from the January 1916 measure, declining recruitment kept the possibility in view: and practically all Irish opinion agreed that such a step would be utterly unacceptable.

Thus wartime conditions conspired to the advantage of radical nationalists; even Redmond's victory in putting Home Rule on the statute book could be written off as a cheque continually post-dated (MacNeill's withering metaphor). The endless war kept it permanently in suspension, and the shifts within wartime government brought Ulster's Unionist friends into the circles of power. The Anglophobic commitment of Casement, and the pro-Boer record of men like John MacBride,[viii] were increasingly influential: further encouraged by a half-hearted government campaign against extreme nationalist newspapers. The time was ripe for the minority of Young Turks within the IRB to make their play: the founders of the Dungannon Clubs, Denis McCullough[ix] and Bulmer Hobson. Significantly originating from Belfast, they represented a tiny, but highly disciplined tradition: puritanical, anti-alcohol, highly selective. The Dungannon Clubs nurtured ruthless revolutionaries like Sean MacDermott[x] ('a weird bird', according even to McCullough); they represented a generational clash as well as a conflict of priorities (McCullough forced his own father to retire from the IRB, for reasons of advanced age and excessive conviviality).

[viii] John MacBride (1865–1916): born in County Mayo; studied medicine; undertook an IRB mission to the USA, 1896; emigrated to South Africa; organized the 1798 centenary celebrations there; joined an Irish Brigade to fight for the Boers, 1899; settled in Paris, where he married Maud Gonne, 1903; member of the Supreme Council of the IRB, but not involved in the planning of the Easter rising; served in it under MacDonagh; executed 5 May.

[ix] Denis McCullough (1883–1968): born in Belfast; joined the IRB, 1901; member of the Supreme Council of the IRB, 1906; imprisoned, August–November 1915; President of the Supreme Council, 1916; supported the Easter rising, but not informed of final details; delegated to bring 132 Volunteers into County Tyrone, but, in the confusion, returned with them to Belfast; imprisoned, May 1916.

[x] John [Sean] MacDermott (1884–1916): born in County Leitrim; emigrated to Glasgow at sixteen; returned to Belfast, 1902; joined the Gaelic League and the Ancient Order of Hibernians; joined the IRB, 1906; co-founder and manager of Irish Freedom, 1910; crippled by polio, 1912; elected to the Provisional Committee of the Irish Volunteers, 1913; imprisoned, 1915; co-opted on to the secret Military Council, 1915; fought in the GPO and a signatory of the Proclamation; executed 12 May.

By 1912 the youth wing had gained control, and with them a new style of commitment; evidenced not only by revamped organization,[xi] but also by a dismissive approach to the convenient Old Fenian doctrine of postponing action until a majority of the 'Irish people' should endorse it. A successor group was evolving that would adapt the IRB formulae to use when the necessary external crisis arrived. But, though they founded a successful youth movement, the Fianna, which drilled boys in physical training and military exercises, their numbers were very small before the war.

In 1914 there were an estimated 1,660 IRB members in all Ireland (850 of them in Leinster); by 1916 numbers may have reached 2,000. By then, however, militancy had come to the fore. The *Irish Volunteer* carried articles about military tactics and 'hedge-fighting'; the broad front of fringe nationalist organizations entered on a similar course, highlighted by the Gaelic League's stormy *ard-fheis*[xii] in July 1915 when Douglas Hyde resigned his presidency because of the politicization of

---

[xi] The clash between the generations is well expressed by Desmond FitzGerald's account of his meeting with two IRB officers in 1915 when he went to live in County Wicklow after being excluded from Dublin under the Defence of the Realm Act:

I was, of course, delighted to see them, and only regretted that they came accompanied by such a strong odour of alcohol. I wanted to talk business with them, but they seemed only to want to tell me of the veneration amounting to awe with which they looked upon a patriot against whom the ever-perfidious enemy had struck with all his venom ... I asked when and where the circle met. They seemed rather vague about that, but told me to lift up my heart, for they and the other members were all united in their admiration of me. I said I required to know, as I supposed that I should attend the meeting. That proposal seemed rather to shock them. They said there was certainly no need for me to attend. Everybody knew that I was staunch. ... As I seemed to be getting nowhere on that line, I asked how many members they had. They both replied at once naming a number, but they did not name the same number. But that was unimportant, except as I pointed out to them, that I was starting a company of Volunteers in that district, and as they knew the Supreme Council had issued an order that all members of the organization should join the Volunteers, it would be useful for me to know so that I could be guaranteed that their full membership would come to the meeting that I would call. They did not seem to be quite sure as to whether they had heard of any such order. I said in any case it didn't matter whether or not the order had been received by their circle, obviously every member would recognize it as his duty to join the company that I proposed to form. They did not seem very convinced about that, but agreed rather inarticulately, and went on to assert the enormous respect they felt for a man like me and what an honour it was for them to be in my presence. ... When they were gone the landlady came in to discuss them. She had a most mordant sense of humour.

(Desmond FitzGerald, *Memoirs*, London, 1968, pp. 73–4)

[xii] *Ard-fheis:* in Irish, 'high assembly' or national convention.

the League in the advanced nationalist interest. The I R B had gained control of the executive, and chose to define 'freedom' in political rather than cultural terms; Tom Clarke,[xiii] now directing appointments within the League, knew no Irish at all. 'My work for twenty-two years was to restore to Ireland her intellectual independence,' Hyde wrote to a friend. 'I would have completed it, if I had been let. These people "queered the pitch" on me, mixed the physical and the intellectual together, interpreted my teaching into terms of bullets and swords – *before the time,* and have reduced me to impotence.'[10]

This was one indication of I R B influence; the growth of the Irish Volunteers provided another. Augustine Birrell, afterwards traduced for not anticipating an insurrection, sent an interesting report to Asquith late in 1915:

During the last few *weeks* I have been reading nothing but uncomfortable figures about the Irish Volunteers, who are steadily month by month *increasing* ... Whenever there is a plucky priest and two or three men with a little courage, the *movement* is *stamped out* – but unluckily such priests and laymen are not always to be found ... the *Revolutionary* propaganda grows in strength and I think, in sincerity of purpose ... The newspapers are poor enough both in circulation and ability, but reading them as I have to do, I think I notice an increasing *exaltation of spirit* and a growth of confidence, in some of the better-written articles which indicates more *belief* in the possibilities of the future than was the case 6 months ago ... and having regard to the uncertainty of our military operations, gloomy possibilities in the East and elsewhere, parliamentary upsets and so on, I feel the *Irish* Situation one of actual menace.[11]

Wartime conditions had produced among extreme nationalists what Birrell correctly saw as 'exaltation of spirit'; correspondingly, the expectations of constitutional nationalists had been baulked by the continuation of the war and the weakening of Asquith's position. The next step, according to I R B convention, would be an emblematic rising at the moment of Britain's adversity.

[xiii] Thomas James Clarke (1857–1916): born in the Isle of Wight of Irish parents; went to the U S A at twenty-one; joined Clan na Gael; sent to England on a dynamiting mission, 1883; arrested and sentenced to life imprisonment; released, 1898; emigrated to the U S A, 1899; became an American citizen, 1905; returned to Ireland, 1907; opened a newsagency that was to be a centre of I R B organization for the next decade; published *Irish Freedom*, 1910; organized the pilgrimage to Wolfe Tone's grave as a counter to a royal visit, 1912; elected to the I R B Supreme Council and urged the setting up of a Military Council, 1915; served in the G P O, 1916; first to sign the Proclamation; executed 3 May.

IV
==

There is a detailed and rather fruitless controversy about how early the 1916 rising was planned, and what form it was intended to take. The picture necessarily remains shadowy: much that was later rationalized as prelude to the rising may have simply been planned resistance to conscription. What matters more is that the web of subterfuge and concealment about insurrection reflected a division even within nationalist circles – in many cases going back to disagreements over Volunteer tactics when faced with Redmond's demands before the war. Not even the IRB was united behind the eventual decision. Thus 1916 was made by a minority of a minority, and many of those involved were pitchforked into action with no notice whatsoever. This owed a good deal to the methods of the reconstituted IRB, and still more to the style of leadership typified by Patrick Pearse.

The ideology of 1916 is inescapably connected with Pearse, whose ideas underwent a notable, though rather obscure, radicalization from 1913 (he probably joined the IRB at the end of that year, having been rejected by them before). His enthusiasm at the sight of armed Ulstermen and his desire to emulate them have been mentioned: 'we may make mistakes in the beginning and shoot the wrong people; but bloodshed is a cleansing and sanctifying thing'. This might variously be interpreted as sinister gibberish, Swiftian irony or rational reaction to the terms set by Ulster. At any rate, the formation of the Irish Volunteers, and still more their split, brought his idealization of violence into the realms of possibility. His messianic and sacrificial notion that the 'Irish' cause was somehow congruent with Christ's sacrifice appealed to MacDonagh and Plunkett as well: the idea of a revolution in consciousness brought about by a symbolic and willed loss of life. Pearse's funeral panegyric on O'Donovan Rossa in August 1915 is correctly seen as its blueprint. 'Life springs from death, and from the graves of patriotic men and women spring living nations.' Pearse's aesthetic frequently celebrated the beauty of boys dying bravely in their prime, rather than growing into the compromises of adulthood. His ecstatic celebration of the sacrifice of death in the European war as a welcome and energizing force may be less comprehensible, but is no less important.

What complicates the picture is the adherence of James Connolly –

far more of an intellectual than Pearse, and up to this an apparent advocate of hard-headed Marxian internationalist socialism. Until shortly before the rising, he had followed his own path: he was not involved in the original plans of the I R B Military Council, but had been drilling his own Citizen Army. There is some evidence that he expected a revolution within Ireland to light a European fuse, a fairly common idea among internationalist socialists during the early months of the war – though, as Lee has cogently pointed out, he might have more profitably tried to analyse the relationship between peasant economies and social revolution contemporarily preoccupying Jaurès, Bernstein and Lenin. He was certainly pressing redistributionist and collectivist ideals, as the blueprint for a social reorganization following a Citizen Army *putsch*. In an abrasive interview recalled by MacNeill, 'he had a notion that once a stand was made, however brief, in Dublin, the country would turn in a mass against the British government and overthrow it'.

What is more important is the extent to which socialist politics in Ireland were already becoming nationalist politics. As early as 1909 the Irish Transport and General Workers' Union had become, in effect, as much a nationalist organization as a labour one; a process that would be facilitated by Pearse's sympathetic language regarding nation-alization and economic protectionism. When the Military Council of the I R B (a subcommittee planning insurrection without the know-ledge of many of the executive) took Connolly into their confidence in January 1916, and he agreed to join their Easter venture, the nationalist rhetoric that had always attracted him won out over Marxian analysis. He, who had said he had always found it easier to explain socialism to the Irish than the Irish to socialists, opted in the end for Irish irrational-ism – though probably with continued misgivings. Tradition has it that as he walked into the GPO in 1916, he warned his Citizen Army, 'If we should win, hold on to your rifles, because the Volunteers may have a different goal.'

The Connolly hagiography has never explained how he came round so far and so fast to the theory of nationalist blood sacrifice. In January 1915 he rejected the concept of war as an 'elevating' or civilizing force. By July he was involved in dealings with the physical-force nationalists (his article on O'Donovan Rossa's funeral suggests as much), though previously he had always stressed 'the immense difference between the socialist republicans and our friends the physical-force men'. In December he riposted to a celebrated article of Pearse's: 'We do not think that the old heart of the earth needs to be warmed with the red wine of millions of lives. We think anyone who does is a blithering idiot.' But in January 1916 he emphasized that 'the time for Ireland's battle is *now*, the place for Ireland's battle is *here*' – Ireland's, not Labour's. And by February he could announce that 'no agency less potent than the red tide of war on Irish soil will ever be able to enable the Irish race to recover its self-respect ... without the slightest trace of irreverence, but in all due humility and awe, we recognize that of us, as of mankind before Calvary, it may truly be said: "Without the shedding of Blood there is no Redemption."' The Marxist who in 1908 had written 'though I have usually posed as a Catholic ... I have not the slightest tincture of faith left' had been effectively captured, not only by the IRB Military Council, but by the religious rhetoric of Pearse.[12] And the real relation between IRB nationalism and social-ism is indicated by Sean MacDermott's view of James Larkin as 'a national danger'. 'All this talk about the friendliness of the English working man and of the Brotherhood of man ... have [sic] a very bad unnational influence.'[13]

Any theoretical contradictions present in the 1916 rising, however, were obscured by the fact that its rhetoric was poetic. Several poets took part, and the most famous reaction to it was a poem: Yeats's 'Easter 1916', written between May and September and strategically published during the Anglo-Irish war four years later. But an intrinsic component of the insurrection (for all the pluralist window-dressing of the Proclamation issued by Pearse) was the strain of mystic Catholicism identifying the Irish soul as Catholic and Gaelic. It could be argued that this was nothing new: literary Fenianism yet again. But the message would be read more clearly than ever in an Ulster heavily committed to the war effort, for whom 1916 would be marked not by the occupation of the GPO, but the terrible carnage on the Somme.

Theory apart, what about the practicalities of insurrection? Given the war scenario, German aid was heavily canvassed through the channels of Clan na Gael and the inevitable John Devoy; more flashily, the dictum of 'Ireland's opportunity is England's adversity' was advo-cated by Roger Casement in his cloak-and-dagger negotiations on the Continent through 1914–15. German support tended to be restricted to the formal and conditional, though arms imports were arranged. As the war lasted on, discussion among Irish Volunteer extremists took the line of when and how a rising should take place – not whether it was advisable in the first place. But the practical necessity of German aid preoccupied some more than others. The way that Pearse deceived the cautious MacNeill and Hobson has used up much ink, though he may not have been the chief conspirator (and was very possibly 'run' by MacDermott). Such differences reflected a strategic IRB disagreement: should the Volunteers be kept in reserve, and weapons stockpiled, for a guerrilla war there was a chance of winning? The pragmatists saw the Irish Volunteers as a military machine, to be built up to a level where it could demand concessions from Britain, or fight for them: they did not want their forces sacrificed by an insurrectionary minority. Ironically, the success of guerrilla war in 1919–21 may owe as much to this efficiency tradition within the Volunteers as to the shift in public support after the rising.

In 1916 Casement believed 50,000 German troops were a *sine qua non* for insurrection; by February MacNeill had decided they should proceed only in circumstances that gave a good chance of success, rather than staking all on a gesture of moral revivalism. In a memorandum drawn up in February 1916, he considered the blood-sacrifice option and dismissed it as intellectually flaccid. 'To my mind, those who feel impelled towards military action on any of the grounds that I have stated are really impelled by a sense of feebleness or despondency or fatalism or by an instinct of satisfying their own emotions or escaping from a difficult and complex and trying situation.'[14] But by now the Military Council subcommittee had taken the initiative: and since they numbered Pearse, Plunkett, Ceannt, MacDermott, Clarke and the convert Connolly, pragmatism and caution were at a discount.

They none the less hoped for German aid, and probably banked heavily on profiting from post-war reorganization of national boundaries. But principally they relied on an emotional and exalted Anglophobia, mobilizing support for a war against the traditional 'English enemy': however little relation this bore to the intentions of an inept, distracted but not malevolent Liberal administration, and to the obstinate fact that the obstruction to the claims of Irish nationalism was now located not across St George's Channel but in Ulster.

German contacts had undertaken to send arms (20,000 rifles and ten machine-guns) to County Kerry 'by' Easter Sunday – a rather vague arrangement. In the event, missed connections and leaked information produced a fiasco, with the arms-steamer captured and scuttled; rendezvous was never made with the German submarine carrying Casement, who was arrested after landing. These events negated the IRB plan to seize strategically placed buildings in Dublin and keep open a corridor to the country. Even before the disasters in Kerry, those who believed in the pragmatic policy were committed against making an attempt – though temporarily shaken by claims of a planned government strike against the Volunteers, which had been resourcefully forged by their extremist colleagues (the 'Castle Document'). None the less, in circumstances of confusion, acrimony and a barrage of countermanding orders, the Military Council went ahead, on Easter Monday instead of the planned Sunday, in a venture that could now be run only on blood-sacrifice lines.

Circumstances had made it a Dublin enterprise – annoying and frustrating supporters in the country who had received countermanding orders by the weekend. There were occasional provincial outbreaks, including an engagement under Thomas Ashe[xiv] in north County Dublin that anticipated the guerrilla tactics adopted three years later; but this was all. In Dublin a force of at most 1,600 (the Irish Volunteers with about 300 Citizen Army) took over key buildings, centred on the GPO in O'Connell Street – where Pearse issued his Proclamation on behalf of 'the Provisional Government of the Irish Republic'. This stressed the responsibility of the IRB, which was the first many Volunteer sympathizers had heard of it, the presence of foreign sympathy and aid, and the continuity of the tradition of armed resistance.[xv]

The whole enterprise dumbfounded general opinion in Dublin; many accounts exist that record astonishment, derision and occasional inspiration, notably the journal by the writer James Stephens.[15] The poet Austin Clarke[xvi] recalled standing tongue-tied outside the GPO on Easter Monday evening, riveted by 'the watchful figures of armed

[xiv] Thomas Ashe (1885–1917): born in County Kerry; Principal of a County Dublin national school, 1908–16; active in the Gaelic League and the Irish Volunteers, 1914; led the County Meath Volunteers, 1916; sentenced to life-imprisonment; released, June 1917; propagandist and campaign organizer for de Valera in County Clare, 1917; rearrested at Mountjoy; organized a hunger strike for political status among Sinn Féin prisoners and died while being force-fed.

[xv] See Appendix, pp. 597–8.

[xvi] Augustine Joseph [Austin] Clarke (1896–1974): born in Dublin; educated at Belvedere College and University College, Dublin; studied Gaelic Literature under Hyde; succeeded MacDonagh as Lecturer in English, University College, Dublin, 1916–21; *The Vengeance of Fionn*, 1917; cast off the burden of Irish history with *Pilgrimage*, 1929; published little between *Night and Morning*, 1938, the last collection concerned with his crisis of faith, and *Ancient Lights*, 1955, the work of an increasingly secure humanist; Hon. D.Litt., Trinity College, Dublin, as Ireland's 'outstanding literary figure', 1966. Major later works: *Flight to Africa*, 1963, *Mnemosyne Lay in the Dust*, 1966, and autobiographies *Twice Round the Black Church*, 1962, and *A Penny in the Clouds*, 1968.

men at the sand-bagged windows'. 'The historic hour existed with all its secret, countless memories of the past, in and of itself, so that even the feeling of suspense and of coming disaster seemed to belong to a lesser experience of reality.'[16] The atmosphere of exaltation inside the building is unforgettably encapsulated in the recollections of Pearse's pupil and aide, Desmond Ryan. The reactions of working-class Dublin concentrated more prosaically on epic feats of looting in the damaged shops, and those of bourgeois Dublin on appalled repudiation of what was generally seen as a German plot and an attempt to stab Redmond in the back. But even among these circles there were those like the eighteen-year-old medical student Ernie O'Malley,[xvii] with no previous record of nationalist involvement, who were strangely stirred. 'In the evening I was in a whirl; my mind jumped from a snatch of song to a remembered page of economic history.'[17] The juxtaposition is significant. O'Malley and a friend acquired a rifle and spent the week in desultory sniping activity; by the age of twenty he would be one of the key organizers of Volunteer military tactics, and a fabled leader in the guerrilla war.

O'Malley's staccato, impressionist memoir records one response that turned rapidly to practical commitment. Even among the rebels, there was already some impatience with the priority given to gestures above practicalities. The pragmatic Michael Collins,[xviii] future mastermind of the guerrilla war, was one of many irritated by Pearse's style: 'I do not think the Rising week was an appropriate time for the issue of memoranda couched in poetic phrases, nor of actions worked out in

[xvii] Ernest O'Malley (1898–1957): born in Mayo; educated at University College, Dublin; joined the Irish Volunteers, 1917; IRA Captain and organizer for Michael Collins, 1919; imprisoned, 1920; escaped, February 1921; first Divisional Commander to reject the Treaty, 1921; appointed to the IRA Army Council, October 1922; severely wounded and captured by Free Staters, November 1922; went on hunger strike; elected abstentionist Sinn Féin TD for North Dublin, 1923; released, July 1924; undertook a fund-raising mission to the USA to promote Fianna Fáil's *Irish Press*, 1927. Wrote two celebrated accounts of post-1916 Ireland: *On Another Man's Wound*, 1936, and *The Singing Flame*, 1978.

[xviii] Michael Collins (1890–1922): born in County Cork; worked as a clerk in London; joined the Gaelic Athletic Association and the IRB; returned to Ireland, 1915; fought in the GPO; interned; released, December 1916; Secretary of the Irish Volunteers' Dependants Fund and Adjutant General of the Provisional Executive; organized the intelligence system that proved so vital in the Anglo-Irish war; Minister of Home Affairs, 1918, and Minister for Finance, 1919–22, in the first Dáil Éireann; organized the National Loan; reluctant member of the Treaty delegation, December 1921; Commander-in-Chief of the government forces in the civil war; shot and killed in County Cork, 22 August 1922.

similar fashion. Looking at it from inside ... it had the air of a Greek tragedy about it, the illusion being more or less completed with the issue of the before mentioned memoranda.'[18] But to Pearse and others inside the G P O, what still mattered was the theology of insurrection, as recalled by Desmond FitzGerald:

Plunkett could forget in conversation the facts that surrounded us. Sometimes when there were only the two of us together we would talk about literature and writers, and he would ask questions about writers who were friends of mine. But with Pearse it was different. Even when he spoke of what might have been, one felt that the major part of his mind was turning over what actually was. Time and again we came back to one favourite topic which could not be avoided. And that was the moral rectitude of what we had undertaken. These can hardly be called discussions for only the one side was taken. We each brought forward every theological argument and quotation that justified the Rising. And if one of us could adduce a point that the other two had not been aware of it was carefully noted. I remember asking to have such points repeated and for exact references. One of the reasons for this was that in talking with others this question so often arose, and any quotation that seemed to be authoritative and that favoured us, was comforting to the questioners. During those talks I probably persuaded myself that we were only interested in being able to give some reassurance to others. But looking back since then I know quite well that as far as I was concerned I was also seeking reassurance for myself. Certainly none of the three gave voice to any argument that might call the rightness of our action into question, unless it was that we had an immediate refutation ready for it.[19]

As the revolutionaries talked, the authorities moved in. The Castle had kept fairly well abreast of plans up to the countermanding orders at the Easter weekend; they then took a breathing-space, though measures would have been taken against the Volunteers by mid-week, following Casement's arrest. Easter Monday took them by surprise; the city was critically undermanned, by guards with empty rifles and an army that was one-fifth the strength it attained after Easter. Inexperienced troops were hastily drafted in; those shot down at the battle of Mount Street Bridge were newly arrived conscripts who believed, according to Dublin folk-memory at least, that they were in France. A week of bitter fighting ensued, taking the form of attacking established rebel positions, rather than streetfighting in its normal sense; much of the city centre was shelled to ruins, despite Connolly's belief that a capitalist government would not destroy urban property. By the next Monday, when fighting was at an end and the inferno of the G P O had been evacuated, 450 had been killed and 2,614 wounded; 116 soldiers and 16 policemen were dead. Committed and exalted

Volunteers had made their mark against army forces who had not hesitated to pulverize the rebels into submission. The first stage of the blood-sacrifice ritual had been accomplished, and the first act of what Collins contemptuously called a 'Greek tragedy' had been played. The form the next act took was up to the British government.

V

The draconian reaction of the authorities to the rebellion should be understood in terms of international war and national security; but it also has to be seen against the background of alienation and Anglo-phobia inherent in so much of the Irish experience. Following the rising, the IRB tactic already defined came into its own: the garrison was forced on to the aggressive, and the Volunteers secured a moral, and on occasion even a military, advantage. Martial law was imposed indefinitely, under a Military Governor (General Maxwell) and extended through Ireland: arrests, trials on a large scale and deportations to prison camps in Britain followed. In dealing with civilians, the statutory powers of the Defence of the Realm Act were generally used: but reprisals against the innocent and defenceless mounted ominously. Already, during the rising, householders in North King Street had been indiscriminately murdered by soldiers; under martial law a succession of appalling incidents took place, notably the murder of the popular and saintly Francis Sheehy-Skeffington[xix] by an officer whom he had seen shoot an unarmed boy. The officer, J. C. Bowen-Colthurst, was after considerable pressure put on trial: he was found guilty but insane, released in 1918, and ended his life as a bank manager.

The Sheehy-Skeffington murder had an enormous effect on public opinion: so had more comic scandals like the ludicrous efforts of Dublin Castle to make MacNeill pin the rising on the parliamentarians Dillon and Devlin. During Easter week, James Stephens had met only one

[xix] Francis [Sheehy-]Skeffington (1878–1916): born in County Cavan; first lay Registrar of University College, Dublin, 1902–4; resigned after a dispute over the rights of women to academic status; married Hanna Sheehy, 1903; member of the Young Ireland branch of the United Irish League, 1905; edited the *Irish Citizen*, 1912; member of the 'peace committee' during the 1913 lock-out; resigned from Irish Citizen Army when it became militarized; imprisoned for campaigning against recruitment, 1914–15; released after a six-day hunger strike; supported the third Home Rule Bill; arrested while attempting to prevent looting and summarily shot.

individual who took a definite side (a maniacally rumour-mongering republican): 'men met and talked volubly, but they said nothing that indicated a personal desire or belief'. Commitment became more decisive: the British authorities behaved more and more in the manner that I R B propaganda desired. Finally, the courts martial and execution of the leaders completed the process: ninety death sentences were passed, seventy-five of them commuted, including that of the commander at Boland's Mills, Eamon de Valera.[xx]

The fifteen grisly executions in early May created as many martyrs. The case in law, given the German connection, was conclusive for the death penalty: but in the circumstances of Ireland during 1916, the decision against commutation was inflammatory.

Rural Ireland, whose attitude towards separatist nationalism in 1915 had been found by Volunteer organizers a mixture of 'incredulity, suspicion and dour hostility',[20] soon rediscovered traditional modes of resistance to established authority. Even more striking was the shift in 'respectable' opinion. The appalled reaction to the rising among the urban middle classes immediately afterwards, preserved in a plethora of resolutions passed by county councils, was rapidly moderated by the behaviour of local garrisons: a survey of County Meath newspapers shows that by early 1917 Cumann na mBan and other extreme nationalist organizations were being given a new kind of respectful

---

[xx] Eamon de Valera (1882–1975): born in New York of a Spanish father and Irish mother; reared in County Limerick; educated at Christian Brothers school, Charleville, Blackrock College and University College, Dublin; joined the Gaelic League, 1908, and the Irish Volunteers, 1913; last commander to surrender, 1916; released, June 1917; Sinn Féin M P for East Clare from 1917; President of Sinn Féin, 1917–26, and of the Volunteers, 1917–22; imprisoned during the German Plot arrests, May 1918; escaped, February 1919; President of the first Dáil Éireann, April 1919; visited America to secure U S and League of Nations recognition of the Republic, 1920; elected President of the Irish Republic, August 1921; resigned 9 January 1922, after the Treaty was ratified by the Dáil; formed the anti-Treaty party Cumann na Poblachta; Adjutant to anti-Treaty I R A Director of Operations in the civil war; arrested by Free State troops, August 1923, and held until July 1924; arrested and imprisoned in Northern Ireland, November 1924; resigned the presidency of Sinn Féin, March 1926, and established Fianna Fáil, November 1926; led the first Fianna Fáil government as President of the Executive Council, 1932–7; opened the thirteenth Assembly of the League of Nations as President of its Council, 1932; removed all reference to the monarch and Governor-General from his Irish constitution, 1937; became Taoiseach and Minister of External Affairs, 1937–48, and Minister of Education, 1939–40; defeated in the election of 1948; returned as Taoiseach, 1951–4 and 1957–9; President of the Irish Republic, 1959–73. His political ideal from 1916 until his death remained a thirty-two-county Gaelic republic.

coverage. The volatile William O'Brien's *Cork Free Press* adopted an implicitly Sinn Féin line early on; George Bernard Shaw mounted a campaign to have the rebel leaders treated as prisoners of war, not traitors; and far more importantly, John Dillon's celebrated speech in the House of Commons on 11 May 1916 implicitly endorsed the rising in moral terms. The message was clear: in order to avoid anarchy the government must enable constitutionalists to extract Home Rule from the rapidly polarizing chaos.

Lloyd George's attempt to do this by conference failed in the summer of 1916, as did the Irish Convention that met from July 1917 under Sir Horace Plunkett. Well-meaning and strenuous, the Convention's deliberations involved parliamentarian nationalists and southern Unionists, but operated in a context that excluded the extreme nationalists; their efforts were condemned to impotence. The Convention's outcome also illustrated Ulster's intransigence: heavily committed to the war effort, with their champions strongly entrenched in Lloyd George's government, the prospect of entering a nationalist Ireland that had tried to stab the Empire in the back was less alluring than ever. By 1917 all that had been clarified was that both moderate nationalists and Unionists accepted the exclusion of a six-county Ulster, including Fermanagh and Tyrone: an admission that reflected Redmond's desperate need to achieve any settlement going. This development infuriated nationalists in the six counties, as well as many Unionists in the south, and provoked a prescient onslaught from William O'Brien.

> If once Ireland were, by the votes of its own representatives, to accept dismemberment, that act could never be undone except by a bloody revolution ... The work, I am afraid, will have to be left to other men and other times. The real cause of the recent rebellion in Ireland was not pro-Germanism or German gold. The real cause was that you have driven all that is best and more unselfish among the young men of Ireland to despair of the constitutional movement by all your own bungling, your ignorance, your double-dealing in reference to Home Rule in this House, but, above all, by the methods by which you have governed Ireland during the last six months. You have thereby filled the hearts of multitudes of the best men of our race with loathing of Parliamentaryism, British or Irish, and by an inevitable reaction you have raised up another more formidable secret society whose ideals are, at all events, pure, and who have proved their courage to fight and die like men for these ideals.[21]

The rebels of 1916, however, were at least as responsible for the inevitability of Partition, as MacNeill had warned them in his February memorandum. Yet the loss of Ulster does not appear to have preoccupied the radical nationalists of the Irish Volunteers, who by now had their attention fixed on the pure and visionary republic of IRB tradition. As Charles Townshend has put it, 1916 had resuscitated a non-parliamentarian ideal:

The rising was certainly a manifestation of political violence, but it was more than this: it was, to a large extent, a manifestation of violence as politics. It was not the prelude to a democratic national movement which led in turn to the establishment of a 'normal' constitutional national polity. It was, rather, a form of politics which may be called 'demonstration politics', the armed propaganda of a self-selected vanguard which claimed the power to interpret the general will. Cathartic action was substituted for methodological debate; ideal types replaced reality; symbols took on real powers. The Irish Republic, 'virtually established', would not now go away, yet it could never exist – not, at any rate, as the 'noble house' of Pearse's thought.[22]

Not only were the executed leaders prayed for (and even prayed *to*); after the rising, even the moderate Irish Parliamentary Party Mayor of Dublin, arrested briefly and mistakenly by General Maxwell, could use the incident to compare himself to Christ. Pearse's poems and addresses, carefully marketed to secure maximum effect, became a sacred book. On every level, martyrolatry had taken over.

The world of symbols and interpretations so dominated politics after 1916 that there is a danger of forgetting the importance of everyday events. For the war continued to impose the conditions in which political action took place; and the exigencies of wartime may be advanced as one of the main reasons for the failure of British policy between 1916 and 1918.[23] The issue of Irish conscription focused this. Whenever the policy was mooted, it was seen, by an increasing number of people in Ireland, as illegitimate. But the idea was repeatedly floated in Cabinet and outside, along with bizarre plans to recruit Irish labourers for agricultural work in France. As the war continued, even intransigent Unionist opinion in Britain began to feel that it would be worth granting Home Rule, possibly approached via federalism, in return for conscription – 'the true Unionist policy in the altered circumstances of the time', according to Austen Chamberlain.

This was one pressure towards a rapid attempt to deliver Home Rule in 1917, independent altogether of the 1916 rising; another was the entry of America into the war in April 1917, with her traditional leaning towards Ireland's case, and the apparent promise of a sympathetic lobby for Irish claims in post-war reorganization. President Wilson's statement that 'no people must be forced under a sovereignty under which it does not wish to live' was seen by many as spelling out an optimistic lesson for Irish nationalist tacticians. The energetic reconstruction of Irish politics from 1917 is usually put down to the change of heart following 1916, and the return to active life of those nationalists interned, and radicalized, in camps like Frongoch. But the stage reached in wartime politics, the threat of conscription, and the possibilities opened up by the American alliance were arguably just as important.

All these developments presaged the emergence of a reconstructed 'broad front' of nationalist politics: called 'Sinn Féin', but a distinctly different formation from the pacific fringe of its early years. The new Sinn Féin swallowed up nascent movements like the Irish National League and represented advanced nationalism in many spheres, including the women's movement. Its own amorphous profile, and Griffith's chameleon political nature, were perfectly adapted to the alteration of circumstances brought about by government policy, by the army's record in Ireland, by the psychological results of large-scale internment, and perhaps most of all by the renewed threat of conscription.

In February 1917, Count Plunkett's[xxi] victory in the strategic Roscommon by-election gave Sinn Féin the impetus for reorganization and attracted several elements hitherto unsympathetic. Sinn Féin rhetoric capitalized on the drama of high-profile tactics like Ashe's hunger strike in 1917; significantly, a member of the hierarchy officiated at his funeral. At the same time, the movement subsumed the more earthy concerns of local agrarian agitators, so much so that by the end of the year the organization of cattle-drives by local Sinn Féin branches was attracting adverse comment, and was disavowed by the leadership in the following months. By October 1917 there were probably 1,200 Sinn Féin Clubs, with about 250,000 members; by 1918 the movement had on many levels succeeded to the position enjoyed by Parnell's Irish Parliamentary Party in the early 1880s. It had become a universal, dynamic, though tightly organized, political corporation, expressing

---

[xxi] George Noble Plunkett (1851–1948): born in Dublin; founding Editor of *Hibernia*, 1882; called to the Irish Bar, 1886; Vice-President of the Royal Irish Academy, 1907–8 and 1911–14, and founder/patron of numerous other educational, scientific and artistic societies; became a political figure in the wake of the 1916 rising in which his son, Joseph Mary, was executed; independent abstentionist MP for North Roscommon, 1917–22; as Minister of Foreign Affairs, 1919–21, in the first Dáil, he attended the Paris Peace Conference and accompanied de Valera to London, July 1921; Minister of Fine Arts, 1921–2; opposed the Treaty; Sinn Féin abstentionist TD for County Roscommon, 1922–7. An hereditary papal count.

a nationalist rhetoric that capitalized on the traditional alienation felt by rural communities towards established authority. And though the incompetent Plunkett was a disastrous leader, he was soon supplanted by a figure many would come to see as Parnell *redivivus*: Eamon de Valera.

The same circumstances encouraged the parallel reconstruction and revival of the I R B, in which Ashe's successor, Michael Collins, came swiftly to the fore: a 27-year-old guerrilla supremo in the making, obsessed with avoiding the confusion that preceded 1916. I R B infiltration of the Irish Volunteers proceeded apace, though their ethos and aims were resented in certain nationalist quarters. Strategic planning and drilling achieved a new importance. Moreover, the national spread of Sinn Féin was obvious to I R B men and Irish Volunteers alike; as the internees returned from Britain, many Volunteers, hitherto 'unpolitical', began to involve themselves in Sinn Féin, with immediate results. At their *ard-fheis* in October 1917, following much uneasy negotiation, Sinn Féin announced that their aim was to have Ireland recognized as 'an independent Republic'; and, 'having achieved that status the Irish People may by Referendum freely choose their own form of government'. 'Independence' first; constitutional debate afterwards. The strategy to be followed involved withdrawal from Westminster and the creation of an alternative Irish parliament – 'Dáil Éireann'. De Valera emerged as President – supported, to the surprise of many, by Arthur Griffith, who withdrew with uncharacteristic grace.

Both political and military organizations were evolving, in preparation for a war that would be fought with the weapons of intimidation and public opinion as well as guerrilla tactics; the separatist option had apparently replaced the Home Rule compromise. From 1917 the abstentionist tactic was adopted by Sinn Féin candidates in by-elections: they were rewarded by some stunning victories like de Valera's landslide in East Clare. Here he stressed that 'religion and patriotism were combined': the Church would respond by tacit support for Sinn Féin in 1918. The Irish Parliamentary Party were losing all their traditional cards; an apparent recovery in their by-election record during the winter of 1917–18 only affected areas where Sinn Féin had never been strong. At the post-war general election, Sinn Féin would inevitably present a dramatic show of strength.

What converted this into a landslide, however, was yet again an extraneous factor: the long-awaited Irish conscription crisis. In April 1918 Lloyd George actually produced a Military Service Bill that could include Ireland, ineptly linked with the revived promise of implementing Home Rule. The bribe was by now manifestly inadequate; the provocation correspondingly intense. A violent reaction brought together Sinn Féin, the Irish Parliamentary Party and every other Irish nationalist group into a massive anti-conscription campaign, based on abstention from Westminster and a broad front of popular agitation. It was backed by the Church, which organized masses of intercession and a national novena, and the trade unions, which produced a one-day general strike (outside Ulster) on 23 April. All this activity was endorsed by even the most conservative county councils. It provided the final legitimization of Sinn Féin as a 'national' political party, and the culmination of the wartime government's record of disastrous Irish decisions.

The seal was set on this last process by Dublin Castle's ill-founded allegations of a 'German Plot' among Sinn Féiners, and subsequent arrests; while Lloyd George administered the *coup de grâce* to the Irish Parliamentary Party by announcing in November 1918 that Home Rule would be withheld 'until the condition of Ireland makes it possible' (for which he relied on Dublin Castle's evaluation). The constitutional nationalists went into the general election a month later with correspondingly low morale and had considerable difficulty in finding candidates; in a sense they had already been replaced by Sinn Féin.

The election results confirmed this; a comparison between individual Irish Parliamentary Party performances in 1910 and 1918 reveals an astoundingly decisive shift, though interesting local studies show the old Irish Parliamentary Party/United Irish League/Ancient Order of Hibernians configuration was more tenacious than sometimes allowed. Sinn Féin won seventy-three seats against the Irish Parliamentary Party's six, with 48 per cent of votes cast – 65 per cent in the twenty-six counties outside what would soon be called 'Northern Ireland'. They were uncontested in twenty-five constituencies. Their programme stressed withdrawal from Westminster, resistance to British power 'by any and every means', and an appeal to the Peace Conference. The IRB was influential in selecting candidates and organizing voters: personation and intimidation were certainly engaged in on a large scale. Several Meath voters later recalled voting '5 or 6 times at least'.[24] But this does not change the fact that a powerful Sinn Féin showing had been perceived as inevitable from the start.

Two-thirds of the electorate were first-time voters, though no particular connection between youth and the Sinn Féin vote is statistically apparent. But community and religion performed their traditional role as cementing factors; Labour took a back seat, promised 'a living wage' by Sinn Féin and unprepared to follow up the confrontation tactics sketched by Larkin before the nationalist deluge. The Sinn Féin platform was studiously unbloodthirsty. They accepted arbitration in disputed Ulster constituencies from Cardinal Logue – yet another indication of nationalist myopia with regard to Ulster's fears. As regarded endorsement of violence, the uses of ambiguity achieved the level of high art. Here as elsewhere, the Parnellite style of post-1917 Sinn Féin has been noted by more than one analyst; and Parnell was the ideal appealed to explicitly in 1918 by both Griffith and de Valera.

In a further echo of previous battles, great capital was made of the land issue; Sinn Féin candidates attacked the failure of graziers to allot the mandatory 10 per cent of their holdings for tillage under wartime regulations. During 1918 Sinn Féin Clubs had marched on such holdings, wielding spades 'in the name of the Irish Republic', worrying those members of the executive who repudiated cattle-driving as 'neither of a national nor of a military character'. Much of the 1918 election campaign fell into a familiar pattern. The ultimate logic of the abstentionist strategy was, as its opponents emphasized, confrontation with the forces of the state; but some advanced nationalists now feared that Sinn Féin had captured the Volunteers for a 'political' policy. Much depended, as throughout the period, on what terms were set by the response of the government.

For the British reactions, after 1916 as before it, still apparently proved the extremists right. In post-war conditions, the combination preached by Bulmer Hobson would begin to work; reliance both on provocation of the British state into repression, and on the Liberal establishment's eventual revulsion from the tactics necessary to contain a guerrilla war. Roughly speaking, the IRB scenario had, with bewildering speed, turned out to be correct. International war had brought about a radicalized and militant insurrectionary movement. Martyrs had been created; though pragmatists like MacNeill thought they saw the nation as 'not so much a thing which they should be satisfied to serve, but rather a stage upon which they might expect to play a part in the drama of heroism'. At the same time, MacNeill astutely pointed out to Hobson during their impotent Easter week, marooned in the suburbs as Dublin burned: 'we would have no political future if we were not arrested'.[25] And this was absolutely true.

To take the IRB version of the mystic rebirth of nationality through an Easter sacrifice, however, is to forget a number of points. One has been intriguingly pointed out by D. George Boyce: what was 'new' about 1916 was not its ideology, which was essentially familiar and recycled, but the nature of its leadership and personnel: the 'advanced' elements of middle-class Catholic Ireland had found an extremist leadership that was not Anglo-Irish. This reflected the advance of Catholic economic, social and political power outside Ulster – and the frustration of a successor class to the Ascendancy, stymied by Ulster resistance and its British Unionist sympathizers. In a sense, just as Anglicization and modernization had enabled the spread of nineteenth-century nationalism, nineteenth-century social and economic developments created the class that came to prominence in the 1916 generation.

The traditionalist version of 1916 also ignores the importance of Ulster. It was Ulster that blocked the way in 1912–14, and helped channel nationalist energies into what became Sinn Féin; it was Ulster resistance that should have provided the target for advanced nationalist aggression in 1916. The leaders of 1916, however, preferred – in classical nineteenth-century nationalist fashion – to ignore the reality of Ulster Unionism in favour of a mirage of 'cultural unity' based on such irrelevancies as memories of Hugh O'Neill, and the Red Branch saga cycle. Ulster's position figured hardly at all in 1918 election propaganda; the ancient enemy, the Saxon oppressor, stood in, as usual, instead. Yet it was the removal of the Ulster difficulty by the implicit acceptance of Partition that would enable the Saxon oppressor to make terms with Irish nationalism in the end.

Arising from this, the intransigence of Sinn Féin rhetoric masked a basic unsureness about identifying the enemy. By 1919 the Irish revolution was an established fact. Sinn Féin had replaced the Irish Parliamentary Party; Irish Unionism, as an Ascendancy monolith, had long been superseded in any real political sense. The revolution had apparently taken place, as in John Adams's America, in the hearts and minds of the people. But, unlike in America, this had followed, rather than preceded, the taking up of arms: it was a correspondingly equivocal process. Who, in fact, had the revolution been against: a British state already committed to Home Rule for twenty-six counties (which until a very late stage most nationalists would accept as a good beginning) or an Irish Parliamentary Party whose forms, practices and, eventually, ethos the new mass movement increasingly came to take over rather than replace? Almost immediately, the intervention of the British army obligingly provided an identifiable enemy, and the heroics of the Anglo-Irish war provided a self-sufficient cause. But when a settlement came to be decided, in 1921, the focus would shift uncomfortably back to the fundamental uncertainty about what was being fought for.

The exaltation of 1916, the immediate appeal of the philosophy of the deed, and the reliance on atavistic Anglophobia had come under stringent examination in Eoin MacNeill's memorandum ruling out insurrection in February 1916.

> The fact that a man is driven back on feelings and instincts to justify an action or course of action, which he has thought over and discussed, is good evidence that what he calls his feelings and his instincts are at variance with his better judgment. A man's feelings or instincts, that is to say his unreasoned propensities in a matter of this kind, are the more dangerous because they are not reducible to reason. They may seem to him to be simple interior voices, when in fact they are the outcome of his own peculiar circumstances, may be shaped by his personal experiences in life or his prospects in life, and may therefore be worthless or dangerous guides in any wider matter involving the fate of his country or his fellow-countrymen.

Over the next five years those few who had seen it must sometimes have uneasily recalled his arguments.

CHAPTER TWENTY

THE TAKEOVER

I

THE ANGLO-IRISH WAR from 1919 to 1921 was the logical result of the politics of exaltation: but how far it was generally desired is less easily established. Once again, the I R B element in the Volunteer movement worked hard to propel affairs towards a point of no return; but the Sinn Féin organization as a whole did not fall easily into line. Many were awaiting the outcome of the Versailles Conference, hoping for American pressure on their behalf; many others were not ready to accept the confrontation tactics of extremist Volunteers, now generally called the Irish Republican Army (I R A). For from 1919 these tactics amounted, essentially, to shooting down policemen, on and off duty, arguing that the Royal Irish Constabulary – however Catholic and Irish in personnel – were objectively the representatives of alien oppression.

Newspaper editorials, and reports of sermons, show that this grisly process was found generally repellent for a long period. Nor were the twelve people killed by government forces up to January 1920 a sufficient response, in I R A terms, to the sixteen policemen assassinated in the same period. It is also worth noting that up to August 1920, when the Restoration of Order Act introduced military courts of inquiry, no murderer had been convicted. The question of violence was a divisive issue in Sinn Féin councils from 1917; the campaign of killing policemen was a deliberate assertion against the 'political' wing, as well as evidence of the continuing effort of a minority to enforce their own alternative reality. In their minds this amounted to a declaration of war on behalf of the legitimate government of a 'virtually established' republic. It also entailed a struggle for 'freedom' that would be total, and different from whatever measure of Home Rule the British government might eventually enact.

Hence their preoccupation with 'sovereignty', which was to have such important long-term consequences when the terms of a treaty were debated. Hence, too, the rigorous adherence to pieties of language, enshrined in determinedly myopic accounts like Tom Barry's *Guerrilla Days in Ireland*. Hence Collins's declared preoccupation with 'forcing the fighting, and creating a general state of disorder through the country', and his attacks on 'weaklings and cowards' who disagreed. Technically this included clerics, who condemned 'gunmen' and 'assassins'; but many of them simultaneously offered tacit support to Dáil Éireann and Sinn Féin, retaining a keen sense of where they had lost ground in the 1880s. Hedged bets and divided allegiances remained the order of the day.

At the same time, the government response became more and more heavy-handed; displays of military force were excitedly noted by, for instance, the American Commission for Irish Freedom on their visit in May 1919, and random and pointless imprisonment of activists helped swing support towards the IRA line. However, the government left the Dáil unproscribed for eight months, during which time the institutions of the visionary republic were able to take root: the Dáil on one side, the IRA on the other, with authority very uncertainly distributed between them. The Dáil set up 'ministries' paralleling those of the official government; it specialized in public declarations and manifestos aimed at the international constituency sympathetic to 'small nations', and sent unsuccessful delegates to Versailles; it also declared a sweeping and woolly commitment to social and economic progressivism that was by no means approved by all the delegates. More importantly, the tactic of withdrawal and secession, so often projected in the past, was being tried at last.

Membership of the Dáil was overwhelmingly young, Catholic and generally lower middle class. Deputies (TDs) also included several women – six after the 1920 elections, including Constance Markievicz as Minister of Labour (a post significantly relegated outside the Cabinet in the second Dáil). It was dominated by de Valera as Príomh Aire (President) – when he was available. Like the others, he followed a twilight life spent 'on the run', as well as withdrawing to America for eighteen months in June 1919. Increasingly, Collins achieved a status to match his, being Minister of Finance in the Dáil 'government' as well as effective Commander (though not Chief of Staff) of the IRA; and, from mid-1919, President of the Supreme Council of the IRB. Here again the question of divided authority arose; for if de Valera was President of the Dáil, the IRB constitution established the President of the Supreme Council as President of the visionary Irish republic.

Sinn Féin had spread fastest in the countryside, and the movement's domination of local politics helped reinforce the Dáil's authority.

496

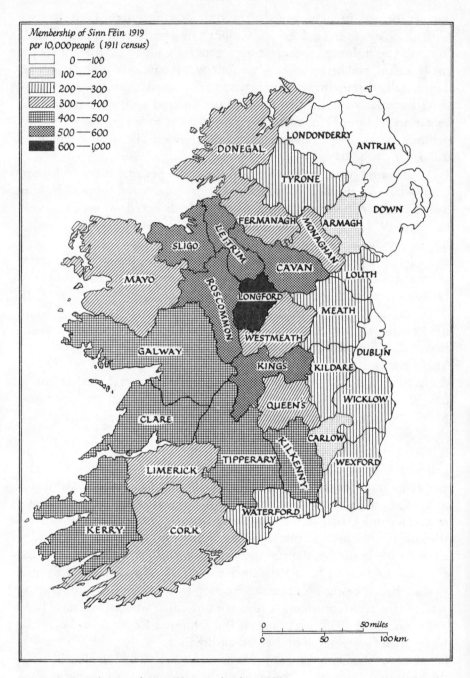

Map 13: *Distribution of Sinn Féin membership 1919*.

Source: David Fitzpatrick, 'The Geography of Irish Nationalism 1910–21', *Past and Present*, no. 78 (February 1978).

However, the local elections of January 1920 do not show a Sinn Féin hegemony; even outside the four counties of north-east Ulster, Sinn Féin captured only 572 seats to the 872 won by other parties. A local study of Meath town councils shows that Sinn Féin captured less than 20 per cent of the electorate, far less than Labour candidates. The glamour of alternative institutions like the Dáil courts, where women often acted as Justices, helped to give the impression of a country perceptibly changing its allegiance. But the strategy of erecting alternative structures was only made effective, as in the Land War, by the sanction of violence in the background. It is also significant that the Dáil courts concerned themselves with controlling cattle-driving and land seizures that would otherwise have turned much respectable opinion against Sinn Féin; and that several local studies show early IRA engagements inspired by land hunger or even labour agitation, rather than by a controlling republican strategy.

In this uncertain way the lines of confrontation shakily came into being. By the summer of 1920 the civil authority in many rural areas was effectively subservient to Sinn Féin – further strengthened by labour agitation like the dock and railway strike of May, declaring an embargo on supplies for troops and police. Resolve was further stiffened when the IRA took to tarring blacklegs. Propaganda stressed the endorsement of public opinion, but armed intimidation was an inextricable part of civil resistance. In courts in County Clare, 'justices were often priests or older, inactive Sinn Féiners of "standing", but the registrars who supervised the working of the courts were almost always active Volunteers. The composition of the courts mirrored the distribution of local power.'[1]

Meanwhile the tally of assassinated policemen mounted. From January 1920 reprisals from the beleaguered police barracks became more savage, and resignations began to reach a critical level. As long as the government refused to accept the republican version of reality as a 'war', they had to rely chiefly on the police; the army were, in any case, a less popular target for IRA squads (160 soldiers had been killed by the time of the truce in July 1921, against 400 policemen). The use of troops as back-up for the police raised sensitive and controversial questions; they were not used as part of an attempted overall offensive until early 1920, after the assassination attempt on the Viceroy, Lord French. Even when drafted into the sort of duties usually accounted police work, they remained inadequate in numbers and training. From mid-1920 their position was even more uncertain; putting them on active service and declaring martial law was seen as too risky, as well as handing a propaganda gift to Sinn Féin. The government – or at least Lloyd George – preferred the policy of unofficial and technically 'unauthorized' reprisals, though much of the advice coming his way, notably from the new administration at Dublin Castle, called for a 'peace policy' and an offer of twenty-six-county dominion Home Rule. Security policy continued indecisive, imposing tough measures on certain areas and lifting them in others. But 'reprisals' continued, and by the autumn had become 'official'. And this was the greatest propaganda gift of all.

The new police reinforcements, nicknamed 'Black and Tans' and 'Auxies',[i] behaved more like independent mercenaries; their brutal regime followed the IRA's policy of killing policemen, and was taken by many to vindicate it. Intimidation never slackened; IRA 'executions' continued, including, for instance, shooting farmers' sons who refused to help dig trenches. Notably in Cork, a bitter pattern of assassination and reprisal took shape; by the end of 1920 IRA flying columns had inflicted considerable losses on police and soldiers, and the Auxiliaries had retaliated by burning some of the city centre. The coercive reaction escalated from late 1920: draconian powers of search and arrest, occasional berserk sackings of villages and towns, and an unrelieved demonstration of hard-line colonial attitudes on the part of the military. 'What probably drove a peacefully inclined man like myself into rebellion,' recalled one Clare man, 'was the British attitude towards us, the assumption that the whole lot of us were a pack of murdering corner-boys.' This is exactly confirmed by the comment of an English Brigade Major after it was all over: 'I think I regarded all civilians as "Shinners", and I never had any dealings with any of them.'[2]

The IRA tactics had provoked the necessary reaction; the government's endorsement of Black and Tan tactics destroyed any credibility that the changes of personnel and organization at Dublin Castle in the summer of 1920 might have conferred. The climax of horrific reprisals is traditionally 21 November 1920, when the IRA killed eleven unarmed British officers in Dublin on suspicion of their being intelligence operatives; later that day, Black and Tans fired into a football crowd, causing twelve deaths, many in the ensuing stampede. Martial law was later introduced, with great doubts; initially for the south-west only, and later extended. To the anger of the security

---

[i] 'Black and Tans' after the hounds of a famous hunt (owing to their khaki-and-black uniforms); 'Auxies' for 'Auxiliaries'.

forces, political considerations were continually enforced upon them, especially regarding the arrest of individuals. But at last Sinn Féin had something that could be presented as a war against England rather than a campaign against local policemen.

The war itself was also conducted by means of public opinion – aided by *engagé* British liberals as much as by Erskine Childers's[ii] tersely efficient propaganda machine, the *Irish Bulletin* (brilliant at scaling up any military activity into a 'notorious' looting or sacking). Other weapons included the hunger strike, its most famous victim the republican Mayor of Cork, Terence MacSwiney,[iii] though this could be claimed as a victory for both sides, since the IRA abandoned the tactic after he had been allowed to die on 24 October 1920. Militarily speaking, IRA organization remained uneven and 'elastic', in Ernie O'Malley's words (his comrades saw him as an eccentric because of his interest in the theory of war). In the countryside, as he noticed, old modes were often relied upon – and something like folk-memory.

I was on the outside. I felt it in many ways, by a diffidence, by an extra courtesy, by a silence. Some were hostile in their minds; others in speech; often the mother would think I was leading her son astray or the father would not approve of what the boys were doing. We of the Volunteers were talked of at first: 'Musha, God help them, but they haven't a stim of sinse.' Yet there was a tradition of armed resistance, dimly felt; it would flare up when we carried out some small successful raid or made a capture. Around the fire it would be discussed; it would heighten the imagination of those who were hostile. In their minds a simple thing became heroic and epical. Perhaps the sense of glory in the people was stirred, and the legend that had been created about myself, whom they did not know, helped them to accept me as part of it.[3]

[ii] Robert Erskine Childers (1870–1922): born in London; reared County Wicklow; educated Haileybury and Cambridge; Clerk of the Commons, 1895–1910; fought in the Boer War, 1899; published *The Riddle of the Sands*, 1903, and works of military history and strategy; converted to Home Rule, 1908; *The Framework of Home Rule*, 1911; involved in Howth gun-running, July 1914; served with Royal Navy Air Services, 1914–19; DSC, 1916; Secretary of the Irish Convention, 1917; Home Rule sympathies hardened into support for republicanism; Minister for Publicity in the Dáil 1919–21; chief secretary to the Treaty delegation; opposed the Treaty and fought with the republicans in the civil war; captured, court-martialled and executed.

[iii] Terence MacSwiney (1879–1920): an accountant; co-founded Cork Dramatic Society, 1908, for which he wrote *The Revolutionist* (performed at the Abbey, 1921) and other plays; co-founded Cork Volunteers, December 1913; published *Fianna Fáil*, 1914; obeyed MacNeill's countermand and persuaded Kerry Volunteers to give up their arms, Easter 1916; imprisoned, 1916–17; elected to first Dáil for West Cork, 1919; helped establish the Dáil's arbitration courts; Lord Mayor of Cork, March 1920; arrested, 12 August 1920; commenced a hunger strike; died seventy-four days later.

There was also reliance on divisive techniques, like boycott and intimidation – already outlined mercilessly by Ernest Blythe[iv] in the campaign against conscription, when he had declared that anyone who 'connived in this crime against us ... merits no more consideration than a wild beast, and should be killed without mercy or hesitation as opportunity offers'. The diverse strategies of the IRA were linked by Collins's legendary intelligence network, often utilizing 'individuals in a fairly high walk of life who openly boasted of their British connection'.[4] In Ernie O'Malley's exalted imagination, as he drilled his flying column in Munster, the immemorial history of struggle took shape all around him:

> Towns built around a King John's keep or a Tudor castle were again garrisons; their influence varying between their armed strength and the people's resistance. The gap between the two was becoming more impenetrable; it was deepened by a steady withdrawal of the factors in which a joint life once met.

O'Malley is a more reliable guide to mentality than to reality, however; and the idea of a 'national' struggle can be exaggerated. The evidence for intensity of operations is necessarily founded on questionable sources. As so often before, central Munster and the Ulster borders were the active areas of disaffection; the west was curiously quiescent in military terms, though levels of participation in organizations, and electoral support, were high.[5] So far as a pattern can be discerned, IRA activists came from the youth of the small towns, and the rural lower middle classes; unlike the Volunteer movement at large, the eldest sons or local notables from the strong-farming and shopkeeping classes were not prominent, whereas the unattached, younger 'men of no property' were. 'For the first time in Irish history, revolutionary leadership had passed into the hands of men without any discernible social peculiarities or distinctions'.[6] Possibly allied to this fact, relationships between provincial detachments and central authority were difficult; local studies indicate a greater degree of

---

[iv] Ernest Blythe (1889–1975): born in County Antrim; clerk in Department of Agriculture; joined Gaelic League and IRB; organizer of Irish Volunteers, 1914; imprisoned during 1916 rising; Minister for Trade and Commerce, 1918–22; accepted the 1921 Treaty; Minister for Local Government, 1922–3, and for Posts and Telegraphs, 1922–32; as Minister for Finance, 1922–31, reduced pensions and gave £1,000 to the Abbey, making it one of the world's first state-sponsored theatres; Vice-President of the Executive Council, 1927–32; Senator, 1933–6; founded An Gúm to publish books in Irish for the government; managing director of the Abbey, 1941–67.

fragmentation (and ineffectuality) than propaganda – or memoirs –
allow. Civil disruption and local feuds provided as much gratification
as actual military enterprises. Many marginalized and rootless people
found a *raison d'être*; and many would cling to it by electing to fight
against the Treaty in 1922.

By the time a truce was called in July 1921, those of the IRA who
supported it had a vested interest in privately claiming that they were
at the end of their tether; after the Treaty, the irreconcilables had an
equally vested interest in claiming that this was not the case. The issue
recurs again and again in the Dáil debates, where the pro-Treaty side
advanced arguments of hard realism. The British *were* still in Ireland;
they had not been driven out of anything except 'a fairly good-sized
police barracks'. Kevin O'Higgins,[v] arguing for the Treaty, stressed
that it was the only alternative to 'a war in which there would have
been no question of military victory'. Even O'Malley, a temperamental
irreconcilable if ever there was one, admitted the dissonance between
perception and reality.[vi] And an IRA document captured early in
1920 summed it up: 'all our training, lectures, etc., drive us to one
conclusion, namely that no matter what strategy we may adopt we
will evidently be beaten in a military sense'. But the last clause is a
vital qualification. Charles Townshend puts it best: the IRA's achievement was 'to find that by matching its operations to its means, it could

[v] Kevin Christopher O'Higgins (1892–1927): joined Sinn Féin while a student;
imprisoned in German Plot arrests, 1918; MP for Queen's County, 1918; Assistant
Minister for Local Government in the 1919 Dáil; advocate of the 1921 Treaty; TD
for South Dublin, 1922; Minister for Economic Affairs, 1922; Minister for Justice and
External Affairs, and Vice-President of the Executive Council, 1922–7; vigorous in
attempts to restore order in the civil war, defending execution of seventy-seven
republicans in 1922–3; shot by an IRA gunman.

[vi] A characteristic reflection:
   Every one of our little fights or attacks was significant, they made panoramic
   pictures of the struggle in the people's eyes and lived on in their minds.
   Only in our country could the details of an individual fight expand to the
   generalizations of a pitched battle. What to me was a defeat, such as the
   destruction of an occupied post without the capture of its arms, would soon be
   sung of as a victory. Our own critical judgements which adjudged action and
   made it grow gigantic through memory and distance, were like to folklore. To
   an outsider, who saw our strivings and their glorification, this flaring imagination
   that lit the stars might make him think of the burglar who shouted at the top
   of his voice to hide the noise of his feet. Actually the people saw the clash
   between two mentalities, two trends in direction, and two philosophies of life;
   between exploiters and exploited. Even the living were quickly becoming
   folklore; I had heard my own name in song at the few dances I had attended.
   (Ernie O'Malley, *On Another Man's Wound*, Tralee, 1979 edition, p. 317)

ensure its survival for long enough to achieve psychological victory out of military stalemate'.[7]

From the other side, a gloomy memorandum from General Macready in May stressed the psychological exhaustion of the army, and alarmed the Cabinet by insisting that a conclusion by October was vital. The numbers of garrisoned troops were always inadequate. By the end of 1921 the total numbers of police were nearly 17,000 (the regular Royal Irish Constabulary had numbered 10,000 in July 1920). The full strength of the I R A may have been about the same, but they were used in much smaller units. 'Active service' members were 5,000 at most. By early 1921 the government forces took to operating in large sweeps, using their own flying columns; reinforcements on a major scale were being arranged from June, when they increased their strength by one-third in less than a month, though the expense of Irish operations had been a very sensitive political issue. The possibility was discussed of drafting in 250,000 troops.

Against this, the I R A had incalculable advantages of terrain; and they also had access to money. De Valera's Irish bond drive raised $5,000,000 in America in 1920, and the Irish Victory Fund had sent $250,000 to Ireland before this. It is difficult to arrive at an overall sense of I R A morale by mid-1921; slackening in some areas, it was hardening in others. Once a truce was called, commitment necessarily weakened, and valuable covers were blown; things would look different afterwards. But they were already vulnerable to losses of men and – even more – *matériel*: there had been a crippling series of arms-raids in March and April, though by May the new Thompson machine-guns were arriving in Dublin from America. It is likely that the republicans could keep making difficulties, without ever 'winning'; Collins knew the value of the gun 'as a propaganda weapon, its power of destruction a headline, its detonation a slogan'.[8] He also saw the I R A hard-pressed in Dublin, whereas the *exaltés* in west Cork and north Tipperary felt they were winning. The real point was: when to start negotiations? And in the end, public and political opinion broke the government's nerve while the I R A were still in the field. This was their victory.

II

But the pressures of liberal opinion abroad, and military demoralization in Ireland, were not the only influences making for peace in 1921. A vital point was that a treaty could now be made with nationalist Ireland, because Unionist Ireland, or at least Ulster Unionist Ireland, had been separately catered for. The Treaty of 1921 did not enable Partition to take place, as sometimes assumed; Partition cleared the way for the Treaty. On 23 December 1920 the Government of Ireland Act had become law – the descendant of the pre-war Home Rule Bill, and essentially constructed to solve the Irish problem as it stood in 1914, not in 1920. It provided for two devolved parliaments in Ireland, one in Belfast for the six counties, and another in Dublin, linked by a notional 'Council of Ireland'. The government had hoped to defuse the Irish situation; but nationalists ignored it, merely using the subsequent elections to produce another mandate for Sinn Féin. Though the government tried for a nine-county Ulster, stressing that the religious balance in such a unit would facilitate eventual reunification, Ulster Unionists insisted on a six-county unit that would contain a heavily weighted Protestant majority. The six north-eastern counties (now called, inaccurately, 'Northern Ireland') accepted secession. It is often said that they did so unwillingly, but this was a tactical reaction: many knew they had gained a near-impregnable position, and saw it as the effective legalization of Carson's pre-war provisional government.

Moreover, the mechanisms of a separate Belfast administration had been created with great care and thoroughness by civil servants during 1920, while the heroics of the 'war' exploded around them. Dublin Castle's last act, in effect, was to create a successor administration for Belfast, embodying much of its experience and resources. A special Under-Secretary for Ulster matters was appointed in September 1920 – Sir Ernest Clark,[vii] later credited with being 'midwife' to the new 'province'. Administrative partition was a reality even before the Government of Ireland Act reached the statute book at the end of the year. This was the actuality behind the window-dressing of inducements to 'unity' that accompanied the Act. Most British politicians were reluctant to admit that Partition might be more than temporary; Irish nationalists oddly connived in this, by ignoring what was hap-

[vii] Ernest Clark (1864–1951): entered the civil service, 1884; CBE, 1918; Assistant Secretary of the Inland Revenue, 1919; Secretary to the Royal Commission on Income Tax, 1919–20; knighted, 1920; Assistant Under-Secretary for Ireland, 1920–21; architect of the Northern Ireland constitution, 1921; head of Northern Ireland civil service and Permanent Secretary of its Ministry of Finance, 1921–5; KCB, 1924; director of Harland & Wolff and other companies, 1925–33; member of the Joint Exchequer Board of Great Britain and Northern Ireland, 1930; Governor of Tasmania, 1933–45.

pening or dismissing it as irrelevant. Meanwhile Ulster Unionists and sympathetic civil servants, by creating a *fait accompli*, helped to copperfasten it. An effective transfer of services had been arranged by the time of the Treaty negotiations, though the timing of the transfer was kept discreetly quiet.[9]

Attempts in 1921 to bring Craig and de Valera together seem less important in this light; everything was different now. The May elections in Northern Ireland had produced a huge Unionist majority and inaugurated what was effectively a one-party state, containing a large, and appalled, one-third minority of Catholics.

To the south, the Government of Ireland machinery was boycotted, leaving Lloyd George with the unpalatable alternative of governing the twenty-six counties as a Crown colony under martial law. It was this situation, and the removal of Ulster, that prepared the government for negotiation, rather than, as sometimes sentimentally assumed, King George V's conciliatory speech opening the new Northern Ireland parliament.[viii] Lloyd George subsequently offered a conference with few strings attached; de Valera cautiously defined the terms of negotiation before entering upon discussions 'with a view to ascertaining how the association of Ireland with the community of nations known as the British Empire may best be reconciled with Irish national aspirations'.

From the British side, the offer of dominion status (pressed by advisers since 1919–20) was on the table, which raised the bidding from Home Rule; it was rejected by de Valera and the Dáil as involving Ireland inextricably in the Empire. De Valera was already working towards his idea of 'free association' (later 'external association') between Ireland and Britain, and covering his flank by judiciously adapting pure-milk republican doctrine in the Dáil. A similar priority was, disastrously, apparent in the team he sent to negotiate terms in London: Collins, Griffith, Robert Barton,[ix] George Gavan Duffy,[x]

[viii] Though the speech was written by Edward Grigg, Lloyd George's advisor, rejecting earlier drafts by Smuts, Balfour and Craig.

[ix] Robert Childers Barton (1881–1975): born in County Wicklow; educated at Rugby and Oxford; progressive landlord; sat on the Committee of the Irish Agricultural Organization Society from 1910; British army officer, 1914; resigned, Easter 1916; joined IRA; Sinn Féin MP for West Wicklow, 1918; Minister for Agriculture, founding the Land Bank, 1921; signatory of the 1921 Treaty, recommending it as 'the lesser of two outrages', but later repudiated it; abstentionist TD, June 1922–7; headed Agricultural Credit Corporation, 1934–54, and Bord na Móna, 1946.

[x] George Gavan Duffy (1882–1951): educated at Stonyhurst and in France; solicitor; Irish Bar, 1917; prepared Casement's defence; helped draft 1919 constitution; Sinn

Eamon Duggan[xi] and the flinty republican convert Erskine Childers as Secretary. To judge by an extraordinary letter written by de Valera to an American ally, his intention was to balance the delegation to a point where it was almost paralysed.[10] It was certainly the case that whoever went to London would have to compromise 'the Republic'. Significantly, he did not entertain the idea of going himself.

The delegates were ready to cede questions of security and defence, like Britain's right to occupy naval bases; more incredibly (though not without a certain amount of Lloyd Georgian chicanery) they were ready to accept that the Ulster question could be passed on to a 'Boundary Commission' that might, or might not, adapt the territory of the Northern Ireland state so far as to make it unviable. Strong claims exist that Lloyd George had guaranteed to Ulster Unionist leaders in 1920 that their borders would remain impregnable. The Prime Minister, however, only produced the Boundary Commission as a *quid pro quo* if the Irish would meet him on what they conceived to be the 'real' questions of sovereignty and allegiance – where the principal difficulties lay. De Valera's concept of 'external association', reciprocal citizenship and republican status within the Commonwealth, was ingenious, but ahead of its time: the contemporary constitutional framework could not incorporate it. The position of the Crown in Irish affairs remained the crux. The British were ready to accept a special Oath of Allegiance for the Irish dominion, which helped sway the delegates; but they would not go so far as de Valera's external-association version enshrined in his suggested alternative 'Document No. 2'.[xii] The delegates eventually accepted a formula based on a draft

Féin representative at Paris Peace Conference, 1919, and envoy in Rome, 1920; last to sign 1921 Treaty; recommended it to the Dáil reluctantly; resigned as Minister for Foreign Affairs, upon abolition of the republican courts, August 1922; resigned from the Dáil, upon its refusal to treat captured republicans as POWs, 1923; judge of the high court, 1936, and President, 1946.

[xi] Edmund John [Eamon] Duggan (1874–1936): born in County Meath; solicitor, 1914; supported Sinn Féin; arrested in 1916 rising; IRA Director of Intelligence; elected to first Dáil, 1918; arrested, 1920; released, July 1921, becoming Chief Liaison Officer for Ireland; signatory to 1921 Treaty; Minister for Home Affairs, 1922; Parliamentary Secretary to the Ministry of Defence and the Executive Council; Senator, 1933.

[xii] The British offered, as an oath:

I . . . do solemnly swear true faith and allegiance to the Constitution of the Irish Free State as by law established, and that I will be faithful to HM King George V, his heirs and successors by law, in virtue of the common citizenship

that had been agreed by a committee of the IRB: presaging that organization's influential support of the Treaty. It was an Oath of Fidelity rather than Allegiance, but it was too much for de Valera. The break with the irreconcilables came on a form of words.

To understand this, it is necessary to look at the substance of the Treaty. What had the republicans got from it which was not on offer before? Twenty-six counties had achieved dominion status – the solution endorsed from 1920 by the British Trades Union Congress, the Labour Party, the Asquithean Liberals, and many of Lloyd George's advisers. Bonar Law had originally, and correctly, argued that this would enable Sinn Féin in the fullness of time to declare a secessionist republic; but by 1921, with Ulster protected, he was prepared to accept the danger. Twenty-six-county dominion-status was in some ways a retraction from the 'colonial Home Rule' bruited in 1917–18, or the dominion Home Rule for all Ireland called for by Horace Plunkett's Irish Dominion League in 1919–20. But the realists, notably Collins, saw that it contained the germ of radical future developments. In a private memorandum at the time, he wrote: 'the only association which it will be satisfactory for Ireland to enter will be based, not on the present technical legal status of the Dominions, but on the real position they claim, and have in fact secured'.[11] He was right. But whether the bloody catalogue of assassination and war from 1919–21 was necessary in order to negotiate thus far may fairly be questioned.

And this explains why the irreconcilables repudiated the Treaty arrangement – not because it failed to provide a united Ireland, but because it failed to deliver the 'Republic'. Though the original, correct tactic had been to break off negotiations on Ulster, in the end the Anglophobic obsession with 'the Crown' outranked everything. In any case, neither the London negotiations nor the armed struggle could ever have delivered a united Ireland, since in at least four counties of the disputed six, Sinn Féin never achieved any kind of footing. Lloyd George's attempts to bring Craig into negotiations, and adapt Northern Ireland's 1920 status, met with a predictably monolithic response. Lloyd George's disingenuousness was conditioned by the changing circumstances of his reliance on Tory (and therefore Unionist) allies; if he ever thought of coercing Craig, that was no longer possible. By

of Ireland with Great Britain and her adherence to and membership of the group of nations forming the British Commonwealth of Nations.

De Valera's formula was:

I ... do solemnly swear true faith and allegiance to the constitution of the Irish Free State, to the Treaty of Association and to recognize the King of Great Britain as head of the Associated States.

the same token, F. S. L. Lyons has pointed out that by 1921 hubris had dictated that Griffith play Redmond's part of 1914. 'If Griffith now forced the resignation of Lloyd George, or if Redmond had then forced that of Asquith, the only consequence would have been the return to power of intransigent Unionism incarnate in the obdurate shape of Bonar Law.'[12]

What the Treaty provided was complete independence in domestic affairs, including full fiscal autonomy (which Cabinet members had wanted built into the Government of Ireland Act in 1920, but which Lloyd George had then opposed). 'External' freedoms were also, given the altering status of the dominions, implicitly wide. As to Ulster, both the Irish delegates and many in the British Cabinet expected the projected Boundary Commission to restore Tyrone and Fermanagh at least; the nationalist Belfast *Irish News*, by its enthusiastic reception of the Treaty, seems to have shared this hope. The idea that this would impair Ulster's economic 'viability' is irrelevant, because it would soon be proved 'unviable' in real terms anyway. What remains extraordinary is the vagueness of what 'Boundary Commission' meant: whether its mechanisms would involve plebiscites, and on what basis, was never defined. Even the anti-Treaty party, however, passed easily over Ulster: de Valera was ready to permit exclusion by county option. What mattered was 'the Oath': whatever about the potential contained in dominion status, in the irreconcilables' eyes, accepting the Oath made the bloodshed of the last two years meaningless.

The delegates had been in essence informed of this, but they signed under duress. Would Lloyd George otherwise have resumed war à *outrance*, as he claimed? Certainly the contingency plans were there; and the government would threaten war again when the arrangements looked like breaking down in 1922. Moreover, in the atmosphere of London, if not in the IRA bivouacs of the Tipperary mountains, the terms could look like an Irish victory. Unionist intransigents like Sir Henry Wilson[xiii] were appalled. 'The agreement is a complete surren-

---

[xiii] Henry Hughes Wilson (1864–1922): born in County Longford; educated at Marlborough; served in Boer War and Burma; War Office Director of Military Operations, 1910–14; Major-General, 1913; backed Curragh mutiny, 1914; Deputy Chief of General Staff, August 1914; Lieutenant-General, 1915; formed close alliance with Lloyd George; British military representative on Supreme War Council, 1917; Chief of Imperial General Staff 1918–22; pressed for Irish conscription, 1918; Field-Marshal and knighthood, July 1919; dissatisfied with Versailles settlement and estranged from Lloyd George; established British Intelligence 'Cairo Gang', 1920; Unionist MP for North Down and Security Adviser to the Northern Irish Government, 1922; assassinated.

der. 1. A farcical oath of allegiance. 2. Withdrawal of our troops. 3. A rebel army, etc., etc. The British Empire is doomed.'[13] Much southern Unionist reaction was even more vehement. And the prophetic and ingenious nature of de Valera's 'external association' should not conceal the fact that in 1921 it was completely unacceptable to *all* the British negotiators.

But in Ireland a split was inevitable. On 7 January 1922 the Dáil ratified the Treaty by a tiny majority of seven seats: de Valera declared against it early on, supported by intransigent republicans like Cathal Brugha[xiv] and Austin Stack.[xv] The lines of fissure were symptomatic of antipathies and power struggles already existing; but the debates of 1921–2 indicate what was theoretically at stake too. Pragmatists lined up against irreconcilables and visionaries. Stack's incomprehension was genuine when he referred to Collins's appeal to ' "the duress of the facts", *whatever he meant by that*'. Those who opposed the Treaty were often implacable revolutionaries like O'Malley, prepared to see a drastic hardening of conditions and of attitudes, including the expulsion from the island of Ireland of anyone who harboured any form of imperial allegiance (whom they imagined to be a tiny minority). 'The Republic' did duty for centuries of Anglophobia.

Also against the Treaty were a considerable element who had thrived on the conditions of lawlessness, notably by cattle-driving: Connacht, quiescent in the campaign for independence, put up marked resistance to the Treaty. O'Higgins roughly defined the opposition to the new government as 20 per cent idealism, 20 per cent crime and 60 per cent 'sheer futility'. The nature of formal opposition, those soon to be called the 'Irregulars', owed much to local conditions; it is hard to produce

---

[xiv] Charles William St John Burgess [Cathal Brugha] (1874–1922): born in Dublin; educated at Belvedere College; co-founded candle-manufacturing business; joined the Gaelic League, 1899, and Irish Volunteers, 1913; Second-in-Command at South Dublin Union in 1916 rising; wounded and permanently crippled; IRA Chief of Staff, October 1917–April 1919; presided at first meeting of the Dáil, January 1919; proposed swearing of allegiance to the Republic and its Dáil, August 1919; Minister for Defence, April 1919–January 1922; most strenuous opponent of the 1921 Treaty; killed in action in second week of the civil war.

[xv] Austin Stack (1880–1929): tax inspector; founder member of Kerry Volunteers, 1913; commandment in 1916 rising; arrested, having failed to make contact with German arms shipment; led prisoners' fight for political status; released, June 1917; Sinn Féin TD for West Kerry in first Dáil; set up republican courts as Minister of Justice, 1920; IRA Deputy Chief of Staff, 1921; Minister for Home Affairs, August 1921–January 1922; leading opponent of the Treaty; captured, April 1923; abstentionist Sinn Féin TD, 1923.

a coherent analysis of why certain elements went one way and others another.[14] In many cases, the line of division broke along issues that long pre-dated the Treaty, and the war; in some localities Irregulars paralleled Ribbonmen. The condition of IRA detachments during the six months of truce should also be noted: increasing indiscipline aggravated by poverty (the picture of O'Malley's Tipperary Brigade given in contemporary records is not that which appears in his memoirs). Raids on barracks and post offices may have taken place with little reference to the issues of the Treaty.

What does seem clear is that feeling in the country at large was far more decisively in favour of the Treaty than in the committed republican atmosphere of the Dáil. Implicit recognition of this prompted de Valera's famous countering claim that he had only 'to examine my own heart and it told me straight off what the Irish people wanted'. Local studies of areas like Meath, however, show an overwhelming consensus in favour of something very different.

In many cases, personality clashes and the manoeuvrings of cliques probably dictated the side taken: while it would be tedious to detail individual cases, it is interesting that both Collins and de Valera ended up on the opposite side to that which might have been expected. Up to late 1921 Collins appeared impeccably extremist, telling American journalists that 'the same effort which would get us Dominion Home Rule will get us a republic', and rejecting any thought of Partition. Over the Treaty issue, however, he emerged as the supreme pragmatist, emphasizing the inevitability of compromise: 'It was the acceptance of the invitation [to negotiate] that formed the compromise.' His position was probably dictated by the IRB line, whose Supreme Council split eleven to four in favour of the Treaty: his subsequent tactic was to try and preserve unity while drafting a constitution for the new Free State that would be republican enough to reconcile the anti-Treaty party.

Unfortunately, this draft effectively negated the Treaty, and was rejected by the British. Collins was left desperately trying to prevent a full-scale split by suggesting bi-partisan agreements with the Irregulars, and offering to campaign on a rigged 'Pact' basis in the elections of 1922, putting up a panel of candidates in an agreed proportion, with a view to an eventual coalition government (and ensuring that political power remained monopolized by the Sinn Féin movement, whether pro- or anti-Treaty). This arrangement – which appalled British opinion – may have given a considerable advantage to the anti-Treaty side, and threatened to deny popular endorsement of the Treaty: Collins gave the impression of personally repudiating it before the election, but by and large it stuck. However, twice as many votes were cast for the Treaty as against it, though more votes were cast for independent parties than either; in only one contested constituency (Sligo–Mayo East) did the anti-Treatyites win a majority of the votes. Not a single anti-Treaty candidate headed the poll in any constituency. Collins's own position remained ambivalent; he continued to co-operate with Irregular units in operations against the authorities in Ulster; he probably arranged the assassination of Sir Henry Wilson in June 1922; and he was unprepared to precipitate confrontation between rival IRA units. There are persistent rumours that he was on his way to negotiate with anti-Treaty forces when he was killed in a Cork skirmish in August 1922. But by then, he was irretrievably trapped in what must have been an uncongenial, and unexpected, position.

Exactly the same could be said about de Valera on the other side. Before the Treaty he had appeared as the ingenious reconciler, infuriating Irish-American zealots by floating ideas such as Britain declaring a 'Monroe Doctrine' with a view to Ireland occupying a position analogous to Cuba; he was prepared to allow Ulster counties to opt out on an individual basis; as was pointed out in the Treaty debates, the formulae that he had suggested were nearly as far from 'the Rock of the Republic' as the Treaty itself. He fought, in the end, not to secure the republic, but for his own tortuous compromise of 'external association': a fact contemptuously noted by some of his more intransigent allies, especially in the IRA, many of whom opposed the Treaty on a basis of exalted separatism. De Valera's endorsement of the anti-Treaty side placed him in odd company: the argument that it was better to go on failing and being martyred, than to settle for anything less than a republic, was essentially alien to him. Like Collins, he was painted into a corner; it is hard not to think that the rivalry and antipathy between the two men had been a major cause in bringing this about.

But the Treaty issue made strange bedfellows, and placed anomalous arguments in their mouths. 'Free Staters' liked to accuse the anti-Treaty side of a contempt for democratic majorities; but when Kevin O'Higgins declared that a man who killed without a constitutional mandate from the people was a murderer, Liam Mellows,[xvi] reasonably

[xvi] Liam Mellows (1892–1922): born in Lancashire; reared in County Wexford; educated at Royal Hibernian Military School; clerk in Dublin, 1905; graduated from the Fianna and sworn into IRB, 1912; influenced by Connolly's socialism; founding member of Irish Volunteers, 1913; deported to England; returned for 1916 rising; escaped to USA; worked with Devoy on *Gaelic American*; agent for de Valera's tour

enough, interjected: 'Easter Week?' The ghosts of Pearse's rhetoric were hard to lay.

III
==

The civil war that followed in 1922–3 looms larger in Irish history than the 'Anglo-Irish' war, because it was both more traumatic and more influential. The result of the Anglo-Irish war, a twenty-six-county dominion within the Empire, was not greatly different to that which was coming into view by 1920 in any case. By contrast, the civil war created a caesura across Irish history, separating parties, interests and even families, and creating the rationale for political divisions that endured.

The vital immediate issue was the army split, between IRA 'Irregulars' and the 'Old IRA', who were soon incorporated into the new Free State army. The uneasy relationship between the IRA's authority and that of the Dáil, always problematical, now came into high relief; so did the localized and often autonomous basis of many IRA squadrons, especially in the south-west. As the government of the Free State took shape under Griffith and then Cosgrave, the army chief Richard Mulcahy[xvii] faced an implacable opposition from old comrades like Rory O'Connor,[xviii] Liam Mellows and Liam Lynch.[xix] A real

of USA, 1920; IRA Director of Purchases, 1921; Sinn Féin TD for Galway, 1921; opposed 1921 Treaty as a great coercion act and a betrayal of the republic; edited *Poblacht na hÉireann*; member of Four Courts garrison, June 1922; arrested, September 1922; executed, 8 December.

[xvii] Richard Mulcahy (1886–1971): born in Waterford; post-office clerk; joined the Irish Volunteers, 1913; fought in 1916 rising; interned until general amnesty, 1917; IRA Chief of Staff; MP for Clontarf Division, 1918, and TD for Dublin constituencies, 1922–43, and Tipperary, 1944–61; supported Treaty; General Officer Commanding of military forces of the Provisional Government, 1922–3; Minister of Defence, 1923–4; Chairman of Gaeltacht Commission, 1925–6; Senator, 1943–4; leader of Fine Gael, 1944–59; Minister of Education, 1948–51 and 1954–7.

[xviii] Rory O'Connor (1883–1922): born in Dublin; railway engineer in Canada, 1911–15; returned at request of the IRB; wounded in 1916 rising; interned; left the IRB, feeling that its policy of secrecy detracted from the possibility of promoting popular agitation; IRA Director of Engineering, 1919–21; rejected 1921 Treaty; led IRA Military Council; repudiated the authority of the Dáil, March 1922; took a leading part in establishing the republican garrison at the Four Courts, April 1922; surrendered, June 1922; executed 8 December 1922.

[xix] Liam Lynch (1893–1923): born in County Limerick; worked in a hardware

threat of social and military anarchy loomed; the recollections of irreconcilables like Ernie O'Malley and Francis Stuart[xx] express an utter commitment to the adversarial position, and a desire to fight to the end against any government at all.

The fact that both wings of the IRA were involved in protecting Catholic areas of Ulster against incursions by the 'security forces' of the new Belfast government provided distraction, and enforced procrastination in moving against Irregular detachments. But in Dublin the Free State army was faced from April 1922 by a defiant Irregular occupation of the Four Courts building. Their leaders refused to recognize the Provisional government and demanded effective control for the IRA. They were not, at this stage, working with de Valera, who was still negotiating the agreed electoral plan with Collins; it is likely that he was still anticipating an essentially political struggle over issues like the new constitution. However, in the circumstances this was rather a luxury. By late June a combination of tension in Dublin, pressure from London and Collins's abandonment of the joint IRA operations in Ulster brought matters to a head: the Four Courts were stormed by the Free State army, and central Dublin once again became a battleground.

A republican broad front evolved, incorporating political intransigents like de Valera as well as independent IRA units. Civil war spread over the country, involving areas that had been quiescent in 1919–21, and continued until the republican rump (grandiosely addressed by de Valera as the 'Legion of the Rearguard') dumped their arms in May 1923. There had been a horrific toll of deaths: about 800 from the Free State army, and far more republicans. The republican tactic had been to provoke destabilization by declaring the Free State government, courts and police illegal, and therefore legitimate targets: the policy of assassinating Dáil TDs and judges produced a breath-

business; reorganized Cork Volunteers, 1919; commanded an effective Brigade in Anglo-Irish war; member of IRA Supreme Council; influential opponent of 1921 Treaty; IRA Chief of Staff; established the IRA Executive, March 1922; resigned over seizure of the Four Courts but joined its garrison, June 1922; commanded first southern division of the Irregulars; sought to hold the 'Munster Republic'; issued 'orders of frightfulness' against Provisional government, November 1922; shot by Provisional government forces while preparing to come to terms with them, April 1923.

[xx] Henry Francis Montgomery Stuart (b. 1902): born in Australia of Ulster descent; reared in County Meath; educated at Rugby; married Iseult Gonne, daughter of Maud, 1920; joined the republicans in the civil war; imprisoned, August 1922–November 1923; *The Coloured Dome*, 1932, his third novel, marked his emergence as

takingly draconian reaction from the Provisional government. Summary executions without trial, on the basis of arbitrary reprisal, were carried out by ex-comrades; seventy-seven such executions were added to the litany of republican martyrs, and thousands of imprisonments created abiding bitterness.

The Free State government had been confronted with a declared policy of shooting on sight elected TDs, legal officials, ex-British army members, and even sympathetic journalists: an extreme reaction was inevitable. The casual basis of reprisal executions, not to mention the sadistic horrors carried out under some local commands (notably in Kerry), still strike an appalled reaction. But it is important to note that public opinion did not repudiate such policies; the Free State government was strongly supported, even at its most coercive, because it was 'Irish'.

Equally striking is the *kind* of order that was being imposed; for the threat posed by the civil war was not only military. Since the 1914–18 war, agrarian unrest had been simmering; the curtailment of land-purchase machinery had led to local agitation, and the conditions of the Anglo-Irish war had encouraged a strong 'back to the land' movement for land redistribution, notable in areas like Meath as well as the congenitally 'congested' west. The government's ban on fairs and markets also created great rural resentment. Much land was, in fact, peaceably purchased and redistributed from 1919 on; but on the fringe of the movement, an older intransigence broke through. The possessors of rural property, essentially the strong-farming element, reacted by committing themselves to the Irish Farmers' Union, a pressure-group that exerted an increasing influence on the direction of policy under the new dispensation. By March 1920 Irish Farmers' Union leaders were considering an armed 'Farmers' Freedom Force' to suppress strikes and act against 'Labour, socialism and Bolshevism'. And this was symptomatic of the kind of interests that would come to the fore under the Free State, and whose influence was entrenched by the outcome of the civil war.

Already, labour organization had, in general terms, been subsumed into the Sinn Féin nationalist image: a process initially helped by the fact that both movements had discovered a common enemy in the

an exciting talent, but subsequent work disappointed; lectured at Berlin University, 1940–45; made broadcasts to Ireland calling for her continued neutrality, 1942–4; detained, November 1945–July 1946; his German experiences infuse *The Pillar of Cloud*, 1948, and *Redemption*, 1949; a twenty-two-year silence preceded an oblique autobiography, *Black List, Section H*, 1971, and several other novels.

Irish Parliamentary Party. In the end, however, Sinn Féin politicians, despite the organization's radical pedigree, would turn out just as antipathetic to the claims of labour. They were further alarmed by the fact that 'in every major industrial sector Irish workers were abnormally likely to go on strike during 1914–18';[15] industrial militancy, apparently defused in 1914, was recovering. This was indicated by the spectacular expansion of the Irish Transport and General Workers' Union, which seemed in 1918–19 to be becoming the One Big Union of the pre-war dream, while pursuing strike policies with more rigour and effectiveness than in its pure syndicalist days. It continued to orchestrate demonstrations in support of the nationalist cause – notably, a general shut-down in support of republican hunger strikers in mid-April 1920. But by 1921 the cause of labour was threatening in many areas to displace that of the republic. The issue of agricultural wages had come up in several places; a fashion for Russia could apparently be reconciled with nationalism by comparing communism to supposed ancient Gaelic forms of social organization, but the idea of rural Irish Soviets was not an entirely welcome one to local leaders. There was a large-scale farm labourers' strike in Meath during the summer of 1919, a year of continued labour unrest, with returned servicemen flooding the market, and persistent threats of wage cuts. Similar activity led to major confrontations with the Irish Farmers' Union in Waterford during 1921–3; strikes and sit-ins increasingly adopted the ominous name of 'Soviet' (famously in Limerick in 1919, but elsewhere, too, in 1920–21).

Before the civil war, in fact, organized labour politics seemed poised for a breakthrough. In the urban local elections of 1920, Labour won majorities in six councils. A local study of Meath shows further notable electoral success in 1922, which saw communist candidates running on platforms of ignoring the national question and highlighting the social and economic issues raised by post-war recession – including the perennial, and dreaded, question of dividing up grasslands. In the Waterford–East Tipperary constituency, by far the largest number of votes (and 31.3 per cent of the poll) was captured by Labour candidates. In the country at large, Labour did spectacularly well in 1922, returning seventeen of its eighteen candidates, and winning 21.4 per cent of the total votes cast: altogether, the Labour Party won more votes than the anti-Treatyites. Their arrival on the scene was not welcomed by the Sinn Féin candidates, one of whom remarked perplexedly that he had never heard of his Labour opponent before the election: 'he had never met him in prison, nor in an ambush'.[16]

On both sides of the Treaty divide, the reaction of conservative rural nationalism was predictably hostile to the Labour renaissance. By 1922 I R A Volunteers were being used in some areas as strike-breakers: recovering cattle driven away by rebellious labourers in Meath, protecting non-unionized workers from attack, and acting as arbitrators for *lower* farm wages in Clare. A violently disillusioned Peadar O'Donnell[xxi] later recalled I R A men being used in the west 'to patrol estate walls, enforce decrees for rent, arrest and even order out of the country leaders of local land agitations'.[17] A long and bitter farm strike convulsed County Waterford during the second half of 1923 – won by the farmers with full-scale military backing from the Free State army. Under the new regime, cattle-drivers and 'back to the land' agitators were controlled as vigorously as I R A Irregulars. In this, as in much else, the leaders of the new state carried through what Fitzpatrick has called the 'thick strand of continuity' already apparent in political leadership at local level, connecting Free Staters back through Sinn Féin to the much-denounced cabals of the Irish Parliamentary Party. Yet again, nationalist politics short-circuited class politics. But the unwritten history of the events from 1916 to 1923 must include the postwar challenge of Irish labour – defused not only by the effects of recession and emigration but also by the polarization of nationalist politics. In this arena exalted leaders first fought out a brutal duel over a form of words, and then constructed a new state around preoccupations that resolutely ignored even the vague social and economic desiderata once outlined for Pearse's visionary republic.

[xxi] Peadar O'Donnell (1893–1986): born in County Donegal; teacher; organizer of Irish Transport and General Workers' Union, 1916; joined I R A, 1918; active in Donegal Brigade, 1921; took republican side in civil war; imprisoned, July 1922–4; *Storm*, 1925; jailed in land annuities agitation, 1927; *Islanders*, 1928; *Adrigoole*, 1929; presided over European Peasant Congress, Berlin, 1930; founder member of Saor Éire, 1931; left I R A, suspecting it of fascist leanings, and founded Republican Congress, 1935; went to Spain and organized the Connolly Column, December 1936. Editor of *An Phoblacht*, 1931–4, and the *Bell*, 1946–54. Also wrote *The Knife*, 1930; *The Gates Flew Open*, 1932; two volumes of autobiography, *Salud! An Irishman in Spain* and *There Will Be Another Day*, 1963; *Proud Island*, 1975.

CHAPTER TWENTY-ONE

===

IN A FREE STATE

I

===

THE RIGOROUS CONSERVATISM of the Irish Free State has become a cliché; what matters most about the atmosphere and mentality of twenty-six-county Ireland in the 1920s is that the dominant pre-occupation of the regime was self-definition against Britain – cultural and political. Other priorities were consciously demoted. British police and military forces were rapidly evacuated; by May 1922 all were gone except the Dublin garrison. A continuing British presence remained in that 'the Crown' was typified by the institution of a Governor-General. But this figure was an Irishman, and both government rhetoric and the constitution itself continually emphasized that the roots of legitimacy lay in popular sovereignty and allegiance to the Treaty.[i]

At the same time, unease persisted about the imperial connection, which provided the republican opposition with a convenient and much-employed debating point; from the early 1920s, Free State representatives followed the policy of adapting these links in order to loosen the bonds of colonial connection. The word 'colonial' itself raised difficulties in the literal, let alone the psychological, sense. Relations with Britain had been formed by the Treaty, supposedly amounting to an international agreement between equals; much was made of the Free State's right to individual representation (and an independent policy line) at League of Nations assemblies; support was anxiously canvassed from other dominions, with a view to extending the autonomy of all. This was achieved by the Statute of Westminster

---

[i] The constitution was reviled by republicans for having sold the republic: but the chief authority on it defined it as an 'essentially republican Constitution on most advanced Continental lines' (Leo Kohn, *The Constitution of the Irish Free State*, London, 1932, p. 80). It emphasized democratic authority and fundamental rights, and references to monarchical authority and Commonwealth membership were perfunctory. At least one contemporary constitutional lawyer thought it was flexible enough to lead to a republic.

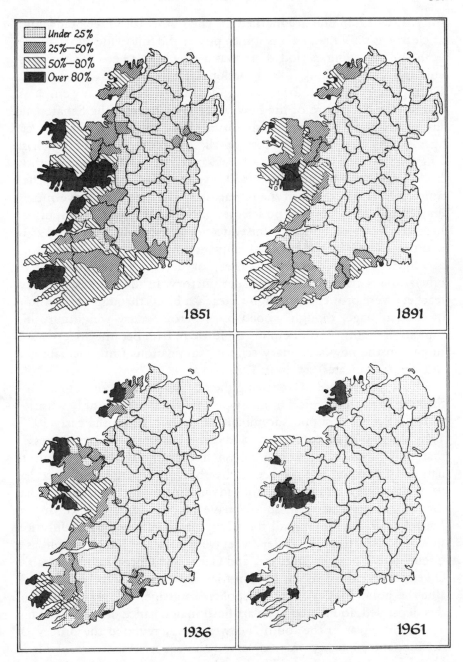

Under 25%	
25%—50%	
50%—80%	
Over 80%	

1851

1891

1936

1961

Map 14: *Irish speakers 1851–1961.*

Source: R. Dudley Edwards, *An Atlas of Irish History.* (Based on maps in B. Ó Cúiv, editor, *A View of the Irish Language.*)

in 1931, which in practice marked the end of the 'Irish Free State' ethos as clearly as de Valera's accession to power the following year.

In the preceding period there was a deeply felt need for the presentation of something like a national philosophy in government. During the 1920s, therefore, the regime necessarily laid heavy emphasis on the 'Gaelic' nature of the new state. The Dáil and the Senate paid lip-service to 'traditional' Irish forms; Irish cultural activities were aggressively proselytized; most of all, the prosecution of the Irish language became the necessary bench-mark of an independent ethos. In 1911 those able to speak Irish at all, let alone speaking it regularly, had numbered 17.6 per cent of the population. The Free State government embarked upon ambitious policies to spread the language. Compulsory measures had been built into the educational system by the early 1930s, and proficiency in 'the national language' was technically mandatory as a qualification for a wide variety of state employments. But its official use remained obstinately perfunctory. In the schools very few teachers were proficient enough to teach subjects through the medium of the language, though wooed by generous salary-weightings and capitation grants. As a discipline on its own, Irish became an 'essential' subject in the new secondary school examinations (Intermediate and Leaving Certificates) set up in 1924.

Outside the schools, Gaelicizing the new state was a preoccupation – the kind of process typical of many post-colonial states, highly sensitive to the influence of a once-dominant neighbour. From the early 1920s a series of important conferences and commissions on education stressed that the chief aim of teaching Irish history should be 'to inculcate national pride and self-respect ... by showing that the Irish race has fulfilled a great mission in the advancement of civilization'; that 'English authors, as such, should have just the limited place due to English literature among all the European literatures'; that education should be structured 'in order to revive the ancient life of Ireland as a Gaelic state, Gaelic in language, and Gaelic and Christian in its ideals'.[1] Given the events of recent Irish history, this was only to be expected. But the policy of reviving the spoken language, on which much of this depended, foundered. The artificial maintenance of Irish-speaking 'Gaeltacht' areas in the south and west never reversed the process of decline, and in many ways deserved the excoriating satire of Flann O'Brien's[ii] *An Béal Bocht* (*The Poor Mouth*); while investigations and

[ii] Brian O'Nolan [Flann O'Brien] (1911–66): born in County Tyrone; educated at University College, Dublin; civil servant, 1932–53; *At Swim Two Birds*, 1938; wrote

reports from the later 1920s gloomily admitted that giving the language an official status and positively discriminating on behalf of Irish-speaking applicants for official positions were not creating an Irish-speaking nation.

This obsession with enforcing public modes of 'Irishness' owed much to the Free State regime's sensitivity about accusations that they had sold out on a separatist republic; it was, in a sense, a continuing result of the civil war. Another, more obvious, result of the recent conflict was a preoccupation with maintaining social and political stability – effectively achieved, though at some considerable cost. In its early years, this was facilitated by the fact that the pro-Treaty party, Cumann na nGaedheal, effectively ran a one-party state – de Valera's republicans staying aloof until 1927, and independent parties remaining in a small minority. Though 'liberal' rights were ostensibly guarded in the constitution, the new government was certainly authoritarian; the regime showed its derivation from latter-day Sinn Féin, never unduly fastidious about democratic procedure. Sinn Féin's air of innovation and experiment, however, was conspicuously absent. As the new power elite settled into place, a covert continuity with the values and priorities of the old Irish Parliamentary Party was, to some eyes at least, more and more evident.

Certainly, the new regime believed in 'strong', not to say ruthless, government. Any ideas of a social-welfare utopia were rigorously dismissed; the old-age pension was actually cut by a shilling a week in 1924. Unemployment and other labour benefits remained minimal, pegged at pre-1922 levels. These spartan measures reflected an adjustment to the realities of fiscal autonomy: the resources of the Free State could come nowhere near funding social expenditure at the levels set by imperial governments since the Liberal administration of 1906. Given the age structure of the Irish population, old-age pensions were an extremely heavy drain on public funds: £3,300,000 out of £20,000,000 state expenditure in 1922–3. But the political effect of such a step was so enormous that it could probably only have been weathered by a government faced by a conveniently abstentionist 'opposition'. Irish poverty, especially in remote rural districts, remained exceptional by contemporary Western standards; the problems of the 'congested districts' obstinately endured. The most notorious statement

an *Irish Times* column as Myles na gCopaleen, 1940–66; *An Béal Bocht*, 1941; *The Hard Life*, 1961; *The Dalkey Archive*, 1964; *The Third Policeman* appeared posthumously. Also *Faustus Kelly*, a satire on Irish politics, for the Abbey, 1943. Uniquely successful in persuading the Irish that they took themselves too seriously.

by a Free State minister remained that of Patrick McGilligan:[iii] 'People may have to die in the country, and die through starvation.' 'Independence' had its price.

Here, as in other areas of Free State government, religious influence was an important factor: the Church was strongly committed to retaining its dominant influence in matters of health and welfare, as in education. Also important was labour's political paralysis: the Irish Transport and General Worker's Union was split in the early 1920s. Larkin became marginalized, and the predominant influence under William O'Brien[iv] was conservative. The 'radical' wing in Irish politics tended to be commandeered by purist republicans, especially after de Valera's followers entered the 'slightly constitutional' sphere in 1926; where a left-wing analysis was adopted by a group like Saor Éire in 1931, it tended to be obscured by gut-level republicanism, necessitating some awkward ideological sleight-of-hand where the Ulster working class were concerned. Under the cautious rule of William Cosgrave,[v]

[iii] Patrick McGilligan (1889–1979): born in County Londonderry; educated at Clongowes and University College, Dublin; joined Sinn Féin, 1910; Secretary to O'Higgins in first Dáil; supported 1921 Treaty; TD for National University of Ireland, 1923–37, and various Dublin constituencies from 1937 to 1965; member of delegation that negotiated the shelving of the Boundary Commission, 1925; co-drafted 1931 Statute of Westminster; Minister of Industry and Commerce, 1924–32; Minister for External Affairs, 1927–32; Minister of Finance, 1948–51; Attorney-General, 1954–7.

[iv] William O'Brien (1881–1968): born in County Cork; joined Irish Socialist Republican Party, 1898, becoming its Treasurer; co-founded Irish Transport and General Workers' Union, 1909; Secretary of Lock-out Committee, 1913; attended IRB conference to discuss the possibility of a rising, 1914; interned, 1916; General Secretary of Labour Party, co-drafting the Democratic Programme, 1919; gave 'unofficial' support to IRA in Anglo-Irish war; interned, 1920; Labour TD for Dublin South, 1922–3, and Tipperary, 1927 and 1932–8; General Secretary of Irish Transport and General Workers' Union, 1923–46, resisting Larkin's attempts to gain control, 1923 and 1943; Financial Secretary to Labour Party, 1931–9, and Chairman of its Administrative Council, 1939–41. President of Irish Trades Union Congress, 1913, 1918, 1925 and 1941.

[v] William Thomas Cosgrave (1880–1965): born in Dublin; educated at Christian Brothers school; attended first Sinn Féin Convention, 1905; member of Irish Volunteers, 1913; fought in 1916; imprisoned, 1916–17; Treasurer of Sinn Féin; Sinn Féin MP for Kilkenny, 1917–18; detained in German Plot arrests, 1918; Minister for Local Government in first Dáil; supported the 1921 Treaty; President of second Dáil and Chairman of Provisional government after the deaths of Griffith and Collins, August 1922; President of Executive Council, 1922–32; also Minister of Finance, 1922–3, agreeing to pay land annuities to the British Treasury (a fact revealed in 1932); founded Cumann na nGaedheal, 1923, which he led until the emergence of Fine Gael; joint Vice-President of Fine Gael, 1933–5, and leader, 1935–44; retired, 1944.

the discourse of Free State politics remained dogmatically buried in the issues over which the civil war had been fought, and practically obsessed by steering a conservative, rural, strongly *petit bourgeois* state through the rocks and shoals raised by fiscal autonomy and international economic instability.

How far was it influenced by the currents of thought affecting other irredentist states? Though there was much admiration in Ireland during the 1920s for Mussolini's Italy, any steps towards corporatism were essentially halting. A cautious clause in the constitution laid some claim to state ownership in natural resources; but O'Higgins lightly referred to Pearse's social ideas as 'largely poetry', and economic notions within the government were too varied to amount to anything like a coherent, let alone radical, framework: The innovative idea of 'semi-state' corporations set up with public money to run certain areas of the economy evolved rather than being invented; a failure of public investment often impelled the government into promoting companies (like the Agricultural Credit Corporation) more comprehensively than originally intended. Where state intervention had a notable effect was in various forms of energy exploitation from the mid-1920s, under the state-controlled Electricity Supply Board: the hydro-electric scheme to harness the River Shannon, carried out with the help of German expertise, became a show-piece of innovation. But it remained exceptional.

The framework of government, as well as its personnel, tended to militate against radical departures. It was conducted by means of carefully defined departments and a powerful, professional civil service, with a strong sense of its independence. Departments were administratively centralized and rigorously controlled. The *corps d'élite* was the authoritative and conservative Department of Finance,[2] which was strongly influenced by the sweeping reforms of the Treasury carried out under the previous dispensation in 1919–20. It also embodied the traditions of the brilliant Collins, whose achievements as Minister of Finance for the Dáil from 1919 were as legendary, and nearly as important, as his military exploits: here as elsewhere he had combined meticulousness and panache.[vi] The Department's spectacular success in

[vi] The government had responded in kind. The flippant diary of one Dublin Castle Under-Secretary describes an incident of late October 1920 featuring Ormonde Winter, head of British Intelligence at the Castle: 'O. came in this evening in a chestnut moustache and wig, trench coat, flannel trousers and bowler hat – looking the most complete swine I ever saw – he had been pinching M C's "war-chest" from the Munster and Leinster Bank – quite illegally I expect – brought in about

floating the first National Loan in 1923 established its position. Senior Finance civil servants continued to take extremely far-ranging decisions, often in circumstances of effective autonomy; while the Department's primacy within government was acknowledged by the practice of submitting bills originating from other departments to Finance for approval before final drafting. Local government, while reorganized to allow for poor relief on a county basis, was not decentralized; ministerial initiatives, and the increasing tendency to appoint professional administrators (like the 'City Managers'), gave it a particular stamp. In some areas, the continuities from the days of British rule were notable: in the early days of the Free State, 98 per cent of civil service personnel had served in the pre-1922 system, and as late as 1934 the proportion was still as high as 45 per cent.

The legal system owed less to the Dáil courts than to the status quo under the Union, creating from 1924 a recognizable hierarchy (district courts, circuit courts, a high court, a court of criminal appeal, a supreme court); for all the rhetoric of cultural zealotry there was not much sign of reviving ancient Brehon practice. The ease and frequency of divorce under the Gaelic social order may have provided one reason, since on that issue the Free State establishment, political and legal, demonstrated its ostentatious commitment to the norms of Catholic social teaching. In this, as in civil administration, the framework of a separate dominion with a recognizably 'Irish' stamp was created; the evolution of dominion autonomy within the Commonwealth would advance the process further on a constitutional level. But, given British proximity and Irish history, how far could 'independence' really be taken?

On the economic level, the logic of the British connection continued; 98 per cent of Irish exports went to the U K in 1924. Equally unchanged was the prevalence, and the favoured position, of the Irish pasture farmer, linked closely to the British market. Partition had skewed the agricultural–industrial balance in both the new states: the proportion of Northern Ireland's population employed in industry was artificially high, while in 1926 more than half of the gainfully employed population in the Free State were directly engaged in agriculture. And the general trends of the post-Famine Irish economy continued – consolidation of medium-sized farms, decline of tillage, and the redistribution process of land purchase. Under the Land Commission, set up in 1923, 450,000 acres were distributed to 24,000 families by 1932.

£4,000. £15,000 more to come.' (Quoted in Ronan Fanning, *The Irish Department of Finance 1922–58*, Dublin, 1978, p. 24)

Agricultural initiatives were taken by the state in areas like livestock-breeding and poultry farming, but agricultural productivity remained abysmally low (half that of Denmark). Cattle-raising remained dominant: so did the interests of the strong farmer, further entrenched by the establishment of the state-sponsored Agricultural Credit Corporation in 1927, advancing working capital to farmers with their properties as security. Politically and economically, the interests of the farming community were seen as vital: maximizing the farmers' incomes was defined as the necessary pre-condition of general prosperity. Significantly, one of the arguments against tariffs produced by the Fiscal Inquiry Committee in 1923 was that they would increase agricultural labourers' wages.

What did not develop, despite the Sinn Féin pedigree of the government's theorists, was a coherent policy of protectionism. Some tariffs were imposed on imported goods, to encourage home production; no overall fiscal readjustments were made with a view to developing new industries. Output figures for industry stayed unspectacular; industrial exports actually declined, though exports overall increased to a peak of £47,300,000 in 1929, when they paid for 77 per cent of imports. But public probity and, yet again, political stability were seen as indissolubly linked to conservative finance; economic nationalism was far too risky a horse to back. A balance of payments crisis was avoided through substantial remittances from emigrants; it should also be stressed that the state began its life with considerable overseas assets. And in yet another way, the heritage of the civil war made itself felt: the direct drain (until 1927) of defence and compensation costs arising from the military efforts of 1922–4, when 30 per cent of all national expenditure had gone to 'defence'. By 1929 it could be brought down to £1,500,000. By then, too, the political advantages of cautious finance were evident: unlike many European countries, Ireland had avoided hyperinflation and maintained an excellent international credit rating.

Thus the Free State government remained cautious about encouraging credit expansion, or funding employment schemes; consequently it did nothing to counter emigration trends, in many ways exacerbated by the priority given to the maintenance of traditional farming structures. Social expenditure remained a low priority, even when defence costs could be lowered; old-age pension payments absorbed much of the money available. Any revenue balance went to keep down income tax, not to build up social services. Much of what had made pre-war Ireland a country to leave was equally true of the new dominion.

In many ways, however, to indict the new regime for cautiousness in social and economic policies is to ignore the constant threat, at least in its early years, of political, or military, anarchy. It was, after all, a post-revolutionary as well as a post-colonial state. An unarmed police force had been created *de novo*: the Garda Síochána (Civic Guard), who rapidly achieved notably good relations with the local community. But the old anomaly of the distribution of power between Dáil and IRA remained, in a different form, and precipitated an army crisis in 1924. The IRA elements who had supported the Treaty had become the Free State army; but the ethos of independent Volunteering (and possibly IRB allegiance) remained powerful. Partly for this reason, some shadowy government squads like the Citizens' Defence Force had been detailed to proceed against Irregulars when the reliability of the army was not considered absolute. The worried Attorney-General of the Free State declared in 1923 that the state was threatened by 'an almost independent army executive', possessing its own 'organization and powers, the direction and control of its policy, the mode and authority of its appointments'; the Minister of Defence was seen as unwilling to press his authority to the explosive point where it might be defined.

In 1924 this point was none the less reached. Old IRA men within the army had remained only edgily reconciled to the post-Treaty world, especially after the death of the charismatic and authoritative Collins. Further resentment at rapid demobilization, as well as pay cuts and removal of perquisites, produced a challenge that became a threatened mutiny against the Army Council. The real issues may well have been jobs and promotion; but it is significant that the unpopular Army Council was tagged as an IRB clique that had forced through the Treaty, and that the mutineers called for a return to Collins's tactic of merely using the Treaty as a stepping-stone towards the republic. 'We are all still revolutionaries,' claimed the Old IRA element who demanded the abolition of the Army Council, 'because our freedom is not yet complete.'

The challenge was defused by O'Higgins's rapid action, giving special powers over the army to the Garda Commissioner Eoin O'Duffy[vii] and enforcing the resignation of Mulcahy and others. In a

[vii] Eoin O'Duffy (1892–1944): born in County Monaghan; engineer; joined IRA, 1917; fought in Anglo-Irish war; supported the 1921 Treaty; TD for Monaghan, 1921–2; IRA Director of Organization, 1921, and Chief of Staff, 1922; first Commander of Garda Síochána, 1922; dismissed by de Valera, 1933; became leader of the Army Comrades Association (the Blueshirts), July 1933; first President of Fine Gael, Sep-

sense, there had been three parties to the struggle: the government's strong men, the dissatisfied Old I R A element in the army (the so-called IR A Organization) and those government members sympathetic to the latter, who did not want to see them go too far, but had been trained in the same school. O'Higgins, characteristically, moved ruthlessly against the last two elements, and used the opportunity to assert the principle of civil over military supremacy in the government as well as army circles. The crisis also indicated an attempt to reclaim the IR B as custodian of the visionary and uncorrupted republic, and to tear it away from its commitment to validating the Treaty; the IR A Organization's secret statement of purpose was significant. They declared an intention to expand their membership until powerful enough 'to demand a strong voice in army policy, with a view of securing complete independence when a suitable occasion arose. It was also decided that the members of the new organization would make every effort to get control of the vital sections of the army and oust those undesirable persons who were and are holding those positions.'[3] This was revolution within the revolution with a vengeance. At least one of Cosgrave's ministers was intimately and sympathetically involved; the episode indicates that the much-reviled Free State government was threatened even from within by those who still yearned for the simplicities of pure-milk republicanism. And simultaneously, of course, they continued to be more overtly threatened by similar elements outside their ranks.

De Valera had embarked, from 1925, on a characteristically tortuous course of adapting his position *vis-à-vis* the institutions of the Free State; but some of his followers among the IR A Irregulars (now generally called the IR A or, almost interchangeably, Sinn Féin) continued an episodically violent policy of attacks on police stations and assassinations of jury members and politicians, with Kevin O'Higgins their most celebrated target in 1927. By 1926 de Valera had convinced enough of his followers in Sinn Féin (as well as himself) that the time had come for a constitutional initiative: he founded a new party, Fianna Fáil,[viii] with the declared intention of entering the Dáil. Though this severed him from the rump of Sinn Féin/IR A irreconcilables, it enabled him to contest the 1927 election: dissatisfaction with five years

tember 1933; resigned, September 1934; launched National Corporate Party, June 1935; led pro-Franco Irish Brigade to Spain, 1936–7; retired from public politics. Afforded a state funeral.

[viii] Literally, 'Soldiers of Destiny': Inis Fáil, the Island of Destiny, being a poetic name for Ireland, and the 'Fianna' a mythological band of warrior-comrades.

of Free State rigour, as well as his own aura of austere and incorruptible authority, helped bring him forty-four seats to the government's forty-seven. The outstanding problem, before entering the Dáil, was inevitably the Oath of Fidelity: Fianna Fáil's manoeuvrings about this were threatening to tip politics into a state of chronic instability when O'Higgins's assassination gave the government the opportunity to pass emergency legislation enforcing the Oath as a *sine qua non* of entering constitutional politics on any level. Fianna Fáil abruptly gave way and took the Oath, while declaring that they viewed it as an empty formula.[ix] For the first time the government party was faced with a real opposition.

The opposition, moreover, succeeded to power in 1932. By a complex convolution, de Valera had reached the position that, logically, he ought to have occupied exactly ten years before: constitutional opposition to the Treaty, relying on the flexibility of constitutional forms (imperial as well as Irish) to enable a reconstruction of Ireland's status *vis-à-vis* the Empire. In the intervening decade, however, his flirtation with the armed and dictatorial powers of intransigent republicanism had conjured up demons that would have a lasting effect. And so, in their different ways, would the policies and priorities dictated by the ethos of the Irish Free State.

II

In Ulster, too, the patterns set in the 1920s cast long shadows to the future. Partition was now a fact, though its British architects had expected it to be temporary, and built in several unrealistic inducements to future unity. The Anglo-Irish war had not, generally, been fought in the north-east; but 1920–22 had seen a violent reaction there, producing large-scale sectarian attacks on Catholic communities. As violence spread to the shipyards and other workplaces, IRA activity escalated; more Catholics than Protestants were killed, but in some areas the confrontation resembled civil war rather than pogrom. In Belfast 455 people were killed, and an estimated 1,766 wounded.

From 1922 the reaction of the Ulster state was to turn in on itself and contain such violence by its own methods – though not immedi-

---

[ix] A solution forecast five years before, appositely enough by the Professor of Metaphysics of University College, Dublin.

ately. The terms of the abortive Craig–Collins pact of 30 March 1922 are interesting in showing what might have been – and how far Northern Ireland was then prepared to go.* Craig's proposal to replace the Council of Ireland with joint meetings of both Cabinets indicates the sort of co-operation technically possible within the Commonwealth framework, which would become out of the question when the Free State converted itself to a republic. But this initiative (especially the idea of a half-Catholic police force) provoked the predictable Ulster Unionist backlash, with attacks on Belfast Catholics. These were *not* investigated by a joint commission, as arranged under the pact, which therefore broke down in recriminations.

Thus Northern Ireland remained a *fait accompli*, its origins indelibly marked by internal violence. The Boundary Commission promised by the Treaty deliberated through 1925, ended in fiasco, and left the border as it was. This was partly due to misunderstanding of his role by Eoin MacNeill, the Free State representative, but it is unlikely that it would have produced any major change. The Free State government went into it no longer expecting anything that could bring about unity; Cosgrave's ideas apparently stopped at some reorganization of boundaries, and alterations that would allow the Catholic minority into the structure of the Northern Ireland state. Craig, for his part, received assurances from sympathizers in the British government that all the Commission would do was produce minor readjustments. The whole enterprise was approached on the basis of Northern Ireland existing *de facto*; the Chairman, who favoured the Ulster line, indicated that the onus of proof lay with those wanting any change in the 1920 arrangements.

The final agreement not only left the existent border recognized by the Free State, but effectively removed the functions theoretically exercised by the Council of Ireland and waived some debts due from the Free State to the British Exchequer under Article 5 of the Treaty. The rather disingenuous argument was advanced that this would increase the Free State's prosperity and therefore make unity more attractive. But in the eyes of Ulster nationalists, it only exacerbated the impression of a corrupt sell-out. They were now, more than ever, a marooned minority.

Certain structures continued to operate across the border (the Irish

---

*It provided for meetings to discuss unity, or failing that, the boundary; the reinstatement of expelled workers in Northern Ireland; the release of prisoners; a weighted committee of Protestants and Catholics to investigate outrages; and a special police force, half Catholics and half Protestants, for mixed districts of Belfast.

Trades Union Congress, the banks, sporting organizations); but the 1920 Act had created an enclave whose two-thirds majority, and whose governing class, representing only that majority, remained obsessively conscious of the need to proclaim their British connection. The tiny parliament was ensconced from 1932 in the grandiose shell of Stormont; executive power for local issues was exercised by a one-party 'Cabinet' of Unionists, though the sovereign and his representative Governor-General were the technical rulers. Because of the over-weighted nature of the state, there was no alternative government-in-waiting, if a Unionist Cabinet resigned; thus London never wanted to precipitate such a crisis by interfering in legislation. This gave free rein to the Unionist conception of the state as representing something *engagé*, embattled against irredentism outside and traitors within. Thus security, for instance, could not, in their view, be 'neutral'. If elements within the bourgeois leadership of Unionism were occasionally dis-posed to conciliate the minority, they were invariably dragged back into line by their grass-roots; a continuing pattern in Ulster political history.

Northern Ireland also sent twelve MPs to Westminster to vote on imperial and external concerns; the Stormont parliament could neither repeal nor alter Westminster statutes. But attitudes to central govern-ment remained problematical. A complicated and argumentative relationship developed over revenue and expenditure.[4] Financial difficulties existed from the beginning, compounded by deepening industrial depression almost from the foundation of the state. By 1925 arrangements were reorganized to ensure that Northern Ireland's expenditure, especially in social welfare, would exercise a prior claim on revenue, above any contribution to the imperial Exchequer. With soaring unemployment, this was the beginning of a running sore. The 'imperial contribution' to be levied for army and navy, servicing the national debt, and so on, dwindled from £8,000,000 per annum to a few thousands by the mid-1930s. The scenario that quickly evolved was a nearly bankrupt Northern Ireland constantly making begging expeditions to the British Treasury: a far cry from the position envis-aged in 1920.

The central state apparatus concerned itself very little with what was done in its truculent and idiosyncratic offshoot. Northern Ireland's local government structures adhered to the English model, but the property franchise weighted representation heavily in favour of the prosperous Protestant community (as, indeed, did the plural business votes they enjoyed for Stormont elections). The abolition of proportional representation for local elections in 1922 entrenched their position still further; proportional representation was also abolished for parliamentary elections in 1929, making dramatic changes in areas like Fermanagh, though the official strategy behind the step had been to marginalize independent Unionist and labour representatives rather than nationalists. Moreover, electoral boundaries in local constituencies were carefully engineered. Belfast's representatives in Stormont went up to sixteen in 1921; but, as in the days when it had been four, only one was a nationalist. And this was emblematic.

The unattractive picture of the statelet was given further prominence by its reliance on draconian special-powers legislation, brought together in a permanent Act in 1933. An armed Special Constabulary was formed, to contain the endemic sectarian violence and impose order on mixed areas. In 1922, 232 people were killed, 1,000 wounded and property worth £3,000,000 destroyed. Given that the notorious 'B-specials' absorbed not only the remnants of the Ulster Volunteer Force, but also unsavoury murder gangs like the United Protestant League, the results were predictable.

Catholic alienation became institutionalized. Their permanent minority status was reflected in the hopelessly small number of nationalist MPs elected, usually abstaining from taking their seats. The new regime was also boycotted in terms of education, leaving the Unionist government free to Protestantize the secular establishment preferred by Whitehall and set up in 1923. Attempts to enforce a non-sectarian principle were fought down by powerful Protestant pressure-groups – though it should be said that both Catholic *and* Protestant opinion were overwhelmingly in favour of the necessity of denominationally controlled education, and continued to be. On this and other levels, a religiously divided society settled into stasis. The immovable (and, in terms of personnel, almost unchanging) Unionist government rested on the formidable class alliance of the 'Protestant people'; Orangeism flourished; labour politics ossified, with trade unions looking to Britain or, occasionally, to the Free State.

The most detailed treatment of the Northern Ireland administration in these years presents the record as 'an argument against devolution'.[5] Certainly few Ulster Catholics would disagree. Their influence was, in practical terms, denied legitimacy. The proportion of Catholics in the Northern Ireland civil service, already small, continued to decline through the 1920s; there are endless unedifying examples of outlandish paranoia, flourishing in the hot-house imagination of the Unionist establishment. One may suffice: Sir Richard Dawson Bates, Minister for Home Affairs, refusing to use the telephone for any important business in 1934, having learned 'with a great deal of surprise, that a Roman Catholic telephonist has been appointed to Stormont'. The telephonist did not last.

This kind of gesture was, of course, conditioned by a public audience that expected constant proofs of probity on the part of its leaders: 'not an inch' must be yielded. And the pattern was reinforced by perceived threats from the South. Devlin, as leader of Ulster nationalists in the late 1920s, began a policy of cautious *rapprochement* by encouraging participation in Stormont; but this was negated by the effect of triumphalist nationalism from Dublin under the de Valera dispensation. In the Free State, nationalist probity could be cheaply demonstrated by rhetorical claims on the North; the realistic arguments of those actually born there, like Ernest Blythe, cut no ice against tactics like the boycott of Belfast goods instituted from Dublin in 1920–22. Ulster traditions, let alone Ulster's sense of separateness, were seen as officially illegitimate: while few pressed republican logic to the point of suggesting mass expulsion of Unionists from Northern Ireland, such suggestions were made.[6] Ulster was invariably described by Southern politicians in terms of its ancient Gaelic identity, from the Red Branch sagas to the O'Neill wars, rather than its centuries of Protestantization and industrialization. The views of the highly influential Professor Timothy Corcoran, a power behind the government's education and Gaelicization policies as well as a constant contributor to the extremist *Catholic Bulletin*, were reflected in that journal's editorial columns, in terms that gave Ulster Unionists every excuse for paranoia:

> The Irish nation is the Gaelic nation; its language and literature is the Gaelic language; its history is the history of the Gael. All other elements have no place in Irish national life, literature and tradition, save as far as they are assimilated into the very substance of Gaelic speech, life and thought. The Irish nation is not a racial synthesis at all; synthesis is not a vital process, and only what is vital is admissible in analogies bearing on the nature of the living Irish nation, speech, literature and tradition. We are not a national conglomerate, nor a national patchwork specimen; the poetry or life of what Aodh de Blacam calls Belfast can only be Irish by being assimilated by Gaelic literature into Gaelic literature.[7]

In fact, the representativeness of the *Bulletin* may reasonably be questioned; and the pragmatic political line taken by the Free State implicitly contradicted this ideology. As already mentioned, at the conclusion of the Boundary Commission the Irish government accepted the border. Cosgrave refused to allow a delegation of Northern nationalists present a petition opposing its outcome (and O'Higgins actually claimed that most Northern nationalists were happy to leave the border as it was). The attitude of the Southern government towards Northern nationalists expressed an embarrassed ambivalence – and, increasingly, a wish that they would accept the necessity to operate in the new six-county context. Even before Collins's death, Blythe and O'Higgins forcefully advised their fellow-ministers that the Northern state was too solidly established to be disrupted by 'minor nagging'; all future pressure should be brought to bear by normal constitutional channels. The Free State government's Northern Advisory Committee arrived at the bleak conclusion that they could do nothing practical to help the beleaguered Catholics in the North.[8] And in June 1922 Collins himself – possibly resigned by now to civil war – expressed what would continue to be the official line of the Southern government in office: 'There can be no question of forcing Ulster into union with the Twenty-Six Counties. I am absolutely against coercion of this kind. If Ulster is going to join us it must be voluntary. Union is our final goal, that is all.'[9] Collins's acceptance of this strategy signals the relegation of a 'united Ireland' under the nationalist banner to the status of a comfortable aspiration.

For those out of office, however, 'verbal republicanism' prevailed – if often inconsistently. De Valera is a celebrated case in point. Up to 1921 he firmly advocated coercion of Ulster's Protestants, refusing to admit any substance to their case for different treatment: 'an accident arising out of the British connection, [which] will disappear with it'. In 1921 he followed a more tortuous path, floating the idea of Ulster counties opting out, if they wished, by individual plebiscites; he also contemplated an interim federal solution. His 'Document No. 2' alternative to the Treaty, as often pointed out, did not dispute the arrangements made for Ulster, though unequivocal evidence seems to show that he also admitted he would consider accepting the Treaty if Ulster came in on its terms. In this as in much else, he reflected nationalist ambivalence about the unanswerable conundrum in the North. It might be added that the twenty-six-county state could not have evolved in the way it did if it had also represented Ulster Protestantism. The removal of that intractable element helped ensure social and cultural coherence to a degree otherwise impossible, an important influence behind the Free State's much-vaunted political stability.

III

This brings us back to a consideration of the nationalist Irish state as it had evolved by 1932, when de Valera succeeded to power. A two-party, British-style democracy had ostensibly developed, though the adoption of proportional representation, and the suppositions of its constitutional architects, reflected an idealized blueprint of myriad small parties and a large degree of independence for parliamentary delegates. Constitutional experiments like 'extern' ministers, and sweeping popular rights of referendum and initiative, were also introduced to this end. But nothing like the envisaged system emerged. Fianna Fáil's entry into politics, and the enduring divide of the civil war, ensured a two-party system, divided by interpretations of 'republicanism' and, indeed, of the very legitimacy of the state. This, as so much else, reflected a continuing insecurity about sovereignty.

Smaller parties, with more mundane preoccupations, failed to develop. The Labour Party, while increasing its seats from fourteen to twenty-two in the 1927 election, only gleaned a low number of first preferences; this election remained their high-water mark for over forty years. And even in the 1927 campaign, a certain ideological defeatism was evident. 'We have had one revolution,' said the Labour leader Thomas Johnson,[xi] 'and one revolution in a generation is enough.' However, in considering why 'class politics' failed to emerge in the new state, the Treaty debate (and the readiness of Cumann na nGaedheal to use red-scare tactics in the early 1920s) does not provide the full answer. It is also necessary to remember the manner in which nineteenth-century political mobilization had occurred, and the interests that it represented, for much of this was transferred to the new order.

[xi] Thomas Johnson (1872–1963): born in Liverpool; first came to Ireland, 1892; commercial traveller; served on Larkin's Strike Committee, 1907; co-founder of Irish Labour Party, 1912, and Vice-Chairman of its executive, 1912–23; Vice-President of Irish Trades Union Congress, 1913, and President, 1915; attended the Socialist International, 1919; co-author of Democratic Programme, 1919; Secretary to Irish Trade Union Congress, 1920–28; T D for County Dublin and leader of Parliamentary Labour Party, 1922–7; denounced Provisional government's execution of republican prisoners, 1922–3; Senator, 1928–36; foundation member of the Labour Court, 1946–56.

The evolution of a conservative bourgeois dominion with a retarded agricultural base was noticeably, if inevitably, different from the imagined brave new world of Sinn Féin visionaries; and criticism was accordingly forthcoming. Francis Stuart, more categoric than most anti-Treatyites, declared that they had 'fought against, and been defeated by, the spirit of liberal democracy'. The new class of Free Stater *haute bourgeoisie* became a target for satire, often identified by the shorthand of salubrious Dublin suburbs (in 1924 Mulcahy discerned a 'Ballsbridge' complex centred round O'Higgins, working to unseat him[xii]). In the withering phrase of one puritanical young republican, 'smoked salmon became the symbol of the risen people'.[10] In Cumann na nGaedheal some family names from the old Redmondite elite began to recur (there was, interestingly, no such continuity in Fianna Fáil). In other areas, too, older patterns reasserted themselves, including the fundamental attitudes to government, well expressed by Tom Garvin: 'the state inherited a tradition of alienation from government combined with an equally ingrained tradition of passive dependence on government aid'.[11]

In what ways did the Free State express its separate identity? One index of 'foreign-ness', carefully cultivated, was neutral status in international affairs. From 1922 the Free State government took a very deliberate decision to follow a policy that would keep it aloof from the strategic designs of larger powers: a policy that involved maintaining good relations with Great Britain itself. An independent but unambitious defence force had to be developed; at the same time, a self-consciously high profile was adopted at the League of Nations, and in the matter of appointing ambassadors abroad. Ministers took every opportunity to emphasize that the right had been won to remain neutral in time of war. Here again there was a desperate necessity to demonstrate that the Treaty had conferred advantages worth fighting for.

Most importantly, though, if the new state was only patchily Gael-icized, it was almost entirely Catholic. Southern Protestant interests were none the less carefully cultivated; their religious and educational freedoms were guarded by statute; they were awarded weighted representation in the Free State Senate (ornamental though its functions became). Many emigrated all the same; by the end of the decade the

---

[xii] This clique included Desmond FitzGerald; and sixty years later, when FitzGerald's son Garret was Taoiseach, the derisory sobriquet for his supposed middle-class-intellectual-professional base was 'Dublin 4', a postal area which in fact includes Ballsbridge.

proportion of Protestants in the twenty-six counties fell by 3 per cent, down to 7.4 per cent. It is interesting, however, to note their occupational proportions in 1926, when they were 8.4 per cent of the population: they still accounted for 28 per cent of farmers with over 200 acres, and 18 per cent of the entire professional class. By 1936 the Protestant proportion of Irish employers and business executives was 20–25 per cent; bank officials, 53 per cent; commercial representatives, 39 per cent; lawyers, 38 per cent. A modest, unofficial form of 'Ascendancy' lingered on.

The Free State constitution, as well as the traditions of separation between Church and state, denied Roman Catholicism the official status of national Church. For all this, the new regime was in a very real sense confessional. From its origins, the Free State government had carefully lined up the Roman Catholic hierarchy on its side, consulting bishops on constitutional matters, and receiving in return powerful support during the edgy days of the civil war, when a joint pastoral branded the IRA Irregulars as murderers. In turn, the Church made its line clear on social policy. It had been flintily against state initiatives in educational and welfare policies under the Westminster regime; and it was no more prepared to see central power aggrandized now. The Central Association of Catholic Clerical School Managers had issued a clear warning in 1921:

We are confident that an Irish government established by the people for the people, while safeguarding the material interests of the new state, will always recognize and respect the principles which must regulate and govern Catholic education. And in view of the impending changes in Irish education we wish to reassert the great fundamental principle that the only satisfactory system of education for Catholics is one wherein Catholic children are taught in Catholic schools by Catholic teachers under Catholic control.[12]

This was the price of support for the new regime: ideas of councils of education, or locally constituted authorities, were vitriolically denounced. In education, as in social law, the state followed the Catholic line: divorce was excluded, birth control outlawed, the Ne Temere decree enforced Catholic conditioning on children of mixed marriages.

If this seemed to the tiny Protestant minority the fulfilment of their most dire prophecies, it should be remembered that they were, in the new state, a dwindling and infinitesimal proportion: while to the vast Catholic majority, these were consensus policies. Moreover, Cosgrave's whole-hearted commitment to endorsing clerical influence in government also reflected a shrewd necessity to guard his flank. His extraordinary idea of a theological senate to evaluate the Catholic orthodoxy of all mooted legislation should be seen in the light of his knowledge that not all the hierarchy were automatically supporters of Cumann na nGaedheal. Some powerful clerics, notably John Hagan, Rector of the Irish College at Rome, and Professor Michael Browne at Maynooth, kept open lines to de Valera and would influence the making of Fianna Fáil. Cosgrave had to bid high: another factor in the emergence of a strongly confessional state.

The cultural chauvinism and insularity of the Free State is easy to deride from a distance, with its official anathematizing of everything from jazz to modern fiction, and the symbolic institution of the much-reviled Censorship Board in 1929. The most vitriolic criticism of the regime came from writers whose work fell foul of it, for the mildest of transgressions: as in contemporary Russia, dissidence was the business of the intelligentsia rather than the politicians. But in common with most ex-colonial countries, the concomitant of nationalist polarization was a need to assert a separate identity, by social and cultural engineering if need be. In the Irish case, it was important to stress the supposed message of Irish history – which involved a necessary degree of deliberate amnesia. Not only was the record of parliamentary nationalism more or less dismissed; the real nature of pre-1916 Irish society had to be glossed over, including, among much else, the hundreds of thousands of Irish who had volunteered in the Great War. The professionalism of the Free State government, and the political stability that ensued from its regime, is impressive; future generations owed them much. But looked at another way, the lopsidedness of developments south as well as north of the new border is striking: and if post-1917 Sinn Féin and its successor organizations had effectively won the Anglo-Irish war, it is tempting to conclude that on other levels they lost the peace.

CHAPTER TWENTY-TWO

THE DE VALERA DISPENSATION

I

WHEN THE MEETING [at which it was decided to abandon military resistance to the Free State] broke up, the chief of staff, Liam Lynch, and de Valera were walking together down from the farm-house where they had come to the agreement when Lynch said: 'I wonder what Tom Clarke would think of this decision.' De Valera stopped in his tracks. 'Tom Clarke is dead,' he said. 'He has not our responsibilities. Nobody will ever know what he would do for this situation did not arise for him. But it has risen for us and we must face it with our intelligence and conscious of our responsibility.'[1]

What this represented was a revolt against the tyranny of the dead; over the next decade de Valera's judicious pragmatism first brought his party to power, and then enabled the reconstruction of Anglo-Irish relations into the form of 'external association', climaxing in the policy of Irish neutrality during the Second World War. In retrospect, the success of these manoeuvres tends to conceal the constraints imposed upon the ex-revolutionary turned constitutional politician. It is salutary to remember that in 1932 many commentators, among the republican left as well as the British sceptics, drew the same analogy: Kerensky, ineffectively holding the ring against the Bolsheviks in 1917.

The comparison would have seemed less apt if it had been more generally realized that de Valera had never really been happy with his IRA associates – and that the external-association ideas of his 'Document No. 2' had always been far nearer to the Commonwealth than to an independent republic. Moreover, in power Fianna Fáil embodied two aspirations: one was to redefine Ireland's relations with the Empire, and the other was to institute a state of 'protectionism', both economic and cultural. The economic aspect of this has been dismissed by historians like Raymond Crotty as the aspiration of the urban classes to share in the economic surplus accruing to ownership of Irish land, by requiring the farming classes to pay higher prices for domestically manufactured goods; but it still had a psychological dimension that was at least as important.

'Protection' might also be linked to the introspection and conservatism of a state where those whose interests were not met by the status quo tended to leave instead of trying to change it. De Valera's Ireland became a twenty-six-county state with thirty-two-county pretensions, institutionalizing a powerful Catholic ethos that was symbolically celebrated in the Eucharistic Congress of 1932, and effectively enshrined in the constitution of 1937. This took precedence over strict adherence to the theories of 1916, or 1919–21; Tom Clarke was, after all, dead. And the construction of the de Valera dispensation created its own satisfactions, its own affirmations and its own precedents: some of which would enforce their own tyranny in the course of time.

II

The social conditions of Ireland – at least, of rural Ireland – during the 1930s have been anatomized in microcosm by a number of classic texts, including an impressionistic anthropological masterpiece, Conrad Arensberg's The Irish Countryman (1937), as well as a series of memoirs from the western islands that rapidly became cult classics. While it is dangerous to generalize from Arensberg's Clare or Peig Sayers's[i] Blaskets, much in 1930s rural Ireland would have been recognizable to a reincarnated Victorian traveller. Housing remained dominated by the single-storey cottage; living conditions were basic; families large; emigration and tuberculosis part of life. (The childhood memoirs of Noel Browne, later a revolutionary Minister of Health, provide a chilling first-hand picture, with no room for nostalgia.[2]) But the two-storey slated farmhouse was appearing alongside the thatched cottage. Land Commission dwellings were raised in considerable numbers through the 1930s, as part of the same policy that encouraged state-sponsored

[i] Peig Sayers (1873–1958): born in County Kerry; lived on Great Blasket Island for over fifty years; came to public attention after a Folklore Commissioner recorded some 400 of her tales and songs of Gaelic Ireland, and her fame spread after the publication of an autobiography, Peig, 1936. The government resettled the few remaining Blasket Islanders on the mainland in 1953, and she spent the last years of her life in a Dingle hospital.

urban housing programmes (though in 1938, a survey found 60 per cent of Dublin's tenements and cottages, containing 65,000 people, unfit for human habitation). The new houses were basic enough, too; and in 1946 only 5 per cent of farm dwellings had an indoor lavatory, while 80 per cent had no 'special facilities' at all. Similarly, some machinery (notably the tractor) was beginning to erode ancient agricultural practices; but demeaning survivals like the hiring fair continued through the 1930s.

Old-fashioned farming and inadequate sanitation did not, in any case, rank high among de Valera's targets; his vision of Ireland, repeated in numerous formulations, was of small agricultural units, each self-sufficiently supporting a frugal family; industrious, Gaelicist and anti-materialist. His ideal, like the popular literary versions, was built on the basis of a fundamentally dignified and ancient peasant way of life. But this had little to do with the objective forces shaping rural existence; in fact, the influential Folklore Commission was founded at the very moment (1935) when the society it celebrated was entering its final stage.

The brokers of an ideal rural Ireland tended to ignore metropolitan Ireland, represented in the large country towns as well as in Dublin and Cork. Here, Anglicized cultural norms had taken firm hold, along with the cinema, the popular press, golf-clubs and race-meetings, and, in some quarters, a repudiation of 'the inhibiting values of farm and shop'.[3] Dublin was a 'professional' city; the 1946 census showed 21.1 per cent working in commerce and finance, 12 per cent in administration, 8.9 per cent in professions, 13.7 per cent in personal services, 32.2 per cent in non-agricultural production. By the war, the electrification of urban Ireland had nearly been achieved (the completion of rural electrification had to wait until the 1970s). Even in industrial development, it has been pointed out that Ireland was not backward by *European* standards, but on a par with Portugal, Scandinavia and Italy. None the less, the inevitable comparison was between 'backward' rural Ireland and 'modern' industrialized England; and the removal of Ulster skewed the picture. The idealization of the Ireland represented by Tomás Ó Criomhthain's *An t-Oileánach* (*The Islandman*) or Muiris Ó Súileabháin's *Fiche Blian ag Fás* (*Twenty Years A-growing*) remained a psychological necessity.

The fundamental reality behind the image of rural Ireland remained that of an emigrating population. The total twenty-six-county population remained about the same, at just under 3,000,000; the pattern of late marriages, but a very high birth-rate within marriage, continued (in 1929, the Irish age of marriage was the highest in the world – 34.9 for men, 29.1 for women – while one-quarter of the female population were unmarried by their forty-fifth birthday). And population growth was counteracted by the rate of emigration: 6 per 1,000 of the total population through 1926–46, with single people, especially women, predominating, and a pronounced rural–urban drift. England remained the chief destination, especially after economic recession struck the USA. The figures were further affected by what appears to be a dramatic rate of Protestant emigration from the twenty-six counties – possibly as much as 26 per cent.

Terence Brown has indicated a change in the perception of emigration from the late 1930s. Up to then, a commitment to sustaining the traditional patterns of farming society was evident: leaving the farm to a sibling represented an affirmation that the old ways must continue. But by the 1940s (at least as indicated by the report of the Commission on Emigration set up in 1948) a more wholesale rejection of rural norms seems apparent. The evidence of previous emigrants, and the improvement of communications, relayed an accessible and sharply contrasting picture to those who stayed behind; discontent with the de Valera vision can be intuited, perhaps most vividly in Patrick Kavanagh's[ii] poem about the sterility and frustration of rural life, *The Great Hunger* (1942). 'If there is a case for viewing a major work of art as an antenna that sensitively detects the shifts of consciousness that determine a people's future, *The Great Hunger* is that work.'[4]

The response of government to the frustrations of rural life was conditioned by the general economic malaise of the early 1930s. Fianna Fáil took over a gloomy financial picture and, to judge by the memoranda produced even before the economic war with Britain, were ready to meet it with the same steely approach as Cumann na nGaedheal. The structure of economic policy, however, was rapidly conditioned by the political relationship with Britain: Fianna Fáil's predisposition to protectionism was augmented by the campaign of economic sanctions that followed de Valera's policy of withholding land annuity payments still due to the British Exchequer under the terms of the Land Purchase Acts. A similar policy might have followed

[ii] Patrick Kavanagh (1904–67): born in County Monaghan; small farmer and cobbler; published his first poems, 1938; went to Dublin, 1939; worked as a journalist; launched *Kavanagh's Weekly*, offering a lively and critical account of the state of Irish life, 1952, further collections of poetry and a novel followed, but only recognized as a major talent with the publication of *Collected Poems*, 1964, and *Collected Pruse* [sic], 1967.

Britain's own shift from free trade in any case; the collapse of the agricultural export market, and the decreased opportunities for emigrants, also enforced a change of approach. It tied in with the Fianna Fáil preoccupation of encouraging a distribution of rural resources and reliance upon small-scale domestic industry, to counterweight the pull towards emigration. Griffith's theory of agricultural and industrial interdependence, and his notion that the country could support an almost infinitely larger number of inhabitants, ideas abandoned by his political heirs, remained articles of faith for those who had opposed him over the Treaty.

Fianna Fáil economic planning in the 1930s stressed the national duty to set up native industries. The growth of a more sophisticated market, and the production processes necessary for the new industries, in fact ensured a continued dependence upon imports. None the less, finance and credit structures to float new businesses were introduced along with quotas, licences and tariffs. And, given the paucity of private venture capital, the 'state-sponsored' corporations started in the 1920s were extended for specific purposes: notably the processing of energy resources, but also various enterprises in transport and commerce. By 1948 eighteen of these organizations had been added to the six inherited.

This did not, however, indicate a commitment to structural reorganization in the interests of a new economic approach. Though many Irish intellectuals were sympathetic to the ideas of corporate government floated in Catholic social theory at the time, the heavy-weight and imaginative report of the Commission on Vocational Organization (1939–43) was politely ignored. It had suggested social, economic and (most dangerous of all) political reorganization, influenced as much by English guild socialism as by Continental examples. The Commission's recommendation that representative non-party boards of employers and workers in various sectors of employment elect a National Assembly, which would manage the national economy through its own governing body and bureaucracy, was met with resounding silence. Vested interests and influential individuals were alienated, including Sean Lemass,[iii] already the most receptive and radical of Fianna Fáil ministers. Nor was the civil service sympathetic;

[iii] Sean Francis Lemass (1899–1971): born in County Dublin; joined the Irish Volunteers, 1915; fought in the GPO, Easter 1916; interned, 1920–21; opposed the Treaty; imprisoned, 1923; TD for Dublin City, 1924–69; a founder and organizer of Fianna Fáil, 1926; Minister for Industry and Commerce in every de Valera administration, 1932–59; Tanaiste, 1945–8; Taoiseach, 1959–65; re-established free trade with Britain, 1965; resigned, 1966. Inspired and served on the committee that sought to revise the

the powerful (and British-derived) bureaucratic structure of Free State government would remain. If recent Irish historiography proves one thing, it is the importance of civil servants in a history whose official records are carefully obscured by the state apparatus, North and South.

Another area in which Fianna Fáil's natural predispositions were encouraged by the economic conditions of the 1930s concerned the policy of reorienting agricultural production away from cattle and towards tillage. Price guarantees and subsidies, bounties and import controls were closely associated with the economic war with Britain, which affected the cattle trade so disastrously. The production of wheat, as so often before, was advocated on a large scale; so was the more novel crop of sugar-beet, under the auspices of the state-sponsored Irish Sugar Company, often the subject of optimistic eulogies.[iv] But – yet again following an iron precedent – the basic pattern of Irish agriculture showed little sign of change. And the increased concentration on tillage did not, contrary to expectation, provide more employment on the land; through the 1930s and 1940s the percentage of males engaged in farm work continued to drop. By another unexpected convolution, Crotty's analysis claims that the effect of state payments to dairy farmers acted as an unintended boost for graziers, by effectively subsidizing lower payments for store cattle and enabling them to expand. Overall, looking at the 1930s, 'an analogy might be drawn between Irish agriculture and primitive zoological or botanical species which, while never achieving a high or productive level of development, are supremely well adapted to survive under extremely adverse biological conditions'.[5]

In many ways, Irish economic conditions before the Second World War presented a variant of the general European dilemma: how to approach the problems of recession in a manner that provided an alternative both to failed free-market capitalism and untried but alarming totalitarianism. The social ideas advanced in papal encyclicals and the theory of economic organization by means of vocational corporations were both tinkered with, and adapted to specifically Irish themes. But what mattered more immediately were the preoccupations

wording of the Republic's constitutional claim to Northern Ireland, making it aspirational.

[iv] But see the sceptical Raymond Crotty: 'It is quite impossible to judge the operating efficiency of this body. Parliamentary control was practically non-existent and the company's accounts have been described as designed to conceal rather than reveal information.' (*Irish Agricultural Production: Its Volume and Structure*, Cork, 1966, p. 148).

of Irish nationalist ideology; Irish history, recent and distant, did much to impose the frameworks that did emerge. In considering this process, the unique nature of de Valera's political party played an important part.

III

Fianna Fáil called itself, as a subtitle, the 'Republican Party', and this constituted an important part of its appeal. But 'Republican' could stand for anything from merely anti-British to agrarian-syndicalist-revolutionary, not to mention exclusivist-Gaelic-Catholic; it was a moral stance as much as a political affiliation. Indeed, a 1929 pamphlet commemorating Austin Stack declared 'the name Republican in Ireland, as used amongst Republicans, bears no political meaning. It stands for the devout lover of his country, trying with might and main for his country's Freedom.' In a sense, republicanism denies politics: another commentary defines the pure faith of republicanism 'above all, [against] those who embrace politics as a family trade and the nation as a prey ... The Republic is not a formula to be dispensed at ballot boxes once in every five years. It is the [sic] way of life.'[6]

Given that Fianna Fáil had accepted the ballot box, this cast some doubt on their acceptability as the 'Republican' party. One way round this was implicitly to redefine republicanism yet again: this time as populist nationalism, with a strong Catholic colouration and a commitment to Gaelic revivalist pieties. Another mechanism involved using the ballot box to alter the Free State's status within the Empire to the point where the technical appellation of 'Republic' was an obvious next step. De Valera instituted both these developments; but there would always be those who adhered to the republic as 'a way of life', and for them Fianna Fáil had betrayed the ideal even more comprehensively than Cumann na nGaedheal.

Thus the new ruling party's relationship with the republican flank was an uncertain one. IRA prisoners were released, and the ban on public drilling and publication of newspapers lifted; but in other areas caution prevailed. For the moment, Fianna Fáil retained credibility by the apparent radicalism of its 'external relations' strategy, as the government steamrollered through constitutional legislation, dismantling various clauses of the Treaty. A 'Republican' profile was aided by the opposition of the Senate, whose powers (and constitution) were accordingly suspended – as were a number of multiple-member constituencies, and university representation in the lower house. Republican credibility was also enhanced by the frosty relations between some government members and their senior civil servants ('a crowd of Free State bastards', in the view of one Fianna Fáil recruit[7]). But for Fianna Fáil to achieve hegemony over Irish politics, it needed more than conciliatory gestures towards its green flank.

The real key to the party's development lay in its local organizations. Though often (and usefully) based on IRA structures, they also inherited the traditional local-versus-central antipathies characteristic of Irish political formations since the Union at least. The vigour of Fianna Fáil's local organization, and the astute use of appointments when in power, enabled the party to represent a geographical spread of influence, unlike the increasingly Dublin-based Cumann na nGaedheal. Garvin interprets the two parties, Fianna Fáil and Fine Gael (as Cumann na nGaedheal eventually became), as factions of the old pan-nationalist party, which continued to exist in a sort of ghostly form beneath the ostensible divide: hence the lack of class differentiation (or, many would say, ideological difference) between the two 'parties' from their origin up to the present. But what was remarkable about Fianna Fáil was its social profile, which gave it an apparently unassailable hegemony over Irish politics by the 1940s. To its original base, small farmer, land-hungry, IRA-oriented, it had added elements of labour, the larger farmers, the business classes and many others.

To make this compatible with de Valera's personal ideology of austere anti-materialism required a certain sleight-of-hand. His belief that 'no man is worth more than £1,000 a year', and his attempt to inaugurate a 'social justice' policy in 1932 by cutting civil service salaries, became moderated by force of circumstance. The powerful and coherent resistance of the civil service, couched in the arguments of a self-conscious elite, was tacitly accepted, though salary cuts for teachers, policemen and army officers continued to be recommended. De Valera would have agreed with the minority report appended to the cuts committee that stated 'an impoverished country with such an elaborate Governmental machine is best likened to a Tin Lizzie fitted with a Rolls-Royce eight-cylinder engine'.[8] But by and large the new regime took on the trappings of the old, while adapting the rhetoric. And in many ways, the triumph of the de Valera dispensation was one of rhetoric, squaring the circle between the mundane limitations of reality and the aspirations of the republic.

This is probably best exemplified by his 1937 constitution. It embodied the language of popular sovereignty, with strong theocratic implications: a popularly elected President appeared as guardian of the people's rights, empowered to refuse to sign a bill if he felt the will of the people ought first to be decided by referendum. The first person to hold this office was, symbolically, Douglas Hyde; later, the office was occupied, no less symbolically, by de Valera himself. Otherwise, the system of government located a great deal of authority in the executive head of government, the Taoiseach; a much-weakened Senate was restored, and proportional representation retained for election to the Dáil.

But the democratic, popular-sovereignty approach was combined with an assumption that the nature and identity of the Irish polity was Catholic, reflected in five articles defining 'rights'. These were much influenced by papal encyclicals and current Catholic social teaching. Divorce was prohibited; the idea of working mothers denounced; the Roman Catholic Church granted a 'special position ... as the guardian of the faith professed by the great majority of the citizens', though the rights of minority Churches were defined. The reaction of the small Protestant minority in the twenty-six counties is symbolized by a sudden rash of pamphlets attempting to stress that the Church of Ireland represented the true, original Church of St Patrick; on more visceral levels, the pervasive fear of mixed marriages leading to total extinction of the Southern Protestant community took an even stronger hold. More to the point, if de Valera's constitution spoke for an overwhelmingly Catholic Ireland, to claim that it also spoke for a thirty-two-county Ireland including a million Ulster Protestants might seem like trying to have it both ways. But that is exactly what the 1937 constitution did.

The constitution also embodied some comment on behalf of equal opportunities, as well as an implication of equitable distribution of resources; though its vague social nostrums were witheringly dismissed by, for instance, the mandarins in the Department of Finance.[v] The

---

[v] The Department of Finance argued that articles dealing with social policy were not of a kind usually enshrined in a Constitution. They will not be helpful to Ministers in the future but will provide a breeding ground for discontent, and so create instability and insecurity. They are consequently objectionable and even dangerous. Their provisions are too vague to be of positive assistance to any Government and are yet sufficiently definite to afford grounds for disaffection to sections of the community, who might claim that the Government were not living up to the Constitution ...

Further, the provisions are mostly unnecessary. Distinct advance along the lines of social and economic policy outlined have already been made without

provisions of the constitution that drastically altered the position of Ireland within the Empire will be considered below. But one breath-takingly comprehensive piece of sleight-of-hand should be noted, for it demonstrates the de Valera habit of squaring rhetorical circles. The first articles of the constitution claimed that 'Ireland' (or, in Irish, 'Éire' – the name 'Free State' was abandoned) included all thirty-two counties; and that therefore, the subsequent provisions applied to the North as well, though only on a platonic level, 'pending the reintegration of the national territory'. Thus was the 'Republic' appeased; and thus was it demonstrated to Ulster Protestants that the institutions of a United Ireland would be, as they had always claimed, oppressively Catholic.

For twenty-six-county purposes, the constitution gratified the aspiration towards a united, republican Ireland, placing a high priority on the restoration of Irish language and culture, and emphasizing that the Commonwealth had no moral claims on Ireland's membership. It was the world view also propagated by the Fianna Fáil newspaper, the *Irish Press* (founded in 1931 and promptly prosecuted by the Free State government, to its advantage). The party's public profile continued to highlight the aspirational (and safe) aspects of republicanism as they had redefined it – notably language revival. The teaching profession had become increasingly restive regarding compulsion, especially about teaching subjects through Irish to children whose home language was English. But Fianna Fáil ministers of education adhered to the party line, Tomás Derrig[vi] declaring in 1943 the necessity of 'waging a most

the aid of these declaratory provisions, some of which are themselves, it should be noted, repugnant to present Government policy, e.g. we do not settle 'as many families as practicable' on the land [see Art. 45, 2, v]. 'Five acres and a cow' would suffice if that were the policy. We create economic holdings of twenty-five acres ...

Also, the provisions are contradictory. The State has established monopolies in important articles such as sugar, electricity, cement, tyres, oil, etc. [despite Art. 45, 2, iii]. The reference to the 'economic domination of the few in what pertains to the control of credit' is not understood [the phrase, in diluted form, appears in Art. 45, 2, iv]. In so far as one can attach any intelligible meaning to it, it is untrue, but it could easily be worked up by agitators as a weapon of attack on the Banks, the Agricultural Credit Corporation, the Industrial Credit Co., or against any large joint-stock concern.

(Quoted in Ronan Fanning, *The Irish Department of Finance 1922–58*, Dublin, 1978, p. 268.)

[vi] Tomás Derrig (1897–1956): born in County Mayo; educated at Christian Brothers school and University College, Galway; joined the Irish Volunteers, 1915; deported, May 1916; joined Sinn Féin, 1917; imprisoned in German Plot arrests, 1918; elected to the Dáil for South Mayo, 1921; rejected the Treaty; TD for Carlow–Kilkenny,

intense war against English, and against human nature itself, for the life of the language'. Many of the intelligentsia had already arrived at a more tolerant and realistic approach: preserving and encouraging Irish as a second language, giving access to Gaelic culture and history, rather than expecting it to reconquer as the 'first national language' – at a time when the number of native speakers in the designated Gaeltacht areas halved between 1922 and 1939. But this, like the campaign against literary censorship in the 1940s, had little effect on the ruling pieties.

During the 1930s, in fact, the compulsory Gaelicization policy was speeded up; a pass in Irish became mandatory for the school-leaving examinations from 1934, and time devoted to other subjects accordingly curtailed. The approach was tacitly recognized as unsuccessful by everyone who had anything to do with it, though education ministers and Gaelic League officials resisted any attempts to quantify or examine the actual results of the policy. 'The system, as developed hastily and *ad hoc* in the 1920s, simply sat atop Irish education for the next forty years. It became in effect a sort of Irish weather, felt, vaguely, to be oppressive but inevitable.'[9]

Otherwise, 'all educational policies', according to one authority, 'were subject to one qualification: they could not interfere with those prerogatives of power which had accrued to the Church in the school system'.[10] And these were considerable. Government policy during the 1930s had encouraged clergy to take on teaching duties, while effectively discouraging the laity; the confessional stamp on Irish society was impressed more and more deeply.

A less predictable inheritance of the Fianna Fáil years was their record in social welfare: less draconian than Cumann na nGaedheal about matters like pension entitlements, and more prepared to extend unemployment insurance. In other areas, the social benefits enshrined in the constitution came strongly through: the 1935 Conditions of Employment Bill imposed a maximum proportion of women workers in industry (and gave the minister the right to prohibit them completely), infuriating the remnant of the Irish feminist movement still active. Articles 40, 41 and 45 of de Valera's constitution implied or declared that a woman's place was in the home; the image of rural utopianism was incompatible with an industrialized female workforce or, it might be added, with any industrialized workforce at all. The

1923–54; founder member of Fianna Fáil, 1926; Minister of Education, 1932–48; Minister for Posts and Telegraphs, 1939, and for Lands, 1951–4.

ideology marketed by Aodh de Blacam,[vii] an important Fianna Fáil propagandist and a close associate of de Valera, postulated the idea that the day of industrialization and urbanization was past and a new, decentralized agrarian order at hand.

Thus the Fianna Fáil Ireland was a nation set apart, by Catholicism and nationality: the interlocking relationships of Church and politics helping to define a unique, God-given way of life. Economic ideals of self-sufficiency could obviously be related to this; state investment in the Irish Sugar Company (1933) and the Turf Development Board (Bord na Moná, 1934) was significant for psychological as much as economic reasons. And 'protectionism' could be cultural, too: a fierce suspicion of cosmopolitanism and what it stood for is evident in many Fianna Fáil manifestos, notably de Valera's St Patrick's Day broadcasts on the new national radio station. Thus in 1935:

Ireland remained a Catholic nation, and as such set the eternal destiny of man high above the 'isms' and idols of the day. Her people would accept no system that decried or imperilled that destiny. So long as that was their attitude none of the forms of state-worship now prevalent could flourish in their land; the state would be confined to its proper functions as guardian of the rights of the individual and the family, co-ordinator of the activities of its citizens.[11]

The curious thing is that Fianna Fáil came to speak, not only for the small-farming, shopkeeping and artisan classes of rural Ireland, but also for many of the bourgeoisie. Between the 1920s and the 1950s the concentration of Fianna Fáil's first-preference votes inexorably moved from west of the Shannon to the more prosperous midlands and east.[12] The party also captured the 'labour' interest, though the left wing of the IRA appropriated the rhetoric of expropriation and class war waged upon 'ranches and banks'. But the IRA, increasingly disgruntled, were marginalized throughout the first decade of Fianna Fáil rule, despite isolated outbreaks and some grisly murders. By the mid-1930s de Valera was arraigning IRA members before military tribunals, using the hated Article 2A introduced by Cumann na nGaedheal; in June 1936 the IRA (though not the more radical Cumann na mBan) was declared an unlawful organization.

[vii] Aodh de Blacam (1890–1951): born in London of Ulster stock; learned Irish; settled in Ireland, 1915; well-known for writings as 'Roddy the Rover'; Sinn Féin publicist in the Anglo-Irish war; interned, 1919; sat on subcommittee on Partition and wrote The Black North, 1938; member of Fianna Fáil national executive, 1938–47; joined Clann na Poblachta. Also Gaelic Literature Surveyed, 1929, and Wolfe Tone, 1935.

The IRA, underground, split over tactics; a rump under Seán Russell[viii] embarked upon a bombing campaign in Britain that sputtered counter-productively through 1938–9. Otherwise, the irreconcilable residue seemed condemned to policies of obscure retaliations and vengeances, bank robberies, odd streetfights, ineffective conspiracy with Nazi Germany, or internment in the appalling conditions of Portlaoise gaol and the Curragh (enlivened by seminars in Irish from the gifted Máirtín Ó Cadhain[ix]). In 1932 the IRA had numbered an estimated 30,000 in the twenty-six counties; by 1944 'there no longer was a Chief of Staff or an Army Council'[13] – hardly even an IRA, though reconstruction came in the late 1940s, and in the North the movement became efficiently organized underground. *An Phoblacht*, particularly under Peadar O'Donnell's editorship, remains the record of an alternative politics in the 1930s and 1940s (much as the *Bell* under Seán O'Faolain[x] stands as the record of an alternative culture); but official republicanism had been vampirized by de Valera. For those who believed they had kept the faith, he was the worst apostate of all: linked by *An Phoblacht* in July 1935 to Churchill, Greenwood, Collins and Cosgrave. For them, the wheel had come full circle.

For de Valera, of course, it had not. In official politics, the old Free State-versus-republican divide could still be presented; and Fianna Fáil

[viii] Seán Russell (1893–1940): born in Dublin; joined Irish Volunteers, 1914; interned after the 1916 rising; member of Sinn Féin; IRA Director of Munitions, 1919–21; rejected the Treaty; remained active in the IRA after the republican surrender, 1923; visited USSR in an attempt to secure arms, 1926; broke with de Valera upon the founding of Fianna Fáil, but also opposed the left-wing tendencies of O'Donnell and Ryan; IRA Quartermaster-General, 1936, and Chief of Staff, April 1938; supported the IRA's bombing campaign in Britain, 1939; visited the USA; sought to re-enter Ireland with German assistance; died *en route* in a U-boat; buried at sea.

[ix] Máirtín Ó Cadhain (1907–70): born in County Galway into a Gaeltacht community; educated at St Patrick's Training School, Dublin; joined the Gaelic League; dismissed from his teaching post and imprisoned for membership of the IRA, 1939–44; joined the translation staff of the Oireachtas, 1949; lecturer in Modern Irish at Trinity College, Dublin, 1956–69; appointed to the chair of Irish, 1969. His major work, the novel *Cré na Cille*, 1949, was chosen by Unesco for translation into several European languages.

[x] Seán O'Faolain (b. 1900): born in Cork; educated Presentation Brothers School and University College, Cork; influenced to take an interest in Gaelic by Corkery; joined the IRA during the Anglo-Irish war; rejected the Treaty; made bombs for the Irregulars during the civil war; acting Director of Publicity, 1922–3; founder member of the Irish Academy of Letters, 1933; founded the *Bell*, 1940, which he edited until 1946. Popular historian and biographer, and author of numerous short stories as well as novels.

had managed to attract many of the anti-Treaty I R A. Moreover, the line of demarcation between government and opposition was pointed up sharply by the development of potentially paramilitary activity in the early 1930s, under the umbrella of the Army Comrades Association: an anti-Fianna Fáil faction that recruited to its leadership the dismissed Police Commissioner, General O'Duffy, in 1933, and subsequently developed into a Fascist-inspired organization called the Blueshirts (later the National Guard).

Their penchant for marches, demonstrations and Italian-inspired anti-democratic rhetoric led to fears of a *coup d'état* – though the enemy they identified tended to be the I R A rather than communists. Opposition also developed from fringe parties representing interest-groups like the farmers. The National Centre Party, founded in 1932, was essentially a pro-Commonwealth, middle-class party under James Dillon[xi] and Frank MacDermot.[xii] Though they embodied distinctive policies on agrarian, economic and Northern policy, they were inevitably tagged as 'pro-British' – an indication of the neo-colonial obsessions prevalent in 'independent' Ireland. Eventually, coalition between the National Centre Party, the National Guard and Cumann na nGaedheal produced the United Ireland Party; after several disastrous initiatives by the hysterical O'Duffy, they were reconstructed into Fine Gael, a party that embodied some corporate-state ideas but remained basically pro-Commonwealth, and apparently represented the Free State priorities continued by other means. O'Duffy departed to fight for Franco, and then declined into insignificance; the Blueshirt flirtation remained an embarrassing episode in the pedigree of Fine Gael (and in that of several sympathetic intellectuals, including W. B. Yeats).

[xi] James Dillon (1902–86): born in Dublin, son of John Dillon; studied business management in London and Chicago; T D for Donegal, 1932–7; co-founded National Centre Party, 1932; Vice-President of Fine Gael, 1933; T D for County Monaghan, 1937–68; disowned by Fine Gael for attacking Irish neutrality, 1941; Minister of Agriculture in coalition governments, 1948–51, and 1954–7; rejoined Fine Gael, 1951, and was its leader, 1959–65.

[xii] Frank MacDermot (1886–1975): born in Dublin; educated at Downside and Oxford; served with the British army, 1914–18; New York banker, 1919–27; unsuccessful Nationalist candidate for West Belfast, 1929; T D for Roscommon, 1932–7; co-founded National Centre Party, 1932; Vice-President of United Ireland Party, 1933; resigned from Fine Gael in protest at O'Duffy's support for Mussolini, 1935; Independent, 1936–7; resigned over 1937 constitution; Senator, 1936–42; Dublin, New York and Paris correspondent of the *Sunday Times*. Wrote a life of Wolfe Tone, 1939. Critic of Irish neutrality, 1941.

'Irish fascism' remains an open question, ideologically speaking – at least for the early 1930s. Threats from extremists, however, enabled Fianna Fáil to demonstrate strong government; and Article 2A, initially used to discipline Blueshirt rowdies, would eventually be used against the IRA. By the end of the decade, the decimated IRA leadership was left clinging to the notion of themselves as the platonic government of a non-existent republic; war on England was declared by means of bombs in suitcases. And the marginalization of intransigent republicanism was both a result, and a reflection, of the fact that by 1939 Fianna Fáil had achieved its own *modus vivendi* with Britain.

IV

In accomplishing this, de Valera's strategy exemplifies the qualities that made him the accepted leader of Irish nationalism in the post-colonial period. From the moment he assumed power, secession from the Commonwealth and the declaration of a republic appeared to be his ultimate objective: but in fact, his policy adhered closely to the lines of 'external association'. And if his strategy looked extreme when seen from London, it was perceived by many of his Irish supporters as the least he could possibly do.

Moreover, constitutional confrontation tactics can be seen as a valuable form of self-definition. Almost his first action was to announce his intention to remove the Oath of Allegiance; the hedges that had been built around the Constitution Act, supposedly protecting the provisions of the Treaty, were ruthlessly trampled down. The Fianna Fáil government proceeded to attack the practice of appeals to the Privy Council (already causing some legal and constitutional resentment), and the position of the Governor-General – though de Valera's celebrated relegation of this post to a shopkeeper in a suburban villa may not have been a deep-laid plan, but a reaction to the previous incumbent's unexpected resignation.

In many ways, the 1931 Statute of Westminster had made all this possible; India was only one dominion that would follow the Irish example in testing the logic to its limit. Nor should the strategy be seen as happening in a vacuum. Deirdre McMahon has shown how the 1933 Oath Bill, the External Relations Act of 1936 (altering the position of the King in the wake of Edward VIII's abdication) and the constitution of 1937 did not operate as an autonomous juggernaut, but interacted closely with British policy and Irish conditions.[14] However, the 1937 constitution deserves close attention in this context, not only as another precedent for restless dominions to follow, but as an example of de Valera's constitutional sleight-of-hand. He wanted it, in his own words eleven years later, 'to be as explicit as it possibly could be, with as few fictions as possible'[15] – a curious, if implicit, admission. Interestingly, the antagonistic head of the Department of Finance used the same image in dismissing the first Articles as

stating at the outset what will be described, and with some justice, as a fiction, and one which will give offence to neighbouring countries with whom we are constantly protesting our desire to live on terms of friendship. Having been at such pains to expel fictions from the existing Constitution ... it seems inconsistent now to import an even greater fiction.[16]

The claim to legislate for Ulster may have been 'fictional', but the articles dealing with Commonwealth relations were not. The Governor-General and the Crown were removed from internal Irish affairs, merely retained as the symbols of 'association' with the Commonwealth. It is worth noting that the King was still accepted as an external authority: old republican repugnance to this should not be underestimated. But the 'external association' of 1936–7 had advanced from that of 1919–21. And even if the King was empowered to act for external purposes, this was a conditional power to be exercised 'as and when advised by the Executive Council so to do'; and only so long as other Commonwealth countries followed similar practices.

The dominion settlement of 1921 was dismantled; the name 'Irish Free State' was replaced by 'Éire' or 'Ireland'; authority in internal affairs resided in the Dáil. Just enough continuity was retained from the Free State dispensation not to re-create civil war divisions, but in practice the new status was not much different from a formal republic within the Commonwealth.

The British reaction, after deliberation, was to bank on that slender thread of continuity, and treat 'Éire' as substantively occupying the Free State's place in the Commonwealth. This had considerable practical advantages for Fianna Fáil, notably in leaving undisturbed the vital emigration-outflow to Britain. On both sides, too, there was a recognition that extreme gestures (a formal declaration of a republic, or the severance of all British links) would finalize Partition. But the diplomatic discussions, conducted at a time when the economic dispute created conditions of considerable tension, were anything but emollient. Each side spoke a different language: the British paying elaborate attention to legal niceties, the Irish stressing the popular will (as Fianna Fáil conceived it) and the burden of history (as de Valera visualized it). From late 1935 a change of tempo is discernible with the arrival of the conciliatory and adroit Malcolm MacDonald[xiii] as Dominions Secretary – a process that was accelerated when Neville Chamberlain came to power. Up to a late stage, however, British policy remained preoccupied by de Valera's supposedly Kerensky-like position, the chances of destabilizing it, and the opportunities for Cumann na nGaedheal's return. These obsessions indicate, yet again, a fatally flawed perception of what was happening in Irish politics.

The same was true for the economic issue. One of de Valera's first actions had been to declare that the land annuity payments made by the Free State to Britain were not legitimate, and should have been included in the general release of Ireland's liability from the UK's public debt. On learning that they had been specifically reserved, he refused to accept the legality of the agreement, and also invoked the moral argument against exacting land purchase payments at all – though they continued to be lodged with the Irish government. The British reaction, especially among Treasury officials, deeply committed to the Treaty and all its works, was initial fury, tempered by caution. Retaliatory duties were imposed on agricultural imports from Ireland – notably a crippling duty on cattle per head (by 1935, running at 68– 88 per cent *ad valorem*). Further duties followed, as well as restrictive quotas on Anglo-Irish trade; this was confidently expected to have a severe effect on the Irish economy.

To some extent, this was the case, though retention of the land annuities helped offset losses, and a budget surplus was maintained until the deadlock was broken in 1935. Moreover, retaliatory Irish restrictions imposed on imports from Britain (notably coal, cement, sugar, iron and steel, and machinery) did more damage to British trade than is often realized. Above all, de Valera used the 'economic war' to brilliant political effect in domestic Irish terms. Traditional Anglophobia responded to the Fianna Fáil rhetoric of sacrifice in the face of foreign oppression; the snap election that returned Fianna Fáil in 1933 was largely fought on this basis. Given that 96 per cent of Irish exports

[xiii] Malcolm MacDonald (1901–81): son of Ramsay MacDonald; MP, 1929–49; Dominions Secretary, 1935–9; negotiated the end of British–Irish trade war, and settled the annuity and 'treaty ports' disputes, 1938; Minister of Health, 1940–41; visited de Valera to discuss Ireland's role in the war, June 1940; High Commissioner to Canada, 1941–6; supervised the granting of self-government to many former colonies after 1946 and remained a roving ambassador for Britain into the 1970s.

went to UK markets, the practical results were necessarily severe; the value of Irish agricultural exports fell by nearly two-thirds between 1929 and 1933 (though these figures are exacerbated by a worldwide collapse of agricultural prices). The balance of payments deficit ate into reserves; by the final settlement in 1938 all sections of the Irish economy had been affected.

However, the interim coal–cattle pact arranged at the end of 1934 had eased the pressure in the two areas most severely affected; and the general lines of the dispute were fortuitously compatible with Fianna Fáil's belief that unlimited live cattle production enforced emigration, and that the cultivation of wheat and sugar-beet should be encouraged in order to reverse the tendency – mistaken though the remedy proved. In many ways, what was most important about the 'economic war' tended to be the assumptions that were wrongly made about its political and social effects. British strategists expected it to destroy de Valera's credibility and return a sympathetic Cumann na nGaedheal to power. Believers in the economics of radical autarky like (for the moment) Sean Lemass thought that the dispute might lead to the desideratum defined in 1928, whereby

Ireland [could] be made a self-contained unit, providing all the necessities of living in adequate quantities for the people residing in the island at the moment and probably for a much larger number ... Until we get a definite national policy decided on in favour of industrial and agricultural protection, and an executive in office prepared to enforce that policy, it is useless to hope for results.[17]

Four years on, the 'definite national policy' was apparently delivered by the conditions of economic war. Lemass was baulked in his plans for reduction of agricultural production, public works, price controls, state credits for industrial expansion and 'drastic restrictions of imports', not only by the powerful opposition of the Department of Finance, but by the monolithic political inertia enforced by respecting the farming interests. But the initiatives that his Department of Industry and Commerce floated throughout the 1930s represented the attempts of at least one Fianna Fáil ideologue to wield a new broom against traditional counsels of caution.

By the time a final agreement with Britain was negotiated in 1938, it is interesting to note that strong conciliatory arguments were advanced from (of all places) the British Treasury – to the effect that Ireland had the moral advantage after centuries of oppression, and the chance of 'a new chapter' was worth some financial generosity. The annuities were cancelled for a £10,000,000 lump payment; trade duties and restrictions were greatly reduced, and some preference allowed to UK goods. From the Irish side, the domestic economy had hardly benefited; the Commission of Inquiry into Banking, Currency and Credit reported in 1938 that cattle and cattle products had declined in value from £54,600,000 in 1929–30 to £31,100,000 in 1935–6: crop production (excluding potatoes) had risen from only £4,100,000 to £5,000,000; though imports from Britain had been reduced from 81 per cent of the total to 50 per cent, other markets had not been developed; and the 96 per cent of Irish exports that had gone to Britain in 1931 had fallen to only 91 per cent. Northern Ireland's imports from Éire had apparently halved, though these figures do not take into account a vigorous smuggling subculture, notably in cattle. De Valera's rhetorical victory did not come cheaply.

These underlying facts, however, were cast into shadow by the brilliant success of 1938: the return of the Irish ports retained by Britain under the Treaty – harbour facilities at Berehaven, Cobh and Lough Swilly, fuel storage at Haulbowline and Rathmullen. These were handed over with curiously little deliberation on the British side; in some ways, their upkeep was seen as a liability, and there was a general expectation (not to be fulfilled) that in time of war they might be made available again. The Chiefs of Staff acquiesced in this gesture of Chamberlainite appeasement as regrettable but inevitable; the infuriated Churchill was in a small minority of parliamentary opposition.

From the Irish side, de Valera saw the 1938 agreement (later in life) as his greatest political achievement. It certainly placed the coping on a decade of brilliant political manoeuvre, which established him as the leader of a reconstructed twenty-six-county state. But, to quote John Bowman, the most striking thing about the 1938 agreement, seen in the wider context, is that 'de Valera's primary concern was not Partition, which he believed intractable in the short term, but the return of the Treaty ports, thus facilitating Southern neutrality in a European war which he believed imminent'.[18] Irredentism, Anglophobia and a determinedly Catholic ethos had paid great political dividends in twenty-six-county terms. The corollary was a blind eye turned to the North.

V

The sovereignty of Éire had been emphatically demonstrated; and the form it had taken was not reconcilable with unity, for all the window-dressing of Articles 2 and 3. Fianna Fáil had remained cautious about Ulster, claiming that they accepted 'existing realities' and were not in favour of 'attacking the North-East', though some of de Valera's American speeches implied otherwise. Partition none the less remained a constant rhetorical target, perceived publicly as a problem of British creation, involving only what de Valera called an 'Ascendancy party' in Down and Antrim. The existence of an invincibly Unionist working class was never mentioned, though there are grounds for believing that de Valera's awareness of the insurmountable nature of the problem increased with time.

Meanwhile, Northern Ireland pursued its own way. Politics there remained in stasis: a permanently weighted, and largely uncontested, Unionist majority was returned regularly to Stormont, enforcing a stultifying continuity. The administration of the province continued to be trapped by the sisyphean task of keeping social benefits up to UK standards, while the Depression eroded industry. A senior Treasury official, explaining yet another plea for assistance from Belfast in 1934, told Neville Chamberlain:

This is not due to extravagance on their part. On the whole I think it could be said that they have economized pretty well. The fact is that they copy all our legislation and that therefore we set their general standard and, for better or worse, in times like these that standard means bankruptcy for a small country which is suffering terribly from unemployment.[19]

Certainly, industrial unemployment, in an area characterized by heavy industry and urban concentrations of population, rapidly became drastic. Ulster's traditional industries, shipping and linen, entered worldwide decline during the 1930s; new-style industry did not re-locate in the province, aircraft production apart. Unemployment in the 1930s averaged 25 per cent, and was often noticeably higher.

Agricultural output diversified and increased during the 1930s, encouraged by British policies of imperial preference (from which Éire was excluded by the economic war). In some ways, administrative devolution worked well for the special conditions of Ulster agriculture.

But agricultural practice remained founded on the small, diversified family farm, and the approach of the farming lobby towards centralized policy did not develop beyond a dogged determination to keep prices up – much resented by urban interests. 'If a farmer wanted somebody to blow his nose some hon. member would get up and raise the question in this House, and a man would be appointed not only to blow the farmer's nose but to wipe it for him.'[20] After indirectly profiting from the economic war between Éire and Britain, Northern Ireland's interests were apparently threatened by the 1938 agreement in areas like butter production – though vociferous complaints met with irritation from the Treasury ('Are we never to be allowed by Ulster to come to terms with the South? Is the tail always going to wag the dog?'[21]). None the less, as in other areas, London's attitude towards Ulster administration opted for complacency and keeping up appearances. And it is suggestive that the most reassuringly sectarian speeches tended to come from Ministers of Agriculture – since they had to cover their flank from criticism for engaging even in limited co-operation with Southern interests.[22] Beneath the surface the irreducible divide remained.

Belfast profited less from administrative devolution. The industrial slums there remained legendary; no clearance scheme was mooted; the response of local authorities to building initiatives was abysmal. House-building subsidies were, in fact, calculated differently from those in Britain: kept at lower.levels, subject to variability, and disastrously reliant upon local builders. The case can be made that demographic patterns were different there, the demand for new houses lower, and that conditions in Scotland may have been worse. But Belfast's health and sanitation standards remained statistically appalling; tuberculosis at epidemic proportions, infant mortality and deaths in childbirth exceptionally high, the threat of the workhouse hanging over the poor. The year 1932 saw the celebrated riots by the poor of both religions against the parsimony of Belfast Poor Law Guardians, specialists in Dickensian rhetoric about undeserving paupers. By 1934 poor relief expenditure in Belfast accounted for more than one-third of all rates income, much resented by the propertied. By 1939 a horrific proportion of the city's working class was living at the degraded level described as 'absolute poverty', faced by an obdurately penny-pinching approach on the part of local authorities determined to peg rates as low as possible.

If lethargy and corruption marked local government, initiatives were not forthcoming from the central authorities either. 'Distributing bones' was the phrase favoured by the ageing Craig (now Lord Craig-avon), as he trundled around his province happily agreeing to classify a road to the Portstewart golf-links as first class, or advocating huge expenditure on Musgrave Street police barracks after an ex-public-school cadet complained about conditions there. Equally characteristic was his solemn warning to Joseph Lyons, the Prime Minister of Australia, to 'watch' his Catholic population – 'they breed like bloody rabbits'. The unfortunate fact that Lyons was himself a Roman Catholic was evidently so inconceivable a thought to Craigavon as not to be worth entertaining.

As for the position of local Catholics, it has been well put by an impartial authority:

Lack of senior positions in the civil service and the judiciary proportionate to their numbers simply highlighted the much broader range of discrimination in the patronage system of public bodies, high and low. Catholics were excluded from power, their political representatives were rendered impotent, their votes were nullified, their children were disadvantaged despite the extra financial sacrifices their parents were called upon to make for their education, and the community was then mocked for not having sufficient qualifications for positions of importance.[23]

The responses of the entrenched Unionist government continued to follow the Pavlovian dictates of sectarian reassurances – exacerbated by the apparent erection of a triumphalist Catholic republic in all but name to the South. Catholic politics in Northern Ireland were effectively trapped in the ghetto. While the extent of overall gerrymandering is by no means easily established, the scandal of Derry's representation – shamelessly rigged for purposes of both parliamentary and local government – was of tremendous symbolic importance. In the 1930s ward boundaries were reconstructed and the size of the Corporation reduced, purely to contain a threatened Catholic pre-ponderance; and even this was a cosmeticized version of the crude readjustment initially proposed by local elements. The outcome, in 1930, was that 9,961 nationalist voters returned eight councillors, and 7,444 Unionists returned twelve.

The religious riots of July 1935 were particularly violent and squalid; the British view of Ulster, even from a National Government that included a rump of fervent Unionist supporters, was often ambivalent. The Treasury certainly perceived Partition as an increasing drain on British resources, though there is some evidence of disagreements in Belfast between those who pressed for hand-outs *ad absurdum* (the

Craigavon line) and the more imperially minded approach of local civil servants like Spender,[xiv] who believed Ulster should budget within its own limitations and adapt British practice to local conditions. The general picture remained that of a dependent economy, operating at a sluggish level, and an administration boosted by injections of central funding. It is true that the picture of 1930s Ulster may be exaggerated simply by the existence of so much specific material relating to the province, while the history of arguably comparable regions has been, in a sense, diluted by absorption into the general British picture. All the same, by the late 1930s many observers (including well-informed civil servants) were wondering how long this state of affairs could continue. What would have happened to Ulster without – yet again – a world war to deliver her?

By 1939 the return of the Treaty ports gave Northern Ireland a vital role in Britain's marine defences, as well as a strategic location for air bases (and eventually American troops). During the war, the numbers employed in the shipyards trebled, strikes notwithstanding; engineering workers doubled; those employed in aircraft production increased fivefold. Northern Ireland produced 140 warships, 10 per cent of the entire merchant shipping of the UK, 1,500 heavy bombers and innumerable quantities of guns, tanks and ammunition. Agricultural productivity was also boosted, by a system of uniform prices; mechanization and fertilization techniques went into a sudden overdrive. Ulster's economic and strategic importance to the British war effort was one vital factor in altering the province's position. Another, of course, was the unparalleled horror of the blitz of Belfast in the spring and early summer of 1941. Both developments affected the relationship of the province to Britain during post-war readjustments.

The central funding authorities, for one thing, looked more benevolently upon Northern Ireland's constant need for subventions. The idea of a notionally 'balanced' Northern Ireland budget was effectively forgotten; the province would share in the new age of welfarism.

[xiv] Wilfrid Bliss Spender (1876–1960): educated Winchester and Staff College, Camberley; signed English form of Ulster Covenant and financed press petition against Home Rule, 1912; resigned from the General Staff over Ulster question, 1913; Ulster Volunteer Force officer, 1913–14; returned to General Staff, 1914; Lieutenant Colonel, 1916; DSO and MC, 1918; commanded Ulster Volunteer Force, 1919, and inaugurated 'B-specials', 1920; CBE, 1921; First Secretary to Northern Ireland Cabinet, 1921–5; Permanent Secretary to the Minister of Finance and Head of the Northern Ireland Civil Service, 1925–44; member of the Joint Exchequer Board, 1933–54.

Living standards, roughly on a par with the Free State in 1930, had advanced nearly 75 per cent above those of Éire by the late 1940s. Post-war agreements, taking effect between 1946 and 1951, established parity between Britain's and Northern Ireland's services and taxation levels; unemployment funds in both areas were amalgamated, relieving Northern Ireland of a great weight of national insurance costs. Similarly the social services agreement spared the province much of the cost of national assistance, family allowance, non-contributory pensions and health-scheme costs. Just as in 1918, Ulster emerged from the war with its position strengthened and its vociferous claims to special treatment ensured a hearing. By the same token, the contrast with the path taken by Éire was thrown into sharper relief than ever.

VI

Irish neutrality in the Second World War should be seen against the background of international politics between the wars, as well as of Anglo-Irish relations. The Free State and Éire had played a leading part in the League of Nations, de Valera serving as President of the Council in 1932, and subsequently as President of the Assembly; the failure of League policies disillusioned him deeply. Neutrality was the traditional policy of small European states, whose example the Irish government rather self-consciously stressed rather than that of other dominions: Éire's special position as the only neutral behind Allied lines was not formally acknowledged, and de Valera affected to see the war as an 'imperial adventure'. Above all, an independent Irish foreign policy was perceived as the *sine qua non* of any real form of independence in the larger sense. Neutrality was, therefore, carefully defined by Frank Aiken,[xv] the Fianna Fáil Minister for the Co-ordination of Defensive Measures in January 1940.

[It] is not like a simple mathematical formula which has only to be announced and demonstrated in order to be believed and respected. It has in fact always been

---

[xv] Frank Aiken (1898–1983): born in County Armagh; joined Irish Volunteers, 1913, and Gaelic League, 1914; Sinn Féin organizer in South Armagh, 1917; IRA Commandant 1919–21; opposed the Treaty; TD for County Louth, 1923–73; IRA Chief of Staff, 1924; founder member of Fianna Fáil, 1926; Minister of Defence, 1932–9, and for Co-ordination of Defensive Measures, 1939–45; Minister of Finance, 1945–8, of Agriculture, 1951, and for External Affairs, 1951–4 and 1957–68; Tanaiste, 1965–9.

one of the difficult problems in human relationship [*sic*]. Instead of earning the respect and goodwill of both belligerents it is regarded by both with hatred and contempt. 'He who is not with me is against me.' In the modern total warfare it is not a condition of peace with both belligerents, but rather a condition of limited warfare with both, a warfare whose limits, under the terrific and all prevailing force of modern total warfare, tend to expand to coincide with those of total warfare. In cold economic and military fact it is becoming more and more difficult to distinguish between the seriousness of the two emergencies called war and neutrality.[24]

'Emergency' became, in fact, the official word for the conditions of 1939–45 in Ireland. The Irish approach amounted to pro-British neutrality (as de Valera had speculatively offered in the 1920 negotiations): secret intelligence and strategic liaisons were made with Britain and the US, not often realized at the time or since. Simultaneously, the strict diplomatic forms of non-belligerence were publicly observed, and Irish politicians never lost sight of the vital importance of establishing sovereignty by maintaining neutrality.

It might be added that this was never perceived by Churchill, who constantly referred to the Irish constitutional position as 'anomalous' and described Irish strategy as 'at war but skulking'. (Eden and others were more sympathetic.) British contingency plans existed to reoccupy the Treaty ports by force if need be; Germany ruled out the option of a direct Irish attack early on, after drawing up detailed plans (and considering a destabilizing invasion of Northern Ireland, imaginatively suggested by Hitler for the twenty-fifth anniversary of Easter 1916). The Reich still retained a strong diplomatic and intelligence presence: 'German spies in Ireland' have entered the folklore. Their activities, however, were more or less confined to inept liaison with the IRA, whom de Valera had defined as traitors to the Irish State in his 1939 Treason Bill.

The position of the partitioned island, at war and not at war, was curious. A diplomatic ballet was danced in 1940 around the chances of North–South co-operation in defence matters, and even around the possibility of Britain supporting Irish unity in return for Éire's open alliance in the war effort; this provoked predictable outrage from Ulster, whose acquiescence was the most unrealistic part of the proposed arrangement, and was in any case rejected by de Valera. Part of the reason may have been his scepticism at Britain's ability to deliver; he was probably further swayed by the belief that she was losing the war; he also remembered how Redmond had forfeited support in 1914. Most of all, though, the principle of neutrality was too closely bound up with Irish identity and Irish sovereignty to be easily relaxed.[xvi]

Much of Éire's wartime experience simply provides harmless diversion for counter-factual speculation (or the writers of might-have-been thrillers). Ulster's war was, by contrast, vivid and committed: and the war effort gave *carte blanche* to Unionist flag-waving. The Home Guard was manned by the B-specials; Unionist leaders made much of being 'King's men'; the Northern Ireland Labour Party was precipitated into a split over the question of commitment to the Union (and, implicitly, the war effort – taken to stand for social progress, unlike 'outworn nationalism'). By November 1941, 23,000 recruits had joined up (conscription was avoided, though Unionist politicians thirsted for it). The disaffected third of the population were, as usual, ignored.

Strategically, it was at first assumed that Ulster was not vulnerable to long-range attack; even German possession of the French seaboard failed to alter this mentality. 1941 changed everything. On 15 April, 180 German planes unloaded more than a hundred tons of bombs over Belfast's residential areas, killing at least 745 in one night. On 4 May, 204 aircraft returned and dropped 95,000 incendiaries on the harbour and shipyards, killing 150 and devastating the war production machine. Altogether, 56,000 houses were damaged, and 3,200 levelled; help came from Éire's fire brigades, a highly symbolic gesture. A generalized fear of further raids persisted, with a nightly exodus from the city to the countryside for months afterwards.

Another symbolic reaction was that of Craig's geriatric Cabinet, spending hours deliberating about how to protect Lord Carson's statue, at a time when the city still had no air-raid shelters, and issuing memoranda about the 'subhuman' habits of slum evacuees – 'unbilletable' people who should be put in 'camps or institutions under suitable supervision'. The inadequacy of Ulster's political leadership was never more vividly demonstrated.

After America's entry into the war, Ireland became less strategically important and Irish neutrality became more openly benevolent; from 1942 stranded Allied air-crews were sent straight to Northern Ireland, while Germans were interned. Ironically, as Irish relations with the USA deteriorated over the neutrality issue, those with Britain improved. But James Dillon remained the only outspoken public voice

---

[xvi] Churchill's famous telegram to de Valera when America entered the war, using the phrase 'A Nation Once Again', had nothing to do with an offer of united Ireland: the intention was, rather obscurely, to convey that Ireland could redeem her soul by entering the war.

against neutrality, and against Hitler, issuing dire warnings about Ireland's fate if Germany won (later corroborated by an ex-Abwehr agent[xvii]). There is still controversy about the number of Éire citizens serving in the war – it may have been about 42,000. But Éire's only direct engagement was an air-raid by German planes led astray through jammed radio signals, killing thirty-four Dubliners on 30 May 1941.

Otherwise, the war affected Ireland in terms of internal transport disruption, fuel shortages, some food and energy rationing; the government assumed sweeping powers of economic organization, and 'planning' was infiltrated into the Department of Supplies under the inevitable Lemass. The Fianna Fáil predisposition towards protectionism and autarky had provided valuable psychological preparation. Tillage was increased, wheat cultivation expanded still further, turf production exploited; mercifully, the meat trade stayed buoyant, though overall economic growth stagnated. Some potentially oppressive legislation was passed: the Wages Standstill Order, in operation from 1941 to 1946, removed legal protection for strikes in pursuance of higher wages, and the 1941 Trade Union Act restricted rights of collective bargaining and even of affiliation to particular unions. The atmosphere of wartime Éire was cautiously authoritarian and necessarily introspective, even solipsistic.

But overall, neutrality was an affirmative rather than a negative stance; even the antagonistic Dillon called it 'a masterly political stroke' on de Valera's part. Elizabeth Bowen astutely noted the national mood in her wartime reports sent back to the British Government:

I find a great readiness, in talkers of all classes, to stress the 'spirituality' of Éire's attitude towards world affairs. At the root, this is not bogus: that this country *is* religious in temperament and disposition as well as practice is, I take it, an accepted fact. Unhappily, religion is used to cover or bolster up a number of bad practices. I ... still see a threat of Catholic-Fascism. And officially the Irish RC Church is opposed to progress, as not good for the people.

The most disagreeable aspect of this official 'spirituality' is its smugness, even

---

[xvii] See Robert Fisk, *In Time of War: Ireland, Ulster and the Price of Neutrality 1939–45* (London, 1983), p. 32, quoting Helmut Clissmann:

Hitler would have sold the Irish down the river. I would have told the Irish that their freedom was coming. I would have been a Lawrence of Arabia. It happened to several friends of mine, with the Bretons and the Walloons. Their freedom was promised but then, when the Germans had what they wanted, the separatist groups were abandoned. Northern Ireland would have been given to a 'Vichy'-type government in London. Hitler did not want to harm the British Empire.

phariseeism. I have heard it said (and have heard it constantly being said) that 'the bombing is a punishment on England for her materialism' . . . Sympathy for Pétainist France (ideas of spiritual rebirth) if not on the increase since last summer is certainly not on the decrease. The equally reconstructive side of the Free French programme seems to be overlooked. And there is still admiration for Franco's Spain . . . The effect of religious opinion in this country (Protestant as well as Catholic) seems still to be, a heavy trend to the Right.[25]

The Dublin government was far from the pro-Nazi cabal imagined in Ulster and elsewhere. But anti-Semitic outbursts were not unknown in the Dáil;[xviii] and Robert Fisk has uncovered a 'grubby neo-Nazi underworld that awaited the Germans in Dublin', meeting for weekly Swastika and oysters sessions at the Red Bank restaurant (and involving the irrepressible General O'Duffy).[26] At the very time when de Valera's celebrated St Patrick's Day broadcast of 1943 called up a vision of an Ireland characterized by cosy homesteads, athletic youths and comely maidens, a more chilling dream was cherished by some at least of his fellow-citizens.

Neutrality remained, observed with 'mathematical consistency' in the phrase of the British envoy: right down to de Valera's punctilious visit expressing formal condolence on the death of Hitler to the German diplomatic representative ('I certainly was not going to add to his humiliation in the hour of defeat'). Revelations of the death camps were already coming in, and the gesture appalled many. Robert Fisk's judgement deserves to be quoted. 'Morally, it was both senseless and deeply wounding to the millions who had suffered in the war; politically, it could have been disastrous. But symbolically, it could not be misunderstood: Éire had not accepted the values of the warring nations and did not intend to do so in the future.'[27]

VII

Emerging from the interlude of 'the emergency', Frank Aiken provided a bleak picture of Irish prospects in the post-war world.

[xviii] Notably by Oliver Flanagan, who in 1943 called for emergency orders 'directed against the Jews, who crucified our Saviour nineteen hundred years ago and who are crucifying us every day in the week . . . There is one thing that Germany did, and that was to rout the Jews out of their country. Until we rout the Jews out of this country, it does not matter what orders you make.' (*Dáil Debates*, vol. 91, cols. 569–72). Flanagan remained a TD (Fine Gael) for over forty years.

This is a small country. It has a small population which is still dwindling, and limited national resources. The age constitution of the population is bad and growing worse. Our economy is mainly agricultural and at that consists chiefly of small farms. Our economic position was relatively stagnant for a long period before the war. It has not since improved. Although there has been a 50 per cent increase in the value of our sterling assets their purchasing power is no greater than before the war owing to the rise in the British price level. It is doubtful if these increased savings will make good the capital deficiency of the war years, but so far as they are used for this purpose the real income from the remainder will be considerably less than before the war.

Exports of industrial products from here have always been limited and show little or no prospect of any material expansion. They are confined for practical purposes to beer, whiskey, textiles and biscuits, where we can spare them after meeting our own requirements.

In the case of agriculture, we have lost the power to compete in butter, bacon and oats. Cattle are the mainstay of our country's export trade, with poultry, eggs and canned meat as subsidiaries.

The excess of imports over exports in the first six months of this year amounted to £15,000,000 which is equal to the total annual excess in the pre-war period ... At the same time our export capacity has been reduced. It is likely to be a long time before we again make our appearance as sellers in the British butter or bacon market ... It is a weakness of our position that we can sell our surplus agricultural products only on the British market and that in any single line we provide only a small proportion of its total requirements ... The volume of agricultural production, excluding turf, shows no tendency to expand. Many farmers are abandoning lines of production which involve hired labour ... There is a tendency to get out of the dairying industry notwithstanding that the country is particularly suited to it, and the production of milk is declining.

A budget of £54,000,000 (excluding provision for capital items and Transition Development Fund) on such a narrow basis resembles an inverted pyramid. Even with this unstable position proposals are still pouring in to the Department of Finance for further expenditure from other Departments and from State-sponsored organizations. Few of the proposals are productive in the economic sense and if adopted they will give rise to increased taxation, even if financed by borrowing at present low rates of interest ...[28]

Agricultural and economic crises loomed; rationing and shortages continued; traumatic strikes involved farm labourers (excluded from the 1936 Conditions of Employment Act) and schoolteachers, as well as industrial workers, and were not defused by the establishment of a labour court under the Industrial Relations Act of 1946. Inflation, and revived emigration, disadvantaged the Fianna Fáil government further; and, given their long tenure of power, the radical ethos that had characterized their early days was no longer evident. Political realignment was on the way.

This was expressed by the proliferation of small parties like Clann na Talmhan, calling for land division and sarcastically reminding Fianna Fáil of the days when they preached the same gospel. In their search for other adversaries to blame, they showed a penchant for discovering Jews and Freemasons. More importantly, a new grouping called Clann na Poblachta brought together old Republicans, anti-Partitionists, socialists and dissident members of Fianna Fáil in what has been called a 'negative consensus': a powerful IRA clique dominated their inner councils. Though a vituperative picture of the new party has been left by Noel Browne,[xix] many personal and professional links with those in other parties enabled them in 1948 to form a coalition government with Fine Gael, Labour and Clann na Talmhan.

The combination of Fine Gael's Mulcahy and McGilligan with hitherto intransigent republicans was as surprising as any *rapprochement* since that of Charles James Fox and Lord North, but it held together through not being Fianna Fáil. The coalition also demonstrated a reassuringly ostentatious piety, assuring the Pope that they 'reposed at the feet of your Holiness the assurance of our filial loyalty and of our devotion to your August Person, as well as our firm resolve to be guided in all our work by the teaching of Christ and to strive for the attainment of a social order in Ireland based on Christian principles'. This may have eased some of the disquiet felt at the spectacle of figures like Seán MacBride,[xx] recently Chief of Staff of the IRA, as Minister for External Affairs.

[xix] Noel Browne (b. 1915): born in County Waterford; educated at Christian Brothers school and England; qualified as a doctor at Trinity College, Dublin; contracted tuberculosis and became leading campaigner for its eradication; Clann na Poblachta TD for Dublin South-east, 1948; Minister of Health, 1948–51; Independent TD, 1951–4 and 1957–8; supported Fianna Fáil outside the Dáil, 1954; co-founder of the National Progressive Democratic Party, for which he sat, 1958–63; joined the Labour Party, and sat, 1969–73; Senator, 1973–7; solitary TD for the Socialist Labour Party, 1977–82; an autobiography, *Against the Tide*, 1986.

[xx] Seán MacBride (1904–88): born in Paris; son of Maud Gonne and Major John MacBride; educated in Paris and University College, Dublin; fought in Anglo-Irish war; opposed the Treaty; imprisoned, 1923–4; leading member of Comhairle na Poblachta, 1929; organized first Saor Éire Convention, 1931; IRA Chief of Staff, 1936–8, but opposed by the Army Council in his call for a republican political party; broke with the IRA in protest at the 1939 bombing campaign; leading barrister defending republicans during the 1940s; founded Clann na Poblachta, 1946; led his party into the 1948–51 coalition, in which he was Minister for External Affairs;

None the less, an incipient radicalism was evident in economic affairs, presenting a challenge to the powerful Department of Finance. Clann na Poblachta's manifesto promised: 'a national monetary authority will be established whose function will be to create currency and credit for the economic needs of full employment, and full production, and to provide credits, free of interest, for full employment and national development'. Though the Department by and large fought off these threats, the beginnings of the debate on economic policy that would characterize the 1950s can be discerned in the coalition's advent to power.

However, the relevance of the coalition experiment to the de Valera dispensation lay in the old obsession with sovereignty *vis-à-vis* Britain: for in 1949 the External Relations Act was repealed and the Republic finally declared. The initiative was taken in a controversial and extra-ordinarily sudden manoeuvre: apparently the result of the Taoiseach, John Costello,[xxi] jumping the gun on a visit to Ottawa in September 1948. But the development was not unexpected. No one in the Cabinet dissented, and if, as alleged, he offered to resign, it was not accepted. The legislation went ahead: arguably dishing Fianna Fáil, but simultaneously dishing any slim chance of ending Partition. The idea that the actualization of the Republic, even a twenty-six-county one, would end a chapter may in any case have been misconceived. Northern nationalists continued, elaborately, to refer to the twenty-six counties as 'the Free State', implying that the constitutional minuets that produced the 'Republic' were irrelevant; the name was platonically preserved for the visionary thirty-two-county separatist state. But this was now further away than ever.

The new Republic retained special citizenship and trade preference arrangements with Britain. But the reaction was the retaliatory Ireland Act passed in 1949 by Westminster providing that Northern Ireland would never leave the UK except by 'consent'. Constitutional bonds were welded even more closely by the practical effects of assurances

Secretary General of the International Community of Jurists, 1963–70; founder member and sometime Chairman of Amnesty International; co-author of the United Nations Declaration of Human Rights; Nobel Peace Prize, 1974; Lenin Peace Prize, 1977.

[xxi] John Aloysius Costello (1891–1976): born in Dublin; educated at University College, Dublin; called to the Bar, 1914; Attorney-General, 1926–32, representing the government at imperial conferences and the League of Nations; TD for County Dublin, 1933, and for other Dublin seats up to 1948; Taoiseach in the first coalition; Taoiseach in 1954–7 coalition; returned to legal practice.

that Northern Ireland's social security benefits and schemes in the post-Beveridge age would not be allowed to fall behind Britain's.

The reaction of the new Republic to the Ireland Act was stunned surprise: a sign of Costello's ineptness, and the insularity of post-war Irish attitudes. As Attlee drily put it, 'the government of Éire considered the cutting of the last tie which united Éire to the British Commonwealth as a more important objective than ending Partition'. Objectively, this seems no more than the truth. However, the official line from Dublin continued to place all the blame for sustaining Partition on London's shoulders. Invitations to join NATO were rejected on the grounds that Partition made it impossible for the Republic to join Britain in such an alliance, though the same arrangement was apparently considered by the coalition in return for a British declaration against Partition. MacBride, visiting the United States in 1949, pledged Ireland to full NATO membership if Britain withdrew from Northern Ireland, assuring Dean Acheson that the British would welcome American intervention to get them off the Partition hook. As so often before, the dissonance between Ireland's and Britain's perceptions of their joint relationship was total.

Where did Ireland stand after 1949? The twenty-six-county Republic retained a special ('external') relationship with Britain, which owed much to de Valera's theoretical precedents.[xxii] Within its borders the Church had achieved the kind of political power where it could not only short-circuit the social-welfare schemes attempted by the coalition government, but could also (during 1936–9) forbid the Labour Party to include in its constitution the aim of 'a Workers' Republic founded on the principles of social justice sustained by democratic institutions and guaranteeing civil and religious liberty and equal opportunities to achieve happiness to all citizens who render service to the community'. A strong minority articulated the case for change; but the intelligentsia tended to be forced *ipso facto* into an adversarial position. The achievement of the Republic did not solve the arguments that had continued throughout the 1930s about what form of government an independent Ireland should adopt.

If the threats of fascism, destabilization and economic collapse had been avoided, so had the possibilities of social democracy. In this process, the Church had played a powerful part, acting as a brake on

[xxii] In July 1945, questioned in the Dáil, de Valera had actually stated that Ireland was, in fact, a republic 'associated as a matter of our external policy with states of the British Commonwealth'; Costello made a more or less similar remark in July 1948.

every secularizing tendency. In 1947 the bishops could publicly condone the boycotting of a divorced Protestant who was elected joint master of a Galway hunt; similar assumptions were writ large in other contemporary statements on issues like a Sunday licensing bill in 1948 ('Largely in deference to our wishes the Bill was decisively rejected'), and on several highly publicized cases regarding adoption law and mixed marriages. By the late 1940s the important point, perhaps, was that these cases were arousing controversy. But the power of the Church to dictate to politicians was formidable. The hierarchy's assumption that this was their right and duty was probably shared by a large majority in the Republic; but this made it all the more sinister when viewed from the North.

In a sense, the priorities thus indicated were firmly in the de Valera tradition. So was the scant attention paid to material progress. He may have believed what he was saying when he remarked in Ennis in 1948 that there was 'probably not in the whole world at the present a country in which there is such a decent standard of living as there is in this part of Ireland' – though statistics of relative incomes refute him. But it cannot have escaped him that, twenty years after Fianna Fáil entered politics, the two things closest to his heart were no nearer achievement: the restoration of the Irish language and the ending of Partition. The fact that these desiderata were, in fact, measurably further from realization than ever owed much to historical forces and contingencies that even a great political shaman like de Valera could do little to control. But the rhetoric of the de Valera dispensation should be evaluated no less stringently for that.

CHAPTER TWENTY-THREE

'MODERN' IRELAND?

I

THE IDEA THAT Ireland underwent a process of 'modernization' (economic, political and social) in the nineteenth century is much contested; certainly, a good deal of what characterized the country in the mid-twentieth century was obdurately pre-modern. Politics remained localist, parochial, clientelist; though it has been suggested that nationalism was a response to the process of modernization, that theory begs the question of how far twentieth-century politics were rooted in early nineteenth-century developments.[i] The Irish case notoriously evades parallels with superficially 'similar' regions, Celtic or Continental. What is striking is how the different layers of the palimpsest of historical experience, laid down over many years, remained distinct in the Irish mind and led to a belief in deliverance. 'Our version of history,' remarked the Bishop of Clonfert in 1957, 'has tended to make us think of freedom as an end in itself and of independent government – like marriage in a fairy story – as the solution of all ills.'[1]

The Irish experience during the 1950s and 1960s illustrates an effort to come to terms with the inadequacy of this expectation. As a conclusion, 1972 may be taken as a year when many old moulds were broken with apparent decisiveness.[ii] During the preceding twenty years, while the political structure remained closely connected to the cultural and social norms of Irish rural society, a 'modernizing' and, according to some, unaccountable bureaucracy steered through initiatives that, by the 1960s, had brought an international dimension into Irish affairs. The effects of internationalizing the economy will be looked at below; more ostentatiously, Irish foreign policy abandoned

[i] See above, pp. 298–9, 316–17.

[ii] The Republic of Ireland was accepted into the EEC; the Stormont parliament and government in Northern Ireland were suspended; the clause in the Republic's constitution, giving the Catholic Church a 'special position', was rescinded.

the solipsistic and counter-productive priority of de Valera's anti-Partition crusade in the early 1950s, and from 1955 achieved a surprising degree of exposure through the United Nations. A predictably pro-Western, anti-Soviet strategy was first adopted, but the influx of Third World members in the 1960s made it easier to take an independent line (though Ireland stayed ostentatiously silent on the subject of Vietnam). Diplomats like Frederick Boland[iii] and Conor Cruise O'Brien[iv] took a prominent part; direct involvement in Cyprus and the Congo heightened the profile. As the British Ambassador had sourly remarked in 1945, 'for the outside world, Dark Rosaleen has a sex appeal, whereas Britannia is regarded as a maiden aunt'.[2]

Significantly, in this process of international exposure, Irish neutrality remained a watchword: originally linked with the anti-Partition campaign from the 1940s, it was reinforced by its status as a 'Third World policy', given increasing relevance by the threat of superpower confrontations. At the UN, Ireland had a stage upon which to conduct a public foreign policy that was ostentatiously not constricted or defined by the Anglo-Irish relationship. The significance of this may have been more psychological than practical; but this made it no less important.

II
==

On the domestic front, the preoccupations stayed local, and the implicit influence of British proximity, historical and contemporary, remained inescapable. But Irish government during the 1950s and

[iii] Frederick H. Boland (1904–85): born in Dublin; educated at Clongowes and Trinity College, Dublin; entered Department of External Affairs, 1929; Assistant Secretary, 1938–46, and Secretary, 1946–50; Ambassador to the UK, 1950–56; Permanent Representative of Éire at the UN, 1956–64, and President of the General Assembly, 1960–61; Chancellor of Trinity College, Dublin, 1964–85.

[iv] Conor Cruise O'Brien (b. 1917): educated at Trinity College, Dublin; served in Irish diplomatic service, 1944–61; publicized anti-Partition propaganda, 1949–51; UN Special Representative, Katanga, 1961; Labour TD, 1969–77; Minister for Posts and Telegraphs, 1973–7; Senator, 1977–9; Editor-in-Chief of the *Observer*, 1978–81. Critic of all who make reflexive and pietistic calls for Irish unity. His writings include *Parnell and His Party*, 1957, a seminal text in the new history of Ireland, *States of Ireland*, 1972, and *Neighbours*, the Ewart-Biggs Memorial Lectures of 1980.

1960s developed, in some respects, away from the British model. A certain degree of power moved from the Dáil to professional committees and advisory bodies; the complaint that interest-groups and bureaucrats were usurping the powers of TDs was increasingly articulated. Government policy was discussed, and to some extent finalized, through mechanisms like the National Economic and Social Council; the institutions of local government tended to be sidetracked as well. Their responsibility for health provisions was moved to eight regional boards in 1970, and the subsequent abolition of local rates left their position hard to define. The division of authority between state-sponsored corporations, employing more than one-third of all state employees by the early 1960s, and the government ministers dealing with allied areas could also become anomalous.

Above all, the adoption of strategic economic planning (cautiously called 'programming'), which is again and again emphasized as the watershed of the post-war era, was not co-ordinated with other areas of government activity, which often remained isolated and haphazard. In 1970–71, following the 1969 Devlin Report, the notion emerged of dividing government departments into policy units and executive units; but it was not wholeheartedly adopted. Meanwhile, the civil service retained its high reputation for independence and lack of corruption, but also, particularly in the Department of Finance, for mandarin authoritarianism in its relations with government. Much as the puritanism of the revolutionary generation of politicians helped moderate the patronage and corruption inseparable from an individualist and localist political culture, the professional *esprit de corps* inherited by the civil service from its previous incarnation remained its hallmark.

In the early 1950s, however, attention was focused on a different area of authoritarianism: the influence of the Church in government. The highly politicized nature of Church authority, in an almost uniformly Catholic state, acted as a powerful cementing factor in the Republic; the rhetoric of nationalism from 1916 had made it clear that the ethos of nationalist Ireland would be unashamedly Catholic, and it was. When the coalition government introduced a state maternity health scheme, to operate without a means test (the 'Mother and Child' scheme), clerical opposition to government intervention in this area was implacable. The Church had a powerfully entrenched interest in the organization of hospitals already threatened by central initiatives. The Mother and Child scheme became a great *cause célèbre*, partly because it revolved around the dynamic socialist minister Noel

Browne, already responsible for the near-eradication of tuberculosis, and innocently prepared to treat the clergy in as offhand a manner as anyone else.

The conflict was not different in kind from previous controversies; the principles of Browne's measure did not differ from those laid down in Fianna Fáil's 1947 Health Act, itself left hanging under an ecclesiastical cloud when the government fell in 1948. But the abandonment of the means test, and probably Browne's record of opposition to the religious orders' monopolies in health care, sharpened the issue. Logic was on Browne's side: the hierarchy in Northern Ireland had not objected to Catholics using Bevan's more sweeping provisions, and the Church could pronounce against the Mother and Child scheme only on the grounds of social teaching, not moral teaching. But once the bishops denounced state health care for all mothers and children as 'a ready-made instrument for future totalitarian aggression ... we have no guarantee that state officials will respect Catholic principles in regard to these matters', Browne was abandoned by all his Cabinet colleagues.

The publicity that the affair attracted was what made it unusual; after his resignation, Browne published his correspondence with the bishops (to the delight of the Ulster Unionist publicity machine, who republished it on their own account as proof of Rome Rule in action). Possibly just as symptomatic was Costello's agonized comment, demonstrating the Dublin approach to freedom of information: 'The public never ought to have become aware of the matter.'

The state did subsequently extend its health-care responsibilities; Fianna Fáil's Social Welfare Act (1952) rationalized and extended national health insurance, unemployment insurance, and widows' and orphans' schemes, though Browne's wider vision of universal social insurance and pensions had to wait. Benefits remained markedly lower than in Northern Ireland and Britain, and available to fewer people; the means test remained, as did nineteenth-century conditions in some 'county homes'.ᵛ And religious authority played a dominant part in

ᵛ Browne describes in his autobiography touring these institutions in the late 1940s:
   Children in workhouses, like old-style criminals, carried numbers on their backs to distinguish one from another. Each destitute family was broken up – the father going this way, the mother that way and the children, according to sex, yet a third and fourth way.* In a workhouse which I visited in Longford, an open sewer ran through the recreation grounds. The food was cooked, as it was in most of the workhouses, in a large vat which had a block and tackle to open and close the vast lids in the open-air kitchens. Whatever was to be stewed for the inmates was poured into these enormous stew pans. The wards were

social welfare, as in education. Clerics had inherited the position of local leaders in many secular matters, as well as that of spiritual mentors. It would, however, be an oversimplification to interpret this as necessarily the result of oppressive authority: as in the nineteenth century, Church leaders were often following their flock, or reinforcing their predispositions, as much as leading them.

As late as 1962 a survey of Catholic attitudes in the Dublin area showed an extraordinarily wide cross-class consensus about the right of the Church to exert social, economic and political authority – and an accompanying distrust of politicians. In the event of a Church–state clash, 87 per cent of those questioned said they would support the Church; 88 per cent endorsed the proposition that the Church was the greatest force for good in the country. Dissent, when it appeared, came from the relatively most educated end of the spectrum, where the survey found an alienated and anti-clerical group of intellectuals. The researcher, an American Jesuit, concluded: 'The Catholic Church has progressively estranged the intellectual class, as our data conclusively indicated, and has deprived itself as well as Ireland of that vitality both so desperately need by almost forcing the talented intellectual to seek his fortunes in some other country.'[3] But the 'intellectual class' made up only a very small minority; nor (with some rarefied and usually temporary exceptions) did they enter politics to articulate their dissatisfaction.

For politics remained, in the 1950s and 1960s, the preserve of the civil war parties. Fianna Fáil exercised an insecure hegemony, managing to form governments consistently throughout the era (apart from the revived coalition of 1954–7), despite being a minority for extended periods (1951–4 and 1961–5). The party retained a certain dynamism, as well as a broadly distributed class profile; with the decline of de Valera into semi-blindness and an austere and enigmatic old age, the successor generation was epitomized by Sean Lemass, a very different kind of ex-revolutionary. Lemass, if not quite the superman claimed by devotees of his brand of economic expansionism, was a tough-

long, the walls had no pictures, the floors were bare and the sky was frequently visible through the broken slates on the roof. The beds were on raised platforms to accommodate straw-filled palliasses, long lines of them on either side of the room, occupied by pale, mummylike human beings lying semicomatose, apathetic and completely uninterested in their surroundings.
(*Against the Tide*, Dublin, 1986, pp. 199–200)

* The persistence of this practice was a bitterly ironic commentary on 'independence': the breaking up of families in workhouses had been Butt's major criticism of the 1837 Poor Law (Ireland) Act. See above, p. 310.

minded meritocrat, energetic and unsentimental to a refreshing degree. He epitomized Fianna Fáil's ability to present itself as the national party, rather in the manner of the nineteenth-century agrarian Leagues, and thus to reinforce its institutionalization as part of national (and local) life. But this effect was also sustained by Fianna Fáil's subtitle, the 'Republican Party'; and there were other elements in the party who retained a subconscious predisposition to legitimize the activities of the increasingly marginalized I R A, while formally outlawing them in practice. This ambivalence would come to the surface with the revival of republicanism in the 1970s.

Meanwhile, the local base of party identification stayed firm. Political scientists identify strong family traditions in membership and voting patterns, characteristic of all major Irish parties. In Fianna Fáil's case, this was accompanied by a certain Americanization and *embourgeoisement*; the traditional policies of ranch redistribution and settling more small farmers on the land were tacitly dropped from the 1940s, and big-business fund-raising adopted from the 1960s through an organization called Taca. The party still, however, remained adept at lining up trade union leadership behind it, especially after the adoption of 'planning' in the late 1950s. Fianna Fáil's unsuccessful attempts to abolish proportional representation by referendum in 1959 and 1968 were interpreted as a cynical attempt to copperfasten their majority; but it should be remembered that the electoral system gave them at least 50 per cent of Dáil seats between 1932 and 1977, in more than half the elections – though they only twice achieved 50 per cent of the votes cast.

Fine Gael remained in almost permanent opposition during this period, having been given artificial resuscitation by their unlikely alliance with the short-lived Clann na Poblachta in the late 1940s. Revival continued, though a lurch towards social democracy was firmly controlled by the implacably conservative Liam Cosgrave[vi] in the 1960s. Their Blueshirt pedigree mattered less and less; so did the executions of the celebrated seventy-seven in the civil war. And the issues that separated the major parties remained dubious. Despite Fianna

[vi] Liam Cosgrave (b. 1920): born in Dublin, son of William T. Cosgrave; educated at Christian Brothers school and King's Inns, Dublin; T D, 1943–81; Minister of Industry and Commerce, 1948, and for External Affairs, 1954–7; Chairman of the Committee of Ministers of the Council of Europe, 1955; Chairman of the first Irish delegation to the U N General Assembly, 1956; leader of Fine Gael, 1965–7; Taoiseach, 1973–7. Signatory to the Sunningdale communiqué, December 1973, but opposed to any changes to the constitution to facilitate better relations with Northern Ireland.

Fáil affectations about their radical roots *vis-à-vis* the bourgeois ante-cedents of Fine Gael, there was next to no difference in the social background of Dáil TDs on each side. Nor was the Taca ethos that of horny-handed sons of toil. It was not until the 1970s that a distinctive Fine Gael strategy emerged, along with the advent to prominence of Garret FitzGerald.[vii] FitzGerald's expertise in the language of modern economics, his attack in 1971 on the government for giving the Catholic Church control of vocational schools, and his criticism of the 'authoritarian desire to enforce private morality by means of public law' as exacerbating the Northern Protestants' fear of unity, set the tone for a face-lifted Fine Gael; as Lemass had done, FitzGerald would change the public rhetoric of Irish politics.

None the less, political scientists remain preoccupied by the Irish political system's combination of a lack of ideological differentiation between the two major parties, powerful competition between local brokerage machines, and firm party allegiances at the base. Politicians appear as brokers between their constituents and the real administrative locations of power, rather than actual distributors of favours on their own account; in the immortal phrase of one disgruntled senator, they allegedly spend their time 'going about persecuting civil servants' in order to arrange particular favours.[viii] Family structures remain powerful; widows inherit political seats; dynasties soldier on. Even the leadership of parties owes much to family tradition: in the 1973 coalition government three out of the sixteen Cabinet members held the same office held by their fathers in 1923 (the use of the word 'clann' – family – by fringe political parties might be noted). One ironic commentator has profiled the 'typical' picture of the Dáil TD, as discovered by political science in the 1960s:

A huge literature has grown up around the theme of the TD as messenger-boy, grievance-man, articulator of local particular interests and, from a more

---

[vii] Garret FitzGerald (b. 1926): born in Dublin; educated at Belvedere College and University College, Dublin; Lecturer in Political Economy at University College, Dublin, 1959–73; Senator, 1965–9; TD for Dublin South-east since 1969; Minister for Foreign Affairs, 1973–7; President of EEC Council of Ministers, January–June, 1975; leader of Fine Gael, 1977–87; Taoiseach, June 1981–March 1982 and December 1982–March 1987. A force behind Fine Gael's 1979 Confederate Ireland scheme, the constitutional crusade of 1981, which sought to make the Republic more attractive to Ulster Protestants, and the 1983 New Ireland Forum.

[viii] It may not be fanciful here to recall the 'mobile structure of client relationships' outlined for seventeenth-century Gaelic society in Chapter 1. And see p. 26 above for the strength of family bonding in Gaelic tribal politics.

jaundiced viewpoint, local political gombeenman. The archetypal backbench TD is seen as the product of the combination of highly centralized bureaucratic government, PR–STV and the parochialism of the culture. He is unconcerned with general issues or the world outside his own constituency; he is conservative, materialist and unintellectual. He leaves policy to the front bench, the civil servants, the interest groups and the clergy; he is deferential to tribal symbols, such as The Language, 1916, the tricolour and anti-Partitionism, but his deference is essentially verbal and is denied by his utterly pragmatic everyday behaviour. Ironically, the frontbenchers are recruited from the back benches and resemble backbenchers closely. The dominance of backbencher concerns in the Dáil is best seen at Question Time, when the structure of Irish representative politics becomes, perhaps, most visible.[4]

Where do the harder lines of ideological commitment fit into this picture – both republican and socialist? In the 1950s and 1960s neither identification was much in evidence. Sinn Féin returned four TDs in the 1957 general election, but this was a temporary upsurge, not repeated; the IRA, which eschewed the use of force in the Republic from 1949, called off its campaign of bombing on the border in 1962 because of an admitted lack of support.[ix] What characterized the republican movement in the 1960s was a rediscovery of socialism – mediated through the Wolfe Tone Society, a ginger-group of republican intellectuals. But the split in 1970 that produced the Provisional IRA also had the effect of rallying elements of disgruntled fundamentalist republicanism in the rural South – more important as a continuing psychological influence than many of the intelligentsia cared to admit.

As for the Labour Party, their profile remained oddly close to elements of Fianna Fáil and Fine Gael, and their electoral appeal correspondingly restricted. The 1960s brought the Labour Party an access of intellectual window-dressing, in the shape of some prominent academic candidates and supporters; in the 1969 election, for the first time they contested every constituency, nominating ninety-nine candidates. Though they gained votes (up to 17 per cent of the national percentage) they lost seats, dropping from twenty-two to eighteen. Just as significantly, their success was overwhelmingly concentrated in Dublin, whereas previously it had been traditionally based on rural Munster and south Leinster. Their relationship with the trade unions continued to be difficult; the credibility of the Party with the labour movement at large remained low, while they were correspondingly

[ix] See below, p. 583.

disadvantaged by gibes from their opponents about 'alien' ideas and inspirations (fuelled in the 1960s when their academic adherents talked romantically about the parallels offered by Cuba). As the 1970s opened, there was no apparent sign that urbanization and industrialization were bringing about a Labour breakthrough; nor that factors differentiating voting patterns were any more rational than they had ever been. The most decisive survey concluded with apposite caution: 'While class has only a small impact on partisanship, everything else has even less impact.'[5] But the weight of the historical palimpsest continued to impose its constricting pattern on the preoccupations of Irish politics.

III

Where a revisionist new departure was spectacularly evident was in economic organization, for the 1950s saw a resounding rejection of economic nationalism, paradoxically spearheaded by Fianna Fáil. Every historian of twentieth-century Ireland looks for some kind of antici-pation of the 1957–8 *démarche* into Keynsian expansionism, and locates it somewhere in the 1940s; even before the evident post-war problems of low growth and increasing deficits, Lemass could float in a 1942 memorandum the necessity for post-war planning in order to ensure expansion. In the post-war climate, interventionism was accepted as a necessary part of economic development; financial theorists kept an eye on the sort of expectations raised by Beveridge in Britain. But from the mid-1950s it was accepted that traditional nationalist assump-tions about the operation of Ireland's economy could no longer be taken as read, since they quite clearly were no longer working.

The implication of Ireland's post-war application for Marshall Aid, raising many delicate questions of political as well as financial policy, implied readiness to engage in economic co-operation within Europe. By 1950 Ireland had received nearly £150,000,000 in grants and loans; the corollary was, in a sense, forced internationalization, and an accompanying realization of backwardness in productivity and output. In order to make a case for the reception of American aid, a recovery programme had to be outlined, involving long-term projections if not actual 'planning'; certainly, the intellectual approach of McGilligan as Minister of Finance in the 1948 coalition government was more recep-tive to Keynsian ideas and capital investment initiatives than any of his predecessors. Involvement in Marshall Aid, however, meant by

implication involvement in Europe, as well as an admission of interdependence with the British economy; by the early 1950s, to some
American observers at least, the extent of Ireland's economic dependence on British markets made nonsense of Irish 'sovereignty'. Even
from Fianna Fáil, there was a more and more open acceptance that the
economic policies of Ireland and Britain would have to be 'dovetailed'
(de Valera's word, *mirabile dictu*) for mutual advantage.

At the same time, emigration provided a painful reminder that more
drastic remedies were needed. In the decade from 1951 to 1961 more
than 400,000 left – many to Britain – bringing the population down
to 2,800,000 by 1961. Rural depopulation inexorably continued; the
dictation of the market abroad and the price-support system at home
meant that extensive farming patterns reasserted themselves. Cattle,
beef and veal made up 70.2 per cent of Irish exports in 1961, having
been 50.8 per cent in 1938. The numbers employed on small farms fell
drastically. By 1956 it appeared to many observers that, despite the
injections of post-war aid, the Irish economy was unfit to cope with
the strains of independence.

From the early 1950s government thinking had been moving
towards the idea of attracting foreign capital – always a sensitive
political issue, given the rhetorical tradition of 'self-sufficiency'. Economic nationalists were ready to attack 'alien institutions ... squeezing
the lifeblood out of our shopkeepers who financed the Land League,
Sinn Féin, and republican movements';[6] this meant that Lemass and
those who shared in his conversion from protectionism had to tread
carefully. But by 1955 economic expansion with foreign capital was
becoming the accepted wisdom among all parties. The coalition
government of 1954–7 first opened up the question of Ireland's admission to the International Monetary Fund and the World Bank; the
Industrial Development Authority and Coras Trachtála (the Export
Board) were already in existence. And the mandarins of the civil service
had become converted, too: for the new departure was spearheaded by
T. K. Whitaker,[x] the influential Secretary of the department of Finance.

In May 1957 Whitaker stressed the need for the Department to
produce some ideas about economic development, faced with the

---

[x]Thomas Kenneth Whitaker (b. 1916): born County Down; educated at Christian
Brothers school and London University; joined the Irish civil service, 1934; Secretary
to Department of Finance, 1956–69; Governor of the Central Bank of Ireland, 1969–
76; Senator, 1977–82; President of the Royal Irish Academy, 1985–7; Chancellor of
the National University of Ireland since 1976; joint Chairman of Anglo-Irish Encounter since 1983.

declining state of public finance, and soaring emigration and unemployment figures. 'One of the biggest problems is how to reshape and redirect the public capital programme so that, in association with developments in agriculture, industry, etc., it will provide *productive* and *self-sustaining* employment.'[7] He was already negotiating with the World Bank, whose representatives saw a first draft of Whitaker's path-breaking *Economic Development* (1958) as well as an early outline of the subsequent first Programme for Economic Expansion. They also made an encouraging visit to Dublin, endorsing Whitaker's approach: international credit followed, bolstering up the approach called for in *Economic Development*.

Whitaker advocated 'an integrated development programme' to staunch the flow of emigration, and attract foreign capital; profitable sectors of agriculture were to be boosted, with a price-support structure for dairying, and competitive efficiency upgraded with a view to taking on international markets. (Domestic reaction was characteristic, in some quarters at least: the *Irish Independent*'s headline on *Economic Development* read: 'Easier Credit Schemes for Farmers Proposed'.) Entrepreneurialism, and 'productive' rather than 'social' investment projects, were stressed, though, in fact, many subsidies to the agricultural sector were continued against Whitaker's advice. Tax holidays and subsidies were to be offered to attract foreign investors, and also to those who lent to foreign firms. The Programmes for Economic Expansion, which built on Whitakerism, were put into practice by the ex-protectionist Lemass. Membership of the EEC was applied for in 1961, and finally succeeded in 1972. In 1965 the establishment of an Anglo-Irish free trade area agreement accepted as an economic reality what would have been politically unthinkable in the pre-war era; though to a certain kind of republican mind, it recalled the Act of Union.

In the meantime, the formula had apparently begun to work. From 1960 to 1969, 350 new foreign companies were established in Ireland; in 1966 the statistics showed the first increase in population since the Famine (62,000). Business management and marketing techniques were professionalized; financial analysis was introduced on a large scale; research councils for economic and industrial affairs attained a new importance. But the traditional industries did not develop a new look or a higher export profile. In the first six years of the Programme 80 per cent of private investment came from foreign capital. Transnational companies that set up between 1962 and 1973, with help from the Industrial Development Authority, would employ 25 per cent of the total manufacturing workforce by 1977; even by 1974 they accounted for 40 per cent of the exports of manufacturing industry, and two-thirds of Irish exports directed outside the U K market. Foreign capital had been attracted with a vengeance; whether native industrialization had been genuinely encouraged was more questionable.

The economic growth rate achieved 4 per cent over the first five years following the adoption of the Whitaker plan; it continued through the Second Programme from 1963 to 1970. By 1971 the population had grown by 100,000; the national growth rate was the highest in western Europe, and the emigration trend had apparently reversed. 'Economic Development' had been an apparent success, though the agricultural growth rate remained sluggish, and later approaches to economic management ignored warning signs. Unemployment remained obstinately high; the Irish economy would be ill-equipped to withstand the onslaught of energy crisis, inflation, recession and soaring unemployment that eventually followed. The boom would peter out in the mid-1970s; Programmes, 'planning' and inter-nationalization may not have had the long-term effect that contemporary analysts confidently expected. And foreign borrowing, according to one gloomy radical economist, played the part in the 1970s and 1980s economy that the potato did in the economic growth of late-Georgian Ireland: possibly threatening similar long-term results.[8]

It is probable that in the boom decade up to the mid-1970s, the distribution of income became more unequal;[9] other ominous pointers apparent in the 1970s included a large and unexpected degree of job-loss in manufacturing industry (while public-sector employment rose dramatically). And throughout the Second and Third Programmes for Economic Expansion, agricultural employment fell at a sharper rate than anticipated.

The long-term effects of economic expansion may be questionable; but the social results were strikingly evident in Ireland during the 1960s. Educational opportunities were broadened by the policy of comprehensive, free post-primary education, put into practice from the early 1960s; the share of the national budget earmarked for education was increased, and the participation rate in second-level education peaked dramatically, outpacing that of Britain by the mid-1970s. The 1960s were also boom years for third-level education, though in the absence of realistic grants this process tended to work to the benefit of the advantaged (and the metropolitan). In the 1960s Trinity College, and more particularly University College, Dublin, acted as crucibles of change, intellectually and politically: the radicalism of the time affected academics as well as students. Fine Gael shifted to the left (or at least to the centre); Labour acquired an intelligentsia; in all parties, a new generation came to prominence.

In some areas of social policy, old moulds were broken; from the mid-1960s, redrawn children's allowance schemes, occupational insurance benefits, and a wide range of state pensions were introduced. The legal and economic position of women continued to be restricted, with a marriage bar in the public service, denial of entry to certain skilled professions, and only a small number of women graduating to third-level scientific and technical education: in 1961, only 29 per cent of all women, and 5 per cent of married women, were registered in the labour force. Here, too, however, the 1960s laid the basis for developments in the subsequent decade.[xi] New areas of debate were opened up by the television boom: a national station was set up in 1962; discussion programmes brought Church spokesmen into the public domain, along with hitherto taboo subjects, notably contraception. In the age of the second Vatican Council, Ireland was exposed to the abandonment of many of the old religious forms – several of them (like the Friday Fast) a particularly traditional part of Irish Catholicism. There were even some halting steps towards ecumenism. But these developments were accompanied by a drastic fall in vocations, just when the population decline was apparently halted.

The overall theme of the 1960s was an exposure to the wider world: through the UN, through international economic initiatives, through the vast expansion in television licences (and the reception of British stations in the east of Ireland), through the cosmopolitan *lingua franca* of student radicalism, and through the tourist boom. Tourist board initiatives in the 1940s had tended to take forms like a plan to turn the North Bull Island bird sanctuary in Dublin Bay into a mini-Blackpool; from the late 1950s Bord Fáilte approached the matter of marketing Ireland with more finesse, and to greater purpose. The development of Shannon Airport led to a huge American influx; the coach-tour industry took over. And the advertising industry 'sold' Ireland as energetically and unrealistically as any seventeenth-century plantation promoter.[xii] Ireland was glossily advertised as a land of Edwardian comforts, limitless Guinness and tangible history – something of an irony, given the continuing cavalier attitude to the capital's architectural heritage. Though the National Monuments legislation of 1952–4

[xi] See below, p. 594.
[xii] See above, p. 66.

protected some ancient buildings, the unique streetscapes of Georgian Dublin were torn down by 'developers' with the tacit encouragement of Fianna Fáil governments. By 1967 receipts from tourism had passed £80,000,000, and a new 'industry' was well-established. It was one more process whereby 'traditional' Ireland was opened up to new influences in the youth-culture decade that came and passed so quickly. And ironically, while the patina of Irish 'history' was marketed by Bord Fáilte as one of the unique features of 'the real Ireland', the 1960s would end in a conflagration that acted as a terrible reminder of what much of that history had really been about.

IV
==

If the classic survey of Clare rural life in the 1930s is Conrad Arensberg's *The Irish Countryman*, the key text for Ulster attitudes in the 1950s is Rosemary Harris's *Prejudice and Tolerance in Ulster*, a sociological study eventually published in 1972. Harris's probing and sympathetic analysis explored a society 'dichotomized' at every level of social life; the institutionalization of social separation at a structural level comes powerfully across. The emphasis falls on how 'normal' life and amicable community relations are sustained through joint recognition of the constraints imposed by religious and cultural polarization. After the whirlwind struck at the end of the 1960s, the recurring lament would be heard: how relaxed relations had been before, how things had been getting better, how old barriers were breaking down. But the idea of a golden age destroyed by an unexpected and counter-productive apocalypse is recurrent in Irish history;[xiii] and Rosemary Harris's analysis of a structurally divided society carries its own implicit message.

'Structural' is a key word; while later surveys made the point that overt discrimination is often exaggerated, the structure of the social divide and different patterns of life between the two communities sustained the impression that social disadvantage adhered to religious lines. An analysis of the 1971 census showed that while both a Protestant and a Catholic middle class existed in Northern Ireland, Catholics were still disproportionately represented in unskilled jobs, and Protestants in skilled employment.[10] Even in middle-class occupations, Catholics, making up 31 per cent of the economically active population in Northern Ireland, accounted for only 6 per cent of mechanical engin-

---

[xiii] See, for instance, Sir John Temple's reflections quoted above, p. 71.

eers, 7 per cent of 'company secretaries and registrars' and 'personal managers', 8 per cent of university teachers, 9 per cent of local authority senior officers, 19 per cent of medical practitioners, and 23 per cent of lawyers.[11] Patterns varied; one survey finds that a 'startlingly high proportion' of alleged discrimination in housing, political representation and employment occurred in the west of the province.[12] There, in a sense, disadvantage had apparently become institutionalized.

Geography continued to matter. As the Northern Ireland government adopted expansionist programmes, investment seemed to favour overwhelmingly Protestant areas east of the Bann; the siting of a new university at Coleraine, a small Protestant town, instead of Derry, a large Catholic city, and the projected new town of 'Craigavon' in the Protestant heartland, fanned resentment. Surveying the background to the outbreaks of 1968–9, the Cameron Commission found patterns of discrimination established in several local authorities and affecting sections of the police force. But this kind of analysis needs to be read in conjunction with work like Rosemary Harris's in order to see how society worked, and lived with, a fundamental polarization within such a tiny space.

The theory that Catholic alienation would in itself have inevitably produced an explosion is not self-evidently demonstrable. The IRA bombing campaign from December 1956 to February 1962 had resulted in nineteen deaths, but even sympathetic commentators point out the complete discrepancy between the republican perception of the campaign, and general Irish opinion. The IRA had some cause to feel disgruntled, given the official Fianna Fáil line on Partition; but few pointed out the double-think.[xiv] The Limerick funeral of one of the activists, killed after a shoot-out, brought on a brief boom of balladry and martyrolatry; but this expressed the traditional psyche of nostalgic

---

[xiv] There were exceptions, notably a prescient pamphlet by Donal Barrington published at this time:

For thirty-five years our leaders have been waging a cold war against the North, and if the cold war has now become a shooting war, those who started and carried on the cold war must accept their share of responsibility. The policy of our leaders has been to coerce the North through the intervention of England, America, the United Nations or some outside power; the policy of the illegal organizations is to do the job themselves. You may call the former policy a constitutional policy, and the latter a physical-force policy, but both are basically policies of coercion. Both policies spring from the same presuppositions concerning the origin of Partition, both refuse to face the facts of the situation, and both are doomed to failure.

(Quoted in Paul Arthur, *Government and Politics in Northern Ireland*, London, 1980, pp. 70–71)

rural republicanism rather than any comprehension of the realities of life in the North. The same might be said of the IRA as a whole during this period; it was ready for the kind of reconsideration that produced the 'socialist republicanism' of the 1960s (though the 1966 detonation of Nelson's Pillar in central Dublin, as a symbolic blow against imperialist monuments, showed a flash of the old spirit). Significantly, several of the IRA leaders of this era would progress via socialist republicanism to the Workers' Party – which by the 1980s took a more sceptical line about irredentist nationalism in general, and verbal anti-Partitionism in particular, than any other party in the Dáil. Equally significantly, however, they were a small minority compared to those who reverted to fundamentalist republicanism when Ulster exploded after 1969.

The way this came about is still debated; it certainly had much to do with the internal economy of the Northern Ireland state, and the social effects of changes in policy from the early 1960s. Welfarism had exacerbated the differences between North and South; by the early 1960s Northern Ireland was costing the British Exchequer £45,000,000 a year. Spectacular differentials existed, not only in the standard of health services available to residents of Northern Ireland, but also in access to higher education, which would be of great importance in the radicalization of student opinion during the late 1960s: Catholics were 22 per cent of the student body at Queen's University in 1961, and 32 per cent in 1971. A large-scale building programme tackled aspects of the province's appalling housing; government funding was pumped into ailing heavy industry. But even in the mid-1960s, unemployment stayed at a constant level (6 per cent of the insured population). At the same time that a newly educated Catholic middle-class and student population were becoming restive about discriminatory structures, unemployment among the Catholic unskilled workers was climbing. And the same process would shortly affect skilled Protestant workers too.

The alteration in Ulster's industrial structure, the shipyard redundancies and linen bankruptcies from the early 1960s, the public demonstrations, the ominously rising Labour vote – all this enforced upon the Unionist government and its Prime Minister, Terence O'Neill,[xv]

xv Terence O'Neill (b. 1914): born in London; educated at Eton; Captain, Irish Guards, 1939–45; Northern Ireland MP for Bannside, 1946–70; Parliamentary Secretary to the Minister of Health, 1948–57; Deputy Speaker of Northern Ireland House of Commons, 1953–6; Minister for Home Affairs, 1956, and of Finance, 1956–63; leader of the Ulster Unionist Party and Prime Minister of Northern Ireland, 1963–9; raised to the peerage as Lord O'Neill of the Maine, 1970; Autobiography, 1972.

a shift to more decisive regional planning, and necessitated access to whatever government funding was available. The situation was exacerbated by pressures to modernize and liberalize the economy, following a critical government survey presented in 1955; there were also expressions of disquiet about the cost of subsidizing Northern Ireland from London, where an unsympathetic Labour government came to power in 1964. But measures like the imposition of a Ministry of Development, taking over local authorities' planning powers, were resented; O'Neill's government was unpopular in various quarters by the mid-1960s. In 1965 he opted for a new rhetoric: friendly meetings with the Republic's Taoiseach, Lemass, possibly with a view to closer economic co-operation.

It is important to remember that this is the most there was at stake: by implicitly 'recognizing' Northern Ireland, Lemass was, in fact, ceding more than O'Neill. But he had covered his flank far more effectively. O'Neill was an unconvincing liberal, as well as an inept tactician who refused to prepare the ground with his resentful colleagues. Subsequent events have created the illusion that he stood for introducing civil rights reform, for which there is no evidence; his 'New Ulster' still excluded Catholics from the Housing Trust, the Lockwood Committee to oversee university expansion, and many public boards. O'Neill's visits to Catholic schools did little to counter this; his jeers at 'jargon words ... like community relations'[13] were more representative, as are his appallingly condescending memoirs. A principal intention of his démarche towards liberalism was to drive the Northern Ireland Labour Party beyond the political pale; as with the abolition of proportional representation decades before, the strategy was not aimed at the Catholic minority as much as at preventing a split in the monolith of Unionist support. As it happened, the Labour advance was halted; this was O'Neill's one success. But within a very few years the Protestant monolith split from top to bottom, as part of the complete destabilization of the Northern Ireland state itself.

Was this inevitable? Seamus Heaney,[xvi] writing with a poet's pre-science in 1966, remarked of Ulster: 'Life goes on, yet people are reluctant to dismiss the possibility of an explosion. A kind of double-

[xvi] Seamus Heaney (b. 1939): born in County Londonderry; educated at Queen's University, Belfast; Lecturer in English at Queen's University, Belfast, 1966–72. Has published a number of highly acclaimed collections of verse that are rooted in the Troubles, but which, in literary terms, transcend them, including *Death of a Naturalist*, 1966; *Wintering Out*, 1972; *North*, 1975; *Field Work*, 1979; *Station Island*, 1984; *The Haw Lantern*, 1987.

think operates; something is rotten, but maybe if we wait it will fester to death.'[14] Lemass evidently believed that economic advance in the Republic was the best way of bringing about long-term unity; O'Neill believed that if Catholics in Ulster made money they would 'live like Protestants'. One-third of the Ulster Catholic community allegedly accepted the Northern Ireland constitution, according to a 1968 survey, while 83 per cent disapproved of the use of force to end Partition. But *embourgeoisement* worked two ways; in January 1964 the Campaign for Social Justice had been set up as a middle-class pressure-group. The forces released by O'Neill's ill-prepared initiative were unpredictable.

After the first O'Neill–Lemass meetings, the nationalist opposition agreed to abandon their policy of abstention from Stormont: a decision that would help to marginalize them as attitudes polarized. But a fundamental fact of O'Neill's strategy was that it lost him more Unionists than it gained him Catholics. Early on, his friendly-neighbour policies attracted the wrath of the fundamentalist cleric Ian Paisley:[xvii] representative of an irreconcilable working-class Protestantism well-established before the 1960s, though subsequent events made him look like a prophet to the faithful. In 1966 O'Neill felt able to dismiss Paisley contemptuously as a fascist eccentric. But what Paisleyism meant was a populist Protestant repudiation of any movement at all: the expression of the fundamentalist need to testify on behalf of righteousness, and an articulation of the unyielding nature of political conflict within a polarized society, as well as a resentment of middle-class Unionist monopolies.[xviii] There were ominous overlaps of

[xvii] Ian Kyle Paisley (b. 1926): born in County Armagh; educated at Barry School of Evangelism; ordained, 1946; co-founder and Moderator of Free Presbyterian Church of Ulster, 1951; founded the Ulster Constitution Defence Committee, Ulster Protestant Volunteers and *Protestant Telegraph*, 1966; imprisoned for obstructing a civil rights march, November 1968; elected Protestant Unionist M P for Bannside in Northern Ireland House of Commons, April 1970, and for North Antrim at Westminster, June 1970; founded Democratic Unionist Party, September 1971; supported anti-Sunningdale Ulster Workers' Council strike, May 1974; drew up a new Ulster covenant and launched a 'Carson trail' to protest against the Thatcher–Haughey 'conspiracy' of December 1980; revived the spirit of Carson again in opposing the Hillsborough agreement of November 1985. Has striven, in his capacity as M P, as member of the various Northern Ireland assemblies set up since 1973, and as M E P for Northern Ireland since 1979, to secure the return of an Ulster parliament without power sharing.

[xviii] Baron Smith's early nineteenth-century definition of Orangeism might be remembered: see above, p. 303. And for the traditional connection between 'no temporizing' in theology and 'no surrender' in politics, see above, p. 159.

membership with the extreme Protestant paramilitary tradition (the Ulster Volunteer Force was refounded in 1966); more ostentatiously, Paisleyism's political profile came into view with Paisley's own prestigious electoral victory in O'Neill's Bannside constituency in 1970. In 1971 he founded the Democratic Unionist Party; a decade later it would be challenging 'official' Unionism for political leadership of Ulster's Protestants.

Writing as early as 1971, Richard Rose pointed out that 'defining Paisleyism at its broadest – at all costs to endeavour to keep Northern Ireland Protestant – would classify slightly more than half the Protestants in the province as Paisleyites'.[15] The growth of unemployment, coupled with what was seen as a Unionist government truckling to Catholics, meant that the reassuring verities of Paisley's fundamentalism capitalized upon a crisis within Unionism. And it was the crisis within Unionism, as much as the radicalization of Catholic politics, which created the explosion of 1969: though the latter process captured the headlines at the time.

The Northern Ireland Civil Rights Association had been founded in January 1967: by 1968 the activists among them were identifying with confrontational political tactics popular in France and America, prepared for the kind of polarization that O'Neillism tried ineffectually to defuse. Notably, the radical People's Democracy movement, born in the crucible of student revolt, adopted the tactics of civil disobedience: media attention would assure leaders like Bernadette Devlin[xix] worldwide prominence. The analogies with student movements elsewhere are easy to make. But sociologists invariably observe the absence of a distinct 'youth culture' in Ulster society: young people there are more likely to identify with traditionalist, adult-dominated activities within their own communities. Given the presence of new-look socialist republicans among the civil rights activists, and the origin of several of their tactics in discussions of the Wolfe Tone Society, the results

---

[xix] Bernadette Josephine Devlin [McAliskey] (b. 1947): born in County Tyrone; educated at Queen's University, Belfast; prominent member of Northern Ireland Civil Rights Association and People's Democracy, 1968; Unity MP for Mid-Ulster, 1969–74, the youngest woman ever elected to Westminster; attacked the sham of O'Neillism in an electrifying maiden speech; sentenced to six months' imprisonment, for inciting riot in the 'Battle of the Bogside', August 1969; called 'an irrelevancy' by Gerry Fitt in 1973, she retorted that the Social Democratic Labour Party were 'political gangsters'; founded the Irish Republican Socialist Party, 1974; stood unsuccessfully for election as an MEP, 1979; spokesperson of the National H-Block Committee, 1980–81; shot by Loyalist gunmen, 1981; unsuccessfully stood in two Irish elections, 1982. *The Price of My Soul*, 1969.

were predictable. When elements among the People's Democracy flew the republican tricolour, they claimed it symbolized Orange and Green united within Ulster. To Protestant observers, already insecure, it represented a less arcane identification. To them, civil rights demonstrations meant that the republican fifth column was on the march again.

The allocation of housing became the flashpoint – though, ironically, levels of inequity were no longer as spectacular as claimed. In 1968 occupations, squattings, marches, might appear the simple mechanics of the international student protest; but within Ulster they represented symbolic invasion of ancient territory, and the assertion of an illegitimate right to 'walk'. And the forces of the Protestant state reacted accordingly. Violence began at a Derry march in October 1968, notably on the part of the police – Royal Ulster Constabulary as well as B-specials. A percussion of violence was set off by the ambush of marchers by Paisleyites at Burntollet Bridge in January 1969, culminating in the terrible 'Battle of the Bogside' in August, and the subsequent onslaught by Protestant mobs and the B-specials on Catholic areas of Belfast. Troops were already being used in aid of the civil power – but reluctantly.[xx] They were now fully committed. The Belfast violence left ten dead, 1,600 injured and property damage of £8,000,000.

By now, O'Neill had resigned, but his successors, James Chichester-Clark[xxi] and Brian Faulkner,[xxii] behaved little differently. Pressed by the

[xx] A Stormont civil servant revealingly recalled:

> You won't believe this, but in fact Westminster made it quite clear to us that not only did we have to commit the whole of the RUC and find ourselves failing but we had to commit the B-specials as well and find ourselves failing. Can you imagine! The most discredited force in the whole of our modern history and we had to commit them before Westminster would agree to commit the army.

(Desmond Hamill, *Pig in the Middle: The Army in Northern Ireland 1969–84*, London, 1985, pp. 20–21)

[xxi] James Dawson Chichester-Clark (b. 1923): educated at Eton; MP for South Derry, the seat vacated by his grandmother, Dame Dehra Parker, 1960; Chief Whip of the Ulster Unionist Party, 1963–9; Minister of Agriculture, 1967–9; resigned over proposed reforms, 23 April 1969; became leader of the Ulster Unionist Party and Prime Minister of Northern Ireland, May 1969; requested the presence of British troops in Northern Ireland, August 1969; unable to contain the violence of the rival paramilitary organizations; resigned, 20 March 1971. Created Lord Moyola.

[xxii] Arthur Brian Deane Faulkner (1921–77): born in County Down; worked in family textile business; active Orangeman; youngest ever MP in Stormont at time of his election for East Down, 1949; Chief Whip of Ulster Unionist Party, 1956–9; Minister of Home Affairs, 1959–63, and of Commerce, 1963–9, successfully attracting foreign investment in Northern Ireland; resigned upon the setting up of the Cameron

British government, a minimal programme of reforms was advanced (including a reformed franchise for local government and consultative committees to involve Catholics in regional decisions); but the 1954 'Flags and Emblems' Act symbolically remained, forbidding display of the tricolour. The minority community's identification with the Republic was still defined as illegitimate; while on their part, consent was withdrawn even further from the governing regime. Though the B-specials were disbanded, the part-time Ulster Defence Regiment, operating from April 1970, became and remained both Protestant and partial. And though the People's Democracy liked to think of themselves as a socialist spearhead, the movement that they had helped to start increasingly took on the complexion of embattled republicanism.

Many Catholic areas, demarcated by community barricades, had become 'no-go' areas, reflecting the process of geographical segregation that solidified as Derry and Belfast burned. The army, originally hailed as their protectors, were unable to cope with the situation; intelligence networks were left to the police, whose idea of 'suspects' was based on atavistic lines of confrontation with republicans. As the Republic's government called for UN intervention, the British sent in more troops – reluctantly, and with unrealistic hopes for an early disengagement. In this storm-centre, the IRA was reborn.

The movement had not initially been ready to capitalize on the crisis of 1969. Though socialist republicans had been involved in the civil rights movement, they did not direct it, even if Unionist wisdom believed otherwise. When the IRA came to the fore, it was as a 'Defenderist' force 'protecting' the Catholic ghettos. Those who took on this role represented the element who had called for guns and split from the woolly radicals dreaming of a national liberation front, North and South; after the IRA convention of 1969, the fundamentalists declared themselves the 'Provisional' IRA, pending the setting up of an executive and army council. They were probably a majority; the 'Officials' were condemned to an odyssey leftwards that meant, for many of them, an eventual repudiation of thirty-two-county repub-

Commission, January 1969; Minister of Development, 1969–71; leader of Ulster Unionist Party and last Prime Minister of Northern Ireland, March 1971–March 1972; introduced internment, August 1971; signed Sunningdale agreement, December 1973; Chief Executive of power-sharing assembly, January–May 1974; founded Unionist Party of Northern Ireland, 1974; retired from politics, 1976; created Baron Faulkner of Downpatrick, January 1977; killed in a riding accident, March 1977. *Memoirs of a Statesman*, 1978.

licanism. For the Provisionals, American money, local support and the army's record in house-to-house searches established them firmly in the urban ghettos. By early 1971 they could go on the offensive against an enemy that could be presented as the military might of British oppression: not the entrenched Ulster Protestant majority who formed, as they had done for a century, the real opposition to a 'united' Ireland.

Nor was this the only realignment taking place in 1970. With the Nationalist Party marginalized, and the Northern Ireland Labour Party hopelessly split along the old fissure of support for the Union, a broad front of moderate nationalists formed the Social Democratic and Labour Party, essentially Catholic, but prepared for cautious co-operation with the regime; its withdrawal of support from Stormont would deliver the death-blow to devolved government. Originally led by the established socialist politician Gerry Fitt,[xxiii] the Social Democratic and Labour Party rapidly brought the civil rights generation into political prominence – notably Fitt's successor, the Derry teacher John Hume.[xxiv] In 1971 polarization was ensured by the policy of internment of 'suspects': 450 arrests were authorized on 9 August, and 346 prisoners rounded up on the basis of out-of-date police lists. None of them was Protestant, despite the rise of the Ulster Volunteer

[xxiii] Gerard Fitt (b. 1926): born in Belfast; educated at Christian Brothers school; merchant seaman, 1941–53; Irish Labour member of Belfast City Council, 1958–81; Republican Labour MP for Belfast Dock at Stormont, 1962–6; Westminster MP for West Belfast, 1966–83; encouraged the Labour government's interest in Northern Ireland, 1966–9; co-founder and first leader of the Social Democratic and Labour Party, 1970; Deputy Chief Executive in power-sharing assembly, 1974; increasingly alienated from even the more moderate Northern nationalists, he resigned from the Social Democratic and Labour Party in 1979 to sit at Westminster as an Independent Socialist; lost his seat to Gerry Adams, the leader of Provisional Sinn Féin, 1983; made a life peer, 1983.

[xxiv] John Hume (b. 1937): born in Derry City; educated at St Columb's College and Maynooth; founded a housing association and a credit union in Derry; member of Northern Ireland Civil Rights Association; Vice-Chairman of the Derry Citizen's Action Committee, 1968–9; MP for Foyle at Stormont, 1969–73, having fought his campaign on the need for a new party in the European democratic socialist tradition; founder member and Deputy Chairman of the Social Democratic Labour Party, 1970, emerging as its chief policy-maker; elected to the power-sharing assembly of 1974, and its Minister of Commerce; spent the mid-1970s attempting to engage the interest of European politicians in the subject of Northern Ireland, believing in the role of the EEC in the 'healing process' for Ireland; MEP for Northern Ireland since 1979; leader of the Social Democratic Labour Party since 1979; architect of the New Ireland Forum, 1983; MP for Foyle since 1983; supporter of the 1985 Hillsborough agreement.

Force to a grisly prominence: by September the numerous Protestant 'defence' organizations were co-ordinated into the Ulster Defence Association. Violence escalated; on 30 January 1972 Catholic alienation was ensured by 'Bloody Sunday', when thirteen civilians were shot dead by paratroopers after a banned civil rights march in Derry. In a subsequent Dublin demonstration, the British embassy was burned to the ground. By the time the year lurched to an end, the death toll had reached 474; 1972 had been marked by a spate of horrific ritual sectarian killings, most of them carried out by Protestant murder gangs, and by the Provisional I R A's adoption of arbitrary bombing blitzes on civilians in crowded city centres. A cease-fire, followed by talks with the Provisional I R A in London, had come to nothing; the urban no-go areas had been forcibly re-entered by the army. And on 24 March, reaching an impasse with the Northern Ireland government over the control of the Royal Ulster Constabulary, Edward Heath had suspended Stormont, replacing the Northern Ireland parliament with direct rule by a Secretary of State. The devolutionary experiment of 1920 had ended in chaos.

The 1920 Act had asserted that the supremacy of the U K Parliament remained 'unaffected and undiminished over all persons, matters and things in Ireland and every part thereof', a fact conveniently forgotten by the outraged Unionist governing class; but up to 1972 the suspension of Stormont was the most decisive act Westminster took. Policies remained makeshift; the Cabinet diaries and memoirs that have surfaced indicate that there was no agreed strategy. Politicians like the ludicrous Reginald Maudling contributed nothing more than the notorious concept of 'an acceptable level of violence'. The Royal Ulster Constabulary was disarmed, and then rearmed; the internment strategy was guaranteed to turn terrorism into communal insurgency; the negotiations with the Provisional I R A in July 1972 were abruptly rescinded; official thinking reverted to the idea that no constitutional rearrangement could be contemplated until the I R A was 'defeated', though the opposite proposition was at least as demonstrably true. Meanwhile the legal system was paralysed by the intimidation (and unwillingness) of jurors and witnesses; the non-jury 'Diplock courts' would follow in 1973. By 1972 the British government was poised to attempt the first of several compromising, power-sharing, internal Ulster 'solutions' with a cautious involvement from the Republic, while Unionist opinion obsessively watched for evidence of a sell-out. The theme remained that of the crisis within Unionism as much as the alienation of the Catholics.

Dublin's policy was, in a sense, equally constricted: the double-think of anti-Partitionism was exposed. The Provisional IRA were condemned, and subject to increasingly coercive legislation. Statements were issued attacking Stormont, but no intervention threatened: as Ronan Fanning has pointed out, much the same as in 1922. But underground ambiguities within the Fianna Fáil camp were highlighted by the 1970 arms trial crisis, when two Cabinet ministers were arrested on suspicion of shipping guns to the Provisional IRA; one of their fellow-defendants said the process raised 'an echo of sadness from the graves of dead generations', a phrase used by de Valera in 1926. Though convictions were not brought, the affair indicated that elements within Fianna Fáil retained 'an each-way bet on force'.[16] The suspension of Stormont, and the power-sharing initiative with an 'Irish dimension' set up in 1973, apparently met Dublin's demands; but the experiment collapsed in the face of Protestant resistance. This proved that populist opposition to closer involvement with the Republic was not manipulated by an elite in Stormont, but had its own dynamism. Which had, after all, been the lesson taught to O'Neill a few eventful years before.

By 1972, then, half a century of the Protestant supremacist state had come to a bloody and chaotic end. The enormous question of the legitimacy of the government had been raised once more; the conflict of British army, Royal Ulster Constabulary and IRA suggested specious parallels with 1919–21 to the exalted republican mind, while the question of majority opinion, in both North and South, was left to one side. Much of the language employed by the British authorities recalled the 'Irish problem' as perceived by administrators in the early nineteenth century; a succession of bewildered Secretaries of State for Northern Ireland resembled the Chief Secretaries of Dublin Castle after the Union. And though riots, ambushes, shootings and kidnappings now took place in raw new suburbs and tenement apartment-blocks, the village names and urban shatter-zones were those of ancient confrontations: Forkhill, Crossmaglen, the Shankill Road, had been familiar to observers of Ulster conflict since the seventeenth century. The special nature of Ulster society, and the imprint of Ulster's peculiar history of partial settlement, evangelical commitment and uneven industrialization, had created a situation for which no glib historical 'precedent' nor any irrelevant colonial 'parallel' could act as guide.

V

For all the rhetoric of anti-Partitionism, opinion in the Republic was covertly realistic about this point, too: the predominant note of modern Ireland in 1972 was that of looking after its own. The mind of the Republic, as frequently measured by opinion polls, made it resoundingly clear that sympathy for the Catholic community in Ulster did not extend to paying the crippling costs that would be necessitated by notional 'unity'. As so often before, nationalist orthodoxy restricted itself to a punctilious observance of names and forms, rather than a commitment to practical policy. 'Ulster' could not be used, as the supposedly 'ancient' province had contained three extra counties. 'Northern Ireland' was repudiated as legitimizing the British statelet, which de Valera had airily referred to as an imaginary confection. 'The North' could be employed; or, more aggressively, 'the Six Counties'. But the obeisance to a thirty-two-county ideal had become increasingly perfunctory, as the Republic evolved its own ethos.

Lemass had sardonically remarked in 1960 that the main weakness of the Irish character was 'an undue disposition to be sorry for ourselves';[17] but looking around the twenty-six-county state in 1972, there seemed little enough to be sorry for. The bourgeois Republic had inherited a powerful state apparatus from the 'oppressor', and built on it. In many ways, what had emerged was the kind of Ireland that intelligent conservatives on both sides of the Irish Sea had drafted in the late nineteenth century: embodying a strong Catholic middle class, powerfully entrenched rights of landed property (including small property), an educational system firmly controlled by the Church, and a stable political system, built on the English model but adapted to Irish preoccupations.

But unlike the nineteenth-century ideal it was not part of the imperial system; it was partitioned (an important reason for the twenty-six-county unit's stability); and there were other unpredictable changes too. Its population was no longer overwhelmingly rural; 31 per cent of the labouring population was engaged in agriculture, but the 1971 census showed that this occupation was in steep decline. The largest occupational increases were in electrical and electronics plants, engineering, and professional and technical work. The proportion of the population dwelling in urban areas had just become a majority (52 per cent, compared to 46 per cent in 1961). Equally significant was the declining proportion of Irish exports going to Britain, and the rising proportion of manufactured exports: developments facilitated by EEC links and international borrowing. And the Republic was economically vulnerable. The dangers of long-term unemployment were pointed out in an Institute of Public Administration survey in 1971; an analysis of the class composition of the workforce by the late 1970s showed 'residual classes stranded in the course of industrial development, especially farmers on marginal holdings or labourers without skills' – considered more characteristic of the southern Mediterranean than western Europe.[18] A destructive escalation in land prices was about to begin; and Ireland had the highest rate of inflation in the EEC, which she had voted to join by an 83 per cent majority in 1972. The limited options available to a small open economy under the conditions of free trade and international recession, along with a potential crisis in external borrowing, would come brutally home a decade later.

This possibility attracted less contemporary attention, however, than optimistic trends in demography. In 1972 the population touched 3,000,000 for the first time in nearly fifty years; the age of marriage for women dropped from 25.9 (1957 figures) to 23.5, and for men from 29.4 to 25.6. At the same time, average family size dropped too: a reversal of all the traditional Irish stereotypes seemed in the offing. Accompanying this trend, the feminist strain evident in early twentieth-century Irish history reasserted itself; agitation produced a government-appointed commission on the status of women in 1972; the marriage bar in public service employment was abolished in 1973; anti-discrimination and employment-equality legislation would shortly follow. In 1971 and 1972, private members' bills legalizing contraception were introduced (and failed) in the Senate and Dáil; by 1974 a supreme court decision would bring the issue into constitutional focus.

Did this mean that traditional Ireland was dead and gone? The country was more overwhelmingly Catholic than ever; in 1971 a survey claimed a 96 per cent mass-going rate among Catholics. The Protestant population in the Republic decreased by 24 per cent between the end of the war and 1971 – from intermarriage and a declining birth rate rather than emigration. The remnants of the 'Anglo-Irish', or an idea of them based on the Dublin Horse Show and the Irish Georgian Society, had become an innocuous part of the advertising industry's Irish package. Trinity College was no longer the bastion of Ascendancy; the hierarchy had lifted their ban on Catholics attending it in

1970, and the college itself drastically restricted its intake of foreign (in effect, British) students. At the same time, the supposition that Church–state ties were liberalizing was easily made; 1972 was also the year when the clause in the constitution giving a special position to the Catholic Church was abolished by referendum. But a number of constitutional confrontations in the subsequent period made it clear that Ireland's Catholic ethos would be defended by a majority of the population as well as a politically powerful Church leadership. And here again what must be emphasized is the low priority given to making reunion with the Republic attractive to Protestant Ulster.

Looking back to 1972 from a slightly later vantage, what is striking is the public commitment to much that had *not* changed. John A. Murphy's sardonic description of the 1916 anniversary celebrations in 1966 deserves quotation: 'On a platform outside the General Post Office in Dublin, the ageing President de Valera spoke of his dreams of a United Ireland and a revived language while behind him his young successors listened uneasily to this embarrassing reminder of their origins.'[19] On the same occasion de Valera described Ulster as 'the land of the O'Neills, the Ó Cathains, the MacDonnells, the Maguires, the MacGuinnesses' – and therefore, to the republican mind, platonically Gaelic and ripe for reunification. This unrealistic world view was still a political stock-in-trade in the 1970s; and increasing cultural self-confidence did not mean the abandonment of nationalistic platitudes. In 1972 Conor Cruise O'Brien published *States of Ireland*, an account of his personal repudiation of nationalist myths; it did not enhance his political career. It is usual to emphasize the scholarly achievements of the *soi-disant* 'revisionist' school of Irish historians, who since the 1940s have been dispassionately re-evaluating the assumptions of the eight-hundred-years-of-struggle version of Irish history; certainly, by 1972 new textbooks were being used in schools and universities, and new questions being asked. But what might seem most striking is how little this affected the popular (and paradoxically Anglocentric) version of Irish history held by the public mind.

And a popular perception of history still mattered – reinforced by the still evidently ancient landscape. Weak and belated planning laws had not halted the ruination of many rural and urban amenities; organizations like An Fóras Forbeartha and An Taisce[xxv] could do little

---

[xxv] An Fóras Forbeartha (National Institute for Physical Planning and Construction Research) incorporated 26 March 1964 and axed 1987; An Taisce, the National Trust for Ireland, approved 18 November 1947 and appointed 15 July 1948.

against combined avarice and apathy, though the ultimate lunacy of a Dublin 'traffic scheme' that suggested concreting in the Grand Canal was dropped. Inner-city Dublin tenements were displaced to high-rise slums in distant suburbs. The Gaeltacht inexorably declined to about 32,000 residents in 1972; compulsory qualifications in the Irish language were dropped for Leaving-Certificate examinations and civil service entry in 1973. But the land still carried the evident marks of conquest and settlement; and Ireland in the early 1970s still retained a powerful sense of national identity, even if the Irish experience had modified or vitiated every general theory of nationalism produced by political scientists.[20] The process had been complex, confused and very far from a linear narrative or an apostolic succession. But the cultural reinforcement of nationalist rhetoric had overridden many implicit contradictions, often finding its strongest affirmation in a negative and sectarian consensus.

This had provided a powerful impetus to political mobilization from the early nineteenth century on; it also meant that the independent state that emerged from the process had little option to be pluralist, for all the oratory of Davis and Tone. The idea of a might-have-been secular Irish nationalism is as much a red herring as the equally ahistorical concept of a platonic 'unity' that Gaelic chiefs in the early modern period are sometimes traduced for never having attained.[xxvi] And this highlights a theme that is evident from the seventeenth century, and recurs in this book: the concept of being 'more' or 'less' Irish than one's neighbour; Irishness as a scale or spectrum rather than a simple national, or residential, qualification; at worst, Irishness as a matter of aggressively displayed credentials.[xxvii] Irish history in the long period since the completion of the Elizabethan conquest concerned a great deal more than the definition of Irishness against Britishness; this survey has attempted to indicate as much. But that sense of difference comes strongly through, though its expression was conditioned by altering circumstances, and adapted for different interest-groups, as the years passed. If the claims of cultural maturity and a new European identity advanced by the 1970s can be substantiated, it may be by the hope of a more relaxed and inclusive definition of Irishness, and a less constricted view of Irish history.

[xxvi] See above, p. 42.

[xxvii] For the seventeenth-century Confederate argument against this approach, see above, p. 96, note xvii.

APPENDIX

===

PROCLAMATION OF THE REPUBLIC

Poblacht na hÉireann

*The Provisional Government of the Irish Republic
to the People of Ireland*

Irishmen and Irishwomen: In the name of God and of the dead generations from which she receives her old tradition of nationhood, Ireland, through us, summons her children to her flag and strikes for her freedom.

Having organized and trained her manhood through her secret revolutionary organization, the Irish Republican Brotherhood, and through her open military organizations, the Irish Volunteers, and the Irish Citizen Army, having patiently perfected her discipline, having resolutely waited for the right moment to reveal itself, she now seizes that moment, and, supported by her exiled children in America and by gallant allies in Europe, but relying in the first on her own strength, she strikes in full confidence of victory.

We declare the right of the people of Ireland to the ownership of Ireland, and to the unfettered control of Irish destinies, to be sovereign and indefeasible. The long usurpation of that right by a foreign people and government has not extinguished the right, nor can it ever be extinguished except by the destruction of the Irish people. In every generation the Irish people have asserted their right to national freedom and sovereignty; six times during the past three hundred years they have asserted it in arms. Standing on that fundamental right and again asserting it in arms in the face of the world, we hereby proclaim the Irish republic as a sovereign independent state, and we pledge our lives and the lives of our comrades-in-arms to the cause of its freedom, of its welfare, and of its exaltation among the nations.

The Irish republic is entitled to, and hereby claims, the allegiance of every Irishman and Irishwoman. The republic guarantees religious and civil liberty, equal rights and equal opportunities to all its citizens, and declares its resolve to pursue the happiness and prosperity of the whole nation and of all its parts, cherishing all the children of the nation equally, and oblivious of the differences carefully fostered by an alien government, which have divided a minority from the majority in the past.

Until our arms have brought the opportune moment for the establishment of a permanent national government, representative of the whole people of Ireland, and elected by the suffrages of all her men and women, the Provisional Government, hereby constituted, will administer the civil and military affairs of the republic in trust for the people. We place the cause of the Irish republic under the protection of the Most High God, whose blessing we invoke upon our arms, and we pray that no one who serves that cause will dishonour it by cowardice, inhumanity, or rapine. In this supreme hour the Irish nation must, by its valour and discipline, and by the readiness of its children to sacrifice themselves for the common good, prove itself worthy of the august destiny to which it is called.

Signed on behalf of the provisional government,

Thomas J. Clarke, Sean MacDiarmada, Thomas MacDonagh, P. H. Pearse, Eamonn Ceannt, James Connolly, Joseph Plunkett.

Issued 24 April 1916. Text reproduced from E. Curtis and R. B. McDowell (editors), *Irish Historical Documents 1172–1922* (London, 1943).

CHRONOLOGY

===

1600   Jan.   O'Neill makes tour of Munster.
         21 Jan.   Mountjoy appointed Lord Deputy.
         Sept./Oct.   Battle at Moyry Pass.

1601   21 Sept.   Spaniards arrive at Kinsale.
         24 Dec.   Battle of Kinsale.

1602   Sept.   Mountjoy breaks O'Neill coronation-stone at Tullahogue.

1603   30 Mar.   O'Neill pardoned in return for surrender at Mellifont.

1606   22 July   Commission for remedying defective land-titles.

1607   4 Sept.   O'Neill and others leave Ireland for the Continent ('flight of the earls': see above, pp. 43–5).
         Dec.   Donegal and Tyrone lands declared forfeit.

1608   18 Apr.   Revolt of Sir Cahir O'Doherty.
         19 July   Commission to survey six Ulster counties.

1610   Apr.–May   Ulster land assigned to British undertakers.

1613   18 May   Opening of parliament at Dublin.

1621   20 Jan.   Patents granted for plantations in Leitrim, King's County, Queen's County, Westmeath.

1625   27 Mar.   Accession of Charles I.

1626   22 Sept.   Charles offers twenty-six 'Graces' to the Irish (see above, pp. 53–5).

1628   24 May   Fifty-one 'Graces' granted in return for financial subsidy.

1633   25 July   Wentworth (later Strafford) sworn in as Lord Deputy.

1635   July   Crown title confirmed over land in Roscommon, Sligo and Mayo (and in Galway, after resistance, Dec. 1636).

1639   21 May   Wentworth's 'Black Oath' of loyalty imposed on Ulster Scots (see above, p. 82).

1640   Aug.   War begins in Scotland.

1641   12 May   Wentworth executed.

9 June   Patrick Darcy argues that Irish parliament possesses independent authority (see above, pp. 84–5).

22–3 Oct.   Outbreak of Ulster rebellion.

Dec.   Old English join the rebels.

1642   19 Mar.   'Adventurers' Act' offers Irish land in return for subsidies.

15 Apr.   Monro's army arrives from Scotland.

10–13 May   First meetings of Catholic leaders in Kilkenny.

8–9 July   Arrival of Owen Roe O'Neill.

Oct.   Confederates assemble at Kilkenny.

1643   Sept.   Truce between Ormond (for the royalists) and Confederates.

13 Nov.   Ormond appointed Lord Lieutenant.

1644   2 July   Royalist defeat at Marston Moor.

1645   14 June   Royalist defeat at Naseby.

25 Aug.   Glamorgan (for the King) makes secret treaty with Confederates.

12 Oct.   Arrival of Rinuccini in Ireland (reaches Kilkenny, 12 Nov.).

1646   28 Mar.   Peace between Confederates and Ormond (formally proclaimed, July–Aug.).

5 June   Battle at Benburb.

12 Aug.   Rinuccini condemns Ormond peace; Waterford Synod (1 Sept.) excommunicates adherents to peace terms.

1647   7 June   Jones lands with parliamentary force at Dublin.

19 June.   Ormond surrenders Dublin.

1648   20 May   Truce between Confederates and Inchiquin (adherents excommunicated by Rinuccini, 27 May).

1649   17 Jan.   Ormond and Confederates sign peace treaty.

30 Jan.   Execution of Charles.

23 Feb.   Rinuccini returns to Rome.

2 Aug.   Ormond defeated by Parliamentarians at Rathmines.

15 Aug.   Oliver Cromwell arrives at Dublin, as civil and military Governor of Ireland.

11 Sept.   Massacre at Drogheda.

11 Oct.   Massacre at Wexford.

20 Oct.   Owen Roe O'Neill and Ormond combine.

6 Nov.   Death of Owen Roe O'Neill.

1650   27 Mar.   Kilkenny surrenders to Cromwell.

26 May   Cromwell returns to England, Ireton taking over.

11 Dec.   Ormond leaves for France.

1652   12 Aug.   'Act for the Settling of Ireland' (see above, pp. 109–10).

1653   June–Sept.   Survey and allocation of forfeited Irish lands, followed by
       arrangements for transplantation ('Act of Satisfaction', 26 Sept.).
       16 Dec.   Cromwell Lord Protector.

1657   9 June   Settlement Act 'for the Assuming, Confirming and Settling of
       Lands and Estates in Ireland'.
       26 June   'Act for Convicting, Discovering and Repressing of Popish
       Recusants'.

1660   Feb.   Parliament restored in Dublin.
       14 May   Charles II proclaimed King.

1662   19 May   Act forbidding export of Irish wool.
       31 July   Act of Settlement, confirming some adventurers' landowning
       rights but also allowing claims from 'innocents' and royalist supporters
       (Court of Claims opened, 20 Sept.; last sitting, Jan. 1669; see above, pp.
       115–16).

1663   27 July   'Cattle Act' restricting Irish trade with colonies and cattle export
       to England (see above, pp. 128–9).

1667   18 Jan.   Cattle exports to England prohibited (see above, p. 128).

1671   18 Jan.   Catholic gentry present petition to Charles.
       22 Apr.   Direct importation from colonies prohibited.

1672   Oct.   *Regium donum* grant to Presbyterian Church initiated.
       Abandonment of presidency system (see above, pp. 138–9).

1678   28 Sept.   Popish Plot alleged, followed by renewed proclamations against
       Catholic clergy and schools.

1679   6 Dec.   Arrest of Oliver Plunkett (executed, 1 July 1681).

1684   Jan.   Foundation of Dublin Philosophical Society.

1685   6 Feb.   Accession of James II.

1686   22 Mar.   Payments to Catholic hierarchy authorized.
       5 June   Tyrconnell arrives as Commander-in-Chief of Irish army.

1687   12 Feb.   Tyrconnell sworn in as Lord Deputy.

1688   10 June   Birth of James, royal heir.
       5 Nov.   William of Orange arrives in England.
       23 Dec.   James flees to France.

1689   12 Mar.   James arrives in Ireland.
       18 Apr.   Siege of Derry begins.

7 May–18 July   Parliament at Dublin; passes (late June) Act of Attainder (see above, pp. 145–6).

22 June   Act for repeal of land settlement.

31 July   Siege of Derry lifted (first relieved, 28 July).

1690   14 June   William arrives in Ireland.

1 July   James defeated at River Boyne.

4 July   James flees to France.

5 Sept.   William leaves Ireland, after failing to capture Limerick.

Sept.–Oct.   Munster surrenders to Marlborough.

1691   9 May   Saint-Ruth arrives from France.

7 July   Ginkel's proclamation offering pardon and security of property to opponents.

12 July   Battle of Aughrim.

3 Oct.   Treaty of Limerick, allowing evacuation of Irish army to France and promising toleration to Irish Catholics (see above, pp. 151–2).

1695   7 Sept.   'Penal Laws': Acts restricting rights of Catholics to education, to bear arms or to possess a horse worth more than five pounds (reinforced, 31 Mar. 1740).

1696   27 Apr.   Act 'for encouraging the linen manufacture of Ireland'.

1697   25 Sept.   Catholic clergy banished by Act of Parliament.

1698   27 June   Westminster Parliament condemns Molyneux's *Case of Ireland being Bound by Acts of Parliament in England Stated* (see above, pp. 161–2).

1699   Jan.–May   Acts (in Irish and English parliaments) restricting Irish woollen exports.

1702   8 Mar.   Accession of Anne.

1704   4 Mar.   Further Penal Law 'to prevent further growth of popery' restricts landholding rights for Catholics and imposes 'tests' for public office holding; amended and strengthened, 30 Aug. 1708 (see above, p. 154).

1713   13 June   Swift becomes Dean of St Patrick's (dies, 19 Oct. 1745).

1714   1 Aug.   Accession of George I.

1719   2 Nov.   Toleration Act for Protestant Dissenters.

1720   7 Apr.   'Declaratory Act' defines right of British Parliament to legislate for Ireland, and denies appellate jurisdiction of Irish House of Lords.

1724   Feb.–Oct.   Swift's *Drapier's Letters*, attacking copper coinage patent granted to William Wood (12 July).

1727   11 June   Accession of George II.

1728   6 May   Act removing franchise from Catholics (see above, p. 206).

1731   25 June   Foundation of Dublin Society for Improving Husbandry, Manu-
       facturing, and Other Useful Arts (from 1820, Royal Dublin Society).

1753   Dec.   Money Bill crisis (see above, p. 237).

1758   29 Apr.   Appointment of Wide Streets Commission (see above, p. 189).

1760   21 Feb.   Thurot lands French force at Carrickfergus in Belfast Lough.
       Mar.   First meetings of Catholic Committee.
       25 Oct.   Accession of George III.

1767   14 Oct.   Beginning of Townshend viceroyalty (recalled, 30 Nov.
       1772).

1768   16 Feb.   Octennial Act (Irish parliament's life limited to eight years).

1772   2 June   Act allowing Catholics to lease bogland.

1774   22 June   'Quebec Act' grants Canadian Catholics religious and civil
       rights.

1778   Apr.   John Paul Jones raids Belfast Lough.
       Volunteering movement begins to spread from Ulster.
       14 Aug.   Catholic Relief Act granting rights of leasing and inheritance.

1779   4 Nov.   Volunteers' demonstration in favour of 'free trade' (see above,
       pp. 243, 245).

1780   24 Feb.   Act opening colonial trade to Irish goods.
       2 May   Act repealing tests imposed on Dissenters.

1782   15 Feb.   Dungannon convention of Volunteers calls for legislative inde-
       pendence.
       27 Mar.   Rockingham forms government (Duke of Portland Irish Lord
       Lieutenant).
       4 May   Catholic Relief Act allows Catholics to own land outside par-
       liamentary boroughs (Dissenters also allowed valid marriage cer-
       emonies).
       21 June   Declaratory Act repealed.
       27 July   Poynings' Law (see p. 23 above) amended.
       Relief Act gives Catholics education rights.

1783   29 Nov.   Parliamentary reform (at Volunteers' behest) rejected by
       College Green (see above, pp. 255–6).

1784   14 May   Foster's Corn Law (sliding scale for export subsidies, varying
       with domestic prices).

1785 3 May   First meeting of Irish Academy (Royal Irish Academy from 28 Jan. 1786).

12 Aug.   Bill to regulate Anglo-Irish trade, adapted from Pitt's original free trade proposals after British protests, introduced at College Green but later abandoned.

1791 Aug.   Wolfe Tone's *Argument on Behalf of the Catholics of Ireland.*

14 Oct.   Foundation of United Irishmen in Belfast (*Northern Star* appears, 4 Jan. 1792).

9 Nov.   First meeting of Dublin United Irishmen.

1792 18 Apr.   Catholic Relief Act allows Catholics to practise law.

25 July   Tone appointed Secretary to Catholic Committee.

1793 2 Jan.   Catholic petition presented to King.

Feb.–Mar.   Legislation restricting movement of arms and suppressing Volunteering.

9 Apr.   Relief Act granting Catholics parliamentary franchise and certain civil and military rights.

Act establishing Irish Militia (afforced, 15 Apr. 1795).

1 Oct.   St Patrick's [Catholic] College, Carlow, opened.

1794 1 Mar.   Catholics statutorily enabled to attend Trinity College, Dublin.

23 May   Suppression of Dublin United Irishmen.

1795 4 Jan.   Earl Fitzwilliam becomes Irish Lord Lieutenant.

23 Feb.   Fitzwilliam dismissed.

10 May   Belfast United Irishmen, meeting underground, adopt new constitution.

5 June   Act providing for establishment of Catholic seminary (opened as Royal College of St Patrick at Maynooth, October).

13 June   Tone leaves for America.

21 Sept.   'Battle of the Diamond' (Loughgall, County Armagh), leading to foundation of Orange Order.

1796 1 Feb.   Tone arrives in France.

24 Mar.   Insurrection Act (curfews, arms searches, death penalty for oath-taking).

16 Sept.   Arrest of Belfast United Irish leaders.

26 Oct.   Habeas Corpus suspended.

Development of Yeomanry corps under commissioned officers.

22–7 Dec.   French fleet, with Tone, in Bantry Bay.

1798 26 Feb.   Abercromby, Commander-in-Chief in Ireland, condemns state of army.

12 Mar.   Arrest of Dublin United Irish leaders (Lord Edward Fitzgerald, 19 May).

30 Mar.   Martial law imposed.

23–4 May   Rebellion begins in Leinster, taking hold in Wexford; Wexford town captured by rebels, 30 May; rebels defeated at New Ross, 5 June.

6–13 June   Outbreaks in Ulster.

21 June   Defeat of Wexford rebels at Vinegar Hill.

22 Aug.   French force under Humbert lands at Killala; humiliates government forces at 'Races of Castlebar', 27 Aug., surrenders at Ballinamuck, 8 Sept.

3 Nov.   Tone arrested after arriving in Lough Swilly with another French force; suicide in prison, 19 Nov.

1799   31 Jan.   Pitt's speech at Westminster advocating the Union between Britain and Ireland.

25 Mar.   Trials by courts martial established (until 1805).

1800   21 May   Bill for Union introduced at College Green.

1 Aug.   Irish Act of Union.

2 Aug.   Last meeting of College Green parliament.

1801   1 Jan.   Act of Union takes effect.

3 Feb.   Pitt resigns as PM over royal veto on Catholic emancipation (returns, 10 May 1804).

1803   23 July   Abortive rising by Robert Emmet (executed, 20 Sept.).

1810   20 June   Unlawful Oaths Act extends powers against secret societies (reinforced 1823, 1839).

1813   12 July   First recorded 'Twelfth of July' sectarian riots in Belfast.

1814   25 July   Peace Preservation Act, policing disturbed areas by local rate-charge.

1815   6 July   'Bianconi car' passenger service opens.

1820   29 Jan.   Accession of George IV.

1822   1 Aug.   Irish Constabulary Act sets up county police forces and salaried magistracy.

1823   12 May   Foundation of Catholic Association.

1824   12 Apr.   Act establishing free trade between Britain and Ireland in manufactured articles.

1825   18 Mar.   Catholic Association dissolved in accordance with Unlawful Societies Act (9 Mar.); reconstituted, 13 July.

18 May   Lords reject Catholic Emancipation Bill (which would disenfranchise Irish forty-shilling freeholders and put clergy on state salaries).

14 Nov.   Catholic pro-cathedral opened in Marlborough St, Dublin.

1826   19–29 June   Catholic electors reject Lord George Beresford in Waterford election.

1828   5 July   Daniel O'Connell elected MP for Clare.
14 Aug.   Foundation of Brunswick Clubs (see above, p. 304).

1829   13 Apr.   Catholic Emancipation Act enables Catholics to enter Parliament and hold civil and military offices.
Forty-shilling freeholders disenfranchised by Irish Parliamentary Elections Act (raising county franchise to ten pounds).

1830   26 June   Accession of William IV.

1831   9 Sept.   £30,000 voted to set up 'national' system of elementary education in Ireland.

1832   7 Aug.   Irish Reform Bill increases seats from 100 to 105 and introduces ten-pound franchise in boroughs.
16 Aug.   Irish Tithe Composition Act allows for commuting tithe payments.

1833   14 Aug.   Irish Church Temporalities Act rationalizes Church of Ireland organization, abolishing ten bishoprics.

1834   22 Apr.   O'Connell introduces debate on Repeal of the Union.

1835   18 Feb.   Alliance between O'Connellites, Whigs and Radicals agreed at Lichfield House.
25 July   Thomas Drummond Under-Secretary (until 15 Apr. 1840).

1836   20 May   Irish Constabulary Act further extends centralized police force and salaried magistracy.

1837   20 June   Accession of Victoria.

1838   10 Apr.   Father Mathew founds abstinence movement.
31 July   Irish Poor Law extends English system to Ireland.

1840   15 Apr.   Repeal Association founded.
10 Aug.   Irish Municipal Reform Act (see above, p. 310).

1841   Mar.–Apr.   Foundation of Dublin Protestant Operative Association (see above, p. 304).
6 June   Census: population, 8,175,124.

1842   15 Oct.   First number of the *Nation*.

1843   7 Oct.   Prohibition and cancellation of 'monster' Repeal meeting at Clontarf.

1844   10 Feb.   O'Connell convicted of 'conspiracy'; fined and sentenced to twelve months' imprisonment, 30 May; judgment reversed by Lords, 4 Sept.

1845   30 June   Maynooth College Act, greatly increasing its endowment.
9 Sept.   Potato blight first noted.
Nov.   Sir Robert Peel, P M, orders import of Indian corn.

1846   Jan.–Mar.   Series of Public Health Acts introducing state-aided public works and public health measures to cope with Famine crisis.
26 June   Repeal of the Corn Laws.
30 June   Peel replaced by Russell and Whig administration, who announce (17 Aug.) decision not to interfere with grain market.
28 July   O'Connell and Young Irelanders split over physical force.

1847   13 Jan.   Foundation of Irish Confederation.
26 Feb.–8 June   Acts setting up soup-kitchens and rate-aided outdoor relief.
15 May   Death of O'Connell.

1848   12 Feb.   John Mitchel starts the *United Irishman*.
13 May   Mitchel arrested; tried and sentenced to transportation, 26–7 May.
29 July   William Smith O'Brien's abortive rising at Ballingarry, County Tipperary; trials and death sentences, Sept.–Oct.; commuted to transportation, 5 June 1849.

1849   28 July   (Second) Encumbered Estates Act, facilitating sales of mortgaged land through a special court.
14 Oct.   First tenant protection society set up at Callan, County Kilkenny.

1850   24 Feb.   Cullen becomes Archbishop of Armagh.
9 Aug.   Irish Tenant League founded.
14 Aug.   Reform Act trebles county electorate (and reduces borough electorate: see above, pp. 343–4).

1851   30 Mar.   Census: population, 6,552,385.

1852   17 Mar.   First St Patrick's Day march in New York.
30 June   Act providing for 'Griffith's valuation' of landholdings throughout Ireland.
8–9 Sept.   Tenant League conference in Dublin.

1854   3 Nov.   Catholic University opened in Dublin (renamed University College, 1882; transferred to Jesuits, 1883).

1855   Feb.   Formation of New York Emmet Monument Association.

1856   Phoenix Society formed at Skibbereen by O'Donovan Rossa.

1858   17 Mar.   James Stephens founds I R B in Dublin.

1859   Apr.   Fenian Brotherhood set up in U S A.

1861   7 Apr.   Census: population, 5,798,967.

1862   1 Jan.   Formation of Harland & Wolff in Belfast.

1863   28 Nov.   Foundation of Fenian newspaper, the *Irish People* (ends 16 Sept. 1865).

1864   29 Dec.   Foundation of National Association of Ireland (see above, p. 394).

1866   Apr.–June   Fenian skirmishes in Canada.
        22 June   Cullen becomes Cardinal.

1867   11–12 Feb.   Fenian disturbances in England and Ireland, including attempted risings in Munster and round Dublin, 5–6 Mar.
        20 June   Clan na Gael founded in New York (see above, p. 359).
        23 Nov.   Execution of Fenian 'Manchester Martyrs'.
        13 Dec.   Fenian explosion at Clerkenwell gaol.

1868   13 July   Irish Reform Act reduces borough franchise to four pounds (occupier) and introduces lodger franchise.
        3 Aug.   Foundation of Amnesty campaign.

1869   26 July   Irish Church Act disestablishes Church of Ireland (see above, p. 396).
        22 Nov.   O'Donovan Rossa contests and wins Tipperary by-election *in absentia*; declared ineligible as convicted felon.

1870   19 May   Isaac Butt founds Home Rule movement (first public meeting of Home Government Association, 1 Sept.).
        1 Aug.   Gladstone's first Land Act (see above, pp. 396–7).

1871   2 Apr.   Census: population, 5,412,377.

1873   8 Jan.   Foundation of Home Rule Confederation of Great Britain.
        12 Mar.   Defeat of Gladstone's Irish University Bill.
        26 May   Religious tests abandoned for Trinity College by Act of Parliament.
        18–21 Nov.   Home Rule League founded at Dublin conference.

1874   Feb.   General election returns sixty Home Rulers.
        2 July   Butt's Home Rule motion defeated 458–61 in Commons.

1876   20 Aug.   I R B Supreme Council withdraw support from Home Rule movement (see above, p. 403).

1877 31 July Minority of Home Rulers begin 'obstruction' tactics in Commons.

28 Aug. Parnell becomes President of Home Rule Confederation of Great Britain.

1878 24–7 Oct. Devoy's overtures to Parnellites suggesting 'New Departure' alliance.

1879 26 Jan. I R B Supreme Council finally reject 'New Departure' strategy.

20 Apr. Irishtown meeting launches land agitation.

16 Aug. Foundation of National Land League of Mayo.

21 Oct. Foundation of Irish National Land League.

1880 2 Jan.–11 Mar. Parnell's American tour.

17 May Parnell elected Chairman of Irish Parliamentary Party.

24 Oct. Foundation in New York of Ladies' Land League.

1881 31 Jan. Ladies' Land League launched in Ireland.

21 Mar. 'Peace Preservation' Act for Ireland.

3 Apr. Census: population, 5,174,836.

22 Aug. Gladstone's Second Land Act (see above, pp. 412–13). Land Commission court opened, Oct.

13 Oct. Parnell arrested.

20 Oct. Land League outlawed.

1882 2 May Parnell released under terms of 'Kilmainham Treaty'.

6 May 'Phoenix Park murders' of Lord Frederick Cavendish and T. H. Burke.

12 July Crime Prevention Act.

17 Oct. Foundation of Irish National League.

1884 1 Oct. Concordat between Irish-Catholic bishops and Parnellite party, whereby the latter agree to press Catholic claims in education issue.

1 Nov. Foundation of Gaelic Athletic Association.

1885 14 Aug. 'Ashbourne' Land Purchase Act.

17 Dec. Newspaper reports of Gladstone's conversion to Home Rule, following general election results giving Parnellites the balance of power.

1886 16 Feb. Irish hierarchy formally endorse Home Rule.

22 Feb. Lord Randolph Churchill's militant speech to loyalists at Ulster Hall, Belfast.

8 June Gladstone's Home Rule Bill defeated (for terms, see above, pp. 424–5).

23 Oct. Announcement of 'Plan of Campaign' to withhold rents on certain estates (proclaimed unlawful, 18 Dec.).

1887   18 Apr.   *The Times* publishes facsimile letter linking Parnell with 'Phoenix Park murders' (Special Investigative Commission appointed, 13 Aug. 1888).

23 Aug.   Land Act gives courts power to revise and fix rents.

1889   20–22 Feb.   Richard Pigott exposed as forger of *The Times* letter in Special Commission proceedings.

24 Dec.   O'Shea divorce petition filed, citing Parnell.

1890   15–17 Nov.   O'Shea divorce hearing.

25 Nov.   Parnell re-elected Chairman of Irish Parliamentary Party; Gladstone then announces this makes his own authority as leader of a party pledged to Home Rule 'almost a nullity'.

28 Nov.   Parnell denounces Liberals and Liberal alliance.

1–6 Dec.   Irish Parliamentary Party debates end in split, majority opposing Parnell.

1891   3 Feb.   Final failure of reconciliation negotiations.

5 Apr.   Census: population, 4,704,750.

5 Aug.   Land Purchase Act further facilitates arrangements.

Congested Districts Board established.

6 Oct.   Parnell dies at Brighton.

1892   16 Aug.   National Literary Society founded.

25 Nov.   Douglas Hyde's address, 'On the Necessity for De-Anglicizing the Irish People'.

1893   31 July   Foundation of Gaelic League.

2 Sept.   Second Home Rule Bill passed by Commons; rejected by Lords, 9 Sept. (see above, pp. 424–5).

1894   18 Apr.   Foundation of Irish Agricultural Organization Society.

27–8 Apr.   Irish Trades Union Congress founded.

1896   29 May   Foundation of James Connolly's Irish Socialist Republican Party.

1898   23 Jan.   Foundation of William O'Brien's United Irish League.

27 June–1 July   Ancient Order of Hibernians revived and strengthened by unity congress in U S A; similar process in Ireland, 4 Mar. 1902.

12 Aug.   Irish Local Government Act setting up elective county and district councils.

1899   8 May   First production of Irish Literary Theatre (see above, pp. 452–3).

9 Aug.   Agricultural and Technical Instruction Act, setting up Department of Agriculture.

1900   30 Jan.   Reunion of Irish Parliamentary Party under John Redmond
       (co-opt United Irish League, 19–20 June).
       30 Sept.   Foundation of Cumann na nGaedheal under Arthur Griffith.

1901   22 Jan.   Accession of Edward VII.
       31 Mar.   Census: population, 4,458,775.

1902   2 Apr.   W. B. Yeats's *Cathleen ni Houlihan* performed.
       20 Dec.   Opening of Land Conference representing landlords and tenants.

1903   11 June   T. H. Sloan forms independent Orange Order.
       14 Aug.   'Wyndham' Land Act following conference recommendation
       that tenants buy out landlords with Treasury loans.

1904   26 Aug.   Foundation of Lord Dunraven's Irish Reform Association
       calling for agreed measure of devolution (leads to Wyndham's resig-
       nation, 6 Mar. 1905).
       2 Dec.   Beginnings of Ulster Unionist MPs' organization (Ulster Union-
       ist Council from Mar. 1905).
       27 Dec.   Abbey Theatre opens.

1905   8 Mar.   Meeting of first Dungannon Club in Belfast.

1907   21 Apr.   Cumann na nGaedheal and Dungannon Clubs become Sinn
       Féin League.
       6 May   James Larkin organizes dock strikes in Belfast.
       21 May   Nationalist conference declares against Birrell's devolutionary
       Irish Council Bill (dropped 3 June).
       5 Sept.   National Council merges with Sinn Féin League; from Sept.
       1908, called Sinn Féin.
       Dec.   Tom Clarke arrives in Ireland (having been imprisoned 1883–98,
       and in USA thereafter).

1908   1 Aug.   Irish Universities Act abolishes Royal University of Ireland
       (examining body only) and establishes two new universities: basis of
       National University of Ireland and Queen's University of Belfast.
       8 Sept.   Pearse opens St Enda's School (Scoil Eanna); moves to The
       Hermitage, Rathfarnham, 1910.
       29 Dec.   Foundation of Irish Transport Workers' Union (later Irish Trans-
       port and General Workers' Union).

1909   16 Aug.   Foundation of Fianna Éireann.
       3 Dec.   Birrell's Land Act extends land purchase facilities.

1910   21 Feb.   Carson becomes leader of Irish Unionists.
       6 May   Accession of George V.

1911   2 Apr.   Census: population, 4,381,951.
       21 Aug.   Formation of Irish Women's Suffrage Federation.

1912 6 Feb.   Exclusion from Home Rule submitted to Cabinet by Churchill and Lloyd George; rejected.

9 Apr.   Bonar Law's unconditional pledge of British Unionist support for Ulster resistance to Home Rule.

11 Apr.   Third Home Rule Bill introduced in Commons.

28 Sept.   Solemn League and Covenant signed in Ulster (see above, pp. 466–7).

1913 16 Jan.   Home Rule Bill passes third reading; defeated in Lords, 30 Jan.; passes Commons again, 7 July; defeated in Lords, 15 July.

31 Jan.   Foundation of Ulster Volunteer Force.

26 Aug.   Beginning of Irish Transport and General Workers' Union strike in Dublin, escalating into general lock-out (gradual return to work from 18 Jan. 1914).

19 Nov.   Formation of Citizen Army.

25 Nov.   Foundation of Irish Volunteers.

Dec.   Pearse joins IRB.

1914 20 Mar.   Curragh 'incident' (see above, p. 469).

24–5 Apr.   Ulster Volunteer Force gun-running.

25 May   Home Rule Bill passes Commons.

23 June   Amending bill allows for temporary exclusion of parts of Ulster.

8 July   Amending bill altered by Lords to exclude all Ulster permanently; shelved by government.

21–4 July   Buckingham Palace conference fails to negotiate Ulster impasse.

26 July   Howth gun-running by Irish Volunteers; four killed in ensuing demonstrations.

3 Aug.   Germany and France go to war; Redmond pledges Irish support for British war effort and Volunteers for defence of Ireland.

4 Aug.   UK and Germany go to war.

9 Sept.   IRB discuss possibility of a rising.

15 Sept.   Home Rule Bill suspended in advance of its enactment (18 Sept.).

20 Sept.   Redmond's Woodenbridge speech commits Volunteers to serve anywhere in field of war.

24 Sept.   Beginning of Volunteer split.

1915 May   Military Committee of IRB Supreme Council constituted.

29 July   Gaelic League taken over by militant nationalists; Hyde stands down.

Dec.   Military Council of IRB formed (future signatories of 1916 proclamation).

1916 Jan.   Supreme Council of IRB decide on early insurrection.

3 Apr. Irish Volunteers ordered to prepare for manoeuvres, Easter Sunday (23 Apr.).

20–21 Apr. The *Aud* captured and scuttled with German arms cargo.

21 Apr. Casement arrives from Germany; arrested; sentenced, 29 June; hanged, 3 Aug.

22 Apr. Countermanding order issued by MacNeill.

23 Apr. Military Council decide to proceed.

24 Apr. Seizure of central Dublin buildings by Irish Volunteers and Citizen Army.

29 Apr. Rebels surrender.

3–12 May Execution of rebel leaders.

12 June Ulster Unionist Council agree to immediate implementation of Home Rule if six Ulster counties temporarily excluded.

22–3 Dec. Return of first interned political prisoners.

1917 5 Feb. Count Plunkett wins Roscommon by-election for Sinn Féin; further victories, 9 May (South Longford), 10 July (East Clare), 10 Aug. (Kilkenny City).

16 May Announcement of Irish Convention as alternative to immediate Home Rule with Ulster exclusion; Convention meets, 25 July–5 Apr. 1918, fruitlessly.

25 Oct. De Valera elected President at Sinn Féin *ard-fheis*; Sinn Féin change constitution, opting for an independent republic.

1918 18 Apr. Military Service Act threatens conscription for Ireland.

Mansion House conference concerts all-Irish opposition.

17–18 May Sinn Féin leaders arrested on grounds of supposed German Plot.

14–28 Dec. General election: Sinn Féin 73, Irish Parliamentary Party 6, Unionists 25, 1 Independent Unionist.

1919 21 Jan. Soloheadbeg ambush by six Irish Volunteers; two policemen killed.

First meeting of Dáil Éireann, in Mansion House; de Valera elected President, 1 Apr.

14–25 Apr. General strike at Limerick.

1 June–23 Dec. 1920 De Valera in USA.

4 July Sinn Féin and other organizations suppressed in Tipperary and later in other troubled areas.

12 Sept. Dáil Éireann declared illegal.

11 Nov. First number of *Irish Bulletin*.

1920 2 Jan. First Black and Tans recruited.

15 Jan. Sinn Féin control 172 out of 206 borough and urban councils in local elections; further successes in June.

23 May Railwaymen's strike begins; refusal to transport troops.

21–4 July   Sectarian riots in Belfast (recurrence, with thirty deaths, in Aug.).

27 July   'Auxiliary' parliamentary force recruited to cope with spreading guerrilla violence.

9 Aug.   Restoration of Order Act.

25 Oct.   Terence MacSwiney dies on hunger strike.

1 Nov.   Execution of Kevin Barry.

Enrolment of Ulster Special Constabulary begins.

21 Nov.   'Bloody Sunday' (see above, p. 498).

10 Dec.   Martial law in Cork, Kerry, Limerick and Tipperary.

23 Dec.   Government of Ireland Act sets up six-county parliament and administration in North; similar provision for South ignored.

1921   4 Feb.   Craig succeeds Carson as Ulster Unionist leader.

25 May   Dublin Customs House burned down.

22 June   Opening of Northern Ireland parliament by George V.

9 July   Truce between I R A and British army.

11 Oct.   Conference opens in London.

6 Dec.   Anglo–Irish Treaty signed (see above, pp. 504–8).

14 Dec.   Debate on Treaty terms begins in Dáil Éireann (ends, 7 Jan. 1922).

1922   7 Jan.   Treaty approved by Dáil Éireann (64 to 57)

9 Jan.   Griffith elected President, succeeding de Valera.

16 Jan.   Provisional government take over from Dublin Castle.

30 Mar.   Craig–Collins pact (see above, p. 527).

7 Apr.   Special Powers Act in Northern Ireland (annually renewed; made permanent, 9 May 1933).

14 Apr.   Anti-Treaty forces seize Four Courts, Dublin.

16 June   General election in Irish Free State: large majority to pro-Treaty Sinn Féin.

28 June   Attack on Four Courts by Provisional government (destroyed, with Public Records Office, 30 June): civil war follows.

9 Sept.   Third Dáil assembles, William Cosgrave president.

11 Sept.   Abolition of proportional representation for local elections in Northern Ireland.

17 Nov.–2 May 1923   Seventy-seven republican prisoners executed.

1923   27 Apr.   De Valera orders suspension of republic campaign; arms dumped in May.

22 June   Northern Ireland Education Act setting up non-denominational schools opposed by Presbyterians and boycotted by Catholics.

24 July   Land Commission replaces Congested Districts Board.

15 Aug.   De Valera arrested.

10 Sept.   Irish Free State enters League of Nations.

1924 6–19 Mar.   Army 'mutiny' (see above, pp. 524–5).

1925 11 Feb.   Effective prohibition of divorce legislation in Irish Free State.
      7 Nov.   Findings of Irish Boundary Commission leaked; agreement to
      maintain existing border, 3 Dec.

1926 18 Apr.   Census: population of Irish Free State, 2,971,992; of Northern
      Ireland, 1,256,561.
      16 May   Foundation of Fianna Fáil.

1927 28 May   Agricultural Credit Corporation established.
      10 July   Assassination of Kevin O'Higgins.
      20 July   Public Safety and Constitution Bills introduced.
      11 Aug.   Electricity Supply Board established.

1929 16 July   Censorship of Publications Act.
      21 Oct.   Shannon hydro-electric scheme commences operations.

1931 26 Sept.   Foundation of Saor Éire.
      11 Dec.   Statute of Westminster, giving effective legislative autonomy
      to dominions.

1932 9 Feb.   Foundation of Army Comrades Association (from 20 July 1933,
      National Guard – nicknamed Blueshirts).
      16 Feb.   Fianna Fáil win general election.
      30 June   Land annuities withheld.
      15–23 July   Retaliatory trade legislation begins 'economic war'.

1933 3 May   Act removing Oath from constitution.
      22 Aug.   Blueshirts outlawed.
      2 Sept.   Cumann na nGaedheal, Centre Party and National Guard join
      to form Fine Gael.
      Nov.   Amending Acts reducing power of Crown representative.

1934 21 Dec.   Coal–cattle pact (see above, p. 553).

1935 28 Feb.   Sale and import of contraceptives made illegal.

1936 26 Apr.   Census: population of Irish Free State, 2,968,420.
      18 June   IRA declared illegal.
      11 Dec.   (following Edward VIII's abdication) Amending Act removes
      references to Crown and Governor-General from constitution.

1937 28 Feb.   Census: population of Northern Ireland, 1,279,745.
      14 June   De Valera's new constitution approved (see above, pp. 543–5,
      550–51).

1938 25 Apr.   Anglo-Irish agreement on trade and finance; Treaty ports to be
      returned.
      25 June   Douglas Hyde becomes President of Ireland.

1939   16 Jan.   IRA begin bombing campaign in England.
2 Sept.   Éire's intention to stay neutral announced (war declared, 3 Sept.).

1940   3 Jan.   Emergency legislation against IRA introduced.
24 Nov.   J. M. Andrews succeeds Craig as PM of Northern Ireland.

1941   7–8 Apr., 15–16 Apr., 4–5 May   Air-raids on Belfast.

1943   28 Apr.   Sir Basil Brooke (from 4 July 1952, Lord Brookeborough) becomes PM of Northern Ireland.

1944   14 Jan.   Irish Labour Party splits.

1945   2 May   De Valera expresses formal condolences to German embassy on death of Hitler.
16 June   Seán T. O'Kelly elected President (installed, 25 June).

1946   12 May   Census: population of Éire, 2,955,167.
6 July   Foundation of Clann na Poblachta.

1947   13 Aug.   Health Act extends powers of county councils and provides maternity care.

1948   4 Feb.   General election: Fianna Fáil loses overall majority; coalition government takes over under J. A. Costello, 18 Feb.
21 Dec.   Republic of Ireland Act (intention announced by Costello in Canada, 7 Sept.): Éire becomes Republic of Ireland and leaves Commonwealth, 18 Apr. 1949.

1949   2 June   Ireland Act passed at Westminster, declaring special relationship of Irish citizens to UK and guaranteeing Northern Ireland will remain within UK unless its parliament decides otherwise.

1950   20 Dec.   Foundation of Industrial Development Authority.

1951   11 Mar.   Ian Paisley forms Free Presbyterian Church.
4 Apr.   Hierarchy condemns 'Mother and Child' scheme (see above, pp. 571–2).
8 Apr.   Census: population of Republic, 2,960,593; Northern Ireland, 1,370,921.
30 May   General election: Fianna Fáil regain power.

1952   3 July   Foundation of Bord Fáilte (Irish Tourist Board).

1954   6 Apr.   Flags and Emblems Act in Northern Ireland legislates against interference with Union Jack and effectively prohibits display of tricolour.
18 May   General election: coalition government regains power.

1955   14 Dec.   Republic of Ireland joins UN.

1956   8 Apr.   Census: population of Republic, 2,898,264.
        12 Dec.   IR A begins campaign on Northern Ireland border (called off,
        26 Feb. 1962).

1957   4 Jan.   Funeral of Seán South, Limerick I R A man killed in border-raid.
        5 Mar.   General election returns Fianna Fáil with large majority (they
        retain power until 1973).

1958   2 July   Industrial Development Act, to encourage inflow of foreign
        capital.
        Dec.   Publication of T. K. Whitaker's *Economic Development* (see above,
        pp. 578–9).

1959   17 June   De Valera elected President; Sean Lemass becomes Taoiseach,
        23 June.

1960   20 Sept.   F. H. Boland becomes President of U N General Assembly.

1961   9 Apr.   Census: population of Republic, 2,818,341.
        23 Apr.   Census: population of Northern Ireland, 1,425,642.
        31 Dec.   R T E television station begins broadcasting.

1963   25 Mar.   Terence O'Neill succeeds Brookeborough as P M of Northern
        Ireland.

1964   Jan.   Campaign for Social Justice founded in Northern Ireland.
        July   Publication of Second Programme for Economic Expansion.

1965   14 Jan.   Lemass and O'Neill meet in Belfast.
        2 Feb.   Nationalist Party in Northern Ireland decide to enter Stormont.
        9 Feb.   Lemass and O'Neill meet in Dublin.
        10 Feb.   Publication of Lockwood Committee Report on higher edu-
        cation in Northern Ireland.
        14 Dec.   Anglo-Irish free trade agreement signed.

1966   8 Mar.   Nelson's Pillar in Dublin detonated.
        Apr.   Commemoration of 1916 rising.
        17 Apr.   Census: population of Republic, 2,884,002.
        26 June   Three sectarian murders by Ulster Volunteer Force.
        19 July   Ian Paisley convicted of unlawful assembly and breach of peace;
        imprisoned 20 July.
        9 Oct.   Census: population of Northern Ireland, 1,484,775.
        10 Nov.   Jack Lynch replaces Lemass as Taoiseach.

1967   Jan.   Foundation of Northern Ireland Civil Rights Association.
        11 July   Censorship Act lifts ban on books prohibited for twelve years.
        11 Dec.   Lynch and O'Neill meet in Belfast.

1968   8 Jan.   Lynch and O'Neill meet in Dublin.

24 Aug.   Northern Ireland Civil Rights Association organize march from Coalisland to Dungannon.

5 Oct.   Police clash with Derry civil rights marchers.

9 Oct.   Origins of People's Democracy in Belfast student demonstrations.

11 Dec.   William Craig dismissed from Northern Ireland government.

1969   4 Jan.   People's Democracy march from Belfast to Derry attacked by Protestants at Burntollet Bridge.

24 Jan.   Brian Faulkner resigns from Northern Ireland government.

Mar.   Publication of Third Programme for Economic Expansion in Republic.

19 Apr.   Riots in Derry: police enter Bogside.

20 Apr.   Sabotage of Silent Valley reservoir.

28 Apr.   O'Neill resigns; succeeded by Chichester-Clark.

12–16 July   Derry riots.

14 July   First death (at Dungiven, County Londonderry).

13 Aug.   Bogside under siege; Lynch announces request to UN and threatens intervention.

14–15 Aug.   Riots in Derry and Belfast; troops assume control.

12 Sept.   Publication of Cameron report on Northern Ireland disturbances.

10 Oct.   Hunt Committee report on Ulster police recommends abolition of B-specials (disbanded, 30 Apr. 1970) and creation of Ulster Defence Regiment (set up, 18 Dec.).

25 Nov.   Electoral reform in Northern Ireland universalizes local government franchise.

1970   11 Jan.   IRA split into Officials and Provisionals (see above, pp. 589–90).

16 Apr.   Paisley returned to Stormont in Bannside by-election.

6 May   Charles Haughey and Neil Blaney dismissed from government; arrested for conspiracy to import arms, 28 May; Blaney discharged, 2 July; Haughey acquitted, 23 Oct.

18 June   Paisley elected to Westminster in North Antrim by-election.

25 June   Hierarchy remove restrictions on Catholics attending Trinity College.

26 June   Bernadette Devlin, MP, arrested.

3 July   Riots in Belfast (six killed).

21 Aug.   Foundation of Social Democratic Labour Party.

1971   6 Feb.   First British soldier killed by Provisionals (following a month of rioting).

20 Mar.   Brian Faulkner succeeds Chichester-Clark as PM of Northern Ireland.

18 Apr.   Census: population of Republic, 2,978,248.

25 Apr.   Census: population of Northern Ireland, 1,536,065.

16 July   Social Democratic Labour Party withdraw from Stormont in protest at failure to inquire into deaths of two civilians killed by army (8 July).

9 Aug.   Internment introduced in Northern Ireland (see above, p. 590).

5 Oct.   Paisley founds Democratic Unionist Party.

1972   22 Jan.   Republic signs treaty of accession to E E C (effective from 1 Jan. 1973).

30 Jan.   'Bloody Sunday': thirteen killed in Derry (see above, p. 591).

2 Feb.   British embassy burned in Dublin.

23 Mar.   Local Government Reform Act in Northern Ireland (district councils).

24 Mar.   Stormont parliament and government suspended: direct rule by Secretary of State, William Whitelaw.

26 May   Republic establishes special criminal court for offences against the state.

22 June   Provisional cease-fire.

7 July   Abortive negotiations between Provisional leaders and Whitelaw in London.

30 Oct.   Whitelaw's Green Paper, 'The Future of Northern Ireland', declares no U K opposition to unity by consent.

7 Dec.   Referendum removes 'special position' of Roman Catholic Church from constitution.

Note: This is a brief catalogue, concentrating on events referred to in the text. For a full chronology, see T. W. Moody, F. X. Martin and F. J. Byrne (editors), *A New History of Ireland V I I I: A Chronology of Irish History to 1976* (Oxford, 1982), to which this chronology is heavily indebted.

REFERENCES

PREFACE

1. Principally Oliver MacDonagh, *States of Mind: A Study of Anglo-Irish Conflict 1780–1980* (London, 1983); P. O'Farrell, *Ireland and England since 1800* (Oxford, 1970); F. S. L. Lyons, *Culture and Anarchy in Ireland 1890–1939* (Oxford, 1979).
2. *The Making of Modern Ireland 1603–1923* (London, 1966); *A Short History of Ireland from Earliest Times to the Present Day* (London, 1952).
3. T. W. Moody, F. X. Martin and F. J. Byrne (editors), *A New History of Ireland. Vol. VIII: A Chronology of Irish History to 1976* (Oxford, 1982) and *Vol. IX: Maps, Genealogies, Lists* (Oxford, 1984).
4. Emile Montegut, quoted on the title-page of Arland Ussher, *The Face and Mind of Ireland* (London, 1949).

PART ONE

PROLOGUE
VARIETIES OF IRISHNESS

1. D. B. Quinn, *The Elizabethans and the Irish* (Ithaca, 1966), p. 5.
2. Fynes Moryson, 'The Commonwealth of Ireland' in C. Litton Falkiner (editor), *Illustrations of Irish History and Topography, Mainly of the Seventeenth Century* (London, 1904), p. 307. This statement is the *leitmotif* of Moryson's absorbing survey.
3. Revd Paul Walsh (editor), *The Life of Red Hugh O'Donnell (Beatha Aodha Ruaidh Uí Dhomhnaill)*, transcribed from the book of Lughaidh Ó Clérigh (Irish Texts Society, Dublin, 1948), part 1, p. 57.
4. Edmund Spenser, *A View of the Present State of Ireland*, edited by W. L. Renwick (Oxford, 1970), p. 151.
5. Aidan Clarke, 'Colonial Identity in Early Seventeenth-century Ireland' in T. W. Moody (editor), *Nationality and the Pursuit of National Independence: Historical Studies XI* (Belfast, 1978), p. 58.
6. N. Canny, *The Upstart Earl: A Study of the Social and Mental World of Richard Boyle, First Earl of Cork, 1566–1643* (Cambridge, 1982), p. 71.

CHAPTER ONE
'WILD SHAMROCK MANNERS': IRELAND IN 1600

1. Maurice Craig, *The Architecture of Ireland from the Earliest Times to 1880* (London, 1982), p. 114.
2. Luke Gernon, 'A Discourse of Ireland' in C. Litton Falkiner, op. cit., p. 353.
3. Fynes Moryson, 'The Commonwealth of Ireland' in C. Litton Falkiner, op. cit., p. 302.
4. J. A. Froude, *The History of England, from the Fall of Wolsey to the Defeat of the Spanish Armada* (London, 1910), vol. X, p. 571.
5. See D. B. Quinn, ' "A Discourse of Ireland" (*c.* 1599): A Sidelight on English Colonial Policy', *Proceedings of the Royal Irish Academy*, vol. xlviii, sect. C, no. 3 (1942), p. 160.
6. Fynes Moryson, 'The Commonwealth of Ireland' in C. Litton Falkiner, op. cit., p. 237.
7. C. Brady, 'Faction and the Origins of the Desmond Rebellion of 1579', *Irish Historical Studies*, vol. xxii, no. 88 (September 1981), p. 300.
8. Josias Bodley, 'A Visit to Lecale, in the County of Down, in the Year 1602–3' in C. Litton Falkiner, op. cit., pp. 342–3.
9. Fynes Moryson, 'The Commonwealth of Ireland' in C. Litton Falkiner, op. cit., p. 248.
10. C. Maxwell (editor), *Irish History from Contemporary Sources 1509–1610* (London, 1923), p. 136.
11. Edmund Spenser, op. cit., pp. 18–19.
12. Fynes Moryson, 'The Commonwealth of Ireland' in C. Litton Falkiner, op. cit., p. 263.

CHAPTER TWO
'NATIONALISM' AND RECUSANCY

1. Barnaby Rich, *A New Description of Ireland* (London, 1610), pp. 90–91. Rich's subtitle is significant: 'Wherein is described the disposition of the Irish, whereunto they are inclined. No less admirable to be perused than credible to be believed; neither unprofitable nor unpleasant to be read and understood by those worthy citizens of London that be now undertakers in Ireland' (i.e., the Ulster settlers).
2. 'The Confession which James Fitz Thomas Gerrald made unto Sir George Carew, the President of Munster, the third day of June 1601', in J. S. Brewer and W. Bullen (eds.), *Calendar of the Carew MSS Preserved in the Archiepiscopal Library at Lambeth, IV, 1601–1603* (London, 1870), p. 78.
3. Robert J. Hunter, 'Catholicism in Meath *c.* 1622', *Collectanea Hibernica*, no. 14 (1971), pp. 7–12.

4. T. Dunne, 'The Gaelic Response to Conquest and Colonization: The Evidence of the Poetry', *Studia Hibernica*, vol. xx (1980), p. 14.

5. See N. Canny, 'The Formation of the Irish Mind: Religion, Politics and Gaelic Irish Literature 1580–1750', *Past and Present*, no. 95 (May 1982), pp. 101–2.

6. Aidan Clarke, 'Colonial Identity in Early Seventeenth-century Ireland' in T. W. Moody, op. cit., p. 63.

7. C. Maxwell, op. cit., p. 150.

8. B. Jennings, 'Miscellaneous Documents 1588–1634' in *Archivium Hibernicum*, vol. xii (1946), p. 150 (spelling slightly modernized in my text).

9. ibid., p. 151.

10. Aidan Clarke, *The Old English in Ireland 1625–42* (London, 1968), p. 61.

11. T. O. Ranger, 'Strafford in Ireland: A Revaluation' in T. H. Aston (editor), *Crisis in Europe 1550–1660* (London, 1965), p. 291.

CHAPTER THREE
PLANTATION: THEORY AND PRACTICE

1. T. W. Moody, *The Londonderry Plantation 1609–41: The City of London and the Plantation of Ulster* (Belfast, 1939), p. 32.

2. George Hill, *An Historical Account of the Plantation of Ulster 1608–20* (Belfast, 1877; reprinted Shannon, 1970), p. 152.

3. ibid., p. 86.

4. T. W. Moody, op. cit., p. 233.

5. T. W. Moody, F. X. Martin and F. J. Byrne (editors), *A New History of Ireland. Vol. III: Early Modern Ireland 1534–1691* (Oxford, 1976), p. 223.

6. See M. MacCarthy-Morrogh, *The Munster Plantation: English Migration to Southern Ireland 1583–1641* (Oxford, 1986).

7. N. Canny, op. cit., p. 138.

8. ibid.; also N. Canny, art. cit., p. 114.

9. P. Livingstone, *The Monaghan Story: A Documented History of the County Monaghan from the Earliest Times to 1976* (Enniskillen, 1980), p. 103.

10. George Hill, op. cit., p. 586.

11. T. W. Moody, op. cit., p. 314.

12. ibid., p. 319.

13. A. T. Q. Stewart, *The Narrow Ground: Aspects of Ulster 1609–1969* (London, 1977), p. 56.

14. R. Gillespie, 'The Origins and Development of an Ulster Urban Network 1600–1641', *Irish Historical Studies*, vol. xxiv, no. 93 (May 1984), p. 28.

15. P. Robinson, 'British Settlement in County Tyrone 1610–66', *Irish Economic and Social History*, vol. v (1978), p. 7.

16. N. Canny, op. cit., p. 129.

CHAPTER FOUR
CONFEDERATE IRELAND

1. P. Adair, *A True Narrative of the Rise and Progress of the Presbyterian Church of Ireland*, quoted in T. C. Barnard, *Cromwellian Ireland: English Government and Reform in Ireland 1649–60* (Oxford, 1975), p. 101.
2. This is as true for those who edited collections (J. T. Gilbert, Mary Hickson, Robert Dunlop, J. P. Prendergast) as for those who provided their own interpretations, like J. A. Froude. Dunlop, reading the 'Depositions' at the time of the Land War of 1879–81, reflects this vividly: 'I began to experience an uncomfortable feeling that my evidence was not so strong as I would have liked it to be. True, the Depositions were very explicit and apparently incontrovertible; but I was living in Dublin at a time when the power of the Land League was at its height, and I could not help asking what value depositions taken by a body of Orange magistrates as to nationalist outrages were likely to possess for an impartial estimate of the state of Ireland during the government of Earl Spencer. Was the state of affairs in 1642 more favourable for an impartial inquiry than it was in 1882?' R. Dunlop, *Ireland under the Commonwealth: Being a Selection of Documents Relating to the Government of Ireland from 1651 to 1659* (Manchester, 1913), pp. i, vii.
3. J. T. Gilbert (editor), *A Contemporary History of Affairs in Ireland from A D 1641 to 1652* (Dublin, 1879), vol. I, p. 465.
4. James Howell, *Mercurius Hibernicus, or a Discourse of the Late Insurrection in Ireland*, quoted in James Touchet, *The Earl of Castlehaven's Memoirs, or His Review of the Civil Wars in Ireland with His Own Engagement and Conduct Therein* (first published 1680; Dublin edition, 1815), pp. 15–16.
5. ibid., p. 19.
6. M. Perceval-Maxwell, 'The Ulster Rising of 1641 and the Depositions', *Irish Historical Studies*, vol. xxi, no. 82 (September 1978), pp. 163, 164.
7. Aidan Clarke, *The Old English in Ireland 1625–42*, p. 179.
8. J. T. Gilbert, *History of the Irish Confederation and the War in Ireland 1641–49 ... Published from Original Manuscripts* (Dublin, 1882–90), vol. V (1889), pp. viii–ix.
9. James Touchet, op. cit., pp. 45–6.

CHAPTER FIVE
CROMWELLIAN IRELAND

1. Pastoral letter of Armagh clergy, August 1651, quoted in 'An Aphorismical Discovery of Treasonable Faction' in J. T. Gilbert, *A Contemporary History of Affairs in Ireland, from A D 1641 to 1652*, vol. II (Dublin, 1880), p. 191.
2. T. C. Barnard, op. cit., p. 14.

3. R. C. Simington (editor), *The Transplantation to Connacht* (Irish Manuscripts Commission, Dublin, 1970), p. xv.

4. K. Bottigheimer, *English Money and Irish Land: The 'Adventurers' in the Cromwellian Settlement of Ireland* (Oxford, 1971).

5. W. J. Smyth, 'Land Values, Land Ownership and Population Patterns in County Tipperary for 1641–60 and 1841–50: Some Comparisons' in L. M. Cullen and F. Furet, *Irlande et France XVII–XX siècles: pour une histoire rurale comparée* (Paris, 1980), pp. 59–84.

6. L. M. Cullen, 'Economic Trends 1660–91' in T. W. Moody, F. X. Martin and F. J. Byrne, op. cit., p. 401.

CHAPTER SIX
RESTORATION IRELAND

1. Quoted in B. Coward, *The Stuart Age: A History of England 1603–1714* (London, 1980), p. 271.

2. R. B. McDowell and D. A. Webb, *Trinity College, Dublin, 1592–1952: An Academic History* (Cambridge, 1982), p. 17.

3. L. M. Cullen in T. W. Moody, F. X. Martin and F. J. Byrne, op. cit., p. 400.

4. M. MacCurtain, 'Rural Society in Post-Cromwellian Ireland' in Art Cosgrove and Donal McCartney (editors), *Studies in Irish History Presented to R. Dudley Edwards* (Dublin, 1979), p. 134.

5. Maurice Craig, op. cit., p. 140.

6. Edward MacLysaght, *Irish Life in the Seventeenth Century: After Cromwell* (Dublin 1939), p. 334. (Appendix B to this pioneering work consists of six fascinating letters by John Dunton from the Rawlinson manuscripts in the Bodleian Library, Oxford.)

CHAPTER SEVEN
SHIPWRECK AND DELIVERANCE: THE FOUNDATIONS OF ASCENDANCY

1. This development is treated in Jeanne Sheehy, *The Rediscovery of Ireland's Past: The Celtic Revival 1830–1930* (London, 1980).

2. William King, *The State of the Protestants of Ireland under the Late King James's Government* (London, 1691), p. 97.

3. Notably the Young Irelander Thomas Davis in the *Dublin Magazine* of 1843: a series of articles published after his death as *The Patriot Parliament of 1689*, edited by C. Gavan Duffy. Davis's thesis was given general currency by W. E. H. Lecky in the influential first volume of his *History of Ireland in the Eighteenth Century* (London, 1892).

4. W. E. H. Lecky, *History of Ireland in the Eighteenth Century*, vol. I, pp. 131–3.

5. J. G. Simms, *Jacobite Ireland 1685–91* (London, 1969), p. 227.

6. The fullest treatment is in J. G. Simms, *The Williamite Confiscation in Ireland 1690–1703* (London, 1956), chapter 5.

7. Literal translation from the Revd John C. MacErlean's edition of *Duanaire Daíbhíd uí Bhruadair*, part 3 (Irish Texts Society, London, 1917). A much freer translation, indeed, adaptation, of these verses by James Stephens may be found in Seán MacReamoinn (editor), *The Pleasures of Gaelic Poetry* (London, 1982), pp. 76–8.

8. See Richard Caulfield (editor), *The Autobiography of Sir Richard Cox* (London, 1860), p. 15; K. T. Hoppen, *The Common Scientist in the Seventeenth Century* (London, 1970), p. 186.

9. A. T. Q. Stewart, op. cit., p. 96.

10. Quoted in D. Hayton, 'The Beginnings of the "Undertaker System" ' in T. Bartlett and D. Hayton (editors), *Penal Era and Golden Age: Essays in Irish History 1690–1800* (Belfast, 1979), p. 37.

11. K. T. Hoppen, op. cit., p. 183.

12. This was a small trade at the best of times, though the measure was considered a particularly high-handed one. It appears not to have caused a trade depression, and its passing had more to do with an opposition crisis in Westminster than with any wider government intention. 'As in the case of the Cattle Acts after the Restoration, the support of the opposition groupings for a sectional economic proposal had managed to carry legislation against a major Irish industry on to the statute book against the will of the executive – a state of affairs made possible in both cases by a tottering ministry at odds with the King.' P. Kelly, 'The Irish Woollen Export Prohibition Act of 1699: Kearney Re-visited', *Irish Economic and Social History*, vol. vii (1980), pp. 22–43.

13. From the 1725 Dublin edition of Molyneux's *The Case of Ireland being Bound by Acts of Parliament in England Stated*, p. 13.

14. For an interesting commentary, see Isolde Victory's Ph.D. thesis (Trinity College, Dublin, 1984): 'Colonial Nationalism in Ireland 1692–1725: From Common Law to Natural Right'.

PART TWO

CHAPTER EIGHT
THE ASCENDANCY MIND

1. Elizabeth Bowen, *Bowen's Court* (London, 1942), p. 172.

2. W. J. McCormack, *Ascendancy and Tradition in Anglo-Irish Literary History from 1789 to 1939* (Oxford, 1985), pp. 67ff.

3. A. P. W. Malcomson, *John Foster: The Politics of the Anglo-Irish Ascendancy* (Oxford, 1978), p. xxix.

4. Emily Charlotte Boyle, Countess of Cork and Orrery (editor), *The Orrery Papers* (London, 1903), vol. I, p. 157.

5. Quoted in Maurice Craig, *Dublin 1660–1860: A Social and Architectural History* (Dublin, 1969), p. 227.

6. Quoted in Isolde Victory, op. cit., p. 147.

7. Emily Charlotte Boyle, op. cit., vol. I, p. 279: letter to William Philips, 12 July 1740.

8. See B. Fitzgerald (editor), *The Correspondence of Emily, Duchess of Leinster (1731–1814)*, (Irish Manuscripts Commission, Dublin, 1949–57), vol. III, p. 322 (18 October 1778) and vol. II, p. 86 (26 January 1760).

9. I. Ehrenpreis, *Swift: The Man, His Works and the Age*, vol. I (London, 1967), p. 8.

10. Jonathan Swift, *Irish Tracts and Sermons*, edited by H. Davis and L. A. Landa (Oxford, 1968), pp. 233–4.

11. J. D. Mahaffy, 'Society in Georgian Dublin' in *Record of the Irish Georgian Society IV* (1912), p. 33.

12. C. Maxwell, *Dublin under the Georges* (London, 1936), p. 74.

13. Maurice Craig, *Dublin 1660–1860: A Social and Architectural History*, p. 4.

14. There is a brilliant discussion of the relationship between the buildings in ibid., chapter 21.

15. Emily Charlotte Boyle, op. cit., vol. II, pp. 227–8: letter to Tom Southern, 28 May 1737.

16. Maurice Craig, *The Architecture of Ireland from the Earliest Times to 1880*, p. 189.

17. ibid., p. 248.

18. W. B. Yeats, 'Introduction' to *The Words upon the Window-pane*, reprinted in *Explorations* (London, 1962), p. 345.

CHAPTER NINE
ECONOMY, SOCIETY AND THE 'HIDDEN' IRELANDS

1. Quoted in D. N. Doyle, *Ireland, Irishmen and Revolutionary America 1760–1820* (Dublin, 1981), p. 11.

2. C. L. and R. E. Ward (editors), *The Letters of Charles O'Conor of Belanagare* (Ann Arbor, Michigan, 1980), vol. I, p. 117: 6 July 1781.

3. C. L. and R. E. Ward, op. cit., vol. II, p. 237: to Joseph Walter, 31 January 1786.

4. P. J. Corish, *The Catholic Community in the Seventeenth and Eighteenth Centuries* (Dublin, 1981), p. 85.

5. Collated by the Revd John Brady as appendices on 'Catholics and Catholicism

in the Eighteenth-century Press' in *Archivium Hibernicum*, vols. xvi–xx and in his *Catholics and Catholicism in the Eighteenth-century Press* (Maynooth, 1965).

6. C. L. and R. E. Ward, op. cit., p. 7: to Denis O'Conor, 17 November 1751.

7. L. A. Clarkson, 'Armagh 1770: Portrait of an Urban Community' in D. W. Harkness and M. O'Dowd (editors), *The Town in Ireland: Historical Studies XIII* (Belfast, 1981), pp. 81–102.

8. L. M. Cullen, 'Problems in the Interpretation and Revision of Eighteenth-century Irish Economic History', *Transactions of the Royal Historical Society*, fifth series, vol. xvii (1967), p. 16.

9. See S. Daultrey, D. Dickson and C. Ó Gráda, 'Hearth Tax, Household Size and Irish Population Change 1672–1821', *Proceedings of the Royal Irish Academy*, vol. lxxxii, sect. C, no. 6 (1982), pp. 125–81.

10. Quoted by D. Dickson, 'Middlemen' in T. Bartlett and D. Hayton, op. cit., p. 173.

11. E. Ledwich, *Statistical Account of the Parish of Aghaboe* (Dublin, 1796), pp. 51–2, quoted in K. H. Connell, *The Population of Ireland 1750–1845* (Oxford, 1950), p. 74.

12. P. Roebuck, 'Rent Movement, Proprietorial Incomes and Agricultural Development 1730–1830' in P. Roebuck (editor), *Plantation to Partition: Essays in Ulster History in Honour of J. L. McCracken* (Belfast, 1981), pp. 82–101.

CHAPTER TEN
THE STRUCTURE OF POLITICS

1. November 1782: quoted in E. M. Johnston, *Great Britain and Ireland 1760–1800* (Edinburgh, 1963), pp. 26–7.

2. Emily Charlotte Boyle, op. cit., vol. II, p. 41: Chesterfield to 'Mr Prior' [n.d.].

3. The question of colonial parallels arises in F. G. James, *Ireland in the Empire 1688–1770* (Cambridge, Mass., 1973), especially pp. 139–41. For an opposing view, see J. C. D. Clark, 'Whig Tradition and Parliamentary Precedent: The English Management of Irish Politics 1754–6', *Historical Journal*, vol. xxi, no. 2 (1978), pp. 275–301.

4. See Charles Phillips, *Curran and His Contemporaries* (London, 1850), p. 53.

5. D. Hayton, 'The Beginnings of the Undertaker System' in T. Bartlett and D. Hayton, op. cit., p. 54.

6. A. P. W. Malcomson, 'Introduction' to *Lord Shannon's Letters to his Son: A Calendar of the Letters Written by the Second Earl of Shannon to His Son, Viscount Boyle, 1790–1802*, edited by Esther Hewitt (Belfast, 1982), p. lxi.

7. R. B. McDowell, *Ireland in the Age of Imperialism and Revolution 1760–1801* (Oxford, 1979), p. 229.

CHAPTER ELEVEN
AMERICANS, VOLUNTEERS AND THE POLITICS
OF 'PATRIOTISM'

1. See D. N. Doyle, op. cit.
2. C. F. Sheridan, *Observation on the Doctrine Laid Down by Sir William Blackstone Respecting the Power of the British Parliament, Particularly with Relation to Ireland* (Dublin, 1779), pp. 34–6.
3. Quoted in R. B. McDowell, op. cit., p. 132.
4. 'Declaration of Irish Rights' 19 April 1780 in D. O. Madden (editor), *Speeches of the Rt. Hon. Henry Grattan*, second edition (Dublin, 1853), pp. 40–44.
5. 'Anglo-Irish Constitutional Relations in the Later Eighteenth Century' in *Confrontations: Studies in Irish History* (London, 1972), p. 125.
6. See P. Kelly, 'British and Irish Politics in 1785', *English Historical Review*, vol. xc, no. 356 (July 1975), pp. 536–63.
7. Quoted in E. M. Johnston, *Ireland in the Eighteenth Century* (Dublin, 1974), p. 161.

CHAPTER TWELVE
'ENTHUSIASM DEFYING PUNISHMENT':
REVOLUTION, REPUBLICANISM AND REACTION

1. R. R. Madden, *The United Irishmen: Their Lives and Times* (London, 1842–5), vol. II, p. 335.
2. R. B. McDowell, op. cit., p. 397.
3. A. P. W. Malcomson, op. cit., p. 357.
4. D. A. Chart (editor), *The Drennan Letters* (Belfast, 1931), p. 178.
5. Originally published by his son in 1826. A fully annotated and inclusive edition is due from Oxford University Press; they have hitherto been most accessible in Seán O'Faolain's abridged edition of 1937.
6. Quoted in Frank MacDermot, *Wolfe Tone and His Times* (second edition, Tralee, 1968), p. 122.
7. Notably in the work of Marianne Elliott; see her definitive *Partners in Revolution: The United Irishmen and France* (London, 1982).
8. See D. Dickson, 'Taxation and Disaffection in Late Eighteenth-century Ireland' in S. Clark and J. Donnelly, Jr (editors), *Irish Peasants: Violence and Political Unrest 1780–1914* (Manchester, 1983), pp. 37–63.
9. See P. Gibbon, *The Origins of Ulster Unionism: The Formation of Popular Protestant Politics and Ideology in Nineteenth-century Ireland* (Manchester, 1975); and D. Miller, 'The Armagh Troubles 1784–95' in S. Clark and J. Donnelly, Jr, op. cit., pp. 155–91.
10. T. Bartlett, 'Select Documents XXXVIII: Defenders and Defenderism in 1795', *Irish Historical Studies*, vol. xxiv, no. 95 (May 1985), p. 375.

11. For this and other Defender oaths and iconography, see ibid.

12. Quoted in H. Senior, *Orangeism in Ireland and Britain 1795–1836* (London, 1966), p. 16.

13. See T. Bartlett, 'Indiscipline and Disaffection in the Armed Forces in Ireland in the 1790s' in P. J. Corish (editor), *Radicals, Rebels and Establishments: Historical Studies XV* (Belfast, 1985), pp. 115–34.

14. Quoted in H. Senior, op. cit., p. 83.

15. See S. Connolly, *Priests and People in Pre-Famine Ireland 1780–1845* (Dublin, 1982), pp. 226–9.

16. Marianne Elliott, op. cit., p. 166.

17. Quoted in Marianne Elliot, 'The Origins and Transformation of Early Irish Republicanism', *International Review of Social History*, vol. xxiii (1978), p. 27.

18. Speech of 5 February 1800, quoted in D. O. Madden, op. cit., p. 255.

19. Quoted in H. Senior, op. cit., p. 126.

20. 17 July 1799; printed as Public Record Office of Northern Ireland Education Facsimile No. 50.

21. T. Bartlett, 'Indiscipline and Disaffection in the Armed Forces in Ireland in the 1790s' in P. J. Corish, op. cit., p. 129.

22. See R. N. C. Vance, 'Text and Tradition: Robert Emmet's Speech from the Dock', *Studies*, vol. lxxi (Summer 1982), pp. 185–91.

PART THREE

CHAPTER THIRTEEN
THE MOBILIZATION OF POPULAR POLITICS

1. An argument advanced stimulatingly in Oliver MacDonagh, *States of Mind: A Study of Anglo-Irish Conflict 1780–1980* and now the subject of much further research.

2. M. Beames, *Peasants and Power: The Whiteboy Movements and Their Control in Pre-Famine Ireland* (Brighton, 1983), p. 30.

3. Quoted in David Fitzpatrick, 'Class, Family and Rural Unrest in Nineteenth-century Ireland' in P. J. Drudy (editor), *Irish Studies 2. Ireland: Land, Politics and People* (Cambridge, 1982), p. 47.

4. Quoted in Fergus O'Ferrall, *Catholic Emancipation: Daniel O'Connell and the Birth of Irish Democracy* (Dublin, 1985), p. 120.

5. Quoted in ibid., p. 144: letter to J. C. Foster, 16 July 1826.

6. Now published *in extenso* by Maurice O'Connell: *The Correspondence of Daniel O'Connell* (eight vols., Irish Manuscripts Commission, Dublin, 1972–80).

7. The figures are from K. T. Hoppen, *Elections, Politics and Society in Ireland 1832–85* (Oxford, 1984): rising to 60,597 after the legislation of 1832.

8. Ian d'Alton, *Protestant Society and Politics in Cork 1812–44* (Cork, 1980), p. 55.
9. Quoted in Fergus O'Ferrall, *Daniel O'Connell* (Dublin, 1981), p. 86.
10. Lady Augusta Gregory (editor), *Mr Gregory's Letter-Box* (Coole edition, Gerrard's Cross, 1981), p. 23: letter of 4 September 1813 to Sir William Gregory.
11. Quoted in K. T. Hoppen, *Elections, Politics and Society in Ireland 1832–85*, p. 279.
12. Quoted in Oliver MacDonagh, op. cit., p. 58: speech to Dublin Corporation, 1843.
13. Debating O'Connell's motion for a pledge repudiating the use of physical force, 27 July 1846.
14. 'Narrative of Thomas Darcy Magee' in Dennis Gwynn, *Young Ireland and 1848* (Cork, 1949), p. 320.

CHAPTER FOURTEEN
THE FAMINE: BEFORE AND AFTER

1. Quoted in Joel Mokyr, *Why Ireland Starved: A Quantitative and Analytical History of the Irish Economy 1800–1850* (London, 1983), p. 145.
2. J. Lee in *Irish Historiography 1970–79* (Cork, 1981), p. 182.
3. See especially R. D. C. Black, *Economic Thought and the Irish Question 1817–70* (Cambridge, 1970): far more enlightening on government policy than Cecil Woodham Smith's popular *The Great Hunger: Ireland 1845–9* (London, 1962).
4. For a sample of disagreements, see Raymond Crotty, *Irish Agricultural Production: Its Volume and Structure* (Cork, 1966); Joel Mokyr, op. cit.; and exchange between Liam Kennedy, Peter Solar and Joel Mokyr in *Irish Economic and Social History*, vol. xi (1984), pp. 101–21.
5. See tables in Joel Mokyr, op. cit., p. 267.
6. ibid., p. 275.
7. Based on hitherto unpublished work by C. Ó Gráda and Phelim Hughes, 'Fertility Trends, Excess Mortality and the Great Irish Famine'. I am grateful to both authors for showing me this paper. Also see C. Ó Gráda and Joel Mokyr, 'New Developments in Irish Population History 1700–1850', *Economic History Review*, vol. xxxvii, no. 4 (November 1984), pp. 473–88.
8. C. Trevelyan (writing anonymously), 'The Irish Crisis', *Edinburgh Review*, vol. clxxv (January 1848), p. 260. For the view from Clare, see S. Kierse, *The Famine Years in the Parish of Killaloe 1845–51* (Killaloe, 1984).
9. Oliver MacDonagh, *Ireland: The Union and Its Aftermath* (London, 1977), p. 37.
10. *Report of Geo. Nicholls, Esq., on Poor Law, Ireland, 1837*, quoted in R. D. C. Black, op. cit., p. 112.
11. ibid., p. 129.
12. Quoted in ibid., pp. 18, 136: H. Trower to David Ricardo, 10 January 1822.
13. S. Kierse, op. cit., p. 18.

14. D. Thomson and M. McGusty (editors), *The Irish Journals of Elizabeth Smith 1840–50* (Oxford, 1980), p. 126: 24 January 1847.

15. M. Doheny, *The Felon's Track, or History of the Attempted Outbreak in Ireland Embracing the Leading Events in the Irish Struggle from the Year 1843 to the Close of 1848* (Dublin, 1914 edition), pp. 234, 259–60.

16. Raymond Crotty estimates that in 1830, 5.06 per cent married under seventeen, and 36.72 per cent under twenty; these figures had dropped to 1.23 per cent and 22.5 per cent by 1840. But this interpretation has been contested.

17. See P. M. A. Bourke, 'The Agricultural Statistics of the 1841 Census of Ireland: A Critical Review', *Economic History Review* second series, vol. xviii (1965), pp. 374–91.

18. Joel Mokyr, op. cit., pp. 92–3.

19. P. M. A. Bourke, op. cit., p. 40, points out that the 1841 figures were in *Irish* acres, which inflated the number of apparently very small holdings *vis-à-vis* those recorded in 1851, when the smaller English acre was used.

20. J. Donnelly, Jr, *The Land and the People of Nineteenth-century Cork: The Rural Economy and the Land Question* (London, 1975), p. 78.

21. D. Thomson and M. McGusty, op. cit., pp. 131, 160.

22. E. Larkin, 'The Devotional Revolution in Ireland 1850–75', *American Historical Review,* vol. lxxvii, no. 3 (June 1972), p. 645.

23. K. H. Connell, 'Peasant Marriage in Ireland: Its Structure and Development Since the Famine', *Economic History Review*, vol. xiv, no. 3 (April 1962), pp. 502–23.

24. S. Kierse, op. cit., p. 57.

25. K. T. Hoppen, *Elections, Politics and Society in Ireland 1832–85*, p. 25.

CHAPTER FIFTEEN
IRELAND ABROAD

1. See Joel Mokyr, *Why Ireland Starved*, chapter 1, for arguments in favour of the higher estimate: see also C. Ó Gráda, 'A Note on Nineteenth-century Emigration Statistics', *Population Studies*, vol. 29, no. 1 (March 1975), pp. 143–9.

2. See Brenda Collins, 'Proto-industrialization and Pre-Famine Emigration', *Social History*, vol. vii, no. 2 (May 1982), pp. 127–46.

3. Padraig Cundun, quoted in Kerby Miller, *Emigrants and Exiles: Ireland and the Irish Exodus to North America* (Oxford, 1985), p. 275.

4. *Cork Constitution*, 6 November 1848, quoted in J. Donnelly, Jr, op. cit., p. 127; also see S. H. Cousens, 'The Regional Pattern of Emigration During the Great Irish Famine 1846–51', *Transactions of the Institute of British Geographers,* no. 28 (1960), pp. 119–34.

5. This has also been connected to the great reputation in Ireland of a York Quaker family, the Tukes, who had been prominent in famine relief in the west.

See F. Finnegan, 'The Irish in York' in R. Swift and S. Gilley (editors), *The Irish in the Victorian City* (London, 1985), pp. 80–81.

6. David Fitzpatrick, *Irish Emigration 1801–1921*, Studies in Irish Economic and Social History No. 1 (Dundalk, 1984), p. 32.

7. D. N. Doyle, quoted in Kerby Miller, 'Emigrants and Exiles: Irish Cultures and Irish Emigration to North America 1790–1922', *Irish Historical Studies*, vol. xxii, no. 86 (September 1980), p. 101.

8. See D. N. Doyle, 'The Regional Bibliography of Irish America: A Review and Addendum', *Irish Historical Studies*, vol. xxiii, no. 91 (May 1983), pp. 254–83.

9. Alan O'Day, *The English Face of Irish Nationalism: Parnellite Involvement in British Politics 1880–86* (Dublin, 1977), p. 109.

10. L. H. Lees, *Exiles of Erin: Irish Migrants in Victorian London* (Manchester, 1979), p. 46.

11. See R. Swift and S. Gilley, op. cit., and, for a useful bibliography, M. Hartigan, *The History of the Irish in Britain: A Bibliography* (London, 1986). The work of Dr Paul Laxton and his students in the Geography Department of Liverpool University queries many of the usual generalizations about segregation, 'ghettos' and occupations.

12. Quoted in T. W. Moody, *Michael Davitt and Irish Revolution 1846–82* (Oxford, 1981), p. 19.

13. See L. P. Curtis, *Anglo-Saxons and Celts: A Study of Anti-Irish Prejudice in Victorian England* (Bridgeport, Conn., 1966); S. Gilley, 'English Attitudes to the Irish in England 1789–1900' in C. Holmes (editor), *Immigrants and Minorities in British Society* (London, 1978), pp. 81–110; G. Ó Tuathaigh, 'The Irish in Nineteenth-century Britain: Problems of Integration', *Transactions of the Royal Historical Society*, fifth series, vol. 31 (1981).

14. S. Gilley, 'English Attitudes to the Irish in England 1789–1900' in C. Holmes, op. cit., p. 82.

15. On this question, see Gerard Connolly, 'Irish and Catholic: Myth or Reality?' in R. Swift and S. Gilley, op. cit., pp. 225–54.

16. By Owen Dudley Edwards, *Burke and Hare* (Edinburgh, 1980).

17. Conrad Arensberg, *The Irish Countryman: An Anthropological Study* (London, 1937), p. 84.

18. The *Irish Peasant*, 7 April 1906, quoted in Martin J. Waters, 'Peasants and Emigrants: Considerations of the Gaelic League as a Social Movement' in Daniel J. Casey and Robert E. Rhodes (editors), *Views of the Irish Peasantry 1800–1916* (Hamden, Conn., 1977), p. 176.

19. Kerby Miller, *Emigrants and Exiles: Ireland and the Irish Exodus to North America*, p. 378.

CHAPTER SIXTEEN
LAND, POLITICS AND NATIONALISM

1. R. V. Comerford, *The Fenians in Context: Irish Politics and Society 1848–82* (Dublin, 1985), p. 21.
2. F. S. L. Lyons, *Ireland Since the Famine* (London, 1971), p. 45. Also see L. P. Curtis, 'Incumbered Wealth: Landlord Indebtedness in Post-Famine Ireland', *American Historical Review*, vol. lxxxv, no. 2 (April 1980), pp. 332–68.
3. See W. E. Vaughan, *Sin, Sheep and Scotsmen: John George Adair and the Derryveagh Evictions 1861* (Belfast, 1983).
4. For hilarious examples, see K. T. Hoppen, *Elections, Politics and Society in Ireland 1832–85*, p. 132.
5. See graph in W. E. Vaughan, *Landlords and Tenants in Ireland 1848–1904*, Studies in Irish Social and Economic History No. 2 (Dundalk 1984), p. 22, reproduced p. 376 above.
6. R. V. Comerford, op. cit., p. 22.
7. K. T. Hoppen, *Elections, Politics and Society in Ireland 1832–85*, p. 382.
8. T. P. O'Connor, *The Parnell Movement* (London, 1887), p. 135, recalling Athlone in the previous generation.
9. Charles Townshend, *Political Violence in Ireland: Government and Resistance since 1848* (Oxford, 1983), p. 25.
10. R. V. Comerford, op. cit., p. 40.
11. ibid.
12. Charles Kickham in the *Irish People*, 21 May 1864, 16 September 1865.
13. Quoted in E. D. Steele, 'Gladstone and Ireland', *Irish Historical Studies*, vol. xvii, no. 65 (March 1970), p. 67: December 1867.
14. *Letter to the Catholic Clergy of the Archdiocese of Armagh*, 1850.
15. Bessborough Commission, I, p. 67, quoted in S. Clark, *Social Origins of the Irish Land War* (Princeton, 1979), p. 180.
16. K. T. Hoppen, *Elections, Politics and Society in Ireland 1832–85*, p. 33.

CHAPTER SEVENTEEN
THE POLITICS OF PARNELLISM

1. Quoted in T. W. Moody, 'Anna Parnell and the Land League', *Hermathena*, vol. cxvii (1974), p. 16. Her book on the Land War has finally been published and is indispensable: *The Tale of a Great Sham*, edited with an introduction by Dana Hearne (Dublin, 1986).
2. See C. C. O'Brien, *Parnell and His Party 1880–90* (Oxford, 1964), p. 10.
3. Michael Davitt, *The Fall of Feudalism in Ireland* (London and New York, 1904), pp. 377–8.

4. C. C. O'Brien, op. cit., p. 350.

5. See C. Ó Gráda, 'Agricultural Head-rents, Pre-Famine and Post-Famine', *Economic and Social Review*, vol. v, no. 3 (April 1974), pp. 385–92.

6. The fullest treatment is in T. W. Moody, *Michael Davitt and Irish Revolution 1846–82*. Davitt's own priority probably remained separatism, if necessary by violence, until well into 1878.

7. A pattern established by Donald Jordan's important work, to be published as *Land and Politics in the West of Ireland: County Mayo 1846–82* (Cambridge, forthcoming 1989).

8. W. E. Vaughan, 'Landlord and Tenant Relations between the Famine and the Land War' in L. M. Cullen and T. C. Smout (editors), *Comparative Aspects of Scottish and Irish Economic and Social History 1600–1900* (Edinburgh, 1977), p. 221.

9. Wilfrid Scawen Blunt, *The Land War in Ireland: Being a Personal Narrative of Events* (London, 1912), p. 281.

10. Quoted in J. V. O'Brien, *William O'Brien and the Course of Irish Politics 1881–1918* (London, 1976), p. 52: R. Butler to A. J. Balfour, 16 August 1887.

11. Charles Townshend, op. cit., chapters 2 and 3.

12. R. V. Comerford, op. cit., p. 231.

13. B. Becker, *Disturbed Ireland: Being the Letters Written During the Winter 1880–81* (London, 1881), p. 180.

14. Donald Jordan, 'Land and Politics in the West of Ireland: County Mayo 1846–82', Ph.D. (U C L A, Davis, 1982), p. 352. The ensuing tension, according to Jordan, ended the effectiveness of the land agitation in Mayo well before 1881.

15. Anna Parnell, op. cit., p. 92.

16. Katharine O'Shea, *Charles Stewart Parnell: His Love Story and Political Life* (London, 1914), vol. I, pp. 235–6.

17. Raymond Crotty, op. cit., pp. 84, 91. His extended comparison with contemporary Denmark is especially striking.

18. Charles Townshend, op. cit., p. 125.

19. B. Becker, op. cit., p. 83.

20. Tom Garvin, *The Evolution of Irish Nationalist Politics* (Dublin, 1981), pp. 80–81.

21. B. Walker, 'The Land Question and Elections in Ulster 1868–86' in S. Clark and J. Donnelly, Jr, op. cit., p. 259.

22. K. T. Hoppen, *Elections, Politics and Society in Ireland 1832–85*, p. 273.

23. Quoted in H. Patterson, *Class Conflict and Sectarianism: The Protestant Working Class and the Belfast Labour Movement 1868–1920* (Belfast, 1980), p. 23: 3 April 1893. Compare Gladstone's speech introducing the first Home Rule Bill, 7 June 1886, where he spoke of 'that wealthy, intelligent and energetic portion of the Irish community which predominates in a certain portion of Ulster' – possibly a deliberate echo.

24. Quoted by L. Kennedy, 'Farmers, Traders and Agricultural Politics in Pre-Independence Ireland' in S. Clark and J. Donnelly, Jr, op. cit., p. 353.

25. Wilfred Scawen Blunt, op. cit., p. 305.

26. Quoted in R. F. Foster, 'To the Northern Counties Station: Lord Randolph Churchill and the Prelude to the Orange Card' in F. S. L Lyons and R. A. J. Hawkins (editors), *Ireland under the Union: Varieties of Tension. Essays in Honour of T. W. Moody* (Oxford, 1980), p. 285.

27. P. O'Farrell, *Ireland's English Question: Anglo-Irish Relations 1534–1970* (New York, 1971), p. 187.

PART FOUR

CHAPTER EIGHTEEN
THE 'NEW' NATIONALISM

1. Reprinted in *Autobiographies* (London, 1955), p. 554.

2. *Things Past Redress* (London, 1937), p. 214.

3. Tom Garvin, op. cit., p. 106.

4. See, for example, Mary Daly, *Dublin, The Deposed Capital: A Social and Economic History 1860–1914* (Cork, 1985) and J. V. O'Brien, *'Dear, Dirty Dublin': A City in Distress 1899–1916* (London, 1985).

5. Mary Daly, op. cit., p. 218.

6. John Gray, *City in Revolt: James Larkin and the Belfast Dock Strike of 1907* (Belfast, 1985), p. 89.

7. H. Patterson, op. cit., p. 67.

8. J. V. O'Brien, op. cit., pp. 222–3.

9. Martin J. Waters, 'Peasants and Emigrants: Considerations of the Gaelic League as a Social Movement' in Daniel J. Casey and Robert E. Rhodes, op. cit., p. 162.

10. Tom Garvin, op. cit., p. 102.

11. Lady Augusta Gregory, *Our Irish Theatre* (London, 1914), p. 20. The original MS is signed by Yeats.

12. J. M. Synge, *Collected Works. Vol. II: Prose*, edited by Alan Price (Oxford, 1960), pp. 399–400.

13. D. P. Moran, *The Philosophy of Irish Ireland* (Dublin, 1905), pp. 11, 48.

14. J. M. Synge, op. cit., p. 283: letter of 13 July 1905 to Stephen MacKenna.

15. Quoted in Michael Tierney, *Eoin MacNeill: Scholar and Man of Action 1867–1945*, edited by F. X. Martin (Oxford, 1980), p. 104.

16. R. M. Henry, *The Evolution of Sinn Féin* (Dublin, 1920), p. 64.

17. Patrick H. Pearse, *The Story of a Success, being a Record of St Enda's College, September 1908 to 1916*, edited by Desmond Ryan (Dublin, 1917), p. 7.

18. Michael MacGowan, *The Hard Road to Klondike*, translated from the Irish by Valentine Iremonger (London, 1962), p. 142.

19. E. O'Malley, *Memories of a Mayoman* (Dublin, 1981), p. 15.

CHAPTER NINETEEN
WAR AND REVOLUTION

1. See P. Jalland, *The Liberals and Ireland: The Ulster Question in British Politics to 1914* (Brighton, 1980) and Ronan Fanning, 'The Irish Policy of Asquith's Government and the Cabinet Crisis of 1910' in Art Cosgrove and Donal McCartney, op. cit., pp. 279–303.
2. Charles Townshend, op. cit., p. 239.
3. Quoted in David Fitzpatrick, *Politics and Irish Life 1913–21: Provincial Experience of War and Revolution* (Dublin, 1977), p. 58.
4. See A. T. Q. Stewart, *The Ulster Crisis* (London, 1967), chapter 8.
5. David Fitzpatrick, *Politics and Irish Life 1913–21: Provincial Experience of War and Revolution*, p. 101.
6. Quoted in A. T. Q. Stewart, *Ulster Crisis*, p. 182.
7. J. R. Vincent (editor), *The Crawford Papers: The Journals of David Lindsay Twenty-seventh Earl of Crawford and Tenth Earl of Balcarres 1821–1940 during the Years 1892–1940* (Manchester, 1984), p. 343.
8. M. Laffan, *The Partition of Ireland 1911–25* (Dublin Historical Association, Dundalk, 1983), p. 48.
9. B. Mac Giolla Choille, *Intelligence Notes 1913–18* (Toronto, 1970), pp. 147–8.
10. Quoted in L. Ó Broin, *Revolutionary Underground: The Story of the Irish Republican Brotherhood 1858–1924* (Dublin, 1976), p. 171.
11. Quoted in J. V. O'Brien, op. cit., p. 258.
12. Quotations from the *Worker*, 30 January 1915; *Workers' Republic*, 22 July 1899, 25 December 1915, 22 January 1916, 5 February 1916. See also James Newsinger, ' "As Catholic as the Pope": James Connolly and the Roman Catholic Church in Ireland', *Saothar*, no. 11 (1986), pp. 7–18.
13. Quoted in Charles Townshend, op. cit., p. 330.
14. F. X. Martin (editor), 'Eoin MacNeill on the 1916 Rising', *Irish Historical Studies*, vol. xii, no. 47 (March 1961), p. 236.
15. James Stephens, *The Insurrection in Dublin* (first published 1916; Gerrard's Cross edition, 1978).
16. E. R. Dodds (editor), *Journals and Letters of Stephen MacKenna* (London, 1936), pp. 50–51.
17. Ernie O'Malley, *On Another Man's Wound* (Tralee, 1979 edition), p. 38.
18. Quoted in Rex Taylor, *Michael Collins* (London, 1958), p. 72.
19. Fergus FitzGerald (editor), *Memoirs of Desmond FitzGerald 1913–16* (London, 1968), pp. 142–3.
20. E. de Blaighid, quoted in 'Ireland in 1915: National Spirit at Its Lowest Ebb', *A tÓglach*, vol. i, no. 5 (Autumn 1962), p. 5.
21. Quoted in J. V. O'Brien, op. cit., pp. 277–8: 24 July 1916.
22. Charles Townshend, op. cit., p. 312.
23. An interpretation convincingly advanced by D. George Boyce in 'British

Opinion, Ireland and the War', *Historical Journal*, vol. xvii, no. 3 (1974), pp. 575–93.

24. One of them recalled: 'I must have voted thirty times at various polling booths in our area. But I was not by any means the only one to do so and even the officials were in on it. From midday onwards I used to be greeted with a friendly smile by the presiding officer at a particular booth, and his poll clerk would laughingly ask: "Whose name is it this time?" ' O. Coogan, *Politics and War in Meath 1913–23* (Dublin, 1983), p. 105 (also see p. 87).

25. Michael Tierney, op. cit., pp. 180, 222.

CHAPTER TWENTY
THE TAKEOVER

1. David Fitzpatrick, *Politics and Irish Life 1913–21: Provincial Experience of War and Revolution*, p. 179.

2. ibid., p. 30.

3. Ernie O'Malley, *On Another Man's Wound*, p. 128.

4. L. Ó Broin, op. cit., p. 46.

5. For a general treatment of these patterns, see E. Rumpf and A. C. Hepburn, *Nationalism and Socialism in Twentieth-century Ireland* (Liverpool, 1977); and for an important critique, David Fitzpatrick, 'The Geography of Irish Nationalism 1910–21', *Past and Present*, no. 78 (1978), pp. 113–44.

6. David Fitzpatrick, op. cit., p. 224. Also see D. G. Boyce, *Nationalism in Ireland* (London, 1982), p. 312.

7. Charles Townshend, op. cit., pp. 66–7.

8. J. Gleeson, *Bloody Sunday* (London, 1962), p. 36.

9. For an effective treatment, see J. McColgan, *British Policy and the Irish Administration 1920–22* (London, 1983).

10. See Seán Cronin, *The McGarrity Papers: Revelations of the Irish Revolutionary Movement in Ireland and America 1900–1940* (Tralee, 1972), pp. 109–11.

11. L. Ó Broin, op. cit., p. 100. Childers too saw the point, but argued, erroneously, that Britain would never allow Ireland to proceed along this path.

12. F. S. L. Lyons, *Ireland since the Famine*, pp. 431–2.

13. Quoted in Joseph M. Curran, *The Birth of the Irish Free State 1921–3* (University, Alabama, 1980), p. 138.

14. See, however, Charles Townshend, op. cit., pp. 368ff. and E. Rumpf and A. C. Hepburn and David Fitzpatrick as in note 5 above.

15. See David Fitzpatrick, 'Strikes in Ireland 1914–21', *Saothar*, no. 6 (1980), p. 28.

16. Quoted in Michael Gallagher, 'The Pact General Election of 1922', *Irish Historical Studies*, vol. xxi, no. 84 (September 1979), p. 41.

17. P. O'Donnell, *There Will Be Another Day* (Dublin, 1963), pp. 19–20.

CHAPTER TWENTY-ONE
IN A FREE STATE

1. E. B. Titley, *Church, State and the Control of Schooling in Ireland 1900–1944* (Dublin, 1983), p. 82; quotes from National Programme Conference on Primary Instruction, meeting from 6 January 1921.
2. The only government department to receive a full historical treatment, in Ronan Fanning's definitive *The Irish Department of Finance 1922–58* (Dublin, 1978).
3. Quoted in Maryann Gialenella Valuilis, *Almost a Rebellion: The Irish Army Mutiny of 1924* (Cork, 1985), p. 35.
4. Most accessibly followed in F. S. L. Lyons, *Ireland Since the Famine*, pp. 688ff; also see P. Buckland, *The Factory of Grievances: Devolved Government in Northern Ireland 1921–39* (Dublin, 1979), pp. 83–4.
5. See P. Buckland, op. cit., pp. 247ff, 264–5, for the abandonment of non-sectarian guidelines in education.
6. See Clare O'Halloran, *Partition and the Limits of Irish Nationalism: An Ideology under Stress* (Dublin, 1987), pp. 34-5.
7. Quoted in Terence Brown, *Ireland: A Social and Cultural History 1922–79* (London, 1981), p. 63. Piquantly, Father Corcoran, a powerful voice in favour of educational Gaelicization, did not himself speak Irish.
8. Ronan Fanning, *Independent Ireland* (Dublin, 1983), pp. 29ff, gives a fuller account of this vital Committee than any other accessible authority.
9. *Belfast Newsletter*, 30 June 1922, quoted in P. Bew and H. Patterson, *The State in Northern Ireland 1921–72: Political Forces and Social Classes* (Manchester, 1971), pp. 65–6.
10. C. S. Andrews, *Man of No Property* (Dublin, 1982), p. 97. See also p. 50 for his recollections of republican mentality in the early 1920s. 'In our estimation, all Republicans lived conspicuously virtuous lives, free from the taint of scandal and proof against character assassination. This may sound like a naïve, self-righteous statement, but it is true. We looked with contempt upon our Free State opponents who, with the pretensions of the *nouveau riche*, had adopted a lifestyle of which dinner parties, card parties, garden parties, dances, and, of course, horse-racing became the favourite ingredients. Many of them to our satisfaction succumbed to drink, debt and fornication. That too sounds priggish, but it is also true.'
11. Tom Garvin, op. cit., p. 146.
12. Quoted in E. B. Titley, op. cit., p. 84.

CHAPTER TWENTY-TWO
THE DE VALERA DISPENSATION

1. Quoted in John Bowman, *De Valera and the Ulster Question 1917–73* (Oxford, 1982), p. 330.

2. Noel Browne, *Against the Tide* (Dublin, 1986), chapters 1 and 2.

3. Terence Brown, op. cit., p. 136.

4. Terence Brown, op. cit., p. 187.

5. Raymond Crotty, *Irish Agricultural Production: Its Volume and Structure*, p. 159.

6. Quoted in Tim Pat Coogan, *The I R A* (second edition, 1980), pp. 281–3.

7. C. S. Andrews, *Man of No Property*, p. 119.

8. Ronan Fanning, *The Irish Department of Finance 1922–58*, p. 235; also see pp. 229ff on the whole question of civil service cuts.

9. O. MacDonagh, *States of Mind: A Study of Anglo-Irish Conflict 1780–1980*, p. 121.

10. E. B. Titley, op. cit., p. 139.

11. Quoted in ibid., p. 127.

12. See E. Rumpf and A. C. Hepburn, op. cit., especially maps on pp. 139–41.

13. J. Bowyer Bell, *The Secret Army: A History of the I R A 1916–70* (London, 1970), p. 279.

14. Deirdre McMahon, *Republicans and Imperialists: Anglo-Irish Relations in the 1930s* (London, 1984), especially pp. 198–202.

15. John Bowman, op. cit., p. 147.

16. Quoted in Ronan Fanning, *The Irish Department of Finance 1922–58*, p. 267.

17. ibid., p. 246.

18. John Bowman, op. cit., p. 181.

19. Quoted in David Harkness, *Northern Ireland since 1920* (Dublin, 1983), p. 55.

20. Quoted in P. Buckland, op. cit., p. 130.

21. ibid., p. 113.

22. A point made in ibid., p. 135.

23. David Harkness, *Northern Ireland since 1920*, p. 75.

24. Quoted in Robert Fisk, *In Time of War: Ireland, Ulster and the Price of Neutrality 1939–45* (London, 1983), pp. 141–2.

25. Quoted in ibid., p. 371.

26. ibid., p. 373–7.

27. ibid., p. 463.

28. Quoted in Ronan Fanning, *The Irish Department of Finance 1922–58*, pp. 394–5.

CHAPTER TWENTY-THREE
'MODERN' IRELAND?

1. Quoted in Ronan Fanning, *Independent Ireland*, p. 192.

2. Quoted in John Bowman, op. cit., p. 259.

3. Tom Garvin, 'Change and the Political System' in Frank Litton (editor), *Unequal Achievement: The Irish Experience 1957–82* (Institute of Public Administration, Dublin, 1982), pp. 30–31.

4. ibid., p. 26.

5. Michael Gallagher, *Political Parties in the Republic of Ireland* (Manchester, 1985), p. 136.

6. Thus the President of the National Agricultural and Industrial Development Association in 1953, quoted in P. Bew and H. Patterson, *Sean Lemass and the Making of Modern Ireland 1945–66* (Dublin, 1982), pp. 70–71.

7. Ronan Fanning, *The Irish Department of Finance 1922–58*, p. 509.

8. Raymond Crotty, *Ireland in Crisis: A Study in Capitalist Colonial Underdevelopment* (Dingle, 1986), p. 80. It should be added that this was never Whitaker's intention. When he left the Department of Finance in 1969, the state's foreign indebtedness totalled only £78,000,000, having been £40,000,000 of outstanding Marshall Aid loans at the beginning of the decade. Whitaker consistently argued against borrowing for everyday needs rather than for productive purposes, and opposed the policies that brought foreign indebtedness up to about £10,000 million by the late 1980s.

9. See John Blackwell, 'Government, Economy and Society,' in Frank Litton, op. cit., p. 45.

10. See E. A. Aunger, 'Religion and Class: An Analysis of 1971 Census Data' in R. J. Cormack and R. D. Osborne (editors), *Religion, Education and Employment: Aspects of Equal Opportunity in Northern Ireland* (Belfast, 1983), pp. 24–41. The whole collection is a good introduction to the subject. Also see J. Whyte, 'How Much Discrimination was there under the Unionist Regime 1921–68?' in Tom Gallagher and James O'Connell (editors), *Contemporary Irish Studies* (Manchester, 1983) and John Darby, *Conflict in Northern Ireland: The Development of a Polarized Community* (Dublin, 1976), pp. 1–35.

11. R. J. Cormack and R. D. Osborne, op. cit., p. 239.

12. J. Whyte, 'How Much Discrimination was there under the Unionist Regime?' in Tom Gallagher and James O'Connell, op. cit., p. 31.

13. Quoted in P. Bew and H. Patterson, op. cit., p. 191.

14. *New Statesman*, 1 July 1966.

15. R. Rose, *Governing without Consensus: An Irish Perspective* (London, 1971), p. 255.

16. John Bowman, op. cit., p. 287.

17. Brian Farrell, *Sean Lemass* (Dublin, 1983), p. 99.

18. David A. Rottman and Philip J. O'Connell, 'The Changing Social Structure' in Frank Litton, op. cit., p. 72.

19. J. A. Murphy, ' "Put them out!" Parties and Elections 1948–69' in J. Lee (editor), *Ireland 1945–70* (Dublin, 1979), p. 10.

20. An observation made by Charles Townshend, 'Modernization and Nationalism: Perspectives in Recent Irish History', *History*, vol. lxvi, no. 217 (June 1981), p. 243.

BIBLIOGRAPHICAL ESSAY

This is intended both as an indication of some of the work referred to obliquely in the text, and as a guide to further reading. It is by no means a comprehensive bibliography for the entire period or, indeed, for this book: more, a personal selection. A glossary of abbreviations will be found at the end.

The most accessible general bibliographies will be found appended to the published volumes of the *New History of Ireland* (particularly that covering the eighteenth century, referred to below, where the bibliography is more up to date than many of the contributions). Also see T. W. Moody (editor), *Irish Historiography 1936–70* (Dublin, 1971); J. Lee (editor), *Irish Historiography 1970–79* (Cork, 1981); and L. A. Clarkson, 'The Writing of Irish Economic and Social History since 1968', *Ec. Hist. Rev.*, vol. xxxiii, no. 1 (February 1980). General and interpretive works that cover large tracts of the period include Oliver MacDonagh, *States of Mind: A Study of Anglo-Irish Conflict 1780–1980* (London, 1983); P. O'Farrell, *England's Irish Question: Anglo-Irish Relations 1534–1970* (London, 1971); L. M. Cullen's *The Emergence of Modern Ireland 1600–1900* (London, 1981), a seminal text of the new history, and *An Economic History of Ireland since 1600* (London, 1972); E. Estyn Evans, *The Personality of Ireland: Habit, Heritage and History* (revised edition, Belfast, 1981); A. T. Q. Stewart, *The Narrow Ground: Aspects of Ulster 1609–1969* (London, 1977); and P. Roebuck (editor), *Plantation to Partition: Essays in Ulster History in Honour of J. L. McCracken* (Belfast, 1981). Irish nationalism (not Irish history in general) throughout the period is dealt with in D. George Boyce's exemplary *Nationalism in Ireland* (London, 1982); Tom Garvin, *The Evolution of Irish Nationalist Politics* (Dublin, 1981); and R. Kee, *The Green Flag: A History of Irish Nationalism* (London, 1972). Useful collections of essays, with a strong social and economic theme, are S. Clark and J. Donnelly, Jr (editors), *Irish Peasants: Violence and Political Unrest 1780–1914* (Manchester, 1983); R. A. Butlin (editor), *The Development of the Irish Town* (London, 1977); and D. Harkness and M. O'Dowd (editors), *The Town in Ireland: Historical Studies XIII* (Belfast, 1981). A comparative aspect is provided by L. M. Cullen and T. C. Smout (editors), *Comparative Aspects of Irish and Scottish Economic and Social History 1600–1900* (Edinburgh, 1977); L. M. Cullen and F. Furet (editors), *Irlande et France XVIIᵉ–XXᵉ siècles: pour une histoire rurale comparée* (Paris, 1980); and T. M. Devine and D. Dickson (editors), *Ireland and Scotland 1600–1980: Parallels and Contrasts in Economic and Social Development* (Edinburgh, 1983). For general treatments of art and architecture, see Maurice Craig, *The Architecture of Ireland from the Earliest Times to 1880* (London, 1982); M. Bence Jones, *Burke's Guide to Country Houses. Vol. I: Ireland* (London, 1978); and Ann Crookshank and the Knight of Glin, *The Painters of Ireland c. 1660–1920* (London, 1978). Aspects of education and culture covering the entire period are dealt with in B. Ó Cuív (editor), *A View of the Irish Language* (Dublin, 1969) and R. B. McDowell and D. A. Webb, *Trinity College, Dublin, 1592–1952: An Academic History* (Cambridge, 1982). R. Dudley Edwards, *An Atlas of Irish History* (second edition, London, 1981) is an essential background work; and there is much useful information gathered together in T. W. Moody, F. X. Martin, F. J. Byrne (editors), *A New History of Ireland. Vol. IX: Maps, Genealogies, Lists. A Companion to Irish History, Part II* (Oxford, 1984).

PART ONE

The contemporary accounts by Moryson, Gernon, Bodley, Davies and others discussed in the text are most easily accessible in C. Litton Falkiner (editor), *Illustrations of Irish History and Topography, Mainly of the Seventeenth Century* (London, 1904); C. Maxwell (editor), *Irish History from Contemporary Sources 1509–1610* (London, 1923); and H. Morley (editor), *Ireland under Elizabeth and James I* (London, 1890). There is a full edition of the first three parts of Moryson's *Itinerary* in four volumes, published in Glasgow 1907–8, and extracts from the fourth part in C. Hughes (editor), *Shakespeare's Europe* (London, 1903). Barnaby Rich's *A New Description of Ireland* (London, 1610) is valuable (but see note 1, p. 622, above). A *Description of Ireland ... in Anno 1598* was edited by Edmund Hogan (London, 1878). Edmund Spenser's *A View of the Present State of Ireland* edited by W. L. Renwick (Oxford, 1970) is essential; for interpretations see C. Brady, 'Spenser's Irish Crisis: Humanism and Experience in the 1590s', *P & P*, no. 111 (May 1986) and ensuing debate. Also see T. Stafford, *Pacata Hibernia*, edited by Standish O'Grady (London, 1896); *Tracts Relating to Ireland Printed for the Irish Archaeological Society*, vol. I (1841) for Richard Payne's 'Brief Description of Ireland' (1590), and vol. II (1842) for John Dymmok's 'Treatise of Ireland *c.* 1600'; Sir John Harington, 'A Short View of Ireland Written in Anno 1605' in *Anecdota Bodleiana*, edited by W. Dunn McCray, no. 1 (Oxford, 1879); D. B. Quinn (editor), ' "A Discourse of Ireland", *c.* 1599: A Sidelight on English Colonial Policy', *RIA Proc.*, vol. xlvii, sect. C., no. 3 (1942).

The most comprehensive general treatment of the seventeenth century is T. W. Moody, F. X. Martin, F. J. Byrne (editors), *A New History of Ireland. Vol. III: Early Modern Ireland 1534–1691* (Oxford, 1976). But it does not make redundant the other works by contributors, notably Aidan Clarke's essential *The Old English in Ireland 1625–42* (London, 1966) and the works of L. M. Cullen and J. G. Simms cited elsewhere. Also see K. W. Nicholls, *Gaelic and Gaelicized Ireland in the Middle Ages* (Dublin, 1972); D. B. Quinn, *The Elizabethans and the Irish* (Ithaca, 1966) and J. H. Andrews, 'Geography and Government in Elizabethan Ireland', *Irish*

Geographical Studies in Honour of E. Estyn Evans, edited by N. Stephens and R. E. Glasscock (Belfast, 1970), which are all relevant to early seventeenth-century Ireland. Further commentary on some themes stressed in this book will be found in Aidan Clarke, 'Colonial Identity in Early Seventeenth-century Ireland' in T. W. Moody (editor), *Nationality and the Pursuit of National Independence: Historical Studies XI* (Belfast, 1978); N. Canny, 'Hugh O'Neill, Earl of Tyrone, and the Changing Face of Gaelic Ulster', *Stud. Hib.*, vol. x (1970); J. Graham, 'Rural Society in Connacht 1600–1640' in N. Stephens and R. E. Glasscock, *Irish Geographical Studies*; A. T. Lucas, 'Irish Food before the Potato' in *Gwerin*, vol. iii, no. 2 (December 1960), which explores an important subject oddly neglected, except by the indefatigable L. M. Cullen. The best general treatments of religion are J. Bossy, 'The Counter-Reformation and the People of Catholic Ireland 1596–1641' in *Historical Studies VIII* (Dublin, 1971) and P. J. Corish, *The Catholic Community in the Seventeenth and Eighteenth Centuries* (Dublin, 1981). Material about the O'Neill wars and their aftermath may be found in C. Falls, *Elizabeth's Irish Wars* (London, 1950); G. A. Hayes-McCoy, *Irish Battles* (London, 1964); J. J. Silke, *Kinsale: The Spanish Intervention in Ireland at the End of the Elizabethan Wars* (New York, 1970); Micheline Walsh's useful commentaries in *Irish Sword*, vols. iii (1957–8), v (1961–2), vii (1965–6), viii (1967–8) and ix (1969–70); N. Canny, 'The Treaty of Mellifont and the Reorganization of Ulster 1603', *Irish Sword*, vol. ix (1969–70) and 'The Flight of the Earls 1607', *IHS*, vol. xvii, no. 67 (March 1971). Important aspects of the economy are dealt with in D. M. Woodward, 'The Anglo-Irish Livestock Trade of the Seventeenth Century', *IHS*, vol. xvii, no. 72 (September 1972); P. J. Dowden, 'Wool Supply and the Woollen Industry', *Ec. Hist. Rev.*, vol. ix, no. 1 (1956); H. F. Kearney, 'Mercantilism and Ireland 1620–40', *Historical Studies I* (1951).

Interpretation of colonization and plantation has been altered by much recent work, though T. W. Moody's *The Londonderry Plantation 1609–41: The City of London and the Plantation of Ulster* (1939) is still indispensable. So is George Hill's *An Historical Account of the Plantation of Ulster 1608–20* (Belfast, 1877; reprinted Shannon, 1970). Also see George O'Brien's edition of H. Bourgchier's promotional *Advertisements for Ireland*, 1623 (Dublin, 1923). For recent interpretations, an invaluable collection is C. Brady and R. Gillespie (editors), *Natives and Newcomers: The Making of Irish Colonial Society 1534–1641* (Dublin, 1986). Other recent perspectives include K. R. Andrews, N. P. Canny, P. E. Hair, et al., *The Westward Enterprise: English Activities in Ireland, the Atlantic and America 1480–1650* (Liverpool, 1978); M. MacCarthy-Morrogh, *The Munster Plantation: English Migration to Southern Ireland 1583–1641* (Oxford, 1986); R. J. Hunter, 'Towns in the Ulster Plantation', *Stud. Hib.*, vol. xi (1971) and 'Ulster Plantation Towns 1609–41' in D. Harkness and M. O'Dowd, *The Town in Ireland: Historical Studies XIII*; M. Perceval-Maxwell, *The Scottish Migration to Ulster in the Reign of James I* (London, 1973); P. Robinson, 'British Settlement in County Tyrone 1610–66', *IESH*, vol. v (1978); R. Gillespie, *Colonial Ulster: The Settlement of East Ulster 1600–1641* (Cork, 1985); P. Roebuck, 'The Making of an Ulster Great Estate:

The Chichesters ... 1599–1648', *RIA Proc.*, vol. lxxix, sect. C., no. 1 (1979). A pioneering attempt to define the planter mentality has been made by N. Canny in *The Upstart Earl: A Study of the Social and Mental World of Richard Boyle, First Earl of Cork 1566–1643* (Cambridge, 1982).

Settlement and colonization after mid-century are illuminated by K. Bottigheimer, *English Money and Irish Land: The 'Adventurers' in the Cromwellian Settlement of Ireland* (Oxford, 1971); R. C. Simington (editor), *The Transplantation to Connacht* (IMC, Dublin, 1970); J. G. Simms, *The Williamite Confiscation in Ireland 1690–1703* (London, 1956). H. P. Prendergast, *The Cromwellian Settlement of Ireland* (second edition Dublin, 1875), remains a source of value. The establishment of a planter family can be traced in Elizabeth Bowen's highly charged *Bowen's Court* (London, 1942).

The political upheavals of the mid-seventeenth century inspired several great Victorian editions of original material – notably J. T. Gilbert's *Contemporary History of Affairs in Ireland from AD 1641 to 1652* (three vols., Dublin, 1879) and *History of the Irish Confederation and the War in Ireland 1641–9* (six vols., Dublin, 1882–90). Also see R. Dunlop, *Ireland under the Commonwealth: Being a Selection of Documents Relating to the Government of Ireland from 1651 to 1659* (two vols., Manchester, 1913); James Hogan (editor), *Letters and Papers Relating to the Irish Rebellion 1642–6* (IMC, Dublin, 1936); and Aidan Clarke (editor), 'A Discourse between Two Councillors of State, the One of England and the Other of Ireland', *Anal. Hib.*, no. 26 (1970).

Of secondary sources, the work of Aidan Clarke already mentioned is essential; so is T. C. Barnard's *Cromwellian Ireland: English Government and Reform in Ireland 1649–60* (Oxford, 1975). The best treatments of Wentworth's controversial Irish career are H. Kearney, *Strafford in Ireland 1633–41: A Study in Absolutism* (Manchester, 1961) and T. O. Ranger, 'Strafford in Ireland: A Revaluation' in T. H. Aston (editor), *Crisis in Europe 1550–1660* (London, 1965). J. C. Beckett's *Confrontations: Studies in Irish History* (London, 1962) contains valuable essays on 'Irish-Scottish Relations in the Seventeenth Century' and 'The Confederation of Kilkenny Reviewed'. David Stevenson's *Scottish Covenanters and Irish Confederates: Scottish-Irish Relations in the Mid-seventeenth Century* (Belfast, 1981) provides a uniquely valuable treatment that spans events in both countries. There are numerous individual military studies in the *Irish Sword*. For the controversies (and historiography) surrounding the 1641 rising see M. Perceval-Maxwell, 'The Ulster Rising of 1641 and the Depositions', *IHS*, vol. xxi, no. 82 (September 1978) and R. Gillespie, 'The End of an Era: Ulster and the Outbreak of the 1641 Rising' in J. Brady and R. Gillespie, *Natives and Newcomers: The Making of Irish Colonial Society, 1534–1641*.

First-hand material on later seventeenth-century Ireland may be found in William Petty, *Political Anatomy of Ireland* (reprinted by IUP, Dublin, 1970); the extracts from James Dineley's 'Tour' in *RSAI Jn.*, vols. iv (1856), v (1858), vii (1862–3), viii (1864–6), ix (1867) and xliii (1913); J. T. Gilbert's edition of *A Jacobite Narrative of the War in Ireland* (Dublin, 1892; reprinted with an Introduction by

J. G. Simms, 1971); and R. H. Murray (editor), *The Journal of John Stevens 1689–91* (Oxford, 1912). Edward MacLysaght's *Irish Life in the Seventeenth Century: After Cromwell* (Dublin, 1939) is a classic study, and reprints John Dunton's absorbing contemporary letters in an appendix. Also see M. MacCurtain, 'Rural Society in Post-Cromwellian Ireland' in Art Cosgrove and Donal McCartney (editors), *Studies in Irish History Presented to R. Dudley Edwards* (Dublin, 1979); J. G. Simms, 'Dublin in 1685', *IHS*, vol. xiv, no. 55 (March 1965); L. M. Cullen, *Anglo-Irish Trade 1660–1800* (Manchester, 1968); T. C. Barnard, 'Sir William Petty, His Kerry Estate and Irish Population', *IESH*, vol. vi (1979); 'Sir William Petty as Kerry Ironmaster', *RIA Proc.*, vol. lxxxii, sect. C, no. 1 (1982); and 'Sir William Petty, Irish Landowner' in H. Lloyd-Jones, V. Pearl, B. Worden (editors), *History and Imagination: Essays in Honour of H. R. Trevor-Roper* (London, 1981). Questions of government economic policy are illuminated in H. Kearney, 'The Political Background to English Mercantilism 1695–1700', *Ec. Hist. Rev.*, vol. xi, no. 3 (1959) and P. Kelly, 'The Irish Woollen Export Prohibition Act of 1699: Kearney Revisited', *IESH*, vol. vii (1980). Rolf Loeber, 'Irish Country Houses and Castles of the Late Caroline Period', *Quarterly Bulletin of the Irish Georgian Society*, vol. xvi (January–June 1973), breaks new ground.

For the Jacobite era, J. G. Simms, *Jacobite Ireland 1685–91* (London, 1969) is lucid and definitive. Also see J. I. McGuire, 'The Irish Parliament of 1692' in T. Bartlett and D. Hayton (editors), *Penal Era and Golden Age: Essays in Irish History 1690–1800* (Belfast, 1979) and 'The Church of Ireland and the Glorious Revolution of 1688' in Art Cosgrove and Donal McCartney, *Studies in Irish History*; and John Miller, 'The Earl of Tyrconnell and James II's Irish Policy 1685–8', *Hist. Jn.*, vol. xx, no. 4 (1977). A rare treatment from the Continental perspective is provided by W. Troost, *William III and the Treaty of Limerick (1691–7): A Study of His Irish Policy* (Leiden, 1983).

Literary and cultural issues throughout the period are dealt with in T. Dunne, 'The Gaelic Response to Conquest and Colonization: The Evidence of the Poetry', *Stud. Hib.*, vol. xx (1980); N. Canny, 'The Formation of the Irish Mind: Religion, Politics and Gaelic Irish Literature 1580–1750', *P & P*, no. 95 (May 1982); O. Bergin, *Irish Bardic Poetry* (Dublin, 1970); C. O'Rahilly, *Five Seventeenth-century Political Poems* (Dublin, 1952); J. J. Silke, 'Irish Scholarship and the Renaissance 1580–1673', *Studies in the Renaissance*, vol. xx (1973); W. B. Stanford, 'Towards a History of Classical Influences in Ireland', *RIA Proc.*, vol. lxx, sect. C, no. 3 (1970); R. B. McDowell and D. A. Webb, *Trinity College, Dublin, 1592–1952: An Academic History* (Cambridge, 1982); K. T. Hoppen, *The Common Scientist in the Seventeenth Century: A Study of the Dublin Philosophical Society 1683–1708* (London, 1970); T. C. Barnard, 'Miles Symner and the New Learning in Seventeenth-century Ireland', *RSAI Jn.*, vol. cii (1972) and 'The Hartlib Circle and the Origins of the Dublin Philosophical Society', *IHS*, vol. xix, no. 74 (March 1974). Geoffrey Keating's *Foras Feasa ar Éirinn: The History of Ireland*, referred to in the text, was edited by David Comyn and P. S. Dineen for the Irish Texts Society in four volumes (London, 1902–14).

PART TWO

The literature of contemporary letters and memoirs for the eighteenth century is overwhelming, and often very vivid – but remember the caveats on pp. 167–70, above. A few of the most accessible sources, which provide material quoted in the text, include H. Williams (editor), *The Correspondence of Jonathan Swift* (five vols., Oxford, 1963–5); Emily Charlotte Boyle, Countess of Cork and Orrery (editor), *The Orrery Papers* (two vols., London, 1902); Lady Llandover (editor), *The Autobiography and Correspondence of Mary Granville, Mrs Delany* (six vols., London, 1861–2); Esther Hewitt (editor), *Lord Shannon's Letters to His Son: A Calendar of the Letters Written by the Second Earl of Shannon to His Son, Viscount Boyle 1790–1802* (P R O N I, Belfast, 1982); B. Fitzgerald (editor), *The Correspondence of Emily, Duchess of Leinster 1731–1814* (three vols., I M C, Dublin, 1949–57); Jonah Barrington, *Personal Sketches of His Own Times* (three vols., London, 1832) and *The Rise and Fall of the Irish Nation* (Paris, 1833; Dublin, 1853); and C. L. and R. E. Ward (editors), *The Letters of Charles O'Conor of Belanagare* (two vols., Ann Arbor, Michigan 1980), a vital source for the life of the Catholic gentry during this period. The condition of the Catholic Church in the early part of the century is interestingly profiled by Revd Hugh Fenning (editor), *The Fottrell Papers 1721–39: An Edition of the Papers Found on the Person of Father John Fottrell, Provincial of the Dominicans in Ireland, at His Arrest in 1739* (P R O N I, Belfast, 1980). There is much Irish material in T. Coupland, R. B. McDowell, *et al.* (editors), *The Correspondence of Edmund Burke* (ten vols., Cambridge and Chicago, 1958–78), especially vols. V I I I and I X. For social background, see Thomas Molyneux's journeys to Connacht and Kerry in 1709, reprinted in *Miscellany of the Irish Archaeological Society* (1846) and Síle ní Chinnéide's invaluable edition of Coquebert de Montbret's Irish journals in 1790–91: *N. Munster Antiq. Jn.*, vols. v (1948) and xiv (1971); *Galway Arch. Soc. Jn.*, vols. xxv (1952–3), xxxv (1976) and xxxvi (1977–8); *Cork Hist. Soc. Jn.*, vols. lxxviii (1973) and lxxix (1974); *Kerry Arch. Soc. Jn.*, vol. vi (1973); *Kildare Arch. Soc. Jn.*, vol. xv (1974); *R S A I Jn.*, vol. civ (1974). More familiar social background is supplied, inevitably, by Arthur Young's *Tour of Ireland 1776–9*, edited by A. W. Hutton (two vols., London, 1892).

Original materials are presented attractively and conveniently by the Public Record Office of Northern Ireland in their Facsimile series, and two of their best productions deal with this period: 'The Act of Union' (nos. 41–60, 1973) and 'Robert Emmet: The Insurrection of July 1803' (nos. 181–200, 1976).

The most apparently comprehensive general work on the eighteenth century is T. W. Moody and W. E. Vaughan (editors), *A New History of Ireland. Vol. I V: Eighteenth-century Ireland 1691–1800* (Oxford, 1986), but it is not necessarily the most stimulating or even the most up to date. The lively collection edited by T. Bartlett and D. Hayton, *Penal Era and Golden Age: Essays in Irish History 1690–1800*, is essential reading, and there is relevant material in P. J. Corish (editor),

Radicals, Rebels and Establishments: Historical Studies X V (Belfast, 1985). Also see W. H. Crawford and B. Trainor (editors), *Aspects of Irish Social History 1750–1800* (PRONI, Belfast, 1969) as well as the more specific works on economic and social history mentioned below. The best general history is D. Dickson, *New Foundations: Ireland 1660–1800* (Dublin, 1987).

Regarding subjects emphasized in the text, Swift's contribution to Ascendancy culture is dealt with in O. W. Ferguson, *Jonathan Swift and Ireland* (Urbana, Illinois, 1962) and L. A. Landa, *Swift and the Church of Ireland* (Oxford, 1954); also see Swift's *Irish Tracts and Sermons*, edited by H. Davis and L. A. Landa (Oxford, 1968). A. P. W. Malcomson's brilliant *John Foster: The Politics of the Anglo-Irish Ascendancy* (Oxford, 1978) is far more than a biography, and is much the best book on the high politics of the period. Malcomson has also illuminated aspects of social history in *The Pursuit of the Heiress: Aristocratic Marriage in Ireland 1750–1820* (Belfast, PRONI, 1982) and 'Absenteeism in Eighteenth-century Ireland', *IESH*, vol. i (1974). On the latter subject, see also D. Large, 'The Wealth of the Greater Irish Landowners 1750–1815', *IHS*, vol. xv, no. 57 (March 1966). Maurice Craig's *Dublin 1660–1860: A Social and Architectural History* (Dublin, 1969) is a chatty classic; and the *Records of Eighteenth-century Domestic Architecture and Decoration in Ireland*, published by the first Irish Georgian Society (five vols., Dublin, 1909–13), are of unique value. Edward McParland, *James Gandon: Vitruvius Hibernicus* (London, 1985) is a definitive work. R. Munter, *The History of the Irish Newspaper 1685–1760* (Cambridge, 1967) covers an important subject; R. B. McDowell's *Irish Public Opinion 1750–1800* (London, 1944) remains indispensable. Anglo-Irish literature is given an idiosyncratic and vigorous treatment in W. J. McCormack, *Ascendancy and Tradition in Anglo-Irish Literary History from 1789 to 1939* (Oxford, 1985).

The economic and social history of the eighteenth century has been influentially reinterpreted on a broad front by L. M. Cullen; besides works by him already cited, see 'Problems in the Reinterpretation and Revision of Eighteenth-century Irish Economic History', *RHS Trans.*, fifth ser., vol. xvii (1967); 'Irish History without the Potato', *P & P*, no. 40 (July 1968); 'The Hidden Ireland: Reassessment of a Concept', *Stud. Hib.*, vol. ix (1969). A vital background work is T. W. Freeman, *Pre-Famine Ireland: A Study in Historical Geography* (Manchester, 1957). Specific economic aspects are dealt with in J. O'Donovan, *The Economic History of Livestock in Ireland* (Cork, 1940); P. Lynch and J. Vaizey, *Guinness's Brewery in the Irish Economy 1759–1876* (Cambridge, 1960); C. Gill, *The Rise of the Irish Linen Industry* (Oxford, 1925; reprinted 1964). The minefield of demographic history was first systematically explored in K. H. Connell's *The Population of Ireland 1750–1845* (Oxford, 1950); for a critique, see articles on marriage and population growth by M. Drake and J. Lee in *Ec. Hist. Rev.*, vol. xvi, no. 2 (1963) and vol. xxi, no. 2 (1968), and for a magisterial recent survey, S. Daultrey, D. Dickson and C. Ó Gráda, 'Hearth Tax, Household Size and Irish Population Change 1672–1821', *RIA Proc.*, vol. lxxxii, sect. C., no. 6 (1982). The same authors have also written 'Eighteenth-century Population: New Perspectives from

Old Sources', *Jn. Econ. Hist.*, vol. xli (1981); also see C. Ó Gráda and Joel Mokyr, 'New Developments in Irish Population History 1700–1850', *Ec. Hist. Rev.*, vol. xxxvii, no. 4 (November 1984). For population movement and emigration, see R. H. Dickson, *Ulster Emigration to Colonial America 1718–85* (Belfast, 1966).

Social history is sensitively, if rather impressionistically, explored in K. H. Connell, *Irish Peasant Society* (Oxford, 1968). For the lives of Catholics in eighteenth-century Ireland, see S. Connolly, *Priests and People in Pre-Famine Ireland 1780–1845* (Dublin, 1982); J. A. Murphy, 'The Support of the Catholic Clergy in Ireland 1750–1850' in *Historical Studies V* (London, 1965); M. Wall, 'The Rise of a Catholic Middle Class in Eighteenth-century Ireland', *IHS*, vol. xi, no. 42 (September 1958); J. Brady, *Catholics and Catholicism in the Eighteenth-century Press* (Maynooth, 1965); P. J. Corish, *The Catholic Community in the Seventeenth and Eighteenth Centuries*. The classic treatment of the Penal Laws is in M. Wall, *The Penal Laws 1691–1760: Church and State from the Treaty of Limerick to the Accession of George III* (Dundalk, 1961), but forthcoming work from S. Connolly will present a different perspective. For an idiosyncratic view, see R. E. Burns, 'The Irish Penal Code and Some of Its Historians', *Rev. of Pols.*, vol. xxi (1959) and 'The Irish Popery Laws: A Study of Eighteenth-century Legislation and Behaviour', ibid., vol. xxiv (1962). An important series of articles by Gerard Lyne on land tenure in Kerry from the late seventeenth to the late eighteenth centuries shows the Catholic position in an interesting light: see *Jn. of Kerry Arch. and Hist. Soc.*, nos. 10–12 (1977–9). For Gaelic culture, see works already cited by B. Ó Cuív and N. Canny; and R. A. Breathnach, 'The End of a Tradition: A Survey of Eighteenth-century Gaelic Literature', *Stud. Hib.*, vol. i (1961).

Articles on popular protest will be found in C. H. E. Philpin (editor), *Nationalism and Popular Protest in Ireland* (Cambridge, 1987), as well as in S. Clark and J. Donnelly, Jr, *Irish Peasants: Violence and Political Unrest 1780–1914*. Also see J. Donnelly, Jr, 'The Whiteboy Movement 1761–5', *IHS*, vol. xxi, no. 81 (March 1978), 'The Rightboy Movement 1765–8', *Stud. Hib.*, vol. xvii (1977) and 'Hearts of Oak, Hearts of Steel', ibid., vol. xxi (1981); and M. Bric, 'Priest, Parson and Politics: The Rightboy Protest in County Cork 1785–88', *P & P*, no. 100 (August 1983).

The background to, and structure of, high political activity is dealt with in D. Hayton, 'The Crisis in Ireland and the Disintegration of Queen Anne's Last Ministry', *IHS*, vol. xxii, no. 87 (March 1981); E. M. Johnston, *Great Britain and Ireland 1760–1800* (Edinburgh, 1963); and A. P. W. Malcomson, *John Foster: The Politics of the Anglo-Irish Ascendancy*. There are numerous pious 'memoirs' of Ascendancy politicians like Grattan, Flood and Charlemont, usually compiled by members of their families in the early nineteenth century, which should be handled gingerly. For an interpretive approach to eighteenth-century political activity, see T. Bartlett and D. Hayton's *Penal Era and Golden Age: Essays in Irish History 1690–1800*; T. Bartlett, 'Opposition in Late Eighteenth-century Ireland: The Case of the Townshend Viceroyalty', *IHS*, vol. xxii, no. 88 (September 1981); A. P. W. Malcomson, 'The Newtown Act of 1748: Revision and Reconstruction', ibid., vol. xviii, no. 71 (March 1973); Paul Kelly, 'British and Irish Politics in 1785', *EHR*, vol. xc, no. 356 (July 1975); J. C. D. Clark, 'Whig Tactics and Parliamentary Precedent: The English Management of Irish Politics 1754–56', *Hist. Jn.*, vol. xxi, no. 2 (1978); J. C. Beckett, 'Anglo-Irish Constitutional Relations in the Later Eighteenth Century' in *Confrontations: Studies in Irish History*; G. C. Bolton, *The Passing of the Irish Act of Union* (Oxford, 1966).

Interactions between Irish and American upheavals in the later eighteenth century are explored in D. N. Doyle, *Ireland, Irishmen and Revolutionary America 1760–1820* (Dublin, 1981). Also see M. R. O'Connell, *Irish Politics and Social Conflict in the Age of the American Revolution* (Philadelphia, 1965) and Owen Dudley Edwards, 'The Impact of the American Revolution in Ireland' in R. R. Palmer, *The Impact of the American Revolution Abroad* (Washington, 1976). For background, and an imperial perspective, see F. G. James, *Ireland in the Empire 1688–1770* (Cambridge, Mass., 1973). The late eighteenth-century crisis is dealt with at rather rambling length in R. B. McDowell, *Ireland in the Age of Imperialism and Revolution 1760–1801* (Oxford, 1979) and with pithy élan in G. Ó Tuathaigh, *Ireland before the Famine 1798–1848* (Dublin, 1972); but for an original focus, and a contribution of real incisiveness and originality, Marianne Elliott's *Partners in Revolution: The United Irishmen and France* (London, 1982) is indispensable. Also see her 'Origins and Transformation of Early Irish Republicanism', *Int. Rev. Soc. Hist.*, vol. xxiii (1978) and A. T. Q. Stewart, ' "A Stable, Unseen Power": Dr William Drennan and the Origins of the United Irishmen' in John Bossy (editor), *Essays Presented to Michael Roberts* (Belfast, 1976). A different perspective on Wolfe Tone is provided by T. Dunne's combative *Wolfe Tone: Colonial Outsider* (Cork, 1981). An essential text remains the *Life of Theobald Wolfe Tone ... Written by Himself and Continued by His Son*, edited by R. B. O'Brien (two vols., London, 1893). Pending Marianne Elliott's biography, Frank MacDermot's *Theobald Wolfe Tone and His Times* (London, 1939; revised edition Dublin, 1968) remains useful.

J. Donnelly, Jr synthesizes recent work on the 1790s in his review article 'Republicanism and Reaction in the 1790s', *IESH*, vol. xi (1984). Important essays by D. Dickson on taxation, and D. Miller on unrest in Armagh, appear in S. Clark and J. Donnelly, Jr, *Irish Peasants: Violence and Political Unrest 1780–1914*; there is also much of relevance in P. J. Corish, *Radicals, Rebels and Establishments: Historical Studies XV*, notably T. Bartlett's piece on 'Indiscipline and Disaffection in the Armed Forces'. See also his 'An End to Moral Economy: The Irish Militia Disturbances of 1793', *P & P*, no. 99 (May 1983). Bartlett has also edited absorbing material on Defenderism in *IHS*, vol. xxiv, no. 95 (May 1985). For the events of 1798, T. Pakenham's *The Year of Liberty* (London, 1969) is unequalled. *Bishop Stock's 'Narrative' of the Year of the French: 1798* has been edited by Grattan Freyer (Ballina, 1982) and is a vivid eye-witness account of Humbert's invasion. Ulster themes are dealt with in A. T. Q. Stewart, *The Narrow Ground: Aspects of Ulster 1609–1969* and J. S. Reid's monumental *History of the Presbyterian Church in Ireland* (three vols., Belfast, 1867). Also see J. C. Beckett, *Protestant Dissent in Ireland 1687–1780* (London, 1948) and D. W. Miller, 'Presbyterianism and "Modernization" in

Ulster', *P & P*, no. 80 (August 1978). The important subject of history-writing in eighteenth-century Ireland is only beginning to be explored, but see Walter Love, 'Charles O'Conor of Belanagare and Thomas Leland's "Philosophical" History of Ireland', *IHS*, vol. xiii, no. 49 (March 1962) and J. Hill, 'Popery and Protestantism, Civil and Religious Liberty: The Disputed Lessons of Irish History, 1690–1812', *P & P*, no. 118 (February 1988).

PART THREE

The great volume of primary materials about nineteenth-century Ireland is too vast to itemize here, though references to some of the first-hand material will be found in footnotes. The many government investigations into Irish conditions are both accessible and absorbing: especially the Whateley Commission of Inquiry into the condition of the poorer classes in Ireland, which reported 1835–6, and the Devon Commission inquiring into occupation of land in Ireland, which reported in 1845. Two ancillary publications of the *New History of Ireland* provide vital statistics: W. E. Vaughan and A. J. Fitzpatrick (editors), *Irish Historical Statistics: Population 1821–71* (Dublin, 1978) and B. M. Walker (editor), *Parliamentary Election Results in Ireland 1801–1922* (Dublin, 1978). The literature of contemporary memoirs, diaries, travellers' accounts and so on bulks large, and is often enlightening; a few accessible examples are listed below.

An excellent survey of the early nineteenth century is provided by G. Ó Tuathaigh, *Ireland before the Famine 1798–1848*; the works cited by Oliver Mac-Donagh and P. O'Farrell at the beginning of this survey provide illuminating and often iconoclastic insights into the whole period of the Union. Also see F. S. L. Lyons and R. A. J. Hawkins (editors), *Ireland under the Union: Varieties of Tension. Essays in Honour of T. W. Moody* (Oxford, 1980). Mary Daly's *Social and Economic History of Ireland since 1800* (Dublin, 1981) is a valuable introduction. The administrative system is delineated in R. B. McDowell, *The Irish Administration 1800–1914* (London, 1964).

For early nineteenth-century politics, tracts like Thomas Moore's *Memoirs of Captain Rock* (anonymously published in London, 1824) and J. W. Croker's *The State of Ireland Past and Present* (London, 1808), which are both referred to in the text, provide vivid perceptions. Maurice O'Connell's great edition of *The Correspondence of Daniel O'Connell* (eight vols., IMC, Dublin, 1972–80) is essential. Fergus O'Ferrall, *Catholic Emancipation: Daniel O'Connell and the Birth of Irish Democracy* (Dublin, 1985) is a work of great thoroughness and insight; and there are useful essays in K. B. Nowlan and M. R. O'Connell (editors), *Daniel O'Connell: Portrait of a Radical* (Belfast, 1984). The definitive biography is, or will be, Oliver MacDonagh's: the first volume is *The Hereditary Bondsman* (London, 1988). Also see A. Macintyre, *The Liberator: Daniel O'Connell and the Irish Party 1830–47* (London, 1965) and K. B. Nowlan, *The Politics of Repeal: A Study in the Relations between Great Britain and Ireland 1841–50* (London, 1965). Other aspects of politics in the period are covered in I. d'Alton, *Protestant Society and Politics in Cork 1812–44* (Cork, 1980); H. Senior, *Orangeism in Ireland and Britain 1795–1836* (London, 1960); Jacqueline Hill, 'National Festivals, the State and "Protestant Ascendancy" in Ireland 1790–1829', *IHS*, vol. xxv, no. 93 (May 1984) and 'The Protestant Response to Repeal: The Case of the Dublin Working Class' in F. S. L. Lyons and R. A. J. Hawkins, *Ireland under the Union: Varieties of Tension. Essays in Honour of T. W. Moody*; R. B. McDowell, *Public Opinion and Government Policy in Ireland 1801–46* (London, 1952); D. Kerr, *Peel, Priests and Politics: Sir Robert Peel's Administration and the Roman Catholic Church in Ireland 1841–6* (Oxford, 1982).

The only modern account of Young Ireland is R. Davis, *The Young Ireland Movement* (Dublin, 1987), and original accounts like C. Gavan Duffy's *Young Ireland: A Fragment of Irish History* (London, 1880) and Michael Doheny's *The Felon's Track* (1849; reprinted Dublin, 1914) must be handled very carefully indeed. For challenging insights see T. Dunne, 'Haunted by History: Irish Romantic Writing 1800–1850' in R. Porter and M. Tich, *Romanticism in National Context* (Cambridge, 1988). For the formation of a cultural and historical idea of Ireland's past, see Walter Love, 'Charles O'Conor of Belanagare and Thomas Leland's "Philosophical" History of Ireland'; N. Vance, 'Celts, Carthaginians and Constitutions: Anglo-Irish Literary Relations 1780–1820', *IHS*, vol. xxii, no. 87 (March 1981); R. F. Foster, 'History and the Irish Question', *RHS Trans.*, fifth ser., vol. xxx (1983); Donal McCartney, 'The Writing of History in Ireland 1800–1830', *IHS*, vol. x, no. 40 (September 1957); and Jeanne Sheehy's luminous and entertaining *The Rediscovery of Ireland's Past: The Celtic Revival 1830–1930* (London, 1980). Forthcoming work by Clare O'Halloran and Jacqueline Hill will elucidate this area further.

On religious affairs, S. Connolly's *Priests and People in Pre-Famine Ireland 1780–1845* is of great importance; he has also written an excellent pamphlet, *Religion and Society in Nineteenth-century Ireland*, Studies in Irish Economic and Social History No. 3 (Dundalk, 1985). Also see Oliver MacDonagh, 'The Politicization of the Irish Catholic Bishops 1800–1850', *Hist. Jn.*, vol. xviii, no. 1 (1975); P. J. Corish (editor), *A History of Irish Catholicism*, vol. V, parts 2 and 3 (Dublin, 1967); D. Bowen, *The Protestant Crusade in Ireland 1800–1870: A Study of Protestant–Catholic Relations between the Act of Union and Disestablishment* (Dublin, 1978) – though more than one important postgraduate thesis has since disputed Bowen's picture of harmonious Catholic–Protestant relations before the 1820s; R. Finley Holmes, *Henry Cooke* (Belfast, 1981); Peter Brooke, 'Religion and Secular Thought 1850–75' in J. C. Beckett, *et al.*, *Belfast: The Making of the City* (Belfast, 1983); and David Hempton's two important articles, 'Methodism in Irish Society 1770–1830', *RHS Trans.*, fifth ser., vol. xxxvi (1986) and 'The Methodist Crusade in Ireland', *IHS*, vol. xxii, no. 85 (March 1980). D. H. Akenson, *The Irish Education Experiment: The National System of Education in the Nineteenth Century* (London, 1970) is also relevant.

There is a growing literature on the subject of secret societies and rural unrest, though George Cornewall Lewis's classic *On the Local Disturbances in Ireland* (London, 1836) remains the indispensable starting-point. C. H. E. Philpin, *Nationalism and Popular Protest in Ireland*, S. Clark and J. Donnelly, Jr, *Irish Peasants: Violence and Political Unrest 1780–1914* and P. J. Corish, *Radicals, Rebels and Establishments: Historical Studies XV* all contain relevant essays. Also see M. Beames, *Peasants and Power: The Whiteboy Movements and Their Control in Pre-Famine Ireland* (Brighton, 1983); David Fitzpatrick, 'Class, Family and Rural Unrest in Nineteenth-century Ireland' in P. J. Drudy (editor), *Irish Studies 2. Ireland: Land, Politics and People* (Cambridge, 1982); G. Broeker, *Rural Disorder and Police Reform in Ireland 1812–36* (London, 1970); P. O'Farrell, 'Millennialism, Messianism and Utopianism in Irish History', *Anglo-Irish Studies*, vol. ii (1976).

Rural conditions in early nineteenth-century Ireland provoked a flood of contemporary and subsequent comment. Besides the reports of the commissions of inquiry mentioned above, see travellers' accounts like that of Mr and Mrs S. C. Hall, *Ireland: Its Scenery, Character, Etc.* (three vols., London 1841–3) and W. M. Thackeray, *The Irish Sketchbook* (London, 1843); less accessible but more enlightening is the account of someone who actually saw life on the inside of the cabins, Asenath Nicolson, *Ireland's Welcome to the Stranger: Or, Excursions through Ireland in 1844 and 1845 for the Purpose of Personally Investigating the Condition of the Poor* (London, 1847). For secondary commentary, many of the works listed above in the eighteenth-century section are relevant, such as the work on Irish population by K. H. Connell, J. Lee, M. Drake and S. Daultrey, D. Dickson and C. Ó Gráda. There are several valuable articles in J. M. Goldstrom and L. A. Clarkson (editors), *Irish Population, Economy and Society. Essays in Honour of the Late K. H. Connell* (Oxford, 1981), which has an indispensable section on 'Demography and Diet'; also see the collections edited by L. M. Cullen and F. Furet, and L. M. Cullen and T. C. Smout, listed at the beginning of this survey. Raymond Crotty's *Irish Agricultural Production: Its Volume and Structure* (Cork, 1966) is vigorous, brilliant and iconoclastic. Also see R. D. C. Black's *Economic Thought and the Irish Question 1817–70* (Cambridge, 1970).

J. Donnelly, Jr's *The Land and the People of Nineteenth-century Cork: The Rural Economy and the Land Question* (London, 1975) is the kind of book that should be written for every Irish county. For landlord–tenant relations in general, see M. J. Winstanley, *Ireland and the Land Question 1800–1922* (London, 1984), a very useful introduction; and for a specific case-study, W. A. Maguire, *The Downshire Estates in Ireland 1801–45* (Oxford, 1972). (Works dealing with landlord–tenant relations after the Famine are listed later.) For Ulster, see L. Kennedy and P. Ollerenshaw (editors), *An Economic History of Ulster 1820–1940* (Manchester, 1985); E. R. R. Green, *The Lagan Valley 1800–1850* (London, 1949); W. A. McCutcheon, *The Industrial Archaeology of Northern Ireland* (Belfast, 1980); W. H. Crawford, 'Landlord–tenant Relations in Ulster 1609–1820', *IESH*, vol. ii (1975) and *Domestic Industry in Ireland* (Dublin, 1972); also see his essays in the collections edited by L. M. Cullen and T. C. Smout, T. Bartlett and D. Hayton, L. M. Cullen and F. Furet, and D. Roebuck. Other works dealing with Ulster in this period include

J. C. Beckett, *et al.*, *Belfast: The Making of the City* and P. Gibbon, *The Origins of Ulster Unionism: The Formation of Popular Protestant Politics and Ideology in Nineteenth-century Ireland* (Manchester, 1975), which is stimulating, but has been much contested. Finally, J. H. Andrews's *A Paper Landscape: The Ordnance Survey in Nineteenth-century Ireland* (Oxford, 1975) is a masterly work, exploring a far wider area than indicated by the title.

The Famine is specifically dealt with in R. D. Edwards and T. D. Williams, *The Great Famine* (London, 1956) and Joel Mokyr, *Why Ireland Starved: A Quantitative and Analytical History of the Irish Economy 1800–1850* (London, 1983); see also the articles discussing Mokyr's conclusions in *IESH*, vol. xi (1984). There is much of relevance in J. M. Goldstrom and L. A. Clarkson, *Irish Population, Economy and Society. Essays in Honour of the Late K. H. Connell*. A valuable local study is S. Kierse, *The Famine Years in the Parish of Killaloe 1845–51* (Killaloe, 1984); and David Thomson and Moyra McGusty (editors), *The Irish Journals of Elizabeth Smith 1840–50* (Oxford, 1980) is full of insight. For social effects, see K. H. Connell, *Irish Peasant Society*; E. Larkin, 'The Devotional Revolution in Ireland 1850–75', *AHR*, vol. xxvii, no. 3 (June 1972), and *The Historical Dimensions of Irish Catholicism* (New York, 1981) for afterthoughts; D. W. Miller, 'Irish Catholicism and the Great Famine', *Jn. Soc. Hist.*, vol. ix, no. 1 (1975); David Fitzpatrick, 'The Disappearance of the Irish Agricultural Labourer 1841–1912', *IESH*, vol. vii (1980).

The subject of emigration is another booming area. Here the vital starting-point is David Fitzpatrick, *Irish Emigration 1801–1921*, Studies in Irish Economic and Social History No. 1 (Dundalk, 1984). Also see C. Ó Gráda, 'A Note on Nineteenth-century Emigration Statistics', *Population Studies*, no. 29 (1975); S. H. Cousens's articles on regional patterns of emigration over the nineteenth century in *Trans. of the Inst. of British Geographers*, nos. 28 (1960), 33 (1963) and 38 (1965); and R. E. Kennedy, Jr, *The Irish: Emigration, Marriage and Fertility* (London, 1973). Irish emigration to America is dealt with exhaustively in Kerby Miller, *Emigrants and Exiles: Ireland and the Irish Exodus to North America* (Oxford, 1985) – but see the combative approach of D. H. Akenson in *Being Had: Historians, Evidence and the Irish in North America* (Port Credit, Ontario, 1985) and 'An Agnostic View of the Historiography of the Irish-Americans', *Labour/Le Travail*, no. 14 (1984). The vast extent of Irish-American study is indicated by D. N. Doyle, 'The Regional Bibliography of Irish America: A Review and an Addendum', *IHS*, vol. xxiii, no. 91 (May 1983); samples of traditionalist but important work include L. J. McCaffrey, *The Irish Diaspora in America* (second edition, Washington, 1984) and A. Schrier, *Ireland and the American Migration 1850–1900* (Minneapolis, 1951). A useful collection is P. J. Drudy (editor), *Irish Studies 4. The Irish in America: Emigration, Assimilation and Impact* (Cambridge, 1985). Irish emigration to Britain is only now beginning to receive academic analysis: see M. Hartigan (editor), *The History of the Irish in Britain: A Bibliography* (London, 1986). Brenda Collins deals with the Irish in Scotland in J. M. Goldstrom and L. A. Clarkson, *Irish Population, Economy and Society. Essays in Honour of the*

Late K. H. Connell; also see Collins's 'Proto-industrialization and Pre-Famine Emigration' in *Social History*, vol. vii, no. 2 (May 1982). For another view of Irish emigrant activity in Scotland, see Owen Dudley Edwards, *Burke and Hare* (Edinburgh, 1980). Also see R. Swift and S. Gilley (editors), *The Irish in the Victorian City* (London, 1985); L. H. Lees, *Exiles of Erin: Irish Migrants in Victorian London* (Manchester, 1979); L. P. Curtis, *Anglo-Saxons and Celts: A Study of Anti-Irish Prejudice in Victorian England* (Bridgeport, Conn., 1968) – but see S. Gilley's article questioning many of his conclusions in the collection edited by R. Swift and S. Gilley, and also G. Ó Tuathaigh's masterly study of 'The Irish in Britain: Problems of Integration', *R H S Trans.*, fifth ser., vol. xxxi (1981), reprinted by R. Swift and S. Gilley.

Of general treatments of Irish history after the Famine, F. S. L. Lyons's magisterial *Ireland since the Famine* (London, 1971) dominates the field. It is well partnered by J. Lee's iconoclastic and stimulating *The Modernization of Irish Society 1848–1918* (Dublin, 1973). Nicholas Mansergh's classic *The Irish Question 1840–1921* (third edition, London, 1975) looks at Irish history in the context of British policy and Anglo-Irish relations. The political and social underpinnings of post-Famine Ireland are marvellously prospected in K. T. Hoppen's masterpiece, *Elections, Politics and Society in Ireland 1832–85* (Oxford, 1984). Another pioneering study is Charles Townshend's *Political Violence in Ireland: Government and Resistance since 1848* (Oxford, 1983). Much Fenian historiography is hagiography, but R. V. Comerford's coruscating *The Fenians in Context: Irish Politics and Society 1848–82* (Dublin, 1985) lets in a burst of light. Also see T. W. Moody (editor), *The Fenian Movement* (Cork and Dublin, 1968); L. Ó Broin, *Revolutionary Underground: The Story of the Irish Republican Brotherhood 1858–1924* (Dublin, 1976); B. Mac Giolla Choille, 'Fenian Documents in the State Paper Office', *I H S*, vol. xvi, no. 62 (September 1962); and T. D. Williams (editor), *Secret Societies in Ireland* (Dublin, 1973). For constitutional politics before Parnell, see D. Thornley, *Isaac Butt and Home Rule* (London, 1964).

For the background to the land question, James Fintan Lalor's writings are of great interest; they are edited by L. Fogarty as *James Fintan Lalor: Patriot and Political Essayist* (Dublin, 1918). The best introduction to landlord–tenant relations in the later nineteenth century is W. E. Vaughan, *Landlords and Tenants in Ireland 1848–1904*, Studies in Irish Economic and Social History No. 2 (Dundalk, 1984); see also B. Solow's elegant and incisive study, *The Land Question and the Irish Economy 1870–1903* (Cambridge, Mass., 1971); S. Clark, *Social Origins of the Irish Land War* (Princeton, 1979); C. Ó Gráda, 'Agricultural Head-rents, Pre-Famine and Post-Famine', *Econ. and Soc. Review*, vol. v, no. 3 (April 1974); L. P. Curtis, 'Incumbered Wealth: Landlord Indebtedness in Post-Famine Ireland', *A H R*, vol. lxxxi, no. 2 (April 1980); R. F. Foster, *Charles Stewart Parnell: The Man and His Family* (Hassocks, 1976); P. Bew, *Land and the National Question in Ireland 1858–82* (Dublin, 1980); Donald Jordan, *Land and Politics in the West of Ireland: County Mayo 1846–82* (Cambridge, forthcoming, 1989); also Raymond Crotty, *Irish Agricultural Production: Its Volume and Structure* and J. Donnelly, Jr, *The Land*

and the People of Nineteenth-century Cork: The Rural Economy and the Land Question. There are countless contemporary views of the Land War of the early 1880s; a few of the more illuminating (not always consciously) are B. Becker, *Disturbed Ireland: Being the Letters Written during the Winter 1880–81* (London, 1881); S. M. Hussey, *Reminiscences of an Irish Land Agent* (London, 1904); W. Bence Jones, *The Life's Work in Ireland of a Landlord Who Tried to Do His Duty* (London, 1880); Michael Davitt, *The Fall of Feudalism in Ireland* (London and New York, 1904); and Anna Parnell's indispensable *The Tale of a Great Sham* edited with an introduction by Dana Hearne (Dublin, 1986).

For the political crisis of the 1880s see articles in F. S. L. Lyons and R. A. J. Hawkins, *Ireland under the Union: Varieties of Tension. Essays in Honour of T. W. Moody*; Conor Cruise O'Brien, *Parnell and His Party 1880–90* (Oxford, 1964); T. W. Moody, *Michael Davitt and Irish Revolution 1846–82* (Oxford, 1981); J. Loughlin, *Gladstone, Home Rule and the Ulster Question 1882–1893* (Dublin, 1986). The foundations of government policy are explored classically in J. L. Hammond, *Gladstone and the Irish Nation* (London, 1938) and sceptically in A. B. Cooke and J. R. Vincent, *The Governing Passion: Cabinet Government and Party Politics in Britain 1885–6* (Hassocks, 1974) – an iconoclastic *tour de force*. Also see J. R. Vincent, 'Gladstone and Ireland', *Proc. Brit. Academy*, vol. lxiii (1977). A more traditional view is given in E. D. Steele, 'Gladstone and Ireland', *IHS*, vol. xvii, no. 65 (March 1970). Also see T. Dunne, 'La Trahison des clercs: British Intellectuals and First Home Rule Crisis', *IHS*, vol. xxiii, no. 90 (November 1982). Conservative policy, the subject of L. P. Curtis's *Coercion and Conciliation in Ireland 1880–92: A Study in Constructive Unionism* (Princeton, 1963) is forcefully reinterpreted by Andrew Gailey in *Ireland and the Death of Kindness: The Experience of Constructive Unionism 1890–1905* (Cork, 1987). The unwritten history of the 1890s and early 1900s is, in fact, just beginning to be tackled – notably by P. Bew in *Conflict and Conciliation in Ireland 1890–1910: Parnellites and Radical Agrarians* (Oxford, 1987). There are numerous biographies of those active in politics at the time; particularly relevant are F. S. L. Lyons, *John Dillon* (London, 1968) and *Charles Stewart Parnell* (London, 1977); T. W. Moody, *Michael Davitt and Irish Revolution 1846–82*; R. F. Foster, *Lord Randolph Churchill: A Political Life* (Oxford, 1981); J. V. O'Brien, *William O'Brien and the Course of Irish Politics 1881–1918* (London, 1976).

PART FOUR

The sources for twentieth-century Irish history are eclectic and uneven; ironically, much of Irish history after 1922 has to be prospected through British sources, because of the restrictive approach taken by Irish governments towards releasing the papers of government departments. For the period following 1919, the Dáil Éireann debates are valuable – note especially the volume covering the Treaty debates, *Dáil Éireann Official Report: Debate on the Treaty between Great Britain and Ireland Signed on 6 December 1921* (Dublin, 1922).

Two short but invaluable general works are J. A. Murphy, *Ireland in the Twentieth Century* (Dublin, 1975) and Ronan Fanning, *Independent Ireland* (Dublin, 1986), the latter of especial value, because it incorporates much of the author's original research in available official records. Terence Brown's *Ireland: A Social and Cultural History 1922–79* (London, 1981) is a vital guide and Conor Cruise O'Brien (editor), *The Shaping of Modern Ireland* (London, 1960) contains essays of great insight on the early twentieth century. Many of the works cited in the last section, such as those on the land question by B. Solow, W. E. Vaughan and S. Clark and J. Donnelly, Jr, are also relevant to the social and economic history of Ireland in the early twentieth century. Also see T. West, *Horace Plunkett, Co-operation and Politics: An Irish Biography* (Gerrard's Cross, 1986).

Irish urban history is in its infancy, but two important studies of Dublin are Mary Daly, *Dublin, The Deposed Capital: A Social and Economic History 1860–1914* (Cork, 1985) and J. V. O'Brien, *'Dear, Dirty Dublin': A City in Distress 1899–1916* (London, 1982). Labour unrest in the early twentieth century is dealt with in John Gray's *City in Revolt: James Larkin and the Belfast Dock Strike of 1907* (Belfast, 1985); also see H. Patterson, *Class Conflict and Sectarianism: The Protestant Working Class and the Belfast Labour Movement 1868–1920* (Belfast, 1980) and A. C. Hepburn, 'Work, Class and Religion in Belfast 1871–1911', *IESH*, vol. x (1983). James Connolly's *Labour in Irish History* (Dublin, 1910, much reprinted) is necessary background. Issue no. 4 of *Saothar*, the journal of the Irish Labour History Society (1978), is a James Larkin number, with several interesting articles; also see E. Larkin, *James Larkin: Irish Labour Leader 1876–1947* (London, 1961) and A. Mitchell, *Labour in Irish Politics 1890–1930* (Dublin, 1974). The important topic of the Irish feminist movement in this period is nowhere treated adequately; see, in default of anything else, M. Ward, *Unmanageable Revolutionaries: Women and Irish Nationalism* (London, 1983).

First-hand accounts of nationalist involvement in the early twentieth century are embarrassing in their number, and require careful decoding; a sample, chosen for their literary quality at least as much as for their factual accuracy, are Desmond Ryan, *Remembering Sion* (London, 1934), W. B. Yeats, *Autobiographies* (London, 1955) and Ernie O'Malley's incomparable *On Another Man's Wound* (Tralee, 1979 edition). Three contemporary texts of great influence (retrospectively speaking) are Douglas Hyde, 'The Necessity for De-Anglicizing Ireland' in *The Revival of Irish Literature: Addresses by Sir Charles Gavan Duffy, KCMG, Dr George Sigerson, and Dr Douglas Hyde* (London, 1894); D. P. Moran, *The Philosophy of Irish Ireland* (Dublin, 1905); and Arthur Griffith, *The Resurrection of Hungary: A Parallel for Ireland* (Dublin, 1904). The same is true of the *Collected Works* of Patrick H. Pearse (five vols., Dublin, 1920–25), particularly *Political Writings and Speeches*.

Of secondary works, F. S. L. Lyons's *Culture and Anarchy in Ireland 1890–1939* has set many of the terms for recent interpretations of cultural nationalism; see also Conor Cruise O'Brien, 'Passion and Cunning: An Essay on the Politics of W. B. Yeats' in A. N. Jeffares and K. C. W. Cross (editors), *In Excited Reverie: A Centenary Tribute to William Butler Yeats 1865–1939* (London, 1965). G. J. Watson, *Irish 'Identity and the Literary Revival: Synge, Yeats, Joyce and O'Casey* (London, 1979) is both perceptive and lucid. The marginalization of the Ascendancy is treated in P. Buckland, *Irish Unionism. Vol. I: The Anglo-Irish and the New Ireland 1885–1922* (Dublin, 1973); also see L. P. Curtis, 'The Anglo-Irish Predicament' in *Twentieth-century Studies 4* (Edinburgh, 1970). For the Gaelic Athletic Association, see W. F. Mandle, *The Gaelic Athletic Association and Irish Nationalist Politics 1884–1924* (London and Dublin, 1987).

There are few worthwhile biographies for the period, one glowing exception being R. Dudley Edwards's *Patrick Pearse: The Triumph of Failure* (London, 1977), which illuminates far more than its subject; also see Brian Inglis, *Roger Casement* (London, 1973). For the pre-war political crisis, see P. Jalland, *The Liberals and Ireland: The Ulster Question in British Politics to 1914* (Brighton, 1980); Ronan Fanning, 'The Irish Policy of Asquith's Government and the Cabinet Crisis of 1910' in Art Cosgrove and Donal McCartney, *Studies in Irish History Presented to R. Dudley Edwards*; Richard Murphy, 'Faction and the Home Rule Crisis 1912–14' in *History*, vol. lxxi, no. 232 (June 1986). A. T. Q. Stewart's *The Ulster Crisis* (London, 1967) is a work of considerable panache. A topic tacitly ignored by much of traditional Irish historiography is broached in David Fitzpatrick (editor), *Ireland and the First World War* (Trinity History Workshop, Dublin, 1986).

The tangled background to 1916 is explored in F. X. Martin, '1916: Myth, Fact and Mystery', *Stud. Hib.*, vol. vii (1967); see also his edition of Eoin MacNeill's absorbing memoir in *IHS*, vol. xii, no. 47 (March 1961). Much the best general treatment is in Charles Townshend, *Political Violence in Ireland*. For vivid first-hand accounts, see Desmond Ryan, *The Rising* (Dublin, 1949) and James Stephens, *The Insurrection in Dublin* (1916; reprinted Gerrard's Cross, 1978). The politics of the subsequent period are clarified by Michael Laffan in 'The Unification of Sinn Féin in 1917', *IHS*, vol. xvii, no. 67 (March 1971); A. T. Ward, 'Lloyd George and the 1918 Irish Conscription Crisis', *Hist. Jn.*, vol. xvii, no. 1 (March 1974); Tom Garvin, *The Evolution of Irish Nationalist Politics* is also of great value for this era. T. D. Williams (editor), *The Irish Struggle 1916–26* (London, 1966) contains some useful essays. David Fitzpatrick's *Politics and Irish Life 1913–1921: Provincial Experience of War and Revolution* (Dublin, 1977) is a pioneering masterpiece. A more modest local study is O. Coogan, *Politics and War in Meath 1913–23* (Dublin, 1983). General patterns of affiliation are treated in E. Rumpf and A. C. Hepburn, *Nationalism and Socialism in Twentieth-century Ireland* (Liverpool, 1977) and David Fitzpatrick, 'The Geography of Irish Nationalism 1910–1921', *P & P*, no. 78 (February 1978). Charles Townshend's *The British Campaign in Ireland 1919–21: The Development of Political and Military Policies* (Oxford, 1975) is impressively lucid and dispassionate; also see his article 'The Irish Republican Army and the Development of Guerrilla Warfare 1916–21', *EHR*, vol. xciv, no. 371 (April 1979). For labour unrest at this time, see David Fitzpatrick, 'Strikes in Ireland 1914–21', *Saothar*, no. 6 (1980); E. O'Connor, 'Agrarian Unrest and the Labour Movement in County Waterford 1917–23', ibid.; A. Mitchell, *Labour in Irish Politics 1890–1930*; C. D. Greaves, *Liam Mellowes and the Irish Revolution* (London, 1971). Ulster is dealt with in P. Buckland, *Irish Unionism, Vol. II: Ulster Unionism and the Origins of Northern Ireland 1886–1922* (Dublin, 1973); M. Laffan, *The Partition of Ireland 1911–25* (Dundalk, 1983); John McColgan, *British Policy and the Irish Administration 1920–22* (London, 1983). David Miller, *Queen's Rebels: Ulster Loyalism in Historical Perspective* (Dublin, 1978) is one of the best studies of the topic. D. George Boyce's *English Men and Irish Troubles: British Public Opinion and the Making of Irish Policy* (London, 1972) is enlightening about a difficult subject.

Independent Ireland and its establishment are dealt with in J. M. Curran, *The Birth of the Irish Free State 1921–3* (University, Alabama, 1980); Frank Pakenham, *Peace by Ordeal*, (third edition, London, 1972); T. Jones, *Whitehall Diary Vol. III: Ireland*, edited by K. Middlemas (London, 1971); Michael Gallagher, 'The Pact General Election of 1922', *IHS*, vol. xxi, no. 84 (September 1979); Eoin Neeson, *The Civil War in Ireland 1921–3* (Cork, 1966). Seán Cronin (editor), *The McGarrity Papers: Revelations of the Irish Revolutionary Movement in Ireland and America 1900–1940* (Tralee, 1972) contains interesting nuggets, especially regarding de Valera's mental processes. The same complex subject is beautifully dissected in John Bowman, *De Valera and the Ulster Question 1917–73* (Oxford, 1982). Biographies of de Valera are, so far, disappointing, though Deirdre McMahon's work is eagerly awaited. Maurice Moynihan (editor), *Speeches and Statements by Eamon de Valera 1917–73* (Dublin, 1980) is an essential source.

Free State politics are dealt with in B. Farrell, *The Founding of Dáil Éireann: Parliament and Nation-Building* (Dublin, 1971) and Jeffrey Prager, *Building Democracy in Ireland: Political Order and Cultural Integration in a Newly Independent Nation* (Cambridge, 1986). The Irish political system is delineated by Basil Chubb in *The Government and Politics of Ireland* (London, 1971); also see R. K. Carty, *Party and Parish Pump: Electoral Politics in Ireland* (Waterloo, Ontario, 1981) and Tom Garvin, 'The Destiny of the Soldiers: Tradition and Modernity in the Politics of de Valera's Ireland', *Pol. Studies*, vol. xxvi, no. 3 (1978). More visceral issues are addressed in M. G. Valuilis, *Almost a Rebellion: The Irish Army Mutiny of 1924* (Cork, 1985) and D. Keogh, *The Vatican, The Bishops and Irish Politics 1919–39* (Cambridge, 1986). Politics outside the establishment during the 1920s and 1930s may be followed in Tim Pat Coogan, *The IRA* (second edition, London, 1980) and the later chapters of Seán Cronin, *Irish Nationalism: A History of Its Roots and Ideology* (Dublin, 1980) – useful as a first-hand account of the modern period, but not reliable as a general treatment. Also see J. Bowyer Bell, *The Secret Army: The IRA 1916–79* (Dublin, 1979); M. Laffan, 'Violence and Terror in Twentieth-century Ireland: IRB and IRA' in W. J. Mommsen and G. Hirschfeld (editors), *Social Protest, Violence and Terror in Nineteenth- and Twentieth-century Europe* (London, 1982); M. Manning, *The Blueshirts* (Dublin, 1970).

Ronan Fanning's *The Irish Department of Finance 1922–58* (IPA, Dublin, 1978) is essential reading, and casts a far wider net than its title implies; it is studded with lengthy and thought-provoking quotations from otherwise inaccessible government sources. J. P. O'Carroll and J. A. Murphy (editors), *De Valera and His Times: Political Development in the Republic of Ireland* (Cork, 1983) has some useful essays. Important social and cultural issues are addressed in J. Whyte, *Church and State in Modern Ireland 1923–79* (second edition, London, 1980); E. B. Titley, *Church, State and the Control of Schooling in Ireland 1900–1944* (Dublin, 1983); M. O'Callaghan, 'Language, Nationality and Cultural Identity in the Irish Free State 1922–7: The *Irish Statesman* and the *Catholic Bulletin* Reappraised', *IHS*, vol. xxiv, no. 94 (November 1984). Conrad Arensberg's *The Irish Countryman: An Anthropological Study* (London, 1937) is necessary reading. Also useful are Seán Glynn, 'Irish Immigration to Britain 1911–51: Patterns and Policy', *IESH*, vol. viii (1981) and T. K. Daniel, 'Griffith on His Noble Head: The Determinants of Cumann na nGaedheal Economic Policy 1922–32', *IESH*, vol. iii (1976). D. S. Johnson, *The Inter-war Economy in Ireland*, Studies in Irish Economic and Social History No. 4 (Dundalk, 1985) is an excellent introduction, with a very useful bibliography; the definitive work on the subject is still J. Meenan, *The Irish Economy since 1922* (Liverpool, 1970). See also Raymond Crotty, *Irish Agricultural Production: Its Volume and Structure* and G. Ó Tuathaigh, 'The Land Question, Politics and Irish Society 1922–60' in P. J. Drudy, *Irish Studies 2: Ireland: Land, Politics and People*. Anglo-Irish relations in the 1920s are definitively surveyed in D. W. Harkness, *The Restless Dominion: The Irish Free State in the British Commonwealth of Nations 1921–31* (London, 1969); for the 1930s, Deirdre McMahon's *Republicans and Imperialists: Anglo-Irish Relations in the 1930s* (London, 1984) is invaluable.

Ireland's wartime experience has attracted much second-rate writing but has also inspired at least one first-rate book: Robert Fisk's massive *In Time of War: Ireland, Ulster and the Price of Neutrality 1939–45* (London, 1983). Foreign policy is definitively treated in Patrick Keatinge, *A Place among the Nations: Issues of Irish Foreign Policy* (Dublin, 1978).

Northern Ireland since 1920 is acerbically surveyed in P. Buckland, *The Factory of Grievances: Devolved Government in Northern Ireland 1921–39* (Dublin, 1979); also see D. W. Harkness, *Northern Ireland since 1920* (Dublin, 1983) and P. Bew and H. Patterson, *The State in Northern Ireland 1921–72: Political Forces and Social Classes* (Manchester, 1971). Michael Farrell's *Arming the Protestants: The Formation of the Ulster Special Constabulary and the Royal Ulster Constabulary 1920–27* (London, 1983) is *engagé* but illuminating. A particularly useful article is J. Whyte's 'How Much Discrimination was there under the Unionist Regime, 1921–68?' in T. Gallagher and J. O'Connell (editors), *Contemporary Irish Studies* (Manchester, 1983); also see R. J. Cormack and R. D. Osborne (editors), *Religion, Education and Employment: Aspects of Equal Opportunity in Northern Ireland* (Belfast, 1983). Graham Walker's *The Politics of Frustration: Harry Midgley and the Failure of Labour in Northern Ireland* (Manchester, 1985) is an absorbing study of a special case. For the roots of the crisis since 1968, Rosemary Harris's *Prejudice and Tolerance in*

Northern Ireland: A Study of Neighbours and 'Strangers' in a Border Community (Manchester, 1972) is one pioneering study, and R. Rose, *Governing without Consensus: An Irish Perspective* (London, 1971) another. Articles about Northern Ireland since then are too numerous to list; for a useful bibliography, see R. Rose, 'Ulster Politics: A Select Bibliography of Political Discord', *Pol. Studies*, vol. xx (1972); also J. Whyte, 'Interpretations of the Northern Ireland Problem' in C. Townshend (editor), *Consensus in Ireland: Approaches and Recessions* (Oxford, 1988). Among recent works, Steve Bruce, *God Save Ulster: The Religion and Politics of Paisleyism* (Oxford, 1986) is a useful and detached study of an underrated phenomenon. Clare O'Halloran, *Partition and the Limits of Irish Nationalism: An Ideology under Stress* (Dublin, 1987) trenchantly analyses attitudes in the Republic. P. Bishop and E. Mallie, *The Provisional I R A* (London, 1987) elucidates the I R A split of the early 1970s.

There are useful essays about post-war Ireland in J. Lee (editor), *Ireland 1945–70* (Dublin, 1979) and Frank Litton (editor), *Unequal Achievement: The Irish Experience 1957–82* (I P A, Dublin, 1982). P. Bew and H. Patterson, *Sean Lemass and the Making of Modern Ireland 1945–66* (Dublin, 1982) questions some received ideas. Finally, a few works of autobiography, memoir and polemic that illuminate aspects of modern Ireland: Seán O'Faolain, *The Irish* (1947; revised edition, 1980); Francis Stuart, *Black List, Section H* (London, 1975); Peadar O'Donnell, *There Will Be Another Day* (Dublin, 1963); C. S. Andrews, *Dublin Made Me* and *Man of No Property* (Dublin and Cork, 1979–82); John Healy, *The Death of an Irish Town* (Cork, 1968); Dervla Murphy, *A Place Apart* (London, 1978); Hubert Butler, *Escape from the Anthill* (Mullingar, 1985); Noel Browne, *Against the Tide* (Dublin, 1986). Like the rest of this guide, these represent a personal choice, made with difficulty from a bewildering range of material.

GLOSSARY OF ABBREVIATIONS

═══

AHR   *American Historical Review*

Anal. Hib.   *Analecta Hibernica*

Arch. Hib.   *Archivium Hibernicum*

Ec. Hist. Rev.   *Economic History Review*

EHR   *English Historical Review*

Hist. Jn.   *Historical Journal*

IESH   *Irish Economic and Social History*

IHS   *Irish Historical Studies*

IMC   Irish Manuscripts Commission

Int. Rev. Soc. Hist.   *International Review of Social History*

IPA   Institute of Public Administration

IUP   Irish University Press

P & P   *Past and Present*

PRONI   Public Record Office of Northern Ireland

Rev. of Pols.   *Review of Politics*

RHS Trans.   *Transactions of the Royal Historical Society*

RIA Proc.   *Proceedings of the Royal Irish Academy*

RSAI Jn.   *Journal of the Royal Society of Antiquaries of Ireland*

Stud. Hib.   *Studia Hibernica*

INDEX OF SUBJECTS

INDEX OF NAMES

(References in italics denote main entries with full biographical footnotes)